Introduction to Fortran 90/95

McGraw-Hill's *BEST*—Basic Engineering Series and Tools

Chapman, *Introduction to Fortran 90/95*
D'Orazio and Tan, *C Program Design for Engineers*
Eide, et al., *Introduction to Engineering Problem Solving*
Eide, et al., *Introduction to Engineering Design*
Eisenberg, *A Beginner's Guide to Technical Communication*
Gottfried, *Spreadsheet Tools for Engineers: Excel '97 Version*
Mathsoft's *Student Edition of Mathcad 7.0*
Palm, *Introduction to MATLAB for Engineers*
Pritchard, *Mathcad: A Tool for Engineering Problem Solving*

Introduction to Fortran 90/95

First Edition

Stephen J. Chapman

British Aerospace Australia

Boston, Massachusetts   Burr Ridge, Illinois   Dubuque, Iowa
Madison, Wisconsin   New York, New York   San Francisco, California   St. Louis, Missouri

WCB/McGraw-Hill

A Division of The McGraw·Hill Companies

INTRODUCTION TO FORTRAN 90/95

This book is printed on acid-free paper.

4 5 6 7 8 9 10 DOC/DOC 0 9 8 7 6 5 4 3 2 1 0

ISBN 0-07-011969-4

Editorial director: *Kevin T. Kane*
Publisher: *Tom Casson*
Sponsoring editor: *Eric Munson*
Developmental editor II: *Holly Stark*
Marketing manager: *John T. Wannemacher*
Project manager: *Kari A. Geltemeyer*
Production supervisor: *Heather D. Burbridge*
Designer: *Kiera Cunningham*
Compositor: *York Graphic Services, Inc.*
Typeface: *10/12 Times Roman*
Printer: *R. R. Donnelley & Sons Company*

Library of Congress Cataloging-in-Publication Data

Chapman, Stephen J.
  Introduction to Fortran 90/95 / Stephen J. Chapman.
    p.   cm.
  Abbreviated form of Fortran 90/95 for scientists and engineers.
  New York : McGraw-Hill, c1998.
    Includes index.
    ISBN 0-07-011969-4
    1. FORTRAN (Computer program language) I. Chapman, Stephen J.
  Fortran 90/95 for scientists and engineers.   II. Title.
  QA76.73.F25C457   1998
  005.13'3--dc21   97-23252

http://www.mhhe.com

Stephen J. Chapman received a BS in Electrical Engineering from Louisiana State University (1975), an MSE in Electrical Engineering from the University of Central Florida (1979), and pursued further graduate studies at Rice University.

From 1975 to 1980, he served as an officer in the U. S. Navy, assigned to teach Electrical Engineering at the U. S. Naval Nuclear Power School in Orlando, Florida. From 1980 to 1982, he was affiliated with the University of Houston, where he ran the power systems program in the College of Technology.

From 1982 to 1988 and from 1991 to 1995, he served as a Member of the Technical Staff of the Massachusetts Institute of Technology's Lincoln Laboratory, both at the main facility in Lexington, Massachusetts, and at the field site on Kwajalein Atoll in the Republic of the Marshall Islands. While there, he did research in radar signal processing systems. He ultimately became the leader of four large operational range instrumentation radars at the Kwajalein field site (TRADEX, ALTAIR, ALCOR, and MMW). Each of the four radars were controlled by large (100,000+ lines) real-time programs written largely in Fortran; the trials and tribulations associated with modifying those radar systems strongly influenced his views about proper design of Fortran programs.

From 1988 to 1991, Mr. Chapman was a research engineer in Shell Development Company in Houston, Texas, where he did seismic signal processing research. The research culminated in a number of large Fortran programs used to process seismic data. He was also affiliated with the University of Houston, where he continued to teach on a part-time basis.

Mr. Chapman is currently Manager of Technical Systems for British Aerospace Australia, in Melbourne, Australia. In this position, he provides technical direction and design authority for the work of younger engineers within the company. He is also continuing to teach at local universities on a part-time basis.

Mr. Chapman is a Senior Member of the Institute of Electrical and Electronic Engineers (and several of its component societies). He is also a member of the Association for Computing Machinery and the Institution of Engineers (Australia).

This book is dedicated to my wife Rosa, the great love of my life and the mother of our seven wonderful children.

Welcome to McGraw-Hill's *BEST*—Basic Engineering Series and Tools

Engineering educators have had long-standing debates over the content of introductory freshman engineering courses. Some schools emphasize computer-based instruction, some focus on engineering analysis, some concentrate on graphics and visualization, while others emphasize hands-on design. Two things, however, appear certain: no two schools do exactly the same thing, and at most schools, the introductory engineering courses frequently change from one year to the next. In fact, the introductory engineering courses at many schools have become a smorgasbord of different topics, some classical and other closely tied to computer software applications. Given this diversity in content and purpose, the task of providing appropriate text material becomes problematic, since every instructor requires something different.

McGraw-Hill has responded to this challenge by creating a series of modularized textbooks for the topics covered in most first-year introductory engineering courses. Written by authors who are acknowledged authorities in their respective fields, the individual modules vary in length, in accordance with the time typically devoted to each subject. For example, modules on programming languages are written as introductory-level textbooks, providing material for an entire semester of study, whereas modules that cover shorter topics such as ethics and technical writing provide less material, as appropriate for a few weeks of instruction. Individual instructors can easily combine these modules to conform to their particular courses. Most modules include numerous problems and/or projects and are suitable for use within an active-learning environment.

The goal of this series is to provide the educational community with text material that is timely, affordable, of high quality, and flexible in how it is used. We ask that you assist us in fulfilling this goal by letting us know how well we are serving your needs. We are particularly interested in knowing what, in your opinion, we have done well, and where we can make improvements or offer new modules.

Byron S. Gottfried
Consulting Editor
University of Pittsburgh

This book is an abbreviated form of *Fortran 90/95 for Scientists and Engineers,* also published by McGraw-Hill. It is intended to serve as a brief introduction to the Fortran 90 and Fortran 95 languages for undergraduate engineering students. Because it is abbreviated, the book covers only the most popular features of modern Fortran. For a discussion of less popular features of modern Fortran, and for a discussion of older features preserved for backwards compatibility with earlier versions of the language, please see my book, *Fortran 90/95 for Scientists and Engineers,* also published by McGraw-Hill.

This book is written with a specific goal in mind. During my time in industry, it became obvious that the strategies and techniques required to write large, *maintainable* Fortran programs were quite different from the skills new engineers were learning in their Fortran programming classes at school. The incredible cost of maintaining and modifying large programs once they are placed into service absolutely demands that they be written to be easily understood and modified by people other than their original programmers. My goal for this book is to teach simultaneously both the fundamentals of the Fortran language and a programming style that results in good, maintainable programs.

It is quite difficult to teach undergraduates the importance of taking extra effort during the early stages of the program design process in order to make their programs more maintainable. By their very nature class programming assignments must be simple enough for one person to complete in a short period of time, and they do not have to be maintained for years. Because the projects are simple, a student can often "wing it" and still produce working code. A student can take a course, perform all of the programming assignments, pass all the tests, and still not learn the habits that are really needed when working on large projects in industry.

From the very beginning, this book teaches Fortran in a style suitable for use on large projects. It emphasizes the importance of going through a detailed design process before any code is written, using a top-down design technique to break the program into logical portions that can be implemented separately. It stresses the use of procedures to implement those individual portions and the importance of unit testing before the procedures are combined into a finished product. Finally, it emphasizes the importance of exhaustively testing the finished program with many different input data sets before it is released for use.

FEATURES OF THIS BOOK

Many features of this book emphasize the proper way to write reliable Fortran programs. The following features should serve a student well as he or she is first learning Fortran and should also be useful to the practitioner on the job.

Emphasis on modern Fortran 90/95

The book consistently teaches the best current practice in all of its examples. Many Fortran 90/95 features duplicate and supersede older features of the Fortran language. In those cases the proper usage of the modern language is presented. For a discussion of older features of the language, please see my larger book.

Emphasis on strong typing

The IMPLICIT NONE statement is used consistently throughout the book to force the explicit typing of every variable used in every program and to catch common typographical errors at compilation time. In conjunction with the explicit declaration of every variable in a program, the book emphasizes the importance of creating a data dictionary that describes the purpose of each variable in a program unit.

Emphasis on top-down design methodology

The book introduces a top-down design methodology in Chapter 3 and then uses it consistently throughout the rest of the book. This methodology encourages a student to think about the proper design of a program *before* beginning to code. This approach emphasizes the importance of clearly defining the problem to be solved and the required inputs and outputs before beginning any other work. Once the problem is properly defined, the top-down methodology teaches the student to employ stepwise refinement to break the task down into successively smaller subtasks and to implement the subtasks as separate subroutines or functions. Finally, this book teaches the importance of testing at all stages of the process, both unit testing of the component routines and exhaustive testing of the final product. Several examples are given of programs that work properly for some data sets and then fail for others.

The formal design process taught by the book may be summarized as follows:

1. *Clearly state the problem that you are trying to solve.*

2. *Define the inputs required by the program and the outputs to be produced by the program.*

3. *Describe the algorithm that you intend to implement in the program.* This step involves top-down design and stepwise decomposition, using pseudocode or flow charts.

4. *Turn the algorithm into Fortran statements.*

5. *Test the Fortran program.* This step includes unit testing of specific subprograms and also exhaustive testing of the final program with many data sets.

Emphasis on procedures

The book emphasizes the use of subroutines and functions to logically decompose tasks into smaller subtasks. It teaches the advantages of procedures for data hiding and emphasizes the importance of unit testing before combining procedures into the final program. In addition, the book teaches how to avoid common mistakes programmers make with procedures (e.g., argument type mismatches and array length mismatches). It emphasizes the advantages associated with explicit interfaces to procedures, which allow the Fortran compiler to catch most common programming errors at compilation time.

Good Programming Practice boxes

These boxes highlight good programming practices when they are introduced and are summarized at the end of the chapter. For example:

Good Programming Practice
Always indent the body of an `IF` structure by two or more spaces to improve the readability of the code.

Programming Pitfalls boxes

These boxes highlight common errors so that they can be avoided. For example:

Programming Pitfalls
Beware of integer arithmetic. Integer division often gives unexpected results.

Fortran 95-only features

Fortran 95-only features are distinguished by a special background. For example:

> Fortran 95 provides an intrinsic function NULL() that can be used to nullify a pointer at the time it is declared (or at any time during the execution of a program). In Fortran 95, pointers can be declared and nullified as follows:
>
> ```
>         REAL, POINTER :: p1 = NULL(), p2 = NULL()
>         INTEGER, POINTER :: i1 = NULL()
>         ...
>         (additional specification statements)
> ```

The details of the NULL() function are described in Appendix B.

Emphasis on pointers and dynamic data structures

Chapter 9 contains a detailed discussion of Fortran pointers, including possible problems resulting from the incorrect use of pointers, such as memory leaks and pointers to deallocated memory. The chapter also discusses allocatable arrays.

PEDAGOGICAL FEATURES

The book includes several features designed to aid student comprehension. A total of 20 quizzes appear scattered throughout the chapters, with answers to all questions included in Appendix F. These quizzes can serve as a useful self-test of comprehension. In addition, there are approximately 205 end-of-chapter exercises. Answers to selected exercises are available at the book's Web site, and of course, answers to all exercises are included in the instructor's manual. Good programming practices are highlighted in all chapters with special Good Programming Practice boxes, and common errors are highlighted in Programming Pitfalls boxes. End of chapter materials include Summaries of Good Programming Practice and Summaries of Fortran Statements and Structures. Finally, an extensive Glossary is included in Appendix E.

The book is accompanied by an instructor's manual, containing the solutions to all end-of-chapter exercises. The instructor's manual comes with a floppy disk containing the source code for all examples in the book, all end-of-chapter exercises, and a few useful utilities such as one to convert a fixed-source-form program to free form.

A FINAL NOTE TO THE USER

No matter how hard I try to proofread a document like this book, it is inevitable that some typographical errors will slip through and appear in print. If you should spot any such errors, please drop me a note via the publisher, and I will do my best to eliminate them from subsequent printings and editions. Thank you very much for your help in this matter.

I will maintain a complete list of errata and corrections at the book's World Wide Web site, which is http://www.mhhe.com/engineering/chapman/intro. Please check that site for any updates and/or corrections.

ACKNOWLEDGMENTS

I would like to thank Mr. Bob Runyan of Lahey Computer Systems, Inc., for providing me with copies of Lahey's Fortran 90 compiler to use while developing this book. I would like to thank Mr. Sunil Alagade of Microsoft Corporation for providing me with a copy of Microsoft Fortran Powerstation 4.0 Professional, and Ms. Margaret Day of NAG, Ltd., for providing me with a copy of the NAGWare Fortran 90 compiler. Finally, I would like to thank Ms. Kathy Appellof of Digital Equipment Corporation for providing me with a copy of DEC Visual Fortran version 5.0. I have been able to ensure that every example is compatible with these compilers.

I would especially like to thank Holly Stark and the staff at McGraw-Hill for their excellent support during the development of this book.

Finally, I would like to thank my wife Rosa, and our children Avi, David, Rachel, Aaron, Sarah, Naomi, and Shira for putting up with me during the two years it took me to finish this book. Sometimes it seems that it would never end. Maybe we'll see more of each other now!

Stephen J. Chapman
Adelaide, South Australia
February 9, 1997

C O N T E N T S

Introduction To Computers And The Fortran Language

The computer is the most important invention of the 20th century. It affects our lives profoundly in very many ways. When we go to the grocery store, computers run the scanners that check out our groceries. Computers maintain our bank balances and run the automatic teller machines that allow us to make banking transactions at any time of the day or night. Computers control our telephone and electric power systems, run our microwave ovens and other appliances, and even control the engines in our cars. Almost any business in the developed world would collapse overnight if it were suddenly deprived of its computers. Considering the importance of electronic computers in our lives, it is almost impossible to believe that they were invented just over 50 years ago.

Just what is this device that has had such an impact on all of our lives? A computer is a special type of machine that stores information and can perform mathematical calculations on that information at speeds much faster than human beings can think. A **program,** which is stored in the computer's memory, tells the computer what sequence of calculations are required and which information to perform the calculations on. Most computers are very flexible. For example, if I load a different program into the computer on which I am writing these words, it can also balance my checkbook.

Computers can store huge amounts of information, and with proper programming they can make that information instantly available. For example, a bank's computer can hold the complete list of all the checks and deposits made by every one of its customers. On a larger scale, credit companies use their computers to hold the credit histories of every person in the United States—literally billions of pieces of information. When requested, those computers can search through the billions of pieces of information to recover the credit records of any single person and present those records to the user in a matter of seconds.

It is important to realize that computers do not think as we understand thinking. They merely follow the steps contained in their programs. When a computer appears to be doing something clever, in reality a clever person has written the program that the computer is executing. Our collective human creativity allows the computer to perform its seeming miracles. This book will help you learn how to write programs so that the computer will do what *you* want it to do.

■ **1.1**

THE COMPUTER

A block diagram of a typical computer is shown in Figure 1–1. The major components of the computer are the *central processing unit* (CPU), *main memory, secondary memory,* and *input* and *output devices*. The following paragraphs describe these components.

1.1.1 The CPU

The central processing unit is the heart of any computer. It is divided into a *control unit,* an *arithmetic logic unit* (ALU), and internal memory. The control unit within the CPU controls all the other parts of the computer, and the ALU performs the actual mathematical calculations. The internal memory within a CPU consists of a series of *memory registers* used for the temporary storage of intermediate results during calculations.

The control unit of the CPU interprets the instructions of the computer program. The control unit fetches data values from input devices or main memory, stores them in the memory registers, and also sends data values from memory registers to output devices or main memory. For example, if a program says to multiply two numbers together and save the result, the control unit will fetch the two numbers from main memory and store them in registers. Then it will present the numbers in the registers to the ALU along with directions to multiply them and store the results in another register. Finally, after the ALU multiplies the numbers, the control unit will take the result from the destination register and store it back into main memory.

1.1.2 Main Memory and Secondary Memory

The memory of a computer is divided into two major types of memory: *main* or *primary memory* and *secondary memory*. **Main memory** usually consists of semiconductor chips. It is very fast and relatively expensive. Data that is stored in main memory can be fetched for use in 100 nanoseconds or less (sometimes *much* less) on a modern computer. Because it is so fast, main memory is used to temporarily store the program currently being executed by the computer, as well as the data that the program requires.

Main memory is not used for the permanent storage of programs or data. Most main memory is *volatile,* meaning that it is erased whenever the computer's power is turned off. Besides, main memory is expensive, so we buy only enough to hold the largest programs actually being executed at any given time.

Secondary memory consists of devices that are slower and less expensive than main memory. They can store much more information for much less money than main memory can. In addition, most secondary memory devices are *nonvolatile,* meaning that they retain the programs and data stored in them whenever the computer's power is turned off.

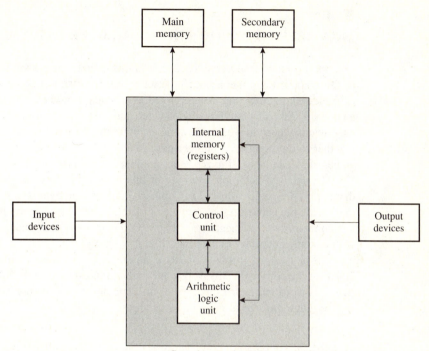

FIGURE 1–1
A block diagram of a typical computer.

Typical secondary memory devices are *hard disks, floppy disks,* and tape drives. Secondary storage devices are normally used to store programs and data that are not needed at the moment but may be needed some time in the future.

1.1.3 Input and Output Devices

Data is entered into a computer through an **input device** and is output through an **output device.** The most common input device on a modern computer is a keyboard. We can use a keyboard to type programs or data into a computer. Other types of input devices found on some computers are scanners and microphones.

Output devices permit us to use the data stored in a computer. The most common output devices on today's computers are CRT screens and printers. Other types of output devices include plotters and speakers.

■ 1.2

DATA REPRESENTATION IN A COMPUTER

Computer memories are composed of millions of individual switches, each of which can be ON or OFF, but not at a state in between. Each switch represents one *binary digit* (also called a **bit**); the ON state is interpreted as a binary 1, and the OFF state is interpreted as a binary 0. Taken by itself, a single switch can only represent the numbers 0 and 1. Since we obviously need to work with numbers other than 0 and 1, a number of bits are grouped together to represent each number used in a computer. When several bits are grouped together, they can be used to represent numbers in the *binary* (base 2) *number system.*

The smallest common grouping of bits is called a **byte.** A *byte* is a group of 8 bits that are used together to represent a binary number. The byte is the fundamental unit used to measure the capacity of a computer's memory. For example, my personal computer has a main memory of 28 megabytes (28,000,000 bytes) and a secondary memory (disk drive) with a storage capacity of 825 megabytes.

The next larger grouping of bits in an computer is called a **word.** A word consists of 2, 4, or more consecutive bytes that are used to represent a single number in memory. The size of a word varies from computer to computer, so words are not a particularly good way to judge the size of computer memories.

1.2.1 The Binary Number System

In the familiar base 10 number system, the smallest (right-most) digit of a number is the one's place (10^0). The next digit is in the 10's place (10^1), and the next one is in the 100's place (10^2), etc. Thus the number 122_{10} is really $(1 \times 10^2) + (2 \times 10^1) + (2 \times 10^0)$. Each digit is worth a power of 10 more than the digit to the right of it in the base 10 system (see Figure 1–2a).

Similarly, in the binary number system, the smallest (right-most) digit is the one's place (2^0). The next digit is in the two's place (2^1), and the next one is in the four's place

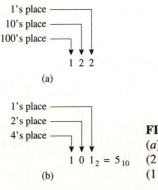

(a)

(b)

FIGURE 1–2
(a) The base 10 number 122 is really $(1 \times 10^2) + (2 \times 10^1) + (2 \times 10^0)$. (b) Similarly, the base 2 number 101_2 is really $(1 \times 2^2) + (0 \times 2^1) + (1 \times 2^0)$.

(2^2), and so on. Each digit is worth a power of two more than the digit to the right of it in the base 2 system. For example, the binary number 101_2 is really $(1 \times 2^2) + (0 \times 2^1) + (1 \times 2^0) = 5$, and the binary number $111_2 = 7$ (see Figure 1–2b).

Note that three binary digits can be used to represent eight possible values: $0 (= 000_2)$ to $7 (= 111_2)$. In general, if n bits are grouped together to form a binary number, then they can represent 2^n possible values. Thus a group of 8 bits (1 byte) can represent 256 possible values, a group of 16 bits (2 bytes) can represent 65,536 possible values, and a group of 32 bits (4 bytes) can represent 4,294,967,296 possible values.

In a typical implementation, half of all possible values are reserved for representing negative numbers, and half of the values are reserved for representing positive numbers. Thus a group of 8 bits (1 byte) is usually used to represent numbers between -128 and $+127$, inclusive, and a group of 16 bits (2 bytes) is usually used to represent numbers between $-32,768$ and $+32,767$, inclusive.

1.2.2 Types of Data Stored In Memory

Three common types of data are stored in a computer's memory: **character data, integer data,** and **real data** (numbers with a decimal point). Each type of data has different characteristics and takes up a different amount of memory in the computer.

Character data

The **character data** type consists of characters and symbols. A typical system for representing character data in a Western language must include the following symbols:

1. The 26 uppercase letters A through Z
2. The 26 lowercase letters a through z
3. The 10 digits 0 through 9
4. Miscellaneous common symbols, such as " , ( ) { } [ ] ! ~ @ # $ % ^ & *.
5. Any special letters or symbols required by the language, such as à ç ë £.

Because the total number of characters and symbols required to write Western languages is less than 256, it is customary to use 1 byte of memory to store each character. Therefore, 10,000 characters would occupy 10,000 bytes of the computer's memory.

The particular bit values corresponding to each letter or symbol may vary from computer to computer, depending on the coding system used for the characters. Two systems are in common use. The most important coding system is **ASCII,** which stands for the American Standard Code for Information Interchange. Most of the computer manufacturers in the world used the ASCII coding system. The other common system is **EBCDIC,** which stands for Extended Binary Coded Decimal Interchange Code. IBM uses EBCDIC on its mainframe computers. The 8-bit codes corresponding to each letter and number in each of the above coding systems are given in Appendix A.

Many countries outside the United States use an international version of the ASCII character set. This set is known as the ISO 646 standard. It is the same as ASCII, except that 10 specific characters may be replaced with the extra symbols needed in a particular country, such as £, å, ñ, and ø. This character set can create problems when a program is moved from one country to another because some symbols will change and printed information might become corrupted.

Some Oriental languages such as Chinese and Japanese contain more than 256 characters (in fact, about 4000 characters are needed to represent each of these languages). To accommodate these languages and all of the other languages in the world, a new coding system called **unicode** has been developed. In the unicode coding system, each character is stored in 2 bytes of memory, so the unicode system supports 65,536 possible different characters. The first 128 unicode characters are identical to the ASCII character set, and other blocks of characters are devoted to various languages such as Chinese, Japanese, Hebrew, Arabic, and Hindi. The unicode coding system can represent character data in any language.

Integer data

The **integer data** type consists of the positive integers, the negative integers, and zero. The amount of memory devoted to storing an integer varies from computer to computer but will usually be 1, 2, 4, or 8 bytes. Four-byte integers are the most common type in modern computers.

Since a finite number of bits is used to store each value, only integers that fall within a certain range can be represented on a computer. Usually, the smallest number that can be stored in an n-bit integer is

$$\text{Smallest Integer Value} = -2^{n-1} \tag{1–1}$$

and the largest number that can be stored in an n-bit integer is

$$\text{Largest Integer Value} = 2^{n-1} - 1 \tag{1–2}$$

For a 4-byte integer, the smallest and largest possible values are $-2,147,483,648$ and $2,147,483,647$, respectively. Attempts to use an integer larger than the largest possible value or smaller than the smallest possible value result in an error called an *overflow condition*.

Real data

The integer data type has two fundamental limitations:

1. It is not possible to represent numbers with fractional parts (0.25, 1.5, 3.14159, etc.) as integer data.
2. It is not possible to represent very large positive integers or very small negative integers because not enough bits are available to represent the value. The largest and smallest possible integers that can be stored in a given memory location are given by Equations (1–1) and (1–2).

To get around these limitations, computers include a **real** or **floating-point** data type.

The real data type stores numbers in a type of scientific notation. We all know that very large or very small numbers can be most conveniently written in scientific notation.

For example, the speed of light in a vacuum is about 299,800,000 meters per second. This number is easier to work with in scientific notation: 2.998×10^8 m/s. The two parts of a number expressed in scientific notation are called the **mantissa** and the **exponent.** The mantissa of the number is 2.998, and the exponent (in the base 10 system) is 8.

The real numbers in a computer are similar to scientific notation except that a computer works in the base 2 system instead of the base 10 system. Real numbers usually occupy 32 bits (4 bytes) of computer memory, divided into two components: a 24-bit mantissa and an 8-bit exponent. (see Figure 1–3) The mantissa contains a number between -1.0 and 1.0, and the exponent contains the power of 2 required to scale the number to its actual value.

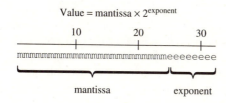

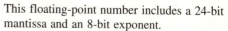

FIGURE 1–3

This floating-point number includes a 24-bit mantissa and an 8-bit exponent.

Real numbers are characterized by two quantities: **precision** and **range.** *Precision* is the number of significant digits that can be preserved in a number, and *range* is the difference between the largest and smallest numbers that can be represented. The precision of a real number depends on the number of bits in its mantissa, whereas the range of the number depends on the number of bits in its exponent. A 24-bit mantissa can represent approximately $\pm 2^{23}$ numbers, or about seven significant decimal digits, so the precision of real numbers is about seven significant digits. An 8-bit exponent can represent multipliers between 2^{-128} and 2^{127}, so the range of real numbers is from about 10^{-38} to 10^{38}. Note that the real data type can represent numbers much larger or much smaller than integers can represent but only with seven significant digits of precision.

When a value with more than seven digits of precision is stored in a real variable, only the most significant seven bits of the number will be preserved. The remaining information will be lost forever. For example, if the value 12,345,678.9 is stored in a real variable on an IBM PC, it will be rounded off to 12,345,680.0. The difference between the original value and the number stored in the computer is known as round-off error.

You will use the real data type in many places throughout this book and in your programs after you finish this course. This data type is quite useful, but you must always remember the limitations associated with round-off error, or your programs might give you an unpleasant surprise. For example, if your program must be able to distinguish between the numbers 1,000,000.0 and 1,000,000.1, then you cannot use the standard real data type. It simply does not have enough precision to tell the difference between these two numbers!

Programming Pitfalls

Always remember the precision and range of the data types that you are working with. Failure to do so can result in subtle programming errors that are very hard to find.

Quiz 1–1

This quiz provides a quick check to see if you understand the concepts introduced in section 1.2. If you have trouble with the quiz, reread the section, ask your instructor, or discuss the material with a fellow student. The answers to this quiz appear in Appendix F.

1. Express the following decimal numbers as their binary equivalents:
    a. 27_{10}
    b. 11_{10}
    c. 35_{10}
    d. 127_{10}

2. Express the following binary numbers as their decimal equivalents:
    a. 1110_2
    b. 01010101_2
    c. 1001_2

3. Is the 4th bit of the number 131_{10} a 1 or a 0?

4. Assume that the following numbers are the contents of a character variable. Find the character corresponding to each number according to the ASCII and EBCDIC coding schemes:
    a. 77_{10}
    b. 01111011_2
    c. 249_{10}

5. Find the maximum and minimum values that can be stored in a 2-byte integer variable.

6. Can a 4-byte variable of the real data type store larger numbers than a 4-byte variable of the integer data type? Why or why not? If it can, what does the real variable give up to make this possible?

■ 1.3

COMPUTER LANGUAGES

When a computer executes a program, it executes a string of very simple operations such as load, store, add, subtract, multiply, and so on. Each such operation has a unique binary pattern called an *operation code (op code)* to specify it. The program that a computer executes is just a string of op codes (and the data associated with the op codes[1]) in the order necessary to achieve a purpose. Op codes are collectively called **machine language,** since they are the actual language that a computer recognizes and executes.

Unfortunately, we humans find machine language very hard to work with. We prefer to work with English-like statements and algebraic equations that are expressed in forms familiar to us, instead of in arbitrary patterns of 0s and 1s. We like to program computers with high-level languages. We write out our instructions in a high-level language and then use special programs called **compilers** and linkers to convert the instructions into the machine language that the computer understands.

Programmers use many different high-level languages, each of which has special characteristics. Some languages are designed to work well for business problems, and others are designed for general scientific use. Still others are especially suited for applications like operating systems programming. It is important to pick a language whose features match the problem that you are trying to solve.

Some common high-level computer languages include Ada, Basic, C, COBOL, Fortran, and Pascal. Of these languages, Fortran is the preeminent language for general scientific computations. It has been around in one form or another for more than 50 years and has been used to implement everything from computer models of nuclear power plants to aircraft design programs to seismic signal processing systems; some Fortran projects have required millions of lines of code. The language is especially useful for numerical analysis and technical calculations. In addition, Fortran is the dominant language in the world of supercomputers and massively parallel computers.

■ 1.4

THE HISTORY OF THE Fortran LANGUAGE

Fortran is the grandfather of all scientific computer languages. The name *Fortran* is derived from FORmula TRANSlation, indicating that the language was intended from the start for translating scientific equations into computer code. IBM developed the first version of the FORTRAN[2] language between 1954 and 1957. Before that time, essentially all computer programs were generated by hand in machine language, which was a slow, tedious, and error-prone process. FORTRAN was a truly revolutionary product. For the

---

[1]The data associated with op codes are called *operands.*

[2]Versions of the language before Fortran 90 were known as FORTRAN (written with all capital letters), while Fortran 90 and later versions are known as Fortran (with only the first letter capitalized).

first time, a programmer could write a desired algorithm as a series of standard algebraic equations, and the FORTRAN compiler would convert the statements into the machine language that the computer could recognize and execute.

The original FORTRAN language was very small compared to our modern versions of Fortran. It contained only a limited number of statement types and supported only the integer and real data types. There were also no subroutines in the first FORTRAN. It was a first effort at writing a high-level computer language, and naturally many deficiencies were found as people started using the language regularly. IBM addressed those problems with its release of FORTRAN II in the spring of 1958.

Further developments continued through 1962, when FORTRAN IV was released. FORTRAN IV was a great improvement, and it became the standard version of Fortran for the next 15 years. In 1966 FORTRAN IV was adopted as an ANSI standard, and it came to be known as FORTRAN 66.

The Fortran language received another major update in 1977. FORTRAN 77 included many new features designed to make structured programs easier to write and maintain, and it quickly became *the* Fortran. FORTRAN 77 introduced such structures as the block IF and was the first version of Fortran in which character variables were truly easy to manipulate.

The next major update of Fortran was Fortran 90.[3] Fortran 90 includes all of FORTRAN 77 as a subset and extends the language in many important new directions. Among the major improvements introduced to the language in Fortran 90 are a new free-source format, array sections, whole-array operations, parameterized data types, derived data types, and explicit interfaces. Fortran 90 is a dramatic improvement over earlier versions of the language.

Fortran 90 was followed in 1997 by a minor update called Fortran 95. Fortran 95 adds a number of new features to the language such as the FORALL construct, pure functions, and some new intrinsic procedures. In addition, it clarifies numerous ambiguities in the Fortran 90 standard.

The subjects of this book are the Fortran 90 and Fortran 95 languages. The vast majority of the book applies to both Fortran 90 and Fortran 95, and we will usually refer to them together as Fortran 90/95. Features that only appear in Fortran 95 are distinguished by the special background shown below. Here is an example of a Fortran 95-specific comment:

> The fixed-source form has been declared obsolescent in Fortran 95, which means that it is a candidate for deletion in future versions of Fortran.

The designers of Fortran 90 and Fortran 95 were careful to make the language backward compatible with FORTRAN 77 and earlier versions. Because of this backward compatibility, most of the millions of programs written in FORTRAN 77 also work with Fortran 90/95. Unfortunately, being backward compatible with earlier versions of Fortran

---

[3] American National Standard Programming Language Fortran, ANSI X3.198-1992; and International Standards Organization ISO/IEC 1539: 1991, Information Technology—Programming Languages—Fortran.

required that Fortran 90/95 retain some archaic features that should never be used in any modern program. *In this text, you will learn to program in* Fortran 90/95 *using only its modern features.* The older features that are retained for backward compatibility are not covered. If you need to know about them, refer to a full-length Fortran book, such as *Fortran 90/95 for Scientists and Engineers.*[4]

■ 1.5
SUMMARY

A computer is a special type of machine that stores information and can perform mathematical calculations on that information at speeds much faster than human beings can think. A program, which is stored in the computer's memory, tells the computer what sequence of calculations are required and which information to perform the calculations on.

The major components of a computer are the central processing unit (CPU), main memory, secondary memory, and input and output devices. The CPU performs all of the control and calculation functions of the computer. Main memory is fast, relatively expensive memory that stores the program being executed and its associated data. Main memory is volatile, meaning that its contents are lost whenever power is turned off. Secondary memory is slower and less expensive than main memory. It is nonvolatile. Hard disks are common secondary memory devices. Input and output devices are used to read data into the computer and to output data from the computer. The most common input device is a keyboard, and the most common output device is a printer.

Computer memories are composed of millions of individual switches, each of which can be ON or OFF, but not at a state in between. These individual switches are binary devices called bits. Eight bits are grouped together to form a byte of memory, and 2 or more bytes (depending on the computer) are grouped together to form a word of memory.

Computer memories can be used to store character, integer, or real data. Each character in most character data sets occupies 1 byte of memory. The 256 possible values in the byte allow for 256 possible character codes. (Characters in the unicode character set occupy 2 bytes, allowing for 65,536 possible character codes.) Integer values occupy 1, 2, 4, or 8 bytes of memory and store integer quantities. Real values store numbers in a kind of scientific notation. They usually occupy 4 bytes of memory. The bits are divided into a separate mantissa and exponent. The precision of the number depends on the number of bits in the mantissa, and the range of the number depends on the number of bits in the exponent.

The earliest computers were programmed in machine language. This process was slow, cumbersome, and error-prone. High-level languages began to appear in about 1954, and they quickly replaced machine language coding for most uses. FORTRAN was one of the earliest high-level languages. The FORTRAN I computer language and compiler were developed between 1954 and 1957. The language has gone through many revisions since then. This book teaches good programming practices using the Fortran 90/95 version of the language.

---

[4]Chapman, *Fortran 90/95 for Scientists and Engineers* (Burr Ridge, IL: McGraw-Hill, 1998).

■ 1.6
EXERCISES

1–1 Express the following decimal numbers as their binary equivalents:

  a. 10_{10}
  b. 32_{10}
  c. 77_{10}
  d. 63_{10}

1–2 Express the following binary numbers as their decimal equivalents:

  a. 01001000_2
  b. 10001001_2
  c. 11111111_2
  d. 0101_2

1–3 Some computers (such as IBM mainframes) implement real data using a 23-bit mantissa and a 9-bit exponent. What precision and range can we expect from real data on these machines?

1–4 Some Cray supercomputers support 46-bit and 64-bit integer data types. What are the maximum and minimum values that we could express in a 46-bit integer? in a 64-bit integer?

1–5 The Fortran language includes a second type of floating-point data known as double precision. A double-precision number usually occupies 8 bytes (64 bits), instead of the 4 bytes occupied by a real number. In the most common implementation, 53 bits are used for the mantissa and 11 bits are used for the exponent. How many significant digits does a double-precision value have? What is the range of double-precision numbers?

Basic Elements of Fortran

■ **2.1**

INTRODUCTION

As engineers and scientists, we design and execute computer programs to accomplish a goal. The goal typically involves technical calculations that would be too difficult or take too long to be performed by hand. Fortran is one of the computer languages commonly used for these technical calculations.

This chapter introduces the basic elements of the Fortran language. By the end of the chapter, you will be able to write simple but functional Fortran programs.

■ **2.2**

THE Fortran CHARACTER SET

Every language, whether it is a natural language such as English or a computer language such as Fortran, Pascal, or C, has its own special alphabet. Only the characters in this alphabet may be used with the language.

The special alphabet used with the Fortran 90/95 language is known as the **Fortran character set.** It consists of the 86 symbols shown in Table 2–1.

■ **TABLE 2–1**
The Fortran 90/95 character set

26	Uppercase letters of the alphabet: A through Z
26	Lowercase letters of the alphabet: a through z
10	Digits: 0 through 9
1	Underscore character: _
5	Arithmetic symbols: + - * / **
18	Miscellaneous symbols: ( ) . = , ' $: ! " % & ; < > ? $ and blank

Note that the uppercase letters of the alphabet are equivalent to the lowercase ones in the Fortran character set. (For example, the uppercase letter A is equivalent to the lowercase letter a.) In other words, Fortran is *case insensitive*. This behavior is in contrast with such case sensitive languages as C in which A and a are two totally different things.

■ **2.3**

THE STRUCTURE OF A Fortran STATEMENT

A Fortran program consists of a series of *statements* designed to accomplish the goal of the programmer. The two basic types of statements are **executable statements** and **nonexecutable statements.** Executable statements describe the actions a program takes when it is executed (e.g., additions, subtractions, multiplications, divisions), while nonexecutable statements provide information necessary for the proper operation of the program. You will see many examples of each type of statement throughout this book.

As I mentioned in Chapter 1, Fortran was one of the first major computer languages to be developed. It originated in the days before terminals and keyboards, when the punched card was the major form of input to the computer. Each punched card had a fixed length of 80 columns, and one character, number, or symbol could be typed in each column. The structure of statements in early versions of Fortran reflected this fixed limitation of 80 characters per line. By contrast, Fortran 90 and Fortran 95 were developed in the age of the terminal and keyboard, so they allow free entry of statements in any column.

In the modern **free-source form,** Fortran statements may be entered anywhere on a line, and each line may be up to 132 characters long. If a statement is too long to fit on a single line, then it may be continued on the next line by ending the current line (and optionally starting the next line) with an ampersand (&) character. For example, the following three Fortran statements are identical:

```
100 output = input1 + input2     ! Sum the inputs
100 output = input1 &
            + input2             ! Sum the inputs
100 output = input1 &
            & + input2           ! Sum the inputs
```

Each statement tells the computer to add the two quantities stored in input1 and input2 and to save the result in output. A statement can continue over 40 lines.

In the preceding statements, the numbers at the beginning of the line are called **statement labels.** A statement label is a number between 1 and 99999. It is the "name" of a Fortran statement and may be used to refer to a statement from other parts of the program. Note that a statement label has no other significance. It is *not* a line number, and it tells nothing about the order in which statements are executed. For example, one line of a program could be labeled 9999, and the very next line of the program could be labeled 1. The two lines would be executed in the same order regardless of the specific label assigned to each statement. Statement labels are optional, and most Fortran 90/95 statements will not have one. If a statement label is used, it must be unique within a given

program unit.[1] For example, if 100 is used as a statement label on a line, it cannot be used again as a statement label on any other line in the same program unit.

Any characters following an exclamation point are **comments** and are ignored by the Fortran compiler. All text from the exclamation point to the end of the line will be ignored, regardless of the position of the exclamation point in the line. Therefore, comments may appear on the same line as an executable statement. Comments are very important because they help us document the proper operation of a program. In the third example, the comment is ignored, so the compiler treats the ampersand as the last character on the line.

■ 2.4

THE STRUCTURE OF A Fortran PROGRAM

Each Fortran program consists of a mixture of executable and nonexecutable statements, which must occur in a specific order. An example of a simple Fortran program is shown in Figure 2–1. This program reads in two numbers, multiplies them together, and prints out the result. An explanation of the significant features of this program follows the figure.

FIGURE 2–1
A simple Fortran program.

```
PROGRAM my_first_program

! Purpose:
!   To illustrate some of the basic features of a Fortran program.
!

! Declare the variables used in this program.
INTEGER :: i, j, k                ! All variables are integers

! Get the variables to multiply together.
WRITE (*,*) 'Enter the numbers to multiply: '
READ (*,*) i, j

! Multiply the numbers together
k = i * j

! Write out the result.
WRITE (*,*) 'Result = ', k

!   Finishup.
STOP
END PROGRAM
```

This Fortran program, like all Fortran program units, is divided into three sections:

---

[1]A *program unit* is a separately compiled piece of Fortran code. You will learn about several other types of program units beginning in Chapter 6.

1. *The declaration section.* This section consists of a group of nonexecutable statements at the beginning of the program that define the name of the program and the number and types of variables referenced in the program.
2. *The execution section.* This section consists of one or more statements describing the actions to be performed by the program.
3. *The termination section.* This section consists of a statement or statements stopping the execution of the program and telling the compiler that the program is complete.

Note that comments may be inserted freely anywhere within, before, or after the program.

2.4.1 The Declaration Section

The declaration section contains the nonexecutable statements at the beginning of the program that define the name of the program and the number and types of variables referenced in the program.

The first statement in this section is the PROGRAM statement. It is a nonexecutable statement that specifies the name of the program to the Fortran compiler. Fortran program names may be up to 31 characters long and contain any combination of alphabetic characters, digits, and the underscore (_) character. However, the first character in a program name must always be alphabetic. If present, the PROGRAM statement must be the first noncomment line of the program. In Figure 2–1 the name of the program is my_first_program.

The next several lines in the program are comments. These comments describe the purpose of the program.

Next comes the INTEGER type declaration statement. This nonexecutable statement is described later in this chapter. It declares that three integer variables called i, j, and k will be used in my_first_program.

2.4.2 The Execution Section

The execution section contains one or more executable statements describing the actions to be performed by the program.

The first executable statement in this program is the WRITE statement, which writes out a message prompting the user to enter the two numbers to be multiplied together. The next executable statement is a READ statement, which reads in the two integers supplied by the user. The third executable statement instructs the computer to multiply the two numbers i and j together and to store the result in variable k. The final WRITE statement prints out the result for the user to see. Comments may be embedded anywhere throughout the execution section.

These statements are explained in detail later in this chapter.

2.4.3 The Termination Section

The termination section consists of the STOP and END PROGRAM statements. The STOP statement is a statement that tells the computer to stop running the program. The END PROGRAM statement is a statement that tells the compiler that there are no more statements to be compiled in the program.

When the STOP statement immediately precedes the END PROGRAM statement as in Figure 2–1, it is optional. The compiler will automatically generate a STOP command when the END PROGRAM statement is reached. The STOP statement is therefore rarely used.

2.4.4 Program Style

my_first_program follows the widely used Fortran convention of capitalizing keywords such as PROGRAM, READ, and WRITE and using lowercase for the program variables. This convention is *not* a Fortran requirement; the program would have worked just as well with all capital letters or all lowercase letters. Because uppercase and lowercase letters are equivalent in Fortran, the program functions identically in either case.

This book follows the convention of capitalizing Fortran keywords and using lowercase for variables, parameters, and so on. Although you do not have to follow this convention, you should always be consistent in the way you write your programs. Establish a standard practice, or adopt the standard practice of the organization in which you work, and then follow it consistently in all of your programs.

> **Good Programming Practice**
> Adopt a programming style and then follow it consistently in all of your programs.

2.4.5 Compiling, Linking, and Executing the Fortran Program

Before the sample program can be run, it must be compiled into object code with a Fortran compiler and then linked with a computer's system libraries to produce an executable program (see Figure 2–2). These two steps are usually done together in response to a single programmer command. The details of compiling and linking are different for every compiler and operating system. You should ask your instructor or consult the appropriate manuals to determine the proper procedure for your system.

Depending on the computer and operating system being used, Fortran programs may be compiled, linked, and run in either *batch mode* or *interactive mode*. In batch mode the commands required to compile, link, and run the program are written into a file along with any data required by the program. This file is then submitted to the *batch processor,*

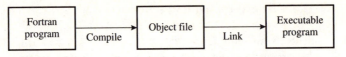

FIGURE 2–2
Creating an executable Fortran program involves two steps, compiling and linking.

which compiles, links, and executes the program without user intervention. In interactive mode, the program is compiled, linked, and executed by commands entered by a user at a terminal or keyboard. A program that is executed in interactive mode can prompt the user for input while it is running. A program under development is usually run in interactive mode so that the programmer can immediately see whether it is working properly.

2.5
CONSTANTS AND VARIABLES

A Fortran **constant** is a data object that is defined before a program is executed and that does not change value during the execution of the program. When a Fortran compiler encounters a constant, it places the value of the constant in a known location in memory and then references that memory location whenever the constant is used in the program.

A Fortran **variable** is a data object that can change value during the execution of a program. (The value of a Fortran variable may or may not be initialized before a program is executed.) When a Fortran compiler encounters a variable, it reserves a known location in memory for the variable and then references that memory location whenever the variable is used in the program.

Each Fortran variable in a program unit must have a unique name. Fortran names may be up to 31 characters long and may contain any combination of alphabetic characters, digits, and the underscore (_) character. However, the first character in a name must always be alphabetic. The following examples are valid variable names:

```
time

distance

z123456789

I_want_to_go_home
```

The following examples are invalid variable names:

```
this_is_a_very_long_variable_name          (Name is too long.)

3_days                                      (First character is a number.)

A$                                          ($ is an illegal character.)

my-help                                     (- is an illegal character.)
```

When writing a program, you should always pick meaningful names for the variables. Meaningful names make a program *much* easier to read and to maintain. Names such as day, month, and year are quite clear even to a person seeing a program for the first time. Because spaces cannot be used in Fortran variable names, underscore characters can be substituted to created meaningful names. For example, *exchange rate* might become exchange_rate.

Good Programming Practice
Use meaningful variable names whenever possible.

You should also include a **data dictionary** in the header of any program that you write. A data dictionary defines each variable used in a program. The definition should include both a description of the contents of the item and the units in which it is measured. A data dictionary may seem unnecessary while the program is being written, but it is invaluable when you or another person have to go back and modify the program at a later time.

Good Programming Practice
Create a data dictionary for each program to make program maintenance easier.

There are five intrinsic or built-in types of Fortran constants and variables. Three of them are numeric (types INTEGER, REAL, and COMPLEX), one is logical (type LOGICAL), and one consists of strings of characters (type CHARACTER). The simplest forms of the INTEGER, REAL, CHARACTER, and LOGICAL data types are discussed in the following sections. A discussion of their more advanced forms and a discussion of the COMPLEX data type are postponed until Chapter 7.

In addition to the intrinsic data types, Fortran permits a programmer to define **derived data types,** which are special data types intended to solve a particular problem. Derived data types are discussed in Chapter 7.

2.5.1 Integer Constants and Variables

An *integer constant* is any number that does not contain a decimal point. These constants can be positive, negative, or zero. If a constant is positive, it may be written either with or without a plus sign. No commas may be embedded within an integer constant. The following examples are valid integer constants:

```
0

-999

123456789

+17
```

The following examples are *not* valid integer constants:

```
1,000,000    (Embedded commas are illegal.)

100.         (If it has a decimal point, it is not an integer constant!)
```

The integer data type was described in Chapter 1.

An *integer variable* is a variable containing a value of the integer data type.

Constants and variables of the integer data type are usually stored in a single word on a computer. Since the length of a word varies from 16 bits up to 64 bits on different computers, the largest integer which can be stored in the computer also varies. Table 2-2 shows the largest and smallest possible integers on several common computers. Note that some computers support more than one length of integer. (The largest and smallest integers can be determined from the number of bits by using Equations 1-1 and 1-2.)

TABLE 2–2
Minimum and maximum possible integers on several computers

Computer	Bits	Minimum value	Maximum value
VAX minicomputer	32	−2,147,483,648	2,147,483,647
IBM 370 mainframe	32	−2,147,483,648	2,147,483,647
PC compatible	32	−2,147,483,648	2,147,483,647
	16*	−32,768*	32,767*

*Indicates optional length. The default length is given first.

Many Fortran 90/95 compilers support integers with more than one length. For example, most PC compilers support both 16-bit integers and 32-bit integers. These different lengths of integers are known as different **kinds** of integers. Fortran 90/95 has an explicit mechanism for choosing which kind of integer is used for a given value. This mechanism is explained in detail in Chapter 7.

2.5.2 Real Constants and Variables

A *real constant* is any number with a decimal point. These numbers can be written with or without an exponent, and they can be positive, negative, or zero. If a constant is positive, it may be written either with or without a plus sign. No commas may be embedded within a real constant. The real data type corresponds to the floating-point number described in Chapter 1.

Real constants may be written with or without an exponent. If used, an exponent consists of the letter E followed by a positive or negative integer that corresponds to the power of 10 used when the number is written in scientific notation. If the exponent is positive, the plus sign may be omitted. The mantissa of the number (the part of the number that precedes the exponent) should contain a decimal point. The following examples are valid real constants:

```
10.

-999.9

1.0E-3        (= 1.0 × 10⁻³, or 0.001)

123.45E20     (= 123.45 × 10²⁰, or 1.2345 × 10²²)

0.12E+1       (= 0.12 × 10¹, or 1.2)
```

The following examples are *not* valid real constants:

```
1,000,000.    (Embedded commas are illegal.)

111E3         (A decimal point is required in the mantissa.)

-12.0E1.5     (Decimal points are not allowed in exponents)
```

A real constant is stored in the computer in two parts: the mantissa and the exponent. The number of bits allocated to the mantissa determines the *precision* of the constant (that is, the number of significant digits to which the constant is known), while the number of bits allocated to the exponent determines the *range* of the constant (that is, the largest and the smallest values that can be represented). For a given word size, the more precise a real number is, the smaller its range is, and vice versa, as described in Chapter 1.

A *real variable* is a variable containing a value of the real data type.

All Fortran 90/95 compilers support real numbers with more than one length. For example, PC compilers support both 32-bit real numbers and 64-bit real numbers. These different lengths of real numbers are different *kinds* of real numbers. You can increase the precision and range of a real constant or variable by selecting the proper kind. You will learn how to specify which particular kind of real number to use for a given value in Chapter 7.

2.5.3 Character Constants and Variables

A *character constant* is a string of characters enclosed in single (') or double (") quotes. The minimum number of characters in a string is 1, while the maximum number of characters in a string varies from compiler to compiler. The maximum number of characters is often as large as 32,767.

The characters between the two single or double quotes are said to be in a **character context.** Any characters representable on a computer are legal in a character context, not just the 86 characters forming the Fortran character set.

The following are valid character constants:

```
'This is a test!'
"This is a test!"
' '                        (A single blank.)
'{^}'                      (These characters are legal in a character
                           context even though they are not a part of
                           the Fortran character set.)
'3.141593'                 (A character string, not a number.)
```

The following are not valid character constants:

```
This is a test!          (No single or double quotes.)
'This is a test!"        (Mismatched quotes.)
''Try this one.'         (Unbalanced single quotes.)
```

If a character string must include an apostrophe, then that apostrophe may be represented by two consecutive single quotes. For example, the string "Man's best friend" would be written in a character constant as

```
'Man''s best friend'
```

Alternatively, the character string containing a single quote can be surrounded by double quotes. For example, the string "Man's best friend" could be written in a character constant as

```
"Man's best friend"
```

Similarly, a character string containing double quotes can be surrounded by single quotes. The character string "Who cares?" could be written in a character constant as

```
'"Who cares?"'
```

Character constants are most often used to print descriptive information using the WRITE statement. For example, the string 'Result = ' in Figure 2–1 is a valid character constant:

```
WRITE (*,*) 'Result = ', k
```

A **character variable** is a variable containing a value of the character data type.

2.5.4 Logical Constants and Variables

A *logical constant* is a constant that can take on one of two possible values: .TRUE. or .FALSE.. (Note that the periods are required on either side of the values to distinguish them from variable names.)

The following are valid logical constants:

```
.TRUE.

.FALSE.
```

The following are not valid logical constants:

        TRUE   (No periods—this is a variable name.)

        .FALSE   (Unbalanced periods.)

Logical constants are rarely used, but logical expressions and variables are commonly used to control program execution (see Chapter 3).

A logical variable is a variable containing a value of the logical data type.

2.5.5 Default and Explicit Variable Typing

When we look at a constant, it is easy to see whether it is an integer, real, character, or logical constant. If a number does not have a decimal point, it is of type integer; if it has a decimal point, it is of type real. If the constant is enclosed in single or double quotes, it is of type character. If it is .TRUE. or .FALSE., it is of type logical. With variables, the situation is not so clear. How do we (or the compiler) know if the variable junk contains an integer, real, character, or logical value?

There are two possible ways in which the type of a variable can be defined: *default typing* and *explicit typing*. If the type of a variable is not explicitly specified in the program, then default typing is used. By default:

Any variable names beginning with the letters I, J, K, L, M, or N are assumed to be of type INTEGER. Any variable names starting with another letter are assumed to be of type REAL.

Therefore, a variable called incr is assumed to be of type integer by default, while a variable called big is assumed to be of type real by default. This default typing convention goes all the way back to the original FORTRAN I in 1954. Note that no variable names are of types character or logical by default because these data types didn't exist in FORTRAN I!

The type of a variable may also be explicitly defined in the declaration section at the beginning of a program. The following Fortran statements can be used to specify the type of variables:

```
INTEGER :: var1, var2, var3, ...
REAL ::    var1, var2, var3, ...
LOGICAL :: var1, var2, var3, ...
```

These nonexecutable statements are called **type declaration statements.** They should be placed after the PROGRAM statement and before the first executable statement in the program, as shown in the following example:

```
PROGRAM example
INTEGER :: day, month, year
REAL :: second
LOGICAL :: test1, test2
(Executable statements)
```

No default names are associated with the character data type, so all character variables must be explicitly typed using the CHARACTER type declaration statement. This statement is a bit more complicated than the previous ones, since character variables may be of different lengths. Its form is

```
CHARACTER(len=<len>) :: var1, var2, var3, ...
```

where <len> is the number of characters in the variables. The (len=<len>) portion of the statement is optional. If only a number appears in the parentheses, then the character variables declared by the statement are of that length. If the parentheses are entirely absent, then the character variables declared by the statement have length 1. For example, the type declaration statements

```
CHARACTER(len=10) :: first, last
CHARACTER :: initial
CHARACTER(15) :: id
```

define two 10-character variables called first and last, a 1-character variable called initial, and a 15-character variable called id.

2.5.6 Keeping Constants Consistent in a Program

You should strive to always keep your physical constants consistent throughout a program. For example, do not use the value 3.14 for π at one point in a program and 3.141593 at another point in the program. Also, you should always write your constants with at least as much precision as your computer will accept. If the real data type on your computer has seven significant digits of precision, then π should be written as 3.141593, *not* as 3.14!

The best way to achieve consistency and precision throughout a program is to assign a name to a constant and then to use that name to refer to the constant throughout the program. If we assign the name pi to the constant 3.141593, then we can refer to pi by name throughout the program and be certain that we are getting the same value everywhere. Furthermore, assigning meaningful names to constants improves the overall readability of our programs because a programmer can tell at a glance just what the constant represents.

Named constants are created using the PARAMETER attribute of a type declaration statement. The form of a type declaration statement with a PARAMETER attribute is

```
type, PARAMETER :: name = value [, name2 = value2, ...]
```

where type is the type of the constant (integer, real, logical, or character), and *name* is the name assigned to constant *value*. Note that more than one named constant may be declared on a single line if they are separated by commas. For example, the following statement assigns the name pi to the constant 3.141593:

```
REAL, PARAMETER :: pi = 3.141593
```

If the named constant is of type character, then it is not necessary to declare the length of the character string. Since the named constant is being defined on the same line as its type declaration, the Fortran compiler can directly count the number of characters in the string. For example, the following statements declare a named constant `error_mes-sage` to be the 14-character string `Unknown error!`.

```
CHARACTER, PARAMETER :: error_message = 'Unknown error!'
```

Good Programming Practice
Keep your physical constants consistent and precise throughout a program. To improve the consistency and understandability of your code, assign a name to all important constants and refer to them by name in the program.

Quiz 2–1

This quiz provides a quick check to see if you understand the concepts introduced in section 2.5. If you have trouble with the quiz, reread the section, ask your instructor, or discuss the material with a fellow student. The answers to this quiz appear in Appendix F.

Questions 1 to 14 contain a list of valid and invalid constants. State whether or not each constant is valid. If the constant is valid, specify its type. If it is invalid, explain why it is invalid.

1. `10.0`

2. `-100,000`

3. `123E-5`

4. `'That's ok!'`

5. `-32768`

6. `3.14159`

7. `"Who are you?"`

8. `.TRUE.`

9. `'3.14159'`

10. `'Distance =`

11. `"That's ok!"`

12. `17.877E+6`

(continued)

(concluded)

13. `FALSE.`

14. `13.0^2`

Questions 15 to 18 contain two real constants each. Tell whether or not the two constants represent the same value within the computer:

15. `4650.; 4.65E+3`

16. `-12.71; -1.27E1`

17. `0.0001; 1.0E4`

18. `3.14159E0; 314.159E-3`

Questions 19 and 20 contain a list of valid and invalid Fortran 90/95 program names. State whether or not each program name is valid. If it is invalid, explain why it is invalid.

19. `PROGRAM new_program`

20. `PROGRAM 3rd`

Questions 21 to 25 contain a list of valid and invalid Fortran 90/95 variable names. State whether or not each variable name is valid. If the variable name is valid, specify its type (assume default typing). If it is invalid, say why it is invalid.

21. `length`

22. `distance`

23. `1problem`

24. `when_does_school_end`

25. `_ok`

Are the following `PARAMETER` declarations correct or incorrect? If a statement is incorrect, state why it is invalid.

26. `REAL, PARAMETER begin = -30`

27. `CHARACTER, PARAMETER :: name = 'Steve'`

■ **2.6**

ASSIGNMENT STATEMENTS AND ARITHMETIC CALCULATIONS

Calculations are specified in Fortran with an **assignment statement** whose general form is

`variable_name = expression`

The assignment statement calculates the value of the expression to the right of the equal sign and *assigns* that value to the variable named on the left of the equal sign. Note that the equal sign does not mean *equality* in the usual sense of the word. Instead, it means "store the value of `expression` into location `variable_name`." For this reason, the equal sign is called the **assignment operator.** A statement such as

$$i = i + 1$$

is complete nonsense in ordinary algebra but makes perfect sense in Fortran. In Fortran it means to take the current value stored in variable `i`, add 1 to it, and store the result back into variable `i`.

The expression to the right of the assignment operator can contain any valid combination of constants, variables, parentheses, and arithmetic or logical operators. The standard arithmetic operators included in Fortran are

+	Addition
–	Subtraction
*	Multiplication
/	Division
**	Exponentiation

Note that the symbols for multiplication (`*`), division (`/`), and exponentiation (`**`) are not the ones used in ordinary mathematical expressions. These special symbols were chosen because they were available in 1950s-era computer character sets and because they were different from the characters being used in variable names.

The five arithmetic operators described above are **binary operators,** which means that they should occur between and apply to two variables or constants, as shown:

```
a + b
a - b
a * b
a / b
a ** b
```

In addition, the + and – symbols can occur as **unary operators,** which means that they apply to one variable or constant, as shown:

```
+23
-a
```

You must be sure to follow certain rules when using Fortran arithmetic operators:

1. No two operators may occur side by side. Thus the expression `a * -b` is illegal. In Fortran it must be written as `a * (-b)`. Similarly, `a ** -2` is illegal and should be written as `a ** (-2)`.

2. Implied multiplication is illegal in Fortran. An expression such as $x(y + z)$ means that we should add y and z and then multiply the result by x. The implied multiplication must be written explicitly in Fortran as x * (y + z).

3. Parentheses may be used to group terms whenever desired. When parentheses are used, the expressions inside the parentheses are evaluated before the expressions outside the parentheses. For example, the expression 2** ((8+2)/5) is evaluated as

$$
\begin{aligned}
2 \text{ ** } ((8+2)/5) &= 2 \text{ ** } (10/5) \\
&= 2 \text{ ** } 2 \\
&= 4
\end{aligned}
$$

2.6.1 Integer Arithmetic

Integer arithmetic is arithmetic involving only integer constants and variables. Integer arithmetic always produces a result that is an integer. Therefore, if the division of two integers is not itself an integer, the computer automatically truncates the fractional part of the answer. This behavior can lead to surprising and unexpected answers. For example, integer arithmetic produces the following strange results:

$$\frac{3}{4} = 0 \quad \frac{4}{4} = 1 \quad \frac{5}{4} = 1 \quad \frac{6}{4} = 1$$

$$\frac{7}{4} = 1 \quad \frac{8}{4} = 2 \quad \frac{9}{4} = 2$$

Because of this behavior, you should *never* use integers to calculate real-world quantities that vary continuously, such as distance, speed, and time. Use integers only for items that are intrinsically integer, such as counters and indices.

Programming Pitfalls

Beware of integer arithmetic. Integer division often gives unexpected results.

2.6.2 Real Arithmetic

Real arithmetic (or **floating-point arithmetic**) is arithmetic involving real constants and variables. Real arithmetic always produces a result that is real. The results of calculations with real numbers are essentially what we would expect. For example, real arithmetic produces the following results:

$$\frac{3.}{4.} = 0.75 \quad \frac{4.}{4.} = 1. \quad \frac{5.}{4.} = 1.25 \quad \frac{6.}{4.} = 1.50$$

$$\frac{7.}{4.} = 1.75 \qquad \frac{8.}{4.} = 2. \qquad \frac{9.}{4.} = 2.25 \qquad \frac{1.}{3.} = 0.3333333$$

However, real numbers do have peculiarities of their own. Because of the finite word length of a computer, some real numbers cannot be represented exactly. For example, the number 1/3 is equal to 0.33333333333 ... , but since the numbers stored in the computer have limited precision, the representation of 1/3 in the computer might be 0.3333333. As a result of this limitation in precision, some quantities that are theoretically equal will not be equal when evaluated by the computer. For example, on some computers 3 . * (1./3.) ≠ 1., but 2 . * (1./2.) = 1. Tests for equality must be performed very cautiously when working with real numbers.

Programming Pitfalls
Beware of real arithmetic: Limited precision can cause two theoretically identical expressions to give slightly different results.

2.6.3 Hierarchy of Operations

Often, many arithmetic operations are combined into a single expression. For example, consider the equation for the distance traveled by an object starting from rest and subjected to a constant acceleration:

```
distance = 0.5 * accel * time ** 2
```

This expression contains two multiplications and an exponentiation. In such an expression, it is important to know the order in which the operations are evaluated. If exponentiation is evaluated before multiplication, this expression is equivalent to

```
distance = 0.5 * accel * (time ** 2)
```

But if multiplication is evaluated before exponentiation, this expression is equivalent to

```
distance = (0.5 * accel * time) ** 2
```

These two equations have different results, and we must be able to unambiguously distinguish between them.

To make the evaluation of expressions unambiguous, Fortran has established a series of rules governing the hierarchy or order in which operations are evaluated within an expression. The Fortran rules generally follow the normal rules of algebra. Arithmetic operations in an expression are evaluated in the following order:

1. The contents of all parentheses are evaluated first, starting from the innermost parentheses and working outward.
2. All exponentials are evaluated, working from right to left.

3. All multiplications and divisions are evaluated, working from left to right.
4. All additions and subtractions are evaluated, working from left to right.

These rules confirm that the first of our two possible interpretations is correct—time is squared before the multiplications are performed.

EXAMPLE 2–1 Variables a, b, c, d, e, f, and g have been initialized to the following values:

$$a = 3. \qquad b = 2. \qquad c = 5. \qquad d = 4.$$
$$e = 10. \qquad f = 2. \qquad g = 3.$$

Evaluate the following Fortran assignment statements:

a. `output = a*b+c*d+e/f**g`
b. `output = a*(b+c)*d+(e/f)**g`
c. `output = a*(b+c)*(d+e)/f**g`

SOLUTION

a. Expression to evaluate: `output = a*b+c*d+e/f**g`

   Fill in numbers: `output = 3.*2.+5.*4.+10./2.**3.`

   Evaluate 2.**3.:   `output = 3.*2.+5.*4.+10./8.`

   Evaluate multiplications
   and divisions from left
   to right: `output = 6. +5.*4.+10./8.`
                                         `output = 6. +20.  +10./8.`
                                         `output = 6. +20.  + 1.25`

   Evaluate additions: `output = 27.25`

b. Expression to evaluate: `output = a* (b+c)*d+(e/f)**g`

   Fill in numbers: `output = 3.*(2.+5.)*4.+(10./2.)**3.`

   Evaluate parentheses: `output = 3.*7.*4.+5.**3.`

   Evaluate exponents: `output = 3.*7.*4.+125.`

   Evaluate multiplications
   and divisions from left
   to right: `output = 21.*4.+125.`
                                         `output = 84. + 125.`

   Evaluate additions: `output = 209.`

c. Expression to evaluate: `output = a*(b+c)*(d+e)/f**g`

   Fill in numbers: `output = 3.*(2.+5.)*(4.+10.)/2.**3.`

Evaluate parentheses:	output = 3.*7.*14./2.**3.
Evaluate exponents:	output = 3.*7.*14./8.
Evaluate multiplications and divisions from left to right:	output = 21.*14./8.
	output = 294./8.
	output = 36.75

As Example 2–1 shows, the order in which operations are performed has a major effect on the final result of an algebraic expression.

EXAMPLE 2–2 Variables a, b, and c have been initialized to the following values:

```
a = 3.    b = 2.    c = 3.
```

Evaluate the following Fortran assignment statements:

a. output = a**(b**c)
b. output = (a**b)**c
c. output = a**b**c

SOLUTION

a. Expression to evaluate: output = a**(b**c)

   Fill in numbers: output = 3.**(2.**3.)

   Evaluate expression in parentheses: output = 3.**8.

   Evaluate remaining expression: output = 6561.

b. Expression to evaluate: output = (a**b)**c

   Fill in numbers: output = (3.**2.)**3.

   Evaluate expression in parentheses: output = 9.**3.

   Evaluate remaining expression: output = 729.

c. Expression to evaluate: output = a**b**c

   Fill in numbers: output = 3.**2.**3.

   Evaluate right-most exponent: output = 3.**8.

   Evaluate remaining exponent: output = 6561.

The results of (*a*) and (*c*) are identical, but the expression in (*a*) is easier to understand and is less ambiguous than the expression in (*c*).

Every expression in a program must be clear so that the program can be maintained and modified when necessary. You should always ask yourself, Will I easily understand this expression if I come back to it in six months? Can another programmer look at my code and easily understand what I am doing? If you have any doubt about the clarity of an expression, use extra parentheses to make the meaning clear.

Good Programming Practice
Use parentheses as necessary to make your expressions clear and easy to understand.

If parentheses are used within an expression, then the parentheses must be balanced. That is, the expression must have an equal number of open parentheses and close parentheses. It is an error to have more of one type than the other. Errors of this sort are usually typographical, and the Fortran compiler will catch them. For example, the expression

```
(2. + 4.) / 2.
```

is legal and evaluates to 3.0, whereas the expression

```
(2. + 4.) / 2.)
```

produces an error during compilation because of the mismatched parentheses.

2.6.4 Mixed-Mode Arithmetic

When an arithmetic operation is performed using two real numbers, its immediate result is of type real. Similarly, when an arithmetic operation is performed using two integers, the result is of type integer. In general, arithmetic operations are only defined between numbers of the same type. For example, the addition of two real numbers is a valid operation, and the addition of two integers is a valid operation, but the addition of a real number and an integer is *not* a valid operation. This behavior is true because real numbers and integers are stored in completely different forms in the computer.

What happens if an operation is between a real number and an integer? Expressions containing both real numbers and integers are called **mixed-mode expressions,** and arithmetic involving both real numbers and integers is called *mixed-mode arithmetic*. In the case of an operation between a real number and an integer, the integer is converted by the computer into a real number, and real arithmetic is used on the numbers. The result is of type real. For example, consider the following equations:

Integer expression:	$\dfrac{3}{2}$	is evaluated to be 1	(integer result)
Real expression:	$\dfrac{3.}{2.}$	is evaluated to be 1.5	(real result)
Mixed-mode expression:	$\dfrac{3.}{2}$	is evaluated to be 1.5	(real result)

The rules governing mixed-mode arithmetic can be confusing to beginning programmers, and even experienced programmers may trip up on them from time to time. Errors are especially common when the mixed-mode expression involves division. Consider the following expressions:

	Expression	Result
1.	`1 + 1/4`	`1`
2.	`1. + 1/4`	`1.`
3.	`1 + 1./4`	`1.25`

Expression 1 contains only integers, so it is evaluated by integer arithmetic. In integer arithmetic, `1/4 = 0` and `1 + 0 = 1`, so the final result is `1` (an integer). Expression 2 is a mixed-mode expression containing both real numbers and integers. However, the first operation to be performed is a division because division comes before addition in the hierarchy of operations. The division is between integers, so the result is `1 / 4 = 0`. Next comes an addition between a floating-point `1.` and an integer `0`, so the compiler converts the integer `0` into a real number and then performs the addition. The resulting number is `1.` (a real number). Expression 3 is also a mixed-mode expression containing both real numbers and integers. The first operation to be performed is a division between a real number and an integer, so the compiler converts the integer `4` into a real number and then performs the division. The result is a real `0.25`. The next operation to be performed is an addition between an integer `1` and a real `0.25`, so the compiler converts the integer `1` into a real number and then performs the addition. The resulting number is `1.25` (a real number).

To summarize:

1. An operation between an integer and a real number is called a mixed-mode operation, and an expression containing one or more such operations is called a mixed-mode expression.
2. When a mixed-mode operation is encountered, Fortran converts the integer into a real number and then performs the operation to get a real result.
3. The automatic mode conversion does not occur until a real number and an integer both appear in the *same* operation. Therefore, a portion of an expression can be evaluated in integer arithmetic, and another portion can be evaluated in real arithmetic.

Automatic type conversion also occurs when the variable to which the expression is assigned is of a different type than the result of the expression. For example, consider the following assignment statement:

$$nres = 1.25 + 9 / 4$$

where `nres` is an integer. The expression to the right of the equal sign evaluates to `3.25`, which is a real number. Since `nres` is an integer, the `3.25` is automatically converted into the integer number `3` before being stored in `nres`.

Now consider the following assignment statement:

$$\text{ave} = \text{(n1 + n2) / 2}$$

where n1 and n2 are integers and ave is a real number. The expression to the right of the equal sign will be performed in integer arithmetic; however, because ave is a real variable, the result will be converted to real form before being stored in ave.

> ### Programming Pitfalls
> Mixed-mode expressions are dangerous because they are hard to understand and may produce misleading results. Avoid them whenever possible.

Later in this chapter, we will learn about type conversion functions, which can force a variable of one type to be converted into a variable of the other type. We will see how to use these functions to make your equations clearer.

2.6.5 Mixed-Mode Arithmetic and Exponentiation

As a general rule, mixed-mode arithmetic operations are undesirable because they are hard to understand and can sometimes lead to unexpected results. However, there is one exception to this rule: exponentiation. For exponentiation, what appears to be mixed-mode operation is actually desirable.

To understand why mixed mode operations are desirable for exponentiation, consider the assignment statement

$$\text{result = y ** n}$$

where result and y are real and n is an integer. The expression y ** n is shorthand for "use y as a factor n times," which is exactly what the computer does when it encounters this expression. Since y is a real number and the computer is multiplying y by itself, the computer is really doing real arithmetic and not mixed-mode arithmetic!

Now consider the assignment statement

$$\text{result = y ** x}$$

where result, y, and x are real. The expression y ** x is shorthand for "use y as a factor x times," but this time x is not an integer. Instead, x might be a number like 2.5. It is not physically possible to multiply a number by itself 2.5 times, so we have to rely on indirect methods to calculate y ** x in this case. The most common approach is to use the standard algebraic formula, which says that

$$y^x = e^{x \ln y} \tag{2-1}$$

Using this equation, we can evaluate y ** x by taking the natural logarithm of y, multiplying by x, and then calculating e to the resulting power. Although this technique certainly works, it takes longer to perform and is less accurate than an ordinary series of multiplications. Therefore, if given a choice, we should try to raise real numbers to integer powers instead of real powers.

Good Programming Practice
Use integer exponents instead of real exponents whenever possible.

Also, note that it is not possible to raise a negative number to a power when using real exponents. Raising a negative number to an integer power is a perfectly legal operation. For example, (-2.0)**2 = 4. However, raising a negative number to a real power will not work, because the natural logarithm of a negative number is undefined. Therefore, the expression (-2.0)**2.0 will produce a run-time error.

Programming Pitfalls
Never raise a negative number to a real power.

Quiz 2–2
This quiz provides a quick check to see if you understand the concepts introduced in section 2.6. If you have trouble with the quiz, reread the section, ask your instructor, or discuss the material with a fellow student. The answers to this quiz appear in Appendix F.

1. In what order are the arithmetic and logical operations evaluated if they appear within an arithmetic expression? How do parentheses modify this order?

2. Are the following expressions legal or illegal? If they are legal, what is their result? If they are illegal, what is wrong with them?

    a. 37 / 3
    b. 37 + 17 / 3
    c. 28 / 3 / 4
    d. (28 / 3) / 4
    e. 28 / (3 / 4)
    f. -3. ** 4. / 2.
    g. 3. ** (-4. / 2.)
    h. 4. ** -3

(continued)

(concluded)

3. Evaluate the following expressions:

    a. `2 + 5 * 2 - 5`
    b. `(2 + 5) * (2 - 5)`
    c. `2 + (5 * 2) - 5`
    d. `(2 + 5) * 2 - 5`

4. Are the following expressions legal or illegal? If they are legal, what is their result? If they are illegal, what is wrong with them?

    a. `2. ** 2. ** 3.`
    b. `2. ** (-2.)`
    c. `(-2) ** 2`
    d. `(-2.) ** (-2.2)`

5. Are the following statements legal or illegal? If they are legal, what is their result? If they are illegal, what is wrong with them?

    ```
    INTEGER :: i, j
    INTEGER, PARAMETER :: k = 4
    i = k ** 2
    j = i / k
    k = i + j
    ```

6. What value is stored in `result` after the following statements are executed?

    ```
    REAL :: a, b, c, result
    a = 10.
    b = 1.5
    c = 5.
    result = a / b + b * c ** 2
    ```

7. What values are stored in `a` and `n` after the following statements are executed?

    ```
    REAL :: a
    INTEGER :: n, i, j
    i = 10.
    j = 3
    n = i / j
    a = i / j
    ```

■ **2.7**

ASSIGNMENT STATEMENTS AND LOGICAL CALCULATIONS

Like arithmetic calculations, logical calculations are performed with an assignment statement, whose form is

```
logical variable name = logical expression
```

The assignment statement calculates the value of the expression to the right of the equal sign and assigns that value to the variable named on the left of the equal sign.

The expression to the right of the equal sign can consist of any combination of valid logical constants, logical variables, and logical operators. A **logical operator** is an operator on numeric, character, or logical data that yields a logical result. The two basic type of logical operators are **relational operators** and **combinational operators.**

2.7.1 Relational Operators

Relational logic operators are operators with two numerical or character operands that yield a logical result. The result depends on the *relationship* between the two values being compared, so these operators are called relational. The general form of a relational operator is

$$a_1 \text{ op } a_2$$

where a_1 and a_2 are arithmetic expressions, variables, constants, or character strings, and op is one of the relational logic operators shown in Table 2–3.

TABLE 2–3
Relational logic operators

Operation	Meaning
==	Equal to
/=	Not equal to
>	Greater than
>=	Greater than or equal to
<	Less than
<=	Less than or equal to

If the relationship between a_1 and a_2 expressed by the operator is true, then the operation returns a value of .TRUE.; otherwise, the operation returns a value of .FALSE..

Some relational operations and their results are

Operation	Result
3 < 4	.TRUE.
3 <= 4	.TRUE.
3 == 4	.FALSE.
3 > 4	.FALSE.
4 <= 4	.TRUE.
'A' < 'B'	.TRUE.

The last logical expression is .TRUE. because characters are evaluated in alphabetical order.

The equivalence relational operator is written with two equal signs, and the assignment operator is written with a single equal sign. The == symbol is a *comparison* operation that returns a logical result, and the = symbol *assigns* the value of the expression to the right of the = sign to the variable on the left of the equal sign. A very common mistake for beginning programmers to make is to use a single equal sign when trying to do a comparison.

Programming Pitfalls
Be careful not to confuse the equivalence relational operator (= =) with the assignment operator (=).

In the hierarchy of operations, relational operators are evaluated after all arithmetic operations have been completed. Therefore, the following two expressions are equivalent (both are .TRUE.).

$$7 + 3 < 2 + 11$$

$$(7 + 3) < (2 + 11)$$

If the comparison is between real and integer values, then the integer value is converted to a real value before the comparison is performed. Comparisons between numerical data and character data are illegal and will cause a compile-time error:

```
4 == 4.      .TRUE. (Integer is converted to real
                     and comparison is made.)

4 <= 'A'     Illegal—produces a compile-time error.
```

2.7.2 Combinational Logic Operators

Combinational logic operators are operators with one or two logical operands that yield a logical result. There are four binary operators, .AND., .OR., .EQV., and .NEQV., and one unary operator, .NOT.. The general form of a binary combinational logic operation is

$$l_1 \text{ .op. } l_2$$

where l_1 and l_2 are logical expressions, variables, or constants and .op. is one of the combinational operators shown in Table 2–4.

■ **TABLE 2–4**
Combinational logic operators

Operator	Function	Definition
l_1 .AND. l_2	Logical AND	Result is TRUE if both l_1 and l_2 are TRUE; otherwise, it is FALSE.
l_1 .OR. l_2	Logical OR	Result is TRUE if either or both of l_1 and l_2 are TRUE; otherwise, it is FALSE.
l_1 .EQV. l_2	Logical equivalence	Result is TRUE if l_1 is the same as l_2 (either both TRUE or both FALSE); otherwise, it is FALSE.
l_1 .NEQV. l_2	Logical non-equivalence	Result is TRUE if one of l_1 and l_2 is TRUE and the other one is FALSE; otherwise, it is FALSE.
.NOT. l_1	Logical NOT	Result is TRUE if l_1 is FALSE, and FALSE if l_1 is TRUE.

The periods are a part of the operator and must always be present. If the relationship between l_1 and l_2 expressed by the operator is true, then the operation returns a value of .TRUE.; otherwise, the operation returns a value of .FALSE..

The results of the combinational logic operators are summarized in the *truth tables* in Tables 2–5a and 2–5b, which show the result of each operation for all possible combinations of l_1 and l_2.

■ **TABLE 2–5(A)**
Truth tables for binary combinational logic operators

l_1	l_2	l_1 .AND. l_2	l_1 .OR. l_2	l_1 .EQV. l_2	l_1 .NEQV. l_2
.FALSE.	.FALSE.	.FALSE.	.FALSE.	.TRUE.	.FALSE.
.FALSE.	.TRUE.	.FALSE.	.TRUE.	.FALSE.	.TRUE.
.TRUE.	.FALSE.	.FALSE.	.TRUE.	.FALSE.	.TRUE.
.TRUE.	.TRUE.	.TRUE.	.TRUE.	.TRUE.	.FALSE.

■ **TABLE 2–5(B)**
Truth table for .NOT. operator

l_1	.NOT. l_1
.FALSE.	.TRUE.
.TRUE.	.FALSE.

In the hierarchy of operations, combinational logic operators are evaluated after all arithmetic operations and all relational operators have been evaluated. The logic operators in an expression are evaluated in the following order:

1. All arithmetic operators are evaluated first in the order previously described.
2. All relational operators (==, /=, >, >=, <, <=) are evaluated from left to right.
3. All .NOT. operators are evaluated.
4. All .AND. operators are evaluated from left to right.
5. All .OR. operators are evaluated from left to right.
6. All .EQV. and .NEQV. operators are evaluated from left to right.

As with arithmetic operations, parentheses can be used to change the default order of evaluation.

Examples of some combinational logic operators and their results are given in Example 2–3.

EXAMPLE 2–3 Assume that the following variables are initialized with the values shown and calculate the result of the specified expressions:

$$L1 = .TRUE.$$
$$L2 = .TRUE.$$
$$L3 = .FALSE.$$

Logical Expression	Result
a. .NOT. L1	.FALSE.
b. L1 .OR. L3	.TRUE.
c. L1 .AND. L3	.FALSE.
d. L2 .NEQV. L3	.TRUE.
e. L1 .AND. L2 .OR. L3	.TRUE.
f. L1 .OR. L2 .AND. L3	.FALSE.
g. .NOT. (L1 .EQV. L2)	.FALSE.

Combinational logical operators are evaluated after all relational logic operators, and the .NOT. operator is evaluated before other combinational logic operators. Therefore, the parentheses in part (*h*) in Example 2–3 are required. If they had been absent, the expression in part (*h*) would have been evaluated in the order (.NOT. L1) .EQV. L2.

In the Fortran 90 and Fortran 95 standards, combinational logic operations involving numerical or character data are illegal and will cause a compile-time error:

$$4 .AND. 3 \quad Error$$

2.7.3 The Significance of Logical Variables and Expressions

Logical variables and expressions are rarely the final product of a Fortran program. Nevertheless, they are absolutely essential to the proper operation of most programs. As we will see in Chapter 3, most of the major branching and looping structures of Fortran are controlled by logical values, so we will have to be able to read and write logical expressions to understand and use Fortran control statements.

■ 2.8

ASSIGNMENT STATEMENTS AND CHARACTER VARIABLES

Character manipulations can be performed with an assignment statement, whose form is

```
character variable name = character expression
```

The assignment statement calculates the value of the character expression to the right of the equal sign and assigns that value to the variable named on the left of the equal sign.

The expression to the right of the equal sign can be any combination of valid character constants, character variables, and character operators. A *character operator* is an operator on character data that yields a character result. The two basic types of character operators are **substring specifications** and **concatenation.**

A character expression may be assigned to a character variable with an assignment statement. If the character expression is *shorter* than the length of the character variable to which it is assigned, then the rest of the variable is padded out with blanks. For example, the statements

```
CHARACTER(len=3) :: file_ext
file_ext = 'f'
```

store the value 'fɸɸ' into variable `file_ext`. (ɸ denotes a blank character.) If the character expression is *longer* than the length of the character variable to which it is assigned, then the excess portion of the character variable is discarded. For example, the statements

```
CHARACTER(len=3) :: file_ext_2
file_extent_2 = 'FILE01'
```

store the value 'FIL' into variable `file_ext_2`, and the characters 'E01' are discarded.

2.8.1 Substring Specifications

A substring specification selects a portion of a character variable and treats that portion as if it were an independent character variable. For example, if the variable `str1` is a six-character variable containing the string '123456', then the substring `str1(2:4)` would be a three-character variable containing the string '234'. Note that the substring `str1(2:4)` really refers to the same memory locations as characters 2 through 4 of `str1`, so if the contents of `str1(2:4)` are changed, the characters in the middle of variable `str1` will also be changed.

A character substring is denoted by placing integer values representing the starting and ending character numbers in parentheses following the variable name. The starting and ending character numbers must be separated by a colon. If the ending character number is less than the starting number, a zero-length character string will be produced.

Example 2–4 illustrates the use of substrings.

EXAMPLE 2–4 What will the contents of variables a, b, and c be at the end of the following program?

```
PROGRAM test
CHARACTER(len=8) :: a, b, c
a = 'ABCDEFGHIJ'
b = '12345678'
c = a(5:7)
b(7:8) = a(2:6)
END PROGRAM
```

SOLUTION

The character manipulations in this program are

1. Line 3 assigns the string 'ABCDEFGHIJ' to a, but only the first eight characters are saved since a is only eight characters long. Therefore, a will contain 'ABCDEFGH'.
2. Line 4 statement assigns the string '12345678' to b.
3. Line 5 assigns the character substring a(5:7) to c. Since c is eight characters long, five blanks will be padded onto variable c, and c will contain 'EFGbbbbb'.
4. Line 6 assigns substring a(2:6) to substring b(7:8). Since b(7:8) is only two characters long, only the first two characters of a(2:6) will be used. Therefore, variable b will contain '123456BC'.

2.8.2 The Concatenation (//) Operator

The operation known as *concatenation* combines two or more strings or substrings into a single large string. The concatenation operator in Fortran is represented by a double slash with no space between the slashes (//). For example, after the following lines are executed

```
PROGRAM test
CHARACTER(len=10) :: a
CHARACTER(len=8) :: b, c
a = 'ABCDEFGHIJ'
b = '12345678'
c = a(1:3) // b(4:5) // a(6:8)
END PROGRAM
```

variable c will contain the string 'ABC45FGH'.

2.8.3 Relational Operators with Character Data

Character strings can be compared in logical expressions using the relational operators ==, /=, <, < =, >, and >=. The result of the comparison is a logical value that is either true or false. For instance, the expression '123' == '123' is true, whereas the expression '123' == '1234' is false. In standard Fortran, character strings may be compared with character strings, and numbers may be compared with numbers; however, character strings may not be compared to numbers.

How are two characters compared to determine if one is greater than the other? The comparison is based on the **collating sequence** of the characters on the computer where the program is being executed. The collating sequence of the characters is the order in which they occur within a specific character set. For example, the character 'A' is character number 65 in the ASCII character set, and the character 'B' is character number 66 in the set (see Appendix A). Therefore, the logical expression 'A' < 'B' is true in the ASCII character set. On the other hand, the character 'a' is character number 97 in the ASCII set, so 'a' < 'A' is false in the ASCII character set. During character comparisons, a lowercase letter is different than the corresponding uppercase letter.

How are two strings compared to determine if one is greater than the other? The comparison begins with the first character in each string. If they are the same, then the second two characters are compared. This process continues until the first difference is found between the strings. For example, 'AAAAAB' > 'AAAAAA'.

What happens if the strings are different lengths? The comparison begins with the first letter in each string and progresses through each letter until a difference is found. If the two strings are the same all the way to the end of one of them, then the other string is considered the larger of the two. Therefore, 'AB' > 'AAAA' and 'AAAAA' > 'AAAA'.

■ 2.9
INTRINSIC FUNCTIONS

In mathematics a **function** is an expression that accepts one or more input values and calculates a single result from them. Scientific and technical calculations usually require functions that are more complex than the simple addition, subtraction, multiplication, division, and exponentiation operations that we have discussed so far. Some of these functions are very common and are used in many different technical disciplines. Others are specific to a single problem or a small number of problems. Examples of very common functions used in scientific calculations are the trigonometric functions, logarithms, and square roots. Examples of rarer functions include the hyperbolic functions and Bessel functions.

The Fortran 90/95 language has mechanisms to support both kinds of functions. Many of the most common functions are built directly into the Fortran language. They are called **intrinsic functions.** Less common functions are not included in the Fortran language, but any function needed to solve a particular problem may be supplied by the user as an **external function.** External functions are described in Chapter 6.

A Fortran function takes one or more input values and calculates a *single* output value from them. The input values to the function are known as **arguments;** they appear in parentheses immediately after the function name. The output of a function is a single number, logical value, or character string, which can be used with other functions, constants, and variables in Fortran expressions. When a function appears in a Fortran statement, the arguments of the function are passed to a separate routine that computes the result of the function, and then the result is used in place of the function in the original calculation. For intrinsic functions, the separate routine to calculate the result of the function is supplied with the Fortran compiler. For external functions, the user must supply the routine.

A list of some common intrinsic functions is given in Table 2–6. A complete list of Fortran 90 and Fortran 95 intrinsic functions is given in Appendix B.

TABLE 2–6
Some common intrinsic functions

Function name and arguments	Function value	Argument type	Result type	Comments
SQRT(X)	$\sqrt{x}$	R	R	Square root of x for $x \geq 0$.
ABS(X)	$\|x\|$	R/I	*	Absolute value of x.
ACHAR(I)		I	CHAR(1)	Returns the character at position I in the ASCII collating sequence.
SIN(X)	$\sin(x)$	R	R	Sine of x (x must be in *radians*).
COS(X)	$\cos(x)$	R	R	Cosine of x (x must be in *radians*).
TAN(X)	$\tan(x)$	R	R	Tangent of x (x must be in *radians*).
EXP(X)	e^x	R	R	e raised to the xth power.
LOG(X)	$\log_e(x)$	R	R	Natural logarithm of x for $x > 0$.
LOG10(X)	$\log_{10}(x)$	R	R	Base 10 logarithm of x for $x > 0$.
IACHAR(C)		CHAR(1)	I	Returns the position of the character C in the ASCII collating sequence.
INT(X)		R	I	Integer part of x (x is truncated).
NINT(X)		R	I	Nearest integer to x (x is rounded).
REAL(I)		I	R	Converts integer value to real.
MOD(A,B)		R/I	*	Remainder or modulo function.
MAX(A,B)		R/I	*	Picks the larger of a and b.
MIN(A,B)		R/I	*	Picks the smaller of a and b.
ASIN(X)	$\sin^{-1}(x)$	R	R	Inverse sine of x (results in *radians*).
ACOS(X)	$\cos^{-1}(x)$	R	R	Inverse cosine of x (results in *radians*).
ATAN(X)	$\tan^{-1}(x)$	R	R	Inverse tangent of x (results in *radians*).

Notes:
* = Result is of the same type as the input argument(s).
R = REAL, I = INTEGER, CHAR(1) = CHARACTER(len = 1)

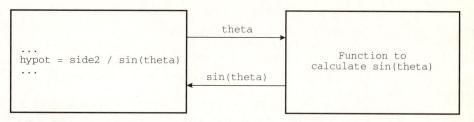

FIGURE 2–3
When a function is included in a Fortran statement, the argument(s) of the function are passed to a separate routine that computes the result of the function. The result is used in place of the function in the original calculation.

Fortran functions are used much like the mathematical functions they are based on. For example, the intrinsic function SIN can be used to calculate the sine of a number. Its form is

$$y = \texttt{SIN(theta)}$$

where theta is the argument of the function SIN. After this statement is executed, the variable y contains the sine of the value stored in variable theta. Note from Table 2–6 that the trigonometric functions expect their arguments to be in radians. If the variable theta is in degrees, then we must convert degrees to radians ($180° = \pi$ radians) before computing the sine. This conversion can be done in the same statement as the sine calculation:

$$y = \texttt{SIN (theta*(3.141593/180.))}$$

The inner set of parentheses is not really required, but it is used to emphasize that 3.141593/180. is a conversion factor. This statement is an example of using extra parentheses for clarity. Alternately, we could create a named constant containing the conversion factor and refer to that constant when the function is executed:

```
INTEGER, PARAMETER :: deg_to_rad = 3.141593 / 180.
    ...
y = SIN (theta * deg_to_rad)
```

The REAL, INT, and NINT functions may be used to avoid undesirable mixed-mode expressions by explicitly converting variable types from one form to another. The REAL function converts an integer into a real number, and the INT and NINT functions convert real numbers into integers. The INT function truncates the real number, while the NINT function rounds it. To understand the distinction between these two operations, consider the real number 2.9995. The result of INT(2.9995) is 2, whereas the result of NINT(2.9995) is 3. The NINT function is very useful when converting back from real to integer form, since the small round-off errors occurring in real calculations will not affect the resulting integer value.

The argument of a function can be a constant, a variable, an expression, or even the result of another function. All of the following statements are legal:

```
y = SIN(3.141593)      (Argument is a constant.)

y = SIN(x)             (Argument is a variable.)

y = SIN(pi*x)          (Argument is an expression.)

y = SIN(SQRT(x))       (Argument is the result of another function.)
```

Functions may be used in expressions anywhere that a constant or variable may be used. However, functions may never appear on the left side of the assignment operator (equal sign); they are not memory locations, and nothing can be stored in them.

The type of argument required by a function and the type of value returned by it are specified in Table 2–6 for the intrinsic functions listed there. Some of these intrinsic functions are **generic functions,** which means that they can use more than one type of input data. The absolute value function ABS is a generic function. If X is a real number, then the type of ABS(X) is real. If X is an integer, then the type of ABS(X) is integer. Some functions are called **specific functions;** they can use only one specific type of input data and produce only one specific type of output value. For example, the function IABS requires an integer argument and returns an integer result. A complete list of all intrinsic functions (both generic and specific) appears in Appendix B.

■ 2.10
LIST-DIRECTED INPUT AND OUTPUT STATEMENTS

An **input statement** reads one or more values from an input device and stores them into variables specified by the programmer. The input device could be a keyboard in an interactive environment or an input disk file in a batch environment. An **output statement** writes one or more values to an output device. The output device could be a CRT screen in an interactive environment or an output listing file in a batch environment.

You saw input and output statements in my_first_program (refer to Figure 2–1). The input statement in the figure was of the form

```
READ (*,*) input_list
```

where input_list is the list of variables into which the values being read in are placed. If multiple variables appear in the list, they should be separated by commas. The parentheses (*,*) in the statement contains control information for the read. The first field in the parentheses specifies the *input/output unit* (or io unit) from which the data is to be read. (The concept of an input/output unit is explained in Chapter 4.) An asterisk in this field means that the data is to be read from the standard input device for the computer— usually the keyboard when running in interactive mode and an input file when running in batch mode. The second field in the parentheses specifies the format in which the data is to be read. (Formats are also explained in Chapter 4.) An asterisk in this field means that list-directed input (sometimes called free-format input) is to be used.

The term **list-directed input** means that the types of the variables in the variable list determine the required format of the input data. For example, consider the following statements:

```
PROGRAM input_example
INTEGER :: i, j
REAL :: a
CHARACTER(len=12) :: chars
READ (*,*) i, j, a, chars
END PROGRAM
```

The input data supplied to the program must consist of two integers, a real number and a character string. Furthermore, they must be in that order. The values may be all on one line separated by commas or blanks, or they may be on separate lines. The list-directed READ statement will continue to read input data until values have been found for all of the variables in the list. If the input data supplied to the program at execution time is

1, 2, 3.,'This one.'

then the variable i will be filled with a 1, j will be filled with a 2, a will be filled with a 3.0, and chars with be filled with 'This one.   '. Since the input character string is only 9 characters long, while the variable chars has room for 12 characters, the string

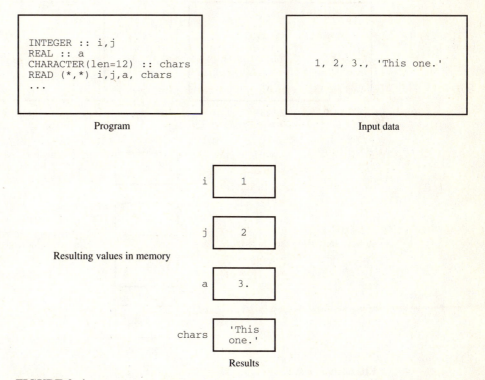

Program

Input data

Resulting values in memory

Results

FIGURE 2–4
For list-directed input, the type and order of the input data values must match the type and order of the supplied input data.

is *left justified* in the character variable, and three blanks are automatically added at the end of it to fill out the remaining space. Also note that for list-directed reads, input character strings must be enclosed in single or double quotes.

When using list-directed input, the values to be read must match the variables in the input list both in order and type. If the input data had been

1, 2, 'This one.', 3.

then a run-time error would have occurred when the program tried to read the data.

Each READ statement in a program begins reading from a new line of input data. If any data is left over on the previous input line, that data is discarded. For example, consider the following program:

```
PROGRAM input_example_2
INTEGER :: i, j, k, l
READ (*,*) i, j
READ (*,*) k, l
END PROGRAM
```

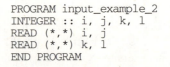

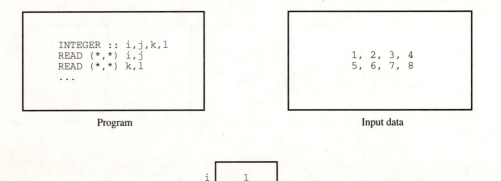

Program   Input data

Resulting values in memory:

Results

FIGURE 2–5
Each list-directed READ statement begins reading from a new line of input data, and any unused data on the previous line is discarded. Here the values 3 and 4 on the first line of input data are never used.

If the input data to this program is

```
1, 2, 3, 4
5, 6, 7, 8
```

then after the READ statements, i will contain a 1, j will contain a 2, k will contain a 5, and l will contain a 6 (see Figure 2–5).

The *list-directed output statement* is of the form

```
WRITE (*,*) output_list
```

where output_list is the list of data items (variables, constants, or expressions) that are to be written. If multiple items appear in the list, then they should be separated by commas. The parentheses (*,*) in the statement contains control information for the write, where the two asterisks have the same meaning as they do for a list-directed read statement.

The term **list-directed output** means that the types of the values in the output list of the write statement determine the format of the output data. For example, consider the following statements:

```
PROGRAM output_example
INTEGER :: ix = 1
LOGICAL :: test = .TRUE.
REAL :: theta = 3.141593
ix = 1
test = .TRUE.
theta = 3.141593
WRITE (*,*) ' IX =          ', ix
WRITE (*,*) ' THETA =       ', theta
WRITE (*,*) ' COS(THETA) = ', COS(theta)
WRITE (*,*) ' TEST =        ', test
WRITE (*,*) REAL(ix), NINT(theta)
END PROGRAM
```

The output resulting from these statements is

```
IX =                        1
THETA =                     3.141593
COS(THETA) =               -1.000000
TEST =              T
          1.000000          3
```

This example illustrates several points about the list-directed WRITE statement:

1. The output list may contain constants (' IX = ' is a constant), variables, functions, and expressions. In each case the value of the constant, variable, function, or expression is output to the standard output device.

2. Note that the format of the output data matches the type of the value being output. For example, even though theta is of type real, NINT(theta) is of type integer. Therefore, the sixth WRITE statement produces an output of three (the nearest integer to 3.141593). Also note that when a logical value is included in a WRITE statement, a single T or F (as appropriate) is written out.

3. The output of list-directed WRITE statements is not very pretty. The values printed out do not line up in neat columns, and there is no way to control the number of signifi-

cant digits displayed for real numbers. We will learn how to produce neatly formatted output in Chapter 4.

Quiz 2–3

This quiz provides a quick check to see if you understand the concepts introduced in sections 2.7 through 2.10. If you have trouble with the quiz, reread the sections, ask your instructor, or discuss the material with a fellow student. The answers to this quiz appear in Appendix F.

Convert the following algebraic equations into Fortran assignment statements:

1. The equivalent resistance R_{eq} of four resistors R_1, R_2, R_3, and R_4 connected in series:

$$R_{eq} = R_1 + R_2 + R_3 + R_4$$

2. The equivalent resistance R_{eq} of four resistors R_1, R_2, R_3, and R_4 connected in parallel:

$$R_{eq} = \cfrac{1}{\cfrac{1}{R_1} + \cfrac{1}{R_2} + \cfrac{1}{R_3} + \cfrac{1}{R_4}}$$

3. The period T of an oscillating pendulum:

$$T = 2\pi\sqrt{\frac{L}{g}}$$

where L is the length of the pendulum and g is the acceleration due to gravity.

4. The equation for damped sinusoidal oscillation:

$$v(t) = V_M e^{-\alpha t} \cos \omega t$$

where V_M is the maximum value of the oscillation, α is the exponential damping factor, and ω is the angular velocity of the oscillation.

Convert the following Fortran assignment statements into algebraic equations:

5. The motion of an object in a constant gravitational field:

```
distance = 0.5 * accel * t**2 + vel_0 * t + pos_0
```

6. The oscillating frequency of a damped RLC circuit:

```
freq = 1. / (2. * pi * sqrt(l * c))
```

where pi is π (3.141592 . . .).

(continued)

7. Energy storage in an inductor:

```
energy = 1.0 / 2.0 * inductance * current**2
```

8. What values will be printed out when the following statements are executed?

```
PROGRAM quiz_1
INTEGER :: i
LOGICAL :: l
REAL :: a
a = 0.05
i = nint ( 2. * 3.141493 / a )
l = i > 100
a = a * (5 / 3)
WRITE (*,*) i, a, l
END PROGRAM
```

9. Suppose that the real variables a, b, and c contain the values $-10.$, 0.1, and 2.1, respectively, and that the logical variable l1, l2, and l3 contain the values .TRUE., .FALSE., and .FALSE., respectively. Is each of the following expressions legal or illegal? If an expression is legal, what will its result be?

   a. a > b .OR. b > c
   b. (.NOT. a) .OR. l1
   c. l1 .AND. .NOT. l2
   d. a < b .EQV. b < c
   e. l1 .OR. l2 .AND. l3
   f. l1 .OR. (l2 .AND. l3)
   g. (l1 .OR. l2) .AND. l3
   h. a .OR. b .AND. l1

10. Suppose that character variables str1, str2 and str3 contain the values 'abc', 'abcd', 'ABC', respectively, and that a computer uses the ASCII character set. Is each of the following expressions legal or illegal? If an expression is legal, what will its result be?

    a. str2(2:4)
    b. str3 // str2(4:4)
    c. str1 > str2
    d. str1 > str3
    e. str2 > 0
    f. IACHAR('C') == 67
    g. 'Z' >= ACHAR(100)

11. If the input data is

```
1, 3
2., 45., 17.
30., 180, 6.
```

(continued)

(concluded)

what will be printed out by the following program?

```
PROGRAM quiz_2
INTEGER :: i, j, k
REAL :: a, b, c
READ (*,*) i, j, a
READ (*,*) b, k
c = SIN ((3.141493 / 180) * a)
WRITE (*,*) i, j, k, a, b, c
END PROGRAM
```

2.11

INITIALIZATION OF VARIABLES

Consider the following program:

```
PROGRAM init
INTEGER :: i
WRITE (*,*) i
END PROGRAM
```

What is the value stored in the variable i? What will be printed out by the WRITE statement? The answer is, We don't know!

The variable i is an example of an **uninitialized variable.** It has been defined by the INTEGER :: i statement, but no value has been placed into it yet. The value of an uninitialized variable is not defined by the Fortran 90/95 standard. Some compilers automatically set uninitialized variables to zero, and some set them to different arbitrary patterns. Some compilers for older versions of Fortran leave in memory whatever values previously existed at the location of the variables. Some compilers even produce a run-time error if a variable is used without first being initialized.

Uninitialized variables can present a serious problem. Since they are handled differently on different machines, a program that works fine on one computer may fail when transported to another one. On some machines, the same program could work sometimes and fail sometimes, depending on the data left behind by the previous program occupying the same memory. Such a situation is totally unacceptable, and we must avoid it by always initializing all of the variables in our programs.

Good Programming Practice
Always initialize all variables in a program before using them.

Three techniques are available to initialize variables in a Fortran program: assignment statements, READ statements, and initialization in type declaration statements. An assignment statement assigns the value of the expression to the right of the equal sign to the variable that appears to the left of the equal sign. In the following code, the variable i is initialized to 1, and we know that a 1 will be printed out by the WRITE statement.

```
PROGRAM init_1
INTEGER :: i
i = 1
WRITE (*,*) i
END PROGRAM
```

A READ statement may be used to initialize variables with values input by the user. In the following code, the variable i is initialized by the READ statement, and we know that whatever value was read by the READ statement will be printed out by the WRITE statement.

```
PROGRAM init_2
INTEGER :: i
READ (*,*) i
WRITE (*,*) i
END PROGRAM
```

The third technique available to initialize variables in a Fortran program is to specify their initial values in the type declaration statement that defines them. This declaration specifies that a value should be preloaded into a variable during the compilation and linking process. Note the fundamental difference between initialization in a type declaration statement and initialization in an assignment statement: A type declaration statement initializes the variable before the program begins to run, whereas an assignment statement initializes the variable during execution.

The form of a type declaration statement used to initialize variables is

```
type :: var1 = value, [var2 = value, ... ]
```

Any number of variables may be declared and initialized in a single type declaration statement provided that they are separated by commas. An example of type declaration statements used to initialize a series of variables is

```
REAL :: time = 0.0, distance = 5128.
INTEGER :: loop = 10
LOGICAL :: done = .FALSE.
CHARACTER(len=12) :: string = 'Characters'
```

Before program execution, time is initialized to 0.0, distance is initialized to 5128., loop is initialized to 10, done is initialized to .FALSE., and string is initialized to 'Characters '.

In the following code, the variable i is initialized by the type declaration statement, so we know that when execution starts, the variable i will contain the value 1. Therefore, the WRITE statement will print out a 1.

```
PROGRAM init_3
INTEGER :: i = 1
WRITE (*,*) i
END PROGRAM
```

■ 2.12

THE IMPLICIT NONE STATEMENT

Fortran has another nonexecutable type declaration statement: the IMPLICIT NONE statement. When it is used, the IMPLICIT NONE statement disables the default typing provisions of Fortran. When the IMPLICIT NONE statement is included in a program, any variable that does not appear in an explicit type declaration statement is considered an error. The IMPLICIT NONE statement should appear after the PROGRAM statement and before any type declaration statements.

When the IMPLICIT NONE statement is included in a program, the programmer must explicitly declare the type of every variable in the program. On first thought, this requirement might seem to be a disadvantage, since the programmer must do more work when he or she first writes a program. This initial impression couldn't be more wrong. In fact, using this statement has several advantages.

The majority of programming errors are simple typographical errors. The IMPLICIT NONE statement catches these errors at compilation time before they can produce subtle errors during execution. For example, consider the following simple program:

```
PROGRAM test_1
REAL :: time
time = 10.0
WRITE (*,*) 'Time = ', tmie
END PROGRAM
```

In this program the variable time is misspelled tmie at one point. When this program is compiled with the Digital Visual Fortran 5.0 compiler and executed, the output is "Time = 0.000000E+00", which is the wrong answer! In contrast, consider the same program with the IMPLICIT NONE statement present:

```
PROGRAM test_1
IMPLICIT NONE
REAL :: time
time = 10.0
WRITE (*,*) 'Time = ', tmie
END PROGRAM
```

When compiled with the same compiler, this program produces the following compile-time error:

```
Source Listing   10-May-1997 11:41:18  DIGITAL Visual Fortran V5.0-408  Page 1
                 10-May-1997 11:41:12  test_1.f90

     1 PROGRAM test_1
     2 IMPLICIT NONE
     3 REAL :: time = 10.0
     4 WRITE (*,*) 'Time = ', tmie
       ......................^
(1) Error: This name does not have a type, and must have an explicit type. [TMIE]

     5 END PROGRAM
```

Instead of having a wrong answer in an otherwise-working program, we have an explicit error message flagging the problem at compilation time. The error message is an enormous advantage when working with longer programs containing many variables.

Another advantage of the IMPLICIT NONE statement is that it makes the code more maintainable. Any program using the statement must include a complete list of all variables in the declaration section of the program. If the program must be modified, a programmer can check the list to avoid using variable names that are already defined in the program. This checking helps to eliminate a very common error in which the modifications to the program inadvertently change the values of some variables used elsewhere in the program.

In general, the use of the IMPLICIT NONE statement becomes more and more advantageous as the size of a programming project increases. The use of IMPLICIT NONE is so important to good program design that we will use it consistently throughout this book.

Good Programming Practice
Always explicitly define every variable in your programs and use the IMPLICIT NONE statement to help you spot and correct typographical errors before they become program execution errors.

■ 2.13

PROGRAM EXAMPLES

Chapter 2 explains the fundamental concepts required to write simple but functional Fortran programs. We will now present a few sample problems in which these concepts are used.

EXAMPLE 2–5   Temperature Conversion: Design a Fortran program that reads an input temperature in degrees Fahrenheit, converts it to an absolute temperature in kelvins, and writes out the result.

SOLUTION

The relationship between temperature in degrees Fahrenheit (°F) and temperature in kelvins (K) can be found in any physics textbook. It is

$$T \text{ (in kelvins)} = \left(\frac{5}{9} T \text{ (in °F)} - 32.0\right) + 273.15 \tag{2–2}$$

The physics books also give us sample values on both temperature scales, which we can use to check the operation of our program. Two such values are

| The boiling point of water | 212° F | 373.15 K |
| The sublimation point of dry ice | −110° F | 194.26 K |

Our program must perform the following steps:

1. Prompt the user to enter an input temperature in °F.
2. Read the input temperature.
3. Calculate the temperature in kelvins from Equation (2–2).
4. Write out the result and stop.

The resulting program is shown in Figure 2–6.

FIGURE 2–6
Program to convert degrees Fahrenheit into kelvins.

```
PROGRAM temp_conversion

! Purpose:
!    To convert an input temperature from degrees Fahrenheit to
!    an output temperature in kelvins.
!
! Record of revisions:
!    Date         Programmer          Description of change
!    ====         ==========          =====================
!    09/03/95  S. J. Chapman          Original code
!
IMPLICIT NONE      ! Force explicit declaration of variables

! Declare variables, and define each variable when it is declared
REAL :: temp_f     ! Temperature in degrees Fahrenheit
REAL :: temp_k     ! Temperature in kelvins

! Prompt the user for the input temperature.
WRITE (*,*) 'Enter the temperature in degrees Fahrenheit: '
READ (*,*) temp_f

! Convert to kelvins.
temp_k = (5. / 9.) * (temp_f - 32.) + 273.15

! Write out the result.
WRITE (*,*) temp_f, ' degrees Fahrenheit = ', temp_k, ' kelvins'

! Finish up.
END PROGRAM
```

To test the completed program, we will run it with the known input values given in this example. Note that user inputs appear in bold face below:

```
C>temp_conversion
Enter the temperature in degrees Fahrenheit:
212
      212.000000 degrees Fahrenheit =      373.150000 kelvins
C>temp_conversion
Enter the temperature in degrees Fahrenheit:
-110
     -110.000000 degrees Fahrenheit =      194.261100 kelvins
```

The results of the program match the values from the physics book.

The program in Figure 2–6 echoes the input values and prints the output values with their units. The results of this program make sense only if the units (degrees Fahrenheit and kelvins) are included with their values. As a general rule, the units associated with any input value should always be printed with the prompt that requests the value, and the units associated with any output value should always be printed with that value.

Good Programming Practice
Always include the appropriate units with any values that you read or write in a program.

The above program exhibits many of the good programming practices that we have described in this chapter. It uses the IMPLICIT NONE statement to force the explicit typing of all variables in the program. It includes a data dictionary defining the meanings of all of the variables in the program. It also uses descriptive variable names. A READ statement initializes the variable temp_f before it is used. Appropriate units are attached to all printed values.

EXAMPLE 2–6 Electrical Engineering: Calculating Real, Reactive, and Apparent Power:

Figure 2–7 shows a sinusoidal ac voltage source with voltage V supplying a load of impedance $Z \angle \theta$ Ω. From simple circuit theory, the rms current I, the real power P, reactive power Q, apparent power S, and power factor PF supplied to the load are given by the equations

$$I = \frac{V}{Z} \tag{2–3}$$

$$P = V I \cos \theta \tag{2–4}$$

$$Q = V I \sin \theta \tag{2–5}$$

$$S = V I \tag{2–6}$$

$$PF = \cos \theta \tag{2–7}$$

where V is the rms voltage of the power source in units of volts (V). The units of current are amperes (A), of real power are watts (W), of reactive power are volt-amperes-reactive (VAR), and of apparent power are volt-amperes (VA). The power factor has no units associated with it.

Given the rms voltage of the power source and the magnitude and angle of the impedance Z, write a program that calculates the rms current I, the real power P, reactive power Q, apparent power S, and power factor PF of the load.

SOLUTION

In this program we need to read in the rms voltage V of the voltage source and the magnitude Z and angle θ of the impedance. The input voltage source will be mea-

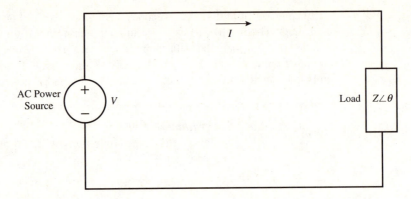

FIGURE 2–7
A sinusoidal ac voltage source with voltage V supplying a load of impedance $Z\angle\theta\ \Omega$.

sured in volts, the magnitude of the impedance Z in ohms, and the angle of the impedance θ in degrees. Once the data is read in, we must convert the angle θ into radians for use with the Fortran trigonometric functions. Next the desired values must
be calculated, and the results must be printed out.

The program must perform the following steps:

1. Prompt the user to enter the source voltage in volts.
2. Read the source voltage.
3. Prompt the user to enter the magnitude and angle of the impedance in ohms and
   degrees.
4. Read the magnitude and angle of the impedance.
5. Calculate the current I from Equation (2–3).
6. Calculate the real power P from Equation (2–4).
7. Calculate the reactive power Q from Equation (2–5).
8. Calculate the apparent power S from Equation (2–6).
9. Calculate the power factor PF from Equation (2–7).
10. Write out the results and stop.

The final Fortran program is shown in Figure 2–8.

FIGURE 2–8
Program to calculate the real power, reactive power, apparent power, and power factor
supplied to a load.

```
PROGRAM power
!
! Purpose:
!   To calculate the current, real, reactive, apparent power,
!   and the power factor supplied to a load.
!
```

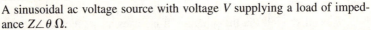

(continued)

(concluded)

```
! Record of revisions:
!   Date          Programmer          Description of change
!   ====          ==========          =====================
!   09/03/95      S. J. Chapman       Original code
!
IMPLICIT NONE

! Declare the constants used in this program.
REAL, PARAMETER :: conv = 0.01745329 ! Degrees to radians cnv factor
! Declare the variables used in this program.
REAL :: amps            ! Current in the load
REAL :: p               ! Real power of load
REAL :: pf              ! Power factor of load
REAL :: q               ! Reactive power of the load
REAL :: s               ! Apparent power of the load
REAL :: theta           ! Impedance angle of the load
REAL :: volts           ! Rms voltage of the power source
REAL :: z               ! Magnitude of the impedance of the load

! Prompt the user for the rms voltage.
WRITE (*,*) 'Enter the rms voltage of the source: '
READ (*,*) volts

! Prompt the user for the magnitude and angle of the impedance.
WRITE (*,*) 'Enter the magnitude and angle of the impedance '
WRITE (*,*) 'in ohms and degrees: '
READ (*,*) z, theta

! Perform calculations
amps = volts / z                        ! Rms current
p = volts * amps * cos (theta * conv)   ! Real power
q = volts * amps * sin (theta * conv)   ! Reactive power
s = volts * amps                        ! Apparent power
pf = cos ( theta * conv)                ! Power factor

! Write out the results.
WRITE (*,*) 'Voltage         = ', volts, ' volts'
WRITE (*,*) 'Impedance       = ', z, ' ohms at ', theta,' degrees'
WRITE (*,*) 'Current         = ', amps, ' amps'
WRITE (*,*) 'Real Power      = ', p, ' watts'
WRITE (*,*) 'Reactive Power  = ', q, ' VAR'
WRITE (*,*) 'Apparent Power  = ', s, ' VA'
WRITE (*,*) 'Power Factor    = ', pf

! Finish up.
END PROGRAM
```

This program also exhibits many of the good programming practices that we have described. It uses the IMPLICIT NONE statement to force the explicit typing of all variables in the program. It includes a variable dictionary defining the uses of all of the variables in the program. It also uses descriptive variable names. (Although the variable names are short, *P*, *Q*, *S*, and *PF* are the standard accepted abbreviations for the corresponding quantities.) All variables are initialized before they are used. The program defines a named constant for the degrees-to-radians conversion factor and then uses that name everywhere throughout the program when the conversion factor is required. All input values are echoed, and appropriate units are attached to all printed values.

To verify the operation of program power, we will do a sample calculation by hand and compare the results with the output of the program for the same input data. If the rms voltage V is 120 V, the magnitude of the impedance Z is 5 Ω, and the angle θ is 30°, then the values are

$$I = \frac{V}{Z} = \frac{120 \text{ V}}{5 \text{ } \Omega} = 24 \text{ A} \tag{2–3}$$

$$P = V I \cos \theta = (120 \text{ V})(24 \text{ A}) \cos 30° = 2494 \text{ W} \tag{2–4}$$

$$Q = V I \sin \theta = (120 \text{ V})(24 \text{ A}) \sin 30° = 1440 \text{ VAR} \tag{2–5}$$

$$S = V I = (120 \text{ V})(24 \text{ A}) = 2880 \text{ VA} \tag{2–6}$$

$$\text{PF} = \cos \theta = \cos 30° = 0.86603 \tag{2–7}$$

When we run program power with the specified input data, the results are identical with the results of our hand calculations:

```
C>power
Enter the rms voltage of the source:
120
Enter the magnitude and angle of the impedance
in ohms and degrees:
5., 30.
Voltage          =        120.000000 volts
Impedance        =          5.000000 ohms at    30.000000 degrees
Current          =         24.000000 amps
Real Power       =       2494.153000 watts
Reactive Power   =       1440.000000 VAR
Apparent Power   =       2880.000000 VA
Power Factor     =          8.660254E-01
```

EXAMPLE 2–7 Carbon 14 Dating: A radioactive isotope of an element is an unstable form of the element that spontaneously decays into another element over a period of time. Radioactive decay is an exponential process. If Q_o is the initial quantity of a radioactive substance at time $t = 0$, then the amount of that substance that will be present at any time t in the future is given by

$$Q(t) = Q_o e^{-\lambda t} \tag{2–8}$$

where λ is the radioactive decay constant.

Because radioactive decay occurs at a known rate, it can be used as a clock to measure the time since the decay started. If we know the initial amount of the radioactive material Q_o present in a sample and the amount of the material Q left at the current time, we can solve for t in Equation (2–8) to determine how long the decay has been going on. The resulting equation is

$$t_{\text{decay}} = -\frac{1}{\lambda} \log \frac{Q}{Q_o} \tag{2–9}$$

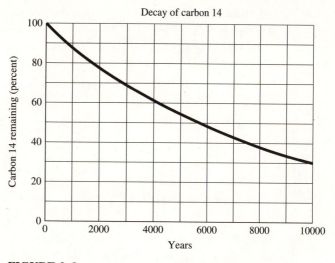

FIGURE 2–9
The radioactive decay of carbon 14 as a function of time.
Notice that 50 percent of the original carbon 14 is left after
about 5730 years have elapsed.

Equation (2–9) has practical applications in many areas of science. For example, archaeologists use a radioactive clock based on carbon 14 to determine the time that has passed since a once-living thing died. Carbon 14 is continually taken into the body while a plant or animal is living, so the amount of it present in the body at the time of death is assumed to be known. The decay constant λ of carbon 14 is well-known to be 0.00012097/year, so if the amount of carbon 14 remaining now can be accurately measured, then Equation (2–9) can be used to determine how long ago the living thing died.

Write a program that reads in the percentage of carbon 14 remaining in a sample, calculates the age of the sample from it, and prints out the result with proper units.

SOLUTION

Our program must perform the following steps:

1. Prompt the user to enter the percentage of carbon 14 remaining in the sample.
2. Read in the percentage.
3. Convert the percentage into the fraction $\dfrac{Q}{Q_0}$.
4. Calculate the age of the sample in years using Equation (2–9).
5. Write out the result and stop.

The resulting code is shown in Figure 2–10.

FIGURE 2–10

Program to calculate the age of a sample from the percentage of carbon 14 remaining in it.

```
PROGRAM c14_date
!
! Purpose:
!   To calculate the age of an organic sample from the percentage
!   of the original carbon 14 remaining in the sample.
!
! Record of revisions:
!      Date        Programmer          Description of change
!      ====        ==========          =====================
!   09/04/95     S. J. Chapman        Original code
!
IMPLICIT NONE

! Declare the constants used in this program.
REAL, PARAMETER :: lamda = 0.00012097   ! The radioactive decay
                                        ! constant of carbon 14,
                                        ! in units of 1/years.

! Declare the variables used in this program.
REAL :: age      ! The age of the sample in years
REAL :: percent  ! The percentage of carbon 14 remaining at the time
                 ! of the measurement
REAL :: ratio    ! The ratio of the carbon 14 remaining at the time
                 ! of the measurement to the original amount of
                 ! carbon 14.

! Prompt the user for the percentage of C-14 remaining.
WRITE (*,*) 'Enter the percentage of carbon 14 remaining:'
READ (*,*) percent

! Echo the user's input value.
WRITE (*,*) 'The remaining carbon 14 = ', percent, ' %.'

! Perform calculations
ratio = percent / 100.                  ! Convert to fractional ratio
age = (-1.0 / lamda) * log(ratio)       ! Get age in years

! Tell the user about the age of the sample.
WRITE (*,*) 'The age of the sample is ', age, ' years.'

! Finish up.
END PROGRAM
```

To test the completed program, we will calculate the time it takes for half of the carbon 14 to disappear. This time is known as the *half-life* of carbon 14.

```
C>c14_date
Enter the percentage of carbon 14 remaining:
50.
The remaining carbon 14 =      50.000000 %.
The age of the sample is      5729.910000 years.
```

The *CRC Handbook of Chemistry and Physics* states that the half-life of carbon 14 is 5730 years, so output of the program agrees with the reference book.

■ 2.14
DEBUGGING Fortran PROGRAMS

There is an old saying that the only sure things in life are death and taxes. We can add one more certainty to that list: If you write a program of any significant size, it won't work the first time you try it! Errors in programs are known as **bugs,** and the process of locating and eliminating them is known as **debugging.** Given that we have written a program and it is not working, how do we debug it?

Three types of errors are found in Fortran programs. The first type of error is a *syntax error.* Syntax errors are errors in the Fortran statement itself, such as spelling errors or punctuation errors. These errors are detected by the compiler during compilation. The second type of error is the *run-time error.* A run-time error occurs when an illegal mathematical operation is attempted during program execution (for example, attempting to divide by 0). These errors cause the program to abort during execution. The third type of error is a *logical error.* Logical errors occur when the program compiles and runs successfully but produces the wrong answer.

The most common mistakes made during programming are *typographical errors.* Some typographical errors create invalid Fortran statements. These errors produce syntax errors that are caught by the compiler. Other typographical errors occur in variable names. For example, the letters in some variable names might have been transposed. If you have used the IMPLICIT NONE statement, then most of these errors will also be caught by the compiler. However, if one legal variable name is substituted for another legal variable name, the compiler cannot detect the error. This sort of substitution might occur if you have two similar variable names. For example, if variables vel1 and vel2 are both used for velocities, then the wrong one might be inadvertently used at some point in the program. This sort of typographical error will produce a logical error. You must check for that sort of error by manually inspecting the code, since the compiler cannot catch it.

Sometimes you can successfully compile and link a program, but run-time errors or logical errors occur when it is executed. In this case either something is wrong with the input data or something is wrong with the logical structure of the program. The first step in locating this sort of bug is to *check the input data to the program.* If your program does not already print out its input data, go back and add WRITE statements to verify that the input values are what you expect them to be.

If the variable names seem to be correct and the input data is correct, then you are probably dealing with a logical error. You should check each of your assignment statements.

1. If an assignment statement is very long, break it into several smaller assignment statements. Smaller statements are easier to verify.
2. Check the placement of parentheses in your assignment statements. A very common error is to have the operations in an assignment statement evaluated in the wrong order. If you have any doubts as to the order in which the variables are being evaluated, add extra sets of parentheses to make your intentions clear.

3. Make sure that you have initialized all the variables properly.
4. Be sure that any functions you use are in the correct units. For example, the input to trigonometric functions must be in units of radians, not degrees.
5. Check for possible errors caused by integer or mixed-mode arithmetic.

If you are still getting the wrong answer, add WRITE statements at various points in your program to see the results of intermediate calculations. If you can locate the point where the calculations go bad, then you know just where to look for the problem, which is 95 percent of the battle.

If you still cannot find the problem after all of the above steps, explain what you are doing to another student or to your instructor and ask him or her to look at the code. People usually see just what they expect to see when they look at their own code. Another person can often quickly spot an error that the programmer has overlooked time after time.

Good Programming Practice
To reduce your debugging effort, make sure to adhere to these practices in your program design:
1. Use the IMPLICIT NONE statement.
2. Echo all input values.
3. Initialize all variables.
4. Use parentheses to make the functions of assignment statements clear.

All modern compilers have special debugging tools called *symbolic debuggers*. A symbolic debugger is a tool that allows you to walk through the execution of your program one statement at a time and to examine the values of any variables at each step along the way. Symbolic debuggers allow you to see all the intermediate results without having to insert a lot of WRITE statements into your code. Symbolic debuggers are powerful and flexible, but unfortunately they are different on every type of compiler. If you will be using a symbolic debugger in your class, your instructor will introduce the debugger appropriate for your compiler and computer.

■ 2.15
SUMMARY

Chapter 2 presents many of the fundamental concepts required to write functional Fortran programs, describes the basic structure of Fortran programs, and introduces four types of Fortran constants and variables: integer, real, logical, and character. This chapter introduces the assignment statement, arithmetic calculations, intrinsic functions, and list-directed input/output statements. The examples throughout the chapter emphasize features of the language that are important for writing understandable and maintainable Fortran code.

The Fortran statements introduced in this chapter must appear in a specific order within a Fortran program. The proper order is summarized in Table 2–7.

TABLE 2–7
The order of Fortran statements in a program

1. PROGRAM statement

2. IMPLICIT NONE statement

3. **Type declaration statements:**
   REAL statement(s)
   INTEGER statement(s)   } Any number in any order.
   LOGICAL statement(s)
   CHARACTER statement(s)

4. **Executable statements:**
   Assignment statement(s)
   READ statement(s)   } Any number in the order
   WRITE statement(s)   required to accomplish the
   STOP statement(s)   desired task.

5. END PROGRAM statement

The order in which Fortran expressions are evaluated follows a fixed hierarchy with operations at a higher level evaluated before operations at lower levels. The order in which expressions are evaluated is summarized in Table 2–8.

TABLE 2–8
Fortran hierarchy of operations

1. Operations within parentheses are evaluated, starting with the innermost parentheses and working outward.

2. All exponential operations are evaluated from *right* to *left.*

3. All multiplications and divisions are evaluated from left to right.

4. All additions and subtractions are evaluated from left to right.

5. All relational operators (==, /=, >, >=, <, <=) are evaluated from left to right.

6. All .NOT. operators are evaluated.

7. All .AND. operators are evaluated from left to right.

8. All .OR. operators are evaluated from left to right.

9. All .EQV. and .NEQV. operators are evaluated from left to right.

The Fortran language includes a number of built-in functions to help us solve problems. These functions are called intrinsic functions, since they are intrinsic to the Fortran language itself. Some common intrinsic functions are summarized in Table 2–6, and a complete listing of intrinsic functions is contained in Appendix B.

The two types of intrinsic functions are specific functions and generic functions. Specific functions require that their input data be of a specific type; if data of the wrong type is supplied to a specific function, the result will be meaningless. In contrast, generic functions can accept input data of more than one type and produce correct results.

2.15.1 Summary of Good Programming Practice

Every Fortran program should be designed so that another person who is familiar with Fortran can easily understand it. Clarity is very important, since a good program may be used for a long period of time. As conditions will change, the program will need to be modified to reflect the changes. The program modifications may be done by someone other than the original programmer. The programmer making the modifications must understand the original program well before attempting to change it.

Designing clear, understandable, and maintainable programs is much harder than simply writing programs. To do so, a programmer must develop the discipline to properly document his or her work. In addition, the programmer must be careful to avoid known pitfalls along the path to good programs. The following guidelines will help you to develop good programs:

1. Use meaningful variable names whenever possible. Use names that can be understood at a glance, like `day`, `month`, and `year`.
2. Always use the `IMPLICIT NONE` statement to catch typographical errors in your program at compilation time.
3. Create a data dictionary in each program that you write. The data dictionary should explicitly declare and define each variable in the program. Be sure to include the physical units associated with each variable, if applicable.
4. Use a consistent number of significant digits in constants. For example, do not use 3.14 for π in one part of your program and 3.141593 in another part of the program. To ensure consistency, a constant may be named, and the constant may be referenced by name wherever it is needed.
5. Be sure to specify all constants with as much precision as your computer will support. For example, specify π as 3.141593, *not* as 3.14.
6. Do not use integer arithmetic to calculate continuously varying real-world quantities such as distance and time. Use integer arithmetic only for things that are intrinsically integral, such as counters.
7. Avoid mixed-mode arithmetic except for exponentiation. If you must mix integer and real variables in a single expression, use the intrinsic functions `REAL`, `INT`, and `NINT` to make the type conversions explicit.
8. Use extra parentheses whenever necessary to improve the readability of your expressions.
9. Initialize all variables in a program before using them. The variables may be initialized with assignment statements, with `READ` statements, or directly in type declaration statements.

10. Always print the physical units associated with any value being written out. The units are important for the proper interpretation of a program's results.

2.15.2 Summary of Fortran Statements

The following summary describes the Fortran statements introduced in this chapter.

Assignment Statement

```
variable = expression
```

Examples:

```
pi = 3.141593
distance = 0.5 * acceleration * time ** 2
side = hypot * cos(theta)
```

Description:
    The left side of the assignment statement must be a variable name. The right side of the assignment statement can be any constant, variable, function, or expression. The value of the quantity on the right side of the equal sign is stored into the variable named on the left side of the equal sign.

CHARACTER Statement

```
CHARACTER(len=<len>) :: variable name[, variable name]
CHARACTER(<len>) :: variable name[, variable name]
CHARACTER :: variable name[, variable name]
```

Examples:

```
CHARACTER(len=10) :: first, last, middle
CHARACTER(10) :: first = 'My Name'
CHARACTER :: middle_initial
```

Description:
    The CHARACTER statement is a type declaration statement that declares variables of the character data type. The length in characters of each variable is specified by (len=<len>) or by <len>. If the length is absent, then the length of the variables defaults to 1.
    The value of a CHARACTER variable may be initialized with a string when it is declared, as shown in the second example.

`END PROGRAM` **Statement**

```
END PROGRAM [name]
```

Description:

The `END PROGRAM` statement must be the last statement in a Fortran program segment. It tells the compiler that there are no further statements to process. Program execution is stopped when the `END PROGRAM` statement is reached. The name of the program is optionally in the `END PROGRAM` statement.

`IMPLICIT NONE` **Statement**

```
IMPLICIT NONE
```

Description:

The `IMPLICIT NONE` statement turns off default typing in Fortran. When it is used in a program, every variable in the program must be explicitly declared in a type declaration statement.

`INTEGER` **Statement**

```
INTEGER :: variable name[, variable name, etc.]
```

Examples:

```
INTEGER :: i, j, count
INTEGER :: day = 4
```

Description:

The `INTEGER` statement is a type declaration statement that declares variables of the integer data type. This statement overrides the default typing specified in Fortran. The value of an `INTEGER` variable may be initialized when it is declared, as shown in the second example.

`LOGICAL` **Statement**

```
LOGICAL :: variable name[, variable name, etc.]
```

Examples:

```
LOGICAL :: initialize, debug
LOGICAL :: debug = .false.
```

(continued)

(concluded)

Description:

The LOGICAL statement is a type declaration statement that declares variables of the logical data type. The value of a LOGICAL variable may be initialized when it is declared, as shown in the second example.

PROGRAM **Statement**

    PROGRAM program_name

Example:

    PROGRAM my_program

Description:

The PROGRAM statement specifies the name of a Fortran program. It must be the first statement in a Fortran program. The name must be unique and cannot be used as a variable name within the program. A program name may have 1 to 31 alphabetic, numeric, and underscore characters, but the first character in the program name *must* be alphabetic.

READ **Statement (list-directed** READ**)**

    READ (*,*) variable name [,variable name, etc.]

Examples:

    READ (*,*) stress
    READ (*,*) distance, time

Description:

The list-directed READ statement reads one or more values from the standard input device and loads them into the variables in the list. The values are stored in the order in which the variables are listed. Data values must be separated by blanks or by commas. As many lines as necessary will be read. Each READ statement begins searching for values with a new line.

REAL **Statement**

    REAL :: variable name[, variable name, etc.]
    REAL :: variable name = value

(continued)

(concluded)

Examples:

```
REAL :: distance, time
REAL :: distance = 100
```

Description:

The REAL statement is a type declaration statement that declares variables of the real data type. This statement overrides the default typing specified in Fortran.

The value of a REAL variable may be initialized when it is declared, as shown in the second example.

STOP **Statement**

```
STOP
```

Description:

The STOP statement stops the execution of a Fortran program. A program can have more than one STOP statement. A STOP statement that immediately precedes an END PRO-GRAM statement may be omitted, since execution is also stopped when the END PROGRAM statement is reached. Since execution ends at an END PROGRAM statement anyway, the STOP statement is rarely used.

WRITE **Statement (list-directed** WRITE**)**

```
WRITE (*,*) expression [,expression, etc.]
```

Examples:

```
WRITE (*,*) stress
WRITE (*,*) distance, time
WRITE (*,*) 'SIN(theta) = ', SIN(theta)
```

Description:

The list-directed WRITE statement writes the values of one or more expressions to the standard output device. The values are written in the order in which the expressions are listed.

■ 2.16
EXERCISES

2–1 State whether or not each of the following Fortran 90/95 constants is valid. If valid, state what type of constant it is. If not, state why it is invalid.
a. `3.14159`
b. `'.TRUE.'`
c. `-123,456.789`
d. `+1E-12`
e. `'Who's coming for dinner?'`
f. `.FALSE`
g. `"Pass / Fail'`
h. `"Enter name:"`

2–2 For each of the following pairs of numbers, state whether they represent the same value or different values within the computer.
a. `123.E+0; 123`
b. `1234.E-3; 1.234E3`
c. `1.41421, 1.41421E0`
d. `0.000005E+6; 5.`

2–3 State whether each of the following program names is valid or not. If not, state why the name is invalid.
a. `junk`
b. `3rd`
c. `Who_are_you?`
d. `time_to_intercept`

2–4 Which of the following expressions are legal in Fortran? If an expression is legal, evaluate it.
a. `2.**3 / 3**2`
b. `2 * 6 + 6 ** 2 / 2`
c. `2 * (-10.)**-3.`
d. `2 / (-10.) ** 3.`
e. `23 / (4 / 8)`

2–5 Which of the following expressions are legal in Fortran? If an expression is legal, evaluate it.
a. `((58/4)*(4/58))`
b. `((58/4)*(4/58.))`
c. `((58./4)*(4/58.))`
d. `((58./4*(4/58.))`

2–6 Evaluate the following expressions.
a. `13 / 5 * 6`
b. `(13 / 5) * 6`
c. `13 / (5 * 6)`
d. `13. / 5 * 6`
e. `13 / 5 * 6.`
f. `INT(13. / 5) * 6`
g. `NINT(13. / 5) * 6`

2–7 Evaluate the following expressions.

    a. 3 ** 3 ** 2
    b. (3 ** 3) ** 2
    c. 3 ** (3 ** 2)

2–8 What values will be output from the following program?

```
PROGRAM sample_1
INTEGER :: i1, i2, i3
REAL :: a1 = 2.4, a2
i1 = a1
i2 = INT ( a1 * i1 )
i3 = NINT ( a1 * i1 )
a2 = a1**i1
WRITE (*,*) i1, i2, i3, a1, a2
END PROGRAM
```

2–9 Which of the following expressions are legal in Fortran? If an expression is legal, evaluate it.

    a. 5.5 >= 5
    b. 20 > 20
    c. .NOT. 6 > 5
    d. 15 <= 'A'
    e. .TRUE. > .FALSE.
    f. 35 / 17. > 35 / 17
    g. 7 <= 8 .EQV. 3 / 2 == 1
    h. 17.5 .AND. (3.3 > 2.)

2–10 Which of the following expressions are legal in Fortran? If an expression is legal, evaluate it. Assume the ASCII collating sequence.

    a. '123' > 'abc'
    b. '9478' == 9478
    c. ACHAR(65) // ACHAR(95) // ACHAR(72)
    d. ACHAR(IACHAR('j') + 5)

2–11 Figure 2–11 shows a right triangle with a hypotenuse of length C and angle θ. From elementary trigonometry, the length of sides A and B are given by

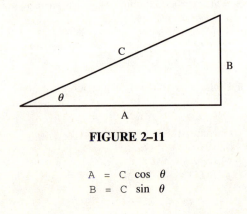

FIGURE 2–11

$$A = C \cos \theta$$
$$B = C \sin \theta$$

The following program is intended to calculate the lengths of sides A and B given the hypotenuse C and angle θ. Will this program run? Will it produce the correct result? Why or why not?

```
PROGRAM triangle
REAL :: a, b, c, theta
WRITE (*,*) 'Enter the length of the hypotenuse C:'
READ (*,*) c
WRITE (*,*) 'Enter the angle THETA in degrees:'
READ (*,*) theta
a = c * COS ( theta )
b = c * SIN ( theta )
WRITE (*,*) 'The length of the adjacent side is ', a
WRITE (*,*) 'The length of the opposite side is ', b
END PROGRAM
```

2–12 What output will be produced by the following program?

```
PROGRAM example
REAL :: a, b, c
INTEGER :: k, l, m
READ (*,*) a, b, c, k
READ (*,*) l, m
WRITE (*,*) a, b, c, k, l, m
END PROGRAM
```

The input data to the program is

```
-3.141592
100, 200., 300, 400
-100, -200, -300
-400
```

2–13 Write a Fortran program that calculates an hourly employee's weekly pay. The program should ask the user for the person's pay rate and the number of hours worked during the week. It should then calculate the total pay from the formula

Total Pay = Hourly Pay Rate × Hours Worked

Finally, it should display the total weekly pay. Check your program by computing the weekly pay for a person earning $7.50 per hour and working for 39 hours.

2–14 The potential energy of an object due to its height above the surface of the Earth is given by the equation

$$PE = mgh \qquad (2\text{–}10)$$

where m is the mass of the object, g is the acceleration due to gravity, and h is the height above the surface of the Earth. The kinetic energy of a moving object is given by the equation

$$KE = \frac{1}{2} mv^2 \qquad (2\text{–}11)$$

where m is the mass of the object and v is the velocity of the object. Write a Fortran statement for the total energy (potential plus kinetic) possessed by an object in the earth's gravitational field.

2–15 If a stationary ball is released at a height h above the surface of the Earth, the velocity of the ball v when it hits the earth is given by the equation

$$v = \sqrt{2gh} \qquad\qquad (2-12)$$

where g is the acceleration due to gravity and h is the height above the surface of the Earth (assuming no air friction). Write a Fortran equation for the velocity of the ball when it hits the Earth.

2–16 Period of a Pendulum The period of an oscillating pendulum T (in seconds) is given by the equation

$$T = 2\pi \sqrt{\frac{L}{g}} \qquad\qquad (2-13)$$

where L is the length of the pendulum in meters and g is the acceleration due to gravity in meters per second squared. Write a Fortran program to calculate the period of a pendulum of length L. The user will specify the length of the pendulum when the program is run. Use good programming practices in your program. (The acceleration due to gravity at the Earth's surface is 9.81 m/sec^2.)

2–17 Write a program to calculate the hypotenuse of a right triangle, given the lengths of its two sides. Use good programming practices in your program.

2–18 Write a program using the IMPLICIT NONE statement and do not declare one of the variables in the program. What sort of error message does your compiler generate?

2–19 The distance between two points ($x1$, $y1$) and ($x2$, $y2$) on the Cartesian coordinate plane in Figure 2–12 is given by the equation

$$d = \sqrt{(x1 - x2)^2 + (y1 - y2)^2} \qquad\qquad (2-14)$$

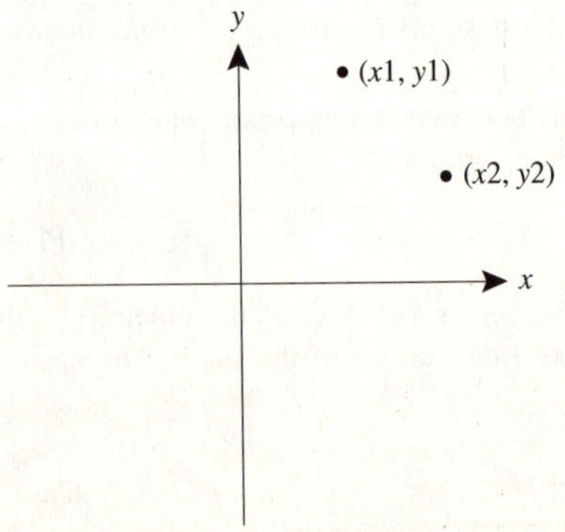

FIGURE 2–12

Write a Fortran program to calculate the distance between any two points $(x1, y1)$ and $(x2, y2)$ specified by the user. Use good programming practices in your program. Use the program to calculate the distance between the points $(2,3)$ and $(8, -5)$.

2–20 **Decibels** Engineers often measure the ratio of two power measurements in *decibels,* or dB. The equation for the ratio of two power measurements in decibels is

$$dB = 10 \log_{10} \frac{P_2}{P_1}$$

where P_2 is the power level being measured, and P_1 is some reference power level. Assume that the reference power level P_1 is 1 milliwatt. Write a program that accepts an input power P_2 and converts it into dB with respect to the 1 milliwatt reference level.

2–21 **Hyperbolic cosine** The hyperbolic cosine function is defined by the equation

$$\cosh x = \frac{e^x + e^{-x}}{2}$$

Write a Fortran program to calculate the hyperbolic cosine of a user-supplied value x. Use the program to calculate the hyperbolic cosine of 3.0. Compare the answer that your program produces to the answer produced by the Fortran intrinsic function COSH(x).

2–22 **Radio Receiver** A simplified version of the front end of an AM radio receiver is shown in Figure 2–13. This receiver consists of an *RLC* tuned circuit containing a resistor, capacitor, and an inductor connected in series. The *RLC* circuit is connected to an external antenna and ground as shown in the picture.

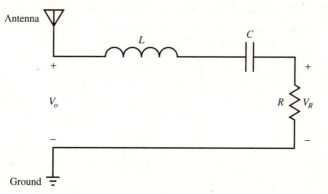

FIGURE 2–13
A simplified representation of an AM radio set.

The tuned circuit allows the radio to select a specific station out of all the stations transmitting on the AM band. At the resonant frequency of the circuit, essentially all of the signal V_o appearing at the antenna appears across the resistor, which represents the rest of the radio. In other words, the radio receives its strongest signal at the resonant frequency. The resonant frequency of the LC circuit is given by the equation

$$f_o = \frac{1}{2\pi \sqrt{LC}} \tag{2–15}$$

where L is inductance in henrys (H) and C is capacitance in farads (F). Write a program that calculates the resonant frequency of this radio set given specific values of L and C. Test your program by calculating the frequency of the radio when $L = 0.1$ mH and $C = 0.25$ nF.

Control Structures and Program Design

In the previous chapter, we developed several complete working Fortran programs. However, the programs were very simple, consisting of a series of Fortran statements that were executed one after another in a fixed order. Such programs are called *sequential* programs. They read input data, process it to produce a desired answer, print out the answer, and quit. There is no way to repeat sections of the program more than once, and there is no way to execute only certain portions of the program depending on values of the input data.

This chapter introduces a number of Fortran statements that allow programmers to control the order in which statements are executed in a program. The two broad categories of control statement are **branches,** which select specific sections of the code to execute, and **loops,** which cause specific sections of the code to be repeated.

Programs with branches and loops tend to become relatively complex; they offer many opportunities for programmers to make mistakes. To help you avoid programming errors, this chapter introduces a formal program-design procedure based on the technique known as *top-down design,* as well as two common algorithm development tools: flowcharts and pseudocode.

3.1
INTRODUCTION TO TOP-DOWN DESIGN TECHNIQUES

Suppose that you are an engineer working in industry and that you need to write a Fortran program to solve some problem. How do you begin?

When given a new problem, the natural tendency is to sit down at a terminal and start programming without "wasting" a lot of time thinking about it first. This "on the fly" approach to programming often works for very small problems, such as many of the examples in this book. In the real world, however, problems are larger, and a programmer using this approach will become hopelessly bogged down. For larger problems, you should always think through the problem and the approach you are going to take to it *before* writing a single line of code.

This section introduces a formal-program design process that we will apply to every major application developed in the remainder of the book. The design process will seem like overkill for some of the simple examples, but as the problems get larger, the process becomes more and more essential to successful programming.

When I was an undergraduate, one of my professors was fond of saying, "Programming is easy. It's knowing what to program that's hard." His point was forcefully driven home to me after I left the university and began working in industry on larger-scale software projects. I found that the most difficult part of my job was to *understand the problem* I was trying to solve. Once I really understood the problem, it became easy to break the problem apart into smaller, more easily manageable pieces with well-defined functions and then to tackle those pieces one at a time.

Top-down design is the process of starting with a large task and breaking it down into smaller, more easily understandable pieces (subtasks) that perform a portion of the desired task. Each subtask may in turn be subdivided into smaller subtasks if necessary. Once the program is divided into small pieces, each piece can be coded and tested independently. We do not attempt to combine the subtasks into a complete task until each subtasks has been verified to work properly by itself.

The concept of top-down design is the basis of our formal program design process. The details of the process are illustrated in Figure 3–1.

Top-down design involves the following steps:

1. *Clearly state the problem that you are trying to solve.*

Programs are usually written to fill some perceived need, but the person requesting the program may not be able to state that need clearly. For example, a user may ask for a program to solve a system of simultaneous linear equations. This request is not clear enough to allow a programmer to design a program to meet the need; he or she must first know much more about the problem to be solved. Is the system of equations to be solved real or complex? What is the maximum number of equations and unknowns that the program must handle? Are there any symmetries in the equations that you can exploit to make the task easier? The program designer will have to talk with the user requesting the program, and the two of them will have to come up with a clear statement of exactly what they are trying to accomplish. A clear statement of the problem will prevent misunderstandings, and it will also help the program designer to organize his or her thoughts. In the example we were describing, a proper statement of the problem might have been:

> Design and write a program to solve a system of simultaneous linear equations having real coefficients and with up to 20 equations in 20 unknowns.

2. *Define the inputs required by the program and the outputs to be produced by the program.*

The inputs to the program and the outputs produced by the program must be specified so that the new program will fit into the overall processing scheme. In the preceding example, the coefficients of the equations to be solved are probably in some preexisting order, and our new program needs to be able to read them in that order. Similarly, the new program needs to produce the answers required by the programs that may follow it in the overall processing scheme and to write out those answers in the proper format.

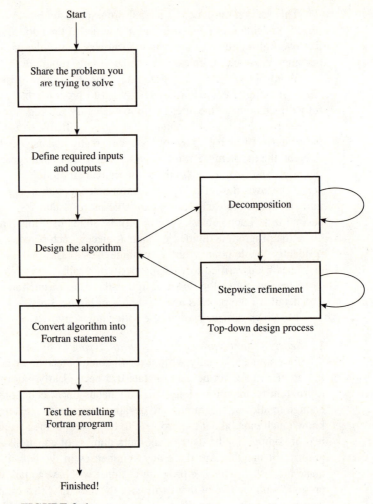

FIGURE 3–1
The program design process used in this book.

3. *Design the algorithm that you intend to implement in the program.*

An **algorithm** is a step-by-step procedure for solving a problem. It is at this stage in the process that top-down design techniques come into play. The designer looks for logical divisions within the problem and divides it up into subtasks along those lines. This process is called *decomposition*. If the subtasks are themselves large, the designer can break them up into even smaller sub-subtasks. This process continues until the problem has been divided into many small pieces, each of which does a simple, clearly understandable job.

After the problem has been decomposed into small pieces, each piece is further refined through a process called *stepwise refinement*. In stepwise refinement, a designer starts with a general description of what the piece of code should do and then defines the functions of the piece in greater and greater detail until they are specific enough to be turned into Fortran statements. Stepwise refinement is usually done with **pseudocode,** which is described in the next section.

A helpful technique is to solve a simple example of the problem by hand during the algorithm development process. If the designer understands the steps that he or she went through in solving the problem by hand, then the designer will be better able to apply decomposition and stepwise refinement to the problem.

4. *Turn the algorithm into* Fortran *statements.*

If the decomposition and refinement process was carried out properly, this step will be very simple. All the programmer will have to do is to replace pseudocode with the corresponding Fortran statements on a one-for-one basis.

5. *Test the resulting* Fortran *program.*

This step is the real killer. The components of the program must first be tested individually, if possible, and then the program as a whole must be tested. When testing a program, we must verify that it works correctly for *all legal input data sets.* It is very common for a program to be written, tested with some standard data set, and released for use, only to find that it produces the wrong answers (or crashes) with a different input data set. If the algorithm implemented in a program has multiple branches, we must test every branch to confirm that the program operates correctly under every possible circumstance.

Large programs typically go through a series of tests before they are released for general use (see Figure 3–2). The first stage of testing is sometimes called **unit testing.** During unit testing, the individual subtasks of the program are tested separately to confirm that they work correctly. After the unit testing is completed, the program goes through a series of *builds* during which the individual subtasks are combined to produce the final program. The first build of the program typically includes only a few of the subtasks. It is used to check the interactions among those subtasks and the functions performed by the combinations of the subtasks. In successive builds, more and more subtasks are added, until the entire program is complete. Testing is performed on each build, and any errors (bugs) that are detected are corrected before moving on to the next build.

Testing continues even after the program is complete. The first complete version of the program is usually called the *alpha release.* It is exercised by the programmers and others very close to them in as many different ways as possible, and the bugs discovered during the testing are corrected. When the most serious bugs have been removed from the program, a new version called the *beta release* is prepared. The beta release is normally given to "friendly" outside users who have a need for the program in their normal day-to-day jobs. These users put the program through its paces under many different conditions and with many different input data sets, and they report any bugs that they find to the programmers. When those bugs have been corrected, the program is ready to be released for general use.

Because the programs in this book are fairly small, we will not go through the sort of extensive testing described above. However, we will follow the basic principles in testing all of our programs.

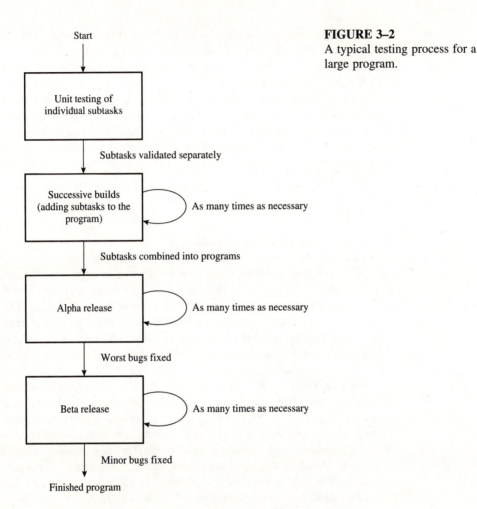

FIGURE 3–2
A typical testing process for a large program.

The program design process may be summarized as follows:

1. Clearly state the problem that you are trying to solve.
2. Define the inputs required by the program and the outputs to be produced by the program.
3. Design the algorithm that you intend to implement in the program.
4. Turn the algorithm into Fortran statements.
5. Test the Fortran program.

Good Programming Practice
Follow the steps of the program-design process to produce reliable, understandable Fortran programs.

In a large programming project, the time actually spent programming is surprisingly small. In his book *The Mythical Man-Month*[1], Frederick P. Brooks Jr. suggests that in a typical large software project, one-third of the time is spent planning what to do (steps 1 through 3), one-sixth of the time is spent actually writing the program (step 4), and fully one-half of the time is spent in testing and debugging the program! Clearly, anything that we can do to reduce the testing and debugging time will be very helpful. We can best reduce the testing and debugging time by doing a very careful job in the planning phase and by using good programming practices. Good programming practices will reduce the number of bugs in the program and will make the ones that do creep in easier to find.

▮ 3.2
PSEUDOCODE AND FLOWCHARTS

Part of the design process is to describe the algorithm that you intend to implement. The description of the algorithm should be in a standard form that is easy for both you and other people to understand, and the description should aid you in turning your concept into Fortran code. The standard forms that we use to describe algorithms are called **constructs,** and an algorithm described using these constructs is called a structured algorithm. When the algorithm is implemented in a Fortran program, the resulting program is called a *structured program.*

The constructs used to build algorithms can be described in two different ways: pseudocode and flowcharts. Pseudocode is a hybrid mixture of Fortran and English. It is structured like Fortran with a separate line for each distinct idea or segment of code, but the descriptions on each line are in English. Each line of the pseudocode should describe its idea in plain, easily understandable English. Pseudocode is very useful for developing algorithms, since it is flexible and easy to modify. Pseudocode is especially useful because it can be written and modified on the same computer terminal used to write the Fortran program—no special graphical capabilities are required.

For example, the pseudocode for the algorithm in Example 2–4 is

```
Prompt user to enter temperature in degrees Fahrenheit
Read temperature in degrees Fahrenheit (temp_f)
temp_k in kelvins ← (5./9.) * (temp_f − 32) + 273.15
Write temperature in kelvins
```

Notice that a left arrow (←) is used instead of an equal sign (=) to indicate that a value is stored in a variable, to avoid any confusion between assignment and equality. Pseudocode is intended to aid you in organizing your thoughts before converting them into Fortran code.

Flowcharts are a way to describe algorithms graphically. In a flowchart, different graphical symbols represent the different operations in the algorithm, and our standard

---

[1] F. P. Brooks Jr., *The Mythical Man-Month,* (New York: Addison-Wesley, 1975.)

constructs are made up of collections of one or more of these symbols. Flowcharts are very useful for describing the algorithm implemented in a program after it is completed. However, since they are graphical, flowcharts tend to be cumbersome to modify, and they are not very useful during the preliminary stages of algorithm definition when rapid changes are occurring. The most common graphical symbols used in flowcharts are shown in Figure 3–3, and the flowchart for the algorithm in Example 2–4 is shown in Figure 3–4.

The examples in this book illustrate the use of both pseudocode and flowcharts. You are welcome to use whichever one of these tools gives you the best results in your own programming projects.

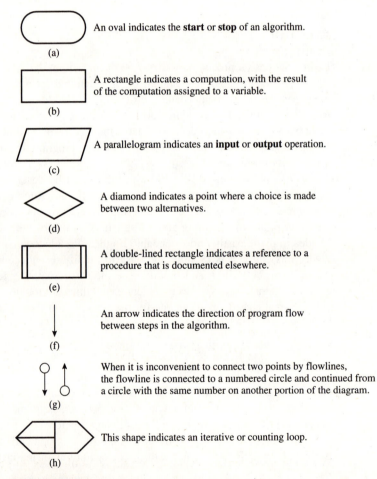

FIGURE 3–3
Common symbols used in flowcharts.

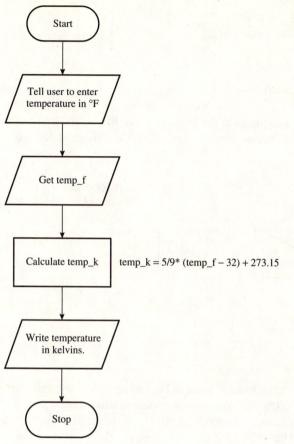

FIGURE 3–4
Flowchart for the algorithm in Example 2–4.

Start

Tell user to enter temperature in °F

Get temp_f

Calculate temp_k $temp\_k = 5/9* (temp\_f - 32) + 273.15$

Write temperature in kelvins.

Stop

■ **3.3**

CONTROL CONSTRUCTS: BRANCHES

Branches are Fortran statements that permit us to select and execute specific sections of code (called *blocks*) while skipping other sections of code. They are variations of the IF statement, plus the SELECT CASE.

3.3.1 The Block IF Construct

The commonest form of the IF statement is the block IF construct. This construct specifies that a block of code will be executed if and only if a certain logical expression is true. The block IF construct has the form

```
IF (logical_expr) THEN
    Statement 1
    Statement 2          }  Block 1
    ...
END IF
```

If the logical expression is true, the program executes the statements in the block between the `IF` and `END IF` statements. If the logical expression is false, then the program skips all of the statements in the block between the `IF` and `END IF` statements and executes the next statement after the `END IF`. The flowchart for a block `IF` construct is shown in Figure 3–5.

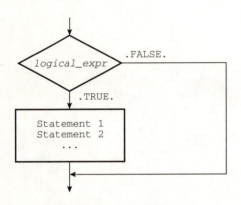

FIGURE 3–5
Flowchart for a simple block `IF` construct.

The `IF (...) THEN` is a single Fortran statement that must be written together on the same line, and the statements to be executed must occupy separate lines below the `IF (...) THEN` statement. An `END IF` statement must follow them on a separate line. The line containing the `END IF` statement must not have a statement number. For readability, the block of code between the `IF` and `END IF` statements is usually indented by two or three spaces, but this convention is not actually required.

Good Programming Practice
Always indent the body of a block `IF` construct by two or more spaces to improve the readability of the code.

As an example of a block `IF` construct, consider the solution of a quadratic equation of the form

$$ax^2 + bx + c = 0 \qquad (3\text{–}1)$$

The solution to this equation is

$$x = \frac{-b \pm \sqrt{b^2 - 4ac}}{2a} \qquad (3\text{–}2)$$

The term $b^2 - 4ac$ is known as the *discriminant* of the equation. If $b^2 - 4ac > 0$, then the quadratic equation has two distinct real roots. If $b^2 - 4ac = 0$, then the equation has a single repeated root; and if $b^2 - 4ac < 0$, then the quadratic equation has two complex roots.

Suppose that we want to examine the discriminant of the quadratic equation and tell a user if the equation has complex roots. In pseudocode the block IF construct would take the form

```
IF (b**2 - 4.*a*c) < 0. THEN
        Write message that equation has two complex roots.
END of IF
```

In Fortran the block IF construct is

```
IF ( (b**2 - 4.*a*c) < 0. ) THEN
      WRITE (*,*) 'There are two complex roots to this equation.'
END IF
```

The flowchart for this construct is shown in Figure 3–6.

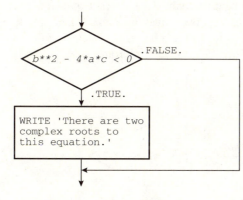

FIGURE 3–6

Flowchart showing structure to determine if a quadratic equation has two complex roots.

3.3.2 The ELSE and ELSE IF Clauses

In the simple block IF construct, a block of code is executed if the controlling logical expression is true. If the controlling logical expression is false, all the statements in the construct are skipped.

Sometimes we may want to execute one set of statements if some condition is true and different sets of statements if other conditions are true. If fact, we might have many different options to consider. An ELSE clause and one or more ELSE IF clauses may be added to the block IF construct for this purpose. The block IF construct with an ELSE clause and an ELSE IF clause has this form:

```
IF (logical_expr_1) THEN
      Statement 1        ⎫
      Statement 2        ⎬  Block 1
      ...                ⎭
```

```
          ELSE IF (logical_expr_2) THEN
             Statement 1
             Statement 2                    } Block 2
             ...
          ELSE
             Statement 1
             Statement 2                    } Block 3
             ...
          END IF
```

If *logical_expr_1* is true, then the program executes the statements in block 1 and skips to the first executable statement following the END IF. Otherwise, the program checks for the status of *logical_expr_2*. If *logical_expr_2* is true, then the program executes the statements in block 2 and skips to the first executable statement following the END IF. If both logical expressions are false, then the program executes the statements in block 3.

The ELSE and ELSE IF statements must occupy lines by themselves. A line containing an ELSE or ELSE IF statement should not have a statement number.

Any number of ELSE IF clauses can appear in a block IF construct. The logical expression in each clause will be tested only if the logical expressions in every clause above it are false. Once one of the expressions proves to be true and the corresponding code block is executed, the program skips to the first executable statement following the END IF.

The flowchart for a block IF construct with an ELSE IF and an ELSE clause is shown in Figure 3–7.

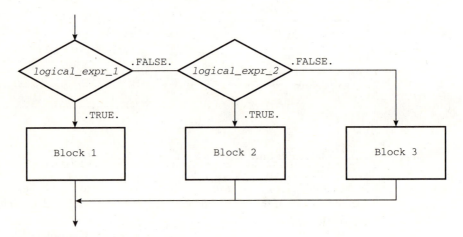

FIGURE 3–7
Flowchart for a block IF construct with an ELSE IF clause and an ELSE clause.

To illustrate the use of the ELSE and ELSE IF clauses, let's reconsider the quadratic equation. Suppose that we want to examine the discriminant of a quadratic equation and to tell a user whether the equation has two complex roots, two identical real roots, or two distinct real roots. In pseudocode this construct would take the form

```
IF (b**2 − 4.*a*c) < 0. THEN
   Write message that equation has two complex roots.
ELSE IF (b**2 − 4.*a*c) == 0. THEN
   Write message that equation has two identical real roots.
ELSE
   Write message that equation has two distinct real roots.
END IF
```

The corresponding Fortran statements are

```
IF ( (b**2 − 4.*a*c) < 0. ) THEN
   WRITE (*,*) 'The equation has two complex roots.'
ELSE IF ( (b**2 − 4.*a*c) == 0. ) THEN
   WRITE (*,*) 'The equation has two identical real roots.'
ELSE
   WRITE (*,*) 'The equation has two distinct real roots.'
END IF
```

The flowchart for this construct is shown in Figure 3–8.

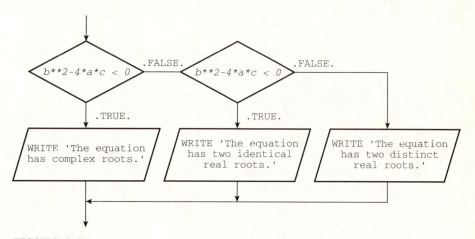

FIGURE 3–8
Flowchart showing structure to determine whether a quadratic equation has two complex roots, two identical real roots, or two distinct real roots.

3.3.3 Examples Using Block IF Constructs

We will now look at two examples that illustrate the use of block IF constructs.

EXAMPLE 3–1 The Quadratic Equation: Design and write a program to solve for the roots of a quadratic equation, regardless of type.

SOLUTION

In solving this problem, we will follow the design steps outlined earlier in the chapter.

1. State the problem.

The problem statement for this example is very simple. We want to write a program that will solve for the roots of a quadratic equation, whether they are distinct real roots, repeated real roots, or complex roots.

2. Define the inputs and outputs.

The inputs required by this program are the coefficients a, b, and c of the quadratic equation

$$ax^2 + bx + c = 0 \qquad\qquad (3\text{--}1)$$

The output from the program will be the roots of the quadratic equation, whether they are distinct real roots, repeated real roots, or complex roots.

3. Design the algorithm.

This task can be broken down into three major sections, whose functions are input, processing, and output:

```
Read the input data
Calculate the roots
Write out the roots
```

We will now break each of the above major sections into smaller, more detailed pieces. There are three possible ways to calculate the roots, depending on the value of the discriminant, so it is logical to implement this algorithm with a three-branched IF statement. The resulting pseudocode is:

```
Prompt the user for the coefficients a, b, and c.
Read a, b, and c.
Echo the input coefficients
discriminant ← b**2 - 4. * a * c.
IF discriminant > 0 THEN
    x1 ← ( -b + sqrt (discriminant) ) / ( 2. * a )
    x2 ← ( -b - sqrt (discriminant) ) / ( 2. * a )
    Write message that equation has two distinct real roots.
    Write out the two roots.
ELSE IF discriminant == 0 THEN
    x1 ← -b / ( 2. * a )
    Write message that equation has two identical real roots.
    Write out the repeated root.
ELSE
    real_part ← -b / ( 2. * a )
    imag_part ← sqrt ( abs ( discriminant ) ) / ( 2. * a )
    Write message that equation has two complex roots.
    Write out the two roots.
END IF
```

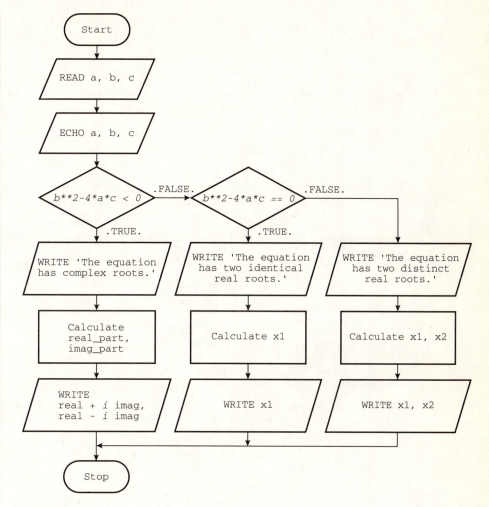

FIGURE 3–9

Flowchart of program roots.

The flowchart for this program is shown in Figure 3–9.

4. **Turn the algorithm into Fortran statements.**

The final Fortran code is shown in Figure 3–10.

FIGURE 3–10

Program to solve for the roots of a quadratic equation.

```
PROGRAM roots
! Purpose:
!   This program solves for the roots of a quadratic equation of the
```
(continued)

(concluded)
```
!    form a*x**2 + b*x + c = 0. It calculates the answers regardless
!    of the type of roots that the equation possesses.
!
! Record of revisions:
!    Date        Programmer        Description of change
!    ====        ==========        =====================
!   9/06/95    S. J. Chapman      Original code
!
IMPLICIT NONE

! Declare the variables used in this program
REAL :: a                ! Coefficient of x**2 term of equation
REAL :: b                ! Coefficient of x term of equation
REAL :: c                ! Constant term of equation
REAL :: discriminant     ! Discriminant of the equation
REAL :: imag_part        ! Imaginary part of equation (for complex roots)
REAL :: real_part        ! Real part of equation (for complex roots)
REAL :: x1               ! First solution of equation (for real roots)
REAL :: x2               ! First solution of equation (for real roots)
! Prompt the user for the coefficients of the equation
WRITE (*,*) 'This program solves for the roots of a quadratic '
WRITE (*,*) 'equation of the form A * X**2 + B * X + C = 0. '
WRITE (*,*) 'Enter the coefficients A, B, and C: '
READ  (*,*) a, b, c

! Echo back coefficients
WRITE (*,*) 'The coefficients A, B, and C are: ', a, b, c

! Calculate discriminant
discriminant = b**2 - 4. * a * c

! Solve for the roots, depending upon the value of the discriminant
IF ( discriminant > 0. ) THEN ! there are two real roots, so...

   x1 = ( -b + sqrt(discriminant) ) / ( 2. * a )
   x2 = ( -b - sqrt(discriminant) ) / ( 2. * a )
   WRITE (*,*) 'This equation has two real roots:'
   WRITE (*,*) 'X1 = ', x1
   WRITE (*,*) 'X2 = ', x2

ELSE IF ( discriminant == 0. ) THEN ! there is one repeated root, so...

   x1 = ( -b ) / ( 2. * a )
   WRITE (*,*) 'This equation has two identical real roots:'
   WRITE (*,*) 'X1 = X2 = ', x1

ELSE ! there are complex roots, so ...

   real_part = ( -b ) / ( 2. * a )
   imag_part = sqrt ( abs ( discriminant ) ) / ( 2. * a )
   WRITE (*,*) 'This equation has complex roots:'
   WRITE (*,*) 'X1 = ', real_part, ' +i ', imag_part
   WRITE (*,*) 'X2 = ', real_part, ' -i ', imag_part

END IF

END PROGRAM
```

5. **Test the program.**

Finally, we must test the program using real input data. Since there are three possible paths through the program, we must test all three paths before we can be certain that the program is working properly. We can verify the solutions to the following equations from Equation (3–2):

$x^2 + 5x + 6 = 0$ $x = -2$, and $x = -3$

$x^2 + 4x + 4 = 0$ $x = -2$

$x^2 + 2x + 5 = 0$ $x = -1 \pm i2$

If this program is compiled and then run three times with the above coefficients, the results are as follows (user inputs are shown in bold face):

```
C> roots
This program solves for the roots of a quadratic
equation of the form A * X**2 + B * X + C = 0.
Enter the coefficients A, B, and C:
1., 5., 6.
The coefficients A, B, and C are:        1.000000        5.000000
    6.000000
This equation has two real roots:
X1 =            -2.000000
X2 =            -3.000000

C> roots
This program solves for the roots of a quadratic
equation of the form A * X**2 + B * X + C = 0.
Enter the coefficients A, B, and C:
1., 4., 4.
The coefficients A, B, and C are:        1.000000        4.000000
        4.000000
This equation has two identical real roots:
X1 = X2 =            -2.000000

C> roots
This program solves for the roots of a quadratic
equation of the form A * X**2 + B * X + C = 0.
Enter the coefficients A, B, and C:
1., 2., 5.
The coefficients A, B, and C are:        1.000000        2.000000
        5.000000
This equation has complex roots:
X1 =        -1.000000 +i        2.000000
X2 =        -1.000000 -i        2.000000
```

The program gives the correct answers for our test data in all three possible cases.

EXAMPLE 3–2 Evaluating a Function of Two Variables: Write a Fortran program to evaluate a function $f(x,y)$ for any two user-specified values x and y. The function $f(x,y)$ is defined as follows.

$$f(x, y) = \begin{cases} x + y & x \geq 0 \text{ and } y \geq 0 \\ x + y^2 & x \geq 0 \text{ and } y < 0 \\ x^2 + y & x < 0 \text{ and } y \geq 0 \\ x^2 + y^2 & x < 0 \text{ and } y < 0 \end{cases}$$

SOLUTION

The function *f(x,y)* is evaluated differently depending on the signs of the two independent variables *x* and *y*. To determine the proper equation to apply, we will have to check for the signs of the *x* and *y* values supplied by the user.

1. **State the problem.**

   This problem statement is very simple: Evaluate the function *f(x,y)* for any user-supplied values of *x* and *y*.

2. **Define the inputs and outputs.**

   The inputs required by this program are the values of the independent variables *x* and *y*. The output from the program will be the value of the function *f(x,y)*.

3. **Design the algorithm.**

   This task can be broken down into three major sections, whose functions are input, processing, and output:

   ```
   Read the input values x and y
   Calculate f(x,y)
   Write out f(x,y)
   ```

We will now break each of the above major sections into smaller, more detailed pieces. There are four possible ways to calculate the function *f(x,y)*, depending on the values of *x* and *y*, so it is logical to implement this algorithm with a four-branched IF statement. The resulting pseudocode is

   ```
   Prompt the user for the values x and y.
   Read x and y
   Echo the input coefficients
   IF x ≥ 0 and y ≥ 0 THEN
       fun ← x + y
   ELSE IF x ≥ 0 and y < 0 THEN
       fun ← x + y**2
   ELSE IF x < 0 and y ≥ 0 THEN
       fun ← x**2 + y
   ELSE
       fun ← x**2 + y**2
   END IF
   Write out f(x,y)
   ```

The flowchart for this program is shown in Figure 3–11.

4. **Turn the algorithm into Fortran statements.**

The final Fortran code is shown in Figure 3–12.

FIGURE 3–12
Program funxy from Example 3–2.

```
PROGRAM funxy
```

(continued)

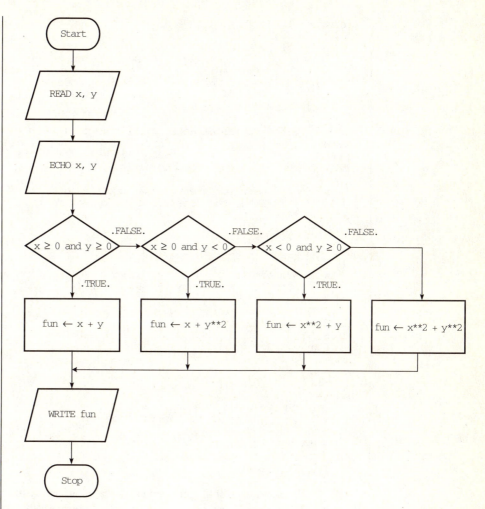

FIGURE 3–11
Flowchart of program funxy.

(continued)
```
!
! Purpose:
!    This program solves the function f(x,y) for a user-specified x and y,
!    where f(x,y) is defined as:
!
!
!              ┌
!              │  X + Y         X >= 0 and Y >= 0
!              │  X + Y**2      X >= 0 and Y < 0
!    F(X,Y) =  │  X**2 + Y      X < 0   and Y >= 0
!              │  X**2 + Y**2   X < 0   and Y < 0
!              └
!
```

(continued)

(concluded)

```
!
! Record of revisions:
!     Date          Programmer         Description of change
!     ====          ==========         =====================
!   09/08/95    S. J. Chapman          Original code
!
IMPLICIT NONE

! Declare the variables used in this program.
REAL :: x                    ! First independent variable
REAL :: y                    ! Second independent variable
REAL :: fun                  ! Resulting function

! Prompt the user for the values x and y
WRITE (*,*) 'Enter the coefficients x and y: '
READ (*,*) x, y

! Write the coefficients of x and y.
WRITE (*,*) 'The coefficients x and y are: ', x, y

! Calculate the function f(x,y) based upon the signs of x and y.
IF ( ( x >= 0. ) .AND. ( y >= 0. ) ) THEN
   fun = x + y
ELSE IF ( ( x >= 0. ) .AND. ( y < 0. ) ) THEN
   fun = x + y**2
ELSE IF ( ( x < 0. ) .AND. ( y >= 0. ) ) THEN
   fun = x**2 + y
ELSE
   fun = x**2 + y**2
END IF

! Write the value of the function.
WRITE (*,*) 'The value of the function is: ', fun

END PROGRAM
```

5. Test the program.

Finally, we must test the program using real input data. Since there are four possible paths through the program, we must test all four paths before we can be certain that the program is working properly. To test all four possible paths, we will execute the program with the four sets of input values $(x,y) = (2,3)$, $(-2,3)$, $(2,-3)$, and $(-2,-3)$. Calculating by hand, we see that

$$f(2,3) = 2 + 3 = 5$$
$$f(2,-3) = 2 + (-3)^2 = 11$$
$$f(-2,3) = (-2)^2 + 3 = 7$$
$$f(-2,-3) = (-2)^2 + (-3)^2 = 13$$

If this program is compiled and then run four times with the above values, the results are

```
C>funxy
Enter the coefficients X and Y:
```

```
2. 3.
The coefficients X and Y are:        2.000000        3.000000
The value of the function is:        5.000000

C>funxy
Enter the coefficients X and Y:
2. -3.
The coefficients X and Y are:        2.000000       -3.000000
The value of the function is:       11.000000

C>funxy
Enter the coefficients X and Y:
-2. 3.
The coefficients X and Y are:       -2.000000        3.000000
The value of the function is:        7.000000

C>funxy
Enter the coefficients X and Y:
-2. -3.
The coefficients X and Y are:       -2.000000       -3.000000
The value of the function is:       13.000000
```

The program gives the correct answers for our test values in all four possible cases.

3.3.4 Named Block IF Constructs

It is possible to assign a name to a block IF construct. The general form of the construct with a name attached is

```
[name:] IF logical_expr_1) THEN
    Statement 1        ⎤
    Statement 2        ⎬ Block 1
    ...                ⎦
ELSE IF (logical_expr_2) THEN [name]
    Statement 1        ⎤
    Statement 2        ⎬ Block 2
    ...                ⎦
ELSE [name]
    Statement 1        ⎤
    Statement 2        ⎬ Block 3
    ...                ⎦
END IF [name]
```

where name may be up to 31 alphanumeric characters long, beginning with a letter. The name given to the IF construct must be unique within each program unit and must not be the same as any constant or variable name within the program unit. If a name is assigned to an IF, then the same name must appear on the associated END IF. Names are optional on the ELSE and ELSE IF statements of the construct, but if they are used, they must be the same as the name on the IF.

Why would we want to name an IF construct? For simple examples like the ones we have seen so far, there is no particular reason to do so. The principal reason for using names is to help us (and the compiler) keep IF constructs straight in our own minds when they get very complicated. For example, suppose that we have a complex IF construct that is hundreds of lines long, spanning many pages of listings. If we name all the parts of such a construct, then we can tell at a glance which construct a particular ELSE or ELSE IF statement belongs to. Names on constructs make a programmer's intentions explicitly clear and can help the compiler flag the specific location of any error.

Good Programming Practice
Assign a name to any large and complicated IF constructs in your program to help you keep track of the parts of the construct.

3.3.5 Notes Concerning the Use of Logical IF Constructs

The block IF construct is very flexible. It must have one IF (...) THEN statement and one END IF statement. In between, it can have any number of ELSE IF clauses and may also have one ELSE clause. With this combination of features, it is possible to implement any desired branching construct.

In addition, block IF constructs may be **nested.** Two block IF constructs are said to be nested if one of them lies entirely within a single code block of the other one. The following two IF constructs are properly nested:

```
outer: IF (x > 0.) THEN
   ...
   inner: IF (y < 0.) THEN
      ...
   END IF inner
   ...
END IF outer
```

It is a good idea to name IF constructs when they are being nested, since the name explicitly indicates which IF a particular END IF is associated with. If the constructs are not named, the Fortran compiler always associates a given END IF with the most recent IF statement. This method works well for a properly written program but can cause the compiler to produce confusing error messages if the programmer makes a coding error. For example, suppose we have a large program containing a construct such as this:

```
PROGRAM mixup
...
IF (test1) THEN
   ...
   IF (test2) THEN
      ...
      IF (test.3) THEN
         ...
      END IF
   ...
```

```
                    END IF
                    ...
              END IF
              ...
              END PROGRAM
```

This program contains three nested `IF` constructs that may span hundreds of lines of code. Now suppose that the first `END IF` statement is accidentally deleted during an editing session. When that happens, the compiler will automatically associate the second `END IF` with the innermost `IF (test3)` construct and the third `END IF` with the middle `IF (test2)`. When the compiler reaches the `END PROGRAM` statement, it will notice that the first `IF (test1)` construct was never ended, and it will generate an error message saying that an `END IF` is missing. Unfortunately, the compiler can't tell *where* the problem occurred, so we will have to go back and manually search the entire program to locate the problem.

In contrast, consider what happens if we assign names to each `IF` construct. The resulting program would be

```
              PROGRAM mixup_1
              ...
              outer: IF (test1) THEN
                 ...
                 middle: IF (test2) THEN
                    ...
                    inner: IF (test3) THEN
                       ...
                    END IF inner
                    ...
                 END IF middle
                 ...
              END IF outer
              ...
              END PROGRAM
```

If the first `END IF` statement is again accidentally deleted during an editing session, the compiler will notice that no `END IF` is associated with the inner `IF`. The compiler will generate an error message as soon as it encounters the `END IF middle` statement. Furthermore, the error message will explicitly state that the problem is associated with the inner `IF` construct, so we know just where to go to fix it.

It is sometimes possible to implement an algorithm using either `ELSE IF` clauses or nested `IF` statements. In that case, a programmer may choose whichever style he or she prefers.

EXAMPLE 3–3 Assigning Letter Grades: Suppose that we are writing a program that reads in a numerical grade and assigns a letter grade to it according to the following table:

$$
\begin{array}{ll}
95 < \text{GRADE} & A \\
86 < \text{GRADE} \le 95 & B \\
76 < \text{GRADE} \le 86 & C \\
66 < \text{GRADE} \le 76 & D \\
0 < \text{GRADE} \le 66 & F \\
\end{array}
$$

Write an IF construct that will assign the grades as described above using (*a*) multiple ELSE IF clauses and (*b*) nested IF constructs.

SOLUTION

(*a*) One possible structure using ELSE IF clauses is

```
IF ( grade > 95.0 ) THEN
   WRITE (*,*) 'The grade is A.'
ELSE IF ( grade > 86.0 ) THEN
   WRITE (*,*) 'The grade is B.'
ELSE IF ( grade > 76.0 ) THEN
   WRITE (*,*) 'The grade is C.'
ELSE IF ( grade > 66.0 ) THEN
   WRITE (*,*) 'The grade is D.'
ELSE
   WRITE (*,*) 'The grade is F.'
END IF
```

(*b*) One possible structure using nested IF constructs is

```
if1: IF ( grade > 95.0 ) THEN
   WRITE (*,*) 'The grade is A.'
ELSE
   if2: IF ( grade > 86.0 ) THEN
      WRITE (*,*) 'The grade is B.'
   ELSE
      if3: IF ( grade > 76.0 ) THEN
         WRITE (*,*) 'The grade is C.'
      ELSE
         if4: IF ( grade > 66.0 ) THEN
            WRITE (*,*) 'The grade is D.'
         ELSE
            WRITE (*,*) 'The grade is F.'
         END IF if4
      END IF if3
   END IF if2
END IF if1
```

As the preceding example shows, a single IF construct with ELSE IF clauses is simpler than a nested IF construct when you have multiple mutually exclusive options.

Good Programming Practice

For branches that have many mutually exclusive options, use a single IF construct with ELSE IF clauses, rather than nested IF constructs.

3.3.6 The Logical IF Statement

An alternative form of the logical IF construct described in section 3.3.5 is a single statement of the form

```
IF (logical_expr) Statement
```

where `Statement` is an executable Fortran statement. If the logical expression is true, the program executes the statement on the same line with it. Otherwise, the program skips to the next executable statement in the program. This form of the logical `IF` is equivalent to a block `IF` construct with only one statement in the `IF` block.

3.3.7 The `CASE` Construct

The `CASE` construct is another form of branching construct. It permits a programmer to select a particular code block to execute based on the value of a single integer, character, or logical expression. The general form of a `CASE` construct is

```
[name:] SELECT CASE (case_expr)
CASE (case_selector_1)  [name]
    Statement1         ⎫
    Statement2         ⎬  Block 1
    ...                ⎭
CASE (case_selector_2)  [name]
    Statement 1        ⎫
    Statement 2        ⎬  Block 2
    ...                ⎭
...

CASE DEFAULT [name]
    Statement 1        ⎫
    Statement 2        ⎬  Block n
    ...                ⎭
END SELECT [name]
```

If the value of *case_expr* is in the range of values included in *case_selector_1*, then the first code block will be executed. Similarly, if the value of *case_expr* is in the range of values included in *case_selector_2*, then the second code block will be executed. The same idea applies for any other cases in the construct. The default code block is optional. If it is present, the default code block will be executed whenever the value of *case_expr* is outside the range of all of the case selectors. If it is not present and the value of *case_expr* is outside the range of all of the case selectors, then none of the code blocks will be executed. The pseudocode for the case construct looks just like its Fortran implementation; a flowchart for this construct is shown in Figure 3–13.

A name may be assigned to a `CASE` construct if desired. The name must be unique within each program unit and must not be the same as any constant or variable name within the program unit. If a name is assigned to a `SELECT CASE` statement, then the same name must appear on the associated `END SELECT`. Names are optional on the `CASE` statements of the construct, but if they are used, they must be the same as the name on the `SELECT CASE` statement.

The *case_expr* may be any integer, character, or logical expression. Each case selector must be an integer, character, or logical value or range of values. All case selectors must be *mutually exclusive;* no single value can appear in more than one case selector.

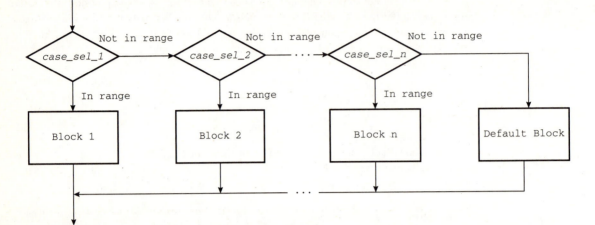

FIGURE 3–13
Flowchart for a CASE construct.

Let's look at a simple example of a CASE construct. This example prints out a message based on the value of an integer variable.

```
INTEGER :: temp_c              ! Temperature in degrees C
...
temp: SELECT CASE (temp_c)
CASE (:-1)
    WRITE (*,*) "It's below freezing today!"
CASE (0)
    WRITE (*,*) "It's exactly at the freezing point."
CASE (1:20)
    WRITE (*,*) "It's cool today."
CASE (21:33)
    WRITE (*,*) "It's warm today."
CASE (34:)
    WRITE (*,*) "It's hot today."
END SELECT temp
```

The value of temp_c controls which case is selected. If the temperature is less than 0, then the first case will be selected, and the message printed out will be "It's below freezing today!" If the temperature is exactly 0, then the second case will be selected and so forth. Note that the cases do not overlap—a given temperature can appear in only one of the cases.

The *case_selector* can take one of four forms:

case_value	Execute block if *case_value* == *case_expr*.
low_value:	Execute block if *low_value* <= *case_expr*.
:high_value	Execute block if *case_expr* <= *high_value*.
low_value:high_value	Execute block if *low_value* <= *case_expr* <= *high_value*.

Or it can be a list of any combination of these forms separated by commas.

The following statements determine whether an integer between 1 and 10 is even or odd and then print out an appropriate message. They illustrate the use of a list of values as case selectors and also the use of the CASE DEFAULT block.

```fortran
INTEGER :: value
...
SELECT CASE (value)
CASE (1,3,5,7,9)
   WRITE (*,*) 'The value is odd.'
CASE (2,4,6,8,10)
   WRITE (*,*) 'The value is even.'
CASE (11:)
   WRITE (*,*) 'The value is too high.'
CASE DEFAULT
   WRITE (*,*) 'The value is negative or zero.'
END SELECT
```

Quiz 3–1

This quiz provides a quick check to see if you understand the concepts introduced in section 3.3. If you have trouble with the quiz, reread the section, ask your instructor, or discuss the material with a fellow student. The answers to this quiz appear in Appendix F.

Write Fortran statements that perform the following functions:

1. If x is greater than or equal to zero, then assign the square root of x to variable sqrt_x and print out the result. Otherwise, print out an error message about the argument of the square root function and set sqrt_x to zero.

2. A variable fun is calculated as numerator / denominator. If the absolute value of denominator is less than 1.0E-10, write "Divide by 0 error." Otherwise, calculate and print out fun.

3. The cost per mile for a rented vehicle is 50 cents for the first 100 miles, 30 cents for the next 200 miles, and 20 cents for all miles in excess of 300 miles. Write Fortran statements that determine the total cost and the average cost per mile for a given number of miles (stored in variable distance).

Examine the following Fortran statements. Are they correct or incorrect? If they are correct, what is the output? If they are incorrect, what is wrong?

4.
```fortran
IF ( volts > 125. ) THEN
   WRITE (*,*) 'WARNING: High voltage on line. '
IF ( volts < 105. ) THEN
   WRITE (*,*) 'WARNING: Low voltage on line.'
ELSE
   WRITE (*,*) 'Line voltage is within tolerances.'
END IF
```

(continued)

(concluded)

5. ```
PROGRAM test
LOGICAL :: warn
REAL :: distance
REAL, PARAMETER :: limit = 100.
warn = .TRUE.
distance = 55. + 10.
IF (distance > limit .OR. warn) THEN
   WRITE (*,*) 'Warning: Distance exceeds limit.'
ELSE
   WRITE (*,*) 'Distance = ', distance
END IF
```

6. ```
REAL, PARAMETER :: pi = 3.141593
REAL :: a = 10.
SELECT CASE ( a * sqrt(pi) )
CASE (0:)
   WRITE (*,*) 'a > 0'
CASE (:0)
   WRITE (*,*) 'a < 0'
CASE DEFAULT
   WRITE (*,*) 'a = 0'
END SELECT
```

7. ```
CHARACTER(len=6) :: color = 'yellow'
SELECT CASE (color)
CASE ('red')
   WRITE (*,*) 'Stop now!'
CASE ('yellow')
   WRITE (*,*) 'Prepare to stop.'
CASE ('green')
   WRITE (*,*) 'Proceed through intersection.'
CASE DEFAULT
   WRITE (*,*) 'Illegal color encountered.'
END SELECT
```

8. ```
IF ( temperature > 37. ) THEN
   WRITE (*,*) 'Human body temperature exceeded.'
ELSE IF ( temperature > 100. )
   WRITE (*,*) 'Boiling point of water exceeded.'
END IF
```

■ **3.4**

CONTROL CONSTRUCTS: LOOPS

Loops are Fortran constructs that permit us to execute a sequence of statements more than once. The two basic forms of loop constructs are while loops and iterative loops (or counting loops). The major difference between these two types of loops is in how the repetition is controlled. The code in an iterative loop is repeated a specified number of times, and the number of repetitions is known before the loops starts. By contrast, the code in a while loop is repeated indefinitely as long as some user-specified condition is satisfied.

3.4.1 The While Loop

A **while loop** is a block of statements that are repeated indefinitely as long as some condition is satisfied. The general form of a while loop in Fortran 90/95 is

```
DO
    ...
    IF (logical_expr) EXIT        } Code block
    ...
END DO
```

The block of statements between the DO and END DO is repeated indefinitely until the *logical_expr* becomes true and the EXIT statement is executed. After the EXIT statement is executed, control transfers to the first statement after the END DO.

The IF statement may be located anywhere within the body of the loop, and it is executed once each time that the loop is repeated. If the *logical_expr* in the IF is false when the statement is executed, the loop continues to execute. If the *logical_expr* in the IF is true when the statement is executed, control transfers immediately to the first statement after the END DO.

If the logical expression is false the first time we reach the while loop, the statements in the loop below the IF will never be executed!

The pseudocode corresponding to a while loop is

FIGURE 3–14
Flowchart for a while loop.

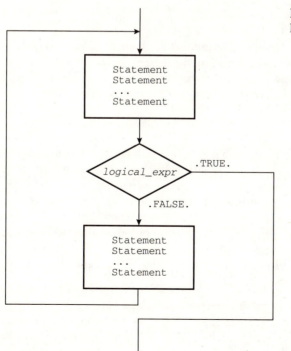

```
WHILE
    ...
    IF logical_expr EXIT
    ...
End of WHILE
```

and the flowchart for this construct is shown in Figure 3–14.

The following example, from statistical analysis, is implemented using a while loop.

EXAMPLE **3–4** *Statistical Analysis:* Scientists and engineers work with large sets of numbers, each of which is a measurement of some particular property. A simple example would be the grades on the first test in this course in which each grade measures how much a particular student has learned in the course to date.

Much of the time, we are not interested in looking closely at every single measurement that we make. Instead, we want to summarize the results of a set of measurements with a few numbers that tell us a lot about the overall data set. Two such numbers are the *average* (or *arithmetic mean*) and the *standard deviation* of the set of measurements. The average or arithmetic mean of a set of numbers is defined as

$$\bar{x} = \frac{1}{N}\sum_{i=1}^{N} x_i \tag{3-3}$$

where x_i is sample i out of N samples. The standard deviation of a set of numbers is defined as

$$s = \sqrt{\frac{N\sum_{i=1}^{N} x_i^2 - \left(\sum_{i=1}^{N} x_i\right)^2}{N(N-1)}} \tag{3-4}$$

Standard deviation is a measure of the amount of scatter on the measurements; the greater the standard deviation, the more scattered the points in the data set are.

Implement an algorithm that reads in a set of measurements and calculates the mean and the standard deviation of the input data set.

SOLUTION

This program must be able to read in an arbitrary number of measurements, and then calculate the mean and standard deviation of those measurements. We will use a while loop to accumulate the input measurements before performing the calculations.

When all the measurements have been read, we must have some way of telling the program that there is no more data to enter. For now, we will assume that all the input measurements are either positive or zero, and we will use a negative input value as a *flag* to indicate that there is no more data to read. If a negative value is entered, then the program will stop reading input values and will calculate the mean and standard deviation of the data set.

1. **State the problem.**

Since we assume that the input numbers must be positive or zero, a proper statement of this problem is

Calculate the average and the standard deviation of a set of measurements, assuming that all the measurements are either positive or zero and that we do not know in advance how many measurements are included in the data set. A negative input value will mark the end of the set of measurements.

2. Define the inputs and outputs.

The inputs required by this program are an unknown number of positive or zero real (floating-point) numbers. The output from this program is a printout of the mean and the standard deviation of the input data set. In addition, we will print out the number of data points input to the program, since this is a useful check that the input data was read correctly.

3. Design the algorithm.

This program can be broken down into three major steps:

```
Accumulate the input data.
Calculate the mean and standard deviation
Write out the mean, standard deviation, and number of points
```

The first major step of the program is to accumulate the input data. To do this, we will have to prompt the user to enter the desired numbers. When the numbers are entered, we will have to keep track of the number of values entered, plus the sum and the sum of the squares of those values. The pseudocode for these steps follows.

```
Initialize n, sum_x, and sum_x2 to 0
WHILE
    Prompt user for next number
    Read in next x
    IF x < 0. EXIT
    n ← n + 1
    sum_x ← sum_x + x
    sum_x2 ← sum_x2 + x**2
End of WHILE
```

Note that we have to read in the first value before the `IF () EXIT` test so that the while loop can have a value to test the first time it executes.

Next we must calculate the mean and standard deviation. The pseudocode for this step is just the Fortran versions of Equations (3–3) and (3–4).

```
x_bar ← sum_x / REAL(n)
std_dev ← SQRT((REAL(n)*sum_x2 − sum_x**2) / (REAL(n)*REAL(n-1)))
```

Finally, we must write out the results:

```
Write out the mean value x_bar
Write out the standard deviation std_dev
Write out the number of input data points n
```

The flowchart for this program is shown in Figure 3–15.

4. Turn the algorithm into Fortran statements.

The final Fortran program is shown in Figure 3–16.

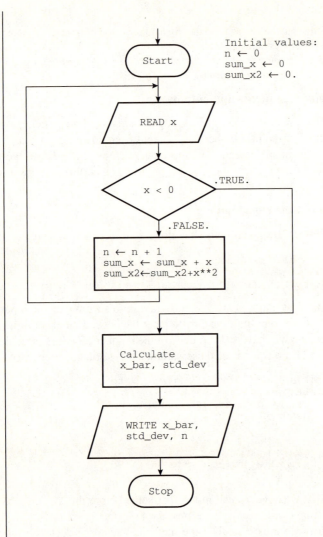

FIGURE 3–15
Flowchart for the statistical analysis program of Example 3–4.

FIGURE 3–16
Program to calculate the mean and standard deviation of a set of nonnegative real numbers.

```
PROGRAM stats_1
!
! Purpose:
!   To calculate mean and the standard deviation of an input
!   data set containing an arbitrary number of input values.
!
! Record of revisions:
!    Date       Programmer      Description of change
!    ====       ==========      =====================
!  09/10/95   S. J. Chapman     Original code
```

(continued)

(concluded)

```
!
IMPLICIT NONE

! Declare and initialize the variables used in this program.
INTEGER :: n = 0        ! The number of input samples.
REAL :: std_dev = 0.    ! The standard deviation of the input samples.
REAL :: sum_x = 0.      ! The sum of the input values.
REAL :: sum_x2 = 0.     ! The sum of the squares of the input values.
REAL :: x = 0.          ! An input data value.
REAL :: x_bar           ! The average of the input samples.

! While loop to read input values.
DO
    ! Read in next value
    WRITE (*,*) 'Enter number:'
    READ  (*,*) x
    WRITE (*,*) 'The number is ', x

    ! Test for loop exit
    IF ( x<0 ) EXIT

    ! Otherwise, accumulate sums.
    n     = n + 1
    sum_x = sum_x + x
    sum_x2 = sum_x2 + x**2
END DO

! Calculate the mean and standard deviation
x_bar = sum_x / real(n)
std_dev = sqrt( (real(n) * sum_x2 - sum_x**2) / (real(n) * real(n-1)) )

! Tell user.
WRITE (*,*) 'The mean of this data set is:', x_bar
WRITE (*,*) 'The standard deviation is: ', std_dev
WRITE (*,*) 'The number of data points is:', n

END PROGRAM
```

5. Test the program.

To test this program, we will calculate the answers by hand for a simple data set and then compare the answers to the results of the program. If we used three input values—3, 4, and 5—then the mean and standard deviation would be

$$\bar{x} = \frac{1}{N} \sum_{i=1}^{N} x_i = \frac{1}{3} 12 = 4$$

$$s = \sqrt{\frac{N \sum_{i=1}^{N} x_i^2 - \left(\sum_{i=1}^{N} x_i \right)^2}{N(N-1)}} = 1$$

When these values are fed into the program, the results are

C>**stats_1**

```
Enter number:
3.
The number is          3.000000
Enter number:
4.
The number is          4.000000
Enter number:
5.
The number is          5.000000
Enter number:
-1.
The number is         -1.000000
The mean of this data set is:        4.000000
The standard deviation is:           1.000000
The number of data points is:           3
```

The program gives the correct answers for our test data set.

In Example 3–4, we failed to follow the design process completely. This failure has left the program with a fatal flaw! Did you spot it?

We failed because *we did not completely test the program for all possible types of inputs.* Look at the example once again. If we enter either no numbers or only one number, then we will be dividing by zero in the preceding equations! The division-by-zero error will cause the program to abort. We need to modify the program to detect this problem, inform the user of it, and stop gracefully.

A modified version of the program called stats_2 is shown Figure 3–17. In this version we check to see if there are enough input values before performing the calculations. If not, the program will print out an intelligent error message and quit. Test the modified program for yourself.

FIGURE 3–17
A modified statistical analysis program that avoids the divide-by-zero problems inherent in program stats_1.

```
PROGRAM stats_2
!
! Purpose:
!   To calculate mean and the standard deviation of an input
!   data set containing an arbitrary number of input values.
!
! Record of revisions:
!      Date        Programmer           Description of change
!      ====        ==========           =====================
!    09/10/95     S. J. Chapman         Original code
! 1. 09/11/95     S. J. Chapman         Correct divide-by-0 error if
!                                       0 or 1 input values given.
!
!
IMPLICIT NONE

! Declare the variables used in this program.
INTEGER :: n = 0          ! The number of input samples.
REAL :: std_dev = 0.  ! The standard deviation of the input samples.
REAL :: sum_x = 0.    ! The sum of the input values.
```

(continued)

```
(concluded)
REAL :: sum_x2 = 0.    ! The sum of the squares of the input values.
REAL :: x = 0.         ! An input data value.
REAL :: x_bar          ! The average of the input samples.

! While loop to read input values.
DO
    ! Read in next value
    WRITE (*,*) 'Enter number: '
    READ  (*,*) x
    WRITE (*,*) 'The number is ', x

    ! Test for loop exit
    IF ( x<0 ) EXIT

    ! Otherwise, accumulate sums.
    n      = n + 1
    sum_x  = sum_x + x
    sum_x2 = sum_x2 + x**2
END DO

! Check to see if we have enough input data.
IF ( n ,< 2 ) THEN ! Insufficient information

    WRITE (*,*) 'At least 2 values must be entered!'

ELSE ! There is enough information, so
     ! calculate the mean and standard deviation

    x_bar = sum_x / real(n)
    std_dev = sqrt( (real(n) * sum_x2 - sum_x**2) / (real(n)*real(n-1)))

    ! Tell user.
    WRITE (*,*) 'The mean of this data set is: ', x_bar
    WRITE (*,*) 'The standard deviation is:    ', std_dev
    WRITE (*,*) 'The number of data points is: ', n

END IF

END PROGRAM
```

3.4.2 The Iterative or Counting Loop

In the Fortran language, a loop that executes a block of statements a specified number of times is called an **iterative DO loop** or a **counting loop.** The counting loop construct has the form

```
DO index = istart, iend, incr
    Statement 1                  ⎫
    ...                          ⎬ Body
    Statement n                  ⎭
END DO
```

index is an integer variable used as the loop counter (also known as the **loop index**). The integer quantities istart, iend, and incr are the *parameters* of the counting loop; they control the values of the variable index during execution. The parameter incr is optional; if it is missing, it is assumed to be 1.

The statements between the DO statement and the END DO statement are known as the *body* of the loop. They are executed repeatedly during each pass of the DO loop.

The counting loop construct functions as follows:

1. Each of the three DO loop parameters istart, iend, and incr may be a constant, a variable, or an expression. If they are variables or expressions, then their values are calculated before the start of the loop and the resulting values are used to control the loop.
2. At the beginning of the execution of the DO loop, the program assigns the value istart to control variable index. If index * incr ≤ iend * incr, the program executes the statements within the body of the loop.
3. After the statements in the body of the loop have been executed, the control variable is recalculated as

$$index = index + incr$$

   If index * incr is still less than or equal to iend * incr, the program executes the statements within the body again.
4. Step 2 is repeated over and over as long as index * incr ≤ iend * incr. When this condition is no longer true, execution skips to the first statement following the end of the DO loop.

Let's look at a number of specific examples to make the operation of the counting loop clearer. First, consider the following example:

```
DO i = 1, 10
    Statement 1
    ...
    Statement n
END DO
```

In this case statements 1 through n will be executed 10 times. The index variable i will be 1 on the first time, 2 on the second time, and so on. The index variable will be 10 on the last pass through the statements. When control is returned to the DO statement after the tenth pass, the index variable i will be increased to 11. Since $11 \times 1 > 10 \times 1$, control will transfer to the first statement after the END DO statement.

Second, consider the following example:

```
DO i = 1, 10, 2
    Statement 1
    ...
    Statement n
END DO
```

In this case statements 1 through n will be executed five times. The index variable i will be 1 on the first time, 3 on the second time, and so on. The index variable will be 9 on the fifth and last pass through the statements. When control is returned to the DO statement after the fifth pass, the index variable i will be increased to 11. Since $11 \times 2 > 10 \times 2$, control will transfer to the first statement after the END DO statement.

Third, consider the following example:

```
DO i = 1, 10, -1
    Statement 1
    ...
    Statement n
END DO
```

Statements 1 through n will never be executed, since index*incr > iend*incr on the very first time that the DO statement is reached. Instead, control will transfer to the first statement after the END DO statement.

Finally, consider the example:

```
DO i = 3, -3, -2
    Statement 1
    ...
    Statement n
END DO
```

In this case statements 1 through n will be executed four times. The index variable i will be 3 on the first time, 1 on the second time, -1 on the third time, and −3 on the fourth time. When control is returned to the DO statement after the fourth pass, the index variable i will be decreased to −5. Since $-5 \times -2 > -3 \times -2$, control will transfer to the first statement after the END DO statement.

The pseudocode corresponding to a counting loop is

```
DO for index = istart to iend by incr
    Statement 1
    ...
    Statement n
End of DO
```

and the flowchart for this construct is shown in Figure 3–18.

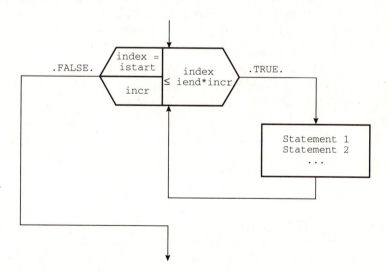

FIGURE 3–18
Flowchart for a DO loop construct.

EXAMPLE 3–5 The Factorial Function: To illustrate the operation of a counting loop, we will use a DO loop to calculate the factorial function. The factorial function is defined as

N! = 1   N = 0
N! = N * (N - 1) * (N-2) * ... * 3 * 2 * 1   N > 0

The Fortran code to calculate N factorial for positive value of N would be

```
n_factorial = 1
DO i = 1, n
    n_factorial = n_factorial * i
END DO
```

Suppose that we wish to calculate the value of 5!. If n is 5, the DO loop parameters will be istart = 1, iend = 5, and incr = 1. This loop will be executed five times, with the variable i taking on values of 1, 2, 3, 4, and 5 in the successive loops. The resulting value of n_factorial will be $1 \times 2 \times 3 \times 4 \times 5 = 120$.

EXAMPLE 3–6 Calculating the Day of Year: The *day of year* is the number of days (including the current day) that have elapsed since the beginning of a given year. It is a number in the range 1 to 365 for ordinary years and 1 to 366 for leap years. Write a Fortran program that accepts a day, month, and year, and calculates the day of year corresponding to that date.

SOLUTION

To determine the day of year, this program will need to sum the number of days in each month preceding the current month, plus the number of elapsed days in the current month. Since the number of days in each month varies, it is necessary to determine the correct number of days to add for each month. We will use CASE construct to determine the proper number of days to add for each month.

During a leap year, an extra day must be added to the day of year for any month after February. This extra day accounts for the presence of February 29 in the leap year. Therefore, to perform the day of year calculation correctly, we must determine which years are leap years. In the Gregorian calendar, leap years are determined by the following rules:

1. Years evenly divisible by 400 are leap years.
2. Years evenly divisible by 100 but not by 400 are not leap years.
3. All years divisible by 4 but *not* by 100 are leap years.
4. All other years are not leap years.

We will use the MOD (for modulo) function to determine whether a year is evenly divisible by a given number. If the result of the MOD function is 0, then the year was evenly divisible.

A program to calculate the day of year is shown in Figure 3–19. Note that the program sums the number of days in each month before the current month and that it uses a CASE construct to determine the number of days in each month.

FIGURE 3–19
A program to calculate the equivalent day of year from a given day, month, and year.

```
PROGRAM doy

! Purpose:
!   This program calculates the day of year corresponding to a
!   specified date. It illustrates the use CASE construct.
```
(continued)

(concluded)

```
!
! Record of revisions:
!      Date         Programmer         Description of change
!      ====         ==========         =====================
!    9/09/95     S. J. Chapman         Original code
!
IMPLICIT NONE

! Declare the variables used in this program
INTEGER :: day              ! Day (dd)
INTEGER :: day_of_year      ! Day of year
INTEGER :: i                ! Index variable
INTEGER :: leap_day         ! Extra day for leap year
INTEGER :: month            ! Month (mm)
INTEGER :: year             ! Year (yyyy)

! Get day, month, and year to convert
WRITE (*,*) 'This program calculates the day of year given the '
WRITE (*,*) 'current date. Enter current month (1-12), day(1-31),'
WRITE (*,*) 'and year in that order:'
READ (*,*) month, day, year

! Check for leap year, and add extra day if necessary
IF ( MOD(year,400) == 0 ) THEN
   leap_day = 1              ! Years divisible by 400 are leap years
ELSE IF ( MOD(year,100) == 0 ) THEN
   leap_day = 0              ! Other centuries are not leap years
ELSE IF ( MOD(year,4) == 0 ) THEN
   leap_day = 1              ! Otherwise every 4th year is a leap year
ELSE
   leap_day = 0              ! Other years are not leap years
END IF

! Calculate day of year
day_of_year = day
DO i = 1, month-1

   ! Add days in months from January to last month
   SELECT CASE (i)
   CASE (1,3,5,7,8,10,12)
      day_of_year = day_of_year + 31
   CASE (4,6,9,11)
      day_of_year = day_of_year + 30
   CASE (2)
      day_of_year = day_of_year + 28 + leap_day
   END SELECT

END DO

! Tell user
WRITE (*,*) 'Day          = ', day
WRITE (*,*) 'Month        = ', month
WRITE (*,*) 'Year         = ', year
WRITE (*,*) 'day of year = ', day_of_year

END PROGRAM
```

We will use the following known results to test the program:

1. Year 1999 is not a leap year. January 1 must be day of year 1, and December 31 must be day of year 365.

2. Year 2000 is a leap year. January 1 must be day of year 1, and December 31 must be day of year 366.
3. Year 2001 is not a leap year. March 1 must be day of year 60, since January has 31 days, February has 28 days, and this is the first day of March.

If this program is compiled and then run five times with the above dates, the results are

```
C>doy

This program calculates the day of year given the
current date. Enter current month (1-12), day(1-31),
and year in that order: 1 1 1999

Day         =              1
Month       =              1
Year        =           1999
day of year =              1

C>doy

This program calculates the day of year given the
current date. Enter current month (1-12), day(1-31),
and year in that order: 12 31 1999

Day         =             31
Month       =             12
Year        =           1999
day of year =            365

C>doy

This program calculates the day of year given the
current date. Enter current month (1-12), day(1-31),
and year in that order: 1 1 2000

Day         =              1
Month       =              1
Year        =           2000
day of year =              1

C>doy

This program calculates the day of year given the
current date. Enter current month (1-12), day(1-31),
and year in that order: 12 31 2000

Day         =             31
Month       =             12
Year        =           2000
day of year =            366

C>doy

This program calculates the day of year given the
current date. Enter current month (1-12), day(1-31),
and year in that order: 3 1 2001

Day         =              1
Month       =              3
Year        =           2001
```

day of year =   60

The program gives the correct answers for our test dates in all five test cases.

EXAMPLE 3–7 *Statistical Analysis:* Implement an algorithm that reads in a set of measurements and calculates the mean and the standard deviation of the input data set, when any value in the data set can be positive, negative, or zero.

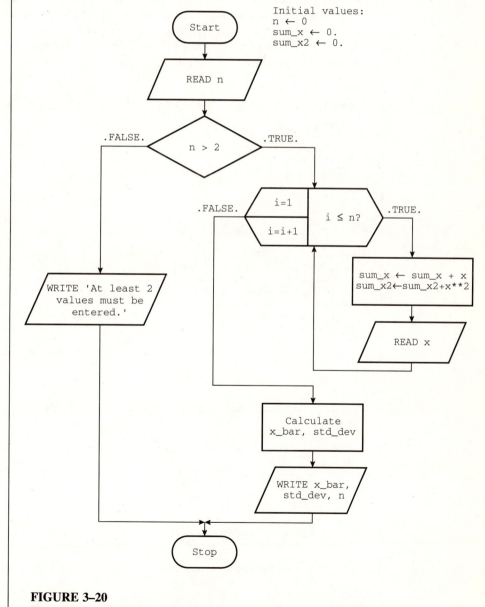

FIGURE 3–20
Flowchart for modified statistical analysis program using a DO loop.

SOLUTION

This program must be able to read in an arbitrary number of measurements and then calculate the mean and standard deviation of those measurements. Each measurement can be positive, negative, or zero.

Since we cannot use a data value as a flag this time, we will ask the user for the number of input values and then use a DO loop to read in those values. A flowchart for this program is shown in Figure 3–20. Note that we are using a counting loop instead of a while loop, so that the input values may be positive, negative, or zero. The modified program that permits the use of any input value is shown in Figure 3–21. Verify its operation for yourself by finding the mean and standard deviation of the following five input values: 3., −1., 0., 1., and −2.

FIGURE 3–21
Modified statistical analysis program that works with both positive and input values.

```
PROGRAM stats_3
!
! Purpose:
!   To calculate the mean and the standard deviation of an input
!   data set, where each input value can be positive, negative,
!   or zero.
!
! Record of revisions:
!    Date          Programmer        Description of change
!    ====          ==========        =====================
!  09/11/95     S. J. Chapman        Original code
!
IMPLICIT NONE

! Declare the variables used in this program.
INTEGER :: i          ! Loop index
INTEGER :: n = 0      ! The number of input samples.
REAL :: std_dev       ! The standard deviation of the input samples.
REAL :: sum_x = 0.    ! The sum of the input values.
REAL :: sum_x2 = 0.   ! The sum of the squares of the input values.
REAL :: x = 0.        ! An input data value.
REAL :: x_bar         ! The average of the input samples.

! Get the number of points to input.
WRITE (*,*) 'Enter number of points: '
READ (*,*) n

! Check to see if we have enough input data.
IF ( n < 2 ) THEN ! Insufficient data

   WRITE (*,*) 'At least 2 values must be entered.'

ELSE ! we will have enough data, so let's get it.

   ! Loop to read input values.
   DO i = 1, n

      ! Read values
      WRITE (*,*) 'Enter number: '
```

(continued)

(concluded)

```
      READ (*,*) x
      WRITE (*,*) 'The number is ', x

      ! Accumulate sums.
      sum_x = sum_x + x
      sum_x2 = sum_x2 + x**2

   END DO

   ! Now calculate statistics.
   x_bar = sum_x / real(n)
   std_dev = sqrt((real(n)*sum_x2 - sum_x**2) / (real(n)*real(n-1)))

   ! Tell user.
   WRITE (*,*) 'The mean of this data set is:', x_bar
   WRITE (*,*) 'The standard deviation is:     ', std_dev
   WRITE (*,*) 'The number of data points is:  ', n

END IF

END PROGRAM
```

Details of Operation

Now that we have seen examples of a counting DO loop in operation, we will examine some of the important details required to use DO loops properly.

1. Fortran does not require us to indent the body of the DO loop (as we have done in the preceding examples). The Fortran compiler will recognize the loop even if every statement starts in column 1. However, the code is much more readable if the body of the DO loop is indented, so you should always indent the bodies of your DO loops.

Good Programming Practice
Always indent the body of a DO loop by two or more spaces to improve the readability of the code.

---

2. Never modify the index variable of a DO loop anywhere within the DO loop because the index variable controls the repetitions in the DO loop. Changing the index variable could produce unexpected results. In the worst case, modifying the index variable could produce an *infinite loop* that never completes. Consider the following example:

```
PROGRAM bad_1
INTEGER :: i
DO i = 1, 4
   i = 2
END DO
END PROGRAM
```

If i is reset to 2 every time through the loop, the loop will never end because the index variable can never be greater than 4! This loop will run forever unless the program containing it is killed. Almost all Fortran compilers will recognize this problem and will generate a compile-time error if a program attempts to modify an index variable within a loop.

Programming Pitfalls
Never modify the value of a DO loop index variable while inside the loop.

3. The following equation calculates the number of iterations a DO loop will perform:

$$\text{iter} = \frac{\text{iend} - \text{istart} + \text{incr}}{\text{incr}} \tag{3–5}$$

Some compilers do permit you to modify the values of istart, iend, and incr within a DO loop. However, you should never modify control values within the loop; for example, changing iend and incr can inadvertently change the number of iterations the loop performs.

Programming Pitfalls
Never modify the control values of a DO loop (istart, iend, incr) while inside the loop.

4. If the number of iterations calculated from Equation (3–5) is less than or equal to 0, the statements within the DO loop are never executed at all. For example, the statements in the following DO loop will never be executed

```
DO i = 3, 2
   . . .
END DO
```

since

$$\text{iter} = \frac{\text{iend} - \text{istart} + \text{incr}}{\text{incr}} = \frac{2 - 3 + 1}{1} = 0$$

5. Counting DO loops can count down as well as up. The following DO loop executes three times with i being 3, 2, and 1 in the successive loops:

```
DO i = 3, 1, -1
   . . .
END DO
```

6. The index variable and control parameters of a DO loop should always be integers.

7. Program execution can branch out of a DO loop at any time while the loop is executing. If program execution does branch out of a DO loop before it would otherwise finish, the loop index variable retains the value that it has when the branch occurs. Consider the following example:

```
INTEGER :: i
DO i = 1, 5
   ...
   IF (i >= 3) EXIT
   ...
END DO
WRITE (*,*) i
```

Execution will branch out of the DO loop and go to the WRITE statement on the third pass through the loop. When execution gets to the WRITE statement, variable i will contain a value of 3.

8. If a DO loop completes normally, the value of the index variable is undefined when the loop is completed. In the following example the value written out by the WRITE statement is not defined in the Fortran standard:

```
INTEGER :: i
DO i = 1, 5
   ...
END DO
WRITE (*,*) i
```

On many computers, after the loop has completed, the index variable i will contain the first value of the index variable to fail the index * incr ≤ iend * incr test. In the preceding code, i should contain a 6 after the loop is finished. However, don't count on it! Since the value is officially undefined in the Fortran standard, some compilers may produce a different result. If your code depends on the value of the index variable after the loop is completed, you may get different results if you run the program on another computer.

Good Programming Practice

Never depend on an index variable to retain a specific value after a DO loop completes normally.

---

9. It is illegal for program execution to branch into the body of a loop. The following code will generate a compile-time error on a Fortran compiler:

```
INTEGER :: i
DO i = 1, 5
   ...
   200 ...
END DO
...
GO TO 200
```

3.4.3 The CYCLE and EXIT Statements

Two additional statements that can control the operation of while loops and counting DO loops are CYCLE and EXIT.

    If the CYCLE statement is executed in the body of a loop, the execution of the body will stop and control will be returned to the top of the loop. The loop index will be incremented, and execution will resume again if the index has not reached its limit. An example of the CYCLE statement in a DO loop follows.

```
PROGRAM test_cycle
INTEGER :: i
DO i = 1, 5
   IF ( i == 3 ) CYCLE
   WRITE (*,*) i
END DO
WRITE (*,*) 'End of loop!'
END PROGRAM
```

The flowchart for this loop is shown in Figure 3–22a. When this program is executed, the output is

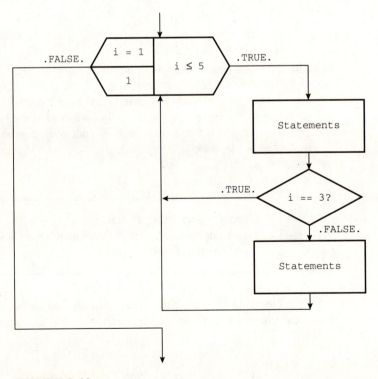

FIGURE 3–22
(a) Flowchart of a DO loop containing a CYCLE statement.

```
C>test_cycle
             1
             2
             4
             5
End of loop!
```

Note that the CYCLE statement was executed on the iteration when i was 3, and control returned to the top of the loop without executing the WRITE statement.

If the EXIT statement is executed in the body of a loop, the execution of the body will stop and control will be transferred to the first executable statement after the loop. An example of the EXIT statement in a DO loop follows.

```
PROGRAM test_exit
INTEGER :: i
DO i = 1, 5
   IF ( i == 3 ) EXIT
   WRITE (*,*) i
END DO
WRITE (*,*) 'End of loop!'
END PROGRAM
```

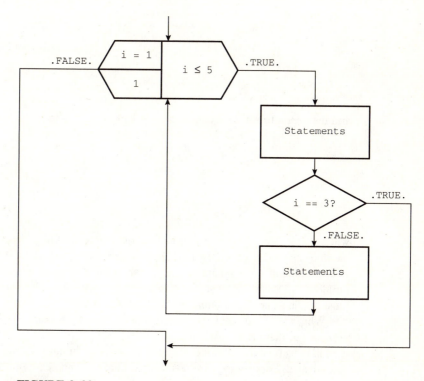

FIGURE 3–22

(b) Flowchart of a DO loop containing an EXIT statement.

The flowchart for this loop is shown in Figure 3–22*b*. When this program is executed, the output is

```
C>test_exit
            1
            2
End of loop!
```

Note that the EXIT statement was executed on the iteration when i was 3, and control returned to the first executable statement after the loop without executing the WRITE statement.

Both the CYCLE and EXIT statements work with both types of Fortran loops: while loops and counting DO loops.

3.4.4 Named Loops

It is possible to assign a name to a loop. The general form of a while loop with a name attached is

```
[name:] DO
        Statement
        Statement
        ...
        IF ( logical_expr ) CYCLE [name]
        ...
        IF ( logical_expr ) EXIT [name]
        ...
END DO [name]
```

and the general form of a counting loop with a name attached is

```
[name:] DO index = istart, iend, incr
        Statement
        Statement
        ...
        IF ( logical_expr ) CYCLE [name]
        ...
END DO [name]
```

where name may be up to 31 alphanumeric characters long, beginning with a letter. The name given to the loop must be unique within each program unit. If a name is assigned to a loop, then the same name must appear on the associated END DO. Names are optional on any CYCLE and EXIT statements associated with the loop, but if they are used, they must be the same as the name on the DO statement.

Why would we want to name a loop? For simple examples like the ones we have seen so far, there is no particular reason to do so. The principal reason for using names is to help us (and the compiler) keep loops straight in our own minds when they get very complicated. For example, suppose that we have a complex loop that is hundreds of lines long, spanning many pages of listings. There may be many smaller loops inside body of that loop. If we name all of the parts of the loop, then we can tell at a glance which construct a particular END DO, CYCLE, or EXIT statement belongs to. Names on constructs make our intentions explicitly clear and can help the compiler flag the specific location of any error.

Good Programming Practice
Assign a name to any large and complicated loops in your program to help you keep track of the parts of the construct.

3.4.5 Nesting Loops and Block IF Constructs

Nesting loops

When one loop is completely inside another loop, the two loops are called **nested loops.** The following example shows two nested DO loops used to calculate and write out the product of two integers.

```
PROGRAM nested_loops
INTEGER :: i, j, product
DO i = 1, 3
   DO j = 1, 3
      product = i * j
      WRITE (*,*) i, ' * ', j, ' = ', product
   END DO
END DO
END PROGRAM
```

In this example the outer DO loop will assign a value of 1 to index variable i, and then the inner DO loop will be executed. The inner DO loop will be executed three times with index variable j having values 1, 2, and 3. When the entire inner DO loop has been completed, the outer DO loop will assign a value of 2 to index variable i and the inner DO loop will be executed again. This process repeats until the outer DO loop has executed three times, and the resulting output is

```
1 *   1 =   1
1 *   2 =   2
1 *   3 =   3
2 *   1 =   2
2 *   2 =   4
2 *   3 =   6
3 *   1 =   3
3 *   2 =   6
3 *   3 =   9
```

Note that the inner DO loop executes completely before the index variable of the outer DO loop is incremented.

When a Fortran compiler encounters an END DO statement, it associates that statement with the innermost currently open loop. Therefore, the first END DO statement in the preceding example closes the DO j = 1, 3 loop, and the second END DO statement closes the DO i = 1, 3 loop. This fact can produce hard-to-find errors if an END DO statement is accidentally deleted somewhere within a nested loop construct. If each nested loop is named, then the error will be much easier to find.

 Programming Pitfalls
The accidental deletion of an END DO statement in a large set of nested DO loops can produce a hard-to-find error. Use names on nested DO loops to avoid this problem.

To illustrate this problem, let's "accidentally" delete the inner END DO statement in the previous example, and compile the program with the Digital Visual Fortran 5.0 compiler.

```
PROGRAM bad_nested_loops_1
INTEGER :: i, j, product
DO i = 1, 3
   DO j = 1, 3
      product = i * j
      WRITE (*,*) i, ' * ', j, ' = ', product
END DO
END PROGRAM
```

The output of the compiler is

```
C>f132 bad_nested_loops_1.f90
DIGITAL Visual Fortran Optimizing Compiler Version: V5.0
Copyright (c) 1997 Digital Equipment Corp. All rights reserved.

bad_nes1.f90
bad_nes1.f90(3) : Error: An unterminated block exists.
DO i = 1, 3
^
```

The compiler reports a problem with the loop construct, but it does not detect the problem until it reaches the END PROGRAM statement, and it cannot tell where the problem occurred. If the program is very large, we would be faced with a difficult task when we tried to locate the problem.

Now let's name each loop and "accidentally" delete the inner END DO statement.

```
PROGRAM bad_nested_loops_2
INTEGER :: i, j, product
outer: DO i = 1, 3
   inner: DO j = 1, 3
      product = i * j
      WRITE (*,*) i, ' * ', j, ' = ', product
END DO outer
END PROGRAM
```

When we compile this program with the Digital Visual Fortran 5.0 compiler, the output is:

```
C>f132 bad_nested_loops_2.f90
DIGITAL Visual Fortran Optimizing Compiler Version: V5.0
Copyright (c) 1997 Digital Equipment Corp. All rights reserved.

bad_nes2.f90
bad_nes2.f90(7) : Error: The block construct names must match, and they do not.
  [OUTER]
END DO outer
-------^
bad_nes2.f90(3) : Error: An unterminated block exists.
```

The compiler reports a problem with the loop construct, and it reports which loops are involved in the problem. This information can be a major aid in debugging the program.

Good Programming Practice
Assign names to all nested loops so that they will be easier to understand and debug.

Remember that it is not possible to change an index variable within the body of a DO loop. Therefore, it is not possible to use the same index variable for two nested DO loops, since the inner loop would be attempting to change the index variable of the outer loop within the body of the outer loop.

Good Programming Practice
Use independent index variables for each loop in a set of nested DO loops.

Good Programming Practice
If two loops are nested, always ensure that one of them lies completely within the other one.

The following DO loops are incorrectly nested, and a compile-time error will be generated for this code.

```
outer: DO i = 1, 3
   ...
   inner: DO j = 1, 3
      ...
END DO outer
   ...
   END DO inner
```

The CYCLE and EXIT statements in nested loops

If a CYCLE or EXIT statement appears inside an *unnamed* set of nested loops, then the CYCLE or EXIT statement refers to the *innermost* of the loops containing it. For example, consider the following program:

```
PROGRAM test_cycle_1
INTEGER :: i, j, product
DO i = 1, 3
   DO j = 1, 3
      IF ( j == 2) CYCLE
      product = i * j
      WRITE (*,*) i, ' * ', j, ' = ', product
   END DO
END DO
END PROGRAM
```

If the inner loop counter j is equal to 2, then the CYCLE statement will be executed. When the cycle statement is executed, the remainder of the code block of the *innermost* DO loop is skipped, and execution of the innermost loop will start over with j increased by 1. The resulting output values are

```
1 *   1 =   1
1 *   3 =   3
2 *   1 =   2
2 *   3 =   6
3 *   1 =   3
3 *   3 =   9
```

Note that each time the inner loop variable had the value 2, execution of the inner loop was skipped.

It is also possible to make the CYCLE or EXIT statement refer to the *outer* loop of a nested construct of *named* loops by specifying a loop name in the statement. In the following example, when the inner loop counter j is equal to 2, the CYCLE outer statement will be executed. When this statement is executed, the remainder of the code block of the *outer* DO loop is skipped, and execution of the outer loop will start over with i increased by 1.

```
PROGRAM test_cycle_2
INTEGER :: i, j, product
outer: DO i = 1, 3
   inner: DO j = 1, 3
      IF ( j == 2) CYCLE outer
      product = i * j
      WRITE (*,*) i, ' * ', j, ' = ', product
   END DO inner
END DO outer
END PROGRAM
```

The resulting output values are

```
1 *   1 =   1
2 *   1 =   2
3 *   1 =   3
```

You should always use loop names with CYCLE or EXIT statements in nested loops to make sure that the statements affected the proper loop.

Good Programming Practice
Use loop names with CYCLE or EXIT statements in nested loops to make sure that the statements affect the proper loop.

Nesting loops within IF constructs and vice versa

It is also possible to nest loops within block IF constructs or block IF constructs within loops. If a loop is nested within a block IF construct, the loop must lie entirely within a single code block of the IF construct. For example, the following statements are illegal because the loop stretches between the IF and the ELSE code blocks of the IF construct:

```
outer: IF ( a<b ) THEN
    ...
    inner: DO i = 1, 3
        ...
ELSE
        ...
    END DO inner
    ...
END IF outer
```

In contrast, the following statements are legal because the loop lies entirely within a single code block of the IF construct.

```
outer: IF ( a < b ) THEN
    ...
    inner: DO i = 1, 3
        ...
    END DO inner
    ...
ELSE
    ...
END IF outer
```

EXAMPLE 3–8 Physics—The Flight of a Ball: If we assume negligible air friction and ignore the curvature of the earth, a ball that is thrown into the air from any point on the earth's surface will follow a parabolic flight path (see Figure 3–23*a*). The height of the ball at any time *t* after it is thrown is given by Equation (3–6)

$$y(t) = y_o + v_{yo} t + \frac{1}{2} gt^2 \tag{3–6}$$

where y_o is the initial height of the object above the ground, V_{yo} is the initial vertical velocity of the object, and g is the acceleration due to the earth's gravity. The horizontal distance (range) traveled by the ball as a function of time after it is thrown is given by Equation (3–7)

$$x(t) = x_o + v_{xo}\, t \tag{3–7}$$

where x_o is the initial horizontal position of the ball on the ground and v_{xo} is the initial horizontal velocity of the ball.

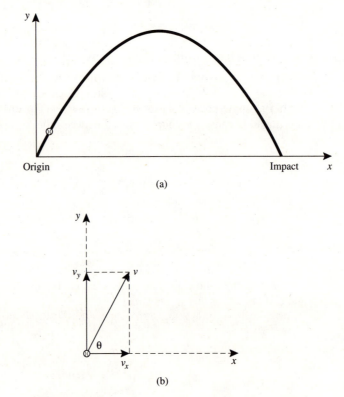

(a)

(b)

FIGURE 3–23
(a) When a ball is thrown upwards, it follows a parabolic trajectory. (b) The horizontal and vertical components of a velocity vector v at an angle θ with respect to the horizontal.

If the ball is thrown with some initial velocity v_o at an angle of θ degrees with respect to the earth's surface (Figure 3-23b), then the initial horizontal and vertical components of velocity will be

$$v_{xo} = v_o \cos \theta \tag{3–8}$$

$$v_{yo} = v_o \sin \theta \tag{3–9}$$

Assume that the ball is initially thrown from position $(x_o, y_o) = (0,0)$ with an initial velocity v_o of 20 meters per second at an initial angle of θ degrees. Design, write, and test a program that will determine the horizontal distance the ball travels from the time it was thrown until it touches the ground again. The program should do this calculation for all angles θ from 0 to 90 degrees in 1-degree steps. Determine the angle θ that maximizes the range of the ball.

SOLUTION

In order to solve this problem, we must determine an equation for the range of the thrown ball. Therefore, start by finding the time that the ball remains in the air and then finding the horizontal distance that the ball can travel during that time.

We can calculate the time that the ball will remain in the air after it is thrown from Equation (3–5). The ball will touch the ground at the time t for which $y(t) = 0$. Remembering that the ball will start from ground level ($y(0) = 0$). Solving for t, we get:

$$y(t) = y_o + v_{yo}\, t + \frac{1}{2}\, g\, t^2 \tag{3–6}$$

$$0 = 0 + v_{yo}\, t + \frac{1}{2}\, g\, t^2$$

$$0 = \left(v_{yo} + \frac{1}{2}\, gt\right) t$$

The ball will be at ground level at time $t_1 = 0$ (when we threw it) and at time

$$t_2 = -\frac{2\, v_{yo}}{g}$$

Then we use Equation (3–7) to find the horizontal distance that the ball will travel in time t_2:

$$range = x(t_2) = x_o + v_{xo}\, t_2 \tag{3–7}$$

$$range = 0 + v_{xo} \left(-\frac{2\, v_{yo}}{g}\right)$$

$$range = -\frac{2\, v_{xo}\, v_{yo}}{g}$$

We can substitute Equations (3–7) and (3–8) for v_{xo} and v_{yo} to get an equation expressed in terms of the initial velocity v and initial angle θ:

$$range = -\frac{2\, (v_o \cos \theta)\, (v_o \sin \theta)}{g}$$

$$range = -\frac{2\, v_o^2 \cos \theta \sin \theta}{g} \tag{3–10}$$

From the problem statement, we know that the initial velocity v_0 is 20 meters per second and that the ball will be thrown at all angles from 0 to 90 degrees in 1-degree steps. Finally, any elementary physics textbook will tell us that the acceleration due to the earth's gravity is -9.81 meters per second squared.

Now let's apply our design technique to this problem.

1. **State the problem.**

   A proper statement of this problem would be

   Calculate the range that a ball would travel when it is thrown with an initial velocity of v_0 at an initial angle θ. Calculate this range for a v_0 of 20 meters per second and at all angles between 0 and 90 degrees, in 1-degree increments. Determine the angle θ that will result in the maximum range for the ball. Assume that there is no air friction.

2. **Define the inputs and outputs**

   This problem does not require any inputs. We know from the problem statement what v_0 and θ will be, so there is no need to read them in. The outputs from this program will be a table showing the range of the ball for each angle θ and the angle θ for which the range is maximum.

3. **Design the algorithm**

   This program can be broken down into the following major steps:

   ```
   DO for theta = 0 to 90 degrees
       Calculate the range of the ball for each angle theta
       Determine if this theta yields the maximum range so far
       Write out the range as a function of theta
   END of DO
   WRITE out the theta yielding maximum range
   ```

An iterative DO loop is appropriate for this algorithm, since we are calculating the range of the ball for a specified number of angles. We will calculate the range for each value of θ, and then compare each range with the maximum range found so far to determine which angle yields the maximum range. Note that the trigonometric functions work in radians, so the angles in degrees must be converted to radians before the range is calculated. The detailed pseudocode for this algorithm follows.

```
Initialize max_range and max_degrees to 0
Initialize v0 to 20 meters/second
DO for theta = 0 to 90 degrees
    radian ← theta * degrees_2_rad        (Convert degrees to radians)
    angle ← (-2. * v0**2 / gravity ) * sin(radian) * cos(radian)
    Write out theta and range
    IF range > max_range then
       max_range ← range
       max_degrees ← theta
```

```
    END of IF
END of DO
Write out max_degrees, max_range
```

The flowchart for this program is shown in Figure 3–24.

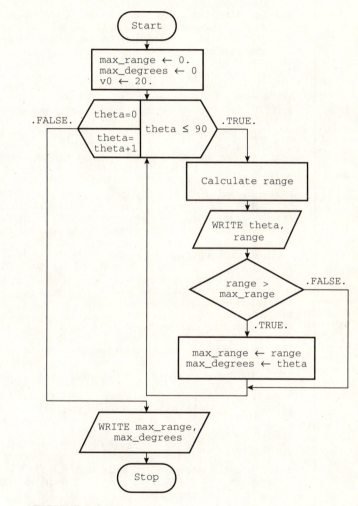

FIGURE 3–24
Flowchart for a program to determine the angle θ at which a ball thrown with an initial velocity v_0 of 20 m/s will travel the farthest.

4. **Turn the algorithm into Fortran statements.**

The final Fortran program is shown in Figure 3–25.

FIGURE 3–25

Program `ball` to determine the angle that maximizes the range of a thrown ball.

```
PROGRAM ball
!
! Purpose:
!   To calculate distance traveled by a ball thrown at a specified
!   angle THETA and at a specified velocity VO from a point on the
!   surface of the earth, ignoring the effects of air friction and
!   the earth's curvature.
!
! Record of revisions:
!    Date        Programmer         Description of change
!    ====        ==========         =====================
! 12/09/95    S. J. Chapman        Original code
!
IMPLICIT NONE
! Declare parameters
REAL, PARAMETER :: degrees_2_rad = 0.01745329 ! Deg ==>rad conv.

! Declare variables
REAL :: gravity = -9.81 ! Accel. due to gravity (m/s)
INTEGER :: max_degrees  ! angle at which the max rng occurs (degrees)
REAL :: max_range       ! Maximum range for the ball at vel v0 (meters)
REAL :: range           ! Range of the ball at a particular angle (meters)
REAL :: radian          ! Angle at which the ball was thrown (in radians)
INTEGER :: theta        ! Angle at which the ball was thrown (in degrees)
REAL :: v0              ! Velocity of the ball (in m/s)

! Initialize variables.
max_range = 0.
max_degrees = 0
v0 = 20.

! Loop over all specified angles.

loop: DO theta = 0, 90

! Get angle in radians
radian = real(theta) * degrees_2_rad

! Calculate range in meters.
range = (-2. * v0**2 / gravity) * sin(radian) * cos(radian)

! Write out the range for this angle.
   WRITE (*,*) 'THETA = ', theta, ' degrees; Range = ', range, &
               ' meters'

! Compare the range to the previous maximum range. If this
! range is larger, save it and the angle at which it occurred.
IF ( range > max_range ) THEN
   max_range = range
   max_degrees = theta
END IF

END DO loop
```

(continued)

(concluded)
```
! Skip a line, and then write out the maximum range and the angle
! at which it occurred.
WRITE (*,*) ' '
WRITE (*,*) 'Max range = ', max_range, ' at ', max_degrees, ' degrees'

END PROGRAM
```

The degrees-to-radians conversion factor is always a constant, so in the program it is given a name using the PARAMETER attribute, and all references to the constant within the program use that name. The acceleration due to gravity at sea level can be found in any physics text. It is about 9.81 m/sec^2, directed downward.

5. Test the program.

To test this program, we will calculate the answers by hand for a few of the angles and then compare the results with the output of the program.

$\theta = 0°$: $\qquad range = -\dfrac{2\,(20^2)}{-9.81}\cos 0 \sin 0 = 0$ meters

$\theta = 5°$: $\qquad range = -\dfrac{2\,(20^2)}{-9.81}\cos\left(\dfrac{5\pi}{180}\right)\sin\left(\dfrac{5\pi}{180}\right) = 7.080$ meters

$\theta = 40°$: $\qquad range = -\dfrac{2\,(20^2)}{-9.81}\cos\left(\dfrac{40\pi}{180}\right)\sin\left(\dfrac{40\pi}{180}\right) = 40.16$ meters

$\theta = 45°$: $\qquad range = -\dfrac{2\,(20^2)}{-9.81}\cos\left(\dfrac{45\pi}{180}\right)\sin\left(\dfrac{45\pi}{180}\right) = 40.77$ meters

When program ball is executed, a 90-line table of angles and ranges is produced. To save space, only a portion of the table is reproduced here:

```
C>ball

Theta =         0 degrees; Range = 0.000000E+00 meters
Theta =         1 degrees; Range =        1.423017 meters
Theta =         2 degrees; Range =        2.844300 meters
Theta =         3 degrees; Range =        4.262118 meters
Theta =         4 degrees; Range =        5.674743 meters
Theta =         5 degrees; Range =        7.080455 meters
     . . .
Theta =        40 degrees; Range =       40.155260 meters
Theta =        41 degrees; Range =       40.377900 meters
Theta =        42 degrees; Range =       40.551350 meters
Theta =        43 degrees; Range =       40.675390 meters
Theta =        44 degrees; Range =       40.749880 meters
Theta =        45 degrees; Range =       40.774720 meters
Theta =        46 degrees; Range =       40.749880 meters
Theta =        47 degrees; Range =       40.675390 meters
Theta =        48 degrees; Range =       40.551350 meters
Theta =        49 degrees; Range =       40.377900 meters
Theta =        50 degrees; Range =       40.155260 meters
     . . .
Theta =        85 degrees; Range =        7.080470 meters
Theta =        86 degrees; Range =        5.674757 meters
Theta =        87 degrees; Range =        4.262130 meters
```

```
Theta =        88 degrees; Range =      2.844310 meters
Theta =        89 degrees; Range =      1.423035 meters
Theta =        90 degrees; Range = 1.587826E-05 meters
```

```
Max range =   40.774720 at          45 degrees
```
The program output matches our hand calculation for the angles calculated above to the four-digit accuracy of the hand calculation. Note that the maximum range occurred at an angle of 45 degrees.

Quiz 3–2

This quiz provides a quick check to see if you understand the concepts introduced in section 3.4. If you have trouble with the quiz, reread the section, ask your instructor, or discuss the material with a fellow student. The answers to this quiz appear in Appendix F.

Examine the following DO loops and determine how many times each loop will be executed. Assume that all the index variables shown are of type integer.

1. `DO index = 7, 10`

2. `DO j = 7, 10, -1`

3. `DO index = 1, 10, 10`

4. `DO loop_counter = -2, 10, 2`

5. `DO time = -2, -10, -1`

6. `DO i = -10, -7, -3`

Examine the following loops and determine the value in `ires` at the end of each loop. Assume that `ires`, `incr`, and all index variables are integers.

7.
```
ires = 0
DO index = 1, 10
   ires = ires + 1
END DO
```

8.
```
ires = 0
DO index = 1, 10
   ires = ires + index
END DO
```

9.
```
ires = 0
DO index = 1, 10
   IF ( ires == 10 ) CYCLE
   ires = ires + index
END DO
```

(continued)

(concluded)

```
10. ires = 0
    DO index1 = 1, 10
       DO index2 = 1, 10
          ires = ires + 1
       END DO
    END DO

11. ires = 0
    DO index1 = 1, 10
       DO index2 = index1, 10
          IF ( index2 > 6 ) EXIT
          ires = ires + 1
       END DO
    END DO
```

Examine the following Fortran statements and tell whether or not they are valid. If they are invalid, indicate the reason why they are invalid.

```
12. loop1: DO i = 1, 10
       loop2: DO j = 1, 10
          loop3: DO i = i, j
             ...
          END DO loop3
       END DO loop2
    END DO loop1

13. loop1: DO i = 1, 10
       loop2: DO j = i, 10
          loop3: DO k = I, j
             ...
          END DO loop3
       END DO loop2
    END DO loop1

14. loopx: DO i = 1, 10
       ...
       loopy: DO j = 1, 10
          ...
       END DO loopx
    END DO loopy
```

■ 3.5

MORE ON DEBUGGING Fortran PROGRAMS

It is much easier to make a mistake when writing a program containing branches and loops than it is when writing simple sequential programs. Even after going through the full design process, a program of any size is almost guaranteed not to be completely correct the first time it is used. Suppose that we have built the program and tested it, only to find that the output values are in error. How do we go about finding the bugs and fixing them?

The best approach to locating the error is to use a symbolic debugger if one is supplied with your compiler. Ask your instructor or check your system's manuals to determine how to use the symbolic debugger supplied with your particular compiler and computer.

An alternate approach to locating the error is to insert WRITE statements into the code to print out important variables at key points in the program. When the program is run, the WRITE statements will print out the values of the key variables. Compare these values to the ones you expect, and the places where the actual and expected values differ will serve as a clue to help you locate the problem. For example, you can add the following WRITE statements to a program to verify the operation of a counting loop:

```
WRITE (*,*) 'At loop1: ist, ien, inc = ', ist, ien, inc
loop1: DO i = ist, ien, inc
    WRITE (*,*) 'In loop1: i = ', i
    ...
END DO loop1
WRITE (*,*) 'loop1 completed'
```

When the program is executed, its output listing will contain detailed information about the variables controlling the DO loop and just how many times the loop was executed. Similar WRITE statements could be used to debug the operation of a block IF construct:

```
WRITE (*,*) 'At if1: var1 = ', var1
if1: IF ( sqrt(var1) > 1. ) THEN
    WRITE (*,*) 'At if1: sqrt(var1) > 1.'
    ...
ELSE IF ( sqrt(var1) < 1. ) THEN
    WRITE (*,*) 'At if1: sqrt(var1) < 1.'
    ...
ELSE
    WRITE (*,*) 'At if1: sqrt(var1) == 1.'
    ...
END IF if1
```

Once you have located the portion of the code in which the error occurs, you can take a look at the specific statements in that area to isolate the problem. Be sure to check for these common errors in your code:

1. *If the problem occurs in an* IF *construct, check to see if you used the proper relational operator in your logical expressions.* For example, did you use > when you really intended >=? Logical errors of this sort can be very hard to spot, since the compiler will not give an error message for them. Be especially careful of logical expressions that are very complex, since they will be hard to understand and very easy to mess up. You should use extra parentheses to make them easier to understand. If the logical expressions are really large, consider breaking them into simpler expressions that are easier to follow by using intermediate logical variables. For example, the construct

```
IF ( (sin(x) > 0.5) .AND. (i < 5) .AND. (depth >= 1000. ) ) THEN
  ...
END IF
```

could be replaced by

```
LOGICAL :: test
test = sin(x) > 0.5
test = test .AND. (i < 5)
test = test .AND. (depth >= 1000.)
IF ( test ) THEN
  ...
END IF
```

2. *Another common problem with* IF *statements occurs when real variables are tested for equality.* Because of small round-off errors during floating-point arithmetic operations, two numbers that theoretically should be equal will differ by a tiny amount and the test for equality will fail. When working with real variables, it is often a good idea to replace a test for equality with a test for *near equality.* For example, instead of testing to see if x is equal to 10., you should test to see if $|x - 10.| < 0.0001$. Any value of x between 9.9999 and 10.0001 will satisfy the latter test, so round-off errors will not cause problems. The Fortran statements

$$IF (x == 10.) THEN$$

would be replaced by

$$IF (abs(x - 10.) <= 0.0001) THEN$$

3. *Most errors in counting* DO *loops involve mistakes with the loop parameters.* If you add WRITE statements to the DO loop, the problem should be fairly clear. Did the DO loop start with the correct value? Did it end with the correct value? Did it increment at the proper step? If not, check the parameters of the DO loop closely. You will probably spot an error in the control parameters.

4. *Another cause of errors in counting* DO *loops is inadvertently modifying the* DO *loop index variable.* Explicit attempts to modify the index variable within a loop will be easy to see, and they will usually produce a compiler error. However, the DO loop index may be modified indirectly within a subprogram (see Chapter 6), and the compiler may not be able to detect the problem. In this case the DO loop will function incorrectly, because the DO loop variable will not increment properly. You can detect this problem by examining the value of the index variable in every iteration of the loop.

5. *Errors in while loops are usually related to errors in the logical expression used to control their function.* You can detect these errors by examining the IF (*logical_expr*) EXIT statement of the while loop with WRITE statements.

■ **3.6**

SUMMARY

Chapter 3 presents the basic types of Fortran branches and loops. The principal type of branch is the block `IF-ELSE IF-ELSE-END IF` construct. This construct is very flexible. It can have as many `ELSE IF` clauses as needed to construct any desired test. Furthermore, block `IF` constructs can be nested to produce more complex tests. A second type of branch is the `CASE` construct. It may be used to select among mutually exclusive alternatives specified by an integer, character, or logical control expression.

The two basic types of loops in Fortran are the while loop and the iterative or counting `DO` loop. The while loop repeats a section of code when we do not know in advance how many times the loop must be repeated. The counting `DO` loop repeats a section of code when we know in advance how many times the loop should be repeated.

It is possible to exit from a loop at any time using the `EXIT` statement. It is also possible to jump back to the top of a loop using the `CYCLE` statement. If loops are nested, an `EXIT` or `CYCLE` statement refers by default to the innermost loop.

3.6.1 Summary of Good Programming Practice

The following guidelines should be adhered to when programming with branch or loop constructs. If you follow them consistently, your code will contain fewer bugs, will be easier to debug, and will be more understandable to others who may need to work with it in the future.

1. Always indent code blocks in block `IF`, `DO`, and `CASE` constructs to make them more readable.
2. Be cautious about testing for equality with real variables in an `IF` construct; round-off errors may cause two variables that should be equal to fail a test for equality. Instead, test to see if the variables are nearly equal within the round-off error to be expected on the computer you are working with.
3. Use a while loop to repeat sections of code when you don't know in advance how many times the loop will be executed.
4. Use a counting `DO` loop to repeat sections of code when you know in advance how many times the loop will be executed.
5. Never attempt to modify the values of `DO` loop index or control variables while inside the loop.
6. Assign names to large and complicated loops or `IF` constructs, especially if they are nested.
7. Use loop names with `CYCLE` and `EXIT` statements in nested loops to make certain that the action of the `CYCLE` or `EXIT` statement affects the proper loop.

3.6.2 Summary of Fortran Statements and Constructs

The following summary describes the Fortran 90/95 statements and constructs introduced in this chapter.

Block `IF` Construct

```
[name:] IF ( logical_expr_1 ) THEN
   Block 1
ELSE IF ( logical_expr_2 ) THEN [name]
   Block 2
ELSE [name]
   Block 3
END IF [name]
```

Description:

The block `IF` construct permits the execution of a code block based on the results of one or more logical expressions. If `logical_expr_1` is true, the first code block will be executed. If `logical_expr_1` is false and `logical_expr_2` is true, the second code block will be executed. If both logical expressions are false, the third code block will be executed. After any block is executed, control jumps to the first statement after the construct.

There must be one and only one `IF ( ) THEN` statement in a block `IF` construct. There may be any number of `ELSE IF` clauses (zero or more), and there may be at most one `ELSE` clause in the construct. The name is optional, but if it is used on the `IF` statement, then it must be used on the `END IF` statement. The name is optional on the `ELSE IF` and `ELSE` statements even if it is used on the `IF` and `END IF` statements.

`CASE` Construct

```
[name:] SELECT CASE (case_expr)
CASE (case_selector_1) [name]
   Block 1
CASE (case_selector_2) [name]
   Block 2
CASE DEFAULT [name]
   Block n
END SELECT [name]
```

Description:

The `CASE` construct executes a specific block of statements based on the value of the `case_expr`, which can be an integer, character, or logical value.
Each case selector specifies one or more possible values for the case expression. If the `case_expr` is a value included in a given case selector, then the corresponding block of statements is executed, and control will jump to the first executable statement after the end of the construct. If no case selector is executed then the `CASE DEFAULT` block will be executed if present and control will jump to the first executable statement after the end of the construct. If `CASE DEFAULT` is not present, the construct does nothing.

(continued)

(concluded)

There must be one SELECT CASE statement and one END SELECT statement in a CASE construct. There will be one or more CASE statements. At most, one CASE DEFAULT statement may be included. Note that all case selectors must be *mutually exclusive*. The name is optional, but if it is used on the SELECT CASE statement, then it must also be used on the END SELECT statement. The name is optional on the CASE statements even if it is used on the SELECT CASE and END SELECT statements.

CYCLE **Statement**

```
CYCLE [name]
```

Example:

```
CYCLE inner
```

Description:

The CYCLE statement may appear within any DO loop. When the statement is executed, all of the statements below it within the loop are skipped and control returns to the top of the loop. In while loops execution resumes from the top of the loop. In counting loops, the loop index is incremented, and if the index is still less than its limit, execution resumes from the top of the loop.

An unnamed CYCLE statement always causes the *innermost* loop containing the statement to cycle. A named CYCLE statement causes the named loop to cycle, even if it is not the innermost loop.

DO **Loop (Iterative or Counting Loop) Construct**

```
[name:] DO index = istart, iend, incr
   ...
END DO [name]
```

Example:

```
loop: DO index = 1, last_value, 3
   ...
END DO loop
```

Description:

The iterative DO loop repeats a block of code a known number of times. During the first iteration of the DO loop, the variable *index* is set to the value *istart*. *index* is incremented by *incr* in each successive loop until $index * incr > iend * incr$, at which time the loop terminates. The loop name is optional, but if it is used on the DO

(continued)

(concluded)

statement, then it must be used on the END DO statement. The loop variable *index* is incremented and tested *before* each loop, so the DO loop code will never be executed at all if *istart * incr > iend * incr*.

EXIT **Statement**

EXIT *[name]*

Example:

EXIT loop1

Description:

The EXIT statement may appear within any DO loop. When an EXIT statement is encountered, the program stops executing the loop and jumps to the first executable statement after the END DO.

An unnamed EXIT statement always causes the *innermost* loop containing the statement to exit. A named EXIT statement causes the named loop to exit, even if it is not the innermost loop.

Logical IF **Statement**

IF (*logical_expr*) statement

Description:

The logical IF statement is a special case of the block IF construct. If *logical_expr* is true, then the statement on the line with the IF is executed. Execution continues at the next line after the IF statement.

This statement may be used instead of the block IF construct if only one statement needs to be executed as a result of the logical condition.

WHILE **Loop Construct**

```
[name:] DO
    ...
IF ( logical_expr ) EXIT [name]
    ...
END DO [name]
```

(continued)

(concluded)

Example:

```
loop1: DO
    ...
    IF ( istatus /= 0 ) EXIT loop1
    ...
END DO loop1
```

Description:
  The while loop repeats a block of code until a specified *logical_expr* becomes true. It differs from a counting DO loop in that we do not know in advance how many times the loop will be repeated. When the IF statement of the loop is executed with the *logical_expr* true, execution skips to the next statement following the end of the loop.
  The name of the loop is optional, but if a name is included on the DO statement, then the same name must appear on the END DO statement. The name on the EXIT statement is optional; it may be left out even if the DO and END DO are named.

■ **3.7**

EXERCISES

3–1 The tangent function is defined as tan θ = sin θ / cos θ. This expression can be evaluated to solve for the tangent as long as the magnitude of cos θ is not too near to 0. (If cos θ is 0, evaluating the equation for tan θ will produce a divide-by-zero error.) Assume that θ is given in degrees and write Fortran statements to evaluate tan θ as long as the magnitude of cos θ is greater than or equal to 10^{-20}. If the magnitude of cos θ is less than 10^{-20}, write out an error message instead.

3–2 Write the Fortran statements required to calculate $y(t)$ from the equation

$$y(t) = \begin{cases} -3t^2 + 5 & t \geq 0 \\ 3t^2 + 5 & t < 0 \end{cases}$$

for values of t between −9 and 9 in steps of 3.

3–3 Write the Fortran statements required to calculate and print out the squares of all the even integers between 0 and 50.

3–4 Write a Fortran program to evaluate the equation $y(x) = x^2 - 3x + 2$ for all values of x between −1 and 3 in steps of 0.1.

3–5 Write a Fortran program to calculate the factorial function, as defined in Example 3–6. Be sure to handle the special cases of 0! and of illegal input values.

3–6 The following Fortran statements are intended to alert a user to dangerously high oral thermometer readings (values are in degrees Fahrenheit). Are they correct or incorrect? If they are incorrect, explain why and correct them.

```
IF ( temp < 97.5 ) THEN
   WRITE (*,*) 'Temperature below normal'
ELSE IF ( temp > 97.5 ) THEN
   WRITE (*,*) 'Temperature normal'
ELSE IF ( temp > 99.5 ) THEN
   WRITE (*,*) 'Temperature slightly high'
ELSE IF ( temp > 103.0 ) THEN
   WRITE (*,*) 'Temperature dangerously high'
END IF
```

3-7 The cost of sending a package by an express delivery service is $10.00 for the first 2 pounds, and $3.75 for each pound or fraction thereof over 2 pounds. If the package weighs more than 70 pounds, a $10.00 excess weight surcharge is added to the cost. No package over 100 pounds will be accepted. Write a program that accepts the weight of a package in pounds and computes the cost of mailing the package. Be sure to handle the case of overweight packages.

3-8 What is the difference in behavior between a CYCLE statement and an EXIT statement?

3-9 The following Fortran statements calculate the square root of the products of all numbers between 1 and 10, taken in any combination. Assume that i and j are integers and that result is real. Is this code correct or incorrect? If it is incorrect, explain why and correct it.

```
loop1: DO i = 1, 10
   loop2: DO j = 1, 10
      result = sqrt ( real (i*j) )
      WRITE (*,*) 'sqrt(', i, '*', j, ') = ', result
   END DO loop1
END DO loop2
```

3-10 The inverse sine function ASIN(x) is only defined for the range $-1.0 \le x \le 1.0$. If x is outside this range, an error will occur when the function is evaluated. The following Fortran statements calculate the inverse sine of a number if it is in the proper range and print an error message if it is not. Assume that x and inverse_sine are real. Is this code correct or incorrect? If it is incorrect, explain why and correct it.

```
test: IF ( ABS(x) <= 1. ) THEN
   inverse_sine = ASIN(x)
ELSE test
   WRITE (*,*) x, ' is out of range!'
END IF test
```

3-11 The program in Example 3-2 evaluates the function $f(x,y)$ for any two user-specified values x and y, where the function $f(x,y)$ is defined as follows.

$$f(x,y) = \begin{cases} x + y & x \ge 0 \text{ and } y \ge 0 \\ x + y^2 & x \ge 0 \text{ and } y < 0 \\ x^2 + y & x < 0 \text{ and } y \ge 0 \\ x^2 + y^2 & x < 0 \text{ and } y < 0 \end{cases}$$

The problem was solved by using a single logical IF construct with four code blocks to calculate $f(x,y)$ for all possible combinations of x and y. Rewrite program funxy to use nested IF constructs, where the outer construct evaluates the value of x and the inner constructs evaluate the value of y. Be sure to assign names to each your construct.

3–12 Suppose that a student has the option of enrolling for a single elective during a term. The student must select a course from a limited list of options: English, History, Astronomy, or Literature. Construct a fragment of Fortran code that will prompt the student for his or her choice, read in the choice, and use the answer as the case expression for a CASE construct. Be sure to include a default case to handle invalid inputs.

3–13 Examine the following DO statements and determine how many times each loop will be executed. (Assume that all loop index variables are integers.)

   a. DO irange = -32768, 32767
   b. DO j = 100, 1, -10
   c. DO kount = 2, 3, 4
   d. DO index = -4, -7
   e. DO i = -10, 10, 10
   f. DO

3–14 Examine the following iterative DO loops. Determine the value of `ires` at the end of each loop and also the number of times each loop executes. Assume that all variables are integers.

a.
```
ires = 0
   DO index = -10, 10
      ires = ires + 1
   END DO
```

b.
```
ires = 0
loop1: DO index1 = 1, 20, 5
   IF ( index1 <= 10 ) CYCLE
   loop2: DO index2 = index1, 20, 5
      ires = ires + index2
   END DO loop2
END DO loop1
```

c.
```
ires = 0
loop1: DO index1 = 10, 4, -2
   loop2: DO index2 = 2, index1, 2
      IF ( index2 > 6 ) EXIT loop2
      ires = ires + index2
   END DO loop2
END DO loop1
```

d.
```
ires = 0
loop1: DO index1 = 10, 4, -2
   loop2: DO index2 = 2, index1, 2
      IF ( index2 > 6 ) EXIT loop1
      ires = ires + index2
   END DO loop2
END DO loop1
```

3–15 Examine the following while loops. Determine the value of `ires` at the end of each of the loops and the number of times each loop executes. Assume that all variables are integers.

```
a. ires = 0
   loop1: DO
       ires = ires + 1
       IF ( (ires / 10 ) * 10 == ires ) EXIT
   END DO loop1

b. ires = 2
   loop2: DO
       ires = ires**2
       IF ( ires > 200 ) EXIT
   END DO loop2

c. ires = 2
   DO WHILE ( ires > 200 )
       ires = ires**2
   END DO
```

3–16 Modify program `ball` from Example 3–8 to read in the acceleration due to gravity at a particular location and to calculate the maximum range of the ball for that acceleration. After modifying the program, run it with accelerations of -9.8 m/sec^2, -9.7 m/sec^2, and -9.6 m/sec^2. What effect does the reduction in gravitational attraction have on the range of the ball? What effect does the reduction in gravitational attraction have on the best angle θ at which to throw the ball?

3–17 Modify program `ball` from Example 3–8 to read in the initial velocity with which the ball is thrown. After modifying the program, run it with initial velocities of 10 m/sec, 20 m/sec, and 30 m/sec. What effect does changing the initial velocity v_o have on the range of the ball? What effect does it have on the best angle θ at which to throw the ball?

3–18 Program `doy` in Example 3–6 calculates the day of year associated with any given month, day, and year. As written, this program does not check to see if the data entered by the user is valid. It will accept nonsense values for months and days and do calculations with them to produce meaningless results. Modify the program so that it checks the input values for validity before using them. If the inputs are invalid, the program should tell the user what is wrong and then quit. The year should be number greater than 0, the month should be a number between 1 and 12, and the day should be a number between 1 and a maximum that depends on the month. Use a `CASE` construct to implement the bounds checking performed on the day.

3–19 Write a Fortran program to evaluate the function

$$y(x) = \ln \frac{1}{1-x}$$

for any user-specified value of x, where ln is the natural logarithm (logarithm to the base e). Write the program with a while loop so that the program repeats the calculation for each legal value of x entered into the program. When an illegal value of x is entered, terminate the program.

3–20 Write a Fortran program to convert all lowercase characters in a user-supplied character string to uppercase without changing the uppercase and nonalphabetic characters in the string. Assume that your computer uses the ASCII collating sequence.

3–21 Current through a Diode The current flowing through the semiconductor diode shown in Figure 3–26 is given by the equation

$$i_D = I_o \left(e^{\frac{-q v_D}{kT}} - 1 \right) \tag{3–11}$$

where

i_D = the voltage across the diode, in volts
v_D = the current flow through the diode, in amps
I_O = the leakage current of the diode, in amps
q = the charge on an electron, 1.602×10^{-19} coulombs
k = Boltzmann's constant, 1.38×10^{-23} joule/K
T = temperature, in kelvins (K)

The leakage current I_O of the diode is 2.0 μA. Write a computer program to calculate the current flowing through this diode for all voltages from -1.0 V to $+0.8$ V in 0.1 V steps. Repeat this process for each of the following temperatures: 75°F and 100°F, and 125°F. Use the program of Example 2–4 to convert the temperatures from °F to kelvins.

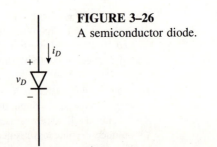

FIGURE 3–26
A semiconductor diode.

3–22 Tension on a Cable A 200-pound object is to be hung from the end of a rigid 8-foot horizontal pole of negligible weight, as shown in Figure 3-27. The pole is attached to a wall by a pivot and is supported by an 8-foot cable that is attached to the wall at a higher point. The tension on this cable is given by the equation

$$T = \frac{W \cdot lc \cdot lp}{d \sqrt{lp^2 - d^2}} \tag{3–12}$$

where T is the tension on the cable, W is the weight of the object, lc is the length of the cable, lp is the length of the pole, and d is the distance along the pole at which the cable is attached. Write a program to determine the distance d at which to attach the cable to the pole in order to minimize the tension on the cable. The program should calculate the tension on the cable at 0.1 foot intervals from $d = 1$ foot to $d = 7$ feet and should locate the position d that produces the minimum tension.

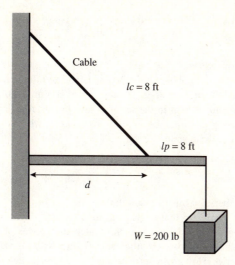

FIGURE 3–27
A 200-pound weight suspended from a rigid bar supported by a cable.

3–23 Bacterial Growth Suppose that a biologist performs an experiment in which he or she measures the rate at which a specific type of bacterium reproduces asexually in different culture media. The experiment shows that in medium A the bacteria reproduce once every 60 minutes, and in medium B the bacteria reproduce once every 90 minutes. Assume that a single bacterium is placed on each culture medium at the beginning of the experiment. Write a Fortran program that calculates and writes out the number of bacteria present in each culture at intervals of 3 hours from the beginning of the experiment until 24 hours have elapsed. How do the numbers of bacteria compare on the two media after 24 hours?

3–24 Decibels Engineers often measure the ratio of two power measurements in *decibels,* or dB. The equation for the ratio of two power measurements in decibels is

$$dB = 10 \log_{10} \frac{P_2}{P_1} \tag{3–13}$$

where P_2 is the power level being measured and P_1 is some reference power level. Assume that the reference power level P_1 is 1 watt, and write a program that calculates the decibel level corresponding to power levels between 1 and 20 watts, in 0.5 W steps.

3–25 Infinite Series Trigonometric functions are usually calculated on computers by using a truncated infinite series. An *infinite series* is an infinite set of terms that together add up to the value of a particular function or expression. For example, one infinite series used to evaluate the sine of a number is

$$\sin x = x - \frac{x^3}{3!} + \frac{x^5}{5!} - \frac{x^7}{7!} + \frac{x^9}{9!} + \ldots \tag{3–14a}$$

or

$$\sin x = \sum_{n=1}^{\infty} (-1)^{n-1} \frac{x^{2n-1}}{(2n-1)!} \tag{3-14b}$$

where x is in units of radians.

Since a computer does not have enough time to add an infinite number of terms for every sine that is calculated, the infinite series is *truncated* after a finite number of terms. The number of terms that should be kept in the series is just enough to calculate the function to the precision of the floating-point numbers on the computer on which the function is being evaluated. The truncated infinite series for $\sin x$ is

$$\sin x = \sum_{n=1}^{N} (-1)^{n-1} \frac{x^{2n-1}}{(2n-1)!} \tag{3-15}$$

where N is the number of terms to retain in the series.

Write a Fortran program that reads in a value for x in degrees and then calculates the sine of x using the sine intrinsic function. Next calculate the sine of x using Equation (3–13) with N = 1, 2, 3, ..., 10. Compare the true value of $\sin x$ with the values calculated using the truncated infinite series. How many terms are required to calculate $\sin x$ to the full accuracy of your computer?

3–26 Geometric Mean The *geometric mean* of a set of numbers x_1 through x_n is defined as the nth root of the product of the numbers:

$$\text{geometric mean} = \sqrt[n]{x_1 \, x_2 \, x_3 \ldots x_n} \tag{3-16}$$

Write a Fortran program that will accept an arbitrary number of positive input values and calculate both the arithmetic mean (*i.e.*, the average) and the geometric mean of the numbers. Use a while loop to get the input values; terminate the inputs if a user enters a negative number. Test your program by calculating the average and geometric mean of the four numbers 10, 5, 2, and 5.

3–27 RMS Average The *root-mean-square* (rms) *average* is another way of calculating a mean for a set of numbers. The rms average of a series of numbers is the square root of the arithmetic mean of the squares of the numbers.

$$\text{rms average} = \sqrt{\frac{1}{N} \sum_{i=1}^{N} x_i^2} \tag{3-17}$$

Write a Fortran program that accepts an arbitrary number of positive input values and calculate the rms average of the numbers. Prompt the user for the number of values to be entered and use a DO loop to read in the numbers. Test your program by calculating the rms average of the four numbers 10, 5, 2, and 5.

3–28 Harmonic Mean The *harmonic mean* is yet another way of calculating a mean for a set of numbers. The harmonic mean of a set of numbers is given by the equation:

$$\text{harmonic mean} = \frac{N}{\dfrac{1}{x_1} + \dfrac{1}{x_2} + \ldots + \dfrac{1}{x_N}} \tag{3-18}$$

Write a Fortran program that will read in an arbitrary number of positive input values and calculate the harmonic mean of the numbers. Use any method that you desire to read in the input values. Test your program by calculating the harmonic mean of the four numbers 10, 5, 2, and 5.

3–29 Write a single Fortran program that calculates the arithmetic mean (average), rms average, geometric mean, and harmonic mean for a set of numbers. Use any method that you desire to read in the input values. Compare these values for each of the following sets of numbers:

a. 4, 4, 4, 4, 4, 4, 4
b. 4, 3, 4, 5, 4, 3, 5
c. 4, 1, 4, 7, 4, 1, 7
d. 1, 2, 3, 4, 5, 6, 7

3–30 **Mean Time between Failure Calculations** The reliability of a piece of electronic equipment is usually measured in terms of mean time between failures (MTBF), where MTBF is the average time that the piece of equipment can operate before a failure occurs in it. For large systems containing many pieces of electronic equipment, it is customary to determine the MTBFs of each component and to calculate the overall MTBF of the system from the failure rates of the individual components. If the system is structured like the one shown in Figure 3–28, every component must work in order for the whole system to work. The overall system MTBF can be calculated as

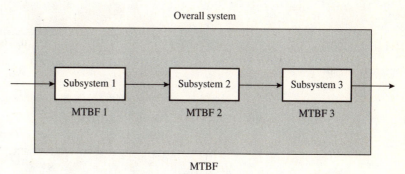

FIGURE 3–28
An electronic system containing three subsystems with known MTBFs.

$$MTBF_{sys} = \frac{1}{\dfrac{1}{MTBF_1} + \dfrac{1}{MTBF_2} + \dots + \dfrac{1}{MTBF_n}} \qquad (3\text{–}19)$$

Write a program that reads in the number of series components in a system and the MTBFs for each component and then calculates the overall MTBF for the system. To test your program, determine the MTBF for a radar system consisting of an antenna subsystem with an MTBF of 2000 hours, a transmitter with an MTBF of 800 hours, a receiver with an MTBF of 3000 hours, and a computer with an MTBF of 5000 hours.

3–31 Refraction When a ray of light passes from a region with an index of refraction n_1 into a region with a different index of refraction n_2, the light ray is bent (see Figure 3–29). The angle at which the light is bent is given by *Snell's Law*

$$n_1 \sin \theta_1 = n_2 \sin \theta_2 \tag{3-20}$$

where θ_1 is the angle of incidence of the light in the first region and θ_2 is the angle of incidence of the light in the second region. You can use Snell's Law to predict the angle of incidence of a light ray in region 2 if the angle of incidence θ_1 in region 1 and the indices of refraction n_1 and n_2 are known. The equation to perform this calculation is

$$\theta_2 = \sin^{-1}\left(\frac{n_1}{n_2} \sin \theta_1\right) \tag{3-21}$$

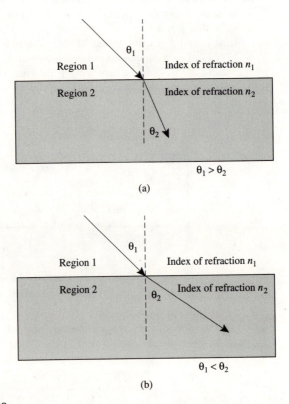

FIGURE 3–29
A ray of light bends as it passes from one medium into another one. (*a*) If the ray of light passes from a region with a low index of refraction into a region with a higher index of refraction, the ray of light bends more towards the vertical. (*b*) If the ray of light passes from a region with a high index of refraction into a region with a lower index of refraction, the ray of light bends away from the vertical.

Write a Fortran program to calculate the angle of incidence (in degrees) of a light ray in region 2 given the angle of incidence θ_1 in region 1 and the indices of refraction n_1 and n_2. (*Note:* If $n_1 > n_2$, then for some angles θ_1, Equation (3–20) will have no real solution because the absolute value of the quantity $\left(\dfrac{n_1}{n_2} \sin \theta_1\right)$ will be greater than 1.0. When this condition occurs, all light is reflected back into region 1 and no light passes into region 2. Your program must be able to recognize and properly handle this condition.)

Test your program by running it for the following cases:

a. $n_1 = 1.0$, $n_2 = 1.7$, and $\theta_1 = 45°$
b. $n_1 = 1.7$, $n_2 = 1.0$, and $\theta_1 = 45°$

Basic I/O Concepts

In the previous chapters, we read values into and wrote them out of our Fortran programs using list-directed READ and WRITE statements. List-directed I/O statements are said to be in **free format.** Free format is specified by the second asterisk in the READ (*,*) and WRITE (*,*) statements. However, the results of writing out data in free format are not always pretty. A large number of extra spaces often appear in the output. In this chapter you learn how to write out data using **formats** that specify the exact way in which the numbers should be printed.

Formats may be used either when writing or when reading data. Because formats are most useful during output, we examine formatted WRITE statements first and postpone formatted READ statements until later in the chapter.

The second major topic introduced in this chapter is disk file processing. You learn the basics of how to read from and write to disk files. Advanced disk file processing is beyond the scope of this text.[1]

■ 4.1

FORMATS AND FORMATTED WRITE STATEMENTS

A format may be used to specify the exact manner in which a program will print out variables. A format can specify both the horizontal and the vertical positions of the variables on the paper and also the number of significant digits to be printed. A typical formatted WRITE statement for an integer i and a real variable result follows.

```
WRITE (*,100) i, result
100 FORMAT (' The result for iteration ', I3,' is ', F7.3)
```

The FORMAT statement contains the formatting information used by the WRITE statement. The number 100 within the parentheses in the WRITE statement is the statement

---

[1]For a detailed discussion of advanced disk file processing, see S.J. Chapman, *Fortran 90/95 for Scientists and Engineers* (Burr Ridge, IL: McGraw-Hill, 1998).

label of the FORMAT statement; the label describes how the values contained in i and result are to be printed out. I3 and F7.3 are the **format descriptors** associated with variables i and result, respectively. In this case the FORMAT statement specifies that the program should first write out the phrase 'The result for iteration ', and then write out the value of variable i. The format descriptor I3 specifies that a space three characters wide should be used to print out the value of variable i. The value of i will be followed by the phrase ' is ' and then the value of the variable result. The format descriptor F7.3 specifies that a space seven characters wide should be used to print out the value of variable result and that it should be printed with three digits to the right of the decimal point. The resulting output line and the same line printed with free format follow.

```
The result for iteration  21 is  3.142                (formatted)
   The result for iteration         21 is   3.141593   (free format)
```

Note that we are able to eliminate both extra blank spaces and undesired decimal places by using format statements. Note also that the value in variable result was rounded before it was printed out in F7.3 format. (Only the value printed out has been rounded; the contents of variable result are unchanged.) Formatted I/O will permit us to create neat output listings from our programs.

In addition to FORMAT statements, formats may be specified in character constants or variables. If a character constant or variable is used to contain the format, then the constant or the name of the variable appears within the parentheses in the WRITE statement. For example, the following three WRITE statements are equivalent:

```
WRITE (*,100) i, x                      ! Format in FORMAT statement
100 FORMAT (1X,I6,F10.2)

CHARACTER(len=20) :: string             ! Format in character variable
string = '(1X,I6,F10.2)'
WRITE (*,string) i, x

WRITE (*,'(1X,I6,F10.2)') i, x          ! Format in character constant
```

In these examples each format descriptor was separated from its neighbors by commas. With a few exceptions multiple format descriptors in a single FORMAT statement must be separated by commas.

■ 4.2
OUTPUT DEVICES

To understand the structure of a FORMAT statement, we must know something about the **output devices** on which our data will be displayed. When we run a Fortran program, the output of the program is displayed on an output device. Many types of output devices are used with computers. Some output devices produce permanent paper copies of the data, while others just display it temporarily for us to see. Common output devices include line printers, laser printers, and terminals.

A common way to get a paper copy of the output of a program is on a **line printer.** A line printer is a type of printer that takes its name from the fact that it prints output data a line at a time. Because the line printer was the first common computer output device, Fortran output specifications were designed with it in mind. Other more modern output devices are generally compatible with the older line printer so that the same output statement can be used for any device.

A line printer prints on computer paper that is divided into pages on a continuous roll. There are perforations between the pages so that it is easy to separate them. The most common size of computer paper in the United States is 11 inches high by 14 7/8 inches wide. Each page is divided into a number of lines, and each line is divided into 132 columns, with one character per column. Since most line printers print either 6 lines per inch or 8 lines per vertical inch, the printers can print either 60 or 72 lines per page. This description assumes a 0.5 inch margin at the top and the bottom of each page; if the margin is larger, fewer lines can be printed. The format specifies where a line will print on a page (vertical position) and also where each variable will print within the line (horizontal position).

The computer builds up a complete image of each line in memory before sending it to an output device. The computer memory containing the image of the line is called the **output buffer** (Figure 4–1). The output buffer for a line printer is usually 133 characters wide. The first character in the buffer is known as the **control character;** it specifies the vertical spacing for the line. The remaining 132 characters in the buffer contain the data to be printed on that line.

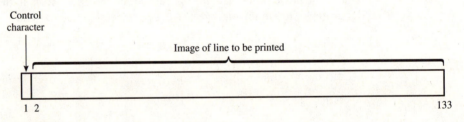

FIGURE 4–1
The output buffer is usually 133 characters long. The first character is the control character, and the next 132 characters are an image of what will be printed on the line.

The control character is not printed on the page. Instead, it provides vertical positioning control information to the printer. Table 4–1 shows the vertical spacing resulting from different control characters.

■ **TABLE 4–1**
Fortran control characters

Control character	Action
1	Skip to new page
blank	Single spacing
0	Double spacing
+	No spacing (print over previous line)

A '1' character causes the printer to skip the remainder of the current page and print the current line at the top of the next page. A blank character causes the printer to print the current line right below the previous one, while a '0' character causes the printer to skip a line before the current line is printed. A '+' character specifies no spacing; in this case the new line will overwrite the previous line. If any other character is used as the control character, the result should be the same as for a blank.

For list-directed output [WRITE (*,*)], a blank control character is automatically inserted at the beginning of each output buffer. Therefore, list-directed output is always printed in single-spaced lines.

The following FORMAT statements illustrate the use of the control character. They will print a heading at the top of a new page, skip one line, and then print column headings for Table 4–1.

```
WRITE (*,100)
100 FORMAT ('1','This heading is at the top of a new page.')
WRITE (*,110)
110 FORMAT ('0','    Control Character    Action ')
WRITE (*,120)
120 FORMAT (' ','    =================    ====== ')
```

The results of executing these Fortran statements are shown in Figure 4–2.

```
This heading is at the top of a new page


Control Character    Action
=================    ======
```

FIGURE 4–2

You must be careful to avoid unpleasant surprises when writing output format statements. For example, the following statements will behave in an unpredictable fashion.

```
WRITE (*,100) n
100 FORMAT (I3)
```

The format descriptor I3 specifies that we want to print the value of variable n in the first three characters of the output buffer. If the value of n is 25, the three positions are filled with ⌀25 (where ⌀ denotes a blank). Because the first character is interpreted as a control character, the printer will space down one line and print out 25 in the first two columns of the new line. On the other hand, if n is 125, then the first three characters of the output buffer are filled with 125. Because the first character is interpreted as a control character, the printer will skip to a new page and print out 25 in the first two columns of the new line. This behavior is certainly not what we intended! You should be very careful not to write any format descriptors that include column 1, since they can produce erratic printing behavior and fail to display the correct results.

> **Programming Pitfalls**
> Never write a format descriptor that includes column 1 of the output line. Erratic paging behavior and incorrectly displayed values may result if you do so.

To help avoid this error, you should write out each control character separately in the FORMAT statement. For example, the following two FORMAT statements are equivalent:

```
100 FORMAT ('1','Count = ', I3)
100 FORMAT ('1Count = ', I3)
```

Both statements produce the same output buffer, containing a 1 in the control character position. However, the control character is more obvious in the first statement than it is in the second one.

■ 4.3
FORMAT DESCRIPTORS

Fortran's many format descriptors fall into four basic categories:

1. Format descriptors that describe the vertical position of a line of text.
2. Format descriptors that describe the horizontal position of data in a line.
3. Format descriptors that describe the output format of a particular value.
4. Format descriptors that control the repetition of portions of a FORMAT statement.

We will deal with some common examples of format descriptors in this chapter. Other less common format descriptors appear in Appendix D. Table 4–2 contains a list of symbols used with format descriptors and their meanings.

■ **TABLE 4–2**
Symbols used with format descriptors

Symbol	Meaning
c	Column number.
d	Number of digits to right of decimal place for real input or output.
m	Minimum number of digits to be displayed
n	Number of spaces to skip
r	**Repeat count**—the number of times to use a descriptor or group of descriptors.
w	**Field width**—the number of characters to use for the input or output.

4.3.1 Integer Output—The I Descriptor

The descriptor used to describe the display format of integer data is the I descriptor. It has the general form

$$rIw \qquad \text{or} \qquad rIw.m$$

where *r*, *w*, and *m* have the meanings given in Table 4–2. Integer values are *right justified* in their fields. (These values are printed out so that the last digit of the integer occupies the right-most column of the field.) If an integer is too large to fit into the field in which it is to be printed, then the field is filled with asterisks. For example, the following statements

```
INTEGER :: index  = -12, junk  = 4, number = -12345
WRITE (*,200) index, index+12, junk, number
WRITE (*,210) index, index+12, junk, number
WRITE (*,220) index, index+12, junk, number
200 FORMAT (' ', 2I5,    I6, I10 )
210 FORMAT (' ', 2I5.0, I6, I10.8 )
220 FORMAT (' ', 2I5.3, I6, I5 )
```

will produce the output

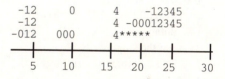

```
-12      0      4    -12345
-12             4 -00012345
-012   000      4*****
```

4.3.2 Real Output—The F Descriptor

One format descriptor used to describe the display format of real data is the F descriptor. It has the form

$$rFw.d$$

where *r*, *w*, and *d* have the meanings given in Table 4–2. Real values are printed *right justified* within their fields. If necessary, the number will be rounded off before it is displayed. For example, suppose that the variable pi contains the value 3.141593. If this variable is displayed using the F7.3 format descriptor, the displayed value will be ᵇᵇ3.142. On the other hand, if the displayed number includes more significant digits than the internal representation of the number, extra zeros will be appended to the right of the decimal point. If the variable pi is displayed with an F10.8 format descriptor, the resulting value will be 3.14159300.

If a real number is too large to fit into the field in which it is to be printed, then the field is filled with asterisks.

For example, the following statements

```
REAL :: a = -12.3, b = .123, c = 123.456
WRITE (*,200) a, b, c
WRITE (*,210) a, b, c
```

```
200 FORMAT (' ', 2F6.3, F8.3 )
210 FORMAT (' ', 3F10.2 )
```

will produce the output

4.3.3   Real Output—The E Descriptor

Real data can also be printed in **exponential notation** using the E descriptor. Scientific notation is a popular way for scientists and engineers to display very large or very small numbers. It consists of expressing a number as a normalized value between 1 and 10 multiplied by 10 raised to a power.

To understand the convenience of scientific notation, consider the following two examples from chemistry and physics. *Avogadro's number* is the number of atoms in a mole of a substance. It can be written out as 602,000,000,000,000,000,000,000, or it can be expressed in scientific notation as 6.02×10^{23}. On the other hand, the charge on an electron is 0.0000000000000000001602 coulombs. This number can be expressed in scientific notation as 1.602×10^{-19}. Scientific notation is clearly a much more convenient way to write these numbers!

The E format descriptor has the form

$$rEw.d$$

where r, w, and d have the meanings given in Table 4–2. Unlike normal scientific notation, the real values displayed in exponential notation with the E descriptor are normalized to a range between 0.1 and 1.0. That is, they are displayed as a number between 0.1 and 1.0 multiplied by a power of 10. For example, the standard scientific notation for the number 4096.0 would be 4.096×10^{3}, while the computer output with the E descriptor would be 0.4096×10^{4}. Because it is not easy to represent exponents on a line printer, the computer output would appear on the printer as `0.4096E+04`.

If a real number cannot fit into its designated field, then the field is filled with asterisks. You should be especially careful with field sizes when working with the E format descriptor, since many items must be considered when sizing the output field. For example, to print out a variable in the E format with four significant digits of accuracy, you need a field width of 11 characters: one character for the sign of the mantissa, two for the zero and decimal point, four for the actual mantissa, one for the E, one for the sign of the exponent, and two for the exponent itself.

$$\pm 0.ddddE\pm ee$$

In general the width of an E format descriptor field must satisfy the expression

$$w \geq d + 7 \qquad\qquad (4\text{--}1)$$

or the field may be filled with asterisks.[2]

For example, the following statements

```
REAL :: a = 1.2346E6, b = 0.001, c = -77.7E10 , d = -77.7E10
WRITE (*,200) a, b, c, d
200 FORMAT (' ', 2E14.4, E13.6, E11.6 )
```

will produce the output

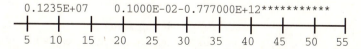

Notice that the fourth field is all asterisks, since the format descriptor does not satisfy Equation (4–1).

4.3.4 True Scientific Notation—The ES Descriptor

The output of the E format descriptor doesn't exactly match conventional scientific notation. Conventional scientific notation expresses a number as a value between 1.0 and 10.0 times a power of 10, while the E format expresses the number as a value between 0.1 and 1.0 times a power of 10.

We can make the computer output match conventional scientific notation by using a slightly modified version of the E descriptor called the ES descriptor. The ES descriptor is exactly the same as the E descriptor except that the number to be output will be displayed with a mantissa in the range between 1 and 10. The ES format descriptor has the form

$$rESw.d$$

where r, w, and d have the meanings given in Table 4–2. The formula for the minimum width of an ES format descriptor is the same as the formula for the width of an E format descriptor, but the ES descriptor can display one more significant digit in a given width because the leading zero is replaced by a significant digit. The ES field must satisfy the expression

$$w \geq d + 7 \tag{4–1}$$

or the field may be filled with asterisks.[3]

For example, the following statements

```
REAL :: a = 1.2346E6, b = 0.001, c = -77.7E10
WRITE (*,200) a, b, c
200 FORMAT (' ', 2ES14.4, ES12.6 )
```

---

[2]If the number to be displayed in the field is positive, then the field width w need only be six characters larger than d. If the number is negative, an extra character is needed for the minus sign. Hence, in general w must be $\geq d + 7$. Also, note that some compilers suppress the leading zero so that one less column is required.

[3]If the number to be displayed in the field is positive, then the field width w need only be six characters larger than d. If the number is negative, an extra character is needed for the minus sign. Hence, in general $w \geq d + 7$.

will produce the output

```
    1.2346E+06    1.0000E-03***********
    +    +    +    +    +    +    +    +
    5   10   15   20   25   30   35   40
```

The third field is all asterisks, since the format descriptor does not satisfy Equation (4–1).

Good Programming Practice
When displaying very large or very small numbers, use the ES format descriptor to cause them to be displayed in conventional scientific notation. This display will help a reader understand the output numbers.

4.3.5 Logical Output—The L Descriptor

The descriptor used to display logical data has the form

$$rLw$$

where r and w have the meanings given in Table 4–2. The value of a logical variable can only be .TRUE. or .FALSE.. The output of logical variable is either a T or an F, right justified in the output field.

For example, the following statements

```
LOGICAL :: output = .TRUE., debug = .FALSE.
WRITE (*,200) output, debug
200 FORMAT (' ', 2L5 )
```

will produce the output

```
    T    F
    +    +    +
    5   10   15
```

4.3.6 Character Output—The A Descriptor

Character data is displayed using the A format descriptor.

$$rA \quad \text{or} \quad rAw$$

where r and w have the meanings given in Table 4–2. The rA descriptor displays character data in a field whose width is the same as the number of characters being displayed, while the rAw descriptor displays character data in a field of fixed width w. If the width w of the field is longer than the length of the character variable, the variable is printed out *right justified* in the field. If the width of the field is shorter than the length of the character variable, only the first w characters of the variable will be printed out in the field.

For example, the following statements

```
CHARACTER(len=17) :: string = 'This is a string.'
WRITE (*,10) string
WRITE (*,11) string
WRITE (*,12) string
10 FORMAT (' ', A)
11 FORMAT (' ', A20)
12 FORMAT (' ', A6)
```

will produce the output

```
This is a string.
    This is a string.
This i
      +    +    +    +    +
      5   10   15   20   25
```

4.3.7 Horizontal Positioning—The X and T Descriptor

Two format descriptors are available to control the spacing of data in the output buffer and, therefore, on the final output line. They are the X descriptor, which inserts spaces into the buffer, and the T descriptor, which "tabs" over to a specific column in the buffer. The X descriptor has the form

$$nX$$

where n is the number of blanks to insert. It is used to add one or more blanks between two values on the output line. The T descriptor has the form

$$Tc$$

where c is the column number to go to. This descriptor is used to jump directly to a specific column in the output buffer. The T descriptor works much like a tab character on a typewriter except that it is possible to jump to any position in the output line, even from beyond that position in the FORMAT statement.

For example, the following statements

```
CHARACTER(len=10) :: first_name = 'James '
CHARACTER :: initial = 'R'
CHARACTER(len=16) :: last_name = 'Johnson '
CHARACTER(len=9) :: class = 'COSC 2301'
INTEGER :: grade = 92
WRITE (*,100) first_name, initial, last_name, grade, class
100 FORMAT (1X, A10, 1X, A1, 1X, A10, 4X, I3, T51, A9)
```

will produce the output

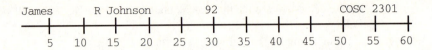

The first 1X descriptor produces a blank control character, so this output line is printed on the next line of the printer. The first name begins in column 1, the middle initial begins in column 12, the last name begins in column 14, the grade begins in column 28, and course name begins in column 50. (The course name begins in column 51 of the buffer, but it is printed in column 50, since the first character in the output buffer is the control character.) This same output structure could have been created with the following statements:

```
WRITE (*,110) first_name, initial, last_name, class, grade
110 FORMAT (1X, A10, T13, A1, T15, A10, T51, A9, T29, I3)
```

In this example we are actually jumping backward in the output line when we print out the grade.

Since you may freely move anywhere in the output buffer with the T descriptor, it is possible to accidentally overwrite portions of your output data before the line is printed. For example, if we change the tab descriptor for class from T51 to T17

```
WRITE (*,120) first_name, initial, last_name, class, grade
120 FORMAT (1X, A10, T13, A1, T15, A10, T17, A9, T29, I3)
```

the program will produce the following output:

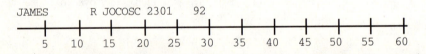

Programming Pitfalls
When using the T descriptor, be careful to make certain that your fields do not overlap.

4.3.8 Repeating Groups of Format Descriptors

We have seen that many individual format descriptors can be repeated by preceding them with a repeat count. For example, the format descriptor 2I10 is the same as the pair of descriptors I10, I10.

We can also repeat whole groups of format descriptors by enclosing the whole group within parentheses and placing a repetition count in front of the parentheses. For example, the following two FORMAT statements are equivalent:

```
320 FORMAT ( 1X, I6, I6, F10.2, F10.2, I6, F10.2, F10.2 )
320 FORMAT ( 1X, I6, 2(I6, 2F10.2) )
```

Groups of format descriptors may be nested if desired. For example, the following two FORMAT statements are equivalent:

```
330 FORMAT ( 1X, I6, F10.2, A, F10.2, A, I6, F10.2, A, F10.2, A )
330 FORMAT ( 1X, 2(I6, 2(F10.2,A)) )
```

However, don't go overboard with nesting. The more complicated you make your FORMAT statements, the harder it will be for you or someone else to understand and debug them.

4.3.9 Changing Output Lines—The Slash (/) Descriptor

The slash (/) descriptor sends the current output buffer to the printer and starts a new output buffer. With slash descriptors, a single WRITE statement can display output values on more than one line. Several slashes can be used together to skip several lines. The slash is one of the special descriptors that does not have to be separated from other descriptors by commas. However, you may use commas if you wish.

For example, suppose that we need to print out the results of an experiment in which we have measured the amplitude and phase of a signal at a certain time and depth. Assume that the integer variable index is 10 and the real variables time, depth, amplitude, and phase are 300., 330., 850.65, and 30., respectively. Then the statements

```
WRITE (*,100) index, time, depth, amplitude, phase
100 FORMAT ('1',T20,'Results for Test Number ',I3,///, &
1X,'Time      = ',F7.0/, &
1X,'Depth     = ',F7.1,' meters',/, &
1X,'Amplitude = ', F8.2/ &,
1X,'Phase     = ',F7.1)
```

generate seven separate output buffers. The first buffer contains a '1' as the control character, so it skips to a new page, and puts a title on the page. The next two output buffers are empty, so two blank lines are printed. The final four output buffers have a blank control character, so the four values for time, depth, amplitude, and phase are printed on successive lines. The resulting output is shown in Figure 4–3.

```
                    Results for Test Number 10



    Time      = 300.
    Depth     = 330.0 meters
    Amplitude = 850.65
    Phase     = 30.2
```

FIGURE 4–3

Notice the 1X descriptors after each slash. These descriptors place a blank in the control character of each output buffer to ensure that the output advances by one line between buffers.

4.3.10 How Format Statements Are Used during WRITEs

Most Fortran compilers verify the syntax of FORMAT statements at compilation time, but do not otherwise process them. Instead, they are saved unchanged as character strings within the compiled program. When the program is executed, the characters in a FORMAT statement are used as a template to guide the operation of the formatted WRITE.

At execution time the list of output variables associated with the WRITE statement is processed together with the format of the statement. The program begins at the left end of the variable list and the left end of the FORMAT statement and scans from left to right, associating the first variable in the output list with the first format descriptor in the format statement, and so on. The variables in the output list must be of the same type and in the same order as the format descriptors in the format statement, or a run-time error will occur.

> **Programming Pitfalls**
> Make sure that a one-to-one correspondence exists between the types of the data in a WRITE statement and the types of the format descriptors in the associated FORMAT statement, or your program will fail at execution time.

As the program moves from left to right through the variable list of a WRITE statement, it also scans from left to right through the associated FORMAT statement. However, you can modify the order in which the contents of a FORMAT statement are used by including repetition counters and parentheses in the statement. FORMAT statements are scanned according to the following rules:

1. FORMAT *statements are scanned in order from left to right.* The first variable format descriptor in the FORMAT statement is associated with the first value in the output list of the WRITE statement and so forth. The type of each format descriptor must match the type of the data being output. In the following example descriptor I5 is associated with variable i, I10 with variable j, I15 with variable k, and F10.2 with variable a.

```
WRITE (*,10) i, j, k, a
10 FORMAT (1X, I5, I10, I15, F10.2)
```

2. *If a format descriptor has a repetition count associated with it, the descriptor will be used the number of times specified in the repetition count before the next descriptor is used.* In the following example descriptor I5 is associated with variable i, and again with variable j. After the descriptor has been used twice, I10 is associated with variable k and F10.2 is associated with variable a.

```
WRITE (*,20) i, j, k, a
20 FORMAT (1X, 2I5, I10, F10.2)
```

3. *If a group of format descriptors included within parentheses has a repetition count associated with it, the entire group will be used the number of times specified in the repetition count before the next descriptor is used.* Each descriptor within the group will be used in order from left to right during each repetition. In the following example descriptor F10.2 is associated with variable a. Next, the group in parentheses is used twice, so I5 is associated with i, E14.6 is associated with b, I5 is associated with j, and E14.6 is associated with c. Finally, F10.2 is associated with d.

```
WRITE (*,30) a, i, b, j, c, d
30 FORMAT (1X, F10.2, 2(I5, E14.6), F10.2)
```

4. If the WRITE statement runs out of variables before the end of the FORMAT statement, *the use of the FORMAT statement stops at the first format descriptor without a corresponding variable, or at the end of the FORMAT statement, whichever comes first.* For example, the statements

```
INTEGER :: m = 1
WRITE (*,40) m
40 FORMAT (1X, 'M = ', I3, 'N = ', I4, 'O = ', F7.2)
```

will produce the output

because the use of the FORMAT statement stops at I4, which is the first unmatched format descriptor. The statements

```
REAL :: voltage = 13800.
WRITE (*,50) voltage / 1000.
50 FORMAT (1X, 'Voltage = ', F8.1, ' kV')
```

will produce the output

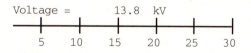

because there are no unmatched descriptors. Therefore, the use of the FORMAT statement stops at the end of the statement.

5. If the scan reaches the end of the FORMAT statement before the WRITE statement runs out of values, the program sends the current output buffer to the printer and starts over

at the right-most open parenthesis in the FORMAT *statement that is not preceded by a repetition count.* For example, the statements

```
INTEGER :: j = 1, k = 1, l = 3, m = 4, n = 5
WRITE (*,60) j, k, l, m, n
60 FORMAT (1X,'value = ', I3)
```

will produce the output

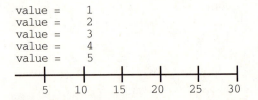

When the program reaches the end of the FORMAT statement after it prints j with the I3 descriptor, it sends that output buffer to the printer and goes back to the right-most open parenthesis not preceded by a repetition count. In this case the right-most open parenthesis without a repetition count is the opening parenthesis of the statement, so the entire statement is used again to print k, l, m, and n. By contrast, the statements

```
INTEGER :: j = 1, k = 1, l = 3, m = 4, n = 5
WRITE (*,60) j, k, l, m, n
60 FORMAT (1X,'Value = ',/, (1X,'New Line',2(3X,I5)))
```

will produce the output

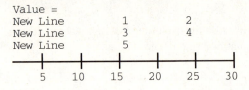

In this case the entire FORMAT statement is used to print values j and k. Since the right-most open parenthesis not preceded by a repetition count is the one just before 1X,'New Line', that part of the statement is used again to print l, m, and n. Note that the open parenthesis associated with (3X,I5) was ignored because it had a repetition count associated with it.

***EXAMPLE 4–1** Generating a Table of Information:* A good way to illustrate the use of formatted WRITE statements is to generate and print out a table of data. The program in Figure 4–4 generates the square roots, squares, and cubes of all integers between 1 and 10 and presents the data in a table with appropriate headings.

FIGURE 4–4

A Fortran program to generate a table of square roots, squares, and cubes.

```
PROGRAM table
!
! Purpose:
!
!   To illustrate the use of formatted WRITE statements. This
!   program generates a table containing the square roots, squares,
!   and cubes of all integers between 1 and 10. The table includes
!   a title and column headings.
!
!   Record of revisions:
!      Date          Programmer          Description of change
!      ====          ==========          =====================
!   09/15/95      S. J. Chapman         Original code
IMPLICIT NONE

INTEGER :: cube        ! The cube of i
INTEGER :: i           ! Index variable
INTEGER :: square      ! The square of i
REAL :: square_root    ! The square root of i

! Print the title of the table on a new page.
WRITE (*,100)
100 FORMAT ('1', T3, 'Table of Square Roots, Squares, and Cubes')

! Print the column headings.
WRITE (*,110)
110 FORMAT ('0',T4,'Number',T13,'Square Root',T29,'Square',T39,'Cube')
WRITE (*,120)
120 FORMAT (1X,T4,'======',T13,'===========',T29,'======',T39,'===='/)

! Generate the required values, and print them out.
DO i = 1, 10
   square_root = SQRT ( REAL(i) )
   square = i**2
   cube = i**3
   WRITE (*,130) i, square_root, square, cube
   130 FORMAT (T4, I4, T13, F10.6, T27, I6, T37, I6)
END DO

END PROGRAM
```

This program uses the tab format descriptor to set up neat columns of data for the table. When this program is compiled and executed on a PC, the result is

```
C>table

Table of Square Roots, Squares, and Cubes

Number   Square Root   Square   Cube
======   ===========   ======   ====
     1      1.000000        1      1
     2      1.414214        4      8
     3      1.732051        9     27
```

4	2.000000	16	64
5	2.236068	25	125
6	2.449490	36	216
7	2.645751	49	343
8	2.828427	64	512
9	3.000000	81	729
10	3.162278	100	1000

EXAMPLE 4–2 *Charge on a Capacitor:* A *capacitor* is an electrical device that stores electric charge. It essentially consists of two flat plates with an insulating material (the *dielectric*) between them (see Figure 4–5).

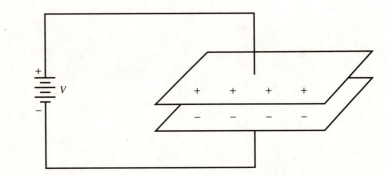

FIGURE 4–5
A capacitor consists of two metal plates separated by an insulating material.

The capacitance of a capacitor is defined as

$$C = \frac{Q}{V} \tag{4–2}$$

where Q is the amount of charge stored in a capacitor in units of coulombs and V is the voltage between the two plates of the capacitor in volts. The units of capacitance are farads (F), with 1 farad = 1 coulomb per volt. When a charge is present on the plates of the capacitor, there is an electric field between the two plates. The energy stored in this electric field is given by the equation

$$E = \frac{1}{2}C V^2 \tag{4–3}$$

where E is the energy in joules. Write a program that will perform one of the following calculations:

1. For a known capacitance and voltage, calculate the charge on the plates, the number of electrons on the plates, and the energy stored in the electric field.
2. For a known charge and voltage, calculate the capacitance of the capacitor, the number of electrons on the plates, and the energy stored in the electric field.

SOLUTION

This program must be able to ask the user which calculation he or she wishes to perform, read in the appropriate values for that calculation, and write out the results in a reasonable format. Note that this problem will require us to work with very small and very large numbers, so we will have to pay special attention to the FORMAT statements in the program. For example, capacitors are typically rated in microfarads (μF or 10^{-6} F) or picofarads (pF or 10^{-12} F), and there are 6.241461×10^{18} electrons per coulomb of charge.

1. **State the problem.**

The problem may be succinctly stated as follows:
a. For a known capacitance and voltage, calculate the charge on a capacitor, the number of electrons stored, and the energy stored in its electric field.
b. For a known charge and voltage, calculate the capacitance of the capacitor, the number of electrons stored, and the energy stored in its electric field.

2. **Define the inputs and outputs.**

This program has two possible sets of input values:
a. Capacitance in farads and voltage in volts, or
b. Charge in coulombs and voltage in volts
The outputs from the program in either mode will be the capacitance of the capacitor, the voltage across the capacitor, the charge on the plates of the capacitor, and the number of electrons on the plates of the capacitor. The output must be printed out in a reasonable and understandable format.

3. **Describe the algorithm.**

This program can be broken down into four major steps:

```
Decide which calculation is required
Get the input data for that calculation
Calculate the unknown quantities
Write out the capacitance, voltage, charge and number of electrons
```

The first major step of the program is to decide which calculation is required. There are two types of calculations: Type 1 requires capacitance and voltage, while type 2 requires charge and voltage. We must prompt the user for the type of input data, read his or her answer, and then read in the appropriate data. The pseudocode for these steps follows.

```
Prompt user for the type of calculation "type"
WHILE
    Read type
    IF type == 1 or type == 2 EXIT
    Tell user of invalid value
End of WHILE
```

```
IF type = 1 THEN
    Prompt the user for the capacitance c in farads
    Read capacitance c
    Prompt the user for the voltage v in volts
    Read voltage v
ELSE IF type = 2 THEN
    Prompt the user for the charge "charge" in coulombs
    Read "charge"
    Prompt the user for the voltage v in volts
    Read voltage v
END IF
```

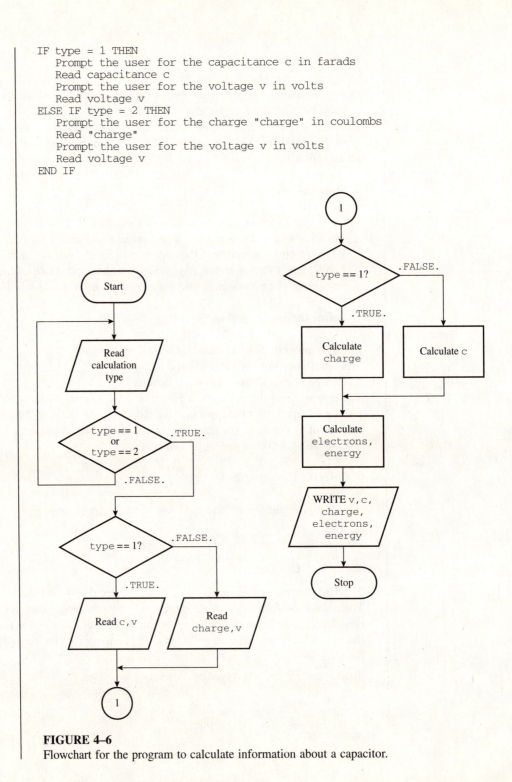

FIGURE 4–6
Flowchart for the program to calculate information about a capacitor.

Next we must calculate unknown values. For type 1 calculations, the unknown values are charge, the number of electrons, and the energy in the electric field; for type 2 calculations, the unknown values are capacitance, the number of electrons, and the energy in the electric field. The pseudocode for this step is

```
IF type == 1 THEN
   charge ← c * v
ELSE
   c ← charge / v
END IF
electrons ← charge * electrons_per_coulomb
energy ← 0.5 * c * v**2
```

where `electrons_per_coulomb` is the number of electrons per coulomb of charge (6.241461×10^{18}). Finally, we must write out the results in a useful format.

```
WRITE v, c, charge, electrons, energy
```

The flowchart for this program is shown in Figure 4–6.

4. **Turn the algorithm into Fortran statements.**

The final Fortran program is shown in Figure 4–7.

FIGURE 4–7
Program to perform capacitor calculations.

```
PROGRAM capacitor
!
! Purpose:
!   To calculate the behavior of a capacitor as follows:
!   1. If capacitance and voltage are known, calculate
!      charge, number of electrons, and energy stored.
!   2. If charge and voltage are known, calculate capa-
!      citance, number of electrons, and energy stored.
!
! Record of revisions:
!    Date          Programmer          Description of change
!    ====          ==========          =====================
!   09/15/95      S. J. Chapman        Original code
!
IMPLICIT NONE

! List of parameters:
REAL, PARAMETER :: electrons_per_coulomb = 6.241461E18

! List of variables:
REAL :: c          ! Capacitance of the capacitor (farads).
REAL :: charge     ! Charge on the capacitor (coulombs).
REAL :: electrons  ! Number of electrons on the plates of the capacitor
REAL :: energy     ! Energy stored in the electric field (joules)
INTEGER :: type    ! Type  of input data available for the calculation:
                   !  1:  C and  V
                   !  2:  CHARGE and   V
REAL :: v          ! Voltage on   the capacitor (volts).
```

(continued)

(concluded)

```fortran
! Prompt user for the type of input data available.
WRITE (*, 100)
100 FORMAT (' This program calculates information about a ' &
            'capacitor.',/, ' Please specify the type of information',&
            ' available from the following list:',/,&
            '    1 -- capacitance and voltage ',/,&
            '    2 -- charge and voltage ',//,&
            ' Select options 1 or 2: ')

! Get response and validate it.
DO
   READ (*,*) type
   IF ( (type == 1) .OR. (type == 2) ) EXIT
   WRITE (*,110) type
   110 FORMAT (' Invalid response: ', I6, '. Please enter 1 or 2:')
END DO

! Get additional data based upon the type of calculation.
input: IF ( type == 1 ) THEN

   WRITE (*,120)                              ! Get capacitance.
   120 FORMAT (' Enter capacitance in farads: ' )
   READ (*,*) c
   WRITE (*,130)                              ! Get voltage.
   130 FORMAT (' Enter voltage in volts: ' )
   READ (*,*) v

ELSE

   WRITE (*,140)                              ! Get charge.
   140 FORMAT (' Enter charge in coulombs: ' )
   READ (*,*) charge
   WRITE (*,130)                              ! Get voltage.
   READ (*,*) v

END IF input

! Calculate the unknown quantities.
calculate: IF ( type == 1 ) THEN
   charge = c * v                             ! Charge
ELSE
   c = charge / v                             ! Capacitance
END IF calculate
electrons = charge * electrons_per_coulomb    ! Electrons
energy = 0.5 * c * v**2                        ! Energy

! Write out answers.
WRITE (*,150) v, c, charge, electrons, energy
150 FORMAT (' For this capacitor: ',/, &
            '    Voltage            = ', F10.2, ' V',/, &
            '    Capacitance        = ',ES10.3, ' F',/, &
            '    Total charge       = ',ES10.3, ' C',/, &
            '    Number of electrons = ',ES10.3,/, &
            '    Total energy       = ', F10.4, ' joules' )

END PROGRAM
```

5. **Test the program.**

    To test this program, we will calculate the answers by hand for a simple data set and then compare the answers to the results of the program. If we use a voltage of 100 V and a capacitance of 100 μF, the resulting charge on the plates of the capacitor is 0.01 C, there are 6.241×10^{16} electrons on the capacitor, and the energy stored is 0.5 joules.

    Running these values through the program using both options 1 and 2 yields the following results:

```
C>capacitor

This program calculates information about a capacitor.
Please specify the type of information available from the following list:
    1 — capacitance and voltage
    2 — charge and voltage

Select options 1 or 2:
1
Enter capacitance in farads:
100.e-6
Enter voltage in volts:
100.
For this capacitor:
   Voltage            =     100.00 V
   Capacitance        = 1.000E-04 F
   Total charge       = 1.000E-02 C
   Number of electrons = 6.241E+16
   Total energy       =     .5000 joules

C>capacitor
This program calculates information about a capacitor.
Please specify the type of information available from the following list:
    1 — capacitance and voltage
    2 — charge and voltage

Select options 1 or 2:
2
Enter charge in coulombs:
0.01
Enter voltage in volts:
100.
For this capacitor:
   Voltage            =     100.00 V
   Capacitance        = 1.000E-04 F
   Total charge       = 1.000E-02 C
   Number of electrons = 6.241E+16
   Total energy       =     .5000 joules
```

The program gives the correct answers for our test data set.

Quiz 4–1

This quiz provides a quick check to see if you understand the concepts introduced sections 4.1 through 4.3. If you have trouble with the quiz, reread

(continued)

(continued)

the sections, ask your instructor, or discuss the material with a fellow student. The answers to this quiz appear in Appendix F. Unless otherwise stated, assume that variables beginning with the letters I through N are integers and that all other variables are reals.

Write Fortran statements that perform the following operations:

1. Skip to a new page and print the title `'This is a test!'` starting in column 25.
2. Skip a line and then display the values of i, j, and data_1 in fields 10 characters wide. Allow two decimal points for the real variable.
3. Beginning in column 12, write out the string `'The result is'` followed by the value of result expressed to five significant digits in correct scientific notation.

    Assume that real variables a, b, and c are initialized with -0.0001, 6.02×10^{23}, and 3.141593, respectively, and that integer variables i, j, and k are initialized with 32767, 24, and -1010101, respectively. What will be printed out by each of the following sets of statements?

4.
```
WRITE (*,10) a, b, c
10 FORMAT (1X,3F10.4)
```
5.
```
WRITE (*,20) a, b, c
20 FORMAT (1X,F10.3, 2X, E10.3, 2X, F10.5)
```
6.
```
WRITE (*,40) a, b, c
40 FORMAT (1X,ES10.4, ES11.4, F10.4)
```
7.
```
WRITE (*,'(I5)') i, j, k
```
8.
```
CHARACTER(len=30) :: fmt
fmt = "(1X,I8, 2X, I8.8, 2X, I8)"
WRITE (*,fmt) i, j, k
```

Assume that string_1 is a 10-character variable initialized with the string `'ABCDEFGHIJ'` and that string_2 is a 5-character variable initialized with the string `'12345'`. What will be printed out by each of the following sets of statements?

9.
```
WRITE (*,"(1X,2A10)") string_1, string_2
```
10.
```
WRITE (*,80) string_1, string_2
80 FORMAT (T21,A10,T24,A5)
```
11.
```
WRITE (*,100) string_1, string_2
100 FORMAT (1X,A5,2X,A5)
```

Examine the following Fortran statements. Are they correct or incorrect? If they are incorrect, why are they incorrect? Assume default typing for variable names where they are not otherwise defined.

12.
```
WRITE (*,100) istart, istop, step
100 FORMAT (2I6,F10.4)
```

(continued)

(concluded)

13.
```
LOGICAL :: test
CHARACTER(len=6) :: name
INTEGER :: ierror
WRITE (*,200) name, test, ierror
200 FORMAT (1X,'Test name: ',A,/,' Completion status : ',&
I6, ' Test results: ', L6 )
```

What output will be generated by each of the following programs? Describe the output from each of these programs, including both the horizontal and vertical position of each output item.

14.
```
INTEGER :: index1 = 1, index2 = 2
REAL :: x1 = 1.2, y1 = 2.4, x2 = 2.4, y2 = 4.8
WRITE (*,120) index1, x1, y1, index2, x2, y2
120 FORMAT ('1',T11,'Output Data',/, &
            ' ',T11,'===========',//,&
         (' ','POINT(',I2,') = ',2F14.6))
```

4.4

FORMATTED READ STATEMENTS

An *input device* is a piece of equipment that can enter data into a computer. The most common input device on a modern computer is a keyboard. As data is entered into the input device, it is stored in an **input buffer** in the computer's memory. Once an entire line has been typed into the input buffer, the user hits the ENTER key on his or her keyboard, and the input buffer is made available for processing by the computer.

A READ statement reads one or more data values from the input buffer associated with an input device. The particular input device to read from is specified by the i/o unit number in the READ statement. It is possible to use a *formatted* READ *statement* to specify the exact manner in which the contents of an input buffer are to be interpreted.

In general a format specifies which columns of the input buffer are to be associated with a particular variable and how those columns are to be interpreted. A typical formatted READ statement follows.

```
READ (*,100) increment
100 FORMAT (6X,I6)
```

This statement specifies that the first six columns of the input buffer are to be skipped, and then the contents of columns 7 through 12 are to be interpreted as an integer, with the resulting value stored in variable increment. As with WRITE statements, formats may be stored in FORMAT statements, character constants, or character variables.

Formats associated with READs use many of the same format descriptors as formats associated with WRITEs. However, the interpretation of those descriptors is somewhat different. The meanings of the format descriptors commonly found with READs are described below.

4.4.1 Integer Input—The I Descriptor

The I descriptor is used to read integer data. It has the general form

$$rIw$$

where *r* and *w* have the meanings given in Table 4–2. An integer value may be placed anywhere within its field, and it will be read and interpreted correctly.

4.4.2 Real Input—The F Descriptor

The F format descriptor is used to describe the input format of real data. It has the form

$$rFw.d$$

where *r*, *w*, and *d* have the meanings given in Table 4–2. The interpretation of real data in a formatted READ statement is rather complicated. The input value in an F input field may be a real number with a decimal point, a real number in exponential notation, or a number without a decimal point. *If a real number with a decimal point or a real number in exponential notation is present in the field, then the number is always interpreted correctly regardless of its position in the input field.* For example, consider the following statement:

```
READ (*,'(3F10.4)') a, b, c
```

Assume that the input data for this statement is

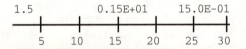

After the statement is executed, all three variables will contain the number 1.5.

If a number *without* a decimal point appears in the field, then a decimal point is assumed to be in the position specified by the *d* term of the format descriptor. For example, if the format descriptor is F10.4, then the four right-most digits of the number are assumed to be the fractional part of the input value; the remaining digits are assumed to be the integer part of the input value. Consider the following Fortran statements:

```
READ (*,110) a, b, c
110 FORMAT (3F10.4)
```

Assume that the input data for these statements is

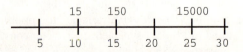

Then after these statements are executed, a will contain 0.0015, b will contain 0.0150, and c will contain 1.5000. The use of values without decimal points in a real input field is very confusing. It is a relic from an earlier version of Fortran that should never be used in your programs.

Good Programming Practice
Always include a decimal point in any real values used with a formatted READ statement.

The E and ES format descriptors are identical to the F descriptor for inputting data and may be used in the place of the F descriptor.

4.4.3 Logical Input—The L Descriptor

The descriptor used to read logical data has the form

$$rLw$$

where *r* and *w* have the meanings given in Table 4–2. The value of a logical variable can only be .TRUE. or .FALSE.. The input value must be either a T or an F, appearing as the first nonblank character in the input field. If any other character is the first nonblank character in the field, a run-time error will occur. The logical input format descriptor is rarely used.

4.4.4 Character Input—The A Descriptor

Character data is read using the A format descriptor.

$$rA \quad \text{or} \quad rAw$$

where *r* and *w* have the meanings given in Table 4–2. The *r*A descriptor reads character data in a field whose width is the same as the length of the character variable being read, while the *r*Aw descriptor reads character data in a field of fixed width *w*. If the width *w* of the field is larger than the length of the character variable, the data from the right-most portion of the field is loaded into the character variable. If the width of the field is smaller than the length of the character variable, the characters in the field will be stored in the left-most characters of the variable and the remainder of the variable will be padded with blanks.

For example, consider the following statements:

```
CHARACTER(len=10) :: string_1, string_2
CHARACTER(len=5)  :: string_3
CHARACTER(len=15) :: string_4, string_5
READ (*,'(A)')    string_1
READ (*,'(A10)')  string_2
READ (*,'(A10)')  string_3
READ (*,'(A10)')  string_4
READ (*,'(A)')    string_5
```

Assume that the input data for these statements is

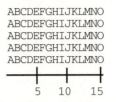

After the statements are executed, variable string_1 will contain 'ABCDEFGHIJ' because string_1 is 10 characters long and the A descriptor will read as many characters as the length of the variable. Variable string_2 will contain 'ABCDEFGHIJ' because string_2 is 10 characters long and the A10 descriptor will read 10 characters. Variable string_3 is only 5 characters long, and the A10 descriptor is 10 characters long; therefore string_3 will contain the 5 right most of the 10 characters in the field: 'FGHIJ'. Variable string_4 will contain 'ABCDEFGHIJ⊅⊅⊅⊅⊅' because string_4 is 15 characters long and the A10 descriptor will read only 10 characters. Finally string_5 will contain 'ABCDEFGHIJKLMNO', since string_5 is 15 characters long and the A descriptor will read as many characters as the length of the variable.

4.4.5 Horizontal Positioning—The X and T Descriptors

The X and T format descriptors may be used when reading formatted input data. The chief use of the X descriptor is to skip over fields in the input data that we do not wish to read. The T descriptor serves the same purpose, but it can also read the same data twice in two different formats. For example, the following code reads the values in characters 1 through 6 of the input buffer twice—once as an integer and once as a character string.

```
CHARACTER(len=6) :: string
INTEGER :: input
READ (*,'(I6,T1,A6)') input, string
```

4.4.6 Vertical Positioning—The Slash (/) Descriptor

The slash (/) format descriptor causes a formatted READ statement to discard the current input buffer, get another one from the input device, and start processing from the beginning of the new input buffer. For example, the following formatted READ statement reads the values of variables a and b from the first input line, skips down two lines, and reads the values of variables c and d from the third input line.

```
REAL :: a, b, c, d
READ (*,300) a, b, c, d
300 FORMAT (2F10.2,//,2F10.2)
```

If the input data for these statements is

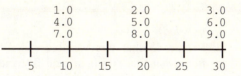

then the contents of variables a, b, c, and d will be 1.0, 2.0, 7.0, and 8.0, respectively.

4.4.7 How Format Statements Are Used during READs

Most Fortran compilers verify the syntax of FORMAT statements at compilation time, but do not otherwise process them. Instead, they are saved unchanged as a character string within the compiled program. When the program is executed, the characters in the FORMAT statement are used as a template to guide the operation of the formatted READ.

At execution time, the list of input variables associated with the READ statement is processed with the format of the statement. The rules for scanning a FORMAT statement are essentially the same for READs as they are for WRITEs. The order of scanning, repetition counts, and the use of parentheses are identical.

When the number of variables to be read and the number of descriptors in the FORMAT statement differ, formatted READs behave as follows:

1. If the READ statement runs out of variables before the end of the FORMAT statement, the use of the FORMAT statement stops after the last variable has been read. The next READ statement will start with a new input buffer, and all of the other data in the original input buffer will be lost.
2. If the scan reaches the end of the FORMAT statement before the READ statement runs out of variables, the program discards the current input buffer. It gets a new input buffer and resumes in the FORMAT statement at the right-most open parenthesis that is not preceded by a repetition count.

Quiz 4–2

This quiz provides a quick check to see if you understand the concepts introduced in section 4.4. If you have trouble with the quiz, reread the section, ask your instructor, or discuss the material with a fellow student. The answers to this quiz appear in Appendix F. Unless otherwise stated, assume that variables beginning with the letters I through N are integers and that all other variables are reals.

Write Fortran statements that perform the following functions:

1. Read the values of a real variable amplitude from columns 10–20, an integer variable count from columns 30–35, and a character variable identity from columns 60–72 of the current input buffer.

(continued)

(concluded)

2. Read a 25-character variable called `title` from columns 10–34 of the first input line and then read five integer variables `i1` through `i5` from columns 5–12 on each of the next five lines.

3. Read columns 11–20 from the current input line into a character variable `string`, skip two lines, and read columns 11–20 into an integer variable `number`. Use a single formatted `READ` statement.

4. `READ (*,'(3I5)') i, j, k`

   With the input data:

5. ```
   CHARACTER(len=5)  :: string_1
   CHARACTER(len=10) :: string_2, string_4
   CHARACTER(len=15) :: string_3
   READ (*,'(4A10)') string_1, string_2, string_3, string_4
   ```

   With the input data:

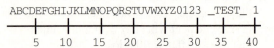

   Examine the following Fortran statements. Are they correct or incorrect? If they are incorrect, why are they incorrect? If they are correct, what do they do?

6. ```
   READ (*,100) nvals, time1, time2
   100 FORMAT (10X,I10,F10.2,F10.4)
   ```

7. ```
   READ (*,220) junk, scratch
   220 FORMAT ( T60,I15,/,E15.3)
   ```

8. ```
   READ (*,220) icount, range, azimuth, elevation
   220 FORMAT ( I6, 4X, F20.2)
   ```

■ 4.5

AN INTRODUCTION TO FILES AND FILE PROCESSING

The programs that we have written up to now have involved relatively small amounts of input and output data. We have typed in the input data from the keyboard each time that a program has been run, and the output data has gone directly to a terminal or printer. This method is acceptable for small data sets, but it rapidly becomes prohibitive when working with large volumes of data. Imagine having to type in 100,000 input values each time a program is run! Such a process would be both time-consuming and prone to typing errors. We need a convenient way to read in and write out large data sets and to be able to use them repeatedly without retyping.

Fortunately, computers have a standard structure for holding data that we will be able to use in our programs. This structure is called a **file.** A file consists of many lines of related data that can be accessed as a unit. Each line of information in a file is called a **record.** Fortran can read information from a file or write information to a file one record at a time.

The files on a computer can be stored on various types of devices, which are collectively know as *secondary memory.* (The computer's RAM is its primary memory.) Secondary memory is slower than the computer's main memory, but it still allows relatively quick access to the data. Common secondary storage devices include hard disk drives, floppy disk drives, and magnetic tapes.

In the early days of computers, magnetic tapes were the most common type of secondary storage device. Computer magnetic tapes store data in a manner similar to the audiocassette tapes that we use to play music. Like them, computer magnetic tapes must be read (or "played") in order from the beginning of the tape to the end of it. When we read data in consecutive order one record after another in this manner, we are using **sequential access.** Other devices such as hard disks have the ability to jump from one record to another anywhere within a file. When we jump freely from one record to another following no specific order, we are using **direct access.** For historical reasons, sequential access is the default access technique in Fortran, even if we are working with devices capable of direct access.

To use files within a Fortran program, we will need some way to select the desired file and to read from or write to it. Fortunately, Fortran has a wonderfully flexible method to read from and write to files, whether they are on disk, magnetic tape, or some other device attached to the computer. This mechanism is known as the **input/output unit (i/o unit,** sometimes called a "logical unit," or simply a "unit"). The i/o unit corresponds to the first asterisk in the `READ (*,*)` and `WRITE (*,*)` statements. If an i/o unit number replaces that asterisk, then the *corresponding read will be from or write will be to the device assigned to that unit* instead of to the standard input or output device. Note that the statements to read from or write to any file or device attached to the computer are exactly the same except for the i/o unit number in the first position, so we already know most of what we need to know to use file i/o. An i/o unit number must be of type `INTEGER`.

Several Fortran statements may be used to control disk file input and output. Table 4–3 summarizes the I/O statements discussed in this chapter.

TABLE 4–3
Fortran control characters

I/O statement	Function
OPEN	Associate a specific disk file with a specific i/o unit number.
CLOSE	End the association of a specific disk file with a specific i/o unit number.
READ	Read data from a specified i/o unit number.
WRITE	Write data to a specified i/o unit number.
REWIND	Move to the beginning of a file.
BACKSPACE	Move back one record in a file.

I/o unit numbers are assigned to disk files or devices using the OPEN statement and detached from them using the CLOSE statement. Once a file is attached to an i/o unit using the OPEN statement, we can read and write in exactly the same manner that we have already learned. When we are through with the file, the CLOSE statement closes the file and releases the i/o unit to be assigned to some other file. The REWIND and BACKSPACE statements may be used to change the current reading or writing position in a file while it is open.

Certain unit numbers are predefined to be connected to certain input or output devices so that we don't need an OPEN statement to use these devices. These predefined units vary from processor to processor.[4] Typically, i/o unit 5 is predefined to be the *standard input device* for your program (that is, the keyboard if you are running at a terminal or the input batch file if you are running in batch mode). Similarly, i/o unit 6 is usually predefined to be the *standard output device* for your program (the screen if you are running at a terminal or the line printer if you are running in batch mode). These assignments date back to the early days of Fortran on IBM computers, so they have been copied by most other vendors in their Fortran compilers. However, you cannot count on these associations always being true for every processor. If you need to read from and write to the standard devices, always use the asterisk instead of the i/o unit number for that device. The asterisk is guaranteed to work correctly on any computer system.

Good Programming Practice
Always use asterisks instead of i/o unit numbers when referring to the standard input or standard output devices. The standard i/o unit numbers vary from processor to processor, but the asterisk works correctly on all processors.

If we want to access any files or devices other than the predefined standard devices, we must first use an OPEN statement to associate the file or device with a specific i/o unit number. Once the association has been established, we can use ordinary Fortran READs and WRITEs with that unit to work with the data in the file.[5]

4.5.1 The OPEN Statement

The OPEN statement associates a file with a given logical unit number. Its form is

```
OPEN (open_list)
```

---

[4]A *processor* is defined as the combination of a specific computer with a specific compiler.

[5]Some Fortran compilers attach default files to logical units that have not been opened. For example, in VAX Fortran, a write to an unopened i/o unit 26 will automatically go into a file called FOR026.DAT. You should never use this feature, since it is nonstandard and varies from processor to processor. Your programs will be much more portable if you always use an OPEN statement before writing to a file.

where *open_list* contains a series of clauses specifying the i/o unit number, the file name, and information about how to access the file. The clauses in the list are separated by commas. The full list of possible clauses in the OPEN statement appears in Appendix D. The five most important items from the list follow.

1. A UNIT= clause indicating the i/o unit number to associate with this file. This clause has the form

$$UNIT=\ int\_expr$$

where *int_expr* can be a nonnegative integer value.

2. A FILE= clause specifying the file name of the file to be opened. This clause has the form

$$FILE=\ char\_expr$$

where *char_expr* is a character value containing the file name to be opened.

3. A STATUS= clause specifying the status of the file to be opened. This clause has the form

$$STATUS=\ char\_expr$$

where *char_expr* is one of the following: 'OLD', 'NEW', 'REPLACE', 'SCRATCH', or 'UNKNOWN'.

4. An ACTION= clause specifying whether a file is to be opened for reading only, for writing only, or for both reading and writing. This clause has the form

$$ACTION=\ char\_expr$$

where *char_expr* is one of the following: 'READ', 'WRITE', or 'READWRITE'. If no action is specified, the file is opened for both reading and writing.

5. An IOSTAT= clause specifying the name of an integer variable in which the status of the open operation can be returned. This clause has the form

$$IOSTAT=\ int\_var$$

where *int_var* is an integer variable. If the OPEN statement is successful, a zero will be returned in the integer variable. If it is not successful, a positive number corresponding to a system error message will be returned in the variable. The system error messages vary from processor to processor, but a zero always means success.

These clauses may appear in any order in the OPEN statement. Some examples of correct OPEN statements follow.

Case 1: Opening a file for input

The following statement opens a file named EXAMPLE.DAT and attaches it to i/o unit 8.

```
INTEGER :: ierror
OPEN (UNIT=8, FILE='EXAMPLE.DAT', STATUS='OLD', ACTION='READ', &
     IOSTAT=ierror)
```

The STATUS='OLD' clause specifies that the file already exists; if it does not exist, then the OPEN statement will return an error code in variable ierror. This statement illustrates the proper form of the OPEN statement for an *input file*. If we are opening a file to read input data from, then the file had better be present with data in it! If the file is not there, something is obviously wrong. By checking the returned value in ierror, we can tell that a problem exists and take appropriate action.

The ACTION='READ' clause specifies that the file should be read only. If an attempt is made to write to the file, an error will occur. This behavior is appropriate for an input file.

Case 2: Opening a file for output

The following statements open a file named OUTDAT and attach it to i/o unit 25.

```
INTEGER :: unit, ierror
CHARACTER(len=6) :: filename
unit = 25
filename = 'OUTDAT'
OPEN (UNIT=unit, FILE=filename, STATUS='NEW', ACTION='WRITE', &
     IOSTAT=ierror)
```

or

```
OPEN (UNIT=unit, FILE=filename, STATUS='REPLACE', ACTION='WRITE', &
     IOSTAT=ierror)
```

The STATUS='NEW' clause specifies that the file is a new file; if it already exists, then the OPEN statement will return an error code in variable ierror. This clause is the proper form of the OPEN statement for an *output file* if we want to make sure that we don't overwrite the data in a file that already exists.

The STATUS='REPLACE' clause specifies that a new file should be opened for output whether a file by the same name exists or not. If the file already exists, the program will delete it, create a new file, and open it for output. The contents of the old file will be lost. If a file does not exist, the program will create a new file by that name and open it. This clause is the proper form of the OPEN statement for an output file if we want to open the file whether or not a previous file exists with the same name.

The ACTION='WRITE' clause specifies that the file should be write only. If an attempt is made to read from the file, an error will occur. This behavior is appropriate for an output file.

Case 3: Opening a scratch file

The following statement opens a *scratch file* and attaches it to i/o unit 12.

```
OPEN (UNIT=12, STATUS='SCRATCH', IOSTAT=ierror)
```

A scratch file is a temporary file that is created by the program and that is deleted automatically when the file is closed or when the program terminates. This type of file may be used for saving intermediate results while a program is running, but it may not be used to save anything that we want to keep after the program finishes. Notice that no file name is specified in the OPEN statement. In fact, it is an error to specify a file name with a scratch file.

The absence of an ACTION= clause indicates that the file has been opened for both reading and writing.

Good Programming Practice
Always be careful to specify the proper status in OPEN statements, depending on whether you are reading from or writing to a file. This practice will help prevent errors such as accidentally overwriting data files that you want to keep.

4.5.2 The CLOSE Statement

The CLOSE statement closes a file and releases the i/o unit number associated with it. Its form is

$$\text{CLOSE } (close\_list)$$

where *close_list* must contain a clause specifying the i/o number and may specify other clauses that are listed in Appendix D. If no CLOSE statement is included in the program for a given file, that file will be closed automatically when the program terminates.

After a nonscratch file is closed, it may be reopened at any time using a new OPEN statement. When it is reopened, it may be associated with the same i/o unit or with a different i/o unit. After the file is closed, the i/o unit that was associated with it is free to be reassigned to any other file in a new OPEN statement.

4.5.3 READs and WRITEs to Disk Files

Once a file has been connected to a logical unit via the OPEN statement, it is possible to read from or write to the file using the same READ and WRITE statements that we have been using. For example, the statements

```
OPEN (UNIT=8, FILE='INPUT.DAT',STATUS='OLD',IOSTAT=ierror)
READ (8,*) x, y, z
```

will read the values of variables x, y, and z in free format from the file INPUT.DAT, and the statements

```
OPEN (UNIT=9, FILE='OUTPUT.DAT',STATUS='REPLACE',IOSTAT=ierror)
WRITE (9,100) x, y, z
100 FORMAT (' X = ', F10.2, ' Y = ', F10.2, ' Z = ', F10.2 )
```

will write the values of variables x, y, and z to the file OUTPUT.DAT in the specified format.

4.5.4 The `IOSTAT=` Clause in the `READ` Statement

The `IOSTAT=` clause is an important additional feature that may be added to the `READ` statement when working with disk files. The form of this clause is

$$IOSTAT= \quad int\_var$$

where *int_var* is an integer variable. If the `READ` statement is successful, a zero will be returned in the integer variable. If the statement fails because of a file or format error, a positive number corresponding to a system error message will be returned in the variable. If the statement fails because the end of the input data file has been reached, a negative number will be returned in the variable.[6]

If no `IOSTAT=` clause is present in a `READ` statement, any attempt to read a line beyond the end of a file will abort the program. This behavior is unacceptable in a well-designed program. The `IOSTAT=` clause enables us to read all the data from a file until the end is reached and then perform some sort of processing on that data. If an `IOSTAT=` clause is present, the program will not abort on an attempt to read a line beyond the end of a file. Instead, the `READ` will complete with the `IOSTAT` variable set to a negative number. We can then test the value of the variable and process the data accordingly.

Good Programming Practice
Always include the `IOSTAT=` clause when reading from a disk file. This clause provides a graceful way to detect end-of-data conditions on the input files.

EXAMPLE **4–3** *Reading Data from a File:* Programs often read a large data set from a file and then process the data in some fashion. Many times the program does not know in advance just how much data is present in the file. In that case the program needs to read the data in a while loop until it reaches the end of the data set; the program, of course, must detect that there is no more data to read. Once it has read in all of the data, the program can process the data in whatever manner is required.

Let's illustrate this process by writing a program that can read in an unknown number of real values from a disk file and detect the end of the data in the disk file.

---

[6]An alternative method of detecting file read errors and end-of-file conditions is to use `ERR=` and `END=` clauses. These clauses of the `READ` statement are summarized in Appendix D.

SOLUTION

This program must open the input disk file and then read the values from it using the IOSTAT= clause to detect problems. If the IOSTAT variable contains a negative number after a READ, then the end of the file has been reached. If the IOSTAT variable contains a zero after a READ, then everything was correct. If the IOSTAT variable contains a positive number after a READ, then a READ error occurred. In this example the program should stop if a READ error occurs.

1. **State the problem.**

The problem may be succinctly stated as follows:

Write a program that can read an unknown number of real values from a user-specified input data file, detecting the end of the data file as it occurs.

2. **Define the inputs and outputs.**

The inputs to this program consist of

a. The name of the file to be opened.
b. The data contained in that file.

The outputs from the program will be the input values in the data file. At the end of the file, the program will write an informative message telling how many valid input values it found.

3. **Describe the algorithm.**

This pseudocode for this program follows.

```
Initialize nvals to 0
Prompt user for file name
Get the name of the input file
OPEN the input file
Check for errors on OPEN

If no OPEN error THEN
   ! Read input data
   WHILE
      READ value
      IF status /= 0 EXIT
      nvals ← nvals + 1
      WRITE valid data to screen
   END of WHILE

   ! Check to see if the WHILE terminated due to end of file
   ! or READ error
   IF status > 0
      WRITE 'READ error occurred on line', nvals
   ELSE
      WRITE number of valid input values nvals
```

```
      END of IF ( status > 0 )
END of IF ( no OPEN error )
END PROGRAM
```

A flowchart for the program is shown in Figure 4–8.

4. Turn the algorithm into Fortran statements.

The final Fortran program is shown in Figure 4–9.

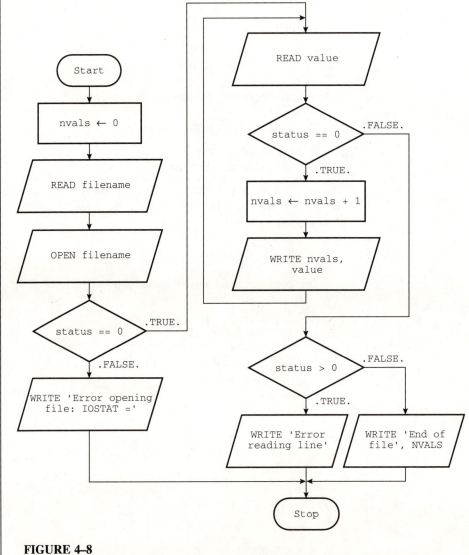

FIGURE 4–8
Flowchart for a program to read an unknown number of values from an input data file.

FIGURE 4–9

Program to read an unknown number of values from a user-specified input disk file.

```
PROGRAM read
!
!   Purpose:
!     To illustrate how to read an unknown number of values from
!     an input data file, detecting both any formatting errors and
!     the end of file.
!
!   Record of revisions:
!       Date          Programmer          Description of change
!       ====          ==========          =====================
!     09/18/95      S. J. Chapman         Original code
!
IMPLICIT NONE

! Declare variables
CHARACTER(len=20) :: filename    ! Name of file to open
INTEGER :: nvals = 0             ! Number of values read in
INTEGER :: status                ! I/O status
REAL :: value                    ! The real value read in

! Get the file name, and echo it back to the user.
WRITE (*,*) 'Please enter input file name: '
READ (*,*) filename
WRITE (*,1000) filename
1000 FORMAT (' ','The input file name is: ', A)

! Open the file, and check for errors on open.
OPEN (UNIT=3, FILE=filename, STATUS='OLD', ACTION='READ', &
      IOSTAT=status )
openif: IF ( status == 0 ) THEN

   ! OPEN was ok. Read values.
   readloop: DO
      READ (3,*,IOSTAT=status) value    ! Get next value
      IF ( status /= 0 ) EXIT           ! EXIT if not valid.
      nvals = nvals + 1                 ! Valid: increase count
      WRITE (*,1010) nvals, value       ! Echo to screen
      1010 FORMAT (' ','Line ', I6, ':Value = ',F10.4 )
   END DO readloop

   ! The WHILE loop has terminated. Was it because of a READ
   ! error or because of the end of the input file?
   readif: IF ( status > 0 ) THEN ! a READ error occurred. Tell user.

      WRITE (*,1020) nvals + 1
      1020 FORMAT ('0','An error occurred reading line ', I6)

   ELSE ! the end of the data was reached. Tell user.

      WRITE (*,1030) nvals
      1030 FORMAT ('0','End of file reached. There were ', I6, &
                   ' values in the file.')
   END IF readif

ELSE openif
   WRITE (*,1040) status
```

(continued)

(concluded)
```
    1040 FORMAT (' ','Error opening file: IOSTAT = ', I6 )
END IF openif

! Close file
CLOSE ( UNIT=8 )

END PROGRAM
```

Note that the input file is opened with `STATUS='OLD'` because we are reading from the file, and the input data must already exist before the program is executed.

5. **Test the program.**

To test this program, we will create two input files, one with valid data and one with an input data error. We will run the program with both input files and verify that it works correctly both for valid data and for data containing input errors. Also, we will run the program with an invalid file name to show that it can properly handle missing input files.

The valid input file is called READ1.DAT. It contains the following lines:

```
-17.0
30.001
1.0
12000.
-0.012
```

The invalid input file is called READ2.DAT. It contains the following lines:

```
-17.0
30.001
ABCDEF
12000.
-0.012
```

Running these files through the program yields the following results:

```
C > read
Please enter input file name:
'read1.dat'
The input file name is: read1.dat
Line      1: Value = -17.0000
Line      2: Value =  30.0010
Line      3: Value =   1.0000
Line      4: Value = 12000.0000
Line      5: Value =    -.0120

End of file reached. There were    5 values in the file.

C > read
Please enter input file name:
'read2.dat'
The input file name is: read2.dat
Line      1: Value = -17.0000
Line      2: Value =  30.0010

An error occurred reading line    3
```

Finally, let's test the program with an invalid input file name:

```
C > read
Please enter input file name:
'JUNK.DAT'
The input file name is: JUNK.DAT
Error opening file: IOSTAT = 602
```

The number of the `IOSTAT` error reported by this program will vary from processor to processor, but it will always be positive. You must consult a listing of the run-time error codes for your particular compiler to find the exact meaning of the error code that your computer reports. For the Fortran compiler used here, run-time error 6416 means "File not found."

This program correctly read all of the values in the input file and detected the end of the data set when it occurred.

4.5.5 File Positioning

As we stated previously, ordinary Fortran files are sequential—they are read in order from the first record in the file to the last record in the file. However, we sometimes need to read a piece of data more than once or to process a whole file more than once during a program. How can we skip around within a sequential file?

Fortran provides two statements to help us move around within a sequential file. They are the `BACKSPACE` statement, which moves back one record each time it is called, and the `REWIND` statement, which restarts the file at its beginning. The forms of these statements are

```
BACKSPACE (UNIT=unit)
```

and

```
REWIND (UNIT=unit)
```

where `unit` is the i/o unit number associated with the file that we want to work with.

Both statements can also include `IOSTAT=` clauses to detect errors during the backspace or rewind operation without causing the program to abort.

EXAMPLE 4–4 Using File-Positioning Commands: We will now illustrate the use of scratch files and file-positioning commands in a simple example problem. Write a program that accepts a series of nonnegative real values and stores them in a scratch file. After the data is input, the program should ask the user what data record he or she wants to retrieve and then recover and display that value from the disk file.

SOLUTION

Since the program is expected to read only positive or zero values, we can use a negative value as a flag to terminate the input to the program. A Fortran program that uses this method is shown in Figure 4–10. This program opens a scratch file and then reads input values from the user. If a value is nonnegative, it is written to the scratch file. When a negative value is encountered, the program asks the user for the record to display. It checks to see if a valid record number was entered. If the record number is valid, it rewinds the file and reads forward to that record number. Finally, it displays the contents of that record to the user.

FIGURE 4–10
Sample program illustrating the use of file-positioning commands.

```
PROGRAM scratch
!
! Purpose:
!   To illustrate the use of a scratch file and positioning
!      commands as follows:
!   1. Read in an arbitrary number of positive or zero
!      values, saving them in a scratch file. Stop
!      reading when a negative value is encountered.
!   2. Ask the user for a record number to display.
!   3. Rewind the file, get that value, and display it.
!
! Record of revisions:
!    Date         Programmer       Description of change
!    ====         ==========       =====================
!  09/18/95   S. J. Chapman        Original code
!
IMPLICIT NONE

! List of parameters:
INTEGER, PARAMETER :: unit = 8 ! i/o unit for scratch file

! List of variables:
REAL :: data                ! Data value stored in a disk file
INTEGER :: icount = 0    ! The number of input data records
INTEGER :: irec             ! Record number to recover and display
INTEGER :: j                ! Loop index

! Open the scratch file
OPEN (UNIT=unit, STATUS='SCRATCH' )

! Prompt user and get input data.
WRITE (*, 100)
100 FORMAT (1X,'Enter positive or zero input values. ',/, &
            1X,'A negative value terminates input.' )

! Get the input values, and write them to the scratch file
DO
   WRITE (*, 110) icount + 1      ! Prompt for next value
   110 FORMAT (1X,'Enter sample ',I4,':' )
   READ (*,*) data                ! Read value
   IF ( data < 0. ) EXIT          ! Exit on negative numbers
   icount = icount + 1            ! Valid value: bump count
   WRITE (unit,120) data          ! Write data to scratch file
   120 FORMAT ( 1X, ES16.6 )
END DO
! Now we have all of the records. Ask which record to see.
! icount records are in the file.
WRITE (*,130) icount
130 FORMAT (1X,'Which record do you want to see (1 to ',I4, ')? ')
READ (*,*) irec
```

(continued)

```
! Do we have a legal record number?  If so,  get the record.
! If not, tell the user and stop.
IF ( (irec >= 1) .AND. (irec <= icount) )  THEN

   ! This is a legal record. Rewind  the scratch file.
   REWIND (UNIT=unit)

   ! Read forward to the desired record.
   DO j = 1, irec
      READ (unit,*) data
   END DO

   ! Tell user.
   WRITE (*,140) irec, data
   140 FORMAT (1X,'The value of record ', I4, ' is ', ES14.5 )

ELSE

   ! We have an illegal record number. Tell user.
   WRITE (*,150) irec
   150 FORMAT (1X,'Illegal record number entered: ', I8)

END IF

END PROGRAM
```

Let us test the program with valid data:

```
C>scratch
Enter positive or zero input values.
A negative input value terminates input.
Enter sample   1:
234.
Enter sample   2:
12.34
Enter sample   3:
0.
Enter sample   4:
16.
Enter sample   5:
11.235
Enter sample   6:
2.
Enter sample   7:
-1
Which record do you want to see (1 to 6)?
5
The value of record   5 is   1.12350E+01
```

Next we should test the program with an invalid record number to confirm that the error condition is handled properly.

```
C>scratch
Enter positive or zero input values.
A negative input value terminates input.
Enter sample   1:
234.
Enter sample   2:
```

(continued)

(concluded)
```
12.34
Enter sample   3:
0.
Enter sample   4:
16.
Enter sample   5:
11.235
Enter sample   6:
2.
Enter sample   7:
-1
Which record do you want to see (1 to    6):
7
Illegal record number entered:           7
```

The program appears to be functioning correctly.

EXAMPLE 4–5 Fitting a Line to a Set of Noisy Measurements: The velocity of a falling object in the presence of a constant gravitational field is given by the equation

$$v(t) = \alpha t + v_o \tag{4-4}$$

where $v(t)$ is the velocity at any time t, α is the acceleration due to gravity, and v_o is the velocity at time 0. This equation is derived from elementary physics—every freshman physics student knows it. If we plot velocity versus time for the falling object, our (v,t) measurement points should fall along a straight line. However, the same freshman physics student also knows that if we go out into the laboratory and attempt to *measure* the velocity versus time of an object, our measurements will *not* fall along a straight line. They may come close, but they will never line up perfectly. Why not? Because we can never make perfect measurements—some *noise* always distorts them.

Many science and engineering problems deal with noisy sets of data such as this, and we want to estimate the straight line that "best fits" the data. This problem is called the *linear regression* problem. Given a noisy set of measurements (x,y) that appear to fall along a straight line, how can we find the equation of the line

$$y = m x + b \tag{4-5}$$

that best fits the measurements? If we can determine the regression coefficients m and b, then we can use this equation to predict the value of y at any given x by evaluating Equation (4–5) for that value of x.

A standard method for finding the regression coefficients m and b is the *method of least squares*. This method is named "least squares" because it produces the line $y = m x + b$ for which the sum of the squares of the differences between the observed y values and the predicted y values is as small as possible. The slope of the least-squares line is given by

$$m = \frac{(\Sigma xy) - (\Sigma x)\bar{y}}{(\Sigma x^2) - (\Sigma x)\bar{x}} \tag{4-6}$$

and the intercept of the least-squares line is given by

$$b = \bar{y} - m\,\bar{x} \qquad\qquad (4\text{--}7)$$

where

Σx is the sum of the x values.
Σx^2 is the sum of the squares of the x values.
Σxy is the sum of the products of the corresponding x and y values.
$\bar{x}$ is the mean (average) of the x values.
$\bar{y}$ is the mean (average) of the y values.

Write a program that will calculate the least-squares slope m and y-axis intercept b for a given set of noisy measured data points (x,y) that are to be found in an input data file.

SOLUTION

1. **State the problem.**

Calculate the slope m and intercept b of a least-squares line that best fits an input data set consisting of an arbitrary number of (x,y) pairs. The input (x,y) data resides in a user-specified input file.

2. **Define the inputs and outputs.**

The inputs required by this program are pairs of points (x,y), where x and y are real quantities. Each pair of points will be located on a separate line in the input disk file. The number of points in the disk file is not known in advance.

The outputs from this program are the slope and intercept of the least-squares fitted line, plus the number of points going into the fit.

3. **Describe the algorithm.**

This program can be broken down into four major steps:

```
Get the name of the input file and open it
Accumulate the input statistics
Calculate the slope and intercept
Write out the slope and intercept
```

The first major step of the program is to prompt the user for the name of the input file and to open the file. After the file is opened, we must check to see that the open was successful. Next we must read the file and keep track of the number of values entered, plus the sums Σx, Σy, Σx^2, and Σxy. The pseudocode for these steps follows.

```
Initialize n, sum_x, sum_x2, sum_y, and sum_xy to 0
Prompt user for input file name
Open file "filename"
Check for error on OPEN
```

(continued)

(concluded)
```
WHILE
    READ x, y from file "filename"
    IF ( end of file ) EXIT
    n ← n + 1
    sum_x ← sum_x + x
    sum_y ← sum_y + y
    sum_x2 ← sum_x2 + x**2
    sum_xy ← sum_xy + x*y
End of WHILE
```

Next we must calculate the slope and intercept of the least-squares line. The pseudocode for this step is just the Fortran versions of Equations (4–5) and (4–6).

```
x_bar ← sum_x / real(n)
y_bar ← sum_y / real(n)
slope ← (sum_xy - sum_x * y_bar) / ( sum_x2 - sum_x * x_bar)
y_int ← y_bar - slope * x_bar
```

Finally we must write out the results.

```
Write out slope "slope" and intercept "y_int".
```

4. **Turn the algorithm into Fortran statements.**

The final Fortran program is shown in Figure 4–11.

FIGURE 4–11
The least-squares fit program of Example 4–5.

```
PROGRAM least_squares_fit
!
! Purpose:
!   To perform a least-squares fit of an input data set
!   to a straight line and to print out the resulting slope
!   and intercept values. The input data for this fit
!   comes from a user-specified input data file.
!
! Record of revisions:
!     Date         Programmer          Description of change
!     ====         ==========          =====================
!   09/28/95    S. J. Chapman         Original code
!
IMPLICIT NONE

! List of parameters:
INTEGER, PARAMETER :: unit = 18 ! I/o unit for disk I/O

! List of variables. Note that cumulative variables are all
! initialized to zero.
CHARACTER(len=24) :: filename ! Input file name (<= 24 chars)
INTEGER :: ierror             ! Status flag from I/O statements
INTEGER :: n = 0              ! Number of input data pairs (x,y)
REAL :: slope                 ! Slope of the line
REAL :: sum_x = 0.            ! Sum of all input X values
REAL :: sum_x2 = 0.           ! Sum of all input X values squared
```

(continued)

(concluded)

```
REAL :: sum_xy = 0.              ! Sum of all input X*Y values
REAL :: sum_y = 0.               ! Sum of all input Y values
REAL :: x                        ! An input X value
REAL :: x_bar                    ! Average X value
REAL :: y                        ! An input Y value
REAL :: y_bar                    ! Average Y value
REAL :: y_int                    ! Y-axis intercept of the line
! Prompt user and get the name of the input file.
WRITE (*,1000)
1000 FORMAT (1X,'This program performs a least-squares fit of an ',/, &
             1X,'input data set to a straight line. Enter the name',/ &
             1X,'of the file containing the input (x,y) pairs: ' )
READ (*,'(A)') filename

! Open the input file
OPEN (UNIT=unit, FILE=filename, STATUS='OLD', ACTION='READ', &
      IOSTAT=ierror )

! Check to see if the OPEN failed.
errorcheck: IF ( ierror > 0 ) THEN

   WRITE (*,1020) filename
   1020 FORMAT (1X,'ERROR: File ',A,' does not exist!')
ELSE

   ! File opened successfully. Read the (x,y) pairs from
   ! the input file.
   DO
      READ (unit,*,IOSTAT=ierror) x, y    ! Get pair
      IF ( ierror /= 0 ) EXIT
      n     = n + 1                        !
      sum_x  = sum_x + x                   ! Calculate
      sum_y  = sum_y + y                   !    statistics
      sum_x2 = sum_x2 + x**2               !
      sum_xy = sum_xy + x * y              !
   END DO

   ! Now calculate the slope and intercept.
   x_bar = sum_x / real(n)
   y_bar = sum_y / real(n)
   slope = (sum_xy - sum_x * y_bar) / ( sum_x2 - sum_x * x_bar)
   y_int = y_bar - slope * x_bar

   ! Tell user.
   WRITE (*, 1030 ) slope, y_int, N
   1030 FORMAT ('0','Regression coefficients for the least-squares line:',&
           /,1X, ' slope (m)     = ', F12.3,&
           /,1X, ' Intercept (b) = ', F12.3,&
           /,1X, ' No of points  = ', I12 )

   ! Close input file, and quit.
   CLOSE (UNIT=unit)

END IF errorcheck

END PROGRAM
```

5. **Test the program.**

To test this program, we will try a simple data set. For example, if every point in the input data set actually falls along a line, then the resulting slope and intercept should be exactly the slope and intercept of that line. Thus the data set

```
1.1, 1.1
2.2, 2.2
3.3, 3.3
4.4, 4.4
5.5, 5.5
6.6, 6.6
7.7, 7.7
```

should produce a slope of 1.0 and an intercept of 0.0. If we place these values in a file called INPUT, and then run the program, the results are

```
C>least_squares_fit

This program performs a least-squares fit of an
input data set to a straight line. Enter the name
of the file containing the input (x,y) pairs:
INPUT
Regression coefficients for the least-squares line:
  slope (m)     =        1.000
  Intercept (b) =         000
  No of points  =           7
```

Now let's add some noise to the measurements. The data set becomes

```
1.1, 1.01
2.2, 2.30
3.3, 3.05
4.4, 4.28
5.5, 5.75
6.6, 6.48
7.7, 7.84
```

If we place these values in a file called INPUT1 and then run the program on that file, the results are

```
C>least_squares_fit

This program performs a least-squares fit of an
input data set to a straight line. Enter the name
of the file containing the input (x,y) pairs:
INPUT1
Regression coefficients for the least-squares line:
  slope (m)     =        1.024
  Intercept (b) =        -.120
  No of points  =           7
```

If we calculate the answer by hand, it is easy to show that the program gives the correct answers for our two test data sets. The noisy input data set and the resulting least-squares fitted line are shown in Figure 4–12.

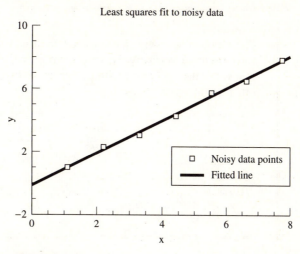

FIGURE 4–12
A noisy input data set and the resulting least-squares fitted line.

The program in this example has a problem—it cannot distinguish between the end
of an input file and a read error (such as character data instead of real data) in the input
file. How would you modify the program to distinguish between these two possible cases?

Quiz 4–3

This quiz provides a quick check to see if you understand the concepts introduced in section 4.5. If you have trouble with the quiz, reread the section,
ask your instructor, or discuss the material with a fellow student. The answers to this quiz appear in Appendix F.

  Write Fortran statements that perform the following functions. Unless
otherwise stated, assume that variables beginning with the letters I through
N are integers and that all other variables are reals.

1. Open an existing file named IN052691 on i/o unit 25 for read-only input, and check the status to see if the OPEN was successful.
2. Open a new output file, making sure that you do not overwrite any existing file by the same name. The name of the output file is stored in
   character variable out_name.
3. Close the file attached to unit 24.
4. Read variables first and last from i/o unit 8 in free format, checking for end of data during the READ.
5. Backspace eight lines in the file attached to i/o unit 13.

(continued)

(concluded)

Examine the following Fortran statements. Are they correct or incorrect? If they are incorrect, why are they incorrect? Unless otherwise stated, assume that variables beginning with the letters I through N are integers and that all other variables are reals.

6. `OPEN (UNIT=35, FILE='DATA1', STATUS='REPLACE',IOSTAT=ierror)`
   `READ (35,*) n, data1, data2`
7. `OPEN (UNIT=11, FILE='DATA1', STATUS='SCRATCH',IOSTAT=ierror)`
8. `OPEN (UNIT=15,STATUS='SCRATCH',ACTION='READ', IOSTAT=ierror)`
9. `OPEN (UNIT=x, FILE='JUNK', STATUS='NEW',IOSTAT=ierror)`
10. `OPEN (UNIT=9, FILE='TEMP.DAT', STATUS='OLD', ACTION='READ', &`
    `       IOSTAT=ierror)`
    `READ (9,*) x, y`

■ 4.6

SUMMARY

Chapter 4 presents a basic introduction to formatted `WRITE` and `READ` statements and to the use of disk files for input and output of data.

In a formatted `WRITE` statement, a `FORMAT` statement number or a character constant or variable containing the format replaces the second asterisk of the unformatted `WRITE` statement (`WRITE (*,*)`). The format describes how the output data is to be displayed. It consists of format descriptors that describe the vertical and horizontal position of the data on a page, as well as the display format for integer, real, logical, and character data types.

The format descriptors discussed in this chapter are summarized in Table 4–4 below.

■ **TABLE 4–4**
Fortran 90/95 format descriptors discussed in chapter 4

FORMAT **descriptors**		Usage
A	Aw	Character data.
Ew.d		Real data in exponential notation.
ESw.d		Real data in scientific notation.
Fw.d		Real data in decimal notation.
Iw	Iw.m	Integer data.
Lw		Logical data.
Tc		Tab: move to column c of current line.
nX		Horizontal spacing: skip n spaces.
/		Vertical spacing: move down 1 line.

where:
c	column number
d	number of digits to right of decimal place
m	minimum number of digits to be displayed
n	number of spaces to skip
w	field width in characters

Formatted READ statements use a format to describe how the program should interpret the input data. The format descriptors in Table 4–4 are also legal in formatted READ statements.

A disk file is opened using the OPEN statement, read and written using READ and WRITE statements, and closed using the CLOSE statement. The OPEN statement associates a file with an i/o unit number, and the READ statements and WRITE statements in the program use that i/o unit number to access the file. When the file is closed, the association is broken.

It is possible to move around within a sequential disk file using the BACKSPACE and REWIND statements. The BACKSPACE statement moves the current position in the file backward by one record whenever it is executed, and the REWIND statement moves the current position back to the first record in the file.

4.6.1 Summary of Good Programming Practice

The following guidelines should be adhered to when programming with formatted output statements or with disk I/O. If you follow these guidelines consistently, your code will contain fewer bugs, will be easier to debug, and will be more understandable to others who may need to work with it in the future.

1. The first column of any output line is reserved for a control character. Never put anything in the first column except for the control character. Be especially careful not to include column 1 in a format descriptor; your program could behave erratically depending on the value of the data being written out.

2. Always be careful to match the type of data in a WRITE statement to the type of descriptors in the corresponding format. Integers should be associated with I format descriptors; reals with E, ES, or F format descriptors; logicals with L descriptors; and characters with A descriptors. A mismatch between data types and format descriptors will result in an error at execution time.

3. Use the ES format descriptor instead of the E descriptor when displaying data in exponential format to make the output data appear to be in conventional scientific notation.

4. Use an asterisk instead of an i/o unit number when reading from the standard input device or writing to the standard output device. This convention makes your code more portable, since the asterisk is the same on all systems, whereas the actual unit numbers assigned to standard input and standard output devices may vary from system to system.

5. Always open input files with STATUS='OLD'. By definition, an input file must already exist if we are to read data from it. If the file does not exist, this condition is an error, and the STATUS='OLD' will catch that error. Input files should also be opened with ACTION='READ' to prevent accidental overwriting of the input data.

6. Open output files with STATUS='NEW' or with STATUS='REPLACE', depending on whether you want to preserve the existing contents of the output file. If the file is opened with STATUS='NEW', it should be impossible to overwrite an existing file, so the program cannot accidentally destroy data. If you don't care about the existing data

in the output file, open the file with STATUS='REPLACE'; the file will be overwritten if it exists. Open scratch files with STATUS='SCRATCH' so that they will be automatically deleted upon closing.

7. Always include the IOSTAT= clause when reading from disk files to detect an end of file or error condition.

4.6.2 Summary of Fortran Statements and Structures

The following summary describes the Fortran statements and structures introduced in this chapter.

BACKSPACE Statement

> BACKSPACE (UNIT=*unit*)

Example:

> BACKSPACE (UNIT=8)

Description:

The BACKSPACE statement moves the current position of a file back by one record.

CLOSE Statement

> CLOSE (*close_list*)

Example:

> CLOSE (UNIT=8)

Description:

The CLOSE statement closes the file associated with an i/o unit number.

FORMAT Statement

> *label* FORMAT (*format descriptor*, ...)

Example:

> 100 FORMAT (' This is a test: ', I6)

(continued)

(concluded)

Description:

      The FORMAT statement describes the position and format of the data being read or written.

Formatted READ Statement

```
READ (unit,format) input_list
```

Examples:

```
READ (1,100) time, speed
100 FORMAT ( F10.4, F18.4 )
READ (1,'(I6)') index
```

Description:

      The formatted READ statement reads data from an input buffer according to the format descriptors specified in the format. The format is a character string that may be specified in a FORMAT statement, a character constant, or a character variable.

Formatted WRITE Statement

```
WRITE (unit,format) output_list
```

Examples:

```
WRITE (*,100) i, j, slope
100 FORMAT ( 1X, 2I10, F10.2 )
  WRITE (*,'( 1X, 2I10, F10.2 )') i, j, slope
```

Description:

      The formatted WRITE statement outputs the data in the output list according to the format descriptors specified in the format. The format is a character string that may be specified in a FORMAT statement, a character constant, or a character variable.

OPEN Statement

```
OPEN (open_list)
```

Example:

```
OPEN (UNIT=8, FILE='IN', STATUS='OLD' ACTION='READ', &
      IOSTAT=ierror)
```

(continued)

(concluded)
Description:
    The OPEN statement associates a file with an i/o unit number so that READ or WRITE statements can access the file.

REWIND Statement

                       REWIND (UNIT=*unit*)

Example:

                       REWIND (UNIT=8)

Description:
    The REWIND statement moves the current position of a file back to the beginning.

■ 4.7
EXERCISES

4–1 What is the purpose of a format? In what three ways can formats be specified?

4–2 What is the effect of each of the following characters when it appears in the control character of the Fortran output buffer? '1'; ' '; '0'; '+'; '2'

4–3 What is printed out by the following Fortran statements?
a.
```
INTEGER :: i
i = -123
WRITE (*,100) i
100 FORMAT ('1','i = ', I6.5)
```
b.
```
REAL :: a, b, sum, difference
a = 1.0020E6
b = 1.0001E6
sum = a + b
difference = a - b
WRITE (*,101) a, b, sum, difference
101 FORMAT (1X,'A = ',ES14.6,' B = ',E14.6, &
' Sum = ',E14.6,' Diff = ', F14.6)
```
c.
```
INTEGER :: i1, i2
i1 = 10
i2 = 4**2
WRITE (*,300) i1 > i2
300 FORMAT (' ', 'Result = ', L6)
```

4-4 What is printed out by the following Fortran statements?

```
REAL :: a = 1.602E-19, b = 57.2957795, c = -1.
WRITE (*,100) a, b, c
100 FORMAT (' ',ES14.7,2(1X,E13.7))
```

4-5 For the following Fortran statements and input data, state what the values of each variable will be when the READ statement has been completed.
Statements:

```
CHARACTER(5) :: a
CHARACTER(10) :: b
CHARACTER(15) :: c
READ (*,'(3A10)') a, b, c
```

Input data:

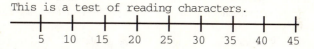

4-6 For the following Fortran statements and input data, state what the values of each variable will be when the READ statements have been completed.
a. Statements:

```
INTEGER :: item1, item2, item3, item4, item5
INTEGER :: item6, item7, item8, item9, item10
READ (*,*) item1, item2, item3, item4, item5, item6
READ (*,*) item7, item8, item9, item10
```

Input data:

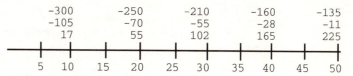

b. Statements:

```
INTEGER :: item1, item2, item3, item4, item5
INTEGER :: item6, item7, item8, item9, item10
READ (*,8) item1, item2, item3, item4, item5, item6
READ (*,8) item7, item8, item9, item10
8 FORMAT (4I10)
```

Input data:

Same as for *a* above.

4-7 **Table of Logarithms** Write a Fortran program to generate a table of the base 10 logarithms between 1 and 10 in steps of 0.1. The table should start on a new page, and it should include a title describing the table and row and column headings. Here's how this table should be organized:

	x.0	x.1	x.2	x.3	x.4	x.5	x.6	x.7	x.8	x.9
1.0	0.000	0.041	0.079	0.114	...					
2.0	0.301	0.322	0.342	0.362	...					
3.0	...									
4.0	...									
5.0	...									
6.0	...									
7.0	...									
8.0	...									
9.0	...									
10.0	...									

4–8 Example 4–3 illustrates the technique of reading an arbitrary amount of real data from an input data file. Modify that program to read in the data from an input data file and to calculate the mean and standard deviation of the samples in the file.

4–9 A real number length is to be displayed in Fw.d format with four digits to the right of the decimal point ($d = 4$). If the number is known to lie within the range $-10000. \leq$ length $\leq$ 10000., what is the minimum field width w that will always be able to display the value of length?

4–10 In what columns will the following characters be printed? Why?

WRITE (*,'(T30,A)') 'Rubbish!'

4–11 Write Fortran statements to perform the functions described below. Assume that variables beginning with I through N are integers and that all other variables are reals.
a. Skip to a new page and print the title 'INPUT DATA' starting in column 40.
b. Skip a line and then display the data point number ipoint in columns 6–10. Display the data point value data_1 in columns 15–26, using scientific notation with seven significant digits.

4–12 What is the minimum field width necessary to display any real data value in E or ES format with six significant bits of accuracy?

4–13 Write a Fortran program that reads in a time in seconds since the start of the day (this value will be somewhere between 0. and 86400.) and writes out the time in the form HH:MM:SS using the 24-hour clock convention. Use the Iw.m format descriptor to ensure that leading zeros are preserved in the MM and SS fields. Be sure to check the input number of seconds for validity. You should also write an appropriate error message if an invalid number is entered.

4–14 Gravitational Acceleration The acceleration due to Earth's gravity at any height h above the surface of Earth is given by the equation

$$g = -G \frac{M}{(R + h)^2} \qquad (4-8)$$

where G is the gravitational constant (6.672×10^{-11} N m^2/kg^2), M is the mass of Earth (5.98×10^{24} kg), R is the mean radius of Earth (6371 km), and h is the height above Earth's surface. If M is measured in kg and R and h in meters, then the resulting acceleration will be in units of meters per second squared. Write a program to calculate the acceleration due to Earth's gravity in 500 km increments at heights from 0 km to 40,000 km above the surface of Earth. Print out the results in a table of height versus acceleration with appropriate labels, including the units of the output values.

4–15 What is the proper STATUS to use when opening a file for reading input data? What is the proper STATUS to use when opening a file for writing output data? What is the proper STATUS to use when opening a temporary storage file?

4–16 What is the proper ACTION to use when opening a file for reading input data? What is the proper ACTION to use when opening a file for writing output data? What is the proper ACTION to use when opening a temporary storage file?

4–17 Is a CLOSE statement always required in a Fortran program that uses disk files? Why or why not?

4–18 Write Fortran statements to perform the following functions. Assume that file INPUT.DAT contains a series of real values organized with one value per record.
a. Open an existing file named INPUT.DAT on logical unit 98 for input and a new file named NEWOUT.DAT on logical unit 99 for output.
b. Read data values from file INPUT.DAT until the end of file is reached. Write all positive data values to the output file.
c. Close the input and output data files.

4–19 Write a program that reads an arbitrary number of real values from a user-specified input data file, rounds the values to the nearest integer, and writes the integers out to a user-specified output file. Open the input and output files with the appropriate status. Be sure to handle the end of file and error conditions properly.

4–20 Write a program that opens a scratch file and writes the integers 1 through 10 in the first 10 records. Move back six records in the file and read the value stored in that record. Save that value in variable x. Move back three records in the file and read the value stored in that record. Save that value in variable y. Multiply the two values x and y together. What is their product?

4–21 Examine the following Fortran statements. Are they correct or incorrect? If they are incorrect, why are they incorrect? (Unless otherwise indicated, assume that variables beginning with I through N are integers and that all other variables are reals.)

a.
```
OPEN (UNIT=1, FILE='INFO.DAT', STATUS='NEW', IOSTAT=ierror)
READ (1,*) i, j, k
```
b.
```
OPEN (UNIT=17, FILE='TEMP.DAT', STATUS='SCRATCH', IOSTAT=ierror)
```
c.
```
OPEN (UNIT=99, FILE='INFO.DAT', STATUS='NEW', &
      ACTION='READWRITE', IOSTAT=ierror)
WRITE (99,*) i, j, k
```

```
d. INTEGER :: unit = 8
   OPEN (UNIT=unit, FILE='INFO.DAT', STATUS='OLD', IOSTAT=ierror)
   READ (8,*) unit
   CLOSE (UNIT=unit)
e. OPEN (UNIT=9, FILE='OUTPUT.DAT', STATUS='NEW', ACTION='WRITE', &
        IOSTAT=ierror)
   WRITE (9,*) mydat1, mydat2
   WRITE (9,*) mydat3, mydat4
   CLOSE (UNIT=9)
```

4–22 Table of Sines and Cosines Write a program to generate a table containing the sine and cosine of θ for θ between 0 and 90 degrees in 1 degree increments. The program should properly label each column in the table.

4–23 Interest Calculations Suppose that you have a sum of money P in an interest-bearing account at a local bank. (P stands for *present value*.) If the bank pays you interest on the money at a rate of i percent per year and compounds the interest monthly, the amount of money that you will have in the bank after n months is given by the equation

$$F = P \left(1 + \frac{i}{1200} \right)^n \tag{4–9}$$

where F is the future value of the account and $\dfrac{i}{12}$ is the monthly percentage interest rate. (The extra factor of 100 in the denominator converts the interest rate from percentages to fractional amounts.) Write a Fortran program that reads an initial amount of money P and an annual interest rate i and then calculates and writes out a table showing the future value of the account every month for the next five years. The table should be written to an output file called INTEREST. Be sure to properly label the columns of your table.

4–24 Write a program to read a set of integers from an input data file and to locate the largest and smallest values within the data file. Print out the largest and smallest values, together with the lines on which they were found. Assume that you do not know the number of values in the file before the file is read.

4–25 Means In exercise 3–29 you wrote a Fortran program that calculated the arithmetic mean (average), rms average, geometric mean, and harmonic mean for a set of numbers. Modify that program to read an arbitrary number of values from an input data file and then calculate the means of those numbers. To test the program, place the following values into an input data file and run the program on that file: 1.0, 2.0, 5.0, 4.0, 3.0, 2.1, 4.7, 3.0.

4–26 Converting Radians to Degrees/Minutes/Seconds Angles are often measured in degrees (°), minutes ('), and seconds ("), with 360 degrees in a circle, 60 minutes in a degree, and 60 seconds in a minute. Write a program that reads angles in radians from an input disk file and converts them into degrees, minutes, and seconds. Test your program by placing the following four angles expressed in radians into an input file and reading that file into the program: 0.0, 1.0, 3.141593, 6.0.

4–27 Program `least_squares_fit` from Example 4–5 has a logical error. The error can cause the program to abort with a divide-by-zero error. It slipped through the example because we did not test the program exhaustively for all possible inputs. Find the error and rewrite the program to eliminate it.

4–28 Dynamically Modifying Format Descriptors Write a program to read a set of four real values in free format from each line of an input data file and print the values out on the standard output device. If a value is exactly zero or if it lies in the range $0.01 \leq |value| < 1000.0$, it should be printed in `F14.6` format; otherwise, it should be printed in `ES14.6` format. (*Hint:* Define the output format in a character variable and modify it to match each line of data as it is printed.) Test your program on the following data set:

4–29 Correlation Coefficient The method of least squares is used to fit a straight line to a noisy input data set consisting of pairs of values x,y. As we saw in Example 4–5, the best fit to equation

$$y = m\,x + b \tag{4–5}$$

is given by

$$m = \frac{(\Sigma xy) - (\Sigma x)\bar{y}}{(\Sigma x^2) - (\Sigma x)\,\bar{x}} \tag{4–6}$$

and

$$b = \bar{y} - m\,\bar{x} \tag{4–7}$$

where

Σx is the sum of the x values.
Σx^2 is the sum of the squares of the x values.

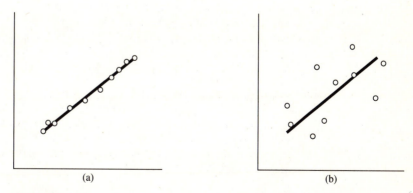

(a)   (b)

FIGURE 4–13
Two least-squares fits: (*a*) with good, low-noise data; (*b*) with very noisy data.

Σxy is the sum of the products of the corresponding x and y values.
$\bar{x}$ is the mean (average) of the x values.
$\bar{y}$ is the mean (average) of the y values.

Figure 4–13 shows two data sets and the least-squares fits associated with each one. As you can see, the low-noise data fits the least-squares line much better than the noisy data does. It would be useful to have some quantitative way to describe how well the data fits the least-squares line given by Equations (4–4), (4–5), and (4–6).

The *correlation coefficient* is a standard statistical measure of the goodness of fit of a data set to a least-squares line. The correlation coefficient is equal to 1.0 when there is a perfect positive linear relationship between data x and y, and it is equal to -1.0 when there is a perfect negative linear relationship between data x and y. The correlation coefficient is 0.0 when there is no linear relationship between x and y at all. The correlation coefficient is given by the equation

$$r = \frac{n(\Sigma xy) - (\Sigma x)(\Sigma y)}{\sqrt{[(n\Sigma x^2) - (\Sigma x)^2][(n\Sigma y^2) - (\Sigma y)^2]}} \tag{4–10}$$

where r is the correlation coefficient and n is the number of data points included in the fit.

Write a program to read an arbitrary number of (x,y) data pairs from an input data file. The program should also calculate and print out both the least-squares fit to the data and the correlation coefficient for the fit. If the correlation coefficient is small ($|r| < 0.3$), write a warning message to the user.

Arrays

An **array** is a group of variables, all of the same type, that is referred to by a single name. The values in the group occupy consecutive locations in the computer's memory (see Figure 5–1). An individual value within the array is called an **array element;** it is identified by the name of the array and a **subscript** pointing to the particular location within the array. For example, the first variable shown in Figure 5–1 is referred to as a(1), and the fifth variable shown in the figure is referred to as a(5). The subscript of an array must be an integer constant or variable.

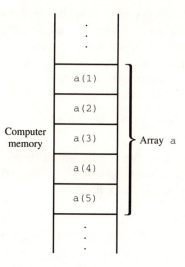

FIGURE 5–1
The elements of an array occupy successive locations in a computer's memory.

As you shall see, arrays can be extremely powerful tools. They permit us to apply the same algorithm repeatedly to many different data items with a simple DO loop. For example, suppose that we need to take the square root of 100 different real numbers. If the numbers are stored as elements of an array a containing 100 real values, then the code

```
DO i = 1, 100
   a(i) = SQRT(a(i))
END DO
```

will take the square root of each real number and store it back into the memory location that it came from. If we wanted to take the square root of 100 real numbers without using arrays, we would have to write out

```
a1    = SQRT(a1)
a2    = SQRT(a2)
   ...
a100 = SQRT(a100)
```

as 100 separate statements! Arrays are obviously a *much* cleaner and shorter way to handle repeated similar operations.

Arrays are very powerful tools for manipulating data in Fortran. We can manipulate and perform calculations with individual elements of arrays one by one, with whole arrays at once, or with various subsets of arrays. We will first learn how to declare arrays in Fortran programs. Then we will learn how to use individual array elements, whole arrays, and array subsets in Fortran statements.

■ 5.1
DECLARING ARRAYS

Before you can use an array, you must declare its type and the number of elements it contains to the compiler in a type declaration statement, which tells the compiler what sort of data is to be stored in the array and how much memory is required to hold it. An array may be of any type: real, integer, logical, or character. The type and size of an array are declared using a type declaration statement. For example, a real array `voltage` containing 16 elements could be declared as follows:

```
REAL, DIMENSION(16) :: voltage
```

The **DIMENSION attribute** in the type declaration statement declares the size of the array being defined. The elements in array `voltage` would be addressed as `voltage(1)`, `voltage(2)`, and so forth, up to `voltage(16)`. Similarly, an array of fifty 20-character-long variables could be declared as follows:

```
CHARACTER(len=20), DIMENSION(50) :: last_name
```

Each of the elements in array `last_name` would be a 20-character-long variable, and the elements would be addressed as `last_name(1)`, `last_name(2)`, and so forth.

Arrays may be declared with more than one subscript, so they may be organized into two or more dimensions. These arrays are convenient for representing data that is normally organized into multiple dimensions, such as map information. The number of subscripts declared for a given array is called the **rank** of the array. Both array `voltage` and array `last_name` are rank-1 arrays, since they have only one subscript. We will use more complex arrays later in the chapter.

The number of elements in a given dimension of an array is called the **extent** of the array in that dimension. The extent of the first (and only) subscript of array `voltage` is 20, and the extent of the first (and only) subscript of array `last_name` is 50. The **shape** of an array is the combination of its rank and the extent of the array in each dimension. Thus two arrays have the same shape if they have the same rank and the same extent in each dimension. Finally, the **size** of an array is the total number of elements declared in that array. For simple rank-1 arrays, the size of the array is the same as the extent of its single subscript. Therefore, the size of array `voltage` is 20, and the size of array `last_name` is 50.

Array constants may also be defined. An array constant is an array consisting entirely of constants. It is defined by placing the constant values between special delimiters called **array constructors.** The starting delimiter of an array constructor is (/, and the ending delimiter of an array constructor is /). For example, the following expression defines an array constant containing five integer elements:

$$(/ \ 1, \ 2, \ 3, \ 4, \ 5 \ /)$$

■ 5.2

USING ARRAY ELEMENTS IN Fortran STATEMENTS

This section contains some of the practical details involved in using arrays in Fortran programs.

5.2.1 Array Elements Are Just Ordinary Variables

Each element of an array is a variable just like any other variable, and you can use an array element in any place where you would use an ordinary variable of the same type. You can include array elements in arithmetic and logical expressions, and you can assign the results of an expression to an array element. For example, assume that arrays `index` and `temp` are declared as follows:

```
INTEGER, DIMENSION(10) :: index
LOGICAL, DIMENSION(2) :: lval
REAL, DIMENSION(3) :: temp
```

Then the following Fortran statements are perfectly valid:

```
index(1) = 1
lval(2) = .TRUE.
temp(3) = REAL(index(1)) / 4.
WRITE (*,*) ' index(1) = ', index(1)
```

5.2.2 Initialization of Array Elements

You must *initialize* the values in an array before you use them, just as with ordinary variables. If an array is not initialized, the contents of the array elements are undefined. In the following Fortran statements, array `j` is an example of an **uninitialized array.**

```
INTEGER, DIMENSION(10) :: j
WRITE (*,*) ' j(1) = ', j(1)
```

The array j has been declared by the type declaration statement, but no values have been placed into it yet. The Fortran standard does not define the values of the elements in an uninitialized array. Some compilers automatically set uninitialized array elements to zero, and some set them to different arbitrary patterns. Other compilers leave in memory whatever values previously existed in the computer's memory at the location of the array elements. Some compilers even produce a run-time error if an array element is used without first being initialized.

Because of these variations, a program that works perfectly well on one processor may fail when it is moved to another one. To ensure that a program performs consistently from processor to processor, always initialize the elements in an array before you use them.

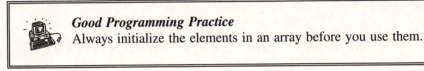

Good Programming Practice
Always initialize the elements in an array before you use them.

You can use one of three techniques to initialize the elements in an array:

1. Initial values may be assigned to the array using assignment statements.
2. Initial values may be declared in type declaration statements and loaded into the array at compilation time.
3. Initial values may be read into the array using Fortran 90/95 READ statements.

Initializing arrays with assignment statements

Initial values may be assigned to the array during program execution by using assignment statements, either element by element in a DO loop or all together with an array constructor. For example, the following DO loop will initialize all of the elements of array array1 to 0.0 one element at a time:

```
REAL, DIMENSION(10) :: array1
DO i = 1, 10
   array1(i) = 0.0
END DO
```

The following assignment statement accomplishes the same function all at once using an array constructor:

```
REAL, DIMENSION(10) :: array1
array1 = (/0.,0.,0.,0.,0.,0.,0.,0.,0.,0./)
```

The simple program shown in Figure 5–2 calculates the squares of the numbers in array number and then prints out the numbers and their squares. Note that the values in array number are initialized element by element with a DO loop.

FIGURE 5–2

A program to calculate the squares of the integers from 1 to 10, using assignment statements to initialize the values in array `number`.

```
PROGRAM squares

IMPLICIT NONE

INTEGER :: i
INTEGER, DIMENSION(10) :: number, square

! Initialize number and calculate square.
DO i = 1, 10
    number(i) = i                       ! Initialize number
    square(i) = number(i)**2            ! Calculate square
END DO

! Write out each number and its square.
DO i = 1, 10
    WRITE (*,100) number(i), square(i)
    100 FORMAT (1X,'Number = ',I6,' Square = ',I6)
END DO

END PROGRAM
```

Initializing arrays in type declaration statements

Initial values may be loaded into the array at compilation time by declaring their values in type declaration statements. To initialize an array in a type declaration statement, we use an array constructor to declare its initial values in that statement. For example, the following statement declares a five-element integer array `array2`, and initializes the elements of `array2` to 1, 2, 3, 4, and 5:

```
INTEGER, DIMENSION(5) :: array2 = (/ 1, 2, 3, 4, 5 /)
```

The five-element array constant `(/ 1, 2, 3, 4, 5 /)` was used to initialize the five-element array `array2`. The number of elements in the constant must match the number of elements in the array being initialized. Either too few or too many elements will result in a compiler error.

This method works well to initialize small arrays, but what do we do if the array has 100 (or even 1000) elements? Writing out the initial values for a 100-element array would be very tedious and repetitive. To initialize larger arrays, we can use an **implied DO loop.** An implied DO loop has the general form

$$(arg1, arg2, \ldots , index = istart, iend, incr)$$

where $arg1$, $arg2$, and so on are values evaluated each time the loop is executed, and $index$, $istart$, $iend$, and $incr$ function in exactly the same way as they do for ordinary counting DO loops. For example, the `array2` declaration above could be written using an implied DO loop as

```
INTEGER, DIMENSION(5) :: array2 = (/ (i, i=1,5) /)
```

and a 1000-element array could be initialized to have the values 1, 2, ..., 1000 using an implied DO loop as follows:

```
INTEGER, DIMENSION(1000) :: array3 = (/ (i, i=1,1000) /)
```

Implied DO loops can be nested or mixed with constants to produce complex patterns. For example, the following statements initialize the elements of array4 to 0 if they are not divisible by five, and to the element number if they are divisible by five.

```
INTEGER, DIMENSION(25) :: array4 = (/ ((0,i=1,4),5*j, j=1,5) /)
```

The inner DO loop (0,i=1,4) executes completely for each step of the outer DO loop, so the pattern of values produced by these nested loops is

```
0, 0, 0, 0, 5, 0, 0, 0, 0, 10, 0, 0, 0, 0, 15, ...
```

Finally, all the elements of an array can be initialized to a single constant value by simply including the constant in the type declaration statement. In the following example, all the elements of array5 are initialized to 1.:

```
REAL, DIMENSION(100) :: array5 = 1.
```

The program in Figure 5–3 illustrates the use of type declaration statements to initialize the values in an array. It calculates the square roots of the numbers in array value and then prints out the numbers and their square roots.

FIGURE 5–3

A program to calculate the square roots of the integers from 1 to 10, using a type specification statement to initialize the values in array value.

```
PROGRAM square_roots

IMPLICIT NONE

INTEGER :: i
REAL, DIMENSION(10) :: value5 (/ (i, i=1,10) /)
REAL, DIMENSION(10) :: square_root

! Calculate the square roots of the numbers.
DO i = 1, 10
   square_root(i) = SQRT(value(i))
END DO

! Write out each number and its square root.
DO i = 1, 10
   WRITE (*,100) value(i), square_root(i)
   100 FORMAT (1X,'Value = ',F5.1,' Square Root = ',F10.4)
END DO

END PROGRAM
```

Initializing arrays with Fortran READ statements

Another way to initialize arrays is with Fortran READ statements. The use of arrays in I/O statements will be described in section 5.4.

5.2.3 Changing the Subscript Range of an Array

The elements of an N-element array are normally addressed using the subscripts 1, 2, ..., N. Thus the elements of array `arr` declared with the statement

```
REAL, DIMENSION(5) :: arr
```

would be addressed as `arr(1)`, `arr(2)`, `arr(3)`, `arr(4)`, and `arr(5)`. In some problems, however, it is more convenient to address the array elements with other subscripts. For example, the possible grades on an exam might range from 0 to 100. One way to accumulate statistics on the number of people scoring any given grade is to have a 101-element array whose subscripts range from 0 to 100, instead of from 1 to 101. If the subscripts range from 0 to 100, each student's exam grade can be used directly as an index into the array.

For such problems, Fortran provides a mechanism to specify the range of numbers that will be used to address the elements of an array. To specify the subscript range, we include the starting and ending subscript numbers in the declaration statement, with the two numbers separated by a colon.

```
REAL, DIMENSION(lower_bound:upper_bound) :: array
```

For example, the following three arrays all consist of five elements:

```
REAL, DIMENSION(5) :: a1
REAL, DIMENSION(-2:2) :: b1
REAL, DIMENSION(5:9) :: c1
```

Array `a1` is addressed with subscripts 1 through 5, array `b1` is addressed with subscripts -2 through 2, and array `c1` is addressed with subscripts 5 through 9. All three arrays have the same shape, since they have the same number of dimensions and the same extent in each dimension. In general, the number of elements in a given dimension of an array can be found from the equation

$$\text{extent} = \text{upper\_bound} - \text{lower\_bound} + 1 \qquad (5\text{-}1)$$

The simple program `squares_2` shown in Figure 5–4 calculates the squares of the numbers in array `number` and then prints out the numbers and their squares. The arrays in this example contain 11 elements, addressed by the subscripts -5, -4, ..., 0, ..., 4, 5.

FIGURE 5–4
A program to calculate the squares of the integers from -5 to 5, using array elements addressed by subscripts -5 through 5.

```
PROGRAM squares_2

IMPLICIT NONE

INTEGER :: i
INTEGER, DIMENSION(-5:5) :: number, square
```

(continued)

(concluded)

```
! Initialize number and calculate square.
DO i = -5, 5
    = i                                ! Initialize number
    square(i) = number(i)**2           ! Calculate square
END DO

! Write out each number and its square.
DO i = -5, 5
    WRITE (*,100) number(i), square(i)
    100 FORMAT (1X,'Number = ',I6,' Square = ',I6)
END DO

END PROGRAM
```

When program `squares_2` is executed, the results are

```
C>squares_2
Number =  -5 Square =  25
Number =  -4 Square =  16
Number =  -3 Square =   9
Number =  -2 Square =   4
Number =  -1 Square =   1
Number =   0 Square =   0
Number =   1 Square =   1
Number =   2 Square =   4
Number =   3 Square =   9
Number =   4 Square =  16
Number =   5 Square =  25
```

5.2.4 Out-of-Bounds Array Subscripts

Each element of an array is addressed using an integer subscript. The range of integers that correspond to elements in the array depends on the size of the array as declared in a program. For a real array declared as

```
REAL, DIMENSION(5) :: a
```

the integer subscripts 1, 2, 3, 4, and 5 would correspond to elements in the array. *Any other integers* (less than 1 or greater than 5) *can not be used as subscripts, since they do not correspond to allocated memory locations.* Such integers subscripts are said to be **out of bounds** for the array. But what happens if we make a mistake and try to access the out-of-bounds element `a(6)` in a program?

The answer to this question is very complicated, since it varies from processor to processor. On some processors, a running Fortran program will check every subscript used to reference an array to see if it is in bounds. If an out-of-bounds subscript is detected, the program will issue an informative error message and stop. Unfortunately, such **bounds checking** requires a lot of computer time, and the program will run very slowly. To make programs run faster, most Fortran compilers make bounds checking optional. If it is turned on, programs run slower, but they are protected from out-of-bounds references.

If it is turned off, programs will run much faster, but out-of-bounds references will not be checked. If your Fortran compiler has a bounds-checking option, you should always turn it on during debugging to help detect programming errors. Once the program has been debugged, bounds checking can be turned off if necessary to increase the execution speed of the final program.

> **Good Programming Practice**
> Always turn on your Fortran compiler's bounds-checking option during program development and debugging to help you catch programming errors producing out-of-bounds references. You may turn off the bounds-checking option if necessary for greater speed in the final program.

What happens in a program if an out-of-bounds reference occurs and the bounds checking option is not turned on? Sometimes the program will abort. Much of the time, though, the computer will simply go to the location in memory at which the referenced array element would have been if it had been allocated and use that memory location. For example, the array a declared at the beginning of this section has five elements. If a(6) were used in a program, the computer would access the first word beyond the end of array a. Since that memory location will be allocated for a totally different purpose, the program can fail in subtle and bizarre ways that can be almost impossible to track down. Be careful with your array subscripts and always use the bounds checker when you are debugging!

5.2.5 The Use of Named Constants with Array Declarations

Many Fortran programs store large amounts of information in arrays. The amount of information that a program can process depends on the size of the arrays included in it. If the arrays are relatively small, the program will be small and will not require much memory to run, but it will only be able to handle a small amount of data. On the other hand, if the arrays are large, the program will be able to handle a lot of information, but it will require a lot of memory to run. The array sizes in such a program are frequently changed to make it run better for different problems or on different processors.

It is a good practice to always declare the array sizes using named constants. As we mentioned in Chapter 2, you can use a named constant in place of an ordinary constant anywhere in a Fortran program. Named constants make it easy to resize the arrays in a Fortran program. In the following code, you can change the sizes of all arrays by simply changing the single constant isize.

```
INTEGER, PARAMETER :: isize = 1000
REAL :: array1(isize)
REAL :: array2(isize)
REAL :: array3(2*isize)
```

Although this point may seem trivial, it is *very* important to the proper maintenance of large Fortran programs. If you declare all related array sizes in a program using named constants and if you use those same named constants in any size tests that occur in the program, then you will simplify the job of modifying the program later. Imagine what it would be like if you had to locate and change every reference to array sizes within a 50,000 line program! The process could take you weeks to complete and debug. By contrast, the size of a well-designed program could be modified in five minutes by changing only one statement in the code.

Good Programming Practice
Always use named constants to declare the sizes of arrays in a Fortran program to make the array sizes easy to change.

EXAMPLE 5–1 *Finding the Largest and Smallest Values in a Data Set:* To illustrate the use of arrays, we will write a simple program that reads in data values supplied by a user and finds the largest and smallest numbers in the data set. The program will then write out the values, with the word LARGEST printed by the largest value and the word SMALLEST printed by the smallest value in the data set.

SOLUTION

This program must be able to ask the user for the number of values to be input and then read the input values into an array. Once the values are all read, the program must go through the data to find the largest and smallest values in the data set. Finally, it must print out the values, with the appropriate annotations beside the largest and smallest values in the data set.

1. **State the problem.**

We have not yet specified the type of data to be processed. If we are processing integer data, then the problem may be stated as follows:

> Develop a program to read a user-specified number of integer values from the standard input device, locate the largest and smallest values in the data set, and write out all of the values with the words 'LARGEST' and 'SMALLEST' printed by the largest and smallest values in the data set.

2. **Define the inputs and outputs.**

This program has two types of inputs:

a. An integer containing the number of integer values to read. This value will come from the standard input device.
b. The integer values in the data set. These values will also come from the standard input device.

The outputs from this program are the values in the data set, with the word 'LARGEST' printed by the largest value and the word 'SMALLEST' printed by the smallest value.

3. Describe the algorithm.

The program can be broken down into four major steps:

```
Get the number of values to read in
Read the input values into an array
Find the largest and smallest values in the array
Write out the data with the words 'LARGEST' and 'SMALLEST' at the
    appropriate places
```

The first two major steps of the program are to get the number of values to read in and to read the values into an input array. We must prompt the user for the number of values to read. If that number is less than or equal to the size of the input array, then we should read in the data values. Otherwise, we should warn the user and quit. The detailed pseudocode for these steps follows.

```
Prompt user for the number of input values nvals
Read in nvals
IF nvals <= max_size then
   DO for j = 1 to nvals
      Read in input values
   End of DO
   ...
   ...(Further processing here)
   ...
ELSE
      Tell user that there are too many values for array size
End of IF
END PROGRAM
```

Next we must locate the largest and smallest values in the data set. We will use variables ilarge and ismall as pointers to the array elements having the largest and smallest values. The pseudocode to find the largest and smallest values is

```
! Find largest value
temp ← input(1)
ilarge ← 1
DO for j = 2 to nvals
   IF input(j) > temp then
      temp ← input(j)
      ilarge ← j
   End of IF
End of DO

! Find smallest value
temp ← input(1)
ismall ← 1
DO for j = 2 to nvals
   IF input(j) < temp then
      temp ← input(j)
      ismall ← j
   End of IF
End of DO
```

The final step is writing out the values with the largest and smallest numbers labeled:

```
DO for j = 1 to nvals
    IF ismall == j then
        Write input(j) and 'SMALLEST'
    ELSE IF ilarge == j then
        Write input(j) and 'LARGEST'
    ELSE
        Write input(j)
End of DO
```

4. **Turn the algorithm into Fortran statements.**

The resulting Fortran program is shown in Figure 5–5.

FIGURE 5–5
A program to read in a data set from the standard input, find the largest and smallest values, and print the values with the largest and smallest values labeled.

```
PROGRAM extremes
!
! Purpose:
!   To find the largest and smallest values in a data set
!   and to print out the data set with the largest and smallest
!   values labeled.
!
! Record of revisions:
!     Date        Programmer          Description of change
!     ====        ==========          =================
!   09/21/95    S. J. Chapman            Original code
!
IMPLICIT NONE

! List of parameters:
INTEGER, PARAMETER :: max_size = 10    ! Max size of data set

! List of variables:
INTEGER, DIMENSION(max_size) :: input ! Input values
INTEGER :: ilarge                     ! Pointer to largest value
INTEGER :: ismall                     ! Pointer to smallest value
INTEGER :: j                          ! DO loop index
INTEGER :: nvals                      ! Number of vals in data set
INTEGER :: temp                       ! Temporary variable

! Get number of values in data set
WRITE (*,*) 'Enter number of values in data set:'
READ (*,*) nvals

! Is the number <= max_size?
size: IF ( nvals <= max_size ) THEN

    ! Get input values.
    in: DO j = 1, nvals
        WRITE (*,100) 'Enter value ', j
        100 FORMAT (' ',A,I3,': ')
        READ (*,*) input(j)
    END DO in
```

(continued)

```
(continued)
    ! Find the largest value.
    temp = input(1)
    ilarge = 1
    large: DO j = 2, nvals
       IF ( input(j) > temp ) THEN
          temp = input(j)
          ilarge = j
       END IF
    END DO large

    ! Find the smallest value.
    temp = input(1)
    ismall = 1
    small: DO j = 2, nvals
       IF ( input(j) < temp ) THEN
          temp = input(j)
          ismall = j
       END IF
    END DO small

    ! Write out list.
    WRITE (*,110)
    110 FORMAT ('0','The values are:')
    out: DO j = 1, nvals
       IF ( j == ilarge ) THEN
          WRITE (*,'(1X,I6,2X,A)') input(j), 'LARGEST'
       ELSE IF ( j == ismall ) THEN
          WRITE (*,'(1X,I6,2X,A)') input(j), 'SMALLEST'
       ELSE
          WRITE (*,'(1X,I6)') input(j)
       END IF
    END DO out
ELSE size

    ! nvals > max_size. Tell user and quit.
    WRITE (*,120) nvals, max_size
    120 FORMAT (1X,'Too many input values: ', I6, '>', I6)
END IF size

END PROGRAM
```

5. Test the program.

To test this program, we will use two data sets, one with 6 values and one with 12 values. Running this program with six values yields the following result:

```
C>extremes
Enter number of values in data set:
6
Enter value 1:
-6
Enter value 2:
5
Enter value 3:
-11
```

(continued)

(concluded)
```
                    Enter value 4:
                    16
                    Enter value 5:
                    9
                    Enter value 6:
                    0

                    The values are:
                       -6
                        5
                      -11     SMALLEST
                       16     LARGEST
                        9
                        0
```

The program correctly labeled the largest and smallest values in the data set. Running this program with 12 values yields the following result:

```
            C>extremes
            Enter number of values in data set:
            12
            Too many input values: 12 > 10
```

The program recognized that there were too many input values, and it quit. Thus the program gives the correct answers for both test data sets.

This program used the named constant `max_size` to declare the size of the array and also in all comparisons related to the array. As a result, we could change this program to process up to 1000 values by simply changing the value of `max_size` from 10 to 1000.

■ 5.3
USING WHOLE ARRAYS AND ARRAY SUBSETS IN Fortran STATEMENTS

When whole arrays and subsets of arrays are used in Fortran statements, the operations are performed on all of the specified array elements simultaneously. This section teaches you how to use whole arrays and subsets of arrays in Fortran statements.

5.3.1 Whole Array Operations

Under certain circumstances, you can use **whole arrays** in arithmetic calculations as though they were ordinary variables. If two arrays are the same shape, you can use them in ordinary arithmetic operations and the operation will be applied on an element-by-element basis. Consider the program in Figure 5–6. Here, arrays a, b, c, and d are all four elements long. Each element in array c is calculated as the sum of the corresponding elements in arrays a and b, using a DO loop. Array d is calculated as the sum of arrays a and b in a single assignment statement (see Figure 5–7).

FIGURE 5–6

A program illustrating both element-by-element addition and whole array addition.

```
PROGRAM add_arrays

IMPLICIT NONE

INTEGER :: i
REAL, DIMENSION(4) :: a = (/ 1., 2., 3., 4./)
REAL, DIMENSION(4) :: b = (/ 5., 6., 7., 8./)
REAL, DIMENSION(4) :: c, d

! Element by element addition
DO i = 1, 4
   c(i) = a(i) + b(i)
END DO

! Whole array addition
d = a + b

! Write out results
WRITE (*,100) 'c', c
WRITE (*,100) 'd', d
100 FORMAT (' ',A,' = ',5(F6.1,1X))

END PROGRAM
```

FIGURE 5–7

When an operation is applied to two arrays of the same shape, the operation is performed on the arrays on an element-by-element basis.

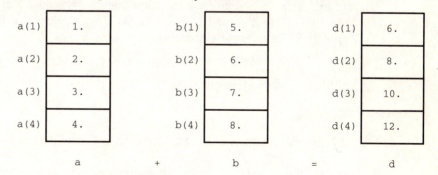

When this program is executed, the results are exactly the same for both calculations:

```
C>add_arrays
c =      6.0 8.0 10.0 12.0
d =      6.0 8.0 10.0 12.0
```

Under what circumstances can two arrays be used as operands in an assignment statement? They can be used if they have the same shape, which means that they have the *same number of dimensions* (the same rank) and *the same number of elements in each dimension* (the same extent). Two arrays of the same shape are said to be **conformable.**

Note that although the two arrays must be the same shape, they do *not* have to have the same subscript range in each dimension. The following arrays can be added freely even though the subscript ranges used to address their elements are different.

```
REAL, DIMENSION(1:4) :: a = (/ 1., 2., 3., 4./)
REAL, DIMENSION(5:8) :: b = (/ 5., 6., 7., 8./)
REAL, DIMENSION(101:104) :: c
c = a + b
```

If two arrays are not conformable, then any attempt to perform arithmetic operations with them will produce a compile-time error.

All Fortran 90/95 intrinsic operations work with conformable arrays: addition, subtraction, multiplication, division, and exponentiation. In each case the operation is performed on an element-by-element basis.

Scalar constants and variables are also conformable with arrays. In that case, the scalar value is applied equally to every element of the array. For example, after the following piece of code is executed, array c will contain the values [10., 20., 30., 40.].

```
REAL, DIMENSION(4) :: a = (/ 1., 2., 3., 4./)
REAL :: b = 10
REAL, DIMENSION(4) :: c
c = a * b
```

Many of the Fortran 90/95 intrinsic functions that are used with scalar values will also accept arrays as input arguments and return arrays as results. The returned arrays will contain the result of applying the function to the input array on an element-by-element basis. These functions are called **elemental intrinsic functions**, since they operate on arrays on a element-by-element basis. Most common functions are elemental, including ABS, SIN, COS, EXP, and LOG. A complete list of elemental functions appears in Appendix B. For example, consider an array a defined as

```
REAL, DIMENSION(4) :: a = (/ -1., 2., -3., 4./)
```

The function ABS(a) would return [1., 2., 3., 4.].

5.3.2 Selecting Subsets of Arrays for Use in Calculations

You have already seen how to use either array elements or entire arrays in arithmetic operations and assignment statements. You can also use subsets of arrays in calculations. A subset of an array is called an **array section.** It is specified by replacing an array subscript with a **subscript triplet** or **vector subscript.**

A subscript triplet has the general form

```
subscript_1 : subscript_2 : stride
```

where *subscript_1* is the first subscript to be included in the array subset, *subscript_2* is the last subscript to be included in the array subset, and *stride* is the subscript increment through the data set. A subscript triplet works much like an implied DO loop. The triplet specifies the ordered set of all array subscripts starting with *subscript_1* and ending with *subscript_2*, advancing at a rate of *stride* between values. For example, let's define an array `array` as

```
INTEGER, DIMENSION(10) :: array = (/1,2,3,4,5,6,7,8,9,10/)
```

Then the array subset `array(1:10:2)` would be an array containing only elements `array(1)`, `array(3)`, `array(5)`, `array(7)`, and `array(9)`.

Array triplets may be written in the following alternative forms, in which some of the components of the triplet are defaulted. If *subscript_1* is missing from the triplet, it defaults to the first subscript in the array. If *subscript_2* is missing from the triplet, it defaults to the last subscript in the array. If *stride* is missing from the triplet, it defaults to 1.

```
subscript_1 : subscript_2 : stride
subscript_1 : subscript_2
subscript_1 :
subscript_1 : : stride
: subscript_2
: subscript_2 : stride
: : stride
:
```

EXAMPLE 5–5 Specifying Array Sections with Subscript Triplets: Assume the following type declarations statements:

```
INTEGER :: i = 3, j = 7
REAL, DIMENSION(10) :: a = (/1.,-2.,3.,-4.,5.,-6.,7.,-8.,9.,-10./)
```

Determine the number of elements in and the contents of the array sections specified by each of the following subscript triplets:

a. `a(:)`
b. `a(i:j)`
c. `a(i:j:i)`
d. `a(i:j:j)`
e. `a(i:)`
f. `a(:j)`
g. `a(::i)`

SOLUTION

a. `a(:)` is identical to the original array: [1.,-2.,3.,-4.,5.,-6.,7.,-8.,9.,-10.].
b. `a(i:j)` is the array subset starting at element 3 and ending at element 7, with a default stride of 1: [3.,-4.,5.,-6.,7.].
c. `a(i:j:i)` is the array subset starting at element 3 and ending at element 7, with a stride of 3: [3.,-6.].
d. `a(i:j:j)` is the array subset starting at element 3 and ending at element 7, with a stride of 7: [3.].

e. `a(i:)` is the array subset starting at element 3 and by default ending at element 10 (the end of the array), with a default stride of 1: [3.,-4.,5.,-6.,7.,-8.,9.,-10.].

f. `a(:j)` is the array subset starting by default at element 1 and ending at element 7, with a default stride of 1: [1.,-2.,3.,-4.,5.,-6.,7.] .

g. `a(::i)` is the array subset starting by default at element 1 and ending by default at element 10, with a stride of 3: [1.,-4.,7.,-10.].

Subscript triplets select ordered subsets of array elements for use in calculations. In contrast, vector subscripts allow arbitrary combinations of array elements to be selected for use in an operation. A *vector subscript* is a one-dimensional integer array specifying the array elements to be used in a calculation. The array elements may be specified in any order, and array elements may be specified more than once. The resulting array will contain one element for each subscript specified in the vector. For example, consider the following type declaration statements:

```
INTEGER, DIMENSION(5) :: vec = (/1, 6, 4, 1, 9 /)
REAL, DIMENSION(10) :: a = (/1.,-2.,3.,-4.,5.,-6.,7.,-8.,9.,-10./)
```

With these definitions, `a(vec)` would be the array [1., -6., -4., 1., 9.].

If a vector subscript includes any array element more than once, then the resulting array section is called a **many-one array section.** Such an array section cannot be used on the left side of an assignment statement, because it would specify that two or more different values should be assigned to the same array element at the same time! For example, consider the following Fortran statements:

```
INTEGER, DIMENSION(5) :: vec = (/1, 2, 1 /)
REAL, DIMENSION(10) :: a = (/10.,20.,30./)
REAL, DIMENSION(2) :: b
b(vec) = a
```

The assignment statement attempts to assign both the value 10. and the value 30. to array element `b(1)`, which is impossible.

■ 5.4
INPUT AND OUTPUT

It is possible to perform I/O operations on either individual array elements or entire arrays. This section describes both types of I/O operations.

5.4.1 Input and Output of Array Elements

An *array element* is a variable just like any other variable and may be used anywhere an ordinary variable of the same type may be used. Therefore, READ and WRITE statements containing array elements are just like READ and WRITE statements for any other variables.

To write out specific elements from an array, just name them in the argument list of the `WRITE` statement. For example, the following code writes out the first five elements of the real array a.

```
WRITE (*,100) a(1), a(2), a(3), a(4), a(5)
100 FORMAT (1X,'a = ', 5F10.2 )
```

5.4.2 The DO Loop

The implied DO loop is also permitted in I/O statements. It permits an argument list to be written many times as a function of an index variable. Every argument in the argument list is written once for each value of the index variable in the implied DO loop. With an implied DO loop, the above statement becomes:

```
WRITE (*,100) ( a(i), i = 1, 5 )
100 FORMAT (1X,'a = ', 5F10.2 )
```

The argument list in this case contains only one item: a(i). This list is repeated once for each value of the index variable i. Since i takes on the values from 1 to 5, the array elements a(1), a(2), a(3), a(4), and a(5) will be written.

The general form of a `WRITE` or `READ` statement with an implied DO loop is

```
WRITE (unit,format) (arg1, arg2, ... , index= istart, iend, incr)
READ  (unit,format) (arg1, arg2, ... , index= istart, iend, incr)
```

where *arg1, arg2,* and so on, are the values to be written or read. Each argument in an output list may be a constant, a variable, an expression, or an array element; each argument in an input list must be a variable. The variable *index* is the DO loop index, and *istart, iend,* and *incr* are respectively the starting value, ending value, and increment of the loop index variable. The index and all the loop control parameters should be of type `INTEGER`.

For a `WRITE` statement containing an implied DO loop, each argument in the argument list is written out once each time the loop is executed. Therefore, a statement like

```
WRITE (*,1000) (i, 2*i, 3*i, i=1, 3)
1000 FORMAT (1X,9I6)
```

will write out nine values on a single line:

$$1\ 2\ 3\ 2\ 4\ 6\ 3\ 6\ 9$$

Now let's look at a slightly more complicated example of using arrays with an implied DO loop. Figure 5–8 shows a program that calculates the square root and cube root of a set of numbers and then prints out a table of square and cube roots. The program computes square roots and cube roots for all numbers between 1 and max_size, where max_size is a named constant. What will the output of this program look like?

FIGURE 5–8

A program that computes the square and cube roots of a set of number and then writes them out using an implied DO loop.

```
PROGRAM square_and_cube_roots
!
! Purpose:
!   To calculate a table of numbers, square roots, and cube roots
!   using an implied DO loop to output the table.
!
! Record of revisions:
!     Date        Programmer          Description of change
!     ====        ==========          =====================
!   08/22/95    S. J. Chapman         Original code
!
IMPLICIT NONE

! List of parameters:
INTEGER, PARAMETER :: max_size = 10

! List of variables:
INTEGER :: j                           ! Loop index
REAL, DIMENSION(max_size) :: value      ! Array of numbers
REAL, DIMENSION(max_size) :: square_root ! Array of square roots
REAL, DIMENSION(max_size) :: cube_root   ! Array of cube roots

! Calculate the square roots & cube roots of the numbers.
DO j = 1, max_size
   value(j) = real(j)
   square_root(j) = sqrt(value(j))
   cube_root(j) = value(j)**(1./3.)
END DO

! Write out each number, its square root, and its cube root.
WRITE (*,100)
100 FORMAT ('0',20X,'Table of Square and Cube Roots',/, &
            4X,' Number Square Root Cube Root', &
            3X,' Number Square Root Cube Root',/, &
            4X,' ==== ======== =======', &
            3X,' ==== ======== =======')
WRITE (*,110) (value(j), square_root(j), cube_root(j), j = 1, max_size)
110 FORMAT (2(4X,F6.0,9X,F6.4,6X,F6.4))

END PROGRAM
```

The implied DO loop in this example will be executed 10 times, with j taking on every value between 1 and 10. (The loop increment is defaulted to 1 here.) During each iteration of the loop, the entire argument list will be written out. Therefore, this WRITE statement will write out 30 values, six per line. The resulting output is

```
                 Table of Square and Cube Roots
    Number   Square Root   Cube Root   Number   Square Root   Cube Root
    ====     ========      ======      ====     ========      ======
     1.       1.0000        1.0000       2.       1.4142        1.2599
     3.       1.7321        1.4422       4.       2.0000        1.5874
     5.       2.2361        1.7100       6.       2.4495        1.8171
     7.       2.6458        1.9129       8.       2.8284        2.0000
     9.       3.0000        2.0801      10.       3.1623        2.1544
```

Like ordinary DO loops, implied DO loops may be *nested*. If they are nested, the inner loop will execute completely for each step in the outer loop. As a simple example, consider the following statements

```
WRITE (*,100) ((i, j, j = 1, 3), i = 1, 2)
100 FORMAT (1X,I5,1X,I5)
```

This WRITE statement contains two implicit DO loops. The index variable of the inner loop is j, and the index variable of the outer loop is i. When the WRITE statement is executed, variable j will take on values 1, 2, and 3 while i is 1, and then it will take on 1, 2, and 3 while i is 2. The output from this statement will be

```
1 1
1 2
1 3
2 1
2 2
2 3
```

Nested implied DO loops are important when working with arrays having two or more dimensions, as you will see later in the chapter.

5.4.3 Input and Output of Whole Arrays and Array Sections

In addition to array elements, entire arrays or array sections may be read or written with READ and WRITE statements. If an array name is mentioned without subscripts in a Fortran I/O statement, then the compiler assumes that every element in the array is to be read in or written out. If an array section is mentioned in a Fortran I/O statement, then the compiler assumes that the entire section is to be read or written. Figure 5–9 shows a simple example of using an array and two array sections in I/O statements.

FIGURE 5–9
Program illustrating array I/O.

```
PROGRAM array_io
!
! Purpose:
!   To illustrate array I/O.
!
! Record of revisions:
!     Date        Programmer              Description of change
!     ====        ==========              =====================
!   10/10/95    S. J. Chapman           Original code
!
!  List of variables:
!     a       -- Name of a 5-element real array
!
IMPLICIT NONE
```

(continued)

(concluded)
```
! List of variables
REAL, DIMENSION(5) :: a = (/1.,2.,3.,20.,10./) ! 5-element test array
INTEGER, DIMENSION(4) :: vec = (/4,3,4,5/)      ! vector subscript

! Output entire array.
WRITE (*,100) a
100 FORMAT ( 2X, 5F8.3 )

! Output array section selected by a triple.
WRITE (*,100) a(2::2)

! Output array section selected by a vector subscript.
WRITE (*,100) a(vec)

END PROGRAM
```

The output from this program is

```
 1.000    2.000    3.000   20.000   10.000
 2.000   20.000
20.000    3.000   20.000  10.000
```

Quiz 5–1

This quiz provides a quick check to see if you understand the concepts introduced in sections 5.1 through 5.4. If you have trouble with the quiz, reread the sections, ask your instructor, or discuss the material with a fellow student. The answers to this quiz appear in Appendix F.

For questions 1 to 3, determine the length of the array specified by each of the following declaration statements and the valid subscript range for each array:

1. `INTEGER :: itemp(15)`
2. `LOGICAL :: test(0:255)`
3. `INTEGER, PARAMETER :: i1 = -20`
   `INTEGER, PARAMETER :: i2 = -1`
   `REAL, DIMENSION(i1:i1*i2) :: a`

Determine which of the following Fortran statements are valid. For each valid statement, specify what will happen in the program. Assume default typing for any variable not explicitly typed.

4. `REAL:: phase(0:11) = (/ 0., 1., 2., 3., 3., 3., &`
   `                        3., 3., 3., 2., 1., 0. /)`
5. `REAL, DIMENSION(10) :: phase = 0.`
6. `INTEGER :: data1(256)`
   `data1 = 0`
   `data1(10:256:10) = 1000`
   `WRITE (*,100) data1`
   `100 FORMAT (1X,10I8)`

(continued)

(concluded)

```
 7. REAL, DIMENSION(21:31) :: array1 = 10.
    REAL, DIMENSION(10) :: array2 = 3.
    WRITE (*,'(1X,10I8)') array1 + array2
 8. INTEGER :: i, j
    INTEGER, DIMENSION(10) :: sub1
    INTEGER, DIMENSION(0:9) :: sub2
    INTEGER, DIMENSION(100) :: in = &
          (/((0,i=1,9),j*10,j=1,10)/)
    sub1 = in(10:100:10)
    sub2 = sub1 / 10
    WRITE (*,100) sub1 * sub2
    100 FORMAT (1X,10I8)
 9. REAL, DIMENSION(-3:0) :: error
    error(-3) = 0.00012
    error(-2) = 0.0152
    error(-1) = 0.0
    WRITE (*,500) error
    500 FORMAT (T6,error = ,/,(3X,I6))
10. INTEGER, PARAMETER :: max = 10
    INTEGER :: I
    INTEGER, DIMENSION(max) :: ivec1 = (/(i,i=1,10)/)
    INTEGER, DIMENSION(max) :: ivec2 = (/(i,i=10,1,-1)/)
    REAL, DIMENSION(max) :: data1
    data1 = real(ivec1)**2
    WRITE (*,500) data1(ivec2)
    500 FORMAT (1X,'Output = ',/,5(3X,F7.1))
11. INTEGER, PARAMETER :: npoint = 10
    REAL, DIMENSION(npoint) :: mydata
    DO i = 1, npoint
       READ (*,*) mydata
    END DO
```

■ **5.5**

EXAMPLES

The following two examples illustrate the use of arrays.

EXAMPLE 5–3 Sorting Data: Many scientific and engineering applications, require you to sort a random input data set so that the numbers in the data set are either all in *ascending order* (lowest to highest) or all in *descending order* (highest to lowest). For example, suppose that you are a zoologist studying a large population of animals and that you want to identify the largest 5 percent of the animals in the population. The most straightforward way to approach this problem is to sort the sizes of all the animals in the population into ascending order and take the top 5 percent of the values.

Sorting data into ascending or descending order seems to be an easy job. We do it all the time. It is simple matter for us to sort the data (10, 3, 6, 4, 9) into the order

(3, 4, 6, 9, 10). How do we do it? We first scan the input data list (10, 3, 6, 4, 9) to find the smallest value in the list (3); then we scan the remaining input data (10, 6, 4, 9) to find the next smallest value (4) and so on until the complete list is sorted.

In fact, sorting can be a very difficult job. As the number of values to be sorted increases, the time required to perform the simple sort described above increases rapidly, since we must scan the input data set once for each value sorted. For very large data sets, this technique just takes too long to be practical. Even worse, how would we sort the data if there were too many numbers to fit into the main memory of the computer? The development of efficient sorting techniques for large data sets is an active area of research, and is the subject of whole courses all by itself.

We will confine this example to the simplest possible algorithm to illustrate the concept of sorting. This simplest algorithm is called the **selection sort.** It is just a computer implementation of the mental math described above. Here is basic algorithm for the selection sort:

1. Scan the list of numbers to be sorted to locate the smallest value in the list. Place that value at the front of the list by swapping it with the value currently at the front of the list. If the value at the front of the list is already the smallest value, then do nothing.
2. Scan the list of numbers from position 2 to the end to locate the next smallest value in the list. Place that value in position 2 of the list by swapping it with the value currently at that position. If the value in position 2 is already the next smallest value, then do nothing.
3. Scan the list of numbers from position 3 to the end to locate the third smallest value in the list. Place that value in position 3 of the list by swapping it with the value currently at that position. If the value in position 3 is already the third smallest value, then do nothing.
4. Repeat this process until the next-to-last position in the list is reached. After the next-to-last position in the list has been processed, the sort is complete.

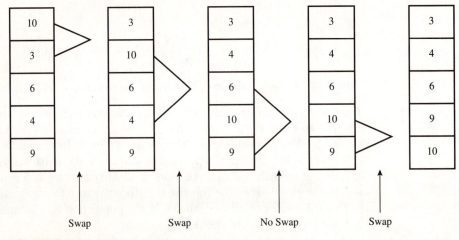

FIGURE 5–10
A problem demonstrating the selection sort algorithm.

Note that if we are sorting N values, this sorting algorithm requires N−1 scans through the data to accomplish the sort.

This process is illustrated in Figure 5–10. Since there are five values in the data set to be sorted, we will make four scans through the data. During the first pass through the entire data set, the minimum value is 3, so the 3 is swapped with the 10, which was in position 1. Pass 2 searches for the minimum value in positions 2 through 5. That minimum is 4, so the 4 is swapped with the 10 in position 2. Pass 3 searches for the minimum value in positions 3 through 5. That minimum is 6, which is already in position 3, so no swapping is required. Finally, pass 4 searches for the minimum value in positions 4 through 5. That minimum is 9, so the 9 is swapped with the 10 in position 4, and the sort is completed.

Programming Pitfalls

The selection sort algorithm is the easiest sorting algorithm to understand, but it is computationally inefficient. You should never use the selection sort to sort really large data sets (say, sets with more than 1000 elements). More efficient algorithms (such as the heapsort or the quicksort) should be used instead.

We will now develop a program to read in a data set from a file, sort it into ascending order, and display the sorted data set.

SOLUTION

This program must be able to ask the user for the name of the file to be sorted, open that file, read the input data, sort the data, and write out the sorted data. The design process for this problem follows.

1. **State the problem.**

We have not yet specified the type of data to be sorted. If the data is real, then the problem may be stated as follows:

Develop a program to read an arbitrary number of real input data values from a user-supplied file, sort the data into ascending order, and write the sorted data to the standard output device.

2. **Define the inputs and outputs.**

This program has two types of inputs:

a. A character string containing the file name of the input data file. This string will come from the standard input device.
b. The real data values in the file.

The outputs from this program are the sorted real data values written to the standard output device.

3. **Describe the algorithm.**

This program can be broken down into five major steps:

```
Get the input file name
Open the input file
Read the input data into an array
Sort the data in ascending order
Write the sorted data
```

The first three major steps of the program are to get the name of the input file, to open the file, and to read in the data. We must prompt the user for the input file name, read in the name, and open the file. If the file open is successful, we must read in the data, keeping track of the number of values that have been read. Since we don't know how many data values to expect, a while loop is appropriate for the READ. A flowchart for these steps is shown in Figure 5–11, and the detailed pseudocode follows the figure.

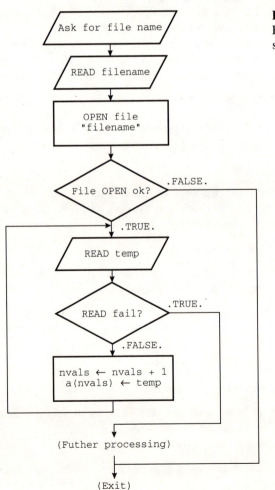

FIGURE 5–11
Flowchart for reading values to sort from an input file.

```
Prompt user for the input file name "filename"
Read the file name "filename"
OPEN file "filename"
IF OPEN is successful THEN
    WHILE
        Read value into temp
        IF read not successful EXIT
        nvals ← nvals + 1
        a(nvals) ← temp
    End of WHILE
    ...
    ...                             (Insert sorting step here)
    ...                             (Insert writing step here)
End of IF
```

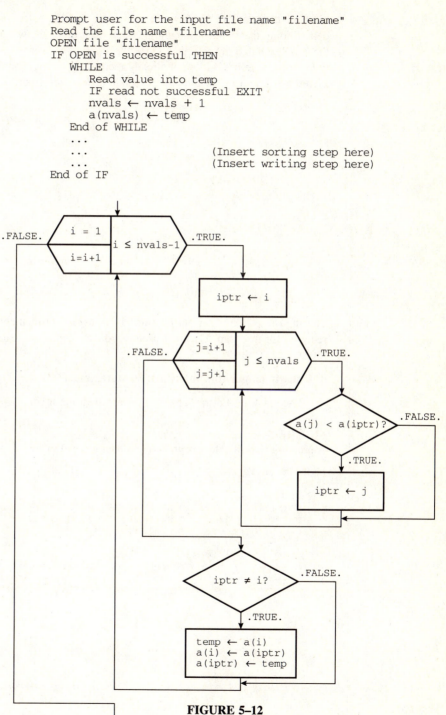

FIGURE 5–12

Flowchart for sorting values with a selection sort.

Next we have to sort the data. We will need to make `nvals-1` passes through the data, finding the smallest remaining value each time. We will use a pointer to locate the smallest value in each pass. Once the smallest value is found, it will be swapped to the top of the list if it is not already there. A flowchart for these steps is shown in Figure 5–12, and the detailed pseudocode follows the figure.

```
DO for i = 1 to nvals-1
    ! Find the minimum value in a(i) through a(nvals)
    iptr ← i
    DO for j = i + 1 to nvals
        IF a(j) < a(iptr) THEN
            iptr ← j
        END of IF
    END of DO

    ! iptr now points to the min value, so swap a(iptr) with
    ! a(i) if iptr /= i.
    IF i /= iptr THEN
        temp ← a(i)
        a(i) ← a(iptr)
        a(iptr) ← temp
    END of IF
END of DO
```

The final step is writing out the sorted values. No refinement of the pseudocode is required for that step. The final pseudocode combines the reading, sorting, and writing steps.

4. **Turn the algorithm into Fortran statements.**

The resulting Fortran program is shown in Figure 5–13.

FIGURE 5–13
A program to read values from an input data file and to sort them into ascending order.

```
PROGRAM sort1
!
! Purpose:
!   To read in a real input data set, sort it into ascending order
!   using the selection sort algorithm, and write the sorted
!   data to the standard output device.
!
! Record of revisions:
!    Date          Programmer          Description of change
!    ====          ==========          =================
!  09/20/95      S. J. Chapman         Original code
!
IMPLICIT NONE

! List of parameters:
INTEGER, PARAMETER :: max_size = 10

! List of variables:
REAL, DIMENSION(max_size) :: a ! Data array to sort
```

(continued)

(continued)

```
CHARACTER(len=20) :: filename   ! Input data file name
INTEGER :: i                    ! Loop index
INTEGER :: iptr                 ! Pointer to smallest value
INTEGER :: j                    ! Loop index
INTEGER :: nvals = 0            ! Number of data values to sort
INTEGER :: status               ! I/O status: 0 for success
REAL :: temp                    ! Temporary variable for swapping

! Get the name of the file containing the input data.
WRITE (*,1000)
1000 FORMAT (1X,'Enter the file name with the data to be sorted: ')
READ (*,'(A20)') filename

! Open input data file. Status is OLD because the input data must
! already exist.
OPEN ( UNIT=9, FILE=filename, STATUS='OLD', ACTION='READ', &
       IOSTAT=status )

! Was the OPEN successful?
fileopen: IF ( status == 0 ) THEN      ! Open successful

   ! The file was opened successfully, so read the data to sort
   ! from it, sort the data, and write out the results.

   ! First read in data.
   DO
      READ (9, *, IOSTAT=status) temp ! Get value
      IF ( status /= 0 ) EXIT         ! Exit on end of data
      nvals = nvals + 1               ! Bump count
      a(nvals) = temp                 ! Save value in array
   END DO

   ! Now, sort the data.
   outer: DO i = 1, nvals-1

      ! Find the minimum value in a(i) through a(nvals)
      iptr = i
      inner: DO j = i+1, nvals
         minval: IF ( a(j) < a(iptr) ) THEN
            iptr = j
         END IF minval
      END DO inner

      ! iptr now points to the minimum value, so swap a(iptr) with a(i)
      ! if i /= iptr.
      swap: IF ( i /= iptr ) THEN
         temp     = a(i)
         a(i)     = a(iptr)
         a(iptr)  = temp
      END IF swap

   END DO outer

   ! Now write out the sorted data.
   WRITE (*,'(A)') ' The sorted output data values are: '
   WRITE (*,1040) ( a(i), i = 1, nvals )
   1040 FORMAT (4X,F10.4)
```

```
(concluded)
ELSE fileopen

    ! Else file open failed. Tell user.
    WRITE (*,1050) status
    1050 FORMAT (1X,'File open failed--status = ', I6)

END IF fileopen

END PROGRAM
```

5. Test the program.

To test this program, we will create an input data file and run the program with it. The data set will contain a mixture of positive and negative numbers as well as at least one duplicated value to see if the program works properly under those conditions. The following data set will be placed in file INPUT2:

```
                    13.3
                    12.
                    -3.0
                     0.
                     4.0
                     6.6
                     4.
                    -6.
```

Running this file through the program yields the following result:

```
C>sort1
Enter the file name containing the data to be sorted:
input2
The sorted output data values are:
        -6.0000
        -3.0000
          .0000
         4.0000
         4.0000
         6.6000
        12.0000
        13.3000
```

The program gives the correct answers for our test data set. Note that it works for both positive and negative numbers as well as for repeated numbers.

To be certain that our program works properly, we must test it for every possible type of input data. This program worked properly for the test input data set, but will it work for *all* input data sets? Study the code now and see if you can spot any flaws before continuing to the next paragraph.

The program has a major flaw that must be corrected. If the input data file has more than 10 values, this program will attempt to store input data in memory locations a(11), a(12), and so on, which have not been allocated in the program. (This result is an out-of-bounds or **array overflow** condition.) If bounds checking is turned on, the program will abort when we try to write to a(11). If bounds checking is not turned on, the results are unpredictable and vary from computer to computer. We must rewrite this program to prevent it from attempting to write into locations beyond the end of the allocated array. One approach is to check whether the number of values exceeds max_size before storing each number into array a. The corrected flowchart for reading in the data is shown in Figure 5–14, and the corrected program is shown in Figure 5–15.

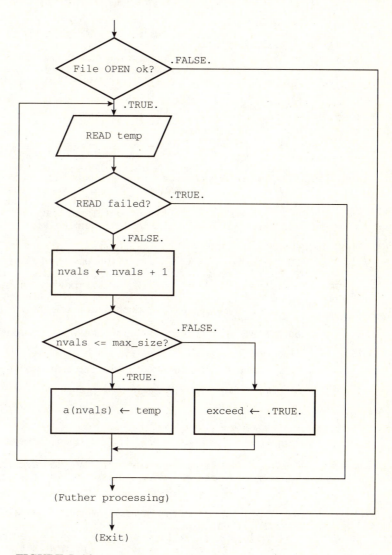

FIGURE 5–14
Corrected flowchart for reading the values to sort from an input file without causing an array overflow.

FIGURE 5-15
The corrected sort program detects array overflows.

```
PROGRAM sort2
!
! Purpose:
!   To read in a real input data set, sort it into ascending order
!   using the selection sort algorithm, and write the sorted
!   data to the standard output device.
!
! Record of revisions:
!    Date        Programmer        Description of change
!    ====        ==========        =================
!   09/20/95   S. J. Chapman     Original code
! 1 09/23/95   S. J. Chapman     Modified to protect against array
!                                  overflow.
!
IMPLICIT NONE

! List of parameters:
INTEGER, PARAMETER :: max_size = 10

! List of variables:
REAL, DIMENSION(max_size) :: a  ! Data array to sort
LOGICAL :: exceed = .FALSE.     ! Logical indicating that array
                                ! limits are exceeded.
CHARACTER(len = 20) :: filename ! Input data file name
INTEGER :: i                    ! Loop index
INTEGER :: iptr                 ! Pointer to smallest value
INTEGER :: j                    ! Loop index
INTEGER :: nvals = 0            ! Number of data values to sort
INTEGER :: status               ! I/O status: 0 for success
REAL :: temp                    ! Temporary variable for swapping

! Get the name of the file containing the input data.
WRITE (*,1000)
1000 FORMAT (1X,'Enter the file name with the data to be sorted: ')
READ (*,'(A20)') filename

! Open input data file. Status is OLD because the input data must
! already exist.
OPEN ( UNIT=9, FILE=filename, STATUS='OLD', ACTION='READ', &
       IOSTAT=status )

! Was the OPEN successful?
fileopen: IF ( status == 0 ) THEN ! Open successful

   ! The file was opened successfully, so read the data to sort
   ! from it, sort the data, and write out the results.
   ! First read in data.
   DO
      READ (9, *, IOSTAT=status) temp       ! Get value
      IF ( status /= 0 ) EXIT               ! Exit on end of data
      nvals = nvals + 1                     ! Bump count
      size: IF ( nvals <= max_size ) THEN   ! Too many values?
         a(nvals) = temp                    ! No: Save value in
                                            !   array

      ELSE
```

(continued)

(concluded)

```
         exceed = .TRUE. ! Yes: Array overflow
         END IF size

      END DO

      ! Was the array size exceeded? If so, tell user and quit.
      toobig: IF ( exceed ) THEN
         WRITE (*,1020) nvals, max_size
         1020 FORMAT (' Maximum array size exceeded: ', I6, '>', I6 )
      ELSE toobig

         ! Limit not exceeded: sort the data.
         outer: DO i = 1, nvals-1

            ! Find the minimum value in a(i) through a(nvals)
            iptr = i
            inner: DO j = i+1, nvals
               minval: IF ( a(j) < a(iptr) ) THEN
                  iptr = j
               END IF minval
            END DO inner

            ! iptr now points to the minimum value, so swap a(iptr) with
            ! a(i) if i /= iptr.
            swap: IF ( i /= iptr ) THEN
               temp = a(i)
               a(i) = a(iptr)
               a(iptr) = temp
            END IF swap

         END DO outer

         ! Now write out the sorted data.
         WRITE (*,'(A)a') ' The sorted output data values are: '
         WRITE (*,1040) ( a(i), i = 1, nvals )
         1040 FORMAT (4X,F10.4)

      END IF toobig

   ELSE fileopen

      ! Else file open failed. Tell user.
      WRITE (*,1050) status
      1050 FORMAT (1X,'File open failed—status = ', I6)

   END IF fileopen

END PROGRAM
```

In the test for array overflow conditions, we have used a logical variable exceed. If the next value to be read into the array would result in an array overflow, then exceed is set to true and the value is not stored. When all values have been read from the input file, the program checks to see if the array size would have been exceeded. If so, it writes out an error message and quits. If not, it sorts the numbers.

This program also illustrates the proper use of named constants to allow the size of a program to be changed easily. The size of array a is set by parameter max_size, and the test for array overflow within the code also uses parameter `max_size`. The maximum sorting capacity of this program could be changed from 10 to 1000 by simply modifying the definition of the named constant `max_size` at the top of the program.

EXAMPLE 5–4 *The Median:* In Chapter 3 we examined two common statistical measures of data: averages (or means) and standard deviations. Another common statistical measure of data is the median. The median of a data set is the value such that half of the numbers in the data set are larger than the value and half of the numbers in the data set are smaller than the value. If the data set contains an even number of values, then it cannot have a value exactly in the middle. In that case the median is usually defined as the average of the two elements in the middle. The median value of a data set is often close to the average value of the data set, but not always. For example, consider the following data set:

```
  1
  2
  3
  4
100
```

The average or mean of this data set is 22, while the median of this data set is 3!

An easy way to compute the median of a data set is to sort it into ascending order and then to select the value in the middle of the data set as the median. If the data set has an even number of values, then average the two middle values to get the median.

Write a program to calculate the mean, median, and standard deviation of an input data set that is read from a user-specified file.

SOLUTION

This program must be able to read in an arbitrary number of measurements from a file and then calculate the mean, median, and standard deviation of those measurements.

1. **State the problem.**

Read in a set of measurements from a user-specified input file; calculate the mean, median, and standard deviation; and write out those values on the standard output device.

2. **Define the inputs and outputs.**

This program has two types of inputs:

a. A character string containing the file name of the input data file. This string will come from the standard input device.
b. The real data values in the file.

The outputs from this program are the average, median, and standard deviation of the input data set. They are written to the standard output device.

3. **Describe the algorithm.**

This program can be broken down into six major steps:

```
Get the input file name
Open the input file
Read the input data into an array
Sort the data in ascending order
Calculate the average, mean, and standard deviation
Write average, median, and standard deviation
```

The detailed pseudocode for the first four steps is similar to that of the previous example:

```
Initialize variables
Prompt user for the input file name "filename"
Read the file name "filename"
OPEN file "filename"
IF OPEN is successful THEN
    WHILE
        Read value into temp
        IF read not successful EXIT
        nvals ← nvals + 1
        IF nvals  <=  max_size then
           a(nvals) ← temp
        ELSE
           exceed ← .TRUE.
        End of IF
    End of WHILE

    ! Notify user if array size exceeded
    IF array size exceeded then
        Write out message to user
    ELSE
       ! Sort the data
       DO for i = 1 to nvals-1
       ! Find the minimum value in a(i) through a(nvals)
       iptr ← i
       DO for j = i+1 to nvals
          IF a(j) < a(iptr) THEN
             iptr ← j
          END of IF
       END of DO (for j = i+1 to nvals)

       ! iptr now points to the min value, so swap A(iptr)
       ! with a(i) if iptr /= i.
       IF i /= iptr THEN
          temp ← a(i)
          a(i) ← a(iptr)
          a(iptr) ← temp
       END of IF
    END of DO (for i = 1 to nvals-1)

    (Add code here)

  End of IF (array size exceeded...)

End of IF (open successful...)
```

The fifth step is to calculate the required average, median, and standard deviation. Therefore, we must first accumulate some statistics on the data (Σx and Σx^2) and then apply the definitions of average, median, and standard deviation given previously. The pseudocode for this step follows.

```
DO for i = 1 to nvals
    sum_x ← sum_x + a(i)
    sum_x2 ← sum_x2 + a(i)**2
End of DO
IF nvals >= 2 THEN
    x_bar ← sum_x / REAL(nvals)
    std_dev ← sqrt((REAL(nvals)*sum_x2-
            sum_x**2)/(REAL(nvals)*REAL(nvals-1)))
    IF nvals is an even number THEN
        median ← (a(nvals/2) + a(nvals/2+1)) / 2.
    ELSE
        median ← a(nvals/2+1)
    END of IF
END of IF
```

We will decide if `nvals` is an even number by using the modulo function `mod(nvals,2)`. If `nvals` is even, this function will return a 0; if `nvals` is odd, it will return a 1. Finally, we must write out the results.

```
Write out average, median, standard deviation, and no. of points
```

4. **Turn the algorithm into Fortran statements.**

The resulting Fortran program is shown in Figure 5–16.

FIGURE 5–16
A program to read in values from an input data file, and to calculate their mean, median, and standard deviation.

```
PROGRAM stat_4
!
! Purpose:
!   To calculate mean, median, and standard deviation of an input
!   data set read from a file.
!
! Record of revisions:
!     Date        Programmer           Description of change
!     ====        ==========           =====================
!   09/26/95    S. J. Chapman          Original code
!
IMPLICIT NONE

! List of parameters:
INTEGER, PARAMETER :: max_size = 100

! List of variables:
REAL, DIMENSION(max_size) :: a ! Data array to sort
LOGICAL :: exceed = .FALSE.    ! Logical indicating that array
                               ! limits are exceeded.
```

(continued)

```
(continued)
CHARACTER(len=20) :: filename   ! Input data file name
INTEGER :: i                    ! Loop index
INTEGER :: iptr                 ! Pointer to smallest value
INTEGER :: j                    ! Loop index
REAL :: median                  ! The median of the input samples
INTEGER :: nvals = 0            ! Number of data values to sort
INTEGER :: status               ! I/O status: 0 for success
REAL :: std_dev                 ! Standard deviation of input samples
REAL :: sum_x = 0.              ! Sum of input values
REAL :: sum_x2 = 0.             ! Sum of input values squared
REAL :: temp                    ! Temporary variable for swapping
REAL :: x_bar                   ! Average of input values

! Get the name of the file containing the input data.
WRITE (*,1000)
1000 FORMAT (1X,'Enter the file name with the data to be sorted: ')
READ (*,1010) filename
1010 FORMAT ( A20 )

! Open input data file. Status is OLD because the input data must
! already exist.
OPEN ( UNIT=9, FILE=filename, STATUS='OLD', ACTION='READ', &
       IOSTAT=status )

! Was the OPEN successful?
fileopen: IF ( status == 0 ) THEN                ! Open successful

   ! The file was opened successfully, so read the data to sort
   ! from it, sort the data, and write out the results.
   ! First read in data.
   DO
      READ (9, *, IOSTAT=status) temp       ! Get value
      IF ( status /= 0 ) EXIT               ! Exit on end of data
      nvals = nvals + 1                      ! Bump count
      size: IF ( nvals <= max_size ) THEN   ! Too many values?
         a(nvals) = temp                     ! No: Save value in array
      ELSE
         exceed = .TRUE.                     ! Yes: Array overflow
      END IF size
END DO

! Was the array size exceeded? If so, tell user and quit.
toobig: IF ( exceed ) THEN
   WRITE (*,1020) nvals, max_size
   1020 FORMAT (' Maximum array size exceeded: ', I6, ' > ', I6 )
ELSE

   ! Limit not exceeded: sort the data.
   outer: DO i = 1, nvals-1

      ! Find the minimum value in a(i) through a(nvals)
      iptr = i
      inner: DO j = i+1, nvals
         minval: IF ( a(j) < a(iptr) ) THEN
            iptr = j
         END IF minval
```

(continued)

(concluded)

```
      END DO inner

      ! iptr now points to the minimum value, so swap A(iptr)
      ! with a(i) if i /= iptr.
      swap: IF ( i /= iptr ) THEN
            temp = a(i)
            a(i) = a(iptr)
         a(iptr) = temp
      END IF swap

   END DO outer

   ! The data is now sorted. Accumulate sums to calculate
   ! statistics.
   sums: DO i = 1, nvals
      sum_x = sum_x + a(i)
      sum_x2 = sum_x2 + a(i)**2
   END DO sums

   ! Check to see if we have enough input data.
   enough: IF ( nvals < 2 ) THEN

      ! Insufficient data.
      WRITE (*,*) ' At least 2 values must be entered.'

   ELSE

      ! Calculate the mean, median, and standard deviation
      x_bar   = sum_x / real(nvals)
      std_dev = sqrt( (real(nvals) * sum_x2 - sum_x**2) &
              / (real(nvals) * real(nvals-1)) )
      even: IF ( mod(nvals,2) == 0 ) THEN
         median = ( a(nvals/2) + a(nvals/2+1) ) / 2.
      ELSE
         median = a(nvals/2+1)
      END IF even

      ! Tell user.
      WRITE (*,*) 'The mean of this data set is:  ', x_bar
      WRITE (*,*) 'The median of this data set is:', median
      WRITE (*,*) 'The standard deviation is:     ', std_dev
      WRITE (*,*) 'The number of data points is: ', nvals

   END IF enough

END IF toobig

ELSE fileopen

   !Else file open failed. Tell user.
   WRITE (*,1050) status
   1050 FORMAT (1X,'File open failed—status = ', I6)

END IF fileopen

END PROGRAM
```

5. **Test the program.**

To test this program, we will calculate the answers by hand for a simple data set and then compare the answers to the results of the program. If we use the five input values 5, 3, 4, 1, and 9, then the mean and standard deviation would be

$$\bar{x} = \frac{1}{N}\sum_{i=1}^{N} x_i = \frac{1}{5} 22 = 4.4$$

$$s = \sqrt{\frac{N\sum_{i=1}^{N} x_i^2 - \left(\sum_{i=1}^{N} x_i\right)^2}{N(N-1)}} = 2.966$$

$$\text{median} = 4$$

If these values are placed in the file INPUT4 and the program is run with that file as an input, the results are

```
C>stat_4
Enter the file name containing the input data:
input4
 The mean of this data set is:    4.400000
 The median of this data set is:  4.000000
 The standard deviation is:       2.966479
 The number of data points is:    5
```

The program gives the correct answers for our test data set.

Note the use of names on loops and branches in the preceding program. Names help us to keep the loops and branches straight, which becomes more and more important as programs get larger. Even in this simple program, loops and branches are nested four deep at some points!

■ 5.6
TWO-DIMENSIONAL OR RANK-2 ARRAYS

The arrays that we have worked with so far in this chapter are *one-dimensional arrays* or **rank-1 arrays** (also known as vectors). These arrays can be visualized as a series of values laid out in a column, with a single subscript used to select the individual array elements (Figure 5–17a). Such arrays are useful to describe data that is a function of one independent variable, such as a series of temperature measurements made at fixed intervals of time.

Some types of data are functions of more than one independent variable. For example, we might wish to measure the temperature at five different locations at four different times. In this case our 20 measurements could logically be grouped into five different columns of four measurements each, with a separate column for each location (Figure

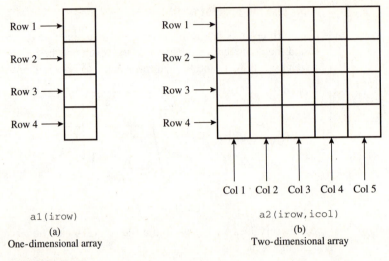

FIGURE 5–17
Representations of one- and two-dimensional arrays.

5–17*b*). Fortran has a mechanism especially designed to hold this sort of data—a *two-di-mensional* or **rank-2 array** (also called a **matrix**).

Rank-2 arrays are arrays whose elements are addressed with two subscripts, and any particular element in the array is selected by simultaneously choosing values for both of them. For example, Figure 5–18*a* shows a set of four generators whose power output has been measured at six different times. Figure 5–18*b* shows an array consisting of the six different power measurements for each of the four generators. In this example, each row specifies a measurement time, and each column specifies a generator number. The array element containing the power supplied by generator 3 at time 4 would be `power(4,3)`; its value is 41.1 MW.

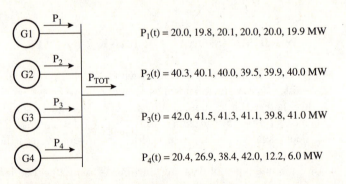

$P_1(t) = 20.0, 19.8, 20.1, 20.0, 20.0, 19.9$ MW

$P_2(t) = 40.3, 40.1, 40.0, 39.5, 39.9, 40.0$ MW

$P_3(t) = 42.0, 41.5, 41.3, 41.1, 39.8, 41.0$ MW

$P_4(t) = 20.4, 26.9, 38.4, 42.0, 12.2, 6.0$ MW

FIGURE 5–18
(*a*) A power generating station consisting of four different generators. The power output of each generator is measured at six different times.

	G1	G2	G3	G4
Time 1	20.0	40.3	42.0	20.4
Time 2	19.8	40.1	41.5	26.9
Time 3	20.1	40.0	41.3	38.4
Time 4	20.0	39.5	41.1	42.0
Time 5	20.0	39.9	39.8	12.2
Time 6	19.9	40.0	41.0	6.0

FIGURE 5–18
(*b*) Two-dimensional matrix of power measurements.

5.6.1 Declaring Rank-2 Arrays

The type and size of a rank-2 array must be declared to the compiler using a type declaration statement. Some sample array declarations follow.

1. `REAL, DIMENSION(3,6) :: sum`

This type statement declares a real array consisting of three rows and six columns, for a total of 18 elements. The legal values of the first subscript are 1 to 3, and the legal values of the second subscript are 1 to 6. Any other subscript values are out of bounds.

2. `INTEGER, DIMENSION(0:100,0:20) :: hist`

This type statement declares an integer array consisting of 101 rows and 21 columns, for a total of 2121 elements. The legal values of the first subscript are 0 to 100, and the legal values of the second subscript are 0 to 20. Any other subscript values are out of bounds.

5.6.2 Rank-2 Array Storage

You already know that a rank-1 array of length N occupies N successive locations in the computer's memory. Similarly, a rank-2 array of size M by N occupies M × N successive locations in the computer's memory. How are the elements of the array arranged in the memory? Fortran always allocates array elements in **column major order.** That is, Fortran allocates the first column in memory, then the second one, then the third one, and so on until all columns have been allocated. Figure 5–19 illustrates this memory allocation scheme for a 3 × 2 array a. As we can see from the picture, the array element a(2,2) is really the fifth location reserved in memory. The order of memory allocation will become important when we discuss data initialization and I/O statements later in this section[1].

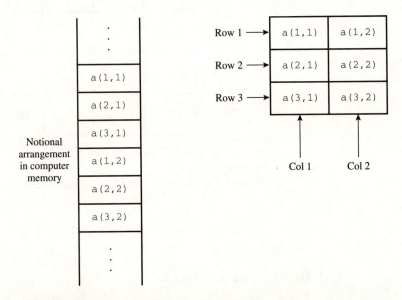

FIGURE 5–19
Notional memory allocation for a 3 × 2 two-dimensional array a.

5.6.3 Initializing Rank-2 Arrays

Rank-2 arrays may be initialized with assignment statements, type declaration statements, or Fortran READ statements.

Initializing rank-2 arrays with assignment statements

You may assign initial values to an array during program execution on an element-by-element basis, using assignment statements in a nested DO loop, or

---

[1]The Fortran 90/95 standard does not actually require the elements of an array to occupy successive locations in memory. The only requirement is that they *appear* to be successive when addressed with appropriate subscripts or when used in operations such as I/O statements. To keep this distinction clear, we will refer to the *notional order* of the elements in memory, with the understanding that the actual order implemented by the processor could be different.

all at once with an array constructor. For example, suppose we want to initialize a 4 × 3 integer array `istat` with the values shown in Figure 5–20a.

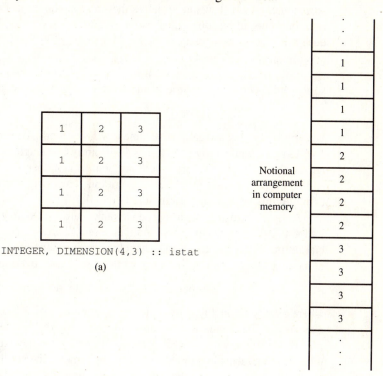

INTEGER, DIMENSION(4,3) :: istat

(a)

Notional arrangement in computer memory

(b)

FIGURE 5–20
(a) Initial values for integer array `istat`. (b) Notional layout of values in memory for array `istat`.

This array could be initialized at run time on an element-by-element with DO loops, as shown:

```
INTEGER, DIMENSION(4,3) :: istat
DO i = 1, 4
   DO j = 1, 3
      istat(i,j) = j
   END DO
END DO
```

Since this array contains the same value in every row for any given column, it is also possible to initialize the array a column at a time using a single DO loop, as shown:

```
INTEGER, DIMENSION(4,3) :: istat
DO j = 1, 3
   istat(:,j) = j
END DO
```

Finally, the array could also be initialized in a single statement with an array constructor. However, this method is not as simple as it might seem. The notional data pattern in memory that would initialize the array is shown in Figure 5–20b. It consists of four 1s, followed by four 2s, followed by four 3s. The array constructor that would produce this pattern in memory is

$$(/\ 1,1,1,1,2,2,2,2,3,3,3,3\ /)$$

so it would seem that the array could be initialized with the assignment statement

$$\texttt{istat}\ =\ (/\ 1,1,1,1,2,2,2,2,3,3,3,3\ /)$$

Unfortunately, this assignment statement will not work. The array constructor produces a 1×12 array, while array `istat` is a 4×3 array. Although they both have the same number of elements, the two arrays are not conformable because they have different shapes and so cannot be used in the same operation. This assignment statement will produce a compile-time error on a Fortran 90/95 compiler.

Array constructors always produce rank-1 arrays. So how can we overcome this limitation to use array constructors to initialize rank-2 arrays? Fortran 90/95 provides the special intrinsic function RESHAPE that changes the shape of an array without changing the number of elements in it. The form of the RESHAPE function is

$$\texttt{output} = \texttt{RESHAPE}\ (\ \texttt{array1},\ \texttt{array2}\ )$$

where `array1` contains the data to reshape and `array2` is a rank-1 array describing the new shape. The number of elements in `array2` is the number of dimensions in the output array, and the value of each element in `array2` is the extent of each dimension. The number of elements in `array1` must be the same as the number of elements in the shape specified in `array2`, or the RESHAPE function will fail. The assignment statement to initialize array `istat` becomes:

$$\texttt{istat} = \texttt{RESHAPE}\ (\ (/\ 1,1,1,1,2,2,2,2,3,3,3,3\ /),\ (/4,3/)\ )$$

The RESHAPE function converts the 1×12 array constructor into a 4×3 array that can be assigned to `istat`.

When RESHAPE changes the shape of an array, it maps the elements from the old shape to the new shape in column major order. Thus the first element in the array constructor becomes `istat(1,1)`, the second one becomes `istat(2,1)`, and so on.

Good Programming Practice
Use the RESHAPE function to change the shape of an array. RESHAPE is especially useful when used with an array constructor to create array constants of any desired shape.

Initializing rank-2 arrays with type declaration statements

Initial values may also be loaded into the array at compilation time using type declaration statements. When a type declaration statement is used to initialize a rank-2 array, the data values are loaded into the array in the order in which memory is notionally allocated by the Fortran compiler. Since arrays are allocated in column order, the values listed in the type declaration statement must be in column order. That is, all the elements in column 1 must be listed in the statement first, then all of the elements in column 2, and so on. Array istat contains four rows and three columns, so to initialize the array with a type declaration statement the four values of column 1 must be listed first, then the four values for column 2, and finally the four values for column 3.

The values used to initialize the array must also have the same shape as the array, so the RESHAPE function must be used as well. Therefore, array istat could be initialized at compilation time with the following statement:

```
INTEGER, DIMENSION(4,3) :: istat(4,3) = &
        RESHAPE ( (/ 1,1,1,1,2,2,2,2,3,3,3,3 /), (/4,3/) )
```

Initializing rank-2 arrays with READ statements

Arrays may be initialized with Fortran READ statements. If an array name appears without subscripts in the argument list of a READ statement, the program will attempt to read values for all of the elements in the array, and the values read will be assigned to the array elements in the order in which they are notionally stored in the computer's memory. Therefore, if file INITIAL.DAT contains the values

```
1 1 1 1 2 2 2 2 3 3 3 3
```

then the following code will initialize istat to have the values shown in Figure 5–20.

```
INTEGER, DIMENSION(4,3) :: istat
OPEN (7, FILE='initial.dat', STATUS='OLD', ACTION='READ')
READ (7,*) istat
```

Implied DO loops may be used in READ statements to change the order in which array elements are initialized or to initialize only a portion of an array. For example, if file INITIAL1.DAT contains the values

```
1 2 3 1 2 3 1 2 3 1 2 3
```

then the following code will initialize istat to have the values shown in Figure 5–20.

```
INTEGER :: i, j
INTEGER, DIMENSION(4,3) :: istat
OPEN (7, FILE='initial1.dat', STATUS='OLD', ACTION='READ')
READ (7,*) ((istat(i,j), j=1,3), i=1,4)
```

The values would have been read from file INITIAL1.DAT in a different order than they were read from the preceding example, but the implied DO loops would ensure that the proper input values went into the proper array elements.

5.6.4 Examples

EXAMPLE 5–5 Electric Power Generation: Figure 5–18*b* shows a series of electrical output power measurements at six different times for four different generators at the Acme Electric Power generating station. Write a program to read these values from a disk file and then to calculate the average power supplied by each generator over the measurement period and the total power supplied by all of the generators at each time in the measurement period.

SOLUTION

1. State the problem.

Calculate the average power supplied by each generator in the station over the measurement period and calculate the total instantaneous power supplied by the generating station at each time within the measurement period. Write those values out on the standard output device.

2. Define the inputs and outputs.

This program has two types of inputs:

a. A character string containing the file name of the input data file. This string will come from the standard input device.
b. The 24 real data values in the file, representing the power supplied by each of the four generators at each of six different times. The data in the input file must be organized so that the six values associated with generator G1 appear first, followed by the six values associated with generator G2, and so on.

The outputs from this program are the average power supplied by each generator in the station over the measurement period and the total instantaneous power supplied by the generating station at each time within the measurement period.

3. Describe the algorithm.

This program can be broken down into six major steps:

```
Get the input file name
Open the input file
Read the input data into an array
Calculate the total instantaneous output power at each time
Calculate the average output power of each generator
Write the output values
```

The detailed pseudocode for the problem is given below:

```
Prompt user for the input file name "filename"
Read file namc "filename"
OPEN file "filename"
IF OPEN is successful THEN
    Read array power

    ! Calculate the instantaneous output power of the station
    DO for itime = 1 to 6
```

```
                    DO for igen = 1 to 4
                       power_sum(itime) ← power(itime,igen) + power_sum(itime)
                    END of DO
                 END of DO

                 ! Calculate the average output power of each generator
                 DO for igen = 1 to 4
                    DO for itime = 1 to 6
                       power_ave(igen) ← power(itime,igen) + power_ave(igen)
                    END of DO
                    power_ave(igen) ← power_ave(igen) / 6
                 END of DO

                 ! Write out the total instantaneous power at each time
                 Write out power_sum for itime = 1 to 6

                 ! Write out the average output power of each generator
                 Write out power_ave for igen = 1 to 4

              End of IF
```

4. **Turn the algorithm into Fortran statements.**

The resulting Fortran program is shown in Figure 5–21.

FIGURE 5–21

Program to calculate the instantaneous power produced by a generating station and the average power produced by each generator within the station.

```
PROGRAM generate
!
! Purpose:
!   To calculate total instantaneous power supplied by a generating
!   station at each instant of time, and to calculate the average
!   power supplied by each generator over the period of measurement.
!
! Record of revisions:
!     Date         Programmer           Description of change
!     ====         ==========           =====================
!   09/27/95     S. J. Chapman          Original code
!
IMPLICIT NONE

! List of parameters:
INTEGER, PARAMETER :: max_gen = 4      ! Max number of generators
INTEGER, PARAMETER :: max_time = 6     ! Max number of times

! List of variables:
CHARACTER(len=20) :: filename          ! Input data file name
INTEGER :: igen                        ! Loop index: generators
INTEGER :: itime                       ! Loop index: time
REAL, DIMENSION(max_time,max_gen) :: power
                                       ! Pwr of each gen at each time
REAL, DIMENSION(max_gen) :: power_ave  ! Ave power of each gen over all times
REAL, DIMENSION(max_time) :: power_sum ! Total power of station at each time
INTEGER :: status                      ! I/O status: 0 = success
```

(continued)

```
(continued)
! Initialize sums to zero.
power_ave = 0.
power_sum = 0.

! Get the name of the file containing the input data.
WRITE (*,1000)
1000 FORMAT (' Enter the file name containing the input data: ')
READ (*,1010) filename
1010 FORMAT ( A20 )

! Open input data file. Status is OLD because the input data must
! already exist.
OPEN ( UNIT=9, FILE=filename, STATUS='OLD', ACTION='READ', &
       IOSTAT=status )

! Was the OPEN successful?
fileopen: IF ( status == 0 ) THEN

   ! The file was opened successfully, so read the data to process.
   READ (9, *, IOSTAT=status) power

   ! Calculate the instantaneous output power of the station at
   ! each time.
   sum1: DO itime = 1, max_time
      sum2: DO igen = 1, max_gen
         power_sum(itime) = power(itime,igen) + power_sum(itime)
      END DO sum2
   END DO sum1

   ! Calculate the average output power of each generator over the
   ! time being measured.
   ave1: DO igen = 1, max_gen
      ave2: DO itime = 1, max_time
         power_ave(igen) = power(itime,igen) + power_ave(igen)
      END DO ave2
      power_ave(igen) = power_ave(igen) / REAL(max_time)
   END DO ave1

   ! Tell user.
   out1: DO itime = 1, max_time
      WRITE (*,1020) itime, power_sum(itime)
      1020 FORMAT (' The instantaneous power at time ', I1, ' is ', &
                     F7.2, ' MW.')
   END DO out1

   out2: DO igen = 1, max_gen
      WRITE (*,1030) igen, power_ave(igen)
      1030 FORMAT (' The average power of generator ', I1, ' is ', &
                     F7.2, ' MW.')
   END DO out2

ELSE fileopen

   ! Else file open failed. Tell user.
   WRITE (*,1050) status
   1050 FORMAT (1X,'File open failed--status = ', I6)
```

(continued)

(concluded)
```
END IF fileopen

END PROGRAM
```

5. Test the program.

To test this program, we will place the data from Figure 5–18*b* into a file called GENDAT. The contents of file GENDAT are:

```
20.0  19.8  20.1  20.0  20.0  19.9
40.3  40.1  40.0  39.5  39.9  40.0
42.0  41.5  41.3  41.1  39.8  41.0
20.4  26.9  38.4  42.0  12.2   6.0
```

Note that each row of the file corresponds to a specific generator and each column corresponds to a specific time. Next we will calculate the answers by hand for one generator and one time and compare the results with those from the program. At time 3, the total instantaneous power being supplied by all the generators is

$$P_{TOT} = 20.1 \text{ MW} + 40.0 \text{ MW} + 41.3 \text{ MW} + 38.4 \text{ MW} = 139.8 \text{ MW}$$

The average power for generator 1 is

$$P_{G1,AVE} = \frac{(20.1 + 19.8 + 20.1 + 20.0 + 20.0 + 19.9)}{6} = 19.98 \text{ MW}$$

The output from the program is

```
C>generate
Enter the file name containing the input data:
gendat
The instantaneous power at time 1 is 122.70 MW.
The instantaneous power at time 2 is 128.30 MW.
The instantaneous power at time 3 is 139.80 MW.
The instantaneous power at time 4 is 142.60 MW.
The instantaneous power at time 5 is 111.90 MW.
The instantaneous power at time 6 is 106.90 MW.
The average power of generator 1 is 19.97 MW.
The average power of generator 2 is 39.97 MW.
The average power of generator 3 is 41.12 MW.
The average power of generator 4 is 24.32 MW.
```

so the numbers match, and the program appears to be working correctly.

Note that the raw data array `power` was organized as a 6 × 4 matrix (6 times by 4 generators), but the input data file was organized as a 4 × 6 matrix (4 generators by 6 times)! This reversal is caused by the fact that Fortran stores array data in columns, but reads in data along lines. In order for the columns to be filled correctly in memory, the data had to be transposed in the input file! Needless to say, this situation can be very confusing for people having to work with the program and its input data.

We need a way to eliminate this source of confusion by making the organization of the data in the input file match the organization of the data within the computer. How can we do that? With implied DO loops! If we were to replace the statement

```
READ (9,*,IOSTAT=status) power
```

with the statement

```
READ (9,*,IOSTAT=status) ((power(itime,igen), igen=1,max_gen), itime=1,max_time)
```

then the data along a row in the input file would go into the corresponding row of the matrix in the computer's memory. With the new READ statement, the input data file could be structured as follows

```
20.0  40.3  42.0  20.4
19.8  40.1  41.5  26.9
20.1  40.0  41.3  38.4
20.0  39.5  41.1  42.0
20.0  39.9  39.8  12.2
19.9  40.0  41.0   6.0
```

and after the READ statement, the contents of array power would be

$$
\text{power} =
\begin{bmatrix}
20.0 & 40.3 & 42.0 & 20.4 \\
19.8 & 40.1 & 41.5 & 26.9 \\
20.1 & 40.0 & 41.3 & 38.4 \\
20.0 & 39.5 & 41.1 & 42.0 \\
20.0 & 39.9 & 39.8 & 12.2 \\
19.9 & 40.0 & 41.0 & 6.0
\end{bmatrix}
$$

Good Programming Practice

Use DO loops and/or implied DO loops when reading or writing rank-2 arrays in order to keep the structure of the matrix in the file the same as the structure of the matrix within the program. This correspondence makes the programs easier to understand.

5.6.5 Whole Array Operations and Array Subsets

Two rank-2 arrays may be used together in arithmetic operations and assignment statements as long as they are conformable (that is, as long as they either have the same shape or one of them is a scalar). If they are conformable, then the corresponding operation will be performed on an element-by-element basis.

Array subsets may be selected from rank-2 arrays using subscript triplets or vector subscripts. A separate subscript triplet or vector subscript is used for each dimension in the array.

For example, consider the following 5×5 array:

$$a = \begin{bmatrix} 1 & 2 & 3 & 4 & 5 \\ 6 & 7 & 8 & 9 & 10 \\ 11 & 12 & 13 & 14 & 15 \\ 16 & 17 & 18 & 19 & 20 \\ 21 & 22 & 23 & 24 & 25 \end{bmatrix}$$

The array subset corresponding to the first column of this array is selected as `a(:,1)`:

$$a(:,1) = \begin{bmatrix} 1 \\ 6 \\ 11 \\ 16 \\ 21 \end{bmatrix}$$

And the array subset corresponding to the first row is selected as `a(1,:)`:

$$a(1,:) = \begin{bmatrix} 1 & 2 & 3 & 4 & 5 \end{bmatrix}$$

Array subscripts may be used independently in each dimension. For example, the array subset `a(1:3,1:5:2)` selects rows 1 through 3 and columns 1, 3, and 5 from array a. This array subset is

$$a(1:3,1:5:2) = \begin{bmatrix} 1 & 3 & 5 \\ 6 & 8 & 10 \\ 11 & 13 & 15 \end{bmatrix}$$

▪ 5.7
MULTIDIMENSIONAL OR RANK-N ARRAYS

Fortran supports more complex arrays with as many as seven different subscripts. These larger arrays are declared, initialized, and used in the same manner as the rank-2 arrays described in the previous section.

Rank-n arrays are notionally allocated in memory in a manner that is an extension of the column order used for rank-2 arrays. Memory allocation for a $2 \times 2 \times 2$ rank-3 array is illustrated in Figure 5–22. The first subscript runs through its complete range before the second subscript is incremented, and the second subscript runs through its complete range before the third subscript is incremented. This process repeats for whatever number of subscripts are declared for the array, with the first subscript always changing most rapidly and the last subscript always changing most slowly. We must keep this allocation structure in mind if we wish to initialize or perform I/O operations with rank-n arrays.

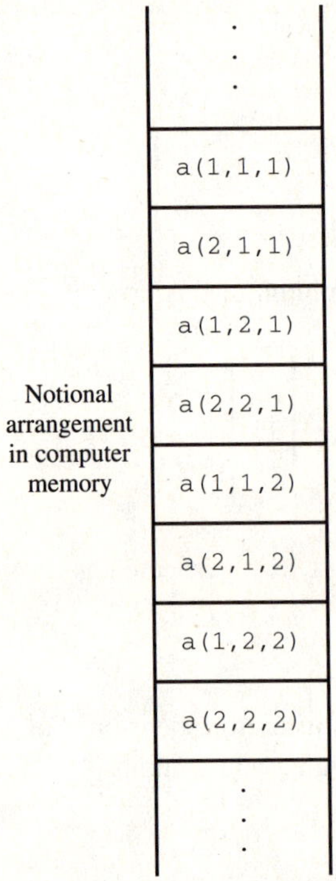

Notional
arrangement
in computer
memory

a(1,1,1)

a(2,1,1)

a(1,2,1)

a(2,2,1)

a(1,1,2)

a(2,1,2)

a(1,2,2)

a(2,2,2)

FIGURE 5–22
Notional memory allocation for a $2 \times 2 \times 2$ array a. Array elements are allocated so that the first subscript changes most rapidly, the second subscript the next most rapidly, and the third subscript the least rapidly.

Quiz 5–2

This quiz provides a quick check to see if you understand the concepts introduced in sections 5.6 and 5.7. If you have trouble with the quiz, reread the sections, ask your instructor, or discuss the material with a fellow student. The answers to this quiz appear in Appendix F.

For questions 1 to 3, determine the number of elements in the array specified by the declaration statements and the valid subscript range(s) for each array.

1. `REAL, DIMENSION(-64:64,0:4) :: data_input`

2. `INTEGER, PARAMETER :: min_u = 1, max_u = 70`
   `INTEGER, PARAMETER :: maxfil = 3`
   `CHARACTER(len=24), DIMENSION(maxfil,min_u:max_u) :: filenm`

3. `INTEGER, DIMENSION(-3:3,-3:3,6) :: in`

Determine which of the following Fortran statements are valid. For each valid statement, specify what will happen in the program. Assume default typing for any variables that are not explicitly typed.

4. `REAL, DIMENSION(0:11,2) :: dist`

(continued)

(continued)
```
    dist = (/ 0.00,   0.25,   1.00,   2.25,   4.00,   6.25, &
             9.00,  12.25,  16.00,  20.25,  25.00,  30.25, &
            -0.00,  -0.25,  -1.00,  -2.25,  -4.00,  -6.25, &
            -9.00,-12.25,-16.00,-20.25,-25.00,-30.25/)
```

5.
```
   REAL, DIMENSION(0:11,2) :: dist
   dist = RESHAPE((/0.00,   0.25,   1.00,   2.25,   4.00,   6.25, &
                    9.00,  12.25,  16.00,  20.25,  25.00,  30.25, &
                    0.00,   0.25,   1.00,   2.25,   4.00,   6.25, &
                    9.00,  12.25,  16.00,  20.25,  25.00,  30.25/)&
                  , (/12,2/))
```

6.
```
   REAL, DIMENSION(-2:2,-1:0) :: data1 = &
            RESHAPE ( (/ 1.0, 2.0, 3.0, 4.0, 5.0, &
                         6.0, 7.0, 8.0, 9.0, 0.0 /), &
                      (/ 5, 2 /) )
   REAL, DIMENSION(0:4,2) :: data2 = &
            RESHAPE ( (/ 0.0, 9.0, 8.0, 7.0, 6.0, &
                         5.0, 4.0, 3.0, 2.0, 1.0 /), &
                      (/ 5, 2 /) )
   REAL, DIMENSION(5,2) :: data_out
   data_out = data1 + data2
   WRITE (*,*) data_out(:,1)
   WRITE (*,*) data_out(3,:)
```

7.
```
   INTEGER, DIMENSION(4) :: list1 = (/1,4,2,2/)
   INTEGER, DIMENSION(3) :: list2 = (/1,2,3/)
   INTEGER, DIMENSION(5,5) :: array
   DO i = 1,5
      DO j = 1,5
         array(i,j) = i + 10 * j
      END DO
   END DO
   WRITE (*,*) array(list1, list2)
```

8.
```
   INTEGER, DIMENSION(4) :: list = (/2,3,2,1/)
   INTEGER, DIMENSION(10) :: vector = (/ (10*k, k = -4,5) /)
   vector(list) = (/ 1, 2, 3, 4 /)
   WRITE (*,*) vector
```

Suppose that a file INPUT contained the following data:

```
    11.2    16.5    31.3     3.1414   16.0    12.0
     1.1     9.0    17.1    11.       15.0    -1.3
    10.0    11.0    12.0    13.0       14.0     5.0
    15.1    16.7    18.9    21.1       24.0   -22.2
```

What data would be read from file INPUT by each of the following statements? What would the value of mydata(2,4) be in each case?

9.
```
   REAL, DIMENSION(3,5) :: mydata
   READ (2,*) mydata
```

10.
```
   REAL, DIMENSION(0:2,2:6) :: mydata
   READ (2,*) mydata
```

(continued)

(concluded)

11. ```
REAL, DIMENSION(3,5) :: mydata
READ (2,*) ((mydata(i,j), j=1,5), i=1,3)
```

12. ```
REAL, DIMENSION(3,5) :: mydata
DO i = 1, 3
    READ (2,*) (mydata(i,j), j=1,5)
END DO
```

Answer the following questions.

13. What is the value of dist(6,2) in question 5 of this quiz?

14. What is the rank of mydata in question 10 of this quiz?

15. What is the shape of mydata in question 10 of this quiz?

16. What is the extent of the first dimension of data_input in question 1 of this quiz?

17. What is the maximum number of dimensions that an array can have in Fortran 90/95?

◼ 5.8
USING FORTRAN INTRINSIC FUNCTIONS WITH ARRAYS

Fortran 90 and Fortran 95 have three classes of intrinsic functions: **elemental functions, inquiry functions,** and **transformational functions.** Some of the functions from each of these classes are designed for use with array arguments. We will now examine a few of them. A summary of all Fortran intrinsic functions and subroutines is found in Appendix B.[2]

5.8.1 Elemental Intrinsic Functions

Elemental intrinsic functions are specified for scalar arguments but may also be applied to array arguments. If the argument of an elemental function is a scalar, then the result of the function will be a scalar. If the argument of the function is an array, then the result of the function will be an array of the same shape as the input array. Note that if the function has multiple input arguments, all of the arguments must have the same shape. If an elemental function is applied to an array, the result will be the same as if the function

---

[2]Appendix B contains tables summarizing all Fortran 90/95 intrinsic procedures. A much more complete description of the operation of each procedure appears in S. J. Chapman, *Fortran 90/95 for Scientists and Engineers* (Burr Ridge, IL: McGraw-Hill, 1998).

were applied to each element of the array on an element-by-element basis. For example, the following two sets of statements are equivalent:

```
REAL, DIMENSION(4) :: x = (/ 0., 3.141592, 1., 2. /)
REAL, DIMENSION(4) :: y
INTEGER :: i

y = SIN(x)                          ! Whole array at once

DO i = 1,4
   y(i) = SIN(x(i))                 ! Element by element
END DO
```

Most of the Fortran intrinsic functions that accept scalar arguments are elemental and so can be used with arrays. This group includes such common functions as ABS, SIN, COS, TAN, EXP, LOG, LOG10, MOD, and SQRT.

5.8.2 Inquiry Intrinsic Functions

Inquiry intrinsic functions are functions whose value depends on the properties of an object being investigated. For example, the function UBOUND(arr) is an inquiry function that returns the largest subscript(s) of array arr. A list of some of the common array inquiry functions is shown in Table 5–1. Any function arguments shown in italics are optional; they may or may not be present when the function is invoked.

These functions are useful for determining the properties of an array, such as its size, shape, extent, and the legal subscript range in each extent. They will be especially important once we begin passing arrays to procedures in Chapter 6.

■ **TABLE 5–1**
Some common array inquiry functions

Function name and calling sequence	Purpose
LBOUND(ARRAY, *DIM*)	Returns all the lower bounds of ARRAY if *DIM* is absent or a specified lower bound of ARRAY if *DIM* is present. The result is a rank-1 array if *DIM* is absent or a scalar if *DIM* is present.
SHAPE(SOURCE)	Returns the shape of array SOURCE.
SIZE(ARRAY, *DIM*)	Returns either the extent of ARRAY along a particular dimension if *DIM* is present; otherwise, it returns the total number of elements in the array.
UBOUND(ARRAY, *DIM*)	Returns all the upper bounds of ARRAY if *DIM* is absent or a specified upper bound of ARRAY if *DIM* is present. The result is a rank-1 array if *DIM* is absent or a scalar if *DIM* is present.

Example 5–6 Determining the Properties of an Array: To illustrate the use of the array inquiry functions, we will declare a two-dimensional array a and use the functions to determine its properties.

Solution

The program in Figure 5–23 invokes the functions SHAPE, SIZE, LBOUND, and UBOUND to determine the properties of the array.

FIGURE 5–23
Program to determine the properties of an array.

```
PROGRAM check_array
!
! Purpose:
!   To illustrate the use of array inquiry functions.
!
! Record of revisions:
!     Date       Programmer          Description of change
!     ====       ==========          =====================
!   04/02/96   S. J. Chapman         Original code
!
IMPLICIT NONE

! List of variables:
REAL,DIMENSION(-5:5,0:3) :: a = 0. ! Array to examine

! Get the shape, size, and bounds of the array.
WRITE (*,'(A,7I6)') ' The shape is:          ', SHAPE(a).
WRITE (*,'(A,I6)')  ' The size is:           ', SIZE(a).
WRITE (*,'(A,7I6)') ' The lower bounds are: ', LBOUND(a).
WRITE (*,'(A,7I6)') ' The upper bounds are: ', UBOUND(a).

END PROGRAM
```

When the program is executed, the results are

```
C>check_array
The shape is:           11    4
The size is:            44
The lower bounds are:   -5    0
The upper bounds are:    5    3
```

These are obviously the correct answers for array a.

5.8.3 Transformational Intrinsic Functions

Transformational intrinsic functions are functions that have one or more array-valued arguments or an array-valued result. Unlike elemental functions, which operate on an element-by-element basis, transformational functions operate on arrays as a whole. The output of a transformational function will often not have the same shape as the input arguments. For example, the function `DOT_PRODUCT` has two vector input arguments of the same size and produces a scalar output. Fortran has *many* transformational intrinsic functions. A few of the more common ones are summarized in Table 5-2; all of them appear in Appendix B.

▪ **TABLE 5–2**
Some common transformational functions

Function name and calling sequence	Purpose
`DOT_PRODUCT(VECTOR_A, VECTOR_B)`	Calculates the dot product of two equal-size vectors.
`MATMUL(MATRIX_A, MATRIX_B)`	Performs matrix multiplication on two conformable matrices.
`RESHAPE(SOURCE,SHAPE)`	Constructs an array of the specified shape from the elements of array `SOURCE`. `SHAPE` is a rank-1 array containing the extents of each dimension in the array to be built.

You have already used the `RESHAPE` function to initialize arrays. A number of other transformational functions appear in the exercises at the end of this chapter.

▪ **5.9**

MASKED ARRAY ASSIGNMENT: THE WHERE CONSTRUCT

We have already seen that Fortran permits us to use either array elements or entire arrays in array assignment statements. For example, we could take the logarithm of the elements in a two-dimensional array `value` in either of the following ways:

```
DO i = 1, ndim1
   DO j = 1, ndim2                              logval = LOG(value)
      logval(i,j) = LOG(value(i,j))
   END DO
END DO
```

Both of these above examples take the logarithm of all of the elements in array `value` and store the result in array `logval`.

Suppose that we want to take the logarithm of some of the elements of array `value`, but not of all of them. For example, suppose that we want to take the logarithm of positive elements only, since the logarithms of zero and negative numbers are not defined and produce run-time errors. One way to accomplish this task is to take the logarithms on an element-by-element basis using a combination of DO loops and an IF construct. For example:

```
DO i = 1, ndim1
   DO j = 1, ndim2
      IF ( value(i,j) > 0. ) THEN
         logval(i,j) = LOG(value(i,j))
      ELSE
```

```
                logval(i,j) = -99999.
            END IF
        END DO
    END DO
```

We could also perform this calculation all at once using a special form of array assignment statement known as **masked array assignment.** A *masked array assignment* statement is an assignment statement whose operation is controlled by a logical array of the *same shape* as the array in the assignment. The assignment operation is performed only for the elements of the array that correspond to true values in the mask. In Fortran 90/95, masked array assignments are implemented using the WHERE construct or statement. The general form of a Fortran 90 WHERE construct is

```
[name:] WHERE (mask_expr)
    Array Assignment Statement(s)    ! Block 1
ELSEWHERE [name:]
    Array Assignment Statement(s)    ! Block 2
END WHERE [name:]
```

where `mask_expr` is a logical array of the same shape as the array(s) being manipulated in the array assignment statements in the construct. This construct applies the operations in block 1 to all the elements of the array for which `mask_expr` is true and applies the operation or set of operations in block 2 to all the elements of the array for which `mask_expr` is false.

A name may be assigned to a WHERE construct if desired. If the WHERE statement at the beginning of a construct is named, then the associated END WHERE statement must have the same name. The name is optional on an ELSEWHERE statement even if it is used on the corresponding WHERE and END WHERE statements.

The example given above could be implemented with a WHERE construct as:

```
WHERE ( value > 0. )
    logval = LOG(value)
ELSEWHERE
    logval = -99999.
END WHERE
```

The expression `value > 0.` produces a logical array whose elements are true where the corresponding elements of `value` are greater than zero, and false where the corresponding elements of `value` are less than or equal zero. This logical array then serves as a mask to control the operation of the array assignment statement.

The WHERE construct is generally more elegant than element-by-element operations, especially for multidimensional arrays.

EXAMPLE 5–7 *Limiting the Maximum and Minimum Values in an Array:* Suppose that we are writing a program to analyze an input data set whose values should be in the range [−1000,1000]. If numbers greater than 1000 or less than −1000 would cause problems with our processing algorithm, we could use a test to limit all data values to the acceptable range. Write such a test for a 10,000-element one-dimensional real array `input` using both DO and IF constructs and a WHERE construct.

SOLUTION

The test using DO and IF constructs is

```
DO i = 1, 10000
   IF ( input(i) > 1000. ) THEN
      input(i) = 1000.
   ELSE IF ( input(i) < -1000. ) THEN
      input(i) = -1000.
   END IF
END DO
```

The test using a WHERE construct is

```
WHERE ( ABS(input) > 1000. )
   input = SIGN(1000.,input)
END WHERE
```

The WHERE construct is simpler than the DO and IF constructs for this example.

Quiz 5–3

This quiz provides a quick check to see if you understand the concepts introduced in sections 5.8 and 5.9. If you have trouble with the quiz, reread the sections, ask your instructor, or discuss the material with a fellow student. The answers to this quiz appear in Appendix F.

For questions 1 to 5, determine what will be printed out by the WRITE statements.

1.
```
REAL, DIMENSION(-3:3,0:50) :: values
WRITE (*,*) LBOUND(values,1)
WRITE (*,*) UBOUND(values,2)
WRITE (*,*) SIZE(values,1)
WRITE (*,*) SIZE(values)
WRITE (*,*) SHAPE(values)
```

2.
```
INTEGER, DIMENSION(2,3) :: arr2
arr2 = RESHAPE( (/3,0,-3,5,-8,2/), (/2,3/) )
WHERE ( arr2 > 0 )
   arr2 = 2 * arr2
END WHERE
WRITE (*,*) arr2
```

Determine if the following set of Fortran statements is valid. If it is, specify what will happen in the program. If not, specify what is wrong.

3.
```
REAL, DIMENSION(6) :: dist1
REAL, DIMENSION(5) :: time
dist1 = (/ 0.00, 0.25, 1.00, 2.25, 4.00, 6.25 /)
time = (/ 0.0, 1.0, 2.0, 3.0, 4.0 /)
WHERE ( time > 0. )
   dist1 = SQRT(dist1)
END WHERE
```

■ **5.10**

WHEN SHOULD YOU USE AN ARRAY?

You have now learned *how* to use arrays in Fortran programs, but you have not yet learned *when* to use them. At this point in a typical Fortran course, many students are tempted to use arrays to solve problems whether they are needed or not just because they know how to do so. How can you decide whether or not it makes sense to use an array in a particular problem?

In general, if much or all of the input data must be in memory at the same time in order to solve a problem efficiently, then the use of arrays to hold that data is appropriate for that problem. Otherwise, arrays are not needed. For example, let's contrast the statistics programs in Examples 3–5 and 5–4. Example 3–5 calculated the mean and standard deviation of a data set, while Example 5–4 calculated the mean, median, and standard deviation of a data set.

Recall that the equations for the mean and standard deviation of a data set are

$$\bar{x} = \frac{1}{N}\sum_{i=1}^{N} x_i \tag{3–3}$$

and

$$s = \sqrt{\frac{N\sum_{i=1}^{N} x_i^2 - \left(\sum_{i=1}^{N} x_i\right)^2}{N(N-1)}} \tag{3-4}$$

The sums in Equations (3–3) and (3–4) that are required to find the mean and standard deviation can easily be formed as data points are read in one by one. There is no need to wait until all the data is read in before starting to build the sums. Therefore, a program to calculate the mean and standard deviation of a data set does not need to use arrays. You could use an array to hold all the input values before calculating the mean and standard deviation, but since the array is not necessary, you should not do so. Example 3–5 works fine and is built entirely without arrays.

On the other hand, finding the median of a data set requires that the data be sorted into ascending order. Since sorting requires all data to be in memory, a program that calculates the median must use an array to hold all the input data before the calculations start. Therefore, Example 5-4 uses an array to hold its input data.

> **Good Programming Practice**
> Do not use arrays to solve a problem unless they are actually needed.

■ 5.11
SUMMARY

Chapter 5 presents an introduction to arrays and to their use in Fortran programs. An array is a group of variables, all of the same type, which are referred to by a single name. An individual variable within the array is called an array element. Array elements are addressed by means of one or more (up to seven) subscripts.

An array is declared using a type declaration statement by naming the array and specifying the maximum (and, optionally, the minimum) subscript values with the DIMEN-SION attribute. The compiler uses the declared subscript ranges to reserve space in the computer's memory to hold the array. The array elements are allocated in memory in an order such that the first subscript of the array changes most rapidly and the last subscript of the array changes most slowly.

As with any variable, an array must be initialized before use. An array may be initialized at compile time using array constructors in the type declaration statements or at run time using array constructors, DO loops, or Fortran READs.

Array elements may be used in a Fortran program just like any other variable. They may appear in assignment statements on either side of the equal sign. Entire arrays and array sections may also be used in calculations and assignment statements as long as the arrays are conformable with each other. Arrays are conformable if they have the same number of dimensions (rank) and the same extent in each dimension. A scalar is also conformable with any array. An operation between two conformable arrays is performed on an element-by-element basis.

Fortran 90/95 contains three types of intrinsic functions: elemental functions, inquiry functions, and transformational functions. Elemental functions are defined for a scalar input and produce a scalar output. When applied to an array, an elemental function produces an output that is the result of applying the operation separately to each element of the input array. Inquiry functions return information about an array, such as its size or bounds. Transformational functions operate on entire arrays and produce an output that is based on all the elements of the array.

The WHERE construct permits an array assignment statement to be performed on only those elements of an array that meet specified criteria. It is useful for preventing errors caused by out-of-range data values in the array.

5.11.1 Summary of Good Programming Practice

The following guidelines should be adhered to when working with arrays.

1. Before writing a program that uses arrays, you should decide whether an array is really needed to solve the problem or not. If arrays are not needed, then don't use them!

2. All array sizes should be declared using named constants. If the sizes are declared using named constants and if those same named constants are used in any size tests within the program, then it will be easy to modify the maximum capacity of the program at a later time.

3. All arrays should be initialized before use. The results of using an uninitialized array are unpredictable and vary from computer to computer.

4. The most common problem when programming with arrays is attempting to read from or write to locations outside the bounds of the array. To detect these problems, the bounds-checking option of your compiler should always be turned on during program testing and debugging. Because bounds checking slows down the execution of a program, the bounds-checking option may be turned off once debugging is completed.

5. Use implicit DO loops to read in or write out two-dimensional arrays so that each row of the array appears as a row of the input or output file. This correspondence helps a programmer to relate the data in the file to the data present within the program.

6. Use the RESHAPE function to change the shape of an array. This function is especially useful when used with an array constructor to create array constants of any desired shape.

7. Use WHERE constructs to modify and assign array elements when you want to modify and assign only those elements that pass some test.

5.11.2 Summary of Fortran Statements and Constructs

Type Declaration Statements with Arrays

```
      type, DIMENSION( [i1:]i2, [j1:]j2, ... ) :: array1, ...
```

Examples:

```
    REAL, DIMENSION(100) :: array
    INTEGER, DIMENSION(-5:5,2) :: i
```

Description:
    These type declaration statements declare both the type and the size of an array.

Implied DO loop structure

```
READ (unit,format) (arg1, arg2, ... , index = istart, iend, incr)
WRITE (unit,format) (arg1, arg2, ... , index = istart, iend, incr)
(/ (arg1, arg2, ... , index= istart, iend, incr) /)
```

Examples:

```
WRITE (*,*) ( array(i), i = 1, 10 )
INTEGER, DIMENSION(100) :: values = (/ (i, i=1,100) /)
```

(continued)

(concluded)

Description:

The implied DO loop repeats the values in an argument list a known number of times. The values in the argument list may be functions of the loop index variable. The loop control parameters `istart`, `iend`, and `incr` function just like those in an ordinary DO loop.

WHERE Construct

```
[name:] WHERE ( mask_expr )
    Block 1
ELSEWHERE [name]
    Block 2
END WHERE [name]
```

Description:

The WHERE construct permits operations to be applied to the elements of an array that match a given criterion. A different set of operations may be applied to the elements that do not match. Each `mask_expr` must be a logical array of the same shape as the arrays being manipulated within the code blocks. If a given element of the `mask_expr` is true, then the array assignment statements in block 1 will be applied to the corresponding element in the arrays being operated on. If the mask expression is false, then the array assignment statements in block 2 will be applied to the corresponding element in the arrays being operated on. The ELSEWHERE clause is optional in this construct.

■ 5.12

EXERCISES

5–1 How may arrays be declared?

5–2 What is the difference between an array and an array element?

5–3 Execute the following Fortran program on your computer with bounds checking turned on and then with bounds checking turned off. What happens in each case?

```
PROGRAM bounds
IMPLICIT NONE
REAL, DIMENSION(5) :: test = (/ 1., 2., 3., 4., 5. /)
REAL, DIMENSION(5) :: test1
INTEGER :: i
DO i = 1, 6
   test1(i) = SQRT(test(i))
   WRITE (*,100) 'SQRT(',test(i), ') = ', test1(i)
```

```
    100 FORMAT (1X,A,F6.3,A,F14.4)
    END DO
    END PROGRAM
```

5–4 Determine the shape and size of the arrays specified by the following declaration statements and the valid subscript range for each dimension of each array.

a. `CHARACTER(len=80), DIMENSION(60) :: line`

b. ```
    INTEGER, PARAMETER :: istart = 32
    INTEGER, PARAMETER :: istop = 256
    INTEGER, DIMENSION(istart:istop) :: char
```

*c.* ```
    INTEGER, PARAMETER :: num_class = 3
    INTEGER, PARAMETER :: num_student = 35
    LOGICAL, DIMENSION(num_student,num_class) :: passfail
```

d. `REAL, DIMENSION(-5:5,-5:5,-5:5,-5:5,-5:5) :: range`

5–5 Determine which of the following Fortran program fragments are valid. For each valid statement, specify what will happen in the program. (Assume default typing for any variables that are not explicitly typed within the program fragments.)

a. ```
    INTEGER, DIMENSION(100) :: icount, jcount
    ...
    icount = (/ (i, i=1, 100) /)
    jcount = icount + 1
```

*b.* ```
    REAL, DIMENSION(6,4) :: b
    ...
    DO i = 1, 6
       DO j = 1, 4
          temp = b(i,j)
          b(i,j) = b(j,i)
          b(j,i) = temp
       END DO
    END DO
```

c. ```
    REAL, DIMENSION(10) :: value
    value(1:10:2) = (/ 5., 4., 3., 2., 1. /)
    value(2:11:2) = (/ 10., 9., 8., 7., 6. /)
    WRITE (*,100) value
    100 FORMAT ('1','Value = ',/,(F10.2))
```

*d.* ```
    INTEGER, DIMENSION(9) :: info
    info = (/1,-3,0,-5,-9,3,0,1,7/)
    WHERE ( info>0 )
       info = -info
    ELSEWHERE
       info = -3 * info
    END WHERE
    WRITE (*,*) info
```

e. ```
    INTEGER, DIMENSION(8) :: info
    info = (/1,-3,0,-5,-9,3,0,7/)
    WRITE (*,*) info <= 0
```

**5–6** Define the following array terms: size, shape, extent, rank, conformable.
```

5–7 Given a 5 x 5 array `my_array` containing the following values, determine the shape and contents of each of the following array sections.

$$my\_array = \begin{bmatrix} 1 & 2 & 3 & 4 & 5 \\ 6 & 7 & 8 & 9 & 10 \\ 11 & 12 & 13 & 14 & 15 \\ 16 & 17 & 18 & 19 & 20 \\ 21 & 22 & 23 & 24 & 25 \end{bmatrix}$$

a. `my_array(3,:)`

b. `my_array(:,2)`

c. `my_array(1:5:2,:)`

d. `my_array(:,2:5:2)`

e. `my_array(1:5:2,1:5:2)`

f. `INTEGER, DIMENSION(3) :: list = (/ 1, 2, 4 /)`
`my_array(:,list)`

5–8 An input data file INPUT1 contains the following values:

```
 27    17    10     8     6
 11    13   -11    12   -21
 -1     0     0     6    14
-16    11    21    26   -16
 04    99   -99    17     2
```

Assume that file INPUT1 has been opened on i/o unit 8 and that array `values` is a 4 × 4 integer array. All array elements have been initialized to zero. What will be the contents of array `values` after each of the following READ statements has been executed?

a. ```
DO i = 1, 4
   READ (8,*) (values(i,j), j = 1, 4)
END DO
```

*b.* `READ (8,*) ((values(i,j), j = 1, 4), i=1,4)`

*c.* ```
DO i = 1, 4
   READ (8,*) values(i,:)
END DO
```

d. `READ (8,*) values`

5–9 What will be printed out by the following program?
```
PROGRAM test
IMPLICIT NONE
INTEGER, PARAMETER :: n = 5, m = 10
INTEGER, DIMENSION(n:m,m-n:m+n) :: info

WRITE (*,100) SHAPE(info)
100 FORMAT (1X,'The shape of the array is:          ',2I6)
WRITE (*,110) SIZE(info)
110 FORMAT (1X,'The size of the array is:           ',I6)
WRITE (*,120) LBOUND(info)
120 FORMAT (1X,'The lower bounds of the array are: ',2I6)
```

```
WRITE (*,130) UBOUND(info)
130 FORMAT (1X,'The upper bounds of the array are: ',2I6)

END PROGRAM
```

5–10 Polar to Rectangular Conversion A scalar quantity is a quantity that can be represented by a single number. For example, the temperature at a given location is a scalar. In contrast, a vector is a quantity that has both a magnitude and a direction associated with it. For example, the velocity of an automobile is a vector, since it has both a magnitude and a direction.

Vectors can be defined either by a magnitude and a direction or by the components of the vector projected along the axes of a rectangular coordinate system. The two representations are equivalent. For two-dimensional vectors, we can convert back and forth between the representations using the following equations:

$$\mathbf{V} = V \angle \theta = V_x \mathbf{i} + V_y \mathbf{j}$$

$$V_x = V \cos \theta$$

$$V_y = V \sin \theta$$

$$V = \sqrt{V_x^2 + V_y^2}$$

$$\theta = \tan^{-1} \frac{V_y}{V_x}$$

where $\mathbf{i}$ and $\mathbf{j}$ are the unit vectors in the x and y directions, respectively. The representation of the vector in terms of magnitude and angle is known as *polar coordinates*, and the representation of the vector in terms of components along the axes is known as *rectangular coordinates*. (See Figure 5–24).

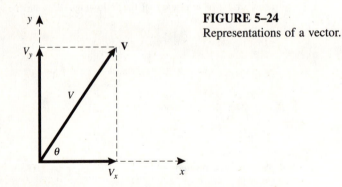

FIGURE 5–24
Representations of a vector.

Write a program that reads the polar coordinates (magnitude and angle) of a vector into a rank-1 array polar (polar(1) will contain the magnitude V and polar(2) will contain the angle θ in degrees) and converts the vector from polar to rectangular form, storing the result in a rank-1 array rect. The first element of rect should contain the x component of the vector, and the second element should contain the y component of the vector. After the conversion, display the contents of array rect. Test your program by converting the following polar vectors to rectangular form:

a. $5/\underline{-36.87°}$

b. $10/\underline{45°}$

c. $25/\underline{233.13°}$

5–11 Rectangular to Polar Conversion Write a program that reads the rectangular components of a dimensional vector into a rank-1 array `rect` and converts the vector from rectangular to polar form, storing the result in a rank-1 array `polar`. The first element of `polar` should contain the magnitude of the vector, and the second element should contain the angle of the vector in degrees. After the conversion, display the contents of array `polar`. (*Hint:* Look up function ATAN2 in Appendix B.) Test your program by converting the following rectangular vectors to polar form:

a. $3\,\mathbf{i} - 4\,\mathbf{j}$

b. $5\,\mathbf{i} + 5\,\mathbf{j}$

c. $-5\,\mathbf{i} + 12\,\mathbf{j}$

5–12 Assume that `values` is a 101-element array containing a list of measurements from a scientific experiment, which has been declared by the statement

```
REAL, DIMENSION(-50:50) :: values
```

Write the Fortran statements that would count the number of positive values, negative values, and zero values in the array and then write out a message summarizing how many values of each type were found.

5–13 Rewrite the Fortran statements of exercise 5–12, taking advantage of the intrinsic function COUNT (see Appendix B).

5–14 Write Fortran statements that would print out every fifth value in the array `values` described in exercise 5–12. The output should take the form

```
values(-50) = xxx.xxxx
values(-45) = xxx.xxxx
...
values( 50) = xxx.xxxx
```

5–15 Write a program that can read in a rank-2 array from an input disk file and calculate the sums of all the data in each row and each column in the array. The size of the array to read will be specified by two numbers on the first line in the input file, and the elements in each row of the array will be found on a single line of the input file. Size the program to handle arrays of up to 100 rows and 100 columns. An example of an input data file containing a 2×4 array follows:

```
    2        4
-24.0    -1121.     812.1      11.1
 35.6      8.1E3   135.23     -17.3
```

Write out the results in the form:

```
Sum of row     1 =
Sum of row     2 =
   ...
Sum of col     1 =
   ...
```

5–16 Test the program that you wrote in exercise 5–15 by running it on the following array:

$$\text{array} = \begin{bmatrix} 33. & -12. & 16. & 0.5 & -1.9 \\ -6. & -14. & 3.5 & 11. & 2.1 \\ 4.4 & 1.1 & -7.1 & 9.3 & -16.1 \\ 0.3 & 6.2 & -9.9 & -12. & 6.8 \end{bmatrix}$$

5–17 Dot Product A three-dimensional vector can be represented in rectangular coordinates as

$$\mathbf{V} = V_x\mathbf{i} + V_y\mathbf{j} + V_z\mathbf{k}$$

where V_x is the component of vector $\mathbf{V}$ in the x direction, V_y is the component of vector $\mathbf{V}$ in the y direction, and V_z is the component of vector $\mathbf{V}$ in the z direction. A three-dimensional vector can be stored in a rank-1 array containing three elements. The same idea applies to an n-dimensional vector. An n-dimensional vector can be stored in a rank-1 array containing n elements.

One common mathematical operation between two vectors is the *dot product*. The dot product of two vectors $\mathbf{V}_1 = V_{x1}\mathbf{i} + V_{y1}\mathbf{j} + V_{z1}\mathbf{k}$ and $\mathbf{V}_2 = V_{x2}\mathbf{i} + V_{y2}\mathbf{j} + V_{z2}\mathbf{k}$ is a scalar quantity defined by the equation

$$\mathbf{V}_1 \cdot \mathbf{V}_2 = V_{x1}V_{x2} + V_{y1}V_{y2} + V_{z1}V_{z2}$$

Write a Fortran program that will read two vectors $\mathbf{V}_1$ and $\mathbf{V}_2$ into two rank-1 arrays in computer memory and then calculate their dot product according to the preceding equation. Test your program by calculating the dot product of vectors $\mathbf{V}_1 = 5\,\mathbf{i} - 3\,\mathbf{j} + 2\,\mathbf{k}$ and $\mathbf{V}_2 = 2\,\mathbf{i} + 3\,\mathbf{j} + 4\,\mathbf{k}$.

5–18 Power Supplied to an Object If an object is being pushed by a force $\mathbf{F}$ at a velocity $\mathbf{v}$, then the power supplied to the object by the force is given by the equation

$$P = \mathbf{F} \cdot \mathbf{v}$$

where the force $\mathbf{F}$ is measured in newtons, the velocity $\mathbf{v}$ is measured in meters per second, and the power P is measured in watts (Figure 5–25). Use the Fortran program written in the exercise 5–17 to calculate the power supplied by a force of $\mathbf{F} = 4\mathbf{i} + 3\mathbf{j} - 2\mathbf{k}$ newtons to an object moving with a velocity of $\mathbf{v} = 4\mathbf{i} - 2\mathbf{j} + 1\,\mathbf{k}$ meters per second.

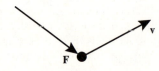

FIGURE 5–25
A force $\mathbf{F}$ applied to an object moving with velocity $\mathbf{v}$.

5–19 Write a set of Fortran statements that would search a rank-3 array `arr` and limit the maximum value of any array element to be less than or equal to 1000. If any element exceeds 1000, its value should be set to 1000. Assume that array `arr` has dimensions $1000 \times 10 \times 30$. Write two sets of statements, one checking the array elements one at a time using DO loops and one using the WHERE construct. Which of the two approaches is easier?

5–20 Cross Product Another common mathematical operation between two vectors is the *cross product*. The cross product of two vectors $\mathbf{V}_1 = V_{x1}\mathbf{i} + V_{y1}\mathbf{j} + V_{z1}\mathbf{k}$ and $\mathbf{V}_2 = V_{x2}\mathbf{i} + V_{y2}\mathbf{j} + V_{z2}\mathbf{k}$ is a vector quantity defined by the equation

$$\mathbf{V}_1 \times \mathbf{V}_2 = (V_{y1}V_{z2} - V_{y2}V_{z1})\mathbf{i} + (V_{z1}V_{x2} - V_{z2}V_{x1})\mathbf{j} + (V_{z1}V_{y2} - V_{z2}V_{y1})\mathbf{k}$$

Write a Fortran program that will read two vectors $\mathbf{V}_1$ and $\mathbf{V}_2$ into arrays in computer memory and then calculate their cross product according to the equation given above. Test your program by calculating the cross product of vectors $\mathbf{V}_1 = 5\,\mathbf{i} - 3\,\mathbf{j} + 2\,\mathbf{k}$ and $\mathbf{V}_2 = 2\,\mathbf{i} + 3\,\mathbf{j} + 4\,\mathbf{k}$.

5–21 Velocity of an Orbiting Object The vector angular velocity ω of an object moving with a velocity $\mathbf{v}$ at a distance $\mathbf{r}$ from the origin of the coordinate system is given by the equation

$$\mathbf{v} = \mathbf{r} \times \omega$$

where $\mathbf{r}$ is the distance in meters, ω is the angular velocity in radians per second, and $\mathbf{v}$ is the velocity in meters per second (Figure 5–26). If the distance from the center of the earth to an orbiting satellite is $\mathbf{r} = 300000\,\mathbf{i} + 400000\,\mathbf{j} + 50000\,\mathbf{k}$ meters and the angular velocity of the satellite is $\omega = -6 \times 10^{-3}\,\mathbf{i} + 2 \times 10^{-3}\,\mathbf{j} - 9 \times 10^{-4}\,\mathbf{k}$ radians per second, what is the velocity of the satellite in meters per second? Use the program written in the previous exercise to calculate the answer.

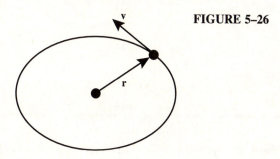

FIGURE 5–26

5–22 Program `stat_4` in Example 5–4 will behave incorrectly if a user enters an invalid value in the input data set. For example, if the user enters the characters `1.o` instead of `1.0` on a line, then the READ statement will return a nonzero status for that line. This nonzero status will be misinterpreted as the end of the data set, and only a portion of the input data will be processed. Modify the program to protect against invalid values in the input data file. If a bad value is encountered in the input data file, the program should display the line number containing the bad value and skip it. The program should process all of the good values in the file, even those after a bad value.

5–23 The location of any point P in a three-dimensional space can be represented by a set of three values (x, y, z), where x is the distance along the x-axis to the point, y is the distance along the y-axis to the point, and z is the distance along the z-axis to the point. If two points P_1 and P_2 are represented by the values (x_1, y_1, z_1) and (x_2, y_2, z_2), then the distance between points and can be calculated from the equation

$$distance = \sqrt{(x_1 - x_2)^2 + (y_1 - y_2)^2 + (z_1 - z_2)^2}$$

Write a Fortran program to read in two points (x_1, y_1, z_1) and (x_2, y_2, z_2) and to calculate the distance between them. Test your program by calculating the distance between the points $(-1, 4, 6)$ and $(1, 5, -2)$.

5–24 **Average Annual Temperature** As a part of a meteorological experiment, average annual temperature measurements were collected at 36 locations specified by latitude and longitude as shown in the following chart.

Write a Fortran program that calculates the average annual temperature along each latitude included in the experiment and the average annual temperature along each longitude included in the experiment. Finally, calculate the average annual temperature for all the locations in the experiment. Take advantage of intrinsic functions where appropriate to make your program simpler.

	90.0° W long	90.5° W long	91.0° W long	91.5° W long	92.0° W long	92.5° W long
30.0° N lat	68.2	72.1	72.5	74.1	74.4	74.2
30.5° N lat	69.4	71.1	71.9	73.1	73.6	73.7
31.0° N lat	68.9	70.5	70.9	71.5	72.8	73.0
31.5° N lat	68.6	69.9	70.4	70.8	71.5	72.2
32.0° N lat	68.1	69.3	69.8	70.2	70.9	71.2
32.5° N lat	68.3	68.8	69.6	70.0	70.5	70.9

5–25 **Matrix Multiplication** Matrix multiplication is defined only for two matrices in which the number of columns in the first matrix is equal to the number of rows in the second matrix. If matrix A is an N × L matrix, and matrix B is an L × M matrix, then the product $C = A × B$ is an N × M matrix whose elements are given by the equation

$$c_{ik} = \sum_{j=1}^{L} a_{ij}b_{jk}$$

For example, if matrices A and B are 2 × 2 matrices

$$A = \begin{bmatrix} 3.0 & -1.0 \\ 1.0 & 2.0 \end{bmatrix} \text{ and } B = \begin{bmatrix} 1.0 & 4.0 \\ 2.0 & -3.0 \end{bmatrix}$$

then the elements of matrix C will be

$$c_{11} = a_{11}b_{11} + a_{12}b_{21} = (3.0)(1.0) + (-1.0)(2.0) = 1.0$$

$$c_{12} = a_{11}b_{12} + a_{12}b_{22} = (3.0)(4.0) + (-1.0)(-3.0) = 15.0$$

$$c_{21} = a_{21}b_{11} + a_{22}b_{21} = (1.0)(1.0) + (2.0)(2.0) = 5.0$$

$$c_{22} = a_{21}b_{12} + a_{22}b_{22} = (1.0)(4.0) + (2.0)(-3.0) = -2.0$$

Write a program that can read in two matrices of arbitrary size from two input disk files and multiply them if they are of compatible sizes. If they are of incompatible sizes, an appropriate error message should be printed. The number of rows and columns in each matrix will be specified by two integers on the first line in each file, and the elements in each row of the matrix will be found on a single line of the input file. Use allocatable arrays to hold both the input matrices and the resulting output matrix. Verify your program by creating two input data files containing matrices of the compatible sizes, calculating the resulting values, and checking the answers by hand. Also, verify the proper behavior of the program if it is given two matrices of incompatible sizes. (Note: Be sure to use the proper form of implied DO statements to read in and write out the data correctly.)

5–26 Use the program produced in exercise 5–25 to multiply the following two matrices A and B:

$$C = A \times B$$
$$\text{where} \quad A = \begin{bmatrix} 1. & -5. & 4. & 2. \\ -6. & -4. & 2. & 2. \end{bmatrix}$$

$$\text{and} \quad B = \begin{bmatrix} 1. & -2. & -1. \\ 2. & 3. & 4. \\ 0. & -1. & 2. \\ 0. & -3. & 1. \end{bmatrix}$$

How many rows and how many columns are present in the resulting matrix C?

5–27 Fortran 90/95 includes an intrinsic function MATMUL to perform matrix multiplication. Rewrite the program of exercise 5–25 to use function MATMUL to multiply the matrices together.

5–28 Relative Maxima A point in a two-dimensional array is said to be a *relative maximum* if it is higher than any of the eight points surrounding it. For example, the element at position (2,2) in the array shown below is a relative maximum, since it is larger than any of the surrounding points.

$$\begin{bmatrix} 11 & 7 & -2 \\ -7 & 14 & 3 \\ 2 & -3 & 5 \end{bmatrix}$$

Write a program to read a matrix A from an input disk file and to scan for all relative maxima within the matrix. The first line in the disk file should contain the number of rows and the number of columns in the matrix, and then the next lines should contain the values in the matrix, with all of the values in a given row on a single line of the input disk file. The program should only consider interior points within the matrix, since any point along an edge of the matrix cannot possibly be completely surrounded by points lower than itself. Test your program by finding the relative maxima in the following matrix, which can be found in file FINDPEAK:

$$A = \begin{bmatrix} 2. & -1. & -2. & 1. & 3. & -5. & 2. & 1. \\ -2. & 0. & -2.5 & 5. & -2. & 2. & 1. & 0. \\ -3. & -3. & -3. & 3. & 0. & 0. & -1. & -2. \\ -4.5 & -4. & -7. & 6. & 1. & -3. & 0. & 5. \\ 3.5 & -3. & -5. & 0. & 4. & 17. & 11. & 5. \\ -9. & -6. & -5. & -3. & 1. & 2. & 0. & 0.5 \\ -7. & -4. & -5. & -3. & 2. & 4. & 3. & -1. \\ -6. & -5. & -5. & -2. & 0. & 1. & 2. & 5. \end{bmatrix}$$

5–29 Temperature Distribution on a Metallic Plate Under steady-state conditions, the temperature at any point on the surface of a metallic plate will be the average of the temperatures of all points surrounding it. This fact can be used in an iterative procedure to calculate the temperature distribution at all points on the plate.

Figure 5–27 shows a square plate divided in 100 squares or nodes by a grid. The temperatures of the nodes form a two-dimensional array T. The temperature in all nodes at the edges of the plate is constrained to be 20°C by a cooling system, and the temperature of the node (3,8) is fixed at 100°C by exposure to boiling water.

A new estimate of the temperature $T_{i,j}$ in any given node can be calculated from the average of the temperatures in all segments surrounding it:

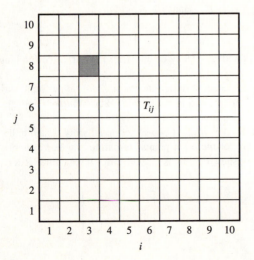

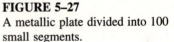

FIGURE 5–27
A metallic plate divided into 100 small segments.

$$T_{ij,new} = \frac{1}{4}(T_{i+1,j} + T_{i-1,j} + T_{i,j+1} + T_{i,j-1}) \tag{5-2}$$

To determine the temperature distribution on the surface of a plate, an initial assumption must be made about the temperatures in each node. Then Equation (5–2) is applied to each node whose temperature is not fixed to calculate a new estimate of the temperature in that node. These updated temperature estimates are used to calculate newer estimates, and the process is repeated until the new temperature estimates in each node differ from the old ones by only a small amount. At that point, a steady-state solution has been found.

Write a program to calculate the steady-state temperature distribution throughout the plate, making an initial assumption that all interior segments are at a temperature of 50°C. Remember that all outside segments are fixed at a temperature of 20°C and segment (3,8) is fixed at a temperature of 100°C. The program should apply Equation (5–2) iteratively until the maximum temperature change between iterations in any node is less than 0.01 degree. What is the steady-state temperature of segment (5,5)?

6

Procedures and Structured Programming

In Chapter 3 you learned the importance of good program design, using the top-down design technique. In *top-down design,* the programmer starts with a statement of the problem to be solved and the required inputs and outputs. Next he or she describes the algorithm to be implemented by the program in broad outline and applies *decomposition* to break the algorithm into logical subdivisions called subtasks. Then the programmer breaks down each subtask until he or she winds up with many small pieces, each of which does a simple, clearly understandable job. Finally the individual pieces are turned into Fortran code.

Although we have followed this design process in our examples, the results have been somewhat restricted because we had to combine the final Fortran code generated for each subtask into a single large program. We did not have a way to code, verify, and test the subtasks independently before combining them into the final program.

Fortunately, Fortran has a special mechanism designed to make subtasks easy to develop and debug independently before building the final program. It is possible to code each subtask as a separate **program unit**[1] called an **external procedure,** and each external procedure can be compiled, tested, and debugged independently of all of the other subtasks (procedures) in the program.

Fortran has two kinds of external procedures: **subroutines** and **function subprograms** (or just **functions**). *Subroutines* are procedures that are invoked by naming them in a separate CALL statement and that can return multiple results through calling arguments. *Function subprogram* are procedures that are invoked by naming them in an expression and whose result is a *single value* that is used in the evaluation of the expression. Both type of procedures are described in this chapter.

Well-designed procedures enormously reduce the effort required on a large programming project. Their benefits include

1. **Independent testing of subtasks.** Each subtask can be coded and compiled as an independent unit. The subtask can be tested separately to ensure that it performs prop-

---

[1] A program unit is a *separately compiled* portion of a Fortran program. Main programs, subroutines, and function subprograms are all program units.

erly by itself before combining it into the larger program. This step is known as *unit testing.* It eliminates a major source of problems before the final program is even built.

2. **Reusable code.** In many cases many parts of a program need the same basic subtask. For example, we may need to sort a list of values into ascending order many times within a program, or even in other programs. It is possible to design, code, test, and debug a *single* procedure to do the sorting and then to reuse that procedure whenever sorting is required. This reusable code has two major advantages: It reduces the total programming effort required, and it simplifies debugging, since the sorting function needs to be debugged only once.

3. **Isolation from unintended side effects.** Subprograms communicate with the main programs that invoke them through a list of variables called an **argument list.** The only variables in the main program that can be changed by the procedure are those in the argument list.

Once a large program is written and released, it has to be maintained. *Program maintenance* involves fixing bugs and modifying the program to handle new and unforeseen circumstances. The programmer who modifies a program during maintenance is often not the person who originally wrote it. The programmer modifying a poorly written program can easily make a change in one region of the code and have that change cause unintended side effects in a totally different part of the program. Unintended side effects happen because the original programmer reused variable names in different portions of the program. When the maintenance programmer changes the values left behind in some of the variables, those values are accidentally picked up and used in other portions of the code.

The use of well-designed procedures minimizes this problem by **data hiding.** All of the variables in the procedure except for those in the argument list are not visible to the main program, and therefore mistakes or changes in those variables cannot accidentally cause unintended side effects in the other parts of the program.

Good Programming Practice

Break large program tasks into procedures whenever practical to achieve the important benefits of independent component testing, reusability, and isolation from undesired side effects.

We will now examine the two types of Fortran 90/95 procedures: subroutines and functions.

■ 6.1
SUBROUTINES

A *subroutine* is a Fortran procedure that is invoked by naming it in a `CALL` statement and that receives its input values and returns its results through an argument list. The general form of a subroutine is

```
SUBROUTINE subroutine_name ( argument_list )
   ...
      (Declaration section)
   ...
      (Execution section)
   ...
RETURN
END SUBROUTINE [name]
```

The SUBROUTINE statement marks the beginning of a subroutine. It specifies the name of the subroutine and the argument list associated with it. The subroutine name must follow standard Fortran conventions: it may be up to 31 characters long and contain both alphabetic characters and digits, but the first character must be alphabetic. The argument list contains a list of the variables and/or arrays that are being passed from the calling program to the subroutine. These variables are called **dummy arguments,** since the subroutine does not actually allocate any memory for them. They are just placeholders for actual arguments that will be passed from the calling program unit when the subroutine is invoked.

Note that like any Fortran program, a subroutine must have a declaration section and an execution section. When a program calls the subroutine, the execution of the calling program is suspended and the execution section of the subroutine is run. When a RETURN or END SUBROUTINE statement is reached in the subroutine, the calling program starts running again at the line following the subroutine call.

Each subroutine is an independent program unit, beginning with a SUBROUTINE statement and terminated by an END SUBROUTINE statement. Each subroutine is compiled separately from the main program and from any other procedures. Because each program unit in a program is compiled separately, statement labels and local variable names may be reused in different routines without causing an error.

Any executable program unit may call a subroutine, including another subroutine. To call a subroutine, the calling program uses a CALL statement. The form of a CALL statement is

```
CALL subroutine_name ( argument_list )
```

where the order and type of the **actual arguments** in the argument list must match the order and type of the dummy arguments declared in the subroutine.

A simple subroutine is shown in Figure 6–1. This subroutine calculates the hypotenuse of a right triangle from the lengths of the other two sides.

FIGURE 6–1

A simple subroutine to calculate the hypotenuse of a right triangle.

```
SUBROUTINE calc_hypotenuse ( side_1, side_2, hypotenuse )
!
! Purpose:
!   To calculate the hypotenuse of a right triangle from the two
!   other sides.
!
```

(continued)

(concluded)

```
! Record of revisions:
!    Date         Programmer             Description of change
!    ====         ==========             =====================
!  08/27/95    S. J. Chapman             Original code
!
IMPLICIT NONE

! Declare calling parameters:
REAL, INTENT(IN) :: side_1          ! Length of side 1
REAL, INTENT(IN) :: side_2          ! Length of side 2
REAL, INTENT(OUT) :: hypotenuse ! Length of hypotenuse

! Declare local variables:
REAL :: temp                        ! Temporary variable

! Calculate hypotenuse
temp = side_1**2 + side_2**2
hypotenuse = SQRT ( temp )

RETURN
END SUBROUTINE
```

This subroutine has three arguments in its dummy argument list. Arguments `side_1` and `side_2` are placeholders for real values containing the lengths of sides 1 and 2 of the triangle. These dummy arguments are used to pass data to the subroutine but are not changed inside the subroutine, so they are declared to be input values with the `INTENT(IN)` attribute. Dummy argument `hypotenuse` is a placeholder for a real variable that will receive the length of the hypotenuse of the triangle. The value of hypotenuse is set in the subroutine, so it is declared to be an output variable with the `INTENT(OUT)` attribute.

The variable `temp` is actually defined within the subroutine. It is used in the subroutine, but it is not accessible to any calling program. Variables used within a subroutine and not accessible by calling programs are called **local variables.**

The `RETURN` statement in the subroutine is optional. Execution automatically returns to the calling program when the `END SUBROUTINE` statement is reached. A `RETURN` statement is necessary only when we wish to return to the calling program before the end of the subroutine is reached. As a result the `RETURN` statement is rarely used.

To test a subroutine, we need to write a program called a **test driver program.** The test driver program is a small program that calls the subroutine with a sample data set for the specific purpose of testing it. A test driver program for subroutine `calc_hypotenuse` is shown in Figure 6–2:

FIGURE 6–2

A test driver program for subroutine `calc_hypotenuse`.

```
PROGRAM test_hypotenuse
!
! Purpose:
!    Program to test the operation of subroutine calc_hypotenuse.
!
```

(continued)

(concluded)

```
! Record of revisions:
!     Date        Programmer        Description of change
!     ====        ==========        =====================
!   08/27/95   S. J. Chapman        Original code
!
IMPLICIT NONE

! Declare variables:
REAL :: s1              ! Length of side 1
REAL :: s2              ! Length of side 2
REAL :: hypot           ! Hypotenuse

! Get the lengths of the two sides.
WRITE (*,*) 'Program to test subroutine calc_hypotenuse: '
WRITE (*,*) 'Enter the length of side 1: '
READ (*,*) s1
WRITE (*,*) 'Enter the length of side 2: '
READ (*,*) s2
```

```
! Call calc_hypotenuse.
CALL calc_hypotenuse ( s1, s2, hypot )
```

```
! Write out hypotenuse.
WRITE (*,1000) hypot
1000 FORMAT (1X,'The length of the hypotenuse is: ', F10.4 )

END PROGRAM
```

This program calls subroutine `calc_hypotenuse` with an actual argument list of variables s1, s2, and hypot. Therefore, wherever the dummy argument side_1 appears in the subroutine, variable s1 is really used instead. Similarly, the hypotenuse is really written into variable hypot.

6.1.1 Sample Problem—Sorting

Let us now reexamine the sorting problem of Example 5–3, using subroutines where appropriate.

EXAMPLE 6–1 *Sorting Data:* Develop a program to read in a data set from a file, sort it into ascending order, and display the sorted data set. Use subroutines where appropriate.

SOLUTION

The program in Example 5–3 read an arbitrary number of real input data values from a user-supplied file, sorted the data into ascending order, and wrote the sorted data to the standard output device. The sorting process would make a good candidate for a subroutine, since only array a and its length nvals are in common between the sorting process and the rest of the program. The rewritten program using a sorting subroutine is shown in Figure 6–3:

FIGURE 6–3

Program to sort real data values into ascending order using a `sort` subroutine

```fortran
PROGRAM sort3
!
! Purpose:
!   To read in a real input data set, sort it into ascending order
!   using the selection sort algorithm, and to write the sorted
!   data to the standard output device. This program calls subroutine
!   "sort" to do the actual sorting.
!
! Record of revisions:
!     Date       Programmer         Description of change
!     ====       ==========         =====================
!   09/28/95    S. J. Chapman       Original code
!
IMPLICIT NONE

! List of parameters:
INTEGER, PARAMETER :: max_size = 10

! List of variables:
REAL, DIMENSION(max_size) :: a ! Data array to sort
LOGICAL :: exceed = .FALSE.    ! Logical indicating that array
                               ! limits are exceeded.
CHARACTER(len=20) :: filename  ! Input data file name
INTEGER :: i                   ! Loop index
INTEGER :: nvals = 0           ! Number of data values to sort
INTEGER :: status              ! I/O status: 0 for success
REAL :: temp                   ! Temporary variable for reading

! Get the name of the file containing the input data.
WRITE (*,*) 'Enter the file name with the data to be sorted: '
READ (*,'(A20)') filename

! Open input data file. Status is OLD because the input data must
! already exist.
OPEN ( UNIT=9, FILE=filename, STATUS='OLD', ACTION='READ', &
       IOSTAT=status )

! Was the OPEN successful?
fileopen: IF ( status == 0 ) THEN      ! Open successful

! The file was opened successfully, so read the data to sort
! from it, sort the data, and write out the results.
! First read in data.
DO
   READ (9, *, IOSTAT=status) temp      ! Get value
   IF ( status /= 0 ) EXIT              ! Exit on end of data
   nvals = nvals + 1                    ! Bump count
   size: IF ( nvals <= max_size ) THEN ! Too many values?
      a(nvals) = temp                   ! No: Save value in array
   ELSE
      exceed = .TRUE.                   ! Yes: Array overflow
   END IF size
END DO
```

(continued)

(continued)

```
      ! Was the array size exceeded?  If so, tell user and quit.
      toobig: IF ( exceed ) THEN
         WRITE (*,1010) nvals, max_size
         1010 FORMAT (' Maximum array size exceeded: ', I6, ' > ', I6 )
      ELSE

         ! Limit not exceeded: sort the data.
         CALL sort (a, nvals)

         ! Now write out the sorted data.
         WRITE (*,1020) ' The sorted output data values are: '
         1020 FORMAT (A)
         WRITE (*,1030) ( a(i), i = 1, nvals )
         1030 FORMAT (4X,F10.4)

      END IF toobig

   ELSE fileopen

      ! Else file open failed.  Tell user.
      WRITE (*,1040) status
      1040 FORMAT (1X,'File open failed--status = ', I6)

   END IF fileopen

   END PROGRAM

SUBROUTINE sort (arr, n)
!
! Purpose:
!   To sort real array "arr" into ascending order using a selection
!   sort.
!
IMPLICIT NONE

! Declare calling parameters:
INTEGER, INTENT(IN) :: n                  ! Number of values
REAL, DIMENSION(n), INTENT(INOUT) :: arr ! Array to be sorted

! Declare local variables:
INTEGER :: i              ! Loop index
INTEGER :: iptr           ! Pointer to smallest value
INTEGER :: j              ! Loop index
REAL :: temp              ! Temp variable for swaps

! Sort the array
outer: DO i = 1, n-1

   ! Find the minimum value in arr(i) through arr(n)
   iptr = i
   inner: DO j = i+1, n
      minval: IF ( arr(j) < arr(iptr) ) THEN
         iptr = j
      END IF minval
   END DO inner
```

(continued)

```
(concluded)
    ! iptr now points to the minimum value, so swap arr(iptr)
    ! with arr(i) if i /= iptr.
    swap: IF ( i /= iptr ) THEN
       temp      = arr(i)
       arr(i)    = arr(iptr)
       arr(iptr)= temp
    END IF swap

END DO outer

END SUBROUTINE sort
```

This new program can be tested just as the original program was, and the results are identical. If the following data set is placed in file INPUT2,

```
13.3
12.
-3.0
 0.
 4.0
 6.6
 4.
-6.
```

then the results of the test run will be

```
C>sort3
Enter the file name containing the data to be sorted:
input2
The sorted output data values are:
      -6.0000
      -3.0000
        .0000
       4.0000
       4.0000
       6.6000
      12.0000
      13.3000
```

The program gives the correct answers for our test data set, as before.

Subroutine sort performs the same function as the sorting code in the original example, but now sort is an independent subroutine that we can reuse unchanged whenever we need to sort any array of real numbers.

Note that the array was declared in the sort subroutine as

```
REAL, DIMENSION(n), INTENT(INOUT) :: arr  ! Array to be sorted
```

The statement tells the Fortran compiler that dummy argument arr is an array whose length is n, where n is also a calling argument. The dummy argument arr is only a placeholder for whatever array is passed as an argument when the subroutine is called. The actual size of the array will be the size of the array that is passed from the calling program.

Also, note that dummy argument `arr` was used both to pass the data to subroutine `sort` and to return the sorted data to the calling program. Since it is used for both input and output, it is declared with the `INTENT(INOUT)` attribute.

6.1.2 The `INTENT` Attribute

Dummy subroutine arguments can have an `INTENT` attribute associated with them. The `INTENT` attribute is associated with the type declaration statement that declares each dummy argument. The attribute can take one of three forms:

`INTENT(IN)`	Dummy argument is used only to pass input data to the subroutine.
`INTENT(OUT)`	Dummy argument is used only to return results to the calling program.
`INTENT(INOUT)` or `INTENT(IN OUT)`	Dummy argument is used both to pass input data to the subroutine and to return results to the calling program.

The purpose of the `INTENT` attribute is to tell the compiler how the programmer intends to use each dummy argument. Some arguments may be intended only to provide input data to the subroutine, and some may be intended only to return results from the subroutine. Finally, some may be intended to both provide data and return results. The appropriate `INTENT` attribute should *always* be declared for each argument.

Once the compiler knows what we intend to do with each dummy argument, it can use that information to help catch programming errors at compile time. For example, suppose that a subroutine accidentally modifies an input argument. Changing that input argument will cause the value of the corresponding variable in the calling program to be changed, and the changed value will be used in all subsequent processing. This type of programming error can be very hard to locate, since it is caused by the interaction between procedures.

In the following example subroutine `sub1` calculates an output value but also accidentally modifies its input value.

```
SUBROUTINE sub1(input,output)
IMPLICIT NONE
REAL, INTENT(IN) :: input
REAL, INTENT(OUT) :: output

output = 2. * input
input = -1.                     ! This line is an error!
END SUBROUTINE
```

By declaring our intent for each dummy argument, the compiler can spot this error for us at compilation time. When this subroutine is compiled with a representative Fortran 90 compiler, the results are

```
1   SUBROUTINE sub1(input,output)
2   IMPLICIT NONE
3   REAL, INTENT(IN) :: input
4   REAL, INTENT(OUT) :: output
5
6   output = 2. * input
7   input = -1.
            |
```
FATAL -- Dummy argument (INPUT) with INTENT(IN) attribute must not be redefined or become undefined within procedure (see "Procedure Arguments" in the Lahey Fortran 90 Language Reference).

```
8   END SUBROUTINE
```
Bytes of stack required for this program unit: 0.

The INTENT attribute is only valid for dummy procedure arguments. As you will see later, declaring the intent of each dummy argument also helps spot errors that occur in the calling sequence *between* procedures. You should always declare the intent of every dummy argument in every procedure.

Good Programming Practice
Always declare the intent of every dummy argument in every procedure.

6.1.3 Passing Arrays to Subroutines

A calling argument is passed to a subroutine by passing a pointer to the memory location of the argument. If the argument happens to be an array, then the pointer points to the first value in the array. However, the subroutine needs to know how big the array is to ensure that it stays within the boundaries of the array and in order to perform array operations. How can we supply this information to the subroutine?

One approach is to pass the bounds of each dimension of the array to the subroutine as arguments in the subroutine call and to declare the corresponding dummy array to be that length. The dummy array is thus an *explicit-shape dummy array,* since each of its bounds is explicitly specified. If this is done, then the subroutine will know the shape of the array. The bounds checkers on most Fortran compilers will be able to report out-of-bounds memory references, and we will be able to use array sections and whole array operations in the subroutine. For example, the following code declares two arrays data1 and data2 to be of extent n, and then processes nvals values in the arrays. If an out-of-bounds reference occurs in this subroutine, it can be detected and reported.

```
SUBROUTINE process ( data1, data2, n, nvals )
INTEGER, INTENT(IN) :: n, nvals
REAL, INTENT(IN), DIMENSION(n) :: data1
REAL, INTENT(OUT), DIMENSION(n) :: data2
```

```
data2 = 3. * data1
END SUBROUTINE process
```

Another approach is to declare all dummy arrays in the subroutine as *assumed-shape dummy arrays* and to create an explicit interface to the subroutine. This approach is explained in section 6.5.2.

EXAMPLE 6–2 Bounds Checking in Subroutines: Write a simple Fortran program containing a subroutine that oversteps the limits of an array in its argument list. Compile and execute the program both with bounds checking turned off and with bounds checking turned on.

SOLUTION

The program in Figure 6–4 allocates a five-element array a. It initializes all the elements of a to zero, and then calls subroutine sub1. Subroutine sub1 modifies six elements of array a, despite the fact that a has only five elements.

FIGURE 6–4
A program illustrating the effect of exceeding the boundaries of an array in a subroutine.

```
PROGRAM array2
!
! Purpose:
!   To illustrate the effect of accessing an out-of-bounds
!   array element.
!
! Record of revisions:
!     Date        Programmer          Description of change
!     ====        ==========          =====================
!   10/03/95    S. J. Chapman         Original code
!
IMPLICIT NONE

! Declare the and initialize the variables used in this program.
INTEGER :: i                           ! Loop index
REAL, DIMENSION(5) :: a = 0.           ! Array

! Call subroutine sub1.
CALL sub1( a, 5, 6 )

! Write out the values of array a
DO i = 1, 6
   WRITE (*,100) i, a(i)
   100 FORMAT ( 1X,'A(', I1, ') = ', F6.2 )
END DO

END PROGRAM

SUBROUTINE sub1 ( a, ndim, n )
IMPLICIT NONE

INTEGER, INTENT(IN) :: ndim              ! size of array
REAL, INTENT(OUT), DIMENSION(ndim) :: a ! Dummy argument
```

(continued)

(concluded)

```
INTEGER, INTENT(IN) :: n                    ! # elements to process
INTEGER :: i                                ! Loop index

DO i = 1, n
   a(i) = i
END DO

END SUBROUTINE sub1
```

When this program is compiled with the Digital Visual Fortran 5.0 compiler with bounds checking turned *off*, the result is

```
C>array2

run-time error F6981: WRITE(CON)
- initial left parenthesis expected in format
```

In this case the subroutine has written beyond the end of array a and has actually written over a part of the main program stored in memory. This result can produce a very subtle and hard to find bug! The subroutine actually destroyed a part of the FORMAT statement by writing beyond the end of array a.

If the program is recompiled with the Digital Visual Fortran 5.0 compiler with bounds checking turned *on*, the result is

```
C>array2

fig6-6.f90(38) : run-time error F6096: $DEBUG
- array or substring subscript expression out of range

Execution traceback:
        from SUB1 in array2.f90(38)
        from main program in array2.f90(19)
```

Here the program detected the out-of-bounds reference and shut down after telling the user where the problem occurred.

6.1.4 Passing Character Variables to Subroutines

When a character variable is used as a dummy subroutine argument, the length of the character variable is declared with an asterisk. Since no memory is actually allocated for dummy arguments, it is not necessary to know the length of the character argument when the subroutine is compiled. Here is a typical dummy character argument:

```
SUBROUTINE sample ( string )
CHARACTER(len=*), INTENT(IN) :: string
...
```

When the subroutine is called, the length of the dummy character argument will be the length of the actual argument passed from the calling program. If we need to know that length during subroutine execution, we can use the intrinsic function LEN() to determine it. For example, the following simple subroutine displays the length of any character argument passed to it.

```
SUBROUTINE sample ( string )
CHARACTER(len=*), INTENT(IN) :: string
WRITE (*,'(1X,A,I3)') 'Length of variable = ', LEN(string)
END SUBROUTINE
```

6.1.5 Error Handling in Subroutines

What happens if a program calls a subroutine with insufficient or invalid data for proper processing? For example, suppose that we are writing a subroutine that subtracts two input variables and takes the square root of the result. What should we do if the difference of the two variables is a negative number?

```
SUBROUTINE process (a, b, result)
IMPLICIT NONE
REAL, INTENT(IN) :: a, b
REAL, INTENT(OUT) :: result
REAL :: temp
temp = a - b
result = SQRT ( temp )
END SUBROUTINE
```

For example, suppose that a is 1 and b is 2. If we just process the values in the subroutine, a run-time error will occur when we attempt to take the square root of a negative number and the program will abort. This result is clearly not acceptable.

An alternative version of the subroutine follows. In this version we test for a negative number, and if one is present, we print out an informative error message and stop.

```
SUBROUTINE process (a, b, result)
IMPLICIT NONE
REAL, INTENT(IN) :: a, b
REAL, INTENT(OUT) :: result
REAL :: temp
temp = a - b
IF ( temp >= 0. ) THEN
   result = SQRT ( temp )
ELSE
   WRITE (*,*) 'Square root of negative value in subroutine PROCESS!'
   STOP
END IF
END SUBROUTINE
```

Although it is better than the previous example, this design is also bad. If temp is ever negative, the program will just stop without ever returning from the call to subroutine process and the user will lose all the data and processing that has occurred up to that point in the program.

A much better way to design the subroutine is to detect the possible error condition and to report it to the calling program by setting a value into an **error flag.** The calling program can then take appropriate actions about the error. For example, the program can be designed to recover from the error if possible. If not, it can at least write out an informative error message, save the partial results calculated so far, and then shut down gracefully.

In the following example, a 0 returned in the error flag means successful completion, and a 1 means that the square-root-of-a-negative-number error occurred.

```
SUBROUTINE process (a, b, result, error)
IMPLICIT NONE
REAL, INTENT(IN) :: a, b
REAL, INTENT(OUT) :: result
INTEGER, INTENT(OUT) :: error
REAL :: temp
temp = a - b
IF ( temp >= 0. ) THEN
   result = SQRT ( temp )
   error = 0
ELSE
   result = 0
   error = 1
END IF
END SUBROUTINE
```

Programming Pitfalls
Never include STOP statements in subroutines. If you do, you might release a working program to users, only to find that it mysteriously halts from time to time on certain unusual data sets.

Good Programming Practice
If error conditions can occur within a subroutine, you should test for them and set an error flag to be returned to the calling program. The calling program should test for the error conditions after a subroutine call and take appropriate actions.

Quiz 6–1
This quiz provides a quick check to see if you understand the concepts introduced in section 6.1. If you have trouble with the quiz, reread the section, ask your instructor, or discuss the material with a fellow student. The answers to this quiz appear in Appendix F.

For questions 1 through 3, determine whether the subroutine calls are correct or not. If they are in error, specify what is wrong with them.

(continued)

(concluded)

1. ```
PROGRAM test1
REAL, DIMENSION(120) :: a
REAL :: average, sd
INTEGER :: n
...
CALL ave_sd (a, n, average, sd)
...
END PROGRAM
SUBROUTINE ave_sd(array, nvals, average, sd)
REAL, INTENT(IN) :: nvals
REAL, INTENT(IN), DIMENSION(nvals) :: array
REAL, INTENT(OUT) :: average, sd
...
END SUBROUTINE
```

2. ```
PROGRAM test2
CHARACTER(len=12) :: str1, str2
str1 = 'ABCDEFGHIJ'
CALL swap_str (str1, str2)
WRITE (*,*) str1, str2
END PROGRAM
SUBROUTINE swap_str (string1, string2)
CHARACTER(len=*),INTENT(IN) :: string1
CHARACTER(len=*),INTENT(OUT) :: string2
INTEGER :: i, length
length = LEN(string1)
DO i = 1, length
   string2(length-i+1:length-i+1) = string1(i:i)
END DO
END SUBROUTINE
```

3. ```
PROGRAM test3
INTEGER, PARAMETER :: len = 25
INTEGER, DIMENSION(len) :: idata
REAL :: sum
...
CALL sub3 (idata, len, sum)
...
END PROGRAM
SUBROUTINE sub3(iarray, len, sum)
INTEGER, INTENT(IN) :: len
INTEGER, INTENT(IN), DIMENSION(len) :: iarray
REAL, INTENT(OUT) :: sum
INTEGER :: i
sum = 0.
DO i = 1, 30
   sum = sum + iarray(i)
END DO
END SUBROUTINE
```

### 6.1.6 Examples

*EXAMPLE 6–3 Statistics Subroutines:* Develop a set of reusable subroutines capable of determining the statistical properties of a data set of real numbers in an array. The set of subroutines should include the following:
```

1. A subroutine to determine the maximum value in a data set and the sample number containing that value.
2. A subroutine to determine the minimum value in a data set and the sample number containing that value.
3. A subroutine to determine the average (mean) and standard deviation of the data set.
4. A subroutine to determine the median of the data set.

SOLUTION

We will be generating four subroutines, each of which works on a common input data set consisting of an array of real numbers.

1. **State the problem.**

    Write four subroutines: `rmax` to find the maximum value and the location of that value in a real array, `rmin` to find the minimum value and the location of that value in a real array, `ave_sd` to find the average and standard deviation of a real array, and `median` to find the median of a real array.

2. **Define the inputs and outputs.**

    The input to each subroutine will be array of values, plus the number of values in the array. The outputs will be as follows:

    a. The output of subroutine `rmax` will be a real variable containing the maximum value in the input array and an integer variable containing the offset in the array at which the maximum value occurred.
    b. The output of subroutine `rmin` will be a real variable containing the minimum value in the input array and an integer variable containing the offset in the array at which the minimum value occurred.
    c. The output of subroutine `ave_sd` will be two real variables containing the average and standard deviation of the input array.
    d. The output of subroutine `median` will be a real variable containing the median value of the input array.

3. **Describe the algorithm.**

The pseudocode for the `rmax` routine is

```
! Initialize "real_max" to the first value in the array
! and "imax" to 1.
real_max ← a(1)
imax ← 1

! Find the maximum value in a(1) through a(n)
DO for i = 2 to n
   IF a(i) > real_max THEN
      real_max ← a(i)
      imax ← i
   END of IF
END of DO
```

The pseudocode for the `rmin` routine is

```
! Initialize "real_min" to the first value in the array
! and "imin" to 1.
real_min ← a(1)
imin ← 1

! Find the maximum value in a(1) through a(n)
DO for i = 2 to n
   IF a(i) < real_min THEN
      real_min ← a(i)
      imin ← i
   END of IF
END of DO
```

The pseudocode for the `ave_sd` routine is essentially the same as that in Example 5–4. It will not be repeated here. For the `median` calculation, we will be able to take advantage of the `sort` subroutine that we have already written. (Here is an example of reusable code saving us time and effort.) The pseudocode for the `median` subroutine is

```
CALL sort ( a, n )
IF n is an even number THEN
   med ← (a(n/2) + a(n/2+1)) / 2.
ELSE
   med ← a(n/2+1)
END of IF
```

4. Turn the algorithm into Fortran statements.

The resulting Fortran subroutines are shown in Figure 6–5.

FIGURE 6–5
The subroutines `rmin`, `rmax`, `ave_sd`, and `median`.

```
SUBROUTINE rmax ( a, n, real_max, imax )
!
! Purpose:
!    To find the maximum value in an array and the location
!    of that value in the array.
!
IMPLICIT NONE

! List of calling arguments:
INTEGER, INTENT(IN) :: n                    ! No. of vals in array a.
REAL, INTENT(IN), DIMENSION(n) :: a         ! Input data.
REAL, INTENT(OUT) :: real_max               ! Maximum value in a.
INTEGER, INTENT(OUT) :: imax                ! Location of max value.

! List of local variables:
INTEGER :: i                                ! Index variable

! Initialize the maximum value to first value in array.
real_max = a(1)
imax = 1
```

(continued)

```
(continued)
! Find the maximum value.
DO i = 2, n
   IF ( a(i) > real_max ) THEN
       real_max  = a(i)
       imax = i
   END IF
END DO

END SUBROUTINE rmax

SUBROUTINE rmin ( a, n, real_min, imin )
!
! Purpose:
!    To find the minimum value in an array and the location
!    of that value in the array.
!
IMPLICIT NONE

! List of calling arguments:
INTEGER, INTENT(IN) :: n                    ! No. of vals in array a.
REAL, INTENT(IN), DIMENSION(N) :: a         ! Input data.
REAL, INTENT(OUT) :: real_min               ! Minimum value in a.
INTEGER, INTENT(OUT) :: imin                ! Location of min value.

! List of local variables:
INTEGER :: i                                ! Index variable

! Initialize the minimum value to first value in array.
real_min  = a(1)
imin = 1

! Find the minimum value.
DO i = 2, n
   IF ( a(i) < real_min ) THEN
       real_min  = a(i)
       imin = i
   END IF
END DO

END SUBROUTINE rmin

SUBROUTINE ave_sd ( a, n, ave, std_dev, error )
!
! Purpose:
!    To calculate the average and standard deviation of an array.
!
IMPLICIT NONE

! List of calling arguments:
INTEGER, INTENT(IN) :: n                    ! No. of vals in array a.
REAL, INTENT(IN), DIMENSION(n) :: a         ! Input data.
REAL, INTENT(OUT) :: ave                    ! Average of a.
REAL, INTENT(OUT) :: std_dev                ! Standard deviation.
INTEGER, INTENT(OUT) :: error               ! Flag: 0 — no error
                                            !       1 — sd invalid
                                            !       2 — ave & sd invalid
```

(continued)

(continued)

```
! List of local variables:
INTEGER :: i                            ! Loop index
REAL :: sum_x                           ! Sum of input values
REAL :: sum_x2                          ! Sum of input values squared

! Initialize the sums to zero.
sum_x  = 0.
sum_x2 = 0.

! Accumulate sums.
DO I = 1, n
   sum_x  = sum_x + a(i)
   sum_x2 = sum_x2 + a(i)**2
END DO

! Check to see if we have enough input data.
IF ( n >= 2 ) THEN ! we have enough data

   ! Calculate the mean and standard deviation
   ave    = sum_x / REAL(n)
   std_dev = SQRT( (REAL(n) * sum_x2 - sum_x**2) &
            / (REAL(n) * REAL(n-1)) )
   error = 0

ELSE IF ( n == 1 ) THEN ! no valid std_dev

   ave = sum_x
   std_dev = 0.                   ! std_dev invalid
   error = 1

ELSE

   ave = 0.                       ! ave invalid
   std_dev = 0.                   ! std_dev invalid
   error = 2

END IF
END SUBROUTINE ave_sd

SUBROUTINE median ( a, n, med )
!
! Purpose:
!   To calculate the median value of an array.
!
IMPLICIT NONE

! List of calling arguments:
INTEGER, INTENT(IN) :: n               ! No. of vals in array a.
REAL, INTENT(IN), DIMENSION(n) :: a ! Input data.
REAL, INTENT(OUT) :: med               ! Median value of a.

! Sort the data into ascending order.
CALL sort ( a, n )

! Get median.
IF ( MOD(n,2) == 0 ) THEN
   med = ( a(n/2) + a(n/2+1) ) / 2.
```

(continued)

(concluded)
```
ELSE
    med = a(n/2+1)
END IF
END SUBROUTINE median
```

5. **Test the resulting Fortran programs.**

To test these subroutines, we need to write a driver program to read the input data, call the subroutines, and write out the results. This test is left as exercise 6–12 at the end of the chapter.

EXAMPLE 6–4 *Gauss-Jordan Elimination:* Many important problems in science and engineering require the solution of a system of N simultaneous linear equations in N unknowns. Some of these problems require the solution of small systems of equations, say 3×3 or 4×4. Such problems are relatively easy to solve. Other problems might require the solution of really large sets of simultaneous equations, like 1000 equations in 1000 unknowns. Those problems are *much* harder to solve, and the solution requires a variety of special iterative techniques. A whole branch of the science of numerical methods is devoted to different ways to solve systems of simultaneous linear equations.

We will now develop a subroutine to solve a system of simultaneous linear equations using the straightforward approach known as Gauss-Jordan elimination. The subroutine that we develop should work fine for systems of up to about 20 equations in 20 unknowns.

Gauss-Jordan elimination depends on the fact that if you multiply one equation in a system of equations by a constant and add it to another equation, the new system of equations will still be equivalent to the original one. In fact, it works in exactly the same way as we solve systems of simultaneous equations by hand.

To understand the technique, consider the following 3×3 system of equations:

$$
\begin{array}{ll}
1.0 \ x1 + 1.0 \ x2 + 1.0 \ x3 = 1.0 & \\
2.0 \ x1 + 1.0 \ x2 + 1.0 \ x3 = 2.0 & \quad (6\text{--}1) \\
1.0 \ x1 + 3.0 \ x2 + 2.0 \ x3 = 4.0 &
\end{array}
$$

We want to manipulate this set of equations by multiplying one of the equations by a constant and adding it to another one until we eventually wind up with a set of equations of the form

$$
\begin{array}{ll}
1.0 \ x1 + 0.0 \ x2 + 0.0 \ x3 = b1 & \\
0.0 \ x1 + 1.0 \ x2 + 0.0 \ x3 = b2 & \quad (6\text{--}2) \\
0.0 \ x1 + 0.0 \ x2 + 1.0 \ x3 = b3 &
\end{array}
$$

When we get to this form, the solution to the system will be obvious: $x1 = b1$, $x2 = b2$, and $x3 = b3$.

To get from Equations (6–1) to Equations (6–2), we must go through three steps:

1. Eliminate all coefficients of x1 except in the first equation.
2. Eliminate all coefficients of x2 except in the second equation.
3. Eliminate all coefficients of x3 except in the third equation.

First we will eliminate all coefficients of x1 except in the first equation. If we multiply the first equation by -2, add it to the second equation, multiply the first equation by -1, and add it to the third equation, the results are

$$
\begin{array}{llll}
1.0 \ x1 + 1.0 \ x2 + 1.0 \ x3 = 1.0 \\
0.0 \ x1 - 1.0 \ x2 - 1.0 \ x3 = 0.0 \\
0.0 \ x1 + 2.0 \ x2 + 1.0 \ x3 = 3.0
\end{array}
\qquad (6\text{–}3)
$$

Next we will eliminate all coefficients of x2 except in the second equation. If we add the second equation as it is to the first equation, multiply the second equation by 2, and add it to the third equation, the results are

$$
\begin{array}{llll}
1.0 \ x1 + 0.0 \ x2 + 0.0 \ x3 = 1.0 \\
0.0 \ x1 - 1.0 \ x2 - 1.0 \ x3 = 0.0 \\
0.0 \ x1 + 0.0 \ x2 - 1.0 \ x3 = 3.0
\end{array}
\qquad (6\text{–}4)
$$

Finally we will eliminate all coefficients of x3 except in the third equation. In this case there is no coefficient of x3 in the first equation, so we don't have to do anything there. If we multiply the third equation by -1 and add it to the second equation, the results are

$$
\begin{array}{llll}
1.0 \ x1 + 0.0 \ x2 + 0.0 \ x3 = 1.0 \\
0.0 \ x1 - 1.0 \ x2 + 0.0 \ x3 = -3.0 \\
0.0 \ x1 + 0.0 \ x2 - 1.0 \ x3 = 3.0
\end{array}
\qquad (6\text{–}5)
$$

The last step is almost trivial. If we divide the equation 1 by the coefficient of x1, equation 2 by the coefficient of x2, and equation 3 by the coefficient of x3, then the solution to the equations will appear on the right side of the equations.

$$
\begin{array}{llll}
1.0 \ x1 + 0.0 \ x2 + 0.0 \ x3 = 1.0 \\
0.0 \ x1 + 1.0 \ x2 + 0.0 \ x3 = 3.0 \\
0.0 \ x1 + 0.0 \ x2 + 1.0 \ x3 = -3.0
\end{array}
\qquad (6\text{–}6)
$$

The final answer is x1 = 1, x2 = 3, and x3 = -3!

Sometimes the technique shown above does not produce a solution. This happens when the set of equations being solved are not all *independent*. For example, consider the following 2×2 system of simultaneous equations:

$$
\begin{array}{ll}
2.0 \ x1 + 3.0 \ x2 = 4.0 \\
4.0 \ x1 + 6.0 \ x2 = 8.0
\end{array}
\qquad (6\text{–}7)
$$

If equation 1 is multiplied by -2 and added to equation 1, we get

$$
\begin{array}{ll}
2.0 \ x1 + 3.0 \ x2 = 4.0 \\
0.0 \ x1 + 0.0 \ x2 = 0.0
\end{array}
\qquad (6\text{–}8)
$$

We cannot solve this system for a unique solution, since an infinite number of values of x1 and x2 satisfy Equations (6–8). These conditions are signified by the fact that the coefficient of x2 in the second equation is 0. The solution to this system of equations is said to be nonunique. Our computer program will have to test for problems like this, and report them with an error code.

SOLUTION

We will now write a subroutine to solve a system of N simultaneous equations in N unknowns. The computer program will work in exactly the manner just shown except that at each step in the process, we will reorder the equations. In the first step, we will reorder the N equations such that the first equation is the one with the largest coefficient (absolute value) of the first variable. In the second step, we will reorder equations 2 through N such that the second equation is the one with the largest coefficient (absolute value) of the second variable. This process is repeated for each step in the solution. Reordering the equations is important, because it reduces round-off errors in large systems of equations and also avoids divide-by-zero errors. (This reordering of equations is called the *maximum pivot* technique in the literature of numerical methods.)

1. **State the problem.**

Write a subroutine to solve a system of N simultaneous equations in N unknowns using Gauss-Jordan elimination and the maximum pivot technique to avoid round-off errors. The subroutine must be able to detect singular sets of equations and set an error flag if they occur.

2. **Define the inputs and outputs.**

The input to the subroutine consists of an N × N matrix a with the coefficients of the variables in the simultaneous equations and a vector b with the contents of the right sides of the equations. The outputs from the subroutine are the solutions to the set of equations (in vector b) and an error flag. Note that the matrix of coefficients a will be destroyed during the solution process.

3. **Describe the algorithm.**

The pseudocode for this subroutine is

```
DO for irow = 1 to n

    ! Find peak pivot for column irow in rows i to n
    ipeak ← irow
    DO for jrow = irow+1 to n
        IF |a(jrow,irow)| > |a(ipeak,irow)| then
            ipeak ← jrow
        END of IF
    END of DO


    ! Check for singular equations
    IF |a(ipeak,irow)| < epsilon THEN
        Equations are singular; set error code & exit
    END of IF
```

```
            ! Otherwise, if ipeak /= irow, swap equations irow & ipeak
            IF ipeak /= irow
                DO for kcol = 1 to n
                    temp ← a(ipeak,kcol)
                    a(ipeak,kcol) ← a(irow,kcol)
                    a(irow,kcol) ← temp
                END of DO
                temp ← b(ipeak)
                b(ipeak) ← b(irow)
                b(irow) ← temp
            END of IF

            ! Multiply equation irow by -a(jrow,irow)/a(irow,irow),
            ! and add it to Eqn jrow
            DO for jrow = 1 to n except for irow
                factor ← -a(jrow,irow)/a(irow,irow)
                DO for kcol = 1 to n
                    a(jrow,kcol) ← a(irow,kcol) * factor + a(jrow,kcol)
                END of DO
                b(jrow) ← b(irow) * factor + b(jrow)
            END of DO
        END of DO

        ! End of main loop over all equations. All off-diagonal
        ! terms are now zero. To get the final answer, we must
        ! divide each equation by the coefficient of its on-diagonal
        ! term.
        DO for irow = 1 to n
            b(irow) ← b(irow) / a(irow,irow)
            a(irow,irow) ← 1.
        END of DO
```

4. Turn the algorithm into Fortran statements.

The resulting Fortran subroutine is shown in Figure 6–6. Note that the subroutine's large outer loops and IF structures are all named to make it easier for us to understand and keep track of them.

FIGURE 6–6
Subroutine simul.

```
SUBROUTINE simul ( a, b, ndim, n, error )
!
! Purpose:
!    Subroutine to solve a set of n linear equations in n
!    unknowns using Gaussian elimination and the maximum
!    pivot technique.
!
! Record of revisions:
!    Date           Programmer              Description of change
!    ====           ==========              =====================
!    10/16/95       S. J. Chapman           Original code
!
IMPLICIT NONE

! Declare calling arguments:
```

(continued)

(continued)

```
INTEGER, INTENT(IN) :: ndim          ! Dimension of arrays a and b
REAL, INTENT(INOUT), DIMENSION(ndim,ndim) :: a
                                     ! Array of coefficients (n x n)
                                     ! This array is of size ndim x
                                     ! ndim, but only n x n of the
                                     ! coefficients are being used
                                     ! The declared dimension ndim
                                     ! must be passed to the sub, or
                                     ! it won't be able to interpret
                                     ! subscripts correctly  (This
                                     ! array is destroyed during
                                     ! processing)
REAL, INTENT(INOUT), DIMENSION(ndim) :: b
                                     ! Input: Right-hand side of eqns
                                     ! Output: Solution vector
INTEGER, INTENT(IN) :: n             ! Number of equations to solve
INTEGER, INTENT(OUT) :: error        ! Error flag:
                                     !    0 -- No error
                                     !    1 -- Singular equations

! Declare local parameters
REAL, PARAMETER :: epsilon = 1.0E-6 ! A "small" number for comparison
                                     ! when determining singular eqns

! Declare local variables:
REAL :: factor                       ! Factor to multiply eqn irow by
                                     ! before adding to eqn jrow
INTEGER :: irow                      ! Number of the equation currently
                                     ! being processed
INTEGER :: ipeak                     ! Pointer to equation containing
                                     ! maximum pivot value
INTEGER :: jrow                      ! Number of the equation compared
                                     ! to the current equation
INTEGER :: kcol                      ! Index over all columns of eqn
REAL :: temp                         ! Scratch value

! Process n times to get all equations...
mainloop: DO irow = 1, n

   ! Find peak pivot for column irow in rows irow to n
   ipeak = irow
   max_pivot: DO jrow = irow+1, n
      IF (ABS(a(jrow,irow)) > ABS(a(ipeak,irow))) THEN
         ipeak = jrow
      END IF
   END DO max_pivot

   ! Check for singular equations.
   singular: IF ( ABS(a(ipeak,irow)) < epsilon ) THEN
      error = 1
      RETURN
   END IF singular

   ! Otherwise, if ipeak /= irow, swap equations irow & ipeak
   swap_eqn: IF ( ipeak /= irow ) THEN
```

(continued)

(concluded)

```
      DO kcol = 1, n
          temp       = a(ipeak,kcol)
          a(ipeak,kcol) = a(irow,kcol)
          a(irow,kcol)  = temp
      END DO
      temp      = b(ipeak)
      b(ipeak) = b(irow)
      b(irow)  = temp
   END IF swap_eqn

   ! Multiply equation irow by -a(jrow,irow)/a(irow,irow),
   ! and add it to Eqn jrow (for all eqns except irow itself)
   eliminate: DO jrow = 1, n
      IF ( jrow /= irow ) THEN
          factor = -a(jrow,irow)/a(irow,irow)
          DO kcol = 1, n
              a(jrow,kcol) = a(irow,kcol)*factor + a(jrow,kcol)
          END DO
          b(jrow) = b(irow)*factor + b(jrow)
      END IF
   END DO eliminate
END DO mainloop

! End of main loop over all equations. All off-diagonal
! terms are now zero. To get the final answer, we must
! divide each equation by the coefficient of its on-diagonal
! term.
divide: DO irow = 1, n
   b(irow)      = b(irow) / a(irow,irow)
   a(irow,irow) = 1.
END DO divide

! Set error flag to 0 and return
error = 0
END SUBROUTINE simul
```

5. Test the resulting Fortran programs.

To test this subroutine, we need to write a driver program. The driver program will open an input data file to read the equations to be solved. The first line of the file will contain the number of equations n in the system, and each of the next n lines will contain the coefficients of one of the equations. To show that the simultaneous equation subroutine is working correctly, we will display the contents of arrays a and b both before and after the call to simul.

The test driver program for subroutine simul is shown in Figure 6–7.

FIGURE 6–7
Test driver routine for subroutine simul.

```
PROGRAM test_simul
!
! Purpose:
!   To test subroutine simul, which solves a set of N linear
```

(continued)

```
(continued)
!     equations in N unknowns.
!
! Record of revisions:
!     Date         Programmer           Description of change
!     ====         ==========           =====================
!     10/15/95     S. J. Chapman        Original code
!
IMPLICIT NONE

! Declare parameters:
INTEGER, PARAMETER :: max_size = 10    ! Max number of eqns

! Declare variables:
INTEGER :: i, j, n, istat, error
REAL, DIMENSION(max_size,max_size) :: a
REAL, DIMENSION(max_size) :: b
CHARACTER(len=20) file_name

! Get the name of the disk file containing the equations.
WRITE (*,1000)
1000 FORMAT (' Enter the file name containing the eqns: ')
READ (*,'(A20)') file_name

! Open input data file. Status is OLD because the input data must
! already exist.
OPEN ( UNIT=1, FILE=file_name, STATUS='OLD', ACTION='READ', &
       IOSTAT=istat )

! Was the OPEN successful?
fileopen: IF ( istat == 0 ) THEN
   ! The file was opened successfully, so read the number of
   ! equations in the system.
   READ (1,*) n
   ! If the number of equations is <= max_size, read them in
   ! and process them.
   size_ok: IF ( n <= max_size ) THEN
      DO i = 1, n
         READ (1,*) (a(i,j), j=1,n), b(i)
      END DO

      ! Display coefficients.
      WRITE (*,1020)
      1020 FORMAT (/,1X,'Coefficients before call:')
      DO i = 1, n
         WRITE (*,1030) (a(i,j), j=1,n), b(i)
         1030 FORMAT (1X,7F11.4)
      END DO

      ! Solve equations.
      CALL simul (a, b, max_size, n, error )

      ! Check for error.
      error_check: IF ( error /= 0 ) THEN

         WRITE (*,1040)
         1040 FORMAT (/1X,'Zero pivot encountered!', &
```

(continued)

(concluded)

```
                                //1X,'There is no unique solution to this system.')

        ELSE error_check

            ! No errors. Display coefficients.
            WRITE (*,1050)
            1050 FORMAT (/,1X,'Coefficients after call:')
            DO i = 1, n
                WRITE (*,1030) (a(i,j), j=1,n), b(i)
            END DO

            ! Write final answer.
            WRITE (*,1060)
            1060 FORMAT (/,1X,'The solutions are:')
            DO i = 1, n
                WRITE (*,1070) i, b(i)
                1070 FORMAT (3X,'X(',I2,') = ',F16.6)
            END DO

        END IF error_check
    END IF size_ok
ELSE fileopen

    ! Else file open failed.  Tell user.
    WRITE (*,1080) istat
    1080 FORMAT (1X,'File open failed—status = ', I6)

END IF fileopen
END PROGRAM
```

To test the subroutine, we need to call it with two different data sets. One of them should have a unique solution, and the other one should be singular. We will test the system with two sets of equations. The original equations that we solved by hand will be placed in file INPUTS1

$$
\begin{array}{l}
1.0\ X1 + 1.0\ X2 + 1.0\ X3 = 1.0 \\
2.0\ X1 + 1.0\ X2 + 1.0\ X3 = 2.0 \\
1.0\ X1 + 3.0\ X2 + 2.0\ X3 = 4.0
\end{array}
\tag{6-1}
$$

and the following set of equations will be placed in file INPUTS2.

$$
\begin{array}{l}
1.0\ X1 + 1.0\ X2 + 1.0\ X3 = 1.0 \\
2.0\ X1 + 6.0\ X2 + 4.0\ X3 = 8.0 \\
1.0\ X1 + 3.0\ X2 + 2.0\ X3 = 4.0
\end{array}
$$

The second equation of this set is a multiple of the third equation, so the second set of equations is singular. When we run program test_simul with these data sets, the results are

```
C>test_simul
Enter the file name containing the eqns:
inputs1

Coefficients before call:
    1.0000      1.0000      1.0000      1.0000
```

```
        2.0000     1.0000     1.0000     2.0000
        1.0000     3.0000     2.0000     4.0000

Coefficients after call:
        1.0000      .0000      .0000     1.0000
         .0000     1.0000      .0000     3.0000
         .0000      .0000     1.0000    -3.0000

The solutions are:
  X( 1) =           1.000000
  X( 2) =           3.000000
  X( 3) =          -3.000000

C>test_simul
Enter the file name containing the eqns:
inputs2

Coefficients before call:
        1.0000     1.0000     1.0000     1.0000
        2.0000     6.0000     4.0000     8.0000
        1.0000     3.0000     2.0000     4.0000

Zero pivot encountered!

There is no unique solution to this system.
```

The subroutine appears to be working correctly for both unique and singular sets of simultaneous equations.

■ 6.2

THE SAVE ATTRIBUTE AND STATEMENT

According to the Fortran 90 and 95 standards, the values of all the local variables and arrays in a procedure become undefined whenever we exit the procedure. The next time that the procedure is invoked, the values of the local variables and arrays in the procedure may or may not be the same as they were the last time we left it, depending on the behavior of the particular compiler being used. If we write a procedure that depends on having its local variables undisturbed between calls, the procedure will work fine on some computers and fail miserably on other ones!

Fortran provides a way to guarantee that local variables and arrays are saved unchanged between calls to a procedure. This is the SAVE attribute. The SAVE attribute appears in a type declaration statement like any other attribute. Any local variables declared with the SAVE attribute will be saved unchanged between calls to the procedure. For example, a local variable sums could be declared with the SAVE attribute as

```
REAL, SAVE :: sums
```

In addition, any local variable that is initialized in a type declaration statement is automatically saved. The SAVE attribute may be specified explicitly, if desired, but the value of the variable will be saved whether or not the attribute is explicitly included. Thus the following two variables are both saved between invocations of the procedure containing them.

```
REAL, SAVE :: sum_x = 0.
REAL :: sum_x2 = 0.
```

Fortran also includes a SAVE statement. The SAVE statement is a nonexecutable statement that goes into the declaration portion of the procedure along with the type declaration statements. Any local variables listed in the SAVE statement will be saved unchanged between calls to the procedure. If no variables are listed in the SAVE statement, then *all* the local variables will be saved unchanged.

The format of the SAVE statement is

```
SAVE :: var1, var2, ...
```

or simply

```
SAVE
```

The SAVE attribute may not appear associated with dummy arguments or with data items declared with the PARAMETER attribute. Similarly, neither of these items may appear in a SAVE statement.

Good Programming Practice

If a procedure requires that the value of a local variable not change between successive invocations of the procedure, include the SAVE attribute in the variable's type declaration statement, include the variable in a SAVE statement, or initialize the variable in its type declaration statement. If you do not do so, the subroutine will work correctly with some processors but will fail with others.

EXAMPLE 6–5 Running Averages: It is sometimes desirable to keep running statistics on a data set as the values are being entered. The subroutine running_average shown in Figure 6–8 accumulates running averages and standard deviations for use in problems where we want to keep statistics on data as it is coming in to the program. As each new data value is added, the running averages and standard deviations of all data up to that point are updated. The running sums used to derive the statistics are reset when the subroutine is called with the logical argument reset set to true. Note that the sums n, sum_x, and sum_x2 are being accumulated in local variables in this subroutine. To ensure that they remain unchanged between subroutine calls, those local variables must appear in a SAVE statement or with a SAVE attribute.

FIGURE 6–8
A subroutine to calculate the running mean and standard deviation of an input data set.

```
SUBROUTINE running_average ( x, ave, std_dev, nvals, reset )
!
! Purpose:
!   To calculate the running average, standard deviation,
!   and number of data points as data values x are received.
```

(continued)

```
(concluded)
!    If "reset" is .TRUE., clear running sums and exit.
!
!   Record of revisions:
!      Date          Programmer          Description of change
!      ====          ==========          =====================
!    10/19/95     S. J. Chapman          Original code
!
IMPLICIT NONE

! List of calling arguments:
REAL, INTENT(IN) :: x                   ! Input data value.
REAL, INTENT(OUT) :: ave                ! Running average.
REAL, INTENT(OUT) :: std_dev            ! Running standard deviation.
INTEGER, INTENT(OUT) :: nvals           ! Current number of points.
LOGICAL, INTENT(IN) :: reset            ! Reset flag: clear sums if true

! List of local variables:
INTEGER, SAVE :: n                      ! Number of input values.
REAL, SAVE :: sum_x                     ! Sum of input values.
REAL, SAVE :: sum_x2                    ! Sum of input values squared.

! If the reset flag is set, clear the running sums at this time.
calc_sums: IF ( reset ) THEN
   n = 0     ; sum_x = 0.   ; sum_x2 = 0.
   ave = 0. ; std_dev = 0. ; nvals = 0
ELSE

   ! Accumulate sums.
   n       = n + 1
   sum_x   = sum_x + x
   sum_x2 = sum_x2 + x**2

   ! Calculate average.
   ave = sum_x / REAL(n)

   ! Calculate standard deviation.
   IF ( n >= 2 ) THEN
      std_dev = SQRT( (REAL(n) * sum_x2 - sum_x**2) &
              / (REAL(n) * REAL(n-1)) )
   ELSE
      std_dev = 0.
   END IF

   ! Number of data points.
   nvals = n

END IF calc_sums

END SUBROUTINE running_average
```

A test driver for this subroutine is shown in Figure 6–9.

FIGURE 6–9

A test driver program to test subroutine running_average.

```
PROGRAM test_running_average
!
!  Purpose:
```

(continued)

(concluded)

```
!    To test running average subroutine.
!
IMPLICIT NONE

! Declare variables:
INTEGER :: istat              ! I/O status
REAL :: ave                   ! Average
REAL :: std_dev               ! Standard deviation
INTEGER :: nvals              ! Number of values
REAL :: x                     ! Input data value
CHARACTER(len=20) file_name   ! Input data file name

! Clear the running sums.
CALL running_average ( 0., ave, std_dev, nvals, .TRUE. )

! Get the name of the file containing the input data.
WRITE (*,*) ' Enter the file name containing the data: '
READ (*,'(A20)') file_name

! Open input data file.  Status is OLD because the input data must
! already exist.
OPEN ( UNIT=21, FILE=file_name, STATUS='OLD', ACTION='READ', &
       IOSTAT=istat )

! Was the OPEN successful?
openok: IF ( istat == 0 ) THEN

   ! The file was opened successfully, so read the data to calculate
   !  running averages for.
   calc: DO
      READ (21,*,IOSTAT=istat) x       ! Get next value
      IF ( istat /= 0 ) EXIT           ! EXIT if not valid.

      ! Get running average & standard deviation
      CALL running_average ( x, ave, std_dev, nvals, .FALSE. )

      ! Now write out the running statistics.
      WRITE (*,1020) 'Value = ', x, ' Ave = ', ave, &
                     ' Std_dev = ', std_dev, &
                     ' Nvals = ', nvals
      1020 FORMAT (1X,3(A,F10.4),A,I6)
   END DO calc

ELSE openok

   ! Else file open failed.  Tell user.
   WRITE (*,1030) istat
   1030 FORMAT (1X,'File open failed—status = ', I6)

END IF openok

END PROGRAM
```

To test this subroutine, we will calculate running statistics by hand for a set of five numbers and compare the hand calculations to the results from the computer program. Recall that the average and standard deviation are defined as

$$\bar{x} = \frac{1}{N} \sum_{i=1}^{N} x_i \tag{3-3}$$

and

$$s = \sqrt{\frac{N \sum_{i=1}^{N} x_i^2 - \left(\sum_{i=1}^{N} x_i\right)^2}{N(N-1)}} \tag{3-4}$$

where x_i is sample i out of N samples. If the five values are

$$3., \quad 2., \quad 3., \quad 4., \quad 2.8$$

then the running statistics calculated by hand would be

Value	n	Σx	Σx^2	Average	Std_dev
3.0	1	3.0	9.0	3.00	0.000
2.0	2	5.0	13.0	2.50	0.707
3.0	3	8.0	22.0	2.67	0.577
4.0	4	12.0	38.0	3.00	0.816
2.8	5	14.8	45.84	2.96	0.713

The output of the test program for the same data set is

```
C>test_running_average
Enter the file name containing the data:
input6
Value =   3.0000   Ave =   3.0000   Std_dev =   0.0000   Nvals =   1
Value =   2.0000   Ave =   2.5000   Std_dev =   0.7071   Nvals =   2
Value =   3.0000   Ave =   2.6667   Std_dev =   0.5774   Nvals =   3
Value =   4.0000   Ave =   3.0000   Std_dev =   0.8165   Nvals =   4
Value =   2.8000   Ave =   2.9600   Std_dev =   0.7127   Nvals =   5
```

so the results check to the accuracy shown in the hand calculations.

6.3
AUTOMATIC ARRAYS

Fortran 90/95 provides a way to automatically create temporary arrays while a procedure is executing and to automatically destroy them when execution returns from the procedure. These arrays are called **automatic arrays.** An *automatic array* is a local explicit-shape array with nonconstant bounds. (The bounds are specified either by dummy arguments or through data from modules, as explained in section 6.4.)

For example, array temp in the following code is an automatic array. Whenever subroutine sub1 is executed, dummy arguments n and m are passed to the subroutine. Note that arrays x and y are explicit-shape dummy arrays of size n × m that have been *passed to* the subroutine, while array temp is an automatic array that is *created within* the subroutine. When the subroutine starts to execute, an array temp of size n × m is automatically created, and when the subroutine ends, the array is automatically destroyed.

```
SUBROUTINE sub1 ( x, y, n, m )
IMPLICIT NONE
INTEGER, INTENT(IN) :: n, m
REAL, INTENT(IN), DIMENSION(n,m) :: x  ! Dummy array
REAL, INTENT(OUT), DIMENSION(n,m) :: y  ! Dummy array
REAL, DIMENSION(n,m) :: temp                  ! Automatic array
temp = 0.
...
END SUBROUTINE
```

Automatic arrays may not be initialized in their type declaration statements, but they may be initialized by assignment statements at the beginning of the procedure in which they are created. They may be passed as calling arguments to other procedures invoked by the procedure in which they are created. However, they cease to exist when the procedure in which they are created executes a RETURN or END statement. It is illegal to specify the SAVE attribute for an automatic array.

EXAMPLE 6–6 *Using Automatic Arrays in a Procedure:* As an example using automatic arrays in a procedure, we will write a new version of subroutine simul that does not destroy its input data while calculating the solution.

To avoid destroying the data, we need to add a new dummy argument to return the solution to the system of equations. This argument is called soln and has INTENT(OUT), since it will be used only for output. Dummy arguments a and b will now have INTENT(IN), since they will not be modified at all in the subroutine. In addition, we will take advantages of array sections to simplify the nested DO loops found in the original subroutine simul.

SOLUTION

The resulting subroutine is shown in Figure 6–10. Note that arrays a1 and temp1 are automatic arrays because they are local to the subroutine, but their bounds are passed to the subroutine as dummy arguments. In contrast, arrays a, b, and soln are explicit-shape dummy arrays because they appear in the argument list of the subroutine.

FIGURE 6–10
A rewritten version of subroutine simul using allocatable arrays. This version does not destroy its input arrays. The declarations of automatic arrays a1 and temp1 and the use of array sections are shown in bold face.

```
SUBROUTINE simul2 ( a, b, soln, ndim, n, error )
!
! Purpose:
!   Subroutine to solve a set of N linear equations in N
!   unknowns using Gaussian elimination and the maximum
!   pivot technique. This version of simul has been
```

(continued)

```
(continued)
!    modified to use array sections and allocatable arrays
!    It DOES NOT DESTROY the original input values.
!
! Record of revisions:
!      Date          Programmer          Description of change
!      ====          ==========          =====================
!    10/16/95     S. J. Chapman          Original code
! 1.03/02/96     S. J. Chapman          Add allocatable arrays
!
IMPLICIT NONE

! Declare calling arguments:
INTEGER, INTENT(IN) :: ndim            ! Dimension of arrays a and b
REAL, INTENT(IN), DIMENSION(ndim,ndim) :: a
                                       ! Array of coefficients (N x N).
                                       ! This array is of size ndim x
                                       ! ndim, but only N x N of the
                                       ! coefficients are being used.
REAL, INTENT(IN), DIMENSION(ndim) :: b
                                       ! Input: Right-hand side of eqns.
REAL, INTENT(OUT), DIMENSION(ndim) :: soln
                                       ! Output: Solution vector.
INTEGER, INTENT(IN) :: n               ! Number of equations to solve.
INTEGER, INTENT(OUT) :: error          ! Error flag:
                                       !    0 — No error
                                       !    1 — Singular equations

! Declare local parameters
REAL, PARAMETER :: epsilon = 1.0E-6    ! A "small" number for comparison
                                       ! when determining singular eqns

! Declare local variables:
REAL, DIMENSION(n,n) :: a1             ! Copy of "a" which will be
                                       ! destroyed during the solution
REAL :: factor                         ! Factor to multiply eqn irow by
                                       ! before adding to eqn jrow
INTEGER :: irow                        ! Number of the equation currently
                                       ! being processed
INTEGER :: ipeak                       ! Pointer to equation containing
                                       ! maximum pivot value
INTEGER :: jrow                        ! Number of the equation compared
                                       ! to the current equation
REAL :: temp                           ! Scratch value
REAL, DIMENSION(n) :: temp1            ! Scratch array

! Make copies of arrays "a" and "b" for local use
a1 = a(1:n,1:n)
soln = b(1:n)

! Process N times to get all equations...
mainloop: DO irow = 1, n

   ! Find peak pivot for column irow in rows irow to N
   ipeak = irow
   max_pivot: DO jrow = irow+1, n
      IF (ABS(a1(jrow,irow)) > ABS(a1(ipeak,irow))) THEN
```

(continued)

(concluded)

```
            ipeak = jrow
         END IF
      END DO max_pivot

      ! Check for singular equations.
      singular: IF ( ABS(a1(ipeak,irow)) < epsilon ) THEN
         error = 1
         RETURN
      END IF singular

      ! Otherwise, if ipeak /= irow, swap equations irow & ipeak
      swap_eqn: IF ( ipeak /= irow ) THEN
         temp1 = a1(ipeak,1:n)
         a1(ipeak,1:n) = a1(irow,1:n)    ! Swap rows in a
         a1(irow,1:n) = temp1
         temp = soln(ipeak)
         soln(ipeak) = soln(irow)        ! Swap rows in b
         soln(irow)  = temp
      END IF swap_eqn

      ! Multiply equation irow by -a1(jrow,irow)/a1(irow,irow),
      ! and add it to Eqn jrow (for all eqns except irow itself).
      eliminate: DO jrow = 1, n
         IF ( jrow /= irow ) THEN
            factor = -a1(jrow,irow)/a1(irow,irow)
            a1(jrow,:) = a1(irow,1:n)*factor + a1(jrow,1:n)
            soln(jrow) = soln(irow)*factor + soln(jrow)
         END IF
      END DO eliminate
   END DO mainloop

   ! End of main loop over all equations. All off-diagonal terms
   ! are now zero. To get the final answer, we must divide
   ! each equation by the coefficient of its on-diagonal term.
   divide: DO irow = 1, n
      soln(irow) = soln(irow) / a1(irow,irow)
      a1(irow,irow) = 1.
   END DO divide

   ! Set error flag to 0 and return.
   error = 0

END SUBROUTINE simul2
```

Testing this subroutine is left as exercise 6–34.

■ **6.4**

SHARING DATA USING MODULES

We have seen that programs exchange data with the subroutines they call through an argument list. Each item in the argument list of the program's CALL statement must be matched by a dummy argument in the argument list of the subroutine being invoked. A pointer to the location of each argument is passed from the calling program to the subroutine for use in accessing the arguments.

In addition to the argument list, Fortran programs, subroutines, and functions can also exchange data through modules. A **module** is a separately compiled program unit that contains the definitions and initial values of the data that we wish to share between program units[2]. If the module's name is included in a USE statement within a program unit, then the data values declared in the module may be used within that program unit. Each program unit that uses a module will have access the same data values, so modules provide a way to share data between program units.

A module begins with a MODULE statement, which assigns a name to the module. The name may be up to 31 characters long and must follow the standard Fortran naming conventions. The module ends with an END MODULE statement, which may optionally include the module's name. The declarations of the data to be shared are placed between these two statements. A sample module is shown in Figure 6–11.

FIGURE 6–11
A simple module used to share data among program units.

```
MODULE test
!
! Purpose:
!   To declare data to share between two routines.

IMPLICIT NONE
SAVE

INTEGER, PARAMETER :: num_vals = 5       ! Max number of values in array
REAL, DIMENSION(num_vals) :: values      ! Data values

END MODULE test
```

The SAVE statement guarantees that all data values declared in the module will be preserved between references in different procedures. It should always be included in any module that declares sharable data.

To use the values in this module, a program unit must declare the module name in a USE statement. The form of a USE statement is

$$USE\ module\_name$$

USE statements must appear before any other statements in a program unit (except for the PROGRAM or SUBROUTINE statement and except for comments, which may appear anywhere). The process of accessing information in a module with a USE statement is known as **USE association.**

An example that uses module test to share data between a main program and a subroutine is shown in Figure 6–12.

---

[2]Modules also have other functions, as you shall see in section 6.5 and in Chapter 9.

FIGURE 6–12
A sample program using a module to share data between a main program and a subroutine.

```
PROGRAM test_module
!
! Purpose:
!   To illustrate sharing data via a module.
!
USE test                        ! Make data in module "test" visible
IMPLICIT NONE

REAL, PARAMETER :: pi = 3.141592  ! Pi

values = pi * (/ 1., 2., 3., 4., 5. /)

CALL sub1                       ! Call subroutine

END PROGRAM
SUBROUTINE sub1
!
! Purpose:
!   To illustrate sharing data via a module.
!
USE test                        ! Make data in module "test" visible
IMPLICIT NONE

WRITE (*,*) values

END SUBROUTINE sub1
```

The contents of module `test` are being shared between the main program and subroutine `sub1`. Any other subroutines or functions within the program could also have access to the data by including the appropriate `USE` statements.

Modules are especially useful for sharing large volumes of data among many program units and for sharing data among a group of related procedures while keeping it invisible from the invoking program unit.

> **Good Programming Practice**
> You may use a module to pass large amounts of data between procedures within a program. If you do so, always include the `SAVE` statement within the module to ensure that the contents of the module remain unchanged between uses. To access the data in a particular program unit, include a `USE` statement as the first noncomment statement after the `PROGRAM`, `SUBROUTINE`, or `FUNCTION` statement within the program unit.

EXAMPLE 6–7 Random Number Generator: It is always impossible to make perfect measurements in the real world. Some *measurement noise* will always be associated with each measurement. This fact is an important consideration in the design of systems to control the operation of such real-world devices as airplanes and refineries. A good engineering design must take these measurement errors into account so that the noise in the measurements will not lead to unstable behavior (no plane crashes or refinery explosions!).

Most engineering designs are tested by running *simulations* of the operation of the system before it is ever built. These simulations involve creating mathematical models of the behavior of the system and feeding the models a realistic string of input data. If the models respond correctly to the simulated input data, then we can have reasonable confidence that the real-world system will respond correctly to the real-world input data.

The simulated input data supplied to the models must be corrupted by a simulated measurement noise, which is just a string of random numbers added to the ideal input data. The simulated noise is usually produced by a *random number generator.*

A random number generator is a procedure that will return a different and apparently random number each time it is called. Since the numbers are in fact generated by a deterministic algorithm, they only appear to be random[3]. However, if the algorithm used to generate them is complex enough, the numbers will be random enough to use in the simulation.

One simple random number generator algorithm follows[4]. It relies on the unpredictability of the modulo function when applied to large numbers. Consider the following equation:

$$n_{i+1} = \text{MOD} \, (8121 \, n_1 + 28411, 134456) \qquad (6\text{–}9)$$

Assume that n_1 is a nonnegative integer. Then because of the modulo function, n_{i+1} will be a number between 0 and 134,455 inclusive. Next, n_{i+1} can be fed into the equation to produce a number n_{i+2} that is also between 0 and 134,455. This process can be repeated forever to produce a series of numbers in the range 0 to 134,455. If we didn't know the numbers 8121; 28,411; and 134,456 in advance, it would be impossible to guess the order in which the values of n would be produced. Furthermore, it turns out that there is an equal (or uniform) probability that any given number will appear in the sequence. Because of these properties, Equation (6–9) can serve as the basis for a simple random number generator with a uniform distribution.

---

[3]Some people refer to these procedures as *pseudorandom number generators.*

[4]This algorithm is adapted from W.H. Press, B.P. Falnnery, S.A. Teukolsky, and W.T. Vetterling, *Numerical Recipes: The Art of Scientific Programming,* (Cambridge University Press, 1986), chapter 7.

We will now use Equation (6–9) to design a random number generator whose output is a real number in the range [0.0, 1.0).[5]

SOLUTION

We will write a subroutine that generates one random number in the range $0 \leq ran < 1.0$ each time that it is called. The random number will be based on the equation

$$ran_i = \frac{n_i}{134456} \qquad (6\text{--}10)$$

where n_i is a number in the range 0 to 134,455 produced by Equation (6–9).

The particular sequence produced by Equations (6–9) and (6–10) will depend on the initial value of n_o (called the *seed*) of the sequence. We must provide a way for the user to specify n_o so that the sequence may be varied from run to run.

1. **State the problem.**

Write a subroutine random0 that will generate and return a single number ran with a uniform probability distribution in the range $0 \leq ran < 1.0$, based on the sequence specified by Equations (6–9) and (6–10). The initial value of the seed n_o will be specified by a call to subroutine seed.

2. **Define the inputs and outputs.**

This problem has two subroutines: seed and random0. The input to subroutine seed is an integer to serve as the starting point of the sequence. There is no output from this subroutine. There is no input to subroutine random0, and the output from the subroutine is a single real value in the range [0.0, 1.0).

3. **Describe the algorithm.**

The pseudocode for subroutine random0 is very simple

```
SUBROUTINE random0 ( ran )
n ← MOD (8121 * n + 28411, 134456 )
ran ← REAL(n) / 134456.
END SUBROUTINE
```

where the value of n is saved between calls to the subroutine. The pseudocode for subroutine seed is also trivial:

```
SUBROUTINE seed ( iseed )
n ← ABS ( iseed )
END SUBROUTINE
```

The absolute value function is used so that the user can enter any integer as the starting point. The user will not have to know in advance that only positive integers are legal seeds.

---

[5]The notation [0.0,1.0) implies that the range of the random numbers is between 0.0 and 1.0, including the number 0.0 but excluding the number 1.0.

The variable n will be placed in a module so that it may be accessed by both subroutines. In addition, we will initialize n to a reasonable value so that we get good results even if subroutine seed is not called to set the seed before the first call to random0.

4. **Turn the algorithm into Fortran statements.**

The resulting Fortran subroutines are shown in Figure 6–13.

FIGURE 6–13
Subroutines to generate a random number sequence and to set the seed of the sequence.

```
MODULE ran001
!
! Purpose:
!   To declare data shared between subs random0 and seed.
!
! Record of revisions:
!     Date          Programmer           Description of change
!     ====          ==========           =====================
!   10/17/95     S. J. Chapman           Original code
!
IMPLICIT NONE
INTEGER, SAVE :: n = 9876
END MODULE ran001

SUBROUTINE random0 ( ran )
!
! Purpose:
!   Subroutine to generate a pseudorandom number with a uniform
!   distribution in the range 0.
!
! Record of revisions:
!     Date          Programmer           Description of change
!     ====          ==========           =====================
!   10/17/95     S. J. Chapman           Original code
!

USE ran001                          ! Shared seed
IMPLICIT NONE

! List of calling arguments:
REAL, INTENT(OUT) :: ran            ! Random number

n = MOD (8121 * n + 28411, 134456 )  ! Next number
ran = REAL(n) / 134456.             ! ran

END SUBROUTINE random0

SUBROUTINE seed ( iseed )
!
! Purpose:
!   To set the seed for random number generator random0.
!
! Record of revisions:
```

(continued)

```
(concluded)
!     Date        Programmer                Description of change
!     ====        ==========                =====================
!   10/17/95    S. J. Chapman               Original code
!
USE ran001                                 ! Shared seed
IMPLICIT NONE

! List of calling arguments:
INTEGER, INTENT(IN) :: iseed               ! Value to initialize sequence

n = ABS ( iseed )                          ! Set seed.

END SUBROUTINE seed
```

5. **Test the resulting Fortran programs.**

   If the numbers generated by these routines are truly uniformly distributed random numbers in the range $0 \le ran < 1.0$, then the average of many numbers should be close to 0.5. To test the results, we will write a test program that prints out the first 10 values produced by random0 to see if they are indeed in the range $0 \le ran < 1.0$. Then the program will average five consecutive 1000-sample intervals to see how close the averages come to 0.5. The test code to call subroutines seed and random0 is shown in Figure 6–14:

FIGURE 6–14
Test driver program for subroutines seed and random0. The results of compiling and running the test program follow.

```
PROGRAM test_random0
!
! Purpose:
!   Subroutine to test the random number generator random0.
!
! Record of revisions:
!     Date        Programmer                Description of change
!     ====        ==========                =====================
!   10/17/95    S. J. Chapman               Original code
!
IMPLICIT NONE

! List of local variables
REAL :: ave              ! Average of random numbers
INTEGER :: i             ! DO loop index
INTEGER :: iseed         ! Seed for random number sequence
INTEGER :: iseq          ! DO loop index
REAL :: ran              ! A random number
REAL :: sum              ! Sum of random numbers

! Get seed.
WRITE (*,*) 'Enter seed: '
READ (*,*) iseed
```

(continued)

```
(concluded)
! Set seed.
CALL SEED ( iseed )

! Print out 10 random numbers.
WRITE (*,*) '10 random numbers:'
DO i = 1, 10
   CALL random0 ( ran )
   WRITE (*,1000) ran
   1000 FORMAT (3X,F16.6)
END DO

! Average 5 consecutive 1000-value sequences.
WRITE (*,*) 'Averages of 5 consecutive 1000-sample sequences:'
DO iseq = 1, 5
   sum = 0.
   DO i = 1, 1000
      CALL random0 ( ran )
      sum = sum + ran
   END DO
   ave = sum / 1000.
   WRITE (*,1000) ave
END DO

END PROGRAM
```

The results of compiling and running the test program follow.

```
C>test_random0
Enter seed:
12
10 random numbers:
                .936091
                .203204
                .431167
                .719105
                .064103
                .789775
                .974839
                .881686
                .384951
                .400086
Averages of 5 consecutive 1000-sample sequences:
                .504282
                .512665
                .496927
                .491514
                .498117
```

The numbers do appear to be between 0.0 and 1.0, and the averages of long sets of these numbers are nearly 0.5, so these subroutines appear to be functioning correctly. You should try them again using different seeds to see if they behave consistently.

Fortran 90/95 includes an intrinsic subroutine `RANDOM_NUMBER` to generate sequences of random numbers. That subroutine will typically produce more nearly random results than the simple subroutine developed in this example. The full details of how to use subroutine `RANDOM_NUMBER` are found in Appendix B.

■ 6.5
MODULE PROCEDURES

In addition to data, modules may also contain complete subroutines and functions, which are known as **module procedures.** These procedures are compiled as a part of the module and are made available to a program unit by including a `USE` statement containing the module name in the program unit.

Procedures that are included within a module must follow any data objects declared in the module and must be preceded by a `CONTAINS` statement. The `CONTAINS` statement tells the compiler that the following statements are included procedures.

In the following simple example of a module procedure, subroutine `sub1` is contained within module `my_subs`.

```
MODULE my_subs
IMPLICIT NONE

(Declare shared data here)

CONTAINS
    SUBROUTINE sub1 ( a, b, c, x, error )
    IMPLICIT NONE
    REAL, DIMENSION(3), INTENT(IN) :: a
    REAL, INTENT(IN) :: b, c
    REAL, INTENT(OUT) :: x
    LOGICAL, INTENT(OUT) :: error
    ...
    END SUBROUTINE sub1
END MODULE my_subs
```

Subroutine `sub1` is made available for use in a calling program unit if the statement `USE my_subs` is included as the first noncomment statement within the program unit. The subroutine can be called with a standard `CALL` statement as shown next.

```
PROGRAM main_prog
USE my_subs
IMPLICIT NONE
    ...
CALL sub1 ( a, b, c, x, error )
    ...
END PROGRAM
```

6.5.1 Using Modules to Create Explicit Interfaces

Why would we bother to include a procedure in a module? We already know that it is possible to separately compile a subroutine and to call it from another program unit, so why go through the extra steps of including the subroutine in a module, compiling the module, declaring the module in a USE statement, and then calling the subroutine?

The answer is that when a procedure is compiled within a module and the module is used by a calling program, all the details of the procedure's interface are made available to the compiler. When the calling program is compiled, the compiler can automatically check the number of arguments in the procedure call, the type of each argument, whether or not each argument is an array, and the INTENT of each argument. In short, the compiler can catch most of the common errors that a programmer might make when using procedures!

A procedure compiled within a module and accessed by USE association is said to have an **explicit interface,** since all the details about every argument in the procedure are explicitly known to the Fortran compiler whenever the procedure is used and the compiler checks the interface to ensure that it is being used properly.

In contrast, procedures not in a module are said to have an **implicit interface.** A Fortran compiler has no information about these procedures when it is compiling a program unit that calls them, so it just *assumes* that the programmer got the number, type, intent, and so on of the arguments right. If the calling sequence is wrong, then the program will fail in strange and hard-to-find ways.

The program in Figure 6–15 illustrates this point. This program contains a main program and a subroutine that is defined inside a module. A real value is passed to the subroutine when an integer argument is expected, so the number will be misinterpreted by the subroutine.

FIGURE 6–15
Example illustrating the effects of a type mismatch when calling a subroutine included within a module.

```
MODULE my_subs
CONTAINS
   SUBROUTINE bad_argument ( i )
   IMPLICIT NONE
   INTEGER, INTENT(IN) :: i        ! Declare argument as integer.
   WRITE (*,*) ' I = ', i          ! Write out i.
   END SUBROUTINE
END MODULE

PROGRAM bad_call
!
!  Purpose:
!  To illustrate misinterpreted calling arguments.
!
USE my_subs
IMPLICIT NONE
REAL :: x = 1.                     ! Declare real variable x.
CALL bad_argument ( x )            ! Call subroutine.
END PROGRAM
```

When this program is compiled, the Fortran compiler will catch the argument mismatch for us.

```
C>f90 fig6-15.f90
DIGITAL Visual Fortran Optimizing Compiler Version: V5.0
Copyright (c) 1997 Digital Equipment Corp. All rights reserved.

fig6-17.f90
fig6-17.f90(18): Error: The type of the actual argument differs from
the type of the dummy argument.   [X]
CALL bad_argument ( x )          ! Call subroutine.
-------------------^
```

6.5.2 Assumed-Shape Arrays

When a procedure has an explicit interface, the full details the type, order, intent, and rank of the procedure's dummy arguments are known to the calling program unit; the full details of the calling program's actual arguments are also known to the procedure. Therefore, the procedure can know the shape and size of actual arrays passed to it and can use that information to manipulate the arrays. Since this information is already known through the explicit interface, there is no need to declare each dummy array argument as an explicit-shape dummy array with the bounds of the array passed as actual arguments.

Instead, the array arguments can be declared as assumed-shape dummy arrays. *Assumed-shape dummy arrays* are special forms of dummy array arguments that assume the shape of the actual calling array arguments when the procedure is invoked. Assumed-shape arrays are declared with a specific type and rank, but with colons in each dimension instead of bounds. For example, array arr1 in the following type declaration statement is an assumed-shape array:

REAL, DIMENSION(:,:) :: arr1

Whole array operations, array sections, and array intrinsic functions can all be used with assumed-shape dummy arrays. If needed, the actual size and extent of an assumed-shape array can be determined by using the array inquiry functions in Table 5–1. However, the upper and lower bounds of each dimension cannot be determined, since only the shape of the actual array but not the bounds are passed to the procedure. If you need the actual bounds for some reason in a particular procedure, then you must use an explicit-shape dummy array.

Assumed-shape dummy arrays are generally better than explicit-shape dummy arrays in that we don't have to pass every bound from the calling program unit to a procedure. However, assumed-shape arrays work only if a procedure has an explicit interface.

EXAMPLE 6–8 Using Assumed-Shape Dummy Arrays: A simple procedure using an assumed-shape dummy array is shown in Figure 6–16. This procedure declares an assumed-shape dummy array array and then determines its size, shape, and bounds using array intrinsic functions. Note that the subroutine is contained in a module, so it has an explicit interface.

FIGURE 6–16

Subroutine to illustrate the use of assumed-shape arrays.

```
MODULE test_module
! Purpose:
!   To illustrate the use of assumed-shape arrays.
!
CONTAINS
   SUBROUTINE test_array(array)
   IMPLICIT NONE
   REAL, DIMENSION(:,:) :: array          ! Assumed-shape array
   INTEGER :: i1, i2                      ! Bounds of first dimension
   INTEGER :: j1, j2                      ! Bounds of second dimension

   ! Get details about array.
   i1 = LBOUND(array,1)
   i2 = UBOUND(array,1)
   j1 = LBOUND(array,2)
   j2 = UBOUND(array,2)
   WRITE (*,100) i1, i2, j1, j2
   100 FORMAT (1X,'The bounds are: (',I2,':',I2,',',I2,':',I2,')')
   WRITE (*,110) SHAPE(array)
   110 FORMAT (1X,'The shape is:     ',2I4)
   WRITE (*,120) SIZE(array)
   120 FORMAT (1X,'The size is:      ',I4)
   END SUBROUTINE test_array
END MODULE test_module

PROGRAM assumed_shape
!
! Purpose:
!   To illustrate the use of assumed-shape arrays.
!
USE test_module
IMPLICIT NONE

! Declare local variables
REAL, DIMENSION(-5:5,-5:5) :: a = 0. ! Array a
REAL, DIMENSION(10,2) :: b = 1.       ! Array b

! Call test_array with array a.
WRITE (*,*) 'Calling test_array with array a:'
CALL test_array(a)

! Call test_array with array b.
WRITE (*,*) 'Calling test_array with array b:'
CALL test_array(b)

END PROGRAM
```

When program `assumed_shape` is executed, the results are

```
C>assumed_shape
Calling test_array with array a:
The bounds are: ( 1:11, 1:11)
The shape is:       11  11
The size is:       121
```

```
Calling test_array with array b:
The bounds are: ( 1:10, 1: 2)
The shape is:        10    2
The size is:         20
```

Note that the subroutine has complete information about the rank, shape, and size of each array passed to it, but not about the bounds used for the array in the calling program. The bounds in the subroutine are just the bounds for an array of that shape whose lower bound is 1.

Good Programming Practice

Use either assumed-shape arrays or explicit-shape arrays as dummy array arguments in procedures. Assumed-shape arrays require an explicit interface. You may use whole array operations, array sections, and array intrinsic functions with the dummy array arguments in either case.

Quiz 6–2

This quiz provides a quick check to see if you understand the concepts introduced in sections 6.2 through 6.5. If you have trouble with the quiz, reread the sections, ask your instructor, or discuss the material with a fellow student. The answers to this quiz appear in Appendix F.

1. When should a SAVE statement or attribute be used in a program or procedure? Why should it be used?
2. What is an automatic array?
3. Why should you gather up the procedures in a program and place them into a module?
4. What are the advantages and disadvantages of assumed-shape dummy arrays?

For questions 5 through 8, determine whether any errors occur in the programs. If possible, tell what the output from each program will be.

5.
```
PROGRAM test1
IMPLICIT NONE
INTEGER, DIMENSION(10) :: i
INTEGER :: j
DO j = 1, 10
   CALL sub1 ( i(j) )
   WRITE (*,*) ' I = ', i(j)
END DO
END PROGRAM test1
SUBROUTINE sub1 ( ival )
IMPLICIT NONE
```

(continued)

```
(concluded)
      INTEGER, INTENT(INOUT) :: ival
      INTEGER :: isum
      isum = isum + 1
      ival = isum
      END SUBROUTINE sub1

6. MODULE mydata
   IMPLICIT NONE
   SAVE
   REAL, DIMENSION(8) :: a
   REAL :: b
   END MODULE mydata

   PROGRAM test2
   USE mydata
   IMPLICIT NONE
   a = (/ 1.,2.,3.,4.,5.,6.,7.,8. /)
   b = 37.
   CALL sub2
   END PROGRAM test2

   SUBROUTINE sub2
   USE mydata
   IMPLICIT NONE
   WRITE (*,*) 'a(5) = ', a(5)
   END SUBROUTINE sub2

7. MODULE mysubs
   CONTAINS
      SUBROUTINE sub3(x,y)
      REAL, INTENT(IN) :: x
      REAL, INTENT(OUT) :: y
      y = 3. * x - 1.
      END SUBROUTINE sub3
   END MODULE

   PROGRAM test3
   USE mysubs
   IMPLICIT NONE
   REAL :: a = 5.
   CALL sub3 (a, -3.)
   END PROGRAM

8. PROGRAM test4
   IMPLICIT NONE
   REAL, DIMENSION(2,2) :: a = 1., b = 2.
   CALL sub4(a, b)
   WRITE (*,*) a
   END PROGRAM
   SUBROUTINE sub4(a,b)
   REAL, DIMENSION(:,:), INTENT(INOUT) :: a
   REAL, DIMENSION(:,:), INTENT(IN) :: b
   a = a + b
   END SUBROUTINE sub4
```

■ 6.6

FORTRAN FUNCTIONS

A Fortran function is a procedure whose result is a single number, logical value, character string, or array. The result of a function is a single value or single array that can be combined with variables and constants to form Fortran expressions. These expressions may appear on the right side of an assignment statement in the calling program. The two types of Fortran functions are **intrinsic functions** and **user-defined functions** (or function subprograms).

Intrinsic functions, such as SIN(X), LOG(X) are built into the Fortran language. Some of these functions were described in Chapters 2 and 5; all of them are listed in Appendix B.

User-defined functions or function subprograms are defined by individual programmers to meet a specific need not addressed by the standard intrinsic functions. They are used just like intrinsic functions in expressions. The general form of a user-defined Fortran function is

```
FUNCTION name ( argument_list )
   ...
   (Declaration section must declare type of name)
   ...
   (Execution section)
   ...
   name = expr
   RETURN
END FUNCTION [name]
```

The function must begin with a FUNCTION statement and end with an END FUNCTION statement. The name of the function may be up to 31 alphabetic, numeric, and underscore characters long, but the first letter must be alphabetic. The name must be specified in the FUNCTION statement and is optional on the END FUNCTION statement.

A function is invoked by naming it in an expression. When a function is invoked, execution begins at the top of the function and ends when either a RETURN statement or the END FUNCTION statement is reached. Because execution ends at the END FUNCTION statement anyway, the RETURN statement is not actually required in most functions and is rarely used. When the function returns, the returned value is used to continue evaluating the Fortran expression that it was named in.

The name of the function must appear on the left side of at least one assignment statement in the function. The value assigned to name when the function returns to the invoking program unit will be the value of the function.

The argument list of the function may be blank if the function can perform its calculations with no input arguments. The parentheses around the argument list are required even if the list is blank.

Since a function returns a value, it is necessary to assign a type to the function. If IMPLICIT NONE is used, the type of the function must be declared both in the function procedure and in the calling programs. If IMPLICIT NONE is not used, the default type of the function will follow the standard rules of Fortran unless they are overridden by a type declaration statement. The type declaration of a user-defined Fortran function can take one of two equivalent forms:

```
INTEGER FUNCTION my_function ( i, j )
```

or

```
FUNCTION my_function ( i, j )
INTEGER :: my_function
```

An example of a user-defined function is shown in Figure 6–17. Function quadf evaluates a quadratic expression with user-specified coefficients at a user-specified value x.

FIGURE 6–17

A function to evaluate a quadratic polynomial of the form $f(x) = a\,x^2 + b\,x + c$.

```
REAL FUNCTION quadf ( x, a, b, c )
!
! Purpose:
!   To evaluate a quadratic polynomial of the form
!   f(x) = a * x**2 + b * x + c.
!
! Record of revisions:
!     Date          Programmer           Description of change
!     ====          ==========           =====================
!   10/22/95      S. J. Chapman          Original code
!
IMPLICIT NONE

! Declare calling arguments.
REAL, INTENT(IN) :: x          ! Value to evaluate expression for
REAL, INTENT(IN) :: a          ! Coefficient of X**2 term
REAL, INTENT(IN) :: b          ! Coefficient of X term
REAL, INTENT(IN) :: c          ! Coefficient of constant term

! Evaluate expression.
quadf = a * x**2 + b * x + c

END FUNCTION
```

This function produces a result of type real. Note that the INTENT attribute is not used with the declaration of the function name quadf, since it must always be used for output only. A simple test program using the function is shown in Figure 6–18.

FIGURE 6–18

A test driver program for function quadf.

```
PROGRAM test_quadf
!
! Purpose:
!   Program to test function quadf.
!
```

(continued)

(concluded)
```
      IMPLICIT NONE

      REAL :: quadf                         ! Declare function
      REAL :: a, b, c, x                    ! Declare local variables

      ! Get input data.
      WRITE (*,*) 'Enter quadratic coefficients a, b, and c: '
      READ  (*,*) a, b, c
      WRITE (*,*) 'Enter location at which to evaluate equation: '
      READ  (*,*) x

      ! Write out result.
      WRITE (*,100) ' quadf(', x, ') = ', quadf(x,a,b,c)
100   FORMAT (A,F10.4,A,F12.4)

      END PROGRAM
```

Notice that function `quadf` is declared as type real both in the function itself and in the test program. In this example function `quadf` was used in the argument list of a `WRITE` statement. It could also have been used in assignment statements or wherever a Fortran expression is permissible. It could *not* be used on the left side of an assignment statement.

Good Programming Practice
Be sure to declare the type of any user-defined functions both in the function itself and in any routines that call the function.

6.6.1 Unintended Side Effects in Functions

Input values are passed to a function through its argument list. Functions use the same argument-passing scheme as subroutines. A function receives pointers to the locations of its arguments, and it can deliberately or accidentally modify the contents of those memory locations. Therefore, it is possible for a function subprogram to modify its own input arguments. If any of the function's dummy arguments appear on the left side of an assignment statement within the function, then the values of the input variables corresponding to those arguments will be changed. A function that modifies the values in its argument list is said to have *side effects*.

By definition, a function should produce a *single output value* using one or more input values, and it should have no side effects. The function should never modify its own input arguments. If a programmer needs to produce more than one output value from a procedure, then the procedure should be written as a subroutine and not as a function. To ensure that a function does not accidentally modify arguments, always declare all dummy arguments with the `INTENT(IN)` attribute.

Good Programming Practice

A well-designed Fortran function should produce a single output value from one or more input values. It should never modify its own input arguments. To ensure that a function does not accidentally modify its input arguments, always declare the arguments with the INTENT(IN) attribute.

Quiz 6–3

This quiz provides a quick check to see if you understand the concepts introduced in section 6.6. If you have trouble with the quiz, reread the section, ask your instructor, or discuss the material with a fellow student. The answers to this quiz appear in Appendix F.

Write a user-defined function to perform the following calculations:

1. $f(x) = \dfrac{x - 1}{x + 1}$

2. The hyperbolic tangent function $\tanh(x) = \dfrac{e^x - e^{-x}}{e^x + e^{-x}}$

3. The factorial function $n! = (n)(n-1)(n-2)...(2)(1)$

4. Write a logical function that has two input arguments, x and y. The function should return a true value if $x^2 + y^2 > 1.0$ or false value otherwise.

For questions 5 to 7, determine whether any errors occur in these functions. If so, show how to correct them.

5.
```fortran
REAL FUNCTION average ( x, n )
IMPLICIT NONE
INTEGER, INTENT(IN) :: n
REAL, DIMENSION(n), INTENT(IN) :: x
INTEGER :: j
REAL :: sum
DO j = 1, n
   sum = sum + x(j)
END DO
average = sum / n
END FUNCTION average
```

6.
```fortran
FUNCTION fun_2 ( a, b, c )
IMPLICIT NONE
REAL, INTENT(IN) :: a, b, c
a = 3. * a
fun_2 = a**2 - b + c
END FUNCTION
```

(continued)

(concluded)

```
7. LOGICAL FUNCTION badval ( x, y )
   IMPLICIT NONE
   REAL, INTENT(IN) :: x, y
   badval = x > y
   END FUNCTION
```

EXAMPLE 6–9 *The Sinc Function:* The sinc function is defined by the equation

$$\text{sinc}(x) = \frac{\sin(x)}{x} \tag{6–11}$$

This function occurs in many types of engineering analysis problems. For example, the sinc function describes the frequency spectrum of a rectangular time pulse. A plot of the function sinc(x) versus x is shown in Figure 6–19.

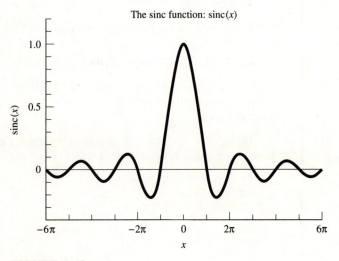

FIGURE 6–19
Plot of sinc(x) versus x.

Write a user-defined Fortran function to calculate the sinc function.

SOLUTION

The sinc function looks easy to implement, but a calculation problem develops when $x = 0$. The value of sinc(0) = 1, since

$$\text{sinc}(0) = \lim_{x \to 0}\left(\frac{\sin(x)}{x}\right) = 1$$

Unfortunately, a computer program would blow up on the division by zero. We must include a logical IF construct in the function to handle the special case where x is nearly zero.

1. **State the problem.**

   Write a Fortran function that calculates sinc(x).

2. **Define the inputs and outputs.**

   The input to the function is the real argument x. The function is of type real, and its output is the value of sinc(x).

3. **Describe the algorithm.**

   The pseudocode for this function is

   ```
   IF |x| > epsilon THEN
       sinc ← SIN(x) / x
   ELSE
       sinc ← 1.
   END IF
   ```

where epsilon is chosen to ensure that the division does not cause divide-by-zero errors. For most computers, a good choice for epsilon might be 1.0E-30.

4. **Turn the algorithm into Fortran statements.**

   The resulting Fortran subroutines are shown in Figure 6–20.

FIGURE 6–20
The Fortran functions sinc(x).

```
FUNCTION sinc ( x )
!
! Purpose:
!   To calculate the sinc function
!   sinc(x) = sin(x)/x.
!
! Record of revisions:
!     Date         Programmer           Description of change
!     ====         ==========           =====================
!   10/22/95     S. J. Chapman          Original code
!
IMPLICIT NONE

! List of calling arguments:
REAL, INTENT(IN) :: x          ! Value for which to evaluate sinc
REAL :: sinc                   ! Output value sinc(x)

! List of local parameters:
REAL, PARAMETER :: epsilon = 1.0E-30 ! the smallest value for which
                                     ! to calculate SIN(x)/x
! Check to see of ABS(x) > epsilon.
IF ( ABS(x) > epsilon ) THEN
```

(continued)

(concluded)
```
   sinc = SIN(x) / x
ELSE
   sinc = 1.
END IF

END FUNCTION sinc
```

5. **Test the resulting Fortran program.**

To test this function, it is necessary to write a driver program to read an input value, call the function, and write out the results. We will calculate several values of sinc(x) on a hand calculator and compare them with the results of the test program. Note that we must verify the function of the program for input values both greater than and less than `epsilon`.

A test driver program is shown in Figure 6–21.

FIGURE 6–21
A test driver program for the function `sinc(x)`.

```
PROGRAM test_sinc
!
! Purpose:
!   To test the sinc function sinc(x)
!
IMPLICIT NONE

! Declare function types:
REAL :: sinc                    ! sinc function

! Declare local variables:
REAL :: x                       ! Input value to evaluate

! Get value to evaluate
WRITE (*,*) 'Enter x: '
READ (*,*) x

! Write answer.
WRITE (*,100) 'sinc(x) = ', sinc(x)
100 FORMAT (1X,A,F8.5)

END PROGRAM
```

Hand calculations yield the following values for sinc(x):

x	sinc(x)
0	1.00000
10^{-29}	1.00000
$\dfrac{\pi}{2}$	0.63662
π	0.00000

The results from the test program for these input values are

```
C>test_sinc
Enter x:
0
sinc(x) =  1.00000

C>test_sinc
Enter x:
1.E-29
sinc(x) =  1.00000

C>test_sinc
Enter x:
1.570796
sinc(x) =  0.63662

C>test_sinc
Enter x:
3.141593
sinc(x) =  0.00000
```

The function appears to be working correctly.

■ 6.7

PASSING FUNCTIONS OR SUBROUTINES AS ARGUMENTS TO PROCEDURES

Fortran allows you to pass a function or subroutine as a calling argument to another procedure. If a user-defined function is named as an actual argument in a procedure call, then
a pointer to that function is passed to the procedure. If the corresponding formal argument in the procedure is used as a function, then when the procedure is executed, the function in the calling argument list will be used in place of the dummy function name in the
procedure. Consider the following example:

```
PROGRAM :: test
REAL, EXTERNAL :: fun_1, fun_2
REAL :: x, y, output
...
CALL evaluate ( fun_1, x, y, output )
CALL evaluate ( fun_2, x, y, output )
...
END PROGRAM
SUBROUTINE evaluate ( fun, a, b, result )
REAL, EXTERNAL :: fun
REAL, INTENT(IN) :: a, b
REAL, INTENT(OUT) :: result
result = b * fun(a)
END SUBROUTINE evaluate
```

Assume that `fun_1` and `fun_2` are two user-supplied functions. Then a pointer to
function `fun_1` is passed to subroutine `evaluate` on the first occasion that it is called,

and function `fun_1` is used in place of the dummy formal argument `fun` in the subroutine. A pointer to function `fun_2` is passed to subroutine `evaluate` the second time that it is called, and function `fun_2` is used in place of the dummy formal argument `fun` in the subroutine.

User-supplied functions may only be passed as calling arguments if they are declared to be external in the calling and the called procedures. When a name in an argument list is declared to be external, this tells the compiler that a separately compiled function is being passed in the argument list instead of a variable. A function may be declared to be external either with an EXTERNAL attribute or in an EXTERNAL statement. The EXTERNAL attribute is included in a type declaration statement, just like any other attribute. For example:

`REAL, EXTERNAL :: fun_1, fun_2`

The EXTERNAL statement is a specification statement of the form

`EXTERNAL fun_1, fun_2`

Either of these forms state that `fun_1` and `fun_2` are names of procedures that are defined outside of the current routine. If used, the EXTERNAL statement must appear in the declaration section before the first executable statement.

EXAMPLE 6–10 Passing Functions to Procedures in an Argument List: The function `ave_value` in Figure 6–22 determines the average amplitude of a function between user-specified limits `first_value` and `last_value` by sampling the function at n evenly spaced points and calculating the average amplitude between those points. The function to be evaluated is passed to function `ave_value` as the dummy argument `func`.

FIGURE 6–22
Function `ave_value` calculates the average amplitude of a function between two points `first_value` and `last_value`. The function is passed to function `ave_value` as a calling argument.

```
REAL FUNCTION ave_value ( func, first_value, last_value, n )
!
! Purpose:
!   To calculate the average value of function "func" over the
!   range [first_value, last_value] by taking n evenly spaced
!   samples over the range and averaging the results.  Function
!   "func" is passed to this routine via a dummy argument.
!
! Record of revisions:
!    Date          Programmer           Description of change
!    ====          ==========           =====================
!   10/25/95    S. J. Chapman           Original code
!
IMPLICIT NONE

! Declare calling arguments:
REAL, EXTERNAL :: func                  ! Function to be evaluated
REAL, INTENT(IN) :: first_value         ! First value in range
```

(continued)

(concluded)
```
REAL, INTENT(IN) :: last_value       ! Last value in range
INTEGER, INTENT(IN) :: n             ! Number of samples to average

! List of local variables:
REAL :: delta              ! Step size between samples
INTEGER :: i               ! Index variable
REAL :: sum                ! Sum of values to average

! Get step size.
delta = ( last_value - first_value ) / REAL(n-1)

! Accumulate sum.
sum = 0.
DO i = 1, n
   sum = sum + func ( REAL(i-1) * delta )
END DO

! Get average.
ave_value = sum / REAL(n)

END FUNCTION
```

A test driver program to test function ave_value is shown in Figure 6–23. In that program, function ave_value is called with the user-defined function my_function as a calling argument. Note that my_function is declared as EXTERNAL in the test driver program test_ave_value. The function my_function is averaged over 101 samples in the interval [0,1], and the results are printed out.

FIGURE 6–23
Test driver program for function ave_value, illustrating how to pass a user-defined function as a calling argument.

```
PROGRAM test_ave_value
!
! Purpose:
!   To test function ave_value by calling it with a user-defined
!   function my_func.
!
! Record of revisions:
!    Date        Programmer            Description of change
!    ====        ==========            =====================
!   10/25/95     S. J. Chapman         Original code
!
IMPLICIT NONE

! Declare functions:
REAL :: ave_value               ! Average value of function
REAL, EXTERNAL :: my_function   ! Function to evaluate

! Declare local variables:
REAL :: ave                     ! Average of my_function
```

(continued)

(concluded)
```
! Call function with func=my_function.
ave = ave_value ( my_function, 0., 1., 101 )
WRITE (*,1000) 'my_function', ave
1000 FORMAT (1X,'The average value of ',A,' between 0. and 1. is ', &
            F16.6,'.')

END PROGRAM

REAL FUNCTION my_function( x )
IMPLICIT NONE
REAL, INTENT(IN) :: x
my_function = 3. * x
END FUNCTION
```

When program `test_ave_value` is executed, the results are

```
C>test_ave_value
The average value of my_function between 0. and 1. is   1.500000.
```

Since for this case `my_function` is a straight line between (0,0) and (1,3), it is obvious that the average value was correctly calculated as 1.5.

Subroutines may also be passed to procedures as calling arguments. If a subroutine is to be passed as a calling argument, it must declared in an `EXTERNAL` statement because subroutine names do not appear in type declaration statements.

■ 6.8
SUMMARY

Chapter 6 presents an introduction to Fortran procedures. Procedures are independently compiled program units with their own declaration sections, execution sections, and termination sections. They are extremely important to the design, coding, and maintenance of large programs. Procedures permit the independent testing of subtasks as a project is being built, allow time savings through reusable code, and improve reliability through variable hiding.

The two types of procedures are subroutines and functions. Subroutines are procedures whose results include one or more values. A subroutine is defined using a `SUBROUTINE` statement and is executed using a `CALL` statement. Input data is passed to a subroutine and results are returned from the subroutine through argument lists on the `SUBROUTINE` statement and `CALL` statement. When a subroutine is called, pointers are passed to the subroutine pointing to the locations of each argument in the argument list. The subroutine reads from and writes to those locations.

The use of each argument in a subroutine's argument list can be controlled by specifying an `INTENT` attribute in the argument's type declaration statement. Each argument can be specified as either input only (`IN`), output only (`OUT`), or both input and output (`INOUT`). The Fortran compiler checks to see that each argument is used properly and can catch many programming errors at compile time.

Data can also be passed to subroutines through modules. A module is a separately compiled program unit that can contain data declarations, procedures, or both. The data and procedures declared in the module are available to any procedure that includes the module with a USE statement. Thus two procedures can share data by placing the data in a module and having both procedures USE the module.

If procedures are placed in a module and that module is used in a program, then the procedures have an explicit interface. The Fortran 90/95 compiler will automatically check to ensure that number, type, and use of all arguments in each procedure call match the argument list specified for the procedure. This feature can catch many common errors.

Fortran functions are procedures whose results are a single number, logical value, character string, or array. Fortran functions are either intrinsic (built in) and user defined. Some intrinsic functions were discussed in Chapters 2 and 5, and all intrinsic functions are included in Appendix B. User-defined functions are declared using the FUNCTION statement and are executed by naming the function as part of a Fortran expression. Data may be passed to a user-defined function through calling arguments or via modules.

A properly designed Fortran function should not change its input arguments. It should *only* change the single output value.

It is possible to pass a function or subroutine to a procedure via a calling argument, provided that the function or subroutine is declared EXTERNAL in the calling program.

6.8.1 Summary of Good Programming Practice

The following guidelines should be adhered to when working with subroutines and functions.

1. Break large program tasks into smaller, more understandable procedures whenever possible.
2. Always specify the INTENT of every dummy argument in every procedure to help catch programming errors.
3. Make sure that the actual argument list in each procedure invocation matches the dummy argument list in number, type, intent, and order. Placing procedures in a module and then accessing the procedures by USE association will create an explicit interface, which will allow the compiler to automatically check that the argument lists are correct.
4. Test for possible error conditions within a subroutine and set an error flag to be returned to the calling program unit. The calling program unit should test for error conditions after the subroutine call and take appropriate actions if an error occurs.
5. If a procedure requires that the value of a local variable not change between successive invocations of the procedure, specify the SAVE attribute in the variable's type declaration statement, include the variable in a SAVE statement, or initialize the variable in its type declaration statement.
6. Modules may be used to pass large amounts of data between procedures within a program. The data values are declared only once in the module, and all procedures needing access to that data use that module. Be sure to include a SAVE statement in the module to guarantee that the data is preserved between accesses by different procedures.

7. Place the procedures that you use in a program in a module. When they are in modules, the Fortran compiler will automatically verify the calling argument list each time that a procedure is used.

8. Be sure to declare the type of any function both in the function itself and in any program units that invoke the function.

9. A well-designed Fortran function should produce a single output value from one or more input values. It should never modify its own input arguments. To ensure that a function does not accidentally modify its input arguments, always declare the arguments with the INTENT(IN) attribute.

6.8.2 Summary of Fortran Statements and Structures

CALL Statement

        CALL *subname(arg1, arg2, ...)*

Example:

        CALL sort (number, data1)

Description:
    This statement transfers execution from the current program unit to the subroutine, passing pointers to the calling arguments. The subroutine executes until either a RETURN or an END SUBROUTINE statement is encountered, and then execution will continue in the calling program unit at the next executable statement following the CALL statement.

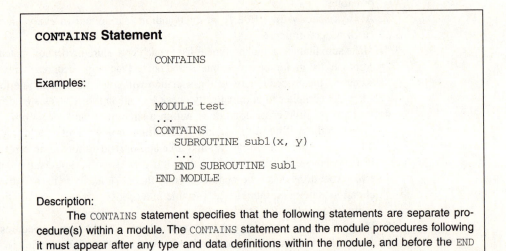

CONTAINS Statement

            CONTAINS

Examples:

            MODULE test
            ...
            CONTAINS
                SUBROUTINE sub1(x, y)
                ...
                END SUBROUTINE sub1
            END MODULE

Description:
    The CONTAINS statement specifies that the following statements are separate procedure(s) within a module. The CONTAINS statement and the module procedures following it must appear after any type and data definitions within the module, and before the END MODULE statement.

END FUNCTION **Statement**

```
                    END FUNCTION [name]
```

Example:

```
                    END FUNCTION my_function
```

Description:

This statement ends a user-defined Fortran function. The name of the function is optional.

END MODULE **Statement**

```
                    END MODULE [name]
```

Example:

```
                    END MODULE my_mod
```

Description:

This statement ends a module. The name of the module is optional.

END SUBROUTINE **Statement**

```
                    END SUBROUTINE [name]
```

Example:

```
                    END SUBROUTINE my_sub
```

Description:

This statement ends a subroutine. The name of the subroutine is optional.

FUNCTION **Statement**

```
                    [type] FUNCTION name( arg1, arg2, ... )
```

Examples:

```
                    INTEGER FUNCTION max_value ( num, iarray )
                    FUNCTION gamma(x)
```

(continued)

(concluded)

Description:
     This statement declares a user-defined Fortran function. The type of the function may be declared in the `FUNCTION` statement, or it may be declared in a separate type declaration statement. The function is executed by naming it in an expression in the calling program. The dummy arguments are placeholders for the calling arguments passed when the function is executed. If a function has no arguments, then it must be declared with an empty pair of parentheses `[name()]`.

`INTENT` Attribute

```
type, INTENT(intent_type) :: name1, name2, ...
```

Example:

```
REAL, INTENT(IN) :: value
INTEGER, INTENT(OUT) :: count
```

Description:
     This attribute declares the intended use of a particular dummy procedure argument. Possible values of *intent_type* are `IN`, `OUT`, and `INOUT`. The `INTENT` attribute allows the Fortran compiler to know the intended use of the argument and to check that it is used in the way intended. This attribute may appear only on dummy arguments in procedures.

`MODULE` Statement

```
MODULE name
```

Example:

```
MODULE my_data_and_subs
```

Description:
     This statement declares a module. The module may contain data, procedures, or both. The data and procedures are made available for use in a program unit by declaring the module name in a `USE` statement (`USE` association).

`RETURN` Statement

```
RETURN
```

(continued)

(concluded)
Example:

```
                    RETURN
```

Description:
　　When this statement is executed in a procedure, control returns to the program unit that invoked the procedure. This statement is optional at the end of a subroutine or function, since execution will automatically return to the calling routine whenever an END SUB-ROUTINE or END FUNCTION statement is reached.

SAVE Attribute

```
          type, SAVE :: name1, name2, ...
```

Example:

```
          REAL, SAVE :: sum
```

Description:
　　This attribute declares that the value of a *local variable* in a procedure must remain unchanged between successive invocations of the procedure. It is equivalent to the naming the variable in a SAVE statement.

SAVE Statement

```
          SAVE [var1, var2, ...]
```

Examples:

```
          SAVE count, index
          SAVE
```

Description:
　　This statement declares that the value of a *local variable* in a procedure must remain unchanged between successive invocations of the procedure. If a list of variables is included, only those variables will be saved. If no list is included, every local variable in the procedure or module will be saved.

SUBROUTINE Statement

```
          SUBROUTINE name ( arg1, arg2, ... )
```

(continued)

(concluded)
Example:

```
              SUBROUTINE sort ( num, data1 )
```

Description:
      This statement declares a Fortran subroutine. The subroutine is executed with a
`CALL` statement. The dummy arguments *arg1, arg2, ...* are placeholders for the calling arguments passed when the subroutine is executed.

USE **Statement**

```
              USE module1, module2, ...
```

Example:

```
              USE my_data
```

Description:
      This statement makes the contents of one or more modules available for use in a pro-
gram unit. `USE` statements must be the first noncomment statements within the program unit
after the `PROGRAM`, `SUBROUTINE`, or `FUNCTION` statement.

■ 6.9
EXERCISES

6–1 What is the difference between a subroutine and a function?

6–2 When a subroutine is called, how is data passed from the calling program to the subroutine?
How are the results of the subroutine returned to the calling program?

6–3 Suppose that a 15-element array a is passed to a subroutine as a calling argument. What will
happen if the subroutine attempts to write to element a(16)?

6–4 Suppose that a real value is passed to a subroutine in an argument that is declared to be an
integer in the subroutine. Is there any way for the subroutine to tell that the argument type is
mismatched? What happens on your computer when the following code is executed?

```
              PROGRAM main
              IMPLICIT NONE
              REAL :: x
              x = -5.
              CALL sub1 ( x )
              END PROGRAM
```

```
                                    SUBROUTINE sub1 ( i )
                                    IMPLICIT NONE
                                    INTEGER, INTENT(IN) :: i
                                    WRITE (*,*) ' I = ', i
                                    END SUBROUTINE
```

6–5 How could the program in exercise 6–4 be modified to ensure that the Fortran compiler catches the argument mismatch between the actual argument in the main program and the dummy argument in subroutine sub1?

6–6 What is the purpose of the INTENT attribute? Where can it be used? Why should it be used?

6–7 Determine whether the following subroutine calls are correct or not. If they are in error, specify what is wrong with them.

a.
```
PROGRAM sum_sqrt
IMPLICIT NONE
INTEGER, PARAMETER :: length = 20
INTEGER :: result
REAL :: test(length) = &
     (/  1., 2., 3., 4., 5., 6., 7., 8., 9.,10., &
        11.,12.,13.,14.,15.,16.,17.,18.,19.,20. /)
...
CALL test_sub ( length, test, result )
...
END PROGRAM sum_sqrt
SUBROUTINE test_sub ( length, array, res )
IMPLICIT NONE
INTEGER, INTENT(IN) :: length
REAL, INTENT(OUT) :: res
INTEGER, INTENT(IN) :: array(length)
INTEGER, INTENT(INOUT) :: i
DO i = 1, length
   res = res + SQRT(array(i))
END DO
END SUBROUTINE test_sub
```

b.
```
PROGRAM test
IMPLICIT NONE
CHARACTER(len=8) :: str = '1AbHz05Z'
CHARACTER :: largest
CALL max_char (str, largest)
WRITE (*,100) str, largest
100 FORMAT (' The largest character in ', A, ' is ', A)
END PROGRAM
SUBROUTINE max_char(string, big)
IMPLICIT NONE
CHARACTER(len=10), INTENT(IN) :: string
CHARACTER, INTENT(OUT) :: big
INTEGER :: i
big = string(1:1)
DO i = 2, 10
   IF ( string(i:i) > big ) THEN
      big = string(i:i)
   END IF
END DO
END SUBROUTINE
```

6–8 What is the purpose of the SAVE statement and attribute? When should they be used?

6–9 Is the following program correct or incorrect? If it is incorrect, what is wrong with it? If it is correct, what values will be printed out?

```
MODULE my_constants
IMPLICIT NONE
REAL, PARAMETER :: pi = 3.141593  ! Pi
REAL, PARAMETER :: g = 9.81       ! Accel. due to gravity
END MODULE my_constants
PROGRAM main
IMPLICIT NONE
USE my_constants
WRITE (*,*) 'SIN(2*pi) = ' SIN(2.*pi)
g = 17.
END PROGRAM
```

6–10 Modify the selection sort subroutine developed in this chapter so that it sorts real values in *descending* order.

6–11 Write a subroutine ucase that accepts a character string and converts any lowercase letter in the string to uppercase without affecting any nonalphabetic characters in the string.

6–12 Write a driver program to test the statistical subroutines developed in Example 6–3. Be sure to test the routines with a variety of input data sets. Did you discover any problems with the subroutines?

6–13 Write a subroutine that uses subroutine random0 to generate a random number in the range [−1.0,1.0).

6–14 **Dice Simulation** It is often useful to be able to simulate the throw of a fair die. Write a Fortran function dice() that simulates the throw of a fair die by returning some random integer between 1 and 6 every time that it is called. (*Hint:* Call random0 to generate a random number. Divide the possible values out of random0 into six equal intervals and return the number of the interval that a given random number falls into.)

6–15 **Road Traffic Density** Subroutine random0 produces a number with a *uniform* probability distribution in the range [0.0, 1.0). This subroutine is suitable for simulating random events if each outcome has an equal probability of occurring. However, in many events the probability of occurrence is *not* equal for every event, and a uniform probability distribution is not suitable for simulating such events.

For example, when traffic engineers studied the number of cars passing a given location in a time interval of length t, they discovered that the probability of k cars passing during the interval is given by the following equation:

$$P(k, t) = e^{-\lambda t} \frac{(\lambda t)^k}{k!} \text{ for } t \geq 0, \lambda > 0, \text{ and } k = 0, 1, 2, \ldots \tag{6–12}$$

This probability distribution is known as the *Poisson distribution;* it occurs in many applications in science and engineering. For example, the number of calls k to a telephone switchboard in time interval t, the number of bacteria k in a specified volume t of liquid, and the number of failures k of a complicated system in time interval t all have Poisson distributions.

Write a function to evaluate the Poisson distribution for any k, t, and λ. Test your function by calculating the probability of 0, 1, 2, . . . , 5 cars passing a particular point on a highway in one minute, given that λ is 1.6 per minute for that highway.

6–16 What are two purposes of a module? What are the special advantages of placing procedures within modules?

6–17 Write three Fortran functions to calculate the hyperbolic sine, cosine, and tangent functions:

$$\sinh(x) = \frac{e^x - e^{-x}}{2} \qquad \cosh(x) = \frac{e^x + e^{-x}}{2} \qquad \tanh(x) = \frac{e^x - e^{-x}}{e^x + e^{-x}}$$

Use your functions to calculate the hyperbolic sines, cosines, and tangents of the following values: -2, -1.5, -1.0, -0.5, -0.25, 0.0, 0.25, 0.5, 1.0, 1.5, and 2.0. Sketch the shapes of the hyperbolic sine, cosine, and tangent functions.

6–18 Cross Product Write a function to calculate the cross product of two vectors and $\mathbf{V}_1$ and $\mathbf{V}_2$:

$$\mathbf{V}_1 \times \mathbf{V}_2 = (V_{y1}V_{z2} - V_{y2}V_{z1})\mathbf{i} + (V_{z1}V_{x2} - V_{z2}V_{x1})\mathbf{j} + (V_{x1}V_{y2} - V_{x2}V_{y1})\mathbf{k}$$

where $\mathbf{V}_1 = V_{x1}\mathbf{i} + V_{y1}\mathbf{j} + V_{z1}\mathbf{k}$ and $\mathbf{V}_2 = V_{x2}\mathbf{i} + V_{y2}\mathbf{j} + V_{z2}\mathbf{k}$. Note that this function will return a real array as its result. Use the function to calculate the cross product of the two vectors $\mathbf{V}_1 = [-2, 4, 0.5]$ and $\mathbf{V}_2 = [0.5, 3, 2]$.

6–19 Matrix Multiplication Write a subroutine to calculate the product of two matrices if they are of compatible sizes and if the output array is large enough to hold the result. If the matrices are not of compatible sizes or if the output array is too small, set an error flag and return to the calling program. The dimensions of all three arrays a, b, and c should be passed to the subroutines from the calling program so that you can use explicit-shape dummy arrays and perform size checking. (*Note:* The definition of matrix multiplication appears in exercise 5–26.) Check your subroutine by multiplying the following two pairs of arrays both with the subroutine and with the intrinsic subroutine MATMUL.

a. $a = \begin{bmatrix} 2 & -1 & 2 \\ -1 & -3 & 4 \\ 2 & 4 & 2 \end{bmatrix}$ $b = \begin{bmatrix} 1 & 2 & 3 \\ 2 & 1 & 2 \\ 3 & 2 & 1 \end{bmatrix}$

b. $a = \begin{bmatrix} 1 & -1 & -2 \\ 2 & 2 & 0 \\ 3 & 3 & 3 \\ 5 & 4 & 4 \end{bmatrix}$ $b = \begin{bmatrix} -2 \\ 5 \\ 2 \end{bmatrix}$

6–20 Write a new version of the matrix multiplication subroutine from exercise 6–19 that uses an explicit interface and assumed-shape arrays. Before multiplying the matrices, this version should check to ensure that the input arrays are compatible and that the output array is large enough to hold the product of the two matrices. It can check for compatibility using the inquiry intrinsic functions found in Table 5–1. If these conditions are not satisfied, the subroutine should set an error flag and return.

6–21 Sort with Carry It is often useful to sort an array `arr1` into ascending order while carrying along a second array `arr2`. In such a sort, each time an element of array `arr1` is exchanged with another element of `arr1`, the corresponding element of array `arr2` is also swapped. When the sort is over, the elements of array `arr1` are in ascending order, and the elements of array `arr2` that were associated with particular elements of array `arr1` are still associated with them. For example, suppose we have the following two arrays:

Element	arr1	arr2
1.	6.	1.
2.	1.	0.
3.	2.	10.

After sorting array `arr1` while carrying along array `arr2`, the contents of the two arrays will be

Element	arr1	arr2
1.	1.	0.
2.	2.	10.
3.	6.	1.

Write a subroutine to sort one real array into ascending order while carrying along a second array. Test the subroutine with the following two nine-element arrays:

```
REAL, DIMENSION(9)  ::  &
    a = (/  1.,  11.,   -6.,  17.,-23.,    0.,    5.,  1., -1.  /)
REAL, DIMENSION(9)  ::  &
    b = (/ 31.,101.,  36.,-17.,   0.,  10.,  -8., -1., -1.  /)
```

6–22 Minima and Maxima of a Function Write a subroutine that attempts to locate the maximum and minimum values of an arbitrary function $f(x)$ over a certain range. The function being evaluated should be passed to the subroutine as a calling argument. The subroutine should have the following input arguments:

`first_value`	The first value of x to search.
`last_value`	The last value of x to search.
`num_steps`	The number of steps to include in the search.
`func`	The name of the function to search.

The subroutine should have the following output arguments:

`xmin`	The value of x at which the minimum was found.
`min_value`	The minimum value of $f(x)$ found.
`xmax`	The value of x at which the maximum was found.
`max_value`	The maximum value $f(x)$ found.

6–23 Write a test driver program for the subroutine generated in the previous problem. The test driver program should pass to the subroutine the user-defined function $f(x) = x^3 - 5x^2 +$

5x + 2 and search for the minimum and maximum in 200 steps over the range $-1 \leq x < 3$. It should print out the resulting minimum and maximum values.

6–24 Histograms A histogram is a plot that shows how many times a particular measurement falls within a certain range of values. For example, consider the students in this class. Suppose that 30 students are in the class and that their scores on the last exam fall within the following ranges:

Range	Number of Students
100–95	3
94–90	6
89–85	9
84–80	7
79–75	4
74–70	2
69–65	1

A plot of the number of students scoring in each range of numbers is a histogram. To create a histogram, we start with a set of data consisting of 30 student grades. We divide the range of possible grades on the test (0 to 100) into a number of bins and then count how many student scores fall within each bin. Then we plot the number of grades in each bin, as shown in Figure 6–24.

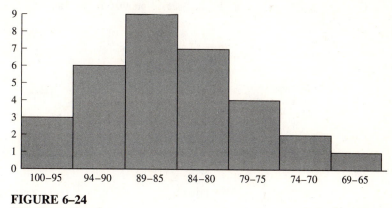

FIGURE 6–24
Histogram of student test scores.

Write a subroutine that will accept an array of real input data values, divide them into a user-specified number of bins over a user-specified range, and accumulate the number of samples that fall within each bin. The subroutine should then plot a histogram of the data values using a line-printer plot.

6–25 Derivative of a Function The derivative of a continuous function f(x) is defined by the equation

$$\frac{d}{dx}f(x) = \lim_{\Delta x \to 0} \frac{f(x + \Delta x) - f(x)}{\Delta x} \qquad (6-13)$$

In a sampled function, this definition becomes

$$f'(x_i) = \frac{f(x_{i+1}) - f(x_i)}{\Delta x} \qquad (6-14)$$

where $\Delta x = x_{i+1} - x_i$. Assume that a vector `vect` contains `nsamp` samples of a function taken at a spacing of `dx` per sample. Write a subroutine that will calculate the derivative of this vector from Equation (6–14). The subroutine should check to make sure that `dx` is greater than zero to prevent divide-by-zero errors in the subroutine.

To check your subroutine, you should generate a data set whose derivative is known and compare the result of the subroutine with the known correct answer. A good choice for a test function is sin x. From elementary calculus, we know that $\frac{d}{dx}(\sin x) = \cos x$. Generate an input vector containing 100 values of the function sin x starting at $x = 0$ and using a step size Δx of 0.05. Take the derivative of the vector with your subroutine and then compare the resulting answers to the known correct answer. How close did your routine come to calculating the correct value for the derivative?

6–26 **Derivative in the Presence of Noise** We will now explore the effects of input noise on the quality of a numerical derivative. First generate an input vector containing 100 values of the function sin x starting at $x = 0$ and using a step size Δx of 0.05, just as you did in the preceding problem. Next use subroutine `random0` to generate a small amount of random noise with a maximum amplitude of ± 0.02 and add that random noise to the samples in your input vector (see Figure 6–25). Note that the peak amplitude of the noise is only 2 percent of

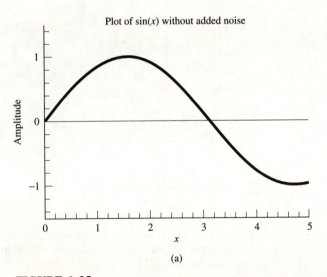

FIGURE 6–25
(a) A plot of sin x as a function of x with no noise added to the data.

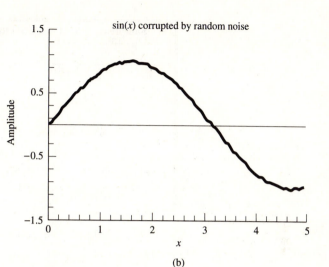

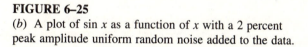

(b)

FIGURE 6–25
(b) A plot of sin x as a function of x with a 2 percent peak amplitude uniform random noise added to the data.

the peak amplitude of your signal, since the maximum value of sin x is 1. Now take the derivative of the function using the derivative subroutine that you developed in the preceding problem. How close to the theoretical value of the derivative did you come?

6–27 **Linear Least-Squares Fit** Develop a subroutine that will calculate slope m and intercept b of the least-squares line that best fits an input data set. The input data points (x,y) will be passed to the subroutine in two input arrays, X and Y. The equations describing the slope and intercept of the least-squares line are

$$y = m\,x + b \qquad\qquad (4\text{–}5)$$

$$m = \frac{(\Sigma xy) - (\Sigma x)\bar{y}}{(\Sigma x^2) - (\Sigma x)\bar{x}} \qquad\qquad (4\text{–}6)$$

and

$$b = \bar{y} - m\,\bar{x} \qquad\qquad (4\text{–}7)$$

where

Σx is the sum of the x values.
Σx^2 is the sum of the squares of the x values.
Σxy is the sum of the products of the corresponding x and y values.
$\bar{x}$ is the mean (average) of the x values.
$\bar{y}$ is the mean (average) of the y values.

Test your routine using a test driver program and the following 20-point input data set:

Sample data to test least-squares fit routine					
No.	x	y	No.	x	y
1	−4.91	−8.18	11	−0.94	0.21
2	−3.84	−7.49	12	0.59	1.73
3	−2.41	−7.11	13	0.69	3.96
4	−2.62	−6.15	14	3.04	4.26
5	−3.78	−5.62	15	1.01	5.75
6	−0.52	−3.30	16	3.60	6.67
7	−1.83	−2.05	17	4.53	7.70
8	−2.01	−2.83	18	5.13	7.31
9	0.28	−1.16	19	4.43	9.05
10	1.08	0.52	20	4.12	10.95

6–28 Correlation Coefficient of Least-Squares Fit Develop a subroutine that will calculate both the slope m and intercept b of the least-squares line that best fits an input data set and also calculate the correlation coefficient of the fit. The input data points (x,y) will be passed to the subroutine in two input arrays X and Y. The equations describing the slope and intercept of the least-squares line are given in the previous problem, and the equation for the correlation coefficient is

$$r = \frac{n(\Sigma xy) - (\Sigma x)(\Sigma y)}{\sqrt{[(n\Sigma x^2) - (\Sigma x)^2]\,[(n\Sigma y^2) - (\Sigma y)^2]}} \tag{4-10}$$

where

Σx is the sum of the x values.
Σy is the sum of the y values.
Σx^2 is the sum of the squares of the x values.
Σy^2 is the sum of the squares of the y values.
Σxy is the sum of the products of the corresponding x and y values.
n is the number of points included in the fit.

Test your routine using a test driver program and the 20-point input data set given in the preceding problem.

6–29 The Birthday Problem If a group of n people are in a room, what is the probability that two or more of them have the same birthday? You can use simulation to answer this question. Write a function that calculates the probability that two or more of n people will have the same birthday, where n is a calling argument. (*Hint:* The function should create an array of size n and generate n birthdays in the range 1 to 365 randomly. It should then check to see if any of the n birthdays are identical. The function should perform this experiment at least 1000 times and calculate the fraction of those times in which two or more people had the same birthday.) Write a main program that calculates and prints out the probability that two or more of n people will have the same birthday for $n = 2, 3, \ldots, 40$.

6–30 Elapsed Time Measurement When testing the operation of procedures, it is very useful to have a set of *elapsed time subroutines*. By starting a timer before a procedure executes and then checking the time after the execution, we can see how fast or slow the procedure is. In this manner, a programmer can identify the time-consuming portions of his or her program and rewrite them if necessary to make them faster.

Write a pair of subroutines named `set_timer` and `elapsed_time` to calculate the elapsed time in seconds between the last time that subroutine `set_timer` was called and the time that subroutine `elapsed_time` is being called. When subroutine `set_timer` is called, it should get the current time and store it into a variable in a module. When subroutine `elapsed_time` is called, it should get the current time and then calculate the difference between the current time and the stored time in the module. The elapsed time in seconds between the two calls should be returned to the calling program unit in an argument of subroutine `elapsed_time`. (*Note:* The intrinsic subroutine to read the current time is called `DATE_AND_TIME`; see Appendix B.)

6–31 Use subroutine `random0` to generate a set of four arrays of random numbers. The four arrays should be 10; 100; 1000; and 10,000 elements long. Then use your elapsed time subroutines to determine the time that it takes subroutine `sort` to sort each array. How does the elapsed time to sort increase as a function of the number of elements being sorted? (*Hint:* On a fast computer, you will need to sort each array many times and calculate the average sorting time in order to overcome the quantization error of the system clock.)

6–32 Evaluating Infinite Series The value of the exponential function e^x can be calculated by evaluating the following infinite series:

$$e^x = \sum_{n=0}^{\infty} \frac{x^n}{n!}$$

Write a Fortran function that calculates e^x using the first 12 terms of the infinite series. Compare the result of your function with the result of the intrinsic function `EXP(x)` for $x = -10, -5., -1., 0., 1., 5., 10.,$ and $15.$

6–33 Use subroutine `random0` to generate an array containing 10,000 random numbers between 0.0 and 1.0. Then use the statistics subroutines developed in this chapter to calculate the average and standard deviation of values in the array. The theoretical average of a uniform random distribution in the range [0,1) is 0.5, and the theoretical standard deviation of the uniform random distribution is $\frac{1}{\sqrt{12}}$. How close does the random array generated by `random0` come to behaving like the theoretical distribution?

6–34 Write a test driver program to test subroutine `simul2` in Figure 6–10. Use the two data sets in Example 6–4 to test the subroutine.

6–35 Gaussian (Normal) Distribution Subroutine `random0` returns a uniformly distributed random variable in the range [0,1), which means that there is an equal probability of any given number in the range occurring on a given call to the subroutine. Another type of random distribution is the Gaussian distribution, in which the random value takes on the classic bell-shaped curve shown in Figure 6–26. A Gaussian distribution with an average of 0.0 and a standard deviation of 1.0 is called a *standardized normal distribution,* and the probability of any given value occurring in the standardized normal distribution is given by the following equation:

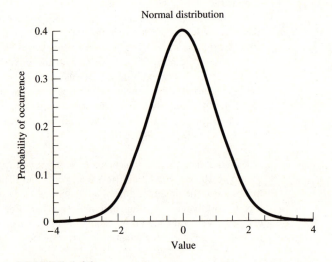

FIGURE 6–26
A normal probability distribution.

$$p(x) = \frac{1}{\sqrt{12}} \, e^{-x^2/2} \tag{6-15}$$

It is possible to generate a random variable with a standardized normal distribution starting from a random variable with a uniform distribution in the range $[-1,1)$ as follows:

1. Select two uniform random variables x_1 and x_2 from the range $[-1,1)$ such that $x_1^2 + x_2^2 < 1$. To do so, generate two uniform random variables in the range $[-1,1)$ and determine whether the sum of their squares is less than 1. If so, use them. If not, try again.
2. Each of the values y_1 and y_2 in the following equations will be a normally distributed random variable.

$$y_1 = \sqrt{\frac{-2 \ln r}{r}} \, x_1 \tag{6-16}$$

$$y_2 = \sqrt{\frac{-2 \ln r}{r}} \, x_2 \tag{6-17}$$

where

$$r = \sqrt{x_1^2 + x_2^2} \tag{6-18}$$

Write a subroutine that returns a normally distributed random value each time that it is called. Test your subroutine by getting 1000 random values and calculating the standard deviation. How close to 1.0 was the result? Plot the resulting distribution with the histogram subroutine from exercise 6–24.

6–36 Gravitational Force The gravitational force F between two bodies of masses m_1 and m_2 is given by the equation

$$F = \frac{Gm_1m_2}{r^2} \qquad (6\text{–}19)$$

where G is the gravitational constant (6.672×10^{-11} N m^2 / kg^2), m_1 and m_2 are the masses of the bodies in kilograms, and r is the distance between the two bodies. Write a function to calculate the gravitational force between two bodies given their masses and the distance between them. Test your function by determining the force on an 800-kg satellite in orbit 38,000 km above the Earth. (The mass of the Earth is 5.98×10^{24} kg.)

7

Additional Data Types

In this chapter we examine alternative kinds of the REAL data type and how to select the desired kind for a particular problem. Then we turn our attention to two additional data types: the COMPLEX data type and the derived data type. The COMPLEX data type is used to store and manipulate complex numbers, which have both real and imaginary components. The derived data type is a mechanism for users to create special new data types to suit the needs of a particular problem that they may be trying to solve.

■ 7.1

ALTERNATIVE KINDS OF THE REAL DATA TYPE

The real data type is used to represent numbers containing decimal points. On most computers a **default real** variable is **single precision,** which is usually 32 bits long. It is divided into two parts: a **mantissa** and an **exponent.** In a typical implementation 24 bits of the number are devoted to the mantissa, and 8 bits are devoted to the exponent. The 24 bits devoted to the mantissa are enough to represent six to seven significant decimal digits, so a real number can have up to about seven significant digits. Similarly, the 8 bits of the exponent are enough to represent numbers as large as 10^{38} and as small as 10^{-38}.

There are times when a 4-byte real number cannot adequately express a value that we need to solve a problem. Scientists and engineers sometimes need to express a number to more than seven significant digits of precision or to work with numbers larger than 10^{38} or smaller than 10^{-38}. In either case we cannot use a single-precision variable to represent the number. Fortran 90/95 includes a longer version of the real data type for use in these circumstances. This longer version of the real data type is also known as **double precision,** in contrast to the default single-precision real.

A double-precision real variable is twice as long as a single-precision real variable, so it is usually 64 bits long. In a typical implementation 53 bits of the number are devoted to the mantissa, and 11 bits are devoted to the exponent. The 53 bits devoted to the mantissa are enough to represent 15 to 16 significant decimal digits. Similarly, the 11 bits of the exponent are enough to represent numbers as large as 10^{308} and as small as 10^{-308}.

7.1.1 Kinds of REAL Constants and Variables

Since Fortran compilers have at least two different kinds of real variables, we need some way to declare which of the types we want to use in a particular problem. The device we use is a **kind type parameter.** Single-precision reals and double-precision reals are different **kinds** of the real data type, each with its own unique kind number. Examples of a real type declaration statement with a kind type parameter follow:

```
REAL(KIND=1) :: value_1
REAL(KIND=4) :: value_2
REAL(KIND=8), DIMENSION(20) :: array
REAL(4) :: temp
```

The kind of a real value is specified in parentheses after the REAL, either with or without the phrase KIND=. A variable declared with a kind type parameter is called a **parameterized variable.** If no kind is specified, then the default kind of real value is used. The default kind may vary from processor to processor but is usually 32-bit single precision.

What do the kind numbers mean? Unfortunately, we do not know. Each compiler vendor is free to assign any kind number to any size of variable. For example, on some compilers a 32-bit real value might be KIND=1 and a 64-bit real value might be KIND=2. On other compilers a 32-bit real value might be KIND=4 and a 64-bit real value might be KIND=8.

Therefore, to make your programs portable between computers, you should always assign kind numbers to a named constant and then use that named constant in all type declaration statements. This approach allows you to modify the program to run on different processors by changing only the value of the named constant. For example:

```
INTEGER, PARAMETER :: single = 4     ! Compiler dependent value
INTEGER, PARAMETER :: double = 8     ! Compiler dependent value
REAL(KIND=single) :: value_1
REAL(KIND=double), DIMENSION(20) :: array
REAL(single) :: temp
```

An even better approach for a large program would be to define the kind parameters within a module and to use that module in each procedure within the program. Then you can change the kind numbers for the entire program by editing a single file.

It is also possible to declare the kind of a real constant. The kind of a real constant is declared by appending an underscore and the kind number to the constant. The following are examples of valid real constants:

```
34.
34._4
34.E3
1234.56789_double
```

The second example is only valid if KIND=4 is a valid kind of real on the particular processor where the program is being executed. The fourth example is only valid if double is a valid previously defined integer named constant, whose value is a valid kind number. A constant without a kind type identifier is assumed to be of the default kind, which is single precision on most processors.

In addition to the preceding examples, a double-precision constant in exponential notation can be declared by using a D instead of an E to declare the exponent of the constant. For example:

3.0E0   is a single-precision constant.

3.0D0   is a double-precision constant.

Good Programming Practice
Always assign kind numbers to a named constant and then use that named constant in all type declaration statements and constant declarations. This practice will make it easier to port the program to different computers that may use different kind numbers. For large programs place the named constants containing the kind parameters in a single module; then use that module in every procedure within the program.

7.1.2 Determining the KIND of a Variable

Fortran 90/95 includes an intrinsic function KIND, which returns the kind number of a given constant or variable. This function can determine the kind numbers in use by your compiler. For example, the program in Figure 7–1 determines the kind numbers associated with single- and double-precision variables on a particular processor.

FIGURE 7–1
Program to determine the kind numbers associated with single- and double-precision real variables on a particular computer system.

```
PROGRAM kinds
!
! Purpose:
!   To determine the kinds of single- and double-precision real
!   values on a particular computer.
!
IMPLICIT NONE

! Write out the kinds of single- and double-precision values
WRITE (*,'(" The KIND for single precision is",I2)') KIND(0.0)
WRITE (*,'(" The KIND for double precision is",I2)') KIND(0.0D0)

END PROGRAM
```

When this program is executed on a 486-based PC using the Digital Visual Fortran compiler, the results are

```
C>kinds
The KIND for single precision is 4
The KIND for double precision is 8
```

Try the program on your own computer/compiler and see what values you get.

7.1.3 Selecting Precision in a Processor-Independent Manner

A major problem encountered when porting a Fortran program from one computer to another one is that the terms *single precision* and *double precision* are not precisely defined. Double-precision values have approximately twice the precision of single-precision values, but the number of bits associated with each kind of real is entirely up to the computer vendor. On most computers a single-precision value is 32 bits long and a double-precision value is 64 bits long. However, on some computers such as Cray Supercomputers and the 64-bit DEC Alpha chip, single precision is 64 bits long and double precision is 128 bits long. Thus a program that runs properly in single precision on a Cray might need double precision to run properly when it is migrated to a 32-bit computer, and a program that requires double precision for proper operation on a 32-bit computer will only need single precision on a computer based on the 64-bit Alpha chip.

How can we write programs so that they can be easily ported between processors with different word sizes and still function correctly? We can use a Fortran 90/95 intrinsic function to automatically select the proper kind of real value to use as the program is moved between computers. This function is called SELECTED_REAL_KIND. When it is executed, it returns the kind number of the smallest type of real value that meets the specified range and precision on that particular processor. The general form of this function is

kind_number = SELECTED_REAL_KIND(p=*precision*,r=*range*)

where *precision* is the number of decimal digits of precision required and *range* is the range of the exponent required in powers of 10. The two arguments *precision* and *range* are called optional arguments; either one or both may be supplied to specify the desired characteristics of the real value. The function returns the kind number of the smallest real kind satisfying the specified requirements. It returns a -1 if the specified precision is not available from any real data type on the processor, a -2 if the specified range is not available from any real data type on the processor, and a -3 if neither is available.

All of the following are legal uses of this function:

```
kind_number = SELECTED_REAL_KIND(p=6,r=37)
kind_number = SELECTED_REAL_KIND(p=12)
kind_number = SELECTED_REAL_KIND(r=100)
kind_number = SELECTED_REAL_KIND(13,200)
kind_number = SELECTED_REAL_KIND(13)
kind_number = SELECTED_REAL_KIND(p=17)
```

On a PC using the Digital Visual Fortran compiler, the first function returns a 4 (the kind number for single precision), and the next four functions return an 8 (the kind number for double precision). The last function returns a -1, since no real data type on an Intel-based PC has 17 decimal digits of precision. Other processors will return different results; try it on yours and see what you get.

Notice from the above example that the p= and r= are optional as long as *precision* and *range* are specified in that order, and the p= is optional if only the precision is specified.

Good Programming Practice
Use the function SELECTED_REAL_KIND to determine the kind numbers of the real variables needed to solve a problem. The function returns the proper kind numbers on any computer, making your programs more portable.

Three other intrinsic functions determine kind of a real value and the precision and range of the real value on a particular computer. These functions are summarized in Table 7–1. The integer function KIND() returns the kind number of a specified value. The integer function PRECISION() returns the number of decimal digits that can be stored in the real value, and the integer function RANGE() returns the exponent range that can be supported by the real value. The use of these functions is illustrated in the program in Figure 7–2.

FIGURE 7–2
Program to illustrate the use of function SELECTED_REAL_KIND() to select desired kinds of real variables in a processor-independent manner and the use of functions KIND(), PRECISION(), and RANGE() to get information about real values.

```
PROGRAM select_kinds
!
! Purpose:
!   To illustrate the use of SELECTED_REAL_KIND to select
!   desired kinds of real variables in a processor-independent
!   manner.
!
! Record of revisions:
!     Date       Programmer        Description of change
!     ====       ==========        =====================
!   12/09/95    S. J. Chapman      Original code
!
IMPLICIT NONE

! Declare parameters:
INTEGER, PARAMETER :: single = SELECTED_REAL_KIND(p=6,r=37)
INTEGER, PARAMETER :: double = SELECTED_REAL_KIND(p=13,r=200)

! Declare variables of each type:
REAL(kind=single) :: var1 = 0.
REAL(kind=double) :: var2 = 0._double

! Write characteristics of selected variables.
WRITE (*,100) 'var1', KIND(var1), PRECISION(var1), RANGE(var1)
```

(continued)

(concluded)
```
     WRITE (*,100) 'var2', KIND(var2), PRECISION(var2), RANGE(var2)
100 FORMAT(1X,A,': kind = ',I2,', Precision = ',I2,', Range = ',I3)

     END PROGRAM
```

When this program is executed on a PC using the Digital Visual Fortran compiler, the results are

```
C>select_kinds
var1: kind =  4, Precision =  6, Range =  37
var2: kind =  8, Precision = 15, Range = 307
```

Note that the program requested 13 decimal digits of precision and a range of 200 powers of 10 for the second variable, but the variable actually assigned by the processor has 15 digits of precision and a range of 307 powers of 10. This type of real variable was the smallest size that met or exceeded the request on the processor.

TABLE 7–1
Common KIND-related intrinsic functions

Function	Description
SELECTED_REAL_KIND(p,r)	Returns the smallest kind of real value with a minimum of p decimal digits of precision and maximum range $\geq 10^r$.
SELECTED_INT_KIND(r)	Returns the smallest kind of integer value with a maximum range $\geq 10^r$.
KIND(X)	Returns kind number of X, where X is a variable or constant of any intrinsic type.
PRECISION(X)	Returns the decimal precision of X, where X is a real or complex value.
RANGE(X)	Returns the decimal exponent range for X, where X is an integer, real, or complex value.

7.1.4 Mixed-Mode Arithmetic

When an arithmetic operation is performed between a double-precision real value and another real or integer value, Fortran converts the other value to double precision and performs the operation in double precision with a double-precision result. However, the automatic mode conversion does not occur until the double-precision number and the other number both appear in the same operation. Therefore, it is possible for a portion of an expression evaluated in integer or single-precision real arithmetic to be followed by another portion evaluated in double-precision real arithmetic.

For example, suppose that we want to add 1/3 to 1/3 and get the answer to 15 significant digits. We might try to calculate the answer with any of the following expressions:

	Expression	Result
1.	`1.D0/3. + 1/3`	`3.333333333333333E-001`
2.	`1./3. + 1.D0/3.`	`6.666666333333333E-001`
3.	`1.D0/3. + 1./3.D0`	`6.666666666666666E-001`

1. In the first expression, the single-precision constant `3.` is converted to double precision before dividing into the double-precision constant `1.D0`, producing the result `3.333333333333333E-001`. Next the integer constant `1` is divided by the integer constant `3`, producing an integer `0`. Finally the integer `0` is converted into double precision and added to first number, producing the final value of `3.333333333333333E-001`.
2. In the second expression, `1./3.` is evaluated in single precision producing the result `3.333333E-01`, and `1./3.D0` is evaluated in double precision, producing the result `3.333333333333333E-001`. Then the single-precision result is converted to double precision and added to the double-precision result to produce the final value of `6.666666333333333E-001`.
3. In the third expression, both terms are evaluated in double precision, leading to a final value of `6.666666666666666E-001`.

As you can see, 1/3 + 1/3 produces significantly different answers depending on the type of numbers used in each part of the expression. The third expression yields the answer that we really wanted while the first two are inaccurate to a greater or lesser degree. This result should serve as a warning: If you really need double-precision arithmetic, you should be very careful to ensure that *all* intermediate portions of a calculation are performed with double-precision arithmetic and that *all* intermediate results are stored in double-precision variables.

7.1.5 Double-Precision Intrinsic Functions

All generic functions that support single-precision real values also support double-precision real values. If the input value is single precision, then the function will be calculated with a single-precision result. If the input value is double precision, then the function will be calculated with a double-precision result.

One important intrinsic function is `DBLE`. This function converts any numeric input argument into double precision.

7.1.6 When to Use High-Precision Real Values

We have seen that double-precision real numbers are better than single-precision real numbers because the former offer more precision and greater range. If double-precision numbers are so good, why bother with single-precision numbers at all? Why don't we just use double-precision numbers all the time?

One good reason for not using double-precision numbers all the time is that every double-precision number requires twice as much memory as a single-precision number. This extra size makes programs using them much larger, and computers with more memory are required to run the programs. Another important consideration is speed. Double-precision calculations are normally slower than single-precision calculations, so computer programs using double-precision calculations run more slowly than computer programs using single-precision calculations. Because of these disadvantages, you should only use double-precision numbers when they are actually needed.

Double-precision numbers are actually needed in three general cases:

1. *When the dynamic range of the calculation requires numbers whose absolute values are smaller than* 10^{-39} *or larger than* 10^{39}. In this case either the problem must be re-scaled or double-precision variables must be used.
2. *When the problem requires numbers of very different sizes to be added to or subtracted from one another.* If two numbers of very different sizes must be added or subtracted from one another, the resulting calculation will lose a great deal of precision. For example, suppose we want to add the number 3.25 to the number 1,000,000.0. In single precision the calculation would be 1000003.0. In double precision the number would be 1,000,003.25.
3. *When the problem requires two numbers of very nearly equal size to be subtracted from one another.* When two numbers of very nearly equal size must be subtracted from each other, small errors in the last digits of the two numbers become greatly exaggerated.

For example, consider two nearly equal numbers that are the result of a series of single-precision calculations. Because of the round-off error in the calculations, each of the numbers is accurate to 0.0001 percent. The first number a1 should be 1.0000000, but through round-off errors in previous calculations is actually 1.0000010; the second number a2 should be 1.0000005, but through round-off errors in previous calculations is actually 1.0000000. The difference between these numbers should be

$$\text{true\_result} = \text{a1} - \text{a2} = -0.0000005$$

but the actual difference between them is

$$\text{actual\_result} = \text{a1} - \text{a2} = 0.0000010$$

Therefore, the error in the subtracted number is

$$\% \text{ ERROR} = \frac{\text{actual\_result-true\_result}}{\text{true\_result}} \times 100\%$$

$$\% \text{ ERROR} = \frac{0.0000010 - (-0.0000005)}{-0.0000005} \times 100\% = -300\%$$

Notice that the single-precision math created a 0.0001 percent error in a1 and a2, and then the subtraction blew up that error into a 300 percent error in the final answer! When two nearly equal numbers must be subtracted as a part of a calculation, then the entire calculation should be performed in double precision to avoid round-off error problems.

EXAMPLE 7–1 *Numerical Calculation of Derivatives:* The derivative of a function is defined mathematically as

$$\frac{d}{dx}f(x) = \lim_{\Delta x \to 0} \frac{f(x + \Delta x) - f(x)}{\Delta x} \tag{7–1}$$

The derivative of a function is a measure of the instantaneous slope of the function at the point being examined. In theory, the smaller Δx, the better the estimate of the derivative. However, the calculation can go bad if there is not enough precision to avoid round-off errors. Note that as Δx gets small, we will be subtracting two numbers that are very nearly equal, and the effects of round-off errors will be multiplied.

To test the effects of precision on our calculations, we will calculate the derivative of the function

$$f(x) = \frac{1}{x} \tag{7–2}$$

for the location $x = 0.15$. This function is shown in Figure 7–3.

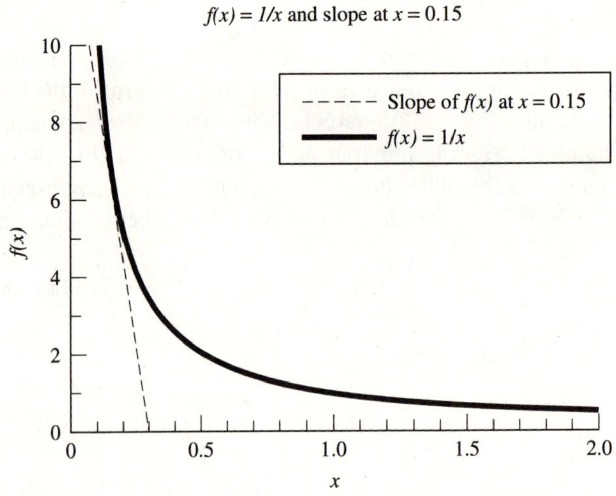

$f(x) = 1/x$ and slope at $x = 0.15$

- - - - - Slope of $f(x)$ at $x = 0.15$
———— $f(x) = 1/x$

FIGURE 7–3
Plot of the function $f(x) = 1/x$, showing the slope at $x = 0.15$.

SOLUTION

From elementary calculus, the derivative of $f(x)$ is

$$\frac{d}{dx}f(x) = \frac{d}{dx}\frac{1}{x} = -\frac{1}{x^2}$$

For $x = 0.15$

$$\frac{d}{dx}f(x) = -\frac{1}{x^2} = -44.44444444444\ldots$$

We will now attempt to evaluate the derivative of Equation (7–2) for sizes of Δx from 10^{-1} to 10^{-10} using both single- and double-precision mathematics. We will print out the results for each case, together with the true analytical solution and the resulting error.

A Fortran program to evaluate the derivative of Equation (7–2) is shown in Figure 7–4.

FIGURE 7–4

Program to evaluate the derivative of the function $f(x) = 1/x$ at $x = 0.15$ using both single-precision and double-precision arithmetic.

```
PROGRAM diff
!
! Purpose:
!   To test the effects of finite precision by differentiating
!   a function with 10 different step sizes, with both single
!   precision and double precision.  The test will be based on
!   the function F(X) = 1./X.
!
! Record of revisions:
!     Date        Programmer       Description of change
!     ====        ==========       =====================
!   12/03/95   S. J. Chapman       Original code
!
IMPLICIT NONE

! Declare parameters
INTEGER, PARAMETER :: single = SELECTED_REAL_KIND(p=6,r=37)
INTEGER, PARAMETER :: double = SELECTED_REAL_KIND(p=13)

! List of local variables:
REAL(KIND=double) :: ans           ! True (analytic) answer
REAL(KIND=double) :: d_ans         ! Double-precision answer
REAL(KIND=double) :: d_error       ! Double-precision percent error
REAL(KIND=double) :: d_fx          ! Double precision F(x)
REAL(KIND=double) :: d_fxdx        ! Double precision F(x+dx)
REAL(KIND=double) :: d_dx          ! Step size
REAL(KIND=double) :: d_x =0.15D0   ! Location to evaluate dF(x)/dx
INTEGER :: i                       ! Index variable
REAL(KIND=single) :: s_ans         ! Single-precision answer
REAL(KIND=single) :: s_error       ! Single-precision percent error
REAL(KIND=single) :: s_fx          ! Single precision F(x)
REAL(KIND=single) :: s_fxdx        ! Single precision F(x+dx)
REAL(KIND=single) :: s_dx          ! Step size
REAL(KIND=single) :: s_x =0.15E0   ! Location to evaluate dF(x)/dx

! Print headings.
WRITE (*,1)
1 FORMAT (1X,'    DX        TRUE ANS      SP ANS          DP ANS ', &
          '      SP ERR    DP ERR ')
```

(continued)

(concluded)
```
! Calculate analytic solution at x=0.15.
ans = - ( 1.D0 / d_x**2 )

! Calculate answer from definition of differentiation
step_size: DO i = 1, 10

   ! Get delta x.
   s_dx = 1.0 / 10.0**i
   d_dx = 1.D0 / 10.D0**i

   ! Calculate single-precision answer.
   s_fxdx = 1. / (s_x + s_dx )
   s_fx   = 1./ s_x
   s_ans  = ( s_fxdx - s_fx ) / s_dx

   ! Calculate single-precision error in percent.
   s_error = ( s_ans - REAL(ans) ) / REAL(ans) * 100.

   ! Calculate double-precision answer.
   d_fxdx = 1.D0 / ( d_x + d_dx )
   d_fx   = 1.D0 / d_x
   d_ans  = ( d_fxdx - d_fx ) / d_dx

   ! Calculate double-precision error in percent.
   d_error = ( d_ans - ans ) / ans * 100.

   ! Tell user.
   WRITE (*,100) d_dx, ans, s_ans, d_ans, s_error, d_error
   100 FORMAT (1X, ES10.3, F12.7, F12.7, ES22.14, F9.3, F9.3)

END DO step_size

END PROGRAM
```

When this program is compiled and executed using Digital Visual Fortran on a PC, the following results are obtained:

```
C>diff
  DX        TRUE ANS     SP ANS          DP ANS                SP ERR   DP ERR
1.000E-01 -44.4444444  -26.6666600  -2.66666666666667D+01   -40.000  -40.000
1.000E-02 -44.4444444  -41.6666500  -4.16666666666667D+01    -6.250   -6.250
1.000E-03 -44.4444444  -44.1498800  -4.41501103752762D+01     -.663    -.662
1.000E-04 -44.4444444  -44.4126100  -4.44148345547379D+01     -.072    -.067
1.000E-05 -44.4444444  -44.4412200  -4.44414816790584D+01     -.007    -.007
1.000E-06 -44.4444444  -44.3458600  -4.44441481501912D+01     -.222    -.001
1.000E-07 -44.4444444  -42.9153400  -4.44441148151035D+01    -3.440     .000
1.000E-08 -44.4444444  -47.6837200  -4.44444416604561D+01     7.288     .000
1.000E-09 -44.4444444    .0000000   -4.44444445690806D+01  -100.000     .000
1.000E-10 -44.4444444    .0000000   -4.44444481217943D+01  -100.000     .000
```

Note that when Δx is fairly large, both the single-precision and double-precision results give essentially the same answer. In that range the accuracy of the result is limited only by the step size. As Δx gets smaller and smaller, the single-precision answer gets better and better until $\Delta x \approx 10^{-5}$. For step sizes smaller than 10^{-5}, round-off errors start to dominate the solution. The double-precision answer gets better and better until $\Delta x \approx 10^{-9}$. For step sizes smaller than 10^{-9}, double-precision round-off errors start to get progressively worse.

7.1.7 Solving Large Systems of Simultaneous Linear Equations

Chapter 6 introduced the method of Gauss-Jordan elimination to solve systems of simultaneous linear equations of the form

$$a_{11}x_1 + a_{12}x_2 + \ldots + a_{1n}x_n = b_1$$
$$a_{21}x_1 + a_{22}x_2 + \ldots + a_{2n}x_n = b_2$$
$$\ldots$$
$$a_{n1}x_1 + a_{n2}x_2 + \ldots + a_{nn}x_n = b_n \tag{7-3}$$

In this Gauss-Jordan method, the first equation in the set is multiplied by a constant and added to all the other equations in the set to eliminate x_1. Then the process is repeated with the second equation in the set multiplied by a constant and added to all the other equations in the set to eliminate x_2, and so forth for all of the equations. This type of solution is subject to cumulative round-off errors that eventually make the answers unusable. Any round-off errors in eliminating the coefficients of x_1 are propagated into even bigger errors when eliminating the coefficients of x_2, which are propagated into even bigger errors when eliminating the coefficients of x_3, and so on. For a large enough system of equations, the cumulative round-off errors will produce unacceptably bad solutions.

How big must a system of equations be before round-off error makes it impossible to solve them using Gauss-Jordan elimination? This question doesn't have an easy answer. Some systems of equations are more sensitive to slight round-off errors than others are. To understand why, let's look at the two simple sets of simultaneous equations shown in Figure 7–5. Figure 7–5a shows a plot of the following simultaneous equations:

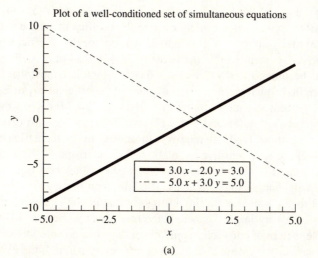

Plot of a well-conditioned set of simultaneous equations

$$3.0\, x - 2.0\, y = 3.0$$
$$5.0\, x + 3.0\, y = 5.0$$

(a)

FIGURE 7–5

(a) Plot of a well-conditioned 2×2 set of equations.

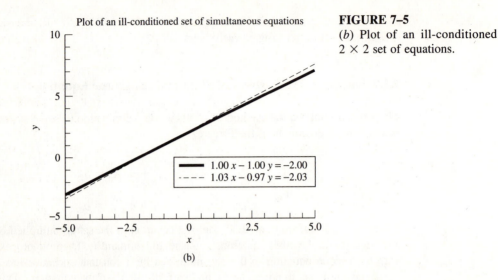

Plot of an ill-conditioned set of simultaneous equations

Legend:
—— $1.00\,x - 1.00\,y = -2.00$
----- $1.03\,x - 0.97\,y = -2.03$

FIGURE 7–5
(*b*) Plot of an ill-conditioned 2×2 set of equations.

(b)

$$3.0\,x - 2.0\,y = 3.0$$
$$5.0\,x + 3.0\,y = 5.0 \tag{7–4}$$

The solution to this set of equations is $x = 1.0$ and $y = 0.0$. The point $(1.0, 0.0)$ is the intersection of the two lines on the plot in Figure 7–5a. Figure 7–5b shows a plot of the following simultaneous equations:

$$1.00\,x - 1.00\,y = -2.00$$
$$1.03\,x - 0.97\,y = -2.03 \tag{7–5}$$

The solution to this set of equations is $x = -1.5$ and $y = 0.5$. The point $(-1.5, 0.5)$ is the intersection of the two lines on the plot in Figure 7–5b.

Now let's compare the sensitivity of Equations (7–4) and (7–5) to slight errors in the coefficients of the equations. (A slight error in the coefficients of the equations is similar to the effect of round-off errors on the equations.) Assume that coefficient a_{11} of Equations (7–3) is in error 1 percent so that a_{11} is really 3.03 instead of 3.00. Then the solution to the equations becomes $x = 0.995$ and $y = 0.008$, which is almost the same as the solution to the original equations. Now let's assume that coefficient a_{11} of Equations (7–4) is in error by 1 percent so that a_{11} is really 1.01 instead of 1.00. Then the solution to the equations becomes $x = 1.789$ and $y = 0.193$, which is a major shift compared to the previous answer. Equations (7–4) are relatively insensitive to small coefficient errors, whereas Equations (7–5) are *very* sensitive to small coefficient errors.

If we examine Figure 7–5b closely, it will be obvious why Equations (7–5) are so sensitive to small changes in coefficients. The lines representing the two equations are almost parallel to each other, so a tiny change in one of the equations moves their intersection point by a very large distance. If the two lines had been exactly parallel to each other, then the system of equations would either have had no solutions or an infinite number of solutions. In the case where the lines are nearly parallel, there is a single unique solution, but its location is very sensitive to slight changes in the coefficients. Therefore, systems like Equations (7–5) will be very sensitive to accumulated round-off noise during Gauss-Jordan elimination.

Systems of simultaneous equations that behave well, such as Equations (7–4), are called **well-conditioned systems,** and systems of simultaneous equations that behave poorly, such as Equations (7–5) are called **ill-conditioned systems.** Well-conditioned systems of equations are relatively immune to round-off error, whereas ill-conditioned systems are very sensitive to round-off error.

When working with very large systems of equations or ill-conditioned systems of equations, it is helpful to work in double-precision arithmetic. Double-precision arithmetic dramatically reduces round-off errors, allowing Gauss-Jordan elimination to produce correct answers even for difficult systems of equations.

EXAMPLE 7–2 Solving Large Systems of Linear Equations: For large and/or ill-conditioned systems of equations, Gauss-Jordan elimination will produce a correct answer only if double-precision arithmetic is used to reduce round-off error. Write a subroutine that uses double-precision arithmetic to solve a system of simultaneous linear equations. Test your subroutine by comparing it to the single-precision subroutine `simul` created in Chapter 6. Compare the two subroutines on both well-defined and ill-defined systems of equations.

SOLUTION

The double-precision subroutine `dsimul` will be essentially the same as the single-precision subroutine `simul2` in Figure 6–10 that we developed in Chapter 6. Subroutine `simul2`, which is renamed `simul` here, is used as the starting point because that version includes both the use of array operations and automatic arrays for simplicity and flexibility and because it does not destroy its input data.

1. **State the problem.**

Write a subroutine to solve a system of N simultaneous equations in N unknowns using Gauss-Jordan elimination, double-precision arithmetic, and the maximum pivot technique to avoid round-off errors. The subroutine must be able to detect singular sets of equations and set an error flag if they occur.

2. **Define the inputs and outputs.**

The input to the subroutine consists of an N × N double-precision matrix `a` with the coefficients of the variables in the simultaneous equations and a double-precision vector `b` with the contents of the right sides of the equations. The outputs from the subroutine are the solutions to the set of equations (in vector `soln`), and an error flag.

3. **Describe the algorithm.**

The pseudocode for this subroutine is the same as the pseudocode for subroutine `simul2` in Chapter 6 and is not repeated here.

4. **Turn the algorithm into Fortran statements.**

The resulting Fortran subroutine is shown in Figure 7–6.

FIGURE 7–6
Subroutine to solve a system of simultaneous equations in double precision.

```
SUBROUTINE dsimul ( a, b, soln, ndim, n, error)
!
!   Purpose:
!     Subroutine to solve a set of N linear equations in N
!     unknowns using Gaussian elimination and the maximum
!     pivot technique.  This version of simul has been
!     modified to use array sections and automatic arrays.
!     It uses double-precision arithmetic to avoid
!     cumulative round-off errors.  It DOES NOT DESTROY the
!     original input values.
!
!   Record of revisions:
!      Date        Programmer          Description of change
!      ====        ==========          =====================
!    10/16/95   S. J. Chapman        Original code
!1.  03/02/96   S. J. Chapman        Add automatic arrays
!2.  05/08/96   S. J. Chapman        Double precision
!
IMPLICIT NONE

! Declare parameters
INTEGER, PARAMETER :: dbl = SELECTED_REAL_KIND(p=13)

! Declare calling arguments:
INTEGER, INTENT(IN) :: ndim              ! Dimension of arrays a and b
REAL(KIND=dbl), INTENT(IN), DIMENSION(ndim,ndim) :: a
                                         ! Array of coefficients (N x N)
                                         ! This array is of size ndim x
                                         ! ndim, but only N x N of the
                                         ! coefficients are being used
REAL(KIND=dbl), INTENT(IN), DIMENSION(ndim) :: b
                                         ! Input: Right-hand side of eqns
REAL(KIND=dbl), INTENT(OUT), DIMENSION(ndim) :: soln
                                         ! Output: Solution vector
INTEGER, INTENT(IN) :: n                 ! Number of equations to solve
INTEGER, INTENT(OUT) :: error            ! Error flag:
                                         !    0 -- No error
                                         !    1 -- Singular equations

! Declare local parameters
REAL(KIND=dbl), PARAMETER :: epsilon = 1.0E-12
                                         ! A "small" number for comparison
                                         ! when determining singular eqns

! Declare local variables:
REAL(KIND=dbl), DIMENSION(n,n) :: a1 ! Copy of "a" that will be
                                     ! destroyed during the solution
REAL(KIND=dbl) :: factor             ! Factor to multiply eqn irow by
                                     ! before adding to eqn jrow
```

(continued)

```
(continued)
INTEGER :: irow                          ! Number of the equation currently
                                         ! being processed
INTEGER :: ipeak                         ! Pointer to equation containing
                                         ! maximum pivot value
INTEGER :: jrow                          ! Number of the equation compared
                                         ! to the current equation
REAL(KIND=dbl) :: temp                   ! Scratch value
REAL(KIND=dbl),DIMENSION(n) :: temp1     ! Scratch array

! Make copies of arrays "a" and "b" for local use
a1 = a(1:n,1:n)
soln = b(1:n)

! Process N times to get all equations...
mainloop: DO irow = 1, n

   ! Find peak pivot for column irow in rows irow to N
   ipeak = irow
   max_pivot: DO jrow = irow+1, n
      IF (ABS(a1(jrow,irow)) > ABS(a1(ipeak,irow))) THEN
         ipeak = jrow
      END IF
   END DO max_pivot

   ! Check for singular equations
   singular: IF ( ABS(a1(ipeak,irow)) < epsilon ) THEN
      error = 1
      RETURN
   END IF singular

   ! Otherwise, if ipeak /= irow, swap equations irow & ipeak
   swap_eqn: IF ( ipeak /= irow ) THEN
      temp1 = a1(ipeak,1:n)
      a1(ipeak,1:n) = a1(irow,1:n)          ! Swap rows in a
      a1(irow,1:n) = temp1
      temp = soln(ipeak)
      soln(ipeak) = soln(irow)     ! Swap rows in b
      soln(irow)  = temp
   END IF swap_eqn

   ! Multiply equation irow by -a1(jrow,irow)/a1(irow,irow),
   ! and add it to Eqn jrow (for all eqns except irow itself).
   eliminate: DO jrow = 1, n
      IF ( jrow /= irow ) THEN
         factor = -a1(jrow,irow)/a1(irow,irow)
         a1(jrow,1:n) = a1(irow,1:n)*factor + a1(jrow,1:n)
         soln(jrow) = soln(irow)*factor + soln(jrow)
      END IF
   END DO eliminate
END DO mainloop

! End of main loop over all equations.  All off-diagonal
! terms are now zero.  To get the final answer, we must
! divide each equation by the coefficient of its on-diagonal
! term.
divide: DO irow = 1, n
```

(continued)

(concluded)
```
    soln(irow) = soln(irow) / a1(irow,irow)
END DO divide

! Set error flag to 0 and return.
error = 0

END SUBROUTINE dsimul
```

5. **Test the resulting Fortran programs.**

To test this subroutine, we must write a driver program. The driver program will open an input data file to read the equations to be solved. The first line of the file will contain the number of equations N in the system, and each of the next N lines will contain the coefficients of one of the equations. The coefficients will be stored in a single-precision array and sent to subroutine simul for solution and will also be stored in a double-precision array and sent to subroutine dsimul for solution. To verify that the solutions are correct, they will be plugged back into the original equations and the resulting errors will be calculated. The solutions and errors for single-precision and double-precision arithmetic will be displayed in a summary table. The test driver program for subroutine dsimul is shown in Figure 7–7.

FIGURE 7–7
Test driver program for subroutine dsimul.

```
PROGRAM test_dsimul
!
!   Purpose:
!     To test subroutine dsimul, which solves a set of N linear
!     equations in N unknowns.  This test driver calls subroutine
!     simul to solve the problem in single precision and subrou-
!     tine dsimul to solve the problem in double precision.  The
!     results of the two solutions together with their errors are
!     displayed in a summary table.
!
!   Record of revisions:
!      Date        Programmer           Description of change
!      ====        ==========           =====================
!    12/12/95    S. J. Chapman          Original code
!
IMPLICIT NONE

! Declare parameters
INTEGER, PARAMETER :: sgl = SELECTED_REAL_KIND(p=6)     ! Single
INTEGER, PARAMETER :: dbl = SELECTED_REAL_KIND(p=13)    ! Double
INTEGER, PARAMETER :: dim = 50 ! max number of equations

! List of local variables
REAL(KIND=sgl),DIMENSION(dim,dim) :: a      ! Single-prec coefs
REAL(KIND=sgl),DIMENSION(dim) :: b          ! Single-prec constants
REAL(KIND=sgl),DIMENSION(dim) :: soln       ! Single-prec solution
REAL(KIND=sgl),DIMENSION(dim) :: serror     ! Single-prec errors
REAL(KIND=sgl) :: serror_max                ! Max single-prec error
```
                                                                          (continued)

(continued)

```fortran
REAL(KIND=dbl),DIMENSION(dim) :: db      ! Double-prec constants
REAL(KIND=dbl),DIMENSION(dim) :: dsoln   ! Double-prec solution
REAL(KIND=dbl),DIMENSION(dim) :: derror  ! Double-prec errors
REAL(KIND=dbl) :: derror_max             ! Max double-prec error
INTEGER :: error_flag                    ! Error flag from subroutines
INTEGER :: i, j                          ! Loop index
INTEGER :: istat                         ! I/O status
INTEGER :: n                             ! Size of system of eqns to solve
CHARACTER(len=20) :: filename            ! Input data file name

! Get the name of the disk file containing the equations.
WRITE (*,*) 'Enter the file name containing the eqns: '
READ (*,'(A20)') filename

! Open input data file.
OPEN ( UNIT=1, FILE=filename, STATUS='OLD', ACTION='READ', &
IOSTAT=istat )

! Was the OPEN successful?
open_ok: IF ( istat == 0 ) THEN

   ! The file was opened successfully, so read the number of
   ! equations in the system.
   READ (1,*) n

   ! If the memory is available, read and solve equations.
   solve: IF ( n <= dim ) THEN

      DO i = 1, n
         READ (1,*) (da(i,j), j=1,n), db(i)
      END DO

      ! Copy the coefficients in single precision for the
      ! single precision solution.
      a = da
      b = db

      ! Display coefficients.
      WRITE (*,1010)
      1010 FORMAT (/,1X,'Coefficients:')
      DO i = 1, n
         WRITE (*,'(1X,7F11.4)') (a(i,j), j=1,n), b(i)
      END DO

      ! Solve equations.
      CALL simul  (a,  b,  soln,  dim, n, error_flag )
      CALL dsimul (da, db, dsoln, dim, n, error_flag )

      ! Check for error.
      error_check: IF ( error_flag /= 0 ) THEN
         WRITE (*,1020)
         1020 FORMAT (/1X,'Zero pivot encountered!', &
               //1X,'There is no unique solution to this system.')

      ELSE error_check
```

(continued)

(concluded)

```
      ! No errors.  Check for round off by substituting into
      ! the original equations and calculate the differences.
      serror_max = 0.
      derror_max = 0._dbl
      serror = 0.
      derror = 0._dbl
      DO i = 1, n
         serror(i) = SUM ( a(i,:)   * soln(:)  ) - b(i)
         derror(i) = SUM ( da(i,:)            * dsoln(:) )   - db(i)
      END DO
      serror_max = MAXVAL ( ABS ( serror ) )
      derror_max = MAXVAL ( ABS ( derror ) )

      ! Tell user about it.
      WRITE (*,1030)
      1030 FORMAT (/1X,'  i     SP x(i)       DP x(i)               ',&
             '        SP Err         DP Err   ')
      WRITE (*,1040)
      1040 FORMAT ( 1X,' ===    =========    =========          ', &
             '    ========      ======== ')
      DO i = 1, n
         WRITE (*,1050) i, soln(i), dsoln(i), serror(i), derror(i)
         1050 FORMAT (1X, I3, 2X, G15.6, G15.6, F15.8, F15.8)
      END DO

         ! Write maximum errors.
         WRITE (*,1060) serror_max, derror_max
         1060 FORMAT (/,1X,'Max single-precision error:',F15.8, &
                /,1X,'Max double-precision error:',F15.8)

      END IF error_check
   END IF solve

ELSE open_ok
   ! Else file open failed.  Tell user.
   WRITE (*,1070) istat
   1070 FORMAT (1X,'File open failed--status = ', I6)
END IF open_ok

END PROGRAM
```

To test the subroutine, we will call it with three data sets. The first should be a well-conditioned system of equations, the second should be an ill-conditioned system of equations, and the third should have no unique solution. The first system of equations that we will use to test the subroutine is the following 6×6 system of equations:

$$
\begin{aligned}
-2.0x_1 + 5.0x_2 + 1.0x_3 + 3.0x_4 + 4.0x_5 - 1.0x_6 &= \ \ 0.0 \\
2.0x_1 - 1.0x_2 - 5.0x_3 - 2.0x_4 + 6.0x_5 + 4.0x_6 &= \ \ 1.0 \\
-1.0x_1 + 6.0x_2 - 4.0x_3 - 5.0x_4 + 3.0x_5 - 1.0x_6 &= -6.0 \\
4.0x_1 + 3.0x_2 - 6.0x_3 - 5.0x_4 - 2.0x_5 - 2.0x_6 &= 10.0 \\
-3.0x_1 + 6.0x_2 + 4.0x_3 + 2.0x_4 - 6.0x_5 + 4.0x_6 &= -6.0 \\
2.0x_1 + 4.0x_2 + 4.0x_3 + 4.0x_4 + 5.0x_5 - 4.0x_6 &= -2.0
\end{aligned}
$$

(7–6)

If this system of equations is placed in a file called SYS6.WEL, and program test_dsimul is run on this file, the results are

```
C>test_dsimul
Enter the file name containing the eqns:
sys6.wel

Coefficients before calls:
    -2.0000     5.0000     1.0000     3.0000     4.0000    -1.0000      .0000
     2.0000    -1.0000    -5.0000    -2.0000     6.0000     4.0000     1.0000
    -1.0000     6.0000    -4.0000    -5.0000     3.0000    -1.0000    -6.0000
     4.0000     3.0000    -6.0000    -5.0000    -2.0000    -2.0000    10.0000
    -3.0000     6.0000     4.0000     2.0000    -6.0000     4.0000    -6.0000
     2.0000     4.0000     4.0000     4.0000     5.0000    -4.0000    -2.0000

   i      SP x(i)      DP x(i)              SP Err       DP Err
  ===    ========     =========           ========     ========
   1      .662556      .662556            .00000173    .00000000
   2     -.132567     -.132567            .00000072    .00000000
   3     -3.01373     -3.01373            .00000286    .00000000
   4      2.83548      2.83548            .00000191    .00000000
   5     -1.08520     -1.08520           -.00000095    .00000000
   6     -.836043     -.836043           -.00000119    .00000000

Max single-precision error:      .00000286
Max double-precision error:      .00000000
```

For this well-conditioned system, the results of single-precision and double-precision calculations were essentially identical. The second system of equations that we will use to test the subroutine is the following 6×6 system of equations. Note that the second and sixth equations are almost identical, so this system is ill-conditioned.

$$
\begin{aligned}
-2.0x_1 + 5.0x_2 \quad\;\; + 1.0x_3 + 3.0x_4 + 4.0x_5 - 1.0x_6 &= 0.0 \\
2.0x_1 - 1.0x_2 \quad\;\; - 5.0x_3 - 2.0x_4 + 6.0x_5 + 4.0x_6 &= 1.0 \\
-1.0x_1 + 6.0x_2 \quad\;\; - 4.0x_3 - 5.0x_4 + 3.0x_5 - 1.0x_6 &= -6.0 \\
4.0x_1 + 3.0x_2 \quad\;\; - 6.0x_3 - 5.0x_4 - 2.0x_5 - 2.0x_6 &= 10.0 \\
-3.0x_1 + 6.0x_2 \quad\;\; + 4.0x_3 + 2.0x_4 - 6.0x_5 + 4.0x_6 &= -6.0 \\
2.0x_1 - 1.00001x_2 - 5.0x_3 - 2.0x_4 + 6.0x_5 + 4.0x_6 &= 1.0001
\end{aligned}
\tag{7-7}
$$

If this system of equations is placed in a file called SYS6.ILL and program test_dsimul is run on this file, the results are.[1]

```
C>test_dsimul
Enter the file name containing the eqns:
sys6.ill

Coefficients before calls:
    -2.0000     5.0000     1.0000     3.0000     4.0000    -1.0000      .0000
     2.0000    -1.0000    -5.0000    -2.0000     6.0000     4.0000     1.0000
    -1.0000     6.0000    -4.0000    -5.0000     3.0000    -1.0000    -6.0000
     4.0000     3.0000    -6.0000    -5.0000    -2.0000    -2.0000    10.0000
    -3.0000     6.0000     4.0000     2.0000    -6.0000     4.0000    -6.0000
     2.0000    -1.0000    -5.0000    -2.0000     6.0000     4.0000     1.0001
```

[1]To reproduce these results with some compilers, you must turn off the optimizer. If the optimizer is used, these compilers store intermediate single-precision results as double-precision values in CPU registers and the calculation is effectively performed in double precision. This practice makes single-precision arithmetic look misleadingly good.

i	SP x(i)	DP x(i)	SP Err	DP Err
===	=========	=========	========	========
1	-44.1711	-38.5295	2.83736500	.00000000
2	-11.1934	-10.0000	-3.96770900	.00000000
3	-52.9274	-47.1554	-2.92594100	.00000000
4	29.8776	26.1372	-4.72323000	.00000000
5	-17.9852	-15.8502	4.52078600	.00000000
6	-5.69733	-5.08561	-3.96770200	.00000000

```
Max single-precision error:     4.72323000
Max double-precision error:      .00000000
```

For this ill-conditioned system, the results of the single-precision and double-precision calculations were dramatically different. The single-precision numbers $x(i)$ differ from the true answers by almost 20 percent, whereas the double-precision answers are almost exactly correct. Double-precision calculations are essential for a correct answer to this problem! The third system of equations that we will use to test the subroutine is the following 6×6 system of equations:

$$
\begin{aligned}
-2.0\,x_1 + 5.0\,x_2 + 1.0\,x_3 + 3.0\,x_4 + 4.0\,x_5 - 1.0\,x_6 &= 0.0 \\
2.0\,x_1 - 1.0\,x_2 - 5.0\,x_3 - 2.0\,x_4 + 6.0\,x_5 + 4.0\,x_6 &= 1.0 \\
-1.0\,x_1 + 6.0\,x_2 - 4.0\,x_3 - 5.0\,x_4 + 3.0\,x_5 - 1.0\,x_6 &= -6.0 \\
4.0\,x_1 + 3.0\,x_2 - 6.0\,x_3 - 5.0\,x_4 - 2.0\,x_5 - 2.0\,x_6 &= 10.0 \\
-3.0\,x_1 + 6.0\,x_2 + 4.0\,x_3 + 2.0\,x_4 - 6.0\,x_5 + 4.0\,x_6 &= -6.0 \\
2.0\,x_1 - 1.0\,x_2 - 5.0\,x_3 - 2.0\,x_4 + 6.0\,x_5 + 4.0\,x_6 &= 1.0
\end{aligned}
\tag{7-8}
$$

If this system of equations is placed in a file called SYS6.SNG and program test_dsimul is run on this file, the results are

```
C>test_dsimul
Enter the file name containing the eqns:
sys6.sng

Coefficients before calls:
    -2.0000     5.0000     1.0000     3.0000     4.0000    -1.0000      .0000
     2.0000    -1.0000    -5.0000    -2.0000     6.0000     4.0000     1.0000
    -1.0000     6.0000    -4.0000    -5.0000     3.0000    -1.0000    -6.0000
     4.0000     3.0000    -6.0000    -5.0000    -2.0000    -2.0000    10.0000
    -3.0000     6.0000     4.0000     2.0000    -6.0000     4.0000    -6.0000
     2.0000    -1.0000    -5.0000    -2.0000     6.0000     4.0000     1.0000

Zero pivot encountered!

There is no unique solution to this system.
```

Since the second and sixth equations of this set are identical, there is no unique solution to this system of equations. The subroutine correctly identified and flagged this situation.

Subroutine dsimul seems to be working correctly for all three cases: well-conditioned systems, ill-conditioned systems, and singular systems. Furthermore, these tests show the clear advantage of the double-precision subroutine over the single-precision subroutine for ill-conditioned systems.

■ 7.2

THE COMPLEX DATA TYPE

Complex numbers occur in many problems in science and engineering. For example, electrical engineers use complex numbers to represent alternating current voltages, currents, and impedances. The differential equations that describe the behavior of most electrical and mechanical systems also give rise to complex numbers. It is impossible to work as an engineer without a good understanding of the use and manipulation of these ubiquitous complex numbers.

A complex number has the general form

$$c = a + bi \tag{7–9}$$

where c is a complex number, a and b are both real numbers, and i is $\sqrt{-1}$. The number a is called the *real part* and b is called the *imaginary part* of the complex number c. Because a complex number has two components, it can be plotted as a point on a plane (see Figure 7–8). The horizontal axis of the plane is the real axis, and the vertical axis of the plane is the imaginary axis; therefore, any complex number $a + bi$ can be represented as a single point a units along the real axis and b units along the imaginary axis. A complex number represented this way is said to be in *rectangular coordinates*, since the real and imaginary axes define the sides of a rectangle.

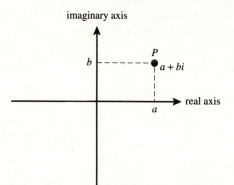

FIGURE 7–8
Representing a complex number in rectangular coordinates.

A complex number can also be represented as a vector of length z and angle θ pointing from the origin of the plane to the point P (see Figure 7–9). A complex number represented this way is said to be in *polar coordinates*.

$$c = a + bi = z \angle \theta$$

The relationships among the rectangular and polar coordinate terms a, b, z, and θ are:

$$a = z \cos \theta \tag{7–10}$$

$$b = z \sin \theta \tag{7–11}$$

$$z = \sqrt{a^2 + b^2} \qquad\qquad (7\text{--}12)$$

$$\theta = \tan^{-1} \frac{b}{a} \qquad\qquad (7\text{--}13)$$

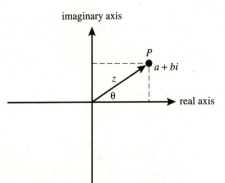

imaginary axis

real axis

FIGURE 7–9
Representing a complex number in polar co-ordinates.

Fortran uses rectangular coordinates to represent complex numbers. Each complex number consists of a pair of real numbers (a,b) occupying successive locations in memory. The first number (a) is the real part of the complex number, and the second number (b) is the imaginary part of the complex number.

If complex numbers c_1 and c_2 are defined as $c_1 = a_1 + b_1 i$ and $c_2 = a_2 + b_2 i$, then the addition, subtraction, multiplication, and division of c_1 and c_2 are defined as follows:

$$c_1 + c_2 = (a_1 + a_2) + (b_1 + b_2)i \qquad\qquad (7\text{--}14)$$

$$c_1 - c_2 = (a_1 - a_2) + (b_1 - b_2)i \qquad\qquad (7\text{--}15)$$

$$c_1 \times c_2 = (a_1 a_2 - b_1 b_2) + (a_1 b_2 + b_1 a_2)i \qquad\qquad (7\text{--}16)$$

$$\frac{c_1}{c_2} = \frac{a_1 a_2 + b_1 b_2}{a_2{}^2 + b_2{}^2} + \frac{b_1 a_2 - a_1 b_2}{a_2{}^2 + b_2{}^2} i \qquad\qquad (7\text{--}17)$$

When two complex numbers appear in a binary operation, Fortran performs the required additions, subtractions, multiplications, or divisions between the two complex numbers using these formulas.

7.2.1 Complex Constants and Variables

A **complex** constant consists of two numeric constants separated by commas and enclosed in parentheses. The first constant is the real part of the complex number, and the second constant is the imaginary part of the complex number. For example, the following complex constants are equivalent to the complex numbers shown next to them:

`(1., 0.)`	$1 + 0i$
`(0.7071,0.7071)`	$0.7071 + 0.7071i$
`(0, -1)`	$-i$
`(1.01E6, 0.5E2)`	$1010000 + 50i$
`(1.12_dbl, 0.1_dbl)`	$1.12 + 0.1i$ (Kind is `dbl`)

The last constant will be valid only if `dbl` is a named constant that has been set to a valid kind number for real data on the particular processor where the constant is used.

A complex variable is declared using a `COMPLEX` type declaration statement. The form of this statement is

$$\text{COMPLEX(KIND=}\textit{kind\_num}) \ :: \ \textit{var1, var2, etc.}$$

The kind of the complex variable is optional; if it is left out, the default kind will be used. For example, the following statement declares a 256-element complex array. Remember that we are actually allocating 512 default-length values because each complex number requires two real values.

```
COMPLEX, DIMENSION(256) :: array
```

There are at least two kinds of complex values on any processor, corresponding to the single-precision and double-precision kinds of real data. The single-precision version of the complex data type will have the same kind number as the single-precision version of the real data type, and the double-precision version of the complex data type will have the same kind number as the double-precision version of the real data type. Therefore, the intrinsic function `SELECTED_REAL_KIND` can also be used to specify the size of complex data in a processor-independent manner.

The **default complex** kind will always be the same as the default real kind on any given processor.

7.2.2 Initializing Complex Variables

Like other variables, complex variables may be initialized by assignment statements, in type declaration statements, or by `READ` statements. The following code initializes all of the elements of array `array1` to `(0.,0.)` using an assignment statement.

```
COMPLEX, DIMENSION(256) :: array1
array1 = (0.,0.)
```

A complex number may also be initialized in a type declaration statement using a complex constant. The following code declares and initializes variable `a1` to `(3.141592, -3.141592)` using a type declaration statement.

```
COMPLEX :: a1 = (3.141592, -3.141592)
```

When a complex number is read or written with a formatted I/O statement, the first format descriptor encountered is used for the real part of the complex number and the second format descriptor encountered is used for the imaginary part of the complex number. The following code initializes variable `a1` using a formatted `READ` statement.

```
COMPLEX :: a1
READ (*,'(2F10.2)') a1
```

The value in the first 10 characters of the input line will be placed in the real part of variable a1, and the value in the second 10 characters of the input line will be placed in the imaginary part of variable a1. Note that no parentheses are included on the input line when we read a complex number using formatted I/O. In contrast, when we read a complex number with a *free-format* I/O statement, the complex number must be typed exactly like a complex constant, parentheses and all. The following READ statement

```
COMPLEX :: a1
READ (*,*) a1
```

requires that the input value be typed as shown: (1.0,0.25). When a complex number is written with a free-format WRITE statement, it is output as a complex value complete with parentheses. For example, the statements

```
COMPLEX :: a1 = (1.0,0.25)
WRITE (*,*) a1
```

produce the result:

```
(1.000000,2.500000E-01)
```

7.2.3 Using Complex Numbers with Relational Operators

We can use the == relational operator to compare two complex numbers to see if they are equal to each other, and we can use the /= operator to see if they are not equal to each other. However, we cannot use the >, <, >=, or <= operators to compare complex numbers. The reason is that complex numbers consist of two parts. Suppose that we have two complex numbers $c_1 = a_1 + b_1 i$ and $c_2 = a_2 + b_2 i$, with $a_1 > a_2$ and $b_1 < b_2$. How can we possibly say which of these numbers is larger?

On the other hand, we can compare the *magnitudes* of two complex numbers. The magnitude of a complex number can be calculated with the CABS intrinsic function (see section 7.2.4) or directly from Equation (7–12).

$$|c| = \sqrt{a^2 + b^2} \tag{7-12}$$

Since the magnitude of a complex number is a real value, we can use any of the relational operators to compare two magnitudes with each other.

7.2.4 COMPLEX Intrinsic Functions

Fortran includes many specific and generic functions that support complex calculations, all of which are listed in Appendix B. These functions fall into three general categories:

1. **Type conversion functions** These functions convert data to and from the complex data type. Function CMPLX(a,b,*kind*) is a generic function that converts real or integer

numbers a and b into a complex number whose real part has value a and whose imaginary part has value b. The kind parameter is optional; if it is specified, then the resulting complex number will be of the specified kind. Functions REAL() and INT() convert the *real part* of a complex number into the corresponding real or integer data type and throw away the imaginary part of the complex number. Function AIMAG() converts the *imaginary part* of a complex number into a real number.

2. **Absolute value function** This function calculates the absolute value of a number. Function CABS(c) is a function that calculates the absolute value of a complex number using the equation

$$\text{CABS}(c) = \sqrt{a^2 + b^2}$$

where $c = a + bi$.

3. **Mathematical functions** These functions include exponential functions, logarithms, trigonometric functions, and square roots. The generic functions SIN, COS, LOG10, SQRT, and so on will work as well with complex data as they will with real data.

EXAMPLE 7–3 *The Quadratic Equation (Revisited):* Write a general program to solve for the roots of a quadratic equation regardless of type. Use complex variables so that no branches will be required based on the value of the discriminant.

SOLUTION

1. **State the problem.**

Write a program that will solve for the roots of a quadratic equation, whether they are distinct real roots, repeated real roots, or complex roots, without requiring tests on the value of the discriminant.

2. **Define the inputs and outputs.**

The inputs required by this program are the coefficients *a*, *b*, and *c* of the quadratic equation

$$ax^2 + bx + c = 0 \tag{3–1}$$

The output from the program will be the roots of the quadratic equation, whether they are real, repeated, or complex.

3. **Describe the algorithm.**

This task can be broken down into three major sections, whose functions are input, processing, and output:

```
Read the input data
Calculate the roots
Write out the roots
```

We will now break each of the above major sections into smaller, more detailed pieces. In this algorithm the value of the discriminant is unimportant in determining how to proceed. The resulting pseudocode is

```
Write 'Enter the coefficients A, B, and C: '
Read in a, b, c
discriminant ← CMPLX( b**2 - 4.*a*c, 0. )
x1 ← ( -b + SQRT(discriminant) ) / ( 2. * a )
x2 ← ( -b - SQRT(discriminant) ) / ( 2. * a )
Write 'The roots of this equation are: '
Write 'x1 = ', REAL(x1), ' +i ', AIMAG(x1)
Write 'x2 = ', REAL(x2), ' +i ', AIMAG(x2)
```

4. Turn the algorithm into Fortran statements.

The final Fortran code is shown in Figure 7–10.

FIGURE 7–10
A program to solve the quadratic equation using complex numbers.

```
PROGRAM roots_2
!
! Purpose:
!   To find the roots of a quadratic equation
!      A * X**2 + B * X + C = 0.
!   using complex numbers to eliminate the need to branch
!   based on the value of the discriminant.
!
! Record of revisions:
!     Date        Programmer            Description of change
!     ====        ==========            =====================
!   12/23/95    S. J. Chapman           Original code
!
IMPLICIT NONE

! List of variables:
REAL :: a                   ! The coefficient of X**2
REAL :: b                   ! The coefficient of X
REAL :: c                   ! The constant coefficient
REAL :: discriminant        ! The discriminant of the quadratic eqn
COMPLEX :: x1               ! First solution to the equation
COMPLEX :: x2               ! Second solution to the equation

! Get the coefficients.
WRITE (*,1000)
1000 FORMAT (' Program to solve for the roots of a quadratic',&
            /,' equation of the form A * X**2 + B * X + C = 0. ' )
WRITE (*,1005)
1005 FORMAT (' Enter the coefficients A, B, and C: ')
READ (*,*) a, b, c

! Calculate the discriminant
discriminant = b**2 - 4. * a * c

! Calculate the roots of the equation
x1 = ( -b + SQRT( CMPLX(discriminant,0.) ) ) / (2. * a)
x2 = ( -b - SQRT( CMPLX(discriminant,0.) ) ) / (2. * a)

! Tell user.
```

(continued)

(concluded)
```
WRITE (*,*) 'The roots are: '
WRITE (*,100) '   x1 = ', REAL(x1), ' + i ', AIMAG(x1)
WRITE (*,100) '   x2 = ', REAL(x2), ' + i ', AIMAG(x2)
100 FORMAT (A,F10.4,A,F10.4)

END PROGRAM roots_2
```

5. Test the program.

Next we must test the program using real input data. We will test cases in which the discriminant is greater than, less than, and equal to zero to be certain that the program is working properly under all circumstances. From Equation (3–1) we can verify the solutions to the following equations:

$$x^2 + 5x + 6 = 0 \qquad x = -2, \text{ and } x = -3$$

$$x^2 + 4x + 4 = 0 \qquad x = -2$$

$$x^2 + 2x + 5 = 0 \qquad x = -1 \pm 2i$$

When the above coefficients are fed into the program, the results are

```
C>roots_2
Program to solve for the roots of a quadratic
equation of the form A * X**2 + B * X + C.
Enter the coefficients A, B, and C:
1,5,6
The roots are:
  X1 =     -2.0000 + i       .0000
  X2 =     -3.0000 + i       .0000

C>roots_2
Program to solve for the roots of a quadratic
equation of the form A * X**2 + B * X + C.
Enter the coefficients A, B, and C:
1,4,4
The roots are:
  X1 =     -2.0000 + i       .0000
  X2 =     -2.0000 + i       .0000

C>roots_2
Program to solve for the roots of a quadratic
equation of the form A * X**2 + B * X + C.
Enter the coefficients A, B, and C:
1,2,5
The roots are:
  X1 =     -1.0000 + i      2.0000
  X2 =     -1.0000 + i     -2.0000
```

The program gives the correct answers for our test data in all three possible cases. Note how much simpler this program is compared to the quadratic root solver in Example 3–1. The use of the complex data type has greatly simplified our program.

Quiz 7–1

This quiz provides a quick check to see if you understand the concepts introduced in sections 7.1 and 7.2. If you have trouble with the quiz, reread the sections, ask your instructor, or discuss the material with a fellow student. The answers to this quiz appear in Appendix F.

1. What kinds of real numbers and integers does your compiler support? What are the kind numbers associated with each one?

2. What will be written out by the following code shown?

```
COMPLEX :: a, b, c, d
a = ( 1.,  -1. )
b = ( -1., -1. )
c = ( 10.,  1. )
d = ( a + b ) / c
WRITE (*,*) d
```

3. Use the definitions in Equations (7–14) through (7–17) given in section 7.2 to write a computer program that evaluates d in the preceding problem without using complex numbers. How much harder is it to evaluate this expression without the benefit of complex numbers?

▪ 7.3
DERIVED DATA TYPES

In addition to Fortran's **intrinsic data types**—integer, real, complex, logical, and character—Fortran permits us to create our own data types to add new features to the language, or to make it easier to solve specifics classes of problems. A user-defined data type may have any number and combination of components, but each component must be either an intrinsic data type or a previously defined user-defined data type. Because user-defined data types must be ultimately derived from intrinsic data types, they are called **derived data types.**

Basically, a derived data type is a convenient way to group together all the information about a particular item. In some ways it is like an array. Like an array, a single derived data type can have many components. Unlike an array, the components of a derived data type may have different types. One component may be an integer while the next component is a real, the next a character string, and so forth. Furthermore, each component is known by a name instead of by a number.

A derived data type is defined by a sequence of type declaration statements beginning with a TYPE statement and ending with an END TYPE statement. Between these two statements are the definitions of the components in the derived data type. The form of a derived data type is

```
TYPE [::] type_name
    component definitions
        ...
END TYPE [type_name]
```

where the double colons and the name on the END TYPE statement are optional. A derived data type may contain as many component definitions as desired.

To illustrate the use of a derived data type, let's suppose that we are writing a grading program. The program contains information about the students in a class such as name, social security number, age, and sex. We could define a special data type called person to contain all the personal information about each person in the program:

```
TYPE :: person
    CHARACTER(len=14) :: first_name
    CHARACTER :: middle_initial
    CHARACTER(len=14) :: last_name
    CHARACTER(len=14) :: phone
    INTEGER :: age
    CHARACTER :: sex
    CHARACTER(len=11) :: ssn
END TYPE person
```

Once the derived type person is defined, variables of that type may be declared as shown:

```
TYPE (person) :: john, jane
TYPE (person), DIMENSION(100) :: people
```

The latter statement declares an array of 100 variables of type person. Each item of a derived data type is known as a **structure.**

It is also possible to create unnamed constants of a derived data type. To do so, we use a **structure constructor.** A structure constructor consists of the name of the type followed by the components of the derived data type in parentheses. The components appear in the order in which they were declared in the definition of the derived type. For example, the variables john and jane could be initialized by constants of type person as follows:

```
john = person('John','R','Jones','323-6439',21,'M','123-45-6789')
jane = person('Jane','C','Bass','332-3060',17,'F','999-99-9999')
```

A derived data type can be used as a component within another derived data type. For example, a grading program could include a derived data type called grade_info containing a component of the type person defined above to contain personal information about the students in the class. The following example defines the derived type grade_info and declares an array class to be 30 variables of this type.

```
TYPE :: grade_info
    TYPE (person) :: student
    INTEGER :: num_quizzes
    REAL, DIMENSION(10) :: quiz_grades
    INTEGER :: num_exams
    REAL, DIMENSION(10) :: exam_grades
    INTEGER :: final_exam_grade
    REAL :: average
END TYPE
TYPE (grade_info), DIMENSION(30) :: class
```

7.3.1 Working with Derived Data Types

Each component in a variable of a derived data type can be addressed independently and can be used just like any other variable of the same type. For example, if the component is an integer, then it can be used just like any other integer. A component is specified by a **component selector,** which consists of the name of the variable followed by a percent sign (%) and followed by the component name. For example, the following statement sets the component `age` of variable `john` to 35:

```
john%age = 35
```

To address a component within an array of a derived data type, place the array subscript after the array name and before the percent sign. For example, to set the final exam grade for student 5 in array `class` at the end of section 7.3, we would write:

```
class(5)%final_exam_grade = 95
```

To address a component of a derived data type that is included within another derived data type, we simply concatenate their names separated by percent signs. Thus, we could set the age of student 5 within the class with the statement:

```
class(5)%student%age = 23
```

As you can see, working with the components of a variable of a derived data type is easy. However, working with variables of derived data types as a whole is *not* easy. It is legal to assign one variable of a given type to another variable of the same type, but that is almost the only defined operation. Other intrinsic operations such as addition, subtraction, multiplication, division, and comparison are not defined by default for these variables. You will learn how to extend these operations to work properly with derived data types in Chapter 8.

7.3.2 Input and Output of Derived Data Types

If a variable of a derived data type is included in a WRITE statement, each of the components of the variable are written out in the order in which they are declared in the type definition. If the WRITE statement uses formatted I/O, then the format descriptors must match the type and order of the components in the variable.

Similarly, if a variable of a derived data type is included in a READ statement, then the input data must be supplied in the order in which each of the components are declared in the type definition. If the READ statement uses formatted I/O, then the format descriptors must match the type and order of the components in the variable.

The program in Figure 7–11 illustrates the output of a variable of type `person` using both formatted and free-format I/O.

FIGURE 7–11

A program to illustrate the output of variables of derived data types.

```
PROGRAM test_io
!
! Purpose:
!   To illustrate I/O of variables of derived data types.
!
! Record of revisions:
!    Date          Programmer          Description of change
!    ====          ==========          =====================
!   12/23/95     S. J. Chapman          Original code
!
IMPLICIT NONE

! Declare type person
TYPE :: person
   CHARACTER(len=14) :: first_name
   CHARACTER :: middle_initial
   CHARACTER(len=14) :: last_name
   CHARACTER(len=14) :: phone
   INTEGER :: age
   CHARACTER :: sex
   CHARACTER(len=11) :: ssn
END TYPE person

! Declare a variable of type person:
TYPE (person) :: john

! Initialize variable
john = person('John','R','Jones','323-6439',21,'M','123-45-6789')

! Output variable using free-format I/O
write (*,*) 'Free format: ', john

! Output variable using formatted I/O
write (*,1000) john
1000 FORMAT (' Formatted I/O:',/,4(1X,A,/),1X,I4,/,1X,A,/,1X,A)

END PROGRAM
```

When this program is executed, the results are

```
C>test_io
Free format: John          RJones          323-6439          21M123-45-6789

Formatted I/O:
John
R
Jones
323-6439
  21
M
123-45-6789
```

7.3.3 Declaring Derived Data Types in Modules

As you have seen, the definition of a derived data type can be fairly bulky. This definition must be included in every procedure that uses variables or constants of the derived type, which can present a painful maintenance problem in large programs. To avoid this problem, programmers usually define all derived data types in a program in a single module and then to use that module in all procedures needing to use the data type. This practice is illustrated in Example 7–4.

Good Programming Practice
For large programs using derived data types, declare the definitions of each data type in a module and then use that module in each procedure of the program that needs to access the derived data type.

EXAMPLE 7–4 Sorting Derived Data Types by Components: To illustrate the use of derived data types, we will create a small customer database program that permits us to read in a database of customer names and addresses and then to sort and display the addresses by last name, by city, or by ZIP code.

SOLUTION

To solve this problem, we will create a simple derived data type containing the personal information about each customer in the database and initialize the customer database from a disk file. Once the database is initialized, we will prompt the user for the desired display order and sort the data into that order.

1. **State the problem.**

Write a program to read a database of customers from a data file and then to sort and display that database in alphabetical order by last name, by city, or by zip code.

2. **Define the inputs and outputs.**

The inputs to the program are the name of the customer database file, the customer database file itself, and an input value from the user specifying the order in which the data is to be sorted. The output from the program is the customer list sorted in order by the selected field.

3. **Describe the algorithm.**

The first step in writing this program is to create a derived data type to hold all the information about each customer. This data type will need to be placed in a module so that it can be used by each procedure in the program. An appropriate data type definition follows.

```
TYPE :: personal_info
   CHARACTER(len=12) :: first          ! First name
  CHARACTER          :: mi             ! Middle Initial
   CHARACTER(len=12) :: last           ! Last name
   CHARACTER(len=26) :: street         ! Street Address
   CHARACTER(len=12) :: city           ! City
   CHARACTER(len=2)  :: state          ! State
   INTEGER           :: zip            ! Zip code
END TYPE personal_info
```

The program can logically be broken up into two sections: a main program that reads and writes the customer database and a separate procedure that sorts the data into the selected order. The top-level pseudocode for the main program is

```
Get name of customer data file
Read customer data file
Prompt for sort order
Sort data in specified order
Write out sorted customer data
```

Now we must expand and refine the pseudocode for the main program. We must describe how the data will be read in, how the sort order is selected, and how the sorting is done in more detail. A detailed version of the pseudocode for the main program follows.

```
Prompt user for the input file name "filename"
Read the file name "filename"
OPEN file "filename"
IF OPEN is successful THEN
   WHILE
      Read value into temp
      IF read not successful EXIT
      nvals ← nvals + 1
      customers(nvals) ← temp
   End of WHILE

   Prompt user for type of sort (1=last name;2=city;3=zip)
   Read choice
   SELECT CASE (choice)
   CASE (1)
      Call sort_database with last_name comparison function
   CASE (2)
      Call sort_database with city comparison function
   CASE (3)
      Call sort_database with zip code comparison function
   CASE DEFAULT
      Tell user of illegal choice
   END of SELECT CASE

   Write out sorted customer data
END of IF
```

The sorting procedure will be a selection sort similar to any of the sorting routines described in Chapters 5 or 6. The procedure will scan the list of values to be sorted to determine the smallest value and place it at the top of the list. Next it will scan the remaining portion of the list and place the next smallest value in the second place on the list, and so forth until the entire list is sorted. The one tricky thing about this particular sorting process is that we do not know in advance what component of the data type we will be sorting on. Sometimes we will be sorting on the last name, but other times we will be sorting on the city or ZIP code. We must do something to make the sort procedure work properly regardless of the component we are sorting on.

The easiest way to get around this problem is to write a series of functions that compare individual components of two variables of the data type to determine the lesser of the two. One function will compare two last names to determine which is the lesser (lower in alphabetical order), another function will compare two city names to determine which is the lesser (lower in alphabetical order), and a third will compare two ZIP codes to determine which is the lesser (lower in numerical sequence). Once the comparison functions are written, we will be able to sort the data in any order by passing the appropriate comparison function to the sorting subroutine as a command-line argument.

The pseudocode for the last name comparison function is

```
LOGICAL FUNCTION lt_last (a, b)
lt_lastname ← a%last < b%last
```

The pseudocode for the city comparison function is

```
LOGICAL FUNCTION lt_city (a, b)
lt_lastname ← a%city < b%city
```

Finally the pseudocode for the ZIP code comparison function is

```
LOGICAL FUNCTION lt_zip (a, b)
lt_zip ← a%zip < b%zip
```

The pseudocode for the sorting subroutine is the same as the pseudocode for subroutine `sort` in Chapter 6 except that the comparison function is passed as a command-line argument. The pseudocode is not reproduced here.

4. **Turn the algorithm into Fortran statements.**

The resulting Fortran subroutine is shown in Figure 7–12.

FIGURE 7–12
Program to sort a customer database according to a user-specified field.

```
MODULE types
!
! Purpose:
!   To define the derived data type used for the customer
!   database.
!
! Record of revisions:
!     Date        Programmer            Description of change
!     ====        ==========            =====================
!   12/27/95    S. J. Chapman          Original code
!
IMPLICIT NONE
```

(continued)

```
(continued)
! Declare type personal_info
TYPE :: personal_info
   CHARACTER(len=12) ::first         ! First name
   CHARACTER          :: mi          ! Middle Initial
   CHARACTER(len=12) :: last         ! Last name
   CHARACTER(len=26) :: street       ! Street Address
   CHARACTER(len=12) :: city         ! City
   CHARACTER(len=2)  :: state        ! State
   INTEGER           :: zip          ! Zip code
END TYPE personal_info

END MODULE types

PROGRAM customer_database
!
! Purpose:
!   To read in a character input data set, sort it into ascending
!   order using the selection sort algorithm, and to write the
!   sorted data to the standard output device.  This program calls
!   subroutine "sort_database" to do the actual sorting.
!
! Record of revisions:
!     Date        Programmer          Description of change
!     ====        ==========          =====================
!   12/27/95    S. J. Chapman         Original code
!
USE types                            ! Declare the module types
IMPLICIT NONE

! List of parameters:
INTEGER, PARAMETER :: max_size = 100 ! Max addresses in database

! List of external functions:
LOGICAL, EXTERNAL :: lt_last         ! Comparison fn for last names
LOGICAL, EXTERNAL :: lt_city         ! Comparison fn for cities
LOGICAL, EXTERNAL :: lt_zip          ! Comparison fn for zip codes

! List of variables:
TYPE(personal_info), DIMENSION(max_size) :: customers
                                     ! Data array to sort
INTEGER :: choice                    ! Choice of how to sort database
LOGICAL :: exceed = .FALSE.          ! Logical indicating that array
                                     !   limits are exceeded.
CHARACTER(len=20) :: filename        ! Input data file name
INTEGER :: i                         ! Loop index
INTEGER :: nvals = 0                 ! Number of data values to sort
INTEGER :: status                    ! I/O status: 0 for success
TYPE(personal_info) :: temp          ! Temporary variable for reading

! Get the name of the file containing the input data.
WRITE (*,*) 'Enter the file name with customer database: '
READ (*,'(A20)') filename

! Open input data file.  Status is OLD because the input data must
! already exist.
OPEN ( UNIT=9, FILE=filename, STATUS='OLD', IOSTAT=status )
```

(continued)

```
(continued)
! Was the OPEN successful?
fileopen: IF ( status == 0 ) THEN              ! Open successful

    ! The file was opened successfully, so read the customer
    ! database from it.
    DO
        READ (9, 1010, IOSTAT=status) temp     ! Get value
        1010 FORMAT (A12,1X,A1,1X,A12,1X,A26,1X,A12,1X,A2,1X,I5)
        IF ( status /= 0 ) EXIT                ! Exit on end of data
        nvals = nvals + 1                      ! Bump count
        size: IF ( nvals <= max_size ) THEN    ! Too many values?
            customers(nvals) = temp            ! No: Save value in array
        ELSE
            exceed = .TRUE.                    ! Yes: Array overflow
        END IF size
    END DO

    ! Was the array size exceeded?  If so, tell user and quit.
    toobig: IF ( exceed ) THEN
        WRITE (*,1020) nvals, max_size
        1020 FORMAT (' Maximum array size exceeded: ', I6, ' > ', I6 )
    ELSE

        ! Limit not exceeded: find out how to sort data.
        WRITE (*,1030)
        1030 FORMAT (1X,'Enter way to sort database:',/, &
                     1X,'  1 — By last name ',/, &
                     1X,'  2 — By city ',/, &
                     1X,'  3 — By zip code ')
        READ (*,*) choice

        ! Sort database
        SELECT CASE ( choice)
        CASE (1)
            CALL sort_database (customers, nvals, lt_last )
        CASE (2)
            CALL sort_database (customers, nvals, lt_city )
        CASE (3)
            CALL sort_database (customers, nvals, lt_zip )
        CASE DEFAULT
            WRITE (*,*) 'Invalid choice entered!'
        END SELECT

        ! Now write out the sorted data.
        WRITE (*,'(A)') ' The sorted database values are: '
        WRITE (*,1040) ( customers(i), i = 1, nvals )
        1040 FORMAT (1X,A12,1X,A1,1X,A12,1X,A26,1X,A12,1X,A2,1X,I5)

    END IF toobig

ELSE fileopen

    ! Status /= 0, so an open error occurred.
    WRITE (*,'(A,I6)') ' File open error: IOSTAT = ', status

END IF fileopen
```

(continued)

```
(continued)
END PROGRAM

SUBROUTINE sort_database (array, n, lt_fun )
!
! Purpose:
!   To sort array "array" into ascending order using a selection
!   sort, where "array" is an array of the derived data type
!   "personal_info."  The sort is based on the the external
!   comparison function "lt_fun," which will differ depending on
!   which component of the derived type array is used for
!   comparison.
!
! Record of revisions:
!     Date          Programmer              Description of change
!     ====          ==========              =====================
!   12/27/95    S. J. Chapman               Original code
!
USE types                                 ! Declare the module types
IMPLICIT NONE

! Declare calling parameters:
INTEGER, INTENT(IN) :: n                             ! Number of values
TYPE(personal_info), DIMENSION(n), INTENT(INOUT) :: array
                                          ! Array to be sorted
LOGICAL, EXTERNAL :: lt_fun               ! Comparison function

! Declare local variables:
INTEGER :: i                    ! Loop index
INTEGER :: iptr                 ! Pointer to smallest value
INTEGER :: j                    ! Loop index
TYPE(personal_info) :: temp     ! Temp variable for swaps

! Sort the array
outer: DO i = 1, n-1

   ! Find the minimum value in array(i) through array(n)
   iptr = i
   inner: DO j = i+1, n
      minval: IF ( lt_fun(array(j),array(iptr)) ) THEN
         iptr = j
      END IF minval
   END DO inner

   ! iptr now points to the minimum value, so swap array(iptr)
   ! with array(i) if i /= iptr.
   swap: IF ( i /= iptr ) THEN
      temp       = array(i)
      array(i)   = array(iptr)
      array(iptr) = temp
      END IF swap

END DO outer
END SUBROUTINE sort_database

LOGICAL FUNCTION lt_last (a, b)
!
```

(continued)

(concluded)
```
! Purpose:
!   To compare variables "a" and "b" and determine which
!   has the smaller last name (lower alphabetical order).
!
USE types                              ! Declare the module types
IMPLICIT NONE

! Declare calling arguments
TYPE (personal_info), INTENT(IN) :: a, b

! Make comparison.
lt_last = a%last < b%last

END FUNCTION lt_last

LOGICAL FUNCTION lt_city (a, b)
!
! Purpose:
!   To compare variables "a" and "b" and determine which
!   has the smaller city (lower alphabetical order).
!
USE types                              ! Declare the module types
IMPLICIT NONE

! Declare calling arguments
TYPE (personal_info), INTENT(IN) :: a, b

! Make comparison.
lt_city = a%city < b%city

END FUNCTION lt_city

LOGICAL FUNCTION lt_zip (a, b)
!
! Purpose:
!   To compare variables "a" and "b" and determine which
!   has the smaller zip code (lower numerical value).
!
USE types                              ! Declare the module types
IMPLICIT NONE

! Declare calling arguments
TYPE (personal_info), INTENT(IN) :: a, b

! Make comparison.
lt_zip = a%zip < b%zip

END FUNCTION lt_zip
```

5. Test the resulting Fortran programs.

To test this program, we will create a sample customer database. A simple customer database is shown in Figure 7–13; it is stored in the disk in a file called `database`.

FIGURE 7–13

Sample customer database used to test the program of Example 7–4.

```
John       Q Public      123 Sesame Street   Anywhere      NY 10035
James      R Johnson     Rt. 5 Box 207C      West Monroe   LA 71291
Joseph     P Ziskend     P. O. Box 433       APO           AP 96555
Andrew     D Jackson     Jackson Square      New Orleans   LA 70003
Jane       X Doe         12 Lakeside Drive   Glenview      IL 60025
Colin      A Jeffries    11 Main Street      Chicago       IL 60003
```

To test the program, we will execute it three times using this database, once with each possible sorting option.

```
C>customer_database
Enter the file name with customer database:
database
Enter way to sort database:
    1 — By last name
    2 — By city
    3 — By zip code
1
The sorted database values are:
Jane       X Doe         12 Lakeside Drive   Glenview      IL 60025
Andrew     D Jackson     Jackson Square      New Orleans   LA 70003
Colin      A Jeffries    11 Main Street      Chicago       IL 60003
James      R Johnson     Rt. 5 Box 207C      West Monroe   LA 71291
John       Q Public      123 Sesame Street   Anywhere      NY 10035
Joseph     P Ziskend     P. O. Box 433       APO           AP 96555


C>customer_database
Enter the file name with customer database:
database
Enter way to sort database:
    1 — By last name
    2 — By city
    3 — By zip code
2
The sorted database values are:
Joseph     P Ziskend     P. O. Box 433       APO           AP 96555
John       Q Public      123 Sesame Street   Anywhere      NY 10035
Colin      A Jeffries    11 Main Street      Chicago       IL 60003
Jane       X Doe         12 Lakeside Drive   Glenview      IL 60025
Andrew     D Jackson     Jackson Square      New Orleans   LA 70003
James      R Johnson     Rt. 5 Box 207C      West Monroe   LA 71291


C>customer_database
Enter the file name with customer database:
database
Enter way to sort database:
    1 — By last name
    2 — By city
    3 — By zip code
3
The sorted database values are:
```

```
John      Q Public        123 Sesame Street    Anywhere       NY 10035
Colin     A Jeffries      11 Main Street       Chicago        IL 60003
Jane      X Doe           12 Lakeside Drive    Glenview       IL 60025
Andrew    D Jackson       Jackson Square       New Orleans    LA 70003
James     R Johnson       Rt. 5 Box 207C       West Monroe    LA 71291
Joseph    P Ziskend       P. O. Box 433        APO            AP 96555
```

Note that the program is working correctly with one minor exception. When it sorted the data by city, it got APO and Anywhere out of order. Can you tell why this happened? You will be asked to rewrite this program to eliminate the problem in exercise 7–10.

Quiz 7–2

This quiz provides a quick check to see if you understand the concepts introduced in section 7.3. If you have trouble with the quiz, reread the sections, ask your instructor, or discuss the material with a fellow student. The answers to this quiz appear in Appendix F.

For questions 1 to 7, assume the following derived data types:

```
TYPE :: position
    REAL :: x
    REAL :: y
    REAL :: z
END TYPE position
TYPE :: time
    INTEGER :: second
    INTEGER :: minute
    INTEGER :: hour
    INTEGER :: day
    INTEGER :: month
    INTEGER :: year
END TYPE time
TYPE :: plot
    TYPE (time) :: plot_time
    TYPE (position) :: plot_position
END TYPE
TYPE (plot), DIMENSION(10) :: points
```

1. Write the Fortran statements to print out the date associated with the seventh plot point in format DD/MM/YYYY   HH:MM:SS.
2. Write the Fortran statements to print out the position associated with the seventh plot point.
3. Write the Fortran statements required to calculate the rate of motion between the second and third plot points. To do this, you will have to calculate the difference in position and the difference in time between the two points. The rate of motion will be $\frac{\Delta\text{pos}}{\Delta\text{time}}$.

(continued)

(concluded)

For questions 4 to 6, state whether each of the following statements is valid. If the statements are valid, describe what they do.

4. `WRITE (*,*) points(1)`

5. `WRITE (*,1000) points(4)`
   `1000 FORMAT (1X, 3ES12.6, 6I6 )`

6. `dpos = points(2).plot_position - points(1).plot_position`

■ 7.4

SUMMARY

This chapter introduced the concept of kinds and kind type parameters. Kinds are versions of the same basic data type, each differing in size, precision, range, and so on.

All Fortran compilers support at least two kinds of real data, which are usually known as single precision and double precision. Double-precision data occupies twice the memory of single-precision data on most computers. Double-precision variables have both a greater range and more significant digits than single-precision variables have.

The choice of precision for a particular real value is specified by the kind type parameter in the type declaration statement. Unfortunately, the numbers associated with each kind of real value vary among different processors. They can be determined by using the KIND intrinsic function on a particular processor, or the desired precision can be specified in a processor-independent manner using the SELECTED_REAL_KIND intrinsic function.

Double-precision real numbers take up more space and require more computer time to calculate than single-precision real numbers do and should not be used indiscriminately. In general, double-precision should be used when:

1. A problem requires many significant digits or a large range of numbers.
2. Numbers of dramatically different sizes must be added or subtracted.
3. Two nearly equal numbers must be subtracted, and the result used in further calculations.

Complex numbers consist of two real numbers in successive locations in memory. These two numbers are treated as though they were the real and imaginary parts of a complex number expressed in rectangular coordinates. They are processed according to the rules for complex addition, subtraction, multiplication, division, and so on. A kind of complex number corresponds to each kind of real number available on a particular processor. The kind numbers are identical for real and complex data, so the desired precision of a complex value may be selected using the SELECTED_REAL_KIND intrinsic function.

Complex constants are written as two numbers in parentheses, separated by commas, for example, `(1.,-1.)`. Complex variables are declared using a COMPLEX type declaration statement. They may be read and written using any type of real format descriptor, for example, E, ES, or F. When reading or writing complex numbers, the real and imaginary parts of the number are processed separately. The first value read will become the real part, and the next value will become the imaginary part. If list-directed input is used with complex numbers, the input value must be typed as a complex constant, complete with parentheses.

Derived data types are data types the programmer defines for use in solving a particular problem. They may contain any number of components, and each component may be of any intrinsic data type or any previously defined derived data type. Derived data types are defined using a `TYPE ... END TYPE` construct, and variables of that type are declared using a `TYPE` statement. Constants of a derived data type may be constructed using structure constructors. A variable or constant of a derived data type is called a structure.

The components of a variable of a derived data type may be used in a program just like any other variables of the same type. They are addressed by naming both the variable and the component separated by a percent sign (e.g., `student%age`). Variables of a derived data type may not be used with any Fortran intrinsic operations except for assignment. Addition, subtraction, multiplication, division, and so on are undefined for these variables. They may be used in I/O statements.

You will learn how to extend intrinsic operations to variables of a derived data type in Chapter 8.

7.4.1 Summary of Good Programming Practice

The following guidelines should be adhered to when working with parameterized variables, complex numbers, and derived data types:

1. Always assign kind numbers to a named constant and then use that named constant in all type declaration statements and constant declarations. For large programs with many procedures, place the kind parameters in a single module and then use that module in every procedure within the program.
2. Use the function `SELECTED_REAL_KIND` to determine the kind numbers of the real values needed to solve a problem. The function will return the proper kind numbers on any processor, making your programs more portable.
3. Use double-precision real numbers instead of single-precision real numbers whenever:

    a. A problem requires many significant digits or a large range of numbers.
    b. Numbers of dramatically different sizes must be added or subtracted.
    c. Two nearly equal numbers must be subtracted, and the result used in further calculations.

4. For large programs using derived data types, declare the definitions of each data type in a module and then use that module in each procedure of the program that needs to access the derived data type.

7.4.2 Summary of Fortran Statements and Structures

COMPLEX Statement

```
COMPLEX(KIND=kind_no) :: var1(, var2, etc.)
```

Examples:

```
COMPLEX(KIND=single) :: volts, amps
```

Description:

The COMPLEX statement declares variables of the complex data type. The kind number is optional and machine dependent. If it is not present, the kind is the default complex kind for the particular machine (usually single precision).

Derived Data Type

```
TYPE [::] type_name
   component 1
   ...
   component n
END TYPE [type_name]
TYPE (type_name) :: var1 (, var2, ...)
```

Example:

```
TYPE :: state_vector
   LOGICAL :: valid            ! Valid data flag
   REAL(kind=single) :: x      ! x position
   REAL(kind=single) :: y      ! y position
   REAL(kind=double) :: time   ! time of validity
   CHARACTER(len=12) :: id     ! Target ID
END TYPE state_vector
TYPE (state_vector), DIMENSION(50) :: objects
```

Description:

The derived data type is a structure containing a combination of intrinsic and previously defined derived data types. The type is defined by a TYPE ... END TYPE construct, and variables of that type are declared with a TYPE() statement.

REAL Statement with KIND parameter

```
REAL(KIND=kind_no) :: var1(, var2, etc.)
```
Examples:

```
REAL(KIND=single) :: distance, time
REAL(KIND=single), DIMENSION(100) :: points
```

(continued)

> *(concluded)*
> Description:
>   The REAL statement is a type declaration statement that declares variables of the real data type. The kind number is optional and machine dependent. If it is not present, the kind is the default real kind for the particular machine (usually single precision).

■ 7.4
EXERCISES

7–1 What are kinds of the REAL data type? How many kinds of real data must a compiler support according to the Fortran 90/95 standard?

7–2 What kind numbers are associated with the different types of real variables available on your compiler/computer? Determine the precision and range associated with each type of real data.

7–3 What are the advantages and disadvantages of double-precision real numbers compared to single-precision real numbers? When should you use double-precision real numbers instead of single-precision real numbers?

7–4 What is an ill-conditioned system of equations? Why is it hard to find the solution to an ill-conditioned set of equations?

7–5 State whether each of the following sets of Fortran statements are legal or illegal. If they are illegal, what is wrong with them? If they are legal, what do they do?

    a. Statements:

```
INTEGER, PARAMETER :: sng = KIND(0.0)
INTEGER, PARAMETER :: dbl = KIND(0.0D0)
REAL(KIND=sng) :: a
REAL(KIND=dbl) :: b
READ (*,'(F18.2)') a, b
WRITE (*,*) a, b
```

  Input Data:

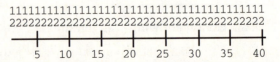

    b. Statements:

```
INTEGER, PARAMETER :: single = SELECTED_REAL_KIND(p=6)
COMPLEX(kind=single), DIMENSION(5) :: a1
INTEGER :: i
```

```
         DO i = 1, 5
             a1(i) = CMPLX ( i, -2*i )
         END DO
         IF (a1(5) > a1(3)) THEN
             WRITE (*,100) (i, a1(i), i = 1, 5)
             100 FORMAT (3X,'a1(',I2,') = (',F10.4,',',F10.4,')')
         END IF
```

7-6 Derivative of a Function Write a subroutine to calculate the derivative of a double-precision real function $f(x)$ at position $x = x_0$. The calling arguments to the subroutine should be the function $f(x)$, the location x_0 at which to evaluate the function, and the step size Δx to use in the evaluation. The output from the subroutine will be the derivative of the function at point $x = x_0$. To make your subroutine machine independent, define double precision as the kind of real value having at least 13 digits of precision. Note that the function to be evaluated should be passed to the subroutine as a calling argument! Test your subroutine by evaluating the function $f(x) = 10 \sin 20x$ at position $x = 0$.

7-7 If you have not done so previously, write a set of elapsed time subroutines for your computer, as described in exercise 6–30. Use the elapsed time subroutines to compare the time required to solve a 10×10 system of simultaneous equations in single precision and in double precision. You will need to write two test driver programs (one single precision and one double precision) that read the coefficients of the equations, start the timer running, solve the equations, and then calculate the elapsed time. How much slower is the double-precision solution than the single-precision solution on your computer?

Test your program on the following system of equations. (This set of equations is contained in file SYS10 in directory CHAP7 at the book's Web site.)

$$
\begin{aligned}
-2x_1 + 5x_2 + x_3 + 3x_4 + 4x_5 - x_6 + 2x_7 - x_8 - 5x_9 - 2x_{10} &= -5 \\
6x_1 + 4x_2 - x_3 + 6x_4 - 4x_5 - 5x_6 + 3x_7 - x_8 + 4x_9 + 3x_{10} &= -6 \\
-6x_1 - 5x_2 - 2x_3 - 2x_4 - 3x_5 + 6x_6 + 4x_7 + 2x_8 - 6x_9 + 4x_{10} &= -7 \\
2x_1 + 4x_2 + 4x_3 + 4x_4 + 5x_5 - 4x_6 + 0x_7 + 0x_8 - 4x_9 + 6x_{10} &= 0 \\
-4x_1 - x_2 + 3x_3 - 3x_4 - 4x_5 - 4x_6 - 4x_7 + 4x_8 + 3x_9 - 3x_{10} &= 5 \\
4x_1 + 3x_2 + 5x_3 + x_4 + x_5 + x_6 + 0x_7 + 3x_8 + 3x_9 + 6x_{10} &= -8 \\
x_1 + 2x_2 - 2x_3 + 0x_4 + 3x_5 - 5x_6 + 5x_7 + 0x_8 + x_9 - 4x_{10} &= 1 \\
-3x_1 - 4x_2 + 2x_3 - x_4 - 2x_5 + 5x_6 - x_7 - x_8 - 4x_9 + x_{10} &= -4 \\
5x_1 + 5x_2 - 2x_3 - 5x_4 + x_5 - 4x_6 - x_7 + 0x_8 - 2x_9 - 3x_{10} &= -7 \\
-5x_1 - 2x_2 - 5x_3 + 2x_4 + x_5 - 3x_6 + 4x_7 - x_8 - 4x_9 + 4x_{10} &= 6
\end{aligned}
$$

7-8 Simultaneous Equations with Complex Coefficients Create a subroutine csimul to solve for the unknowns in a system of simultaneous linear equations that have complex coefficients. Test your subroutine by solving the following system of equations:

$$
\begin{aligned}
(-2+i5)\, x_1 + (1+i3)\, x_2 + (4-i1)\, x_3 &= (7+i5) \\
(2-i1)\, x_1 + (-5-i2)\, x_2 + (6+i4)\, x_3 &= (-10-i8) \\
(-1+i6)\, x_1 + (-4-i5)\, x_2 + (3-i1)\, x_3 &= (-3-i3)
\end{aligned}
$$

7-9 Amplitude and Phase of a Complex Number Write a subroutine that will accept a complex number $c = a + ib$ stored in a variable of type COMPLEX and then return the amplitude amp and the phase theta (in degrees) of the complex number in two real variables. (*Hint:* Use intrinsic function ATAN2 to help calculate the phase.)

7–10 When the database was sorted by city in Example 7–4, APO was placed ahead of Anywhere. Why did this happen? Rewrite the program in this example to eliminate this problem.

7–11 Create a derived data type called polar to hold a complex number expressed in polar (z,θ) format as shown in Figure 7–9. The derived data type will contain two components: a magnitude z and an angle θ, with the angle expressed in degrees. Write a function that converts an ordinary complex number into a polar number and a function that converts a polar number into an ordinary complex number.

7–12 If two complex numbers are expressed in polar form, the two numbers may be multiplied by multiplying their magnitudes and adding their angles. That is, if $P_1 = z_1 \angle \theta_1$ and $P_2 = z_2 \angle \theta_2$, then $P_1 \cdot P_2 = z_1 z_2 \angle \theta_1 + \theta_2$. Write a function that multiplies two variables of type polar together using this expression and returns a result in polar form. Note that the resulting angle θ should be in the range $-180° < \theta \le 180°$.

7–13 **Euler's Equation** Euler's equation defines e raised to an imaginary power in terms of sinusoidal functions as follows:

$$e^{i\theta} = \cos \theta + i \sin \theta \tag{7–18}$$

Write a function to evaluate $e^{i\theta}$ for any θ using Euler's equation. Also, evaluate $e^{i\theta}$ using the intrinsic complex exponential function CEXP. Compare the answers that you get by the two methods for the cases where $\theta = 0, \dfrac{\pi}{2}$, and π.

7–14 A point can be located in a Cartesian plane by two coordinates (x,y), where x is the displacement of the point along the x-axis from the origin and y is the displacement of the point along the y-axis from the origin. Create a derived data type called point whose components are x and y. A line can be represented in a Cartesian plane by the equation

$$y = mx + b \tag{7–19}$$

where m is the slope of the line and b is the y-axis intercept of the line. Create a derived data type called line whose components are m and b.

7–15 The distance between two points (x_1,y_1) and (x_2,y_2) is given by the equation

$$distance = \sqrt{(x_2 - x_1)^2 + (y_2 - y_1)^2} \tag{7–20}$$

Write a function that calculates the distance between two values of type point as defined in exercise 7–14. The inputs should be two points, and the output should be the distance between the two points expressed as a real number.

7–16 From elementary geometry, we know that two points uniquely determine a line as long as they are not coincident. Write a function that accepts two values of type point, and returns a value of type line containing the slope and y-intercept of the line. If the two points are identical, the function should return zeros for both the slope and the intercept. Figure 7–14 shows that the slope of the line can be calculated from the equation

$$m = \frac{y_2 - y_1}{x_2 - x_1} \tag{7–21}$$

and that the intercept can be calculated from the equation

$$b = y1 - mx1 \qquad (7\text{--}22)$$

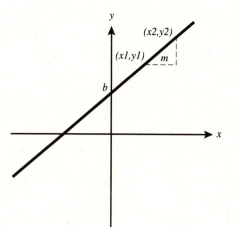

FIGURE 7–14

The slope and intercept of a line can be determined from two points (x_1, y_1) and (x_2, y_2) that lie along the line.

Advanced Features of Procedures and Modules

This chapter introduces some more advanced features of Fortran 90/95 procedures and modules. These features permit us to have better control over access to the information contained in procedures and modules, allow us to write more flexible procedures that support optional arguments and varying data types, and allow us to extend the Fortran language to support new operations on both intrinsic and derived data types.

■ 8.1
INTERNAL PROCEDURES

An *internal procedure* is entirely contained within another program unit, called the **host program unit,** or just the **host.** The internal procedure is compiled with the host, and it can only be invoked from the host program unit. Like module procedures, internal procedures are introduced by a CONTAINS statement. An internal procedure must follow all the executable statements within the host procedure and must be introduced by a CONTAINS statement.

Why would we want to use internal procedures? In some problems, there are low-level manipulations which must be performed repeatedly as a part of the solution. These low-level manipulations can be simplified by defining an internal procedure to perform them.

A simple example of an internal procedure is shown in Figure 8–1. This program accepts an input value in degrees and uses an internal procedure to calculate the secant of that value. Although this example invokes the internal procedure secant only once, it could have been invoked repeatedly in a larger problem to calculate secants of many different angles.

FIGURE 8–1
Program to calculate the secant of an angle in degrees using an internal procedure.

```
PROGRAM test
!
! Purpose:
!   To illustrate the use of an internal procedure.
!
```

(continued)

(concluded)

```
! Record of revisions:
!     Date        Programmer          Description of change
!     ====        ==========          =====================
!   12/28/95    S. J. Chapman         Original code
!
IMPLICIT NONE

! Declare parameters:
INTEGER, PARAMETER :: single = KIND(0.0)    ! Single precision
REAL(KIND=single), PARAMETER :: pi = 3.141592

! Declare local variables:
REAL(kind=single) :: theta                      ! Angle in degrees

! Get desired angle
WRITE (*,*) 'Enter desired angle in degrees: '
READ (*,*) theta

! Calculate and display the result.
WRITE (*,'(A,F10.4)') ' The secant is ', secant(theta)

! Note that the WRITE above was the last executable statement.
! Now, declare internal procedure secant:
CONTAINS
    REAL FUNCTION secant(angle_in_degrees)
    !
    ! Purpose:
    !    To calculate the secant of an angle in degrees.
    !
    REAL(KIND=single) angle_in_degrees

    ! Calculate secant
    secant = 1. / cos( angle_in_degrees * pi / 180. )

    END FUNCTION secant

END PROGRAM test
```

Note that the internal function `secant` appears after the last executable statement in program `test`. It is not a part of the executable code of the host program. When program `test` is executed, the user is prompted for an angle and the internal function `secant` is called to calculate the secant of the angle as a part of the final `WRITE` statement. When this program is executed, the results are

```
C>test
Enter desired angle in degrees:
45
The secant is      1.4142
```

An internal procedure functions exactly like an external procedure with the following three exceptions:

1. The internal procedure can *only* be invoked from the host procedure. No other procedure within the program can access it.

2. The name of an internal procedure may not be passed as a command-line argument to another procedure.

3. An internal procedure inherits all the data entities (parameters and variables) of its host program unit by **host association.**

The last point requires more explanation. When an internal procedure is defined within a host program unit, all the parameters and variables within the host program unit are also usable within the internal procedure. Look at Figure 8–1 again. Note that an IM-PLICIT NONE statement does not occur within the internal procedure, because the one in the host program applies to the internal procedure as well. Note also that both the named constants single and pi, which are defined in the host program, are used in the internal procedure.

The only time when an internal procedure cannot access a data entity defined in its host is when the internal procedure defines a different data entity with the same name. In that case the data entity defined in the host is not accessible in the procedure, and manipulations that occur within the internal procedure will not affect the data entity in the host.

■ 8.2
RECURSIVE PROCEDURES

An ordinary Fortran 90/95 procedure may not invoke itself either directly or indirectly (that is, by either invoking itself or invoking another procedure that then invokes the original procedure). In other words, Fortran 90/95 procedures are not **recursive.**

However, certain classes of problems are most easily solved recursively. For example, the factorial function can be defined as

$$N! = \begin{cases} N(N - 1)! & N \geq 1 \\ 1 & N = 0 \end{cases} \tag{8-1}$$

This definition can most easily be implemented recursively, with the procedure that calculates $N!$ calling itself to calculate $(N - 1)!$, and that procedure calling itself to calculate $(N - 2)!$, and so on until finally the procedure is called to calculate $0!$.

To accommodate such problems, Fortran allows subroutines and functions to be declared recursive. If a procedure is declared recursive, then the Fortran compiler will implement it so that it can invoke itself either directly or indirectly as often as desired.

A subroutine is declared recursive by adding the keyword RECURSIVE to the SUB-ROUTINE statement. Figure 8–2 shows an example subroutine that calculates the factorial function directly from Equation (8–1). It looks just like any other subroutine except that it is declared to be recursive. You will be asked to verify the proper operation of this subroutine in exercise 8–3.

FIGURE 8–2

A subroutine to recursively implement the factorial function.

```
RECURSIVE SUBROUTINE factorial ( n, result )
!
! Purpose:
!   To calculate the factorial function
!           | n(n-1)!    n >= 1
!     n! = |
!           | 1          n = 0
!
! Record of revisions:
!    Date        Programmer              Description of change
!    ====        ==========              =====================
!   10/31/95    S. J. Chapman            Original code
!
IMPLICIT NONE

! List of calling arguments:
INTEGER, INTENT(IN) :: n                ! Value to calculate
INTEGER, INTENT(OUT) :: result          ! Result

! Local variable
INTEGER :: temp                         ! Temporary variable

IF ( n >= 1 ) THEN
   CALL factorial ( n-1, temp )
   result = n * temp
ELSE
   result = 1
END IF

END SUBROUTINE factorial
```

We can also define recursive Fortran functions. However, an extra complication occurs when working with recursive functions. Remember that we invoke a function by naming the function in an expression, while we specify the value to be returned from the function by assigning it to the function name. Thus, if a function were to invoke itself, the function's name would appear on the left side of an assignment statement when its return value is being set and on the right hand side of an assignment statement when it invoking itself recursively. This double use of the function name could certainly cause confusion.

To avoid confusion between the two uses of the function name in a recursive function, Fortran allows us to specify two different names for invoking the function recursively and for returning its result. We use the actual name of the function whenever we want the function to invoke itself, and we use a special *dummy argument* whenever we want to specify a value to return. The name of this special dummy argument is specified in a RESULT clause in the FUNCTION statement. For example, the following line declares a recursive function fact that uses the dummy argument answer for the value returned to the invoking program unit:

```
RECURSIVE FUNCTION fact(n) RESULT(answer)
```

If a RESULT clause is included in a function, then the function name *may not* appear in a type declaration statement in the function. The name of the dummy result variable is declared instead. For example, Figure 8–3 shows a recursive function that calculates the factorial function directly from Equation (8–1). Note that the type of the result variable answer is declared, not the type of the function name fact. You will be asked to verify the proper operation of this function in exercise 8–3.

FIGURE 8–3
A function to recursively implement the factorial function.

```
RECURSIVE FUNCTION fact(n) RESULT(answer)
!
! Purpose:
!   To calculate the factorial function
!            | n(n-1)!    n >= 1
!     n ! = |
!            | 1           n = 0
!
! Record of revisions:
!    Date        Programmer            Description of change
!    ====        ==========            =====================
!   10/31/95     S. J. Chapman         Original code
!
IMPLICIT NONE

! List of calling arguments:
INTEGER, INTENT(IN) :: n           ! Value to calculate
INTEGER :: answer                   ! Result variable

IF ( n >= 1 ) THEN
   answer = n * fact(n-1)
ELSE
   answer = 1
END IF

END FUNCTION fact
```

■ **8.3**

KEYWORD ARGUMENTS AND OPTIONAL ARGUMENTS

In Chapter 6 you learned that the actual argument list used to invoke a procedure must match the dummy argument list exactly in number, type, and order. If the first dummy argument is a real array, then the first actual argument must also be a real array and so on. If the procedure has four dummy arguments, then the procedure invocation must have four actual arguments.

This statement is usually true in Fortran 90/95. However, it is possible to change the order of the calling arguments in the list or to specify actual arguments for only some of the procedure's dummy arguments provided that the interface to the procedure is explicit.

You can make a procedure interface explicit by placing the procedure in a module and accessing that module in the invoking program by USE association.

If a procedure's interface is explicit, then it is possible to use **keyword arguments** in the calling program to provide increased flexibility. A keyword argument is an argument of the form

```
keyword = actual_argument
```

where keyword is the name of the dummy argument that is being associated with the actual argument. If the procedure invocation uses keyword arguments, then the calling arguments can be arranged in any order because the keywords enable the compiler to determine which actual argument goes with which dummy argument.

Let's illustrate this idea with an example. Figure 8–4 shows a function calc that takes three real arguments first, second, and third. The function is contained inside a module to make its interface explicit. The main program invokes this function in four different ways using the same arguments. The first time that the function is invoked, we use the conventional method; that is, the actual arguments match the dummy arguments in type, number, and order:

```
WRITE (*,*) calc ( 3., 1., 2. )
```

The next two times that the function is invoked, we use keyword arguments:

```
WRITE (*,*) calc ( first=3., second=1., third=2. )
WRITE (*,*) calc ( second=1., third=2., first=3. )
```

The final time that the function is called, we use a mixture of conventional arguments and keyword arguments. The first argument is conventional, and so it is associated with the first dummy argument. The later arguments are keyword arguments, so they are associated with dummy arguments by their keywords. In general, it is legal to mix conventional calling arguments and keyword arguments, but once a keyword argument appears in the list, the remaining arguments must also be keyword arguments.

```
WRITE (*,*) calc ( 3., third=2., second=1.)
```

FIGURE 8–4

Program to illustrate the use of keyword arguments.

```
MODULE procs
CONTAINS
   REAL FUNCTION calc ( first, second, third )
   IMPLICIT NONE
   REAL, INTENT(IN) :: first, second, third
   calc = ( first - second ) / third
   END FUNCTION calc
END MODULE procs

PROGRAM test_keywords
```

(continued)

(concluded)
```
              USE procs
              IMPLICIT NONE

              WRITE (*,*) calc ( 3., 1., 2. )
              WRITE (*,*) calc ( first=3., second=1., third=2. )
              WRITE (*,*) calc ( second=1., third=2., first=3. )
              WRITE (*,*) calc ( 3., third=2., second=1.)

              END PROGRAM test_keywords
```

When the program in Figure 8–4 is executed, the results are

```
C>test_keywords
              1.000000
              1.000000
              1.000000
              1.000000
```

The function calculated the same value every time regardless of the order in which the arguments were presented.

Keyword arguments allow us to change the order in which actual arguments are presented to a procedure, but by itself that technique is not very useful. All we are doing here is creating extra typing to accomplish the same goal! However, keyword arguments are useful when used with optional arguments.

An **optional argument** is a dummy procedure argument that does not always have to be present when the procedure is invoked. If it is present, then the procedure will use it. If not, then the procedure will function without it. Optional arguments are possible only in procedures with explicit interfaces. They are specified by including the OPTIONAL attribute in the declaration of a dummy argument:

```
              INTEGER, INTENT(IN), OPTIONAL :: upper_limit
```

The procedure containing an optional argument uses the logical intrinsic function PRESENT to determine whether the optional argument is present when the procedure is executed. PRESENT returns a true value if the optional argument is present and a false value if it is not present. For example, a procedure could take some action based on the presence or absence of an optional argument upper_limit as follows:

```
              IF ( PRESENT(upper_limit) ) THEN
                 ...
              ELSE
                 ...
              END IF
```

Keywords are very useful for procedures with optional arguments. If the optional arguments are present and in order in the calling sequence, then no keywords are required. If only some of the optional arguments are present, but the ones that are present are in order, then no keywords are required. However, if optional arguments are out of order, or if some of the earlier optional arguments are missing while later ones are supplied, then keywords must be supplied; the compiler will use the keywords to sort out which optional arguments are present and which ones are absent.

Incidentally, we have already met an intrinsic function that uses keywords and optional arguments. Recall that the function SELECTED_REAL_KIND accepts two arguments for the desired precision p and the desired range r of the real number. The default order for the two arguments is (p, r), so if the arguments are specified in that order no keywords are necessary. If they are specified out of order or if only the range is specified, then the keywords must be used. Examples of legal uses of the function include

```
kind_num = SELECTED_REAL_KIND(13,100)
kind_num = SELECTED_REAL_KIND(13)
kind_num = SELECTED_REAL_KIND(r=100,p=13)
kind_num = SELECTED_REAL_KIND(r=100)
```

EXAMPLE 8–1 Finding the Extreme Values in a Data Set: Suppose that we want to write a subroutine that searches through a real array to locate the minimum and/or maximum values in the array and the locations where the minimum and/or maximum values occur. This subroutine could be used in many different applications. On some occasions we might be looking for only the maximum value in the array. At other times we might only care about the minimum value. On still other occasions we might be interested in both values (for example, if we were setting the limits on a plotting program). Sometimes we will care where the extreme values occur within an array, and other times it will not matter.

To accommodate all these possibilities in a single subroutine, we will write a subroutine that has four optional output arguments: the maximum value, the location of the maximum value, the minimum value, and the location of the minimum value. The values returned will depend on the arguments the user specifies in the subroutine call.

SOLUTION

The subroutine shown in Figure 8–5 can return from one to four optional results in any possible combination. Note that the subroutine is placed inside a module because it must have an explicit interface in order to support optional arguments.

FIGURE 8–5

A subroutine to locate the extreme values in a real array. The subroutine is embedded in a module to make its interface explicit.

```
MODULE procs

CONTAINS
    SUBROUTINE extremes(a, n, maxval, pos_maxval, minval, pos_minval)
    !
    ! Purpose:
    !   To find the maximum and minimum values in an array and
    !   the location of those values in the array.  This subroutine
    !   returns its output values in optional arguments.
```

(continued)

(continued)

```
!
! Record of revisions:
!    Date        Programmer          Description of change
!    ====        ==========          =====================
!  12/31/95    S. J. Chapman         Original code
!
IMPLICIT NONE

! List of calling arguments:
INTEGER, INTENT(IN) :: n                          ! # vals in array a
REAL, INTENT(IN), DIMENSION(n) :: a               ! Input data.
REAL, INTENT(OUT), OPTIONAL :: maxval             ! Maximum value.
INTEGER, INTENT(OUT), OPTIONAL :: pos_maxval      ! Pos of maxval
REAL, INTENT(OUT), OPTIONAL :: minval             ! Minimum value.
INTEGER, INTENT(OUT), OPTIONAL :: pos_minval      ! Pos of minval

! List of local variables:
INTEGER :: i                          ! Index
REAL :: real_max                      ! Max value
INTEGER :: pos_max                    ! Pos of max value
REAL :: real_min                      ! Min value
INTEGER :: pos_min                    ! Pos of min value

! Initialize the values to first value in array.
real_max = a(1)
pos_max = 1
real_min = a(1)
pos_min = 1

! Find the extreme values in a(2) through a(n).
DO i = 2, n
   max: IF ( a(i) > real_max ) THEN
      real_max = a(i)
      pos_max = i
   END IF max
   min: IF ( a(i) < real_min ) THEN
      real_min = a(i)
      pos_min = i
   END IF min
END DO

! Report the results
IF ( PRESENT(maxval) ) THEN
   maxval = real_max
END IF
   IF ( PRESENT(pos_maxval) ) THEN
   pos_maxval = pos_max
END IF
IF ( PRESENT(minval) ) THEN
   minval = real_min
END IF
IF ( PRESENT(pos_minval) ) THEN
   pos_minval = pos_min
END IF
```

(continued)

(concluded)
```
    END SUBROUTINE extremes
END MODULE procs
```

You will be asked to verify the proper operation of this subroutine in exercise 8–8 at the end of this chapter.

Quiz 8–1

This quiz provides a quick check to see if you understand the concepts introduced in sections 8.1 through 8.3. If you have trouble with the quiz, reread the sections, ask your instructor, or discuss the material with a fellow student. The answers to this quiz appear in Appendix F.

1. What are the major differences between an internal subroutine and an external subroutine? When should you use an internal subroutine?

2. What are recursive procedures? How are they declared?

3. Is the following function legal or illegal? Why?

```
RECURSIVE FUNCTION sum_1_n(n) RESULT(sum)
IMPLICIT NONE
INTEGER, INTENT(IN) :: n
INTEGER :: sum_1_n
IF ( n > 1 ) THEN
    sum = n + sum_1_n(n-1)
ELSE
    sum = 1
END IF
END FUNCTION
```

4. What are keyword arguments? What requirement(s) must be met before they can be used? Why would you want to use a keyword argument?

5. What are optional arguments? What requirement(s) must be met before they can be used? Why would you want to use an optional argument?

■ 8.4

GENERIC PROCEDURES

The Fortran 90/95 language includes both generic and specific intrinsic functions. A **generic function** is a function that can operate properly with many different types of input data, while a **specific function** is a function that requires one specific type of input data. For example, Fortran includes a generic function ABS() to take the absolute value of a number. It can function with integer data, single-precision real data, double-precision real data, or complex data. The language also includes the specific functions IABS(), which requires an integer input value; ABS(), which requires a single-precision real input value; DABS(), which requires a double-precision real input value; and CABS() which requires a complex input value.

Now for a little secret: The generic function ABS() does not actually exist anywhere within a Fortran compiler. Instead, whenever the compiler encounters the generic function, it examines the arguments of the function and invokes the appropriate specific function for those arguments. For example, if the compiler detects the generic function ABS(-34) in a program, it will generate a call to the specific function IABS() because the calling argument of the function is an integer. When we use generic functions, we are allowing the compiler to do some of the detail work for us.

8.4.1 User-Defined Generic Procedures

Fortran 90/95 allows us to define our own generic procedures in addition to the standard ones built into the compiler. For example, we might want to define a generic subroutine sort that sorts integer data, single-precision real data, double-precision real data, or character data, depending on the arguments supplied to it. We could use that generic subroutine in our programs instead of worrying about the specific details of the calling arguments each time that we want to sort a data set.

We can achieve this type of flexibility by placing the specific procedures to be included in the generic procedure into a module and adding a **generic interface block** to the module. The form of a generic interface block is

```
INTERFACE generic_name
    MODULE PROCEDURE specific_procedure_1
    MODULE PROCEDURE specific_procedure_2
    ...
END INTERFACE
```

When the compiler encounters the generic procedure name in a program unit using the module that defines the generic procedure, it will examine the arguments associated with the call to the generic procedure to decide which of the specific procedures it should use.

In order for the compiler to determine which specific procedure to use, each of the specific procedures in the block must be *unambiguously* distinguished from the others. For example, one specific procedure might have real input data while another one has integer input data. The compiler can then compare the generic procedure's calling sequence to the calling sequences of each specific procedure to decide which one to use. The following rules apply to the specific procedures in a generic interface block:

1. Either all the procedures in a generic interface block must be subroutines or all the procedures in the block must be functions. They cannot be mixed, because the generic procedure being defined must either be a subroutine or a function—it cannot be both.
2. Every procedure in the block must be distinguishable from all other procedures in the block by the type, number, and position of its non-optional arguments. As long as each procedure is distinguishable from all other procedures in the block, the compiler will

be able to decide which procedure to use by comparing the type, number, and position of the generic procedure's calling arguments with the type, number, and position of each specific procedure's dummy arguments.

Good Programming Practice
Use generic interface blocks to define procedures that can function with different types of input data. Generic procedures will add to the flexibility of your programs, making it easier for them to handle different types of data.

As an example, suppose that a programmer has written the following four subroutines to sort data into ascending order:

Subroutine	Function
SUBROUTINE sorti (array, nvals)	Sorts integer data.
SUBROUTINE sortr (array, nvals)	Sorts single-precision real data.
SUBROUTINE sortd (array, nvals)	Sorts double-precision real data.
SUBROUTINE sortc (array, nvals)	Sorts character data.

Now he or she wishes to create a generic subroutine sort to sort any of these types of data into ascending order. This can be done by placing the four subroutines into a module and adding a generic interface block as shown:

```
MODULE my_sort
IMPLICIT NONE

! Generic interface block
INTERFACE sort
    MODULE PROCEDURE sorti
    MODULE PROCEDURE sortr
    MODULE PROCEDURE sortd
    MODULE PROCEDURE sortc
END INTERFACE

CONTAINS
    (Add subroutines here)

END MODULE
```

This generic procedure satisfies the requirements stated earlier because all the procedures are subroutines and they can be distinguished from one another by the type of the array in their calling sequences.

EXAMPLE 8–2 *Creating a Generic Subroutine:* Create a subroutine maxval that returns the maximum value in an array and optionally the location of that maximum value. This subroutine should work correctly for integer, single-precision real, double-precision real, single-precision complex, or double-precision complex data. Since relational comparisons of complex data values are meaningless, the complex versions of the subroutine should look for the maximum absolute value in the array.

SOLUTION

We will produce a generic subroutine that can work with five types of input data, so in fact we must create five different subroutines and relate them together using a generic interface block. Note that the subroutines must have an explicit interface in order to support optional arguments, so they will all be placed in a module.

1. **State the problem.**

Write a generic subroutine to find the maximum value in an array and optionally the location of that maximum value. The subroutine should work for integer, single-precision real, double-precision real, single-precision complex, or double-precision complex data. For complex data, the comparisons should be based on the magnitude of the values in the array.

2. **Define the inputs and outputs.**

This problem contains five subroutines. The input to each subroutine will be an array of values of the appropriate type plus the number of values in the array. The outputs will be as follows:

1. A variable containing the maximum value in the input array.
2. An optional integer variable containing the offset in the array at which the maximum value occurred.

The types of the input and output arguments for each subroutine are specified in the following table:

Specific name	Input array type	Array length type	Output maximum value	Optional location of max value
maxval_i	integer	integer	integer	integer
maxval_r	single-precision real	integer	single-precision real	integer
maxval_d	double-precision real	integer	double-precision real	integer
maxval_c	single-precision complex	integer	single-precision real	integer
maxval_dc	double-precision complex	integer	double-precision real	integer

3. **Describe the algorithm.**

The pseudocode for the first three specific subroutines is identical:

```
! Initialize "value_max" to a(1) and "pos_max" to 1.
value_max ← a(1)
```

```
       pos_max ← 1

       ! Find the maximum values in a(2) through a(nvals)
       DO for i = 2 to nvals
          IF a(i) > value_max THEN
             value_max ← a(i)
             pos_max ← i
          END of IF
       END of DO

       ! Report results
       IF argument pos_maxval is present THEN
          pos_maxval ← pos_max
       END of IF
```

The pseudocode for the two complex subroutines is slightly different because comparisons must be with the absolute values:

```
       ! Initialize "value_max" to ABS(a(1)) and "pos_max" to 1.
       value_max ← ABS(a(1))
       pos_max ← 1

       ! Find the maximum values in a(2) through a(nvals)
       DO for i = 2 to nvals
          IF ABS(a(i)) > value_max THEN
             value_max ← ABS(a(i))
             pos_max ← i
          END of IF
       END of DO

       ! Report results
       IF argument pos_maxval is present THEN
          pos_maxval ← pos_max
       END of IF
```

4. **Turn the algorithm into Fortran statements.**

The resulting Fortran subroutine is shown in Figure 8–6.

FIGURE 8–6
A generic subroutine `maxval` that finds the maximum value in an array and optionally the location of that maximum value.

```
MODULE generic_maxval
!
! Purpose:
!   To produce a generic procedure maxval that returns the
!   maximum value in an array and optionally the location
!   of that maximum value for the following input data types:
!   integer, single-precision real, double-precision real,
!   single-precision complex, and double-precision complex.
!   Complex comparisons are done on the absolute values of
!   values in the input array.
!
! Record of revisions:
!    Date         Programmer              Description of change
```

(continued)

(continued)

```
!     ====        ==========              =====================
!   01/03/96    S. J. Chapman             Original code
!
IMPLICIT NONE

! Declare parameters:
INTEGER, PARAMETER :: sgl = SELECTED_REAL_KIND(p=6)
INTEGER, PARAMETER :: dbl = SELECTED_REAL_KIND(p=13)

! Declare generic interface.
INTERFACE maxval
   MODULE PROCEDURE maxval_i
   MODULE PROCEDURE maxval_r
   MODULE PROCEDURE maxval_d
   MODULE PROCEDURE maxval_c
   MODULE PROCEDURE maxval_dc
END INTERFACE

CONTAINS
   SUBROUTINE maxval_i ( array, nvals, value_max, pos_maxval )
   IMPLICIT NONE

   ! List of calling arguments:
   INTEGER, INTENT(IN) :: nvals                         ! # vals
   INTEGER, INTENT(IN), DIMENSION(nvals) :: array    ! Input data
   INTEGER, INTENT(OUT) :: value_max                 ! Max value
   INTEGER, INTENT(OUT), OPTIONAL :: pos_maxval      ! Position

   ! List of local variables:
   INTEGER :: i                                  ! Index
   INTEGER :: pos_max                            ! Pos of max value

   ! Initialize the values to first value in array.
   value_max = array(1)
   pos_max = 1

   ! Find the extreme values in array(2) through array(nvals).
   DO i = 2, nvals
      IF ( array(i) > value_max ) THEN
         value_max = array(i)
         pos_max = i
      END IF
   END DO

   ! Report the results
   IF ( PRESENT(pos_maxval) ) THEN
      pos_maxval = pos_max
   END IF

   END SUBROUTINE maxval_i

   SUBROUTINE maxval_r ( array, nvals, value_max, pos_maxval )
   IMPLICIT NONE

   ! List of calling arguments:
   INTEGER, INTENT(IN) :: nvals
```

(continued)

(continued)

```
      REAL(KIND=sgl), INTENT(IN), DIMENSION(nvals) :: array
      REAL(KIND=sgl), INTENT(OUT) :: value_max
      INTEGER, INTENT(OUT), OPTIONAL :: pos_maxval

      ! List of local variables:
      INTEGER :: i                                      ! Index
      INTEGER :: pos_max                                ! Pos of max value

      ! Initialize the values to first value in array.
      value_max = array(1)
      pos_max = 1

      ! Find the extreme values in array(2) through array(nvals).
      DO i = 2, nvals
         IF ( array(i) > value_max ) THEN
            value_max = array(i)
            pos_max = i
         END IF
      END DO

      ! Report the results
      IF ( PRESENT(pos_maxval) ) THEN
         pos_maxval = pos_max
      END IF

      END SUBROUTINE maxval_r

      SUBROUTINE maxval_d ( array, nvals, value_max, pos_maxval )
      IMPLICIT NONE

      ! List of calling arguments:
      INTEGER, INTENT(IN) :: nvals
      REAL(KIND=dbl), INTENT(IN), DIMENSION(nvals) :: array
      REAL(KIND=dbl), INTENT(OUT) :: value_max
      INTEGER, INTENT(OUT), OPTIONAL :: pos_maxval

      ! List of local variables:
      INTEGER :: i                                      ! Index
      INTEGER :: pos_max                                ! Pos of max value

      ! Initialize the values to first value in array.
      value_max = array(1)
      pos_max = 1

      ! Find the extreme values in array(2) through array(nvals).
      DO i = 2, nvals
         IF ( array(i) > value_max ) THEN
            value_max = array(i)
            pos_max = i
         END IF
      END DO

      ! Report the results
      IF ( PRESENT(pos_maxval) ) THEN
         pos_maxval = pos_max
      END IF
```

(continued)

(continued)
```
      END SUBROUTINE maxval_d

      SUBROUTINE maxval_c ( array, nvals, value_max, pos_maxval )
      IMPLICIT NONE

      ! List of calling arguments:
      INTEGER, INTENT(IN) :: nvals
      COMPLEX(KIND=sgl), INTENT(IN), DIMENSION(nvals) :: array
      REAL(KIND=sgl), INTENT(OUT) :: value_max
      INTEGER, INTENT(OUT), OPTIONAL :: pos_maxval

      ! List of local variables:
      INTEGER :: i                              ! Index
      INTEGER :: pos_max                        ! Pos of max value

      ! Initialize the values to first value in array.
      value_max = ABS(array(1))
      pos_max = 1

      ! Find the extreme values in array(2) through array(nvals).
      DO i = 2, nvals
         IF ( ABS(array(i)) > value_max ) THEN
            value_max = ABS(array(i))
            pos_max = i
         END IF
      END DO

      ! Report the results
      IF ( PRESENT(pos_maxval) ) THEN
         pos_maxval = pos_max
      END IF

      END SUBROUTINE maxval_c

      SUBROUTINE maxval_dc ( array, nvals, value_max, pos_maxval )
      IMPLICIT NONE

      ! List of calling arguments:
      INTEGER, INTENT(IN) :: nvals
      COMPLEX(KIND=dbl), INTENT(IN), DIMENSION(nvals) :: array
      REAL(KIND=dbl), INTENT(OUT) :: value_max
      INTEGER, INTENT(OUT), OPTIONAL :: pos_maxval

      !  List of local variables:
      INTEGER :: i                              ! Index
      INTEGER :: pos_max                        ! Pos of max value

      ! Initialize the values to first value in array.
      value_max = ABS(array(1))
      pos_max = 1

      ! Find the extreme values in array(2) through array(nvals).
      DO i = 2, nvals
         IF ( ABS(array(i)) > value_max ) THEN
            value_max = ABS(array(i))
```

(continued)

(concluded)

```
            pos_max = i
        END IF
    END DO

    ! Report the results
    IF ( PRESENT(pos_maxval) ) THEN
        pos_maxval = pos_max
    END IF

    END SUBROUTINE maxval_dc

END MODULE generic_maxval
```

5. Test the resulting Fortran programs.

To test this generic subroutine, we must write a test driver program to call the subroutine with the five types of data that it supports and to display the results. The test driver program will also illustrate the use of keyword and optional arguments by calling the subroutine with different combinations and orders of arguments. Figure 8–7 shows an appropriate test driver program.

FIGURE 8–7

Test driver program for generic subroutine `maxval`.

```
PROGRAM test_maxval
!
! Purpose:
!   To test the generic subroutine maxval with five types
!   of input data sets.
!
! Record of revisions:
!     Date        Programmer          Description of change
!     ====        ==========          =====================
!   01/03/96    S. J. Chapman         Original code
!
USE generic_maxval
IMPLICIT NONE

! List of variables:
INTEGER, DIMENSION(6) :: array_i                    ! Integer array
REAL(KIND=single), DIMENSION(6) :: array_r          ! Sng-prec real arr
REAL(KIND=double), DIMENSION(6) :: array_d          ! Dbl-prec real arr
COMPLEX(KIND=single), DIMENSION(6) :: array_c       ! Sng-prec cx arr
COMPLEX(KIND=double), DIMENSION(6) :: array_dc      ! Sng-prec cx arr
INTEGER :: value_max_i                              ! Max value
REAL(KIND=single) :: value_max_r                    ! Max value
REAL(KIND=double) :: value_max_d                    ! Max value
INTEGER :: pos_maxval                               ! Pos of max value

! Initialize arrays
```

(continued)

```fortran
(concluded)
array_i  = (/ -13,   3,   2,   0,   25,   -2   /)
array_r  = (/ -13., 3., 2., 0., 25., -2. /)
array_d  = (/ -13._double, 3._double, 2._double, 0._double, &
             25._double, -2._double /)
array_c  = (/ (1.,2.), (-4.,-6.), (4.,-7), (3.,4.), &
             (0.,1.), (6.,-8.) /)
array_dc = (/ (1._double,2._double), (-4._double,-6._double), &
             (4._double,-7._double), (3._double,4._double), &
             (0._double,1._double), (6._double,-8._double) /)

! Test integer subroutine.  Include optional argument.
CALL maxval ( array_i, 6, value_max_i, pos_maxval )
WRITE (*,1000) value_max_i, pos_maxval
1000 FORMAT (' Integer args: max value = ',I3, &
            '; position = ', I3 )

! Test single-prec real subroutine.  Leave out optional arg.
CALL maxval ( array_r, 6, value_max_r )
WRITE (*,1010) value_max_r
1010 FORMAT (' Single prec real args: max value = ',F7.3)

! Test double-prec real subroutine.  Use keywords.
CALL maxval ( ARRAY=array_d, NVALS=6, VALUE_MAX=value_max_d )
WRITE (*,1020) value_max_d
1020 FORMAT (' Double prec real args: max value = ',F7.3)

! Test single-prec complex subroutine.  Use scrambled keywords.
CALL maxval ( NVALS=6, ARRAY=array_c, VALUE_MAX=value_max_r, &
              POS_MAXVAL=pos_maxval )
WRITE (*,1030) value_max_r, pos_maxval
1030 FORMAT (' Single-precision complex args:' &
            ' max abs value = ',F7.3, &
            '; position = ', I3 )

! Test double-prec complex subroutine.  Leave out optional arg.
CALL maxval ( array_dc, 6, value_max_d )
WRITE (*,1040) value_max_r
1040 FORMAT (' Double precision complex args:' &
            ' max abs value = ',F7.3 )

END PROGRAM
```

When the test driver program is executed, the results are

```
C>test_maxval
Integer arguments: max value =   25;  position =  5
Single-precision real arguments: max value =   25.000
Double-precision real arguments: max value =   25.000
Single-precision complex arguments: max abs value =  10.000; position =  6
Double-precision complex arguments: max abs value =  10.000
```

It is obvious from inspection that the subroutine picked out the proper maximum values and locations for each data type.

■ 8.5

EXTENDING Fortran WITH USER-DEFINED OPERATORS AND ASSIGNMENTS

When you were introduced to derived data types in Chapter 7, you learned that none of the intrinsic unary and binary operators are defined for derived data types. In fact, the only operation that was defined for derived data types was the assignment of one item of a derived data type to another variable of the same type. You were able to work freely with the *components* of derived data types, but not with the derived data types themselves. This serious limitation reduces the usefulness of derived data types.

Fortunately, there is a way around this limitation. Fortran 90/95 is an *extensible* language, which means that an individual programmer can add new features to it to accommodate special types of problems. The first examples of this extensibility were derived data types themselves. In addition, Fortran permits the programmer to define new unary and binary operators for both intrinsic and derived data types and to define new extensions to standard operators for derived data types. With appropriate definitions, the Fortran language can be made to add, subtract, multiply, divide, compare, etc. two operators of a derived data type.

How can we define new operators or extend existing ones? The first step is to write a function that performs the desired task and place it into a module. For example, if we want to add two values of a derived data type, we would first create a function whose arguments are the two values to be added and whose result is the sum of the two values. The function will implement the instructions required to perform the addition. The next step is to associate the function with a user-defined or intrinsic operator using an **interface operator block.** The form of an interface operator block is

```
INTERFACE OPERATOR (operator_symbol)
   MODULE PROCEDURE function_1
   ...
END INTERFACE
```

where *operator_symbol* is any standard intrinsic operator (e.g., +, -, *, /, >, <), or any user-defined operator. A user-defined operator is a sequence of up to 31 letters surrounded by periods. (Numbers and underscore characters are not allowed in an operator name.) For example, a user-defined operator might be named .INVERSE. Each function *must* have an explicit interface.

More than one function can be associated with the same operator symbol, but the functions must be distinguishable from one another by having different types of dummy arguments. When the compiler encounters the operator symbol in a program, it invokes the function whose dummy arguments match the operands associated with the operator symbol. If no associated function has dummy arguments that match the operands, then a compilation error results.

If the function associated with an operator has two dummy arguments, then the resulting operator will be a binary operator. If the function has only one dummy argument, then the operator will be a unary operator. Once defined, the operator will be treated as a reference to the function. For binary operations, the left-hand operand will become the first argument of the function and the right-hand operand will become the second argument of the function. The function must not modify its calling arguments. To ensure this condition, it is customary to declare all function arguments with `INTENT(IN)`.

If the operator being defined by the interface is one of Fortran's intrinsic operators then we must consider two additional constraints:

1. It is not possible to change the meaning of an intrinsic operator for predefined intrinsic data types. For example, it is not possible to change the meaning of the addition operator (+) when it is applied to two integers. It is possible to *extend* the meaning of the operator only by defining the actions to perform when the operator is applied to derived data types or to combinations of derived data types and intrinsic data types.
2. The number of arguments in a function must be consistent with the normal use of the operator. For example, multiplication (*) is a binary operator, so any function extending its meaning must have two arguments.

It is possible to extend the meaning of the assignment operator (=) in a similar fashion. To define extended meanings for the assignment operator, we use an **interface assignment block:**

```
INTERFACE ASSIGNMENT (=)
    MODULE PROCEDURE subroutine_1
    ...
END INTERFACE
```

For an assignment operator, the interface body must refer to a *subroutine* instead of a function. The subroutine must have two arguments. The first argument is the output of the assignment statement and must have `INTENT(OUT)`. The second dummy argument is the input to the assignment statement and must have `INTENT(IN)`. The first argument corresponds to the left side of the assignment statement, and the second argument corresponds to the right side of the assignment statement.

More than one subroutine can be associated with the assignment symbol, but the subroutines must be distinguishable from one another by having different types of dummy arguments. When the compiler encounters the assignment symbol in a program, it invokes the subroutine whose dummy arguments match the types of the values on either side of the equal sign. If no associated subroutine has dummy arguments that match the values, then a compilation error results.

Good Programming Practice

Use interface operator blocks and interface assignment blocks to create new operators and to extend the meanings of existing operators to work with derived data types. Once proper operators are defined, working with derived data types can be very easy.

The best way to explain the use of user-defined operators and assignments is by an example. We will now define a new derived data type and create appropriate user-defined operations and assignments for it.

EXAMPLE 8–3 Vectors: The study of the dynamics of objects in motion in three dimensions is an important area of engineering. In the study of dynamics, the position and velocity of objects, forces, torques, and so forth are usually represented by three-component vectors $\mathbf{v} = x\,\hat{\mathbf{i}} + y\,\hat{\mathbf{j}} + z\,\hat{\mathbf{k}}$, where the three components (x, y, z) represent the projection of the vector $\mathbf{v}$ along the x-, y-, and z-axes, respectively, and $\hat{\mathbf{i}}$, $\hat{\mathbf{j}}$, and $\hat{\mathbf{k}}$ are the unit vectors along the x-, y-, and z-axes (see Figure 8–8). The solutions of many mechanical problems involve manipulating these vectors in specific ways.

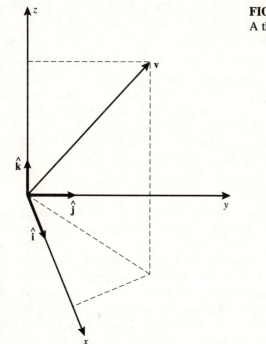

FIGURE 8–8
A three-dimensional vector.

The most common operations performed on these vectors follow.

1. **Addition.** Two vectors are added together by separately adding their x, y, and z components. If $\mathbf{v}_1 = x_1\,\hat{\mathbf{i}} + y_1\,\hat{\mathbf{j}} + z_1\,\hat{\mathbf{k}}$ and $\mathbf{v}_2 = x_2\,\hat{\mathbf{i}} + y_2\,\hat{\mathbf{j}} + z_2\,\hat{\mathbf{k}}$, then $\mathbf{v}_1 + \mathbf{v}_2 = (x_1 + x_2)\hat{\mathbf{i}} + (y_1 + y_2)\hat{\mathbf{j}} + (z_1 + z_2)\hat{\mathbf{k}}$.

2. **Subtraction.** Two vectors are subtracted by separately subtracting their x, y, and z components. If $\mathbf{v}_1 = x_1\,\hat{\mathbf{i}} + y_1\,\hat{\mathbf{j}} + z_1\,\hat{\mathbf{k}}$ and $\mathbf{v}_2 = x_2\,\hat{\mathbf{i}} + y_2\,\hat{\mathbf{j}} + z_2\,\hat{\mathbf{k}}$, then $\mathbf{v}_1 - \mathbf{v}_2 = (x_1 - x_2)\hat{\mathbf{i}} + (y_1 - y_2)\hat{\mathbf{j}} + (z_1 - z_2)\hat{\mathbf{k}}$.

3. **Multiplication by a scalar.** A vector is multiplied by a scalar by separately multiplying each component by the scalar. If $\mathbf{v} = x\,\hat{\mathbf{i}} + y\,\hat{\mathbf{j}} + z\,\hat{\mathbf{k}}$, then $a\mathbf{v} = ax\,\hat{\mathbf{i}} + ay\,\hat{\mathbf{j}} + az\,\hat{\mathbf{k}}$.

4. **Division by a scalar.** A vector is divided by a scalar by separately dividing each component by the scalar. If $\mathbf{v} = x\,\hat{\mathbf{i}} + y\,\hat{\mathbf{j}} + z\,\hat{\mathbf{k}}$, then $\dfrac{\mathbf{v}}{a} = \dfrac{x}{a}\,\hat{\mathbf{i}} + \dfrac{y}{a}\,\hat{\mathbf{j}} + \dfrac{z}{a}\,\hat{\mathbf{k}}$.

5. **The dot product.** The dot product of two vectors is one form of multiplication operation performed on vectors. It produces a scalar that is the sum of the products of the vector's components. If $\mathbf{v}_1 = x_1\,\hat{\mathbf{i}} + y_1\,\hat{\mathbf{j}} + z_1\,\hat{\mathbf{k}}$ and $\mathbf{v}_2 = x_2\,\hat{\mathbf{i}} + y_2\,\hat{\mathbf{j}} + z_2\,\hat{\mathbf{k}}$, then the dot product of the vectors is $\mathbf{v}_1 \cdot \mathbf{v}_2 = x_1 x_2 + y_1 y_2 + z_1 z_2$.

6. **The cross product.** The cross product is another multiplication operation that appears frequently between vectors. The cross product of two vectors is another vector whose direction is perpendicular to the plane formed by the two input vectors. If $\mathbf{v}_1 = x_1\,\hat{\mathbf{i}} + y_1\,\hat{\mathbf{j}} + z_1\,\hat{\mathbf{k}}$ and $\mathbf{v}_2 = x_2\,\hat{\mathbf{i}} + y_2\,\hat{\mathbf{j}} + z_2\,\hat{\mathbf{k}}$, then the cross product of the two vectors is defined as $\mathbf{v}_1 \times \mathbf{v}_2 = (y_1 z_2 - y_2 z_1)\hat{\mathbf{i}} + (z_1 x_2 - z_2 x_1)\hat{\mathbf{j}} + (x_1 y_2 - x_2 y_1)\hat{\mathbf{k}}$.

Create a derived data type called `vector`, having three components x, y, and z. Define functions to create vectors from arrays, to convert vectors to arrays, and to perform the six vector operations defined above. Extend the intrinsic operators +, -, *, and / to have valid meanings when working with vectors and create a new operator `.DOT.` for the dot product of two vectors. Finally, extend the assignment operator (=) to allow three-element arrays to be assigned to vectors and to allow vectors to be assigned to three-element arrays.

Solution

To make it easy to work with vectors, we should place the definition of the data type, the manipulating functions, and the operator definitions in a single module. Any programs wanting to manipulate vectors can then use that one module.

Note that six operations were defined for vectors, but more than six functions must be written to implement them. For example, the multiplication of a vector by a scalar could occur in either order: vector times scalar or scalar times vector. Both orders produce the same result, but the order of command-line arguments for an implementing function is different in either case. Also, a scalar could be either an integer or a single-precision real number. To allow for all four possibilities (either order and either type of scalar), we actually have to write four functions!

1. State the problem.

Create a derived data type called `vector`, having three single-precision real components x, y, and z. Write the following functions and subroutines for manipulating vectors:

1. Create a vector from a three-element single-precision real array.
2. Convert a vector into a three-element single-precision real array.

3. Add two vectors.
4. Subtract two vectors.
5. Multiply a single-precision real scalar by a vector.
6. Multiply a vector by a single-precision real scalar.
7. Multiply an integer scalar by a vector.
8. Multiply a vector by an integer scalar.
9. Divide a vector by a single-precision real scalar.
10. Divide a vector by an integer scalar.
11. Calculate the dot product of two vectors.
12. Calculate the cross product of two vectors.

Associate these functions and subroutines with the appropriate operators using the interface operator constructs and interface assignment constructs.

2. **Define the inputs and outputs.**

Each of the procedures described in step 1 has its own inputs and outputs. The types of the input and output arguments for each function are specified in the following table:

Specific function / subroutine name	Input argument 1 type	Input argument 2 type	Output type
array_to_vector (subroutine)	three-element single-precision real array	N/A	vector
vector_to_array (subroutine)	vector	N/A	three-element single-precision real array
vector_add	vector	vector	vector
vector_subtract	vector	vector	vector
vector_times_real	vector	single-precision real	vector
real_times_vector	single-precision real	vector	vector
vector_times_int	vector	integer	vector
int_times_vector	integer	vector	vector
vector_div_real	vector	single-precision real	vector
vector_div_int	vector	integer	vector
dot_product	vector	vector	single-precision real
cross_product	vector	vector	vector

3. **Describe the algorithm.**

The following definitions apply in the pseudocode for the preceding routines:

1. `vec_1`   First input argument (vector).

2. `vec_2`   Second input argument (vector).

3. `real_1`   First input argument (single-precision real).

4. `real_2`   Second input argument (single-precision real).

5. `int_1`   First input argument (integer).

6. `int_2`   Second input argument (integer).

7. `array`   Input argument (single-precision real array).

8. `vec_result`   Function result (vector).

9. `real_result`   Function result (single-precision real).

10. `array_result` Function result (single-precision real array).

Given these definitions, the pseudocode for the `array_to_vector` subroutine is

```
vec_result%x ← array(1)
vec_result%y ← array(2)
vec_result%z ← array(3)
```

The pseudocode for the `vector_to_array` subroutine is

```
array_result(1) ← vec_1%x
array_result(2) ← vec_1%y
array_result(3) ← vec_1%z
```

The pseudocode for the `vector_add` function is

```
vec_result%x ← vec_1%x + vec_2%x
vec_result%y ← vec_1%y + vec_2%y
vec_result%z ← vec_1%z + vec_2%z
```

The pseudocode for the `vector_subtract` function is

```
vec_result%x ← vec_1%x - vec_2%x
vec_result%y ← vec_1%y - vec_2%y
vec_result%z ← vec_1%z - vec_2%z
```

The pseudocode for the `vector_times_real` function is

```
vec_result%x ← vec_1%x * real_2
vec_result%y ← vec_1%y * real_2
vec_result%z ← vec_1%z * real_2
```

The pseudocode for the `real_times_vector` function is

```
vec_result%x ← real_1 * vec_2%x
vec_result%y ← real_1 * vec_2%y
vec_result%z ← real_1 * vec_2%z
```

The pseudocode for the `vector_times_int` function is

```
vec_result%x ← vec_1%x * REAL(int_2)
vec_result%y ← vec_1%y * REAL(int_2)
vec_result%z ← vec_1%z * REAL(int_2)
```

The pseudocode for the `int_times_vector` function is

```
vec_result%x ← REAL(int_1) * vec_2%x
vec_result%y ← REAL(int_1) * vec_2%y
vec_result%z ← REAL(int_1) * vec_2%z
```

The pseudocode for the `vector_div_real` function is

```
vec_result%x ← vec_1%x / real_2
vec_result%y ← vec_1%y / real_2
vec_result%z ← vec_1%z / real_2
```

The pseudocode for the `vector_div_int` function is

```
vec_result%x ← vec_1%x / REAL(int_2)
vec_result%y ← vec_1%y / REAL(int_2)
vec_result%z ← vec_1%z / REAL(int_2)
```

The pseudocode for the `dot_product` function is

```
real_result ← vec_1%x*vec_2%x + vec_1%y*vec_2%y + vec_1%z*vec_2%z
```

The pseudocode for the `cross_product` function is

```
vec_result%x ← vec_1%y*vec_2%z - vec_1%z*vec_2%y
vec_result%y ← vec_1%z*vec_2%x - vec_1%x*vec_2%z
vec_result%z ← vec_1%x*vec_2%y - vec_1%y*vec_2%x
```

These twelve functions will be assigned to operators in interface operator and interface assignment blocks as follows:

Function	Operator
array_to_vector	=
vector_to_array	=
vector_add	+
vector_subtract	-
vector_times_real	*
real_times_vector	*
vector_times_int	*
int_times_vector	*
vector_div_real	/
vector_div_int	/
dot_product	.DOT.
cross_product	*

4. **Turn the algorithm into Fortran statements.**

   The resulting Fortran module is shown in Figure 8–9.

FIGURE 8–9
A module to create a derived data type `vector` and to define mathematical operations
that can be performed on values of type `vector`.

```
MODULE vectors
!
! Purpose:
!   To define a derived data type called vector and the
!   operations that can be performed on it.  The module
!   defines eight operations that can be performed on vectors:
!
!                       Operation                    Operator
!                       =========                    ========
!     1.  Creation from a real array                    =
!     2.  Conversion to real array                      =
!     3.  Vector addition                               +
!     4.  Vector subtraction                            -
!     5.  Vector-scalar multiplication (4 cases)        *
!     6.  Vector-scalar division (2 cases)              /
!     7.  Dot product                                 .DOT.
!     8.  Cross product                                 *
!
!   It contains a total of 12 procedures to implement those
!   operations:  array_to_vector, vector_to_array, vector_add,
!   vector_subtract, vector_times_real, real_times_vector,
!   vector_times_int, int_times_vector, vector_div_real,
!   vector_div_int, dot_product, and cross_product.
!
! Record of revisions:
!     Date          Programmer            Description of change
!     ====          ==========            =====================
!   01/05/96     S. J. Chapman            Original code
!
IMPLICIT NONE

! Declare vector data type:
TYPE :: vector
   REAL :: x
   REAL :: y
   REAL :: z
END TYPE

! Declare interface operators
INTERFACE ASSIGNMENT (=)
   MODULE PROCEDURE array_to_vector
   MODULE PROCEDURE vector_to_array
END INTERFACE

INTERFACE OPERATOR (+)
   MODULE PROCEDURE vector_add
END INTERFACE
```

(continued)

```
(continued)
INTERFACE OPERATOR (-)
   MODULE PROCEDURE vector_subtract
END INTERFACE

INTERFACE OPERATOR (*)
   MODULE PROCEDURE vector_times_real
   MODULE PROCEDURE real_times_vector
   MODULE PROCEDURE vector_times_int
   MODULE PROCEDURE int_times_vector
   MODULE PROCEDURE cross_product
END INTERFACE

INTERFACE OPERATOR (/)
   MODULE PROCEDURE vector_div_real
   MODULE PROCEDURE vector_div_int
END INTERFACE

INTERFACE OPERATOR (.DOT.)
   MODULE PROCEDURE dot_product
END INTERFACE

! Now define the implementing functions.
CONTAINS
   SUBROUTINE array_to_vector(vec_result, array)
      TYPE (vector), INTENT(OUT) :: vec_result
      REAL, DIMENSION(3), INTENT(IN) :: array
      vec_result%x = array(1)
      vec_result%y = array(2)
      vec_result%z = array(3)
   END SUBROUTINE array_to_vector

   SUBROUTINE vector_to_array(array_result, vec_1)
      REAL, DIMENSION(3), INTENT(OUT) :: array_result
      TYPE (vector), INTENT(IN) :: vec_1
      array_result(1) = vec_1%x
      array_result(2) = vec_1%y
      array_result(3) = vec_1%z
   END SUBROUTINE vector_to_array

   FUNCTION vector_add(vec_1, vec_2)
      TYPE (vector) :: vector_add
      TYPE (vector), INTENT(IN) :: vec_1, vec_2
      vector_add%x = vec_1%x + vec_2%x
      vector_add%y = vec_1%y + vec_2%y
      vector_add%z = vec_1%z + vec_2%z
   END FUNCTION vector_add

   FUNCTION vector_subtract(vec_1, vec_2)
      TYPE (vector) :: vector_subtract
      TYPE (vector), INTENT(IN) :: vec_1, vec_2
      vector_subtract%x = vec_1%x - vec_2%x
      vector_subtract%y = vec_1%y - vec_2%y
      vector_subtract%z = vec_1%z - vec_2%z
   END FUNCTION vector_subtract

   FUNCTION vector_times_real(vec_1, real_2)
```

(continued)

(continued)

```
      TYPE (vector) :: vector_times_real
      TYPE (vector), INTENT(IN) :: vec_1
      REAL, INTENT(IN) :: real_2
      vector_times_real%x = vec_1%x * real_2
      vector_times_real%y = vec_1%y * real_2
      vector_times_real%z = vec_1%z * real_2
   END FUNCTION vector_times_real

   FUNCTION real_times_vector(real_1, vec_2)
      TYPE (vector) :: real_times_vector
      REAL, INTENT(IN) :: real_1
      TYPE (vector), INTENT(IN) :: vec_2
      real_times_vector%x = real_1 * vec_2%x
      real_times_vector%y = real_1 * vec_2%y
      real_times_vector%z = real_1 * vec_2%z
   END FUNCTION real_times_vector

   FUNCTION vector_times_int(vec_1, int_2)
      TYPE (vector) :: vector_times_int
      TYPE (vector), INTENT(IN) :: vec_1
      INTEGER, INTENT(IN) :: int_2
      vector_times_int%x = vec_1%x * REAL(int_2)
      vector_times_int%y = vec_1%y * REAL(int_2)
      vector_times_int%z = vec_1%z * REAL(int_2)
   END FUNCTION vector_times_int

   FUNCTION int_times_vector(int_1, vec_2)
      TYPE (vector) :: int_times_vector
      INTEGER, INTENT(IN) :: int_1
      TYPE (vector), INTENT(IN) :: vec_2
      int_times_vector%x = REAL(int_1) * vec_2%x
      int_times_vector%y = REAL(int_1) * vec_2%y
      int_times_vector%z = REAL(int_1) * vec_2%z
   END FUNCTION int_times_vector

   FUNCTION vector_div_real(vec_1, real_2)
      TYPE (vector) :: vector_div_real
      TYPE (vector), INTENT(IN) :: vec_1
      REAL, INTENT(IN) :: real_2
      vector_div_real%x = vec_1%x / real_2
      vector_div_real%y = vec_1%y / real_2
      vector_div_real%z = vec_1%z / real_2
   END FUNCTION vector_div_real

   FUNCTION vector_div_int(vec_1, int_2)
      TYPE (vector) :: vector_div_int
      TYPE (vector), INTENT(IN) :: vec_1
      INTEGER, INTENT(IN) :: int_2
      vector_div_int%x = vec_1%x / REAL(int_2)
      vector_div_int%y = vec_1%y / REAL(int_2)
      vector_div_int%z = vec_1%z / REAL(int_2)
   END FUNCTION vector_div_int

   FUNCTION dot_product(vec_1, vec_2)
      REAL :: dot_product
      TYPE (vector), INTENT(IN) :: vec_1, vec_2
```

(continued)

```
(concluded)
      dot_product = vec_1%x*vec_2%x + vec_1%y*vec_2%y &
                  + vec_1%z*vec_2%z
   END FUNCTION dot_product

   FUNCTION cross_product(vec_1, vec_2)
      TYPE (vector) :: cross_product
      TYPE (vector), INTENT(IN) :: vec_1, vec_2
      cross_product%x = vec_1%y*vec_2%z - vec_1%z*vec_2%y
      cross_product%y = vec_1%z*vec_2%x - vec_1%x*vec_2%z
      cross_product%z = vec_1%x*vec_2%y - vec_1%y*vec_2%x
   END FUNCTION cross_product

END MODULE vectors
```

5. **Test the resulting Fortran programs.**

   The testing of this data type and its associated operations is left as an exercise to the student (exercise 8–14).

What would happen in a program if we tried to perform an operation with vectors that was not defined in the module? For example, what would happen if we tried to multiply a vector by a double-precision real scalar? A compilation error would result because the compiler does not know how to perform the operation. When defining a new data type and its operations, be careful to define *every* combination of operations that you might wish to use.

■ 8.6
RESTRICTING ACCESS TO THE CONTENTS OF A MODULE

When a module is accessed by USE association, by default all the entities defined within that module become available for use in the program unit containing the USE statement. We have already used this fact to share data between program units, to make procedures with explicit interfaces available to program units, to create new operators, and to extend the meanings of existing operators.

   In Example 8–3 we created a module called vectors to extend the Fortran language. Any program unit that accesses module vectors can define its own vectors and can manipulate them using the binary operators +, -, *, /, and .DOT.. Unfortunately, the program will also be able to invoke such functions as vector_add, vector_subtract, even though it should only be using them indirectly through the use of the defined operators. These procedure names are not needed in any program unit, but they are declared and might conflict with a procedure name defined in the program. A similar problem could occur when many data items are defined within a module, but only a few of them are needed by a particular program unit. All the unnecessary data items will also be available in the program unit, making it possible for a programmer to modify them by mistake.

   In general, you should restrict access to any procedures or data entities in a module to only those program units that must know about them. This process is known as **data**

hiding. The more access is restricted, the less chance there is of a programmer using or modifying an item by mistake. Restricting access makes programs more modular and easier to understand and maintain.

How can we restrict access to the entities in a module? Fortran 90/95 provides a way to control the access to a particular item in a module by program units *outside* that module: the PUBLIC and PRIVATE attributes and statements. If the PUBLIC attribute or statement is specified for an item, then the item will be available to program units outside the module. If the PRIVATE attribute or statement is specified, then the item will not be available to program units outside the module, although procedures inside the module still have access to it. The default attribute for all data and procedures in a module is PUBLIC, so by default any program unit that uses a module can have access to every data item and procedure within it.

We can declare the PUBLIC or PRIVATE status of a data item or procedure in one of two ways: as an attribute in a type definition statement or in an independent Fortran statement. Examples in which the attributes are declared as a part of a type definition statement are

```
INTEGER, PRIVATE :: count
REAL, PUBLIC :: voltage
TYPE (vector), PRIVATE :: scratch_vector
```

We can use this type of declaration for data items and for functions, but not for subroutines. A PUBLIC or PRIVATE statement can also specify the status of data items, functions, and subroutines. The form of a PUBLIC or PRIVATE statement is

```
PUBLIC [::] list of public items
PRIVATE [::] list of private items
```

If a module contains a PRIVATE statement without a list of private items, then by default every data item and procedure in the module is private. Any items that should be public must be explicitly listed in a separate PUBLIC statement. This is the preferred way to design modules, since only the items which are actually required by programs are exposed to them.

> **Good Programming Practice**
> It is good programming practice to hide any module data items or procedures that do not need to be directly accessed by external program units. The best way to do so is to include a PRIVATE statement in each module and then to list the specific items you wish to expose in a separate PUBLIC statement.

As an example of the proper use of data hiding, let's reexamine module vectors from Example 8–3. Programs accessing this module need to define variables of type vector and need to perform operations involving vectors. However, the programs do not need direct access to any of the subroutines or functions in the module. The proper declarations for this circumstance are shown in Figure 8–10.

FIGURE 8–10

The first part of module `vector` now hides all nonessential items from external program units. Changes to the module are shown in bold type.

```
MODULE vectors
!
! Purpose:
!    To define a derived data type called vector and the
!    operations that can be performed on it.  The module
!    defines eight operations that can be performed on vectors:
!
!                         Operation                      Operator
!                         =========                      ========
!       1.  Creation from a real array                      =
!       2.  Conversion to real array                        =
!       3.  Vector addition                                 +
!       4.  Vector subtraction                              -
!       5.  Vector-scalar multiplication (4 cases)          *
!       6.  Vector-scalar division (2 cases)                /
!       7.  Dot product                                   .DOT.
!       8.  Cross product                                   *
!
!    It contains a total of 12 procedures to implement those
!    operations:  array_to_vector, vector_to_array, vector_add,
!    vector_subtract, vector_times_real, real_times_vector,
!    vector_times_int, int_times_vector, vector_div_real,
!    vector_div_int, dot_product, and cross_product.  These
!    procedures are private to the module; they can only be
!    accessed from the outside via the defined operators.
!
! Record of revisions:
!      Date          Programmer            Description of change
!      ====          ==========            =====================
!    01/05/96     S. J. Chapman            Original code
! 1. 01/06/96     S. J. Chapman            Modified to hide non-
!                                              essential items.
!
IMPLICIT NONE

! Declare all items to be private except for type vector and
! the operators defined for it.
PRIVATE
PUBLIC :: vector, assignment(=), operator(+), operator(-), &
          operator(*), operator(/), operator(.DOT.)

! Declare vector data type:
TYPE :: vector
    REAL :: x
    REAL :: y
    REAL :: z
END TYPE
```

Quiz 8–2

This quiz provides a quick check to see if you understand the concepts introduced in sections 8.4 to 8.6. If you have trouble with the quiz, reread the

(continued)

(concluded)

sections, ask your instructor, or discuss the material with a fellow student. The answers to this quiz appear in Appendix F.

1. How is a generic procedure defined?

2. What is a `MODULE PROCEDURE` statement? What is its purpose?

3. What is the difference in structure between a user-defined operator and a user-defined assignment? How are they implemented?

4. How can access to the contents of a module be controlled? Why would we want to limit the access to some data items or procedures in a module?

5. What is the default type of access for items in a module?

■ 8.7

SUMMARY

This chapter introduces several advanced features of procedures and modules of Fortran 90/95. None of these features were available in earlier versions of Fortran.

An internal procedure is a procedure defined entirely within another program unit, which is called the host program unit, and is only accessible from the host program unit. Internal procedures are included in the host program unit after the executable statements of the program unit and are preceded by a `CONTAINS` statement. An internal procedure has access to all the data items defined in its host program unit by host association unless the internal procedure contains a data item of the same name as a data item in the host. In that case the data item in the host is not accessible to the internal procedure.

Ordinarily Fortran 90/95 subroutines and functions are not recursive—they cannot call themselves either directly or indirectly. However, they can be made recursive if they are declared to be recursive in the corresponding `SUBROUTINE` or `FUNCTION` statement. A recursive function declaration includes a `RESULT` clause specifying the name to be used to return the function result.

If a procedure has an explicit interface, then keyword arguments may be used to change the order in which calling arguments are specified. A keyword argument consists of the dummy argument's name followed by an equal sign and the value of the argument. Keyword arguments are very useful in supporting optional arguments.

If a procedure has an explicit interface, then optional arguments may be declared and used. An optional argument is an argument that may or may not be present in the procedure's calling sequence. An intrinsic function `PRESENT()` is provided to determine whether or not a particular optional argument is present when the procedure gets called.

Keyword arguments are commonly used with optional arguments because optional arguments often appear out of sequence in the calling procedure.

Generic procedures are procedures that can function properly with different types of input data. A generic procedure is declared using a generic interface block, which looks like an ordinary interface block with the addition of a generic procedure name. One or more specific procedures may be declared within the body of the generic interface block. Each specific procedure must be distinguishable from all other specific procedures by the type and sequence of its non-optional dummy arguments. When a generic procedure is referenced in a program, the compiler uses the sequence of calling arguments associated with the reference to decide which of the specific procedures to execute.

New operators may be defined and intrinsic operators may be extended to have new meanings in Fortran 90/95. A new operator may have a name consisting of up to 31 characters surrounded by periods. New operators and extended meanings of intrinsic operators are defined using an interface operator block. The first line of the interface operator block specifies the name of the operator to be defined or extended, and its body specifies the Fortran functions that are invoked to define the extended meaning. For binary operators, each function must have two input arguments; for unary operators, each function must have a single input argument. If several functions are present in the interface body, then they must be distinguishable from one another by the type and/or order of their dummy arguments. When the Fortran compiler encounters a new or extended operator, it uses the type and order of the operands to decide which of the functions to execute. This feature is commonly used to extend operators to support derived data types.

The assignment statement (=) may also be extended to work with derived data types by using an interface assignment block. The body of the interface assignment block must refer to one or more subroutines. Each subroutine must have exactly two dummy arguments, with the first argument having INTENT(OUT) and the second argument having IN-TENT(IN). The first argument corresponds to the left side of the equal sign, and the second argument corresponds to the right side of the equal sign. All subroutines in the body of an interface assignment block must be distinguishable from one another by the type and order of their dummy arguments.

It is possible to control access to the data items, operators, and procedures in a module by using the PUBLIC and PRIVATE statements or attributes. If an entity in a module is declared PUBLIC, then it will be available to any program unit that accesses the module by USE association. If an entity is declared PRIVATE, then it will not be available to any program unit that accesses the module by USE association. However, the entity will remain available to any procedures defined within the module.

8.7.1 Summary of Good Programming Practice

The following guidelines should be adhered to when working with the advanced features of procedures and modules:

1. Use user-defined generic procedures to define procedures that can function with different types of input data. Generic procedures will make your programs flexible and improve their ability to handle different types of data.
2. Use interface operator blocks and interface assignment blocks to create new operators and to extend the meanings of existing operators to work with derived data types. Once proper operators are defined, working with derived data types can be very easy.
3. Hide any module data items or procedures that external program units do not need to access directly. The best way to do so is to include a PRIVATE statement in each module and then to list the specific items that you wish to expose in separate PUBLIC statement(s).

8.7.2 Summary of Fortran Statements and Structures

CONTAINS Statement

```
                CONTAINS
```

Example:

```
        PROGRAM main
        ...
        CONTAINS
           SUBROUTINE sub1(x, y)
           ...
           END SUBROUTINE sub1
        END PROGRAM
```

Description:
    The CONTAINS statement specifies that the following statements are one or more separate procedures within the host unit. When used within a module, the CONTAINS statement marks the beginning of one or more module procedures. When used within a main program or an external procedure, the CONTAINS statement marks the beginning of one or more internal procedures. The CONTAINS statement must appear after any type, interface, and data definitions within a module and must follow the last executable statement within a main program or an external procedure.

Generic Interface Block

```
        INTERFACE generic_name
           MODULE PROCEDURE procedure_1
           MODULE PROCEDURE procedure_2
           ...
        END INTERFACE
```

(continued)

(concluded)

Example:

```
INTERFACE sort
    MODULE PROCEDURE sorti
    MODULE PROCEDURE sortr
END INTERFACE
```

Description:

A generic procedure is declared using a generic interface block. A generic interface block declares the name of the generic procedure on the first line and then lists the specific procedures associated with the generic procedure in the interface body.

Interface Assignment Block

```
INTERFACE Assignment (=)
    MODULE PROCEDURE subroutine_1
    ...
END INTERFACE
```

Example:

```
INTERFACE ASSIGNMENT (=)
    MODULE PROCEDURE vector_to_array
    MODULE PROCEDURE array_to_vector
END INTERFACE
```

Description:

An interface assignment block extends the meaning of the assignment statement to support assignment operations between two different derived data types or between derived data types and intrinsic data types. Each procedure in the interface body must be a subroutine with two arguments. The first argument must have INTENT(OUT), and the second one must have INTENT(IN). All subroutines in the interface body must be distinguishable from each other by the order and type of their arguments.

Interface Operator Block

```
INTERFACE OPERATOR (operator_symbol)
    MODULE PROCEDURE function_1
    ...
END INTERFACE
```

(continued)

(concluded)

Example:

```
          INTERFACE OPERATOR (*)
             MODULE PROCEDURE real_times_vector
             MODULE PROCEDURE vector_times_real
          END INTERFACE
```

Description:

An interface operator block is used to define a new operator or to extend the meaning of an intrinsic operator to support derived data types. Each procedure in the interface must be a function whose arguments are INTENT(IN). If the operator is a binary operator, then the function must have two arguments. If the operator is a unary operator, then the function must have only one argument. All functions in the interface body must be distinguishable from each other by the order and type of their arguments and results.

MODULE PROCEDURE Statement

```
   MODULE PROCEDURE module_procedure_1 (, module_procedure_2, ...)
```

Examples:

```
   MODULE PROCEDURE sorti
```

Description:

The MODULE PROCEDURE statement is used in interface blocks to specify that a procedure contained in a module is to be associated with the generic procedure, operator, or assignment defined by the interface.

Recursive FUNCTION Statement

```
   RECURSIVE [type] FUNCTION name( arg1, arg2, ... ) RESULT (res)
```

Example:

```
   RECURSIVE FUNCTION fact( n ) RESULT (answer)
   INTEGER :: answer
```

Description:

This statement declares a recursive Fortran function. A recursive function is one that can invoke itself. The type of the function may be declared either in the FUNCTION statement or in a separate type declaration statement. (The type of the result variable *res* is declared, not the type of the function name.) The value returned by the function call is the value assigned to *res* within the body of the function.

■ 8.8
EXERCISES

8–1 What are the differences between internal procedures and external procedures? When should an internal procedure be used instead of an external procedure?

8–2 In Example 7–4 the logical function lt_city failed to sort APO and Anywhere in proper order because all capital letters appear before all lowercase letters in the ASCII collating sequence. Add an internal procedure to function lt_city to avoid this problem by shifting both city names to uppercase before the comparison. Note that this procedure should *not* shift the names in the database to uppercase. It should only shift the names to uppercase while they are being used for the comparison.

8–3 Write test driver programs for the recursive subroutine factorial and the recursive function fact, which were introduced in section 8.2. Test both procedures by calculating 5! and 10! with each one.

8–4 What is printed out when the following code is executed? What are the values of x, y, i, and j at each point in the program? If a value changes during execution, explain why it changes.

```
PROGRAM exercise8_4
IMPLICIT NONE
REAL :: x = 12., y = -3., result
INTEGER :: i = 6, j = 4
WRITE (*,100) ' Before call: x, y, i, j = ', x, y, i, j
100 FORMAT (A,2F6.1,2I6)
result = exec(y,i)
WRITE (*,*) 'The result is ', result
WRITE (*,100) ' After call:  x, y, i, j = ', x, y, i, j
CONTAINS
    REAL FUNCTION exec(x,i)
    REAL, INTENT(IN) :: x
    INTEGER, INTENT(IN) :: i
    WRITE (*,100) ' In exec:     x, y, i, j = ', x, y, i, j
    100 FORMAT (A,2F6.1,2I6)
    exec = ( x + y ) / REAL ( i + j )
    j = i
    END FUNCTION exec
END PROGRAM
```

8–5 Is the following program correct or not? If it is correct, what is printed out when it executes? If not, what is wrong with it?

```
PROGRAM junk
IMPLICIT NONE
REAL :: a = 3, b = 4, output
INTEGER :: i = 0
call sub1(a, i, output)
WRITE (*,*) 'The output is ', output

CONTAINS
    SUBROUTINE sub1(x, j, junk)
```

```
               REAL, INTENT(IN) :: x
               INTEGER, INTENT(IN) :: j
               REAL, INTENT(OUT) :: junk
               junk = (x - j) / b
               END SUBROUTINE sub1
          END PROGRAM
```

8-6 What is a keyword argument? Under what circumstances can keyword arguments be used?

8-7 Assuming the following subroutine definition, are calls (*a*) through (*f*) legal or illegal? Assume that all calling arguments are of type real and assume that the subroutine interface is explicit. Explain why each illegal call is illegal.

```
          SUBROUTINE my_sub (a, b, c, d, e )
          REAL, INTENT(IN) :: a, d
          REAL, INTENT(OUT) :: b
          REAL, INTENT(IN), OPTIONAL :: c, e
          IF ( PRESENT(c) ) THEN
             b = (a - c) / d
          ELSE
             b = a / d
          END IF
          IF ( PRESENT(e) ) b = b - e
          END SUBROUTINE
```

    a. CALL my_sub (1., x, y, 2., z)
    b. CALL my_sub (10., 21., x, y, z)
    c. CALL my_sub (x, y, 25.)
    d. CALL my_sub (p, q, d=r)
    e. CALL my_sub (a=p, q, d=r, e=s)
    f. CALL my_sub (b=q, a=p, c=t, d=r, e=s)

8-8 Write a test driver program to test subroutine `extremes` from Example 8-1. Be sure to call the subroutine with and without keyword arguments, with keyword arguments in different orders, and with and without the optional arguments.

8-9 What is a generic procedure? How can a generic procedure be defined?

8-10 **Simulating Dice Throws** Assume that a programmer is writing a game program. Part of the program simulates the throw of a pair of dice. Write a subroutine called `throw` to return two random values from 1 to 6 each time it is called. The subroutine should contain an internal function called `die` to actually calculate the result of each toss of a die, and the subroutine should call that function twice to get the two results to return to the calling routine. (*Note:* You can generate a random die result by using the intrinsic subroutine RANDOM_NUMBER.)

8-11 How can a new Fortran operator be defined? What rules apply to the procedures in the body of an interface operator block?

8-12 How can an intrinsic Fortran operator be extended to have new meanings? What special rules apply to procedures in an interface operator block if an intrinsic operator is being extended?

8–13 How can the assignment operator be extended? What rules apply to the procedures in the body of an interface assignment block?

8–14 Write a test driver program to test the vector data type created in Example 8–3 and to also test the user-defined operations associated with it. Verify that the data type and operations are functioning properly.

8–15 Polar Complex Numbers A complex number may be represented in one of two ways: rectangular or polar (see Figure 8–11). The rectangular representation takes the form $c = a + bi$, where a is the real component and b is the imaginary component of the complex number. The polar representation is of the form $z\angle\theta$, where z is the magnitude of the complex number and θ is the angle of the number. The relationship between these two representations of complex numbers is

$$a = z \cos \theta \tag{7–10}$$

$$b = z \sin \theta \tag{7–11}$$

$$z = \sqrt{a^2 + b^2} \tag{7–12}$$

$$\theta = \tan^{-1}\frac{b}{a} \tag{7–13}$$

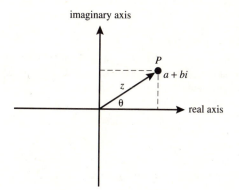

FIGURE 8–11
Representing a complex number in both rectangular and polar coordinates.

The COMPLEX data type represents a complex number in rectangular form. Define a new data type called POLAR that represents a complex number in polar form. Then write a module containing an interface assignment block and the supporting procedures to allow complex numbers to be assigned to polar numbers, and vice versa. (*Hint:* Use function ATAN2 when implementing Equation (7–13).)

8–16 If two complex numbers $P_1 = z_1\angle\theta_1$ and $P_2 = z_2\angle\theta_2$ are expressed in polar form, then the product of the numbers is $P_1 \cdot P_2 = z_1 z_2 \angle\theta_1 + \theta_2$. Similarly P_1 divided by P_2 is $\dfrac{P_1}{P_2} = \dfrac{z_1}{z_2}\angle\theta_1 - \theta_2$. Extend the module created in exercise 8–15 to add an interface operator block and the supporting procedures to allow two POLAR numbers to be multiplied and divided.

8–17 How can you control access to data items and procedures in a module?

8–18 Are the following programs legal or illegal? Why?

    a.
```
MODULE my_module
IMPLICIT NONE
PRIVATE
REAL, PARAMETER :: pi = 3.141592
REAL, PARAMETER :: two_pi = 2 * pi
END MODULE
PROGRAM test
USE my_module
IMPLICIT NONE
WRITE (*,*) 'Pi/2 =', pi / 2.
END PROGRAM
```

    b.
```
MODULE my_module
IMPLICIT NONE
PUBLIC
REAL, PARAMETER :: pi = 3.141592
REAL, PARAMETER :: two_pi = 2 * pi
END MODULE
PROGRAM test
USE my_module
IMPLICIT NONE
REAL :: two_pi
WRITE (*,*) 'Pi/2 =', pi / 2.
two_pi = 2. * pi
END PROGRAM
```

8–19 Modify the module in exercise 8–16 to allow access only to the definition of the POLAR type, the assignment operator, and to the multiplication and division operators. Restrict access to the functions that implement the operator definitions.

9

Dynamic Memory Allocation and Pointers

In earlier chapters we created and used variables of the five intrinsic Fortran data types and of derived data types. These variables had two characteristics in common: They all stored some form of data, and they were almost all **static,**[1] meaning that the number and types of variables in a program were declared when the program was compiled and remained the same throughout program execution.

Fortran 90/95 also includes two ways to allocate memory dynamically at execution time: **allocatable arrays** and **pointers.** *Allocatable arrays* are arrays whose *rank* is specified at compilation time, but whose *shape* is not specified until the program is executed. *Pointers* are variables that contain the *address in memory* of another variable where data is actually stored. Pointers can also be used for dynamic memory allocation.

■ 9.1

ALLOCATABLE ARRAYS

A Fortran array using dynamic memory is declared using the ALLOCATABLE attribute in the type declaration statement and is actually allocated with the ALLOCATE statement. When the program is through using the memory, it should free up the memory for other uses with the DEALLOCATE statement. The structure of a typical array declaration with the ALLOCATABLE attribute is

```
REAL, ALLOCATABLE, DIMENSION(:,:) :: arr1
```

Note that colons are used as placeholders in the declaration, since we do not know how big the array will actually be. The rank of the array is declared in the type declaration statement, but not the size of the array.

An array declared with colons for dimensions is known as a **deferred-shape array** because the actual shape of the array is deferred until the memory for the array is allocated.

---

[1]Automatic arrays in Chapter 6 were the exception.

When the program executes, the actual size of the array will be determined with an ALLOCATE statement. The general form of an ALLOCATE statement is

ALLOCATE (*list of arrays to allocate*, STAT=*status*)

For example:

ALLOCATE (arr1(100,0:10), STAT=status)

This statement allocates a 100×11 array arr1 at execution time. The STAT= clause is optional. If it is present, it returns an integer status. The status will be 0 for successful allocation and a compiler-dependent positive number if the allocation process fails. The most common source of failure is not having enough free memory to allocate the array. If the allocation fails and the STAT= clause is not present, then the program will abort. You should always use the STAT= clause so that the program can terminate gracefully if there is not enough memory available to allocate the array.

Good Programming Practice
Always include the STAT= clause in any ALLOCATE statement and always check the returned status so that a program can be shut down gracefully if there is insufficient memory to allocate the necessary arrays.

An allocatable array may not be used in any way in a program until memory is allocated for it. Any attempt to use an allocatable array that does not currently have memory allocated will produce a run-time error and cause the program to abort. Fortran 90/95 includes the logical intrinsic function ALLOCATED() to allow a program to test the allocation status of an array before attempting to use it. For example, the following code tests the status of allocatable array input_data before attempting to reference it:

```
REAL, ALLOCATABLE, DIMENSION(:) :: input_data
...
IF ( ALLOCATED(input_data) ) THEN
    READ (8,*) input_data
ELSE
    WRITE (*,*) 'Warning-Array not allocated!'
END IF
```

This function can be very helpful in large programs involving many procedures, in which memory is allocated in one procedure and used in a different one.

When the allocatable array is no longer needed in the program, you should *deallocate* the memory to make it available for reuse with a DEALLOCATE statement. The structure of a DEALLOCATE statement is

DEALLOCATE (*list of arrays to deallocate*, STAT=*status*)

For example:

DEALLOCATE (arr1, STAT=status)

where the status clause has the same meaning as it has in the ALLOCATE statement. After a DEALLOCATE statement is executed, the data in the deallocated arrays is no longer available for use. You should always deallocate any arrays when you are finished with them.

Good Programming Practice
Always deallocate dynamic arrays with a DEALLOCATE statement as soon as you are through using them.

You can always use the ALLOCATED intrinsic function to check the **allocation status** of an allocatable array. The function will return a true value of the array is allocated and a false value if the array is not allocated.

EXAMPLE 9–1 Using Allocatable Arrays: To illustrate the use of allocatable arrays, we will rewrite the statistical analysis program of Example 5–4 to dynamically allocate only the amount of memory needed to solve the problem. To determine how much memory to allocate, the program will read the input data file and count the number of values. It will then allocate the array, rewind the file, read in the values, and calculate the statistics.

SOLUTION

The modified program with allocatable arrays is shown in Figure 9–1.

FIGURE 9–1
A statistics program that uses allocatable arrays.

```
PROGRAM stat_5
!
! Purpose:
!   To calculate mean, median, and standard deviation of an input
!   data set read from a file.  This program uses allocatable arrays
!   to use only the memory required to solve each problem.
!
! Record of revisions:
!     Date          Programmer          Description of change
!     ====          ==========          =====================
!   09/26/95     S. J. Chapman          Original code
! 1. 09/30/96    S. J. Chapman          Modified for dynamic memory
!
IMPLICIT NONE

! List of variables:
REAL,ALLOCATABLE,DIMENSION(:) :: a ! Data array to sort
CHARACTER(len=20) :: filename       ! Input data file name
INTEGER :: i                        ! Loop index
INTEGER :: iptr                     ! Pointer to smallest value
INTEGER :: j                        ! Loop index
```

(continued)

(continued)

```
REAL :: median                      ! The median of the input samples
INTEGER :: nvals = 0                 ! Number of values to process
INTEGER :: status                    ! Status: 0 for success
REAL :: std_dev                      ! Standard deviation of input samples
REAL :: sum_x = 0.                   ! Sum of input values
REAL :: sum_x2 = 0.                  ! Sum of input values squared
REAL :: temp                         ! Temporary variable for swapping
REAL :: x_bar                        ! Average of input values

! Get the name of the file containing the input data.
WRITE (*,1000)
1000 FORMAT (1X,'Enter the file name with the data to be sorted:')
READ (*,'(A20)') filename

! Open input data file.  Status is OLD because the input data must
! already exist.
OPEN ( UNIT=9, FILE=filename, STATUS='OLD', ACTION='READ', &
       IOSTAT=status )

! Was the OPEN successful?
fileopen: IF ( status == 0 ) THEN          ! Open successful

   ! The file was opened successfully, so read the data to find
   ! out how many values are in the file and allocate the
   ! required space.
   DO
      READ (9, *, IOSTAT=status) temp       ! Get value
      IF ( status /= 0 ) EXIT                ! Exit on end of data
      nvals = nvals + 1                      ! Bump count
   END DO

   ! Allocate memory
   WRITE (*,*) ' Allocating a: size = ', nvals
   ALLOCATE ( a(nvals), STAT=status )    ! Allocate memory

   ! Was allocation successful?  If so, rewind file, read in
   ! data, and process it.
   allocate_ok: IF ( status == 0 ) THEN

      REWIND ( UNIT=9 )                      ! Rewind file

      ! Now read in the data.  We know that there are enough
      ! values to fill the array.
      READ (9, *) a                          ! Get value

      ! Sort the data.
      outer: DO i = 1, nvals-1

         ! Find the minimum value in a(i) through a(nvals)
         iptr = i
         inner: DO j = i+1, nvals
            minval: IF ( a(j) < a(iptr) ) THEN
               iptr = j
            END IF minval
         END DO inner

         ! iptr now points to the minimum value, so swap a(iptr)
```

(continued)

(concluded)

```
            ! with a(i) if i /= iptr.
         swap: IF ( i /= iptr ) THEN
            temp     = a(i)
            a(i)     = a(iptr)
            a(iptr) = temp
         END IF swap

      END DO outer

      ! The data is now sorted.  Accumulate sums to calculate
      ! statistics.
      sums: DO i = 1, nvals
         sum_x  = sum_x + a(i)
         sum_x2 = sum_x2 + a(i)**2
      END DO sums

      ! Check to see if we have enough input data.
      enough: IF ( nvals < 2 ) THEN

         ! Insufficient data.
         WRITE (*,*) ' At least 2 values must be entered.'

      ELSE

         ! Calculate the mean, median, and standard deviation
         x_bar   = sum_x / real(nvals)
         std_dev = sqrt( (real(nvals) * sum_x2 - sum_x**2) &
                   / (real(nvals) * real(nvals-1)) )
         even: IF ( mod(nvals,2) == 0 ) THEN
            median = ( a(nvals/2) + a(nvals/2+1) ) / 2.
         ELSE
            median = a(nvals/2+1)
         END IF even

         ! Tell user.
         WRITE (*,*) ' The mean of this data set is:  ', x_bar
         WRITE (*,*) ' The median of this data set is:', median
         WRITE (*,*) ' The standard deviation is:     ', std_dev
         WRITE (*,*) ' The number of data points is:  ', nvals

      END IF enough

      ! Deallocate the array now that we are done.
      DEALLOCATE ( a, STAT=status )

   END IF allocate_ok

ELSE fileopen

   ! Else file open failed.  Tell user.
   WRITE (*,1050) status
   1050 FORMAT (1X,'File open failed--status = ', I6)

END IF fileopen

END PROGRAM
```

To test this program, we will run it with the data set we used in Example 5–4.

```
C>stat_5
Enter the file name containing the input data:
input4
  Allocating a: size =                    5
  The mean of this data set is:               4.400000
  The median of this data set is:             4.000000
  The standard deviation is:                  2.966479
  The number of data points is:                      5
```

The program gives the correct answers for our test data set.

■ 9.2

POINTERS

A pointer is a variable that contains the address in memory of another variable where data is actually stored. The difference between a pointer and an ordinary variable is illustrated in Figure 9–2. Both pointers and ordinary variables have names, but pointers store the addresses of ordinary variables, while ordinary variables store data values.

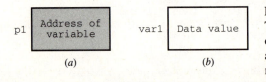

(a)   (b)

FIGURE 9–2
The difference between a pointer and an ordinary variable: (*a*) A pointer stores the address of an ordinary variable in its memory location. (*b*) An ordinary variable stores a data value.

Pointers are primarily used when variables and arrays must be created and destroyed dynamically during the execution of a program and when we do not know before the program executes just how many of any given type of variable will be needed during a run. For example, suppose that a mailing list program must read in an unknown number of names and addresses, sort them into a user-specified order, and then print mailing labels in that order. The names and addresses will be stored in variables of a derived data type. If this program is implemented with static arrays, then the arrays must be as large as the largest possible mailing list ever to be processed. Most of the time the mailing lists will be much smaller, and a large static array would waste valuable computer memory. If the program is implemented with allocatable arrays, then we can allocate just the required amount of memory, but we must still know in advance how many addresses there will be before the first one is read. By contrast, pointers enable us to dynamically allocate a variable for each address as it is read in and to manipulate those addresses in any desired fashion. This flexibility will produce a much more efficient program.

You will first learn the basics of creating and using pointers and then see a few examples of how they can be used to write flexible and powerful programs.

9.2.1 Pointers and Targets

A Fortran variable is declared to be a pointer by including the POINTER attribute in its type definition statement. For example, the following statement declares a pointer p1 that must point to a real variable:

```
REAL, POINTER :: p1
```

Note that the *type* of a pointer must be declared, even though the pointer does not contain any data of that type. Instead, it contains the *address* of a variable of the declared type. A pointer is only allowed to point to variables of its declared type. Any attempt to point to a variable of a different type will produce a compilation error.

Pointers to variables of derived data types may also be declared. For example:

```
TYPE (vector), POINTER :: vector_pointer
```

declares a pointer to a variable of derived data type vector. Pointers may also point to an array. A pointer to an array is declared with a deferred-shape array, meaning that the rank of the array is specified, but the actual extent of the array in each dimension is indicated by colons. Two pointers to arrays are

```
INTEGER, DIMENSION(:), POINTER :: ptr1
REAL, DIMENSION(:,:), POINTER :: ptr2
```

The first pointer can point to any rank-1 integer array, while the second pointer can point to any rank-2 real array.

A pointer can point to any variable or array of the pointer's type as long as the variable or array has been declared to be a **target.** A *target* is a data object whose address has been made available for use with pointers. A Fortran variable or array is declared to be a target by including the TARGET attribute in its type definition statement. For example, the following set of statements declares two targets to which pointers may point:

```
REAL, TARGET :: a1 = 7
INTEGER, DIMENSION(10), TARGET :: int_array
```

They declare a real scalar value a1 and a rank-1 integer array int_array. Variable a1 may be pointed to by any real scalar pointer (such as the pointer p1 declared earlier), and int_array may be pointed to by any integer rank-1 integer pointer (such as pointer ptr1).

Pointer assignment statements

A pointer can be **associated** with a given target by means of a **pointer assignment statement.** A pointer assignment statement takes the form

```
pointer => target
```

where *pointer* is the name of a pointer and *target* is the name of a variable or array of the same type as the pointer. Note that the pointer assignment operator consists of an equal sign followed by a greater than sign with no space in between. When this statement is executed, the memory address of the target is stored in the pointer. After the pointer assignment statement, any reference to the pointer will actually be a reference to the data stored in the target.

If a pointer is already associated with a target by a pointer assignment statement and another pointer assignment statement is executed using the same pointer, then the association with the first target is lost and the pointer now points to the second target. Any reference to the pointer after the second pointer assignment statement will actually be a reference to the data stored in the second target.

For example, the program in Figure 9–3 defines a real pointer p and two target variables t1 and t2. The pointer is first associated with variable t1 by a pointer assignment statement, and p is written out by a WRITE statement (see Figure 9–4a). Then the pointer is associated with variable t2 by another pointer assignment statement, and p is written out by a second WRITE statement (see Figure 9–4b).

FIGURE 9–3
Program to illustrate pointer assignment statements.

```
PROGRAM test_ptr
IMPLICIT NONE
REAL, POINTER :: p
REAL, TARGET :: t1 = 10., t2 = -17.
p => t1
WRITE (*,*) 'p, t1, t2 = ', p, t1, t2
p => t2
WRITE (*,*) 'p, t1, t2 = ', p, t1, t2
END PROGRAM
```

When this program is executed, the results are

```
C>test_ptr
p, t1, t2 =        10.000000       10.000000      -17.000000
p, t1, t2 =       -17.000000       10.000000      -17.000000
```

Note that p never contains either 10. or −17. Instead, it contains the addresses of the variables in which those values were stored, and the Fortran compiler treats a reference to the pointer as a reference to those addresses. Also, note that a value could be accessed either through a pointer to a variable or through the variable's name, and the two forms of access can be mixed even within a single statement.

It is also possible to assign the value of one pointer to another pointer in a pointer assignment statement.

$$pointer1 \Rightarrow pointer2$$

After such a statement, both pointers point directly and independently to the same target. If either pointer is changed in a later assignment, the other one will be unaffected and will continue to point to the original target. If *pointer2* is disassociated (does not point to a target) at the time the statement is executed, then *pointer1* also becomes disassociated.

For example, the program in Figure 9–5 defines two real pointers p1 and p2 and two target variables t1 and t2. The pointer p1 is first associated with variable t1 by a pointer assignment statement, and then pointer p2 is assigned the value of pointer p1 by another

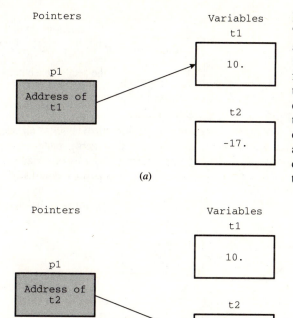

(a)

(b)

FIGURE 9–4
The relationship between the pointer and the variables in program test_ptr. (*a*) The situation after the first executable statement: p contains the address of variable t1, and a reference to p is the same as a reference to t1. (*b*) The situation after the third executable statement: p contains the address of variable t2, and a reference to p is the same as a reference to t2.

pointer assignment statement. After these statements, both pointers p1 and p2 are independently associated with variable t1 (Figure 9–6*a*). When pointer p1 is later associated with variable t2, pointer p2 remains associated with t1 (Figure 9–6*b*).

FIGURE 9–5
Program to illustrate pointer assignment between two pointers.

```
        PROGRAM test_ptr2
        IMPLICIT NONE
        REAL, POINTER :: p1, p2
        REAL, TARGET :: t1 = 10., t2 = -17.
        p1 => t1
        p2 => p1
     WRITE (*,'(A,4F8.2)') ' p1, p2, t1, t2 = ', p1, p2, t1, t2
        p1 => t2
        WRITE (*,'(A,4F8.2)') ' p1, p2, t1, t2 = ', p1, p2, t1, t2
        END PROGRAM
```

When this program is executed, the results are

```
        C>test_ptr2
        p1, p2, t1, t2 =     10.00    10.00    10.00   -17.00
        p1, p2, t1, t2 =    -17.00    10.00    10.00   -17.00
```

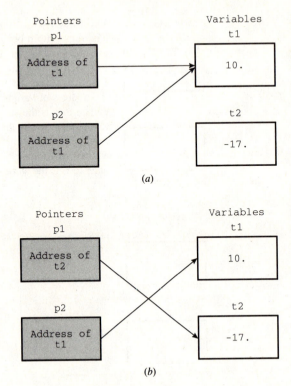

Pointers

p1

Variables

t1

FIGURE 9–6

The relationship between the pointer and the variables in program `test_ptr2`. (*a*) The situation after the second executable statement: p1 and p2 both contain the address of variable t1, and a reference to either one is the same as a reference to t1. (*b*) The situation after the fourth executable statement: p1 contains the address of variable t2, and p2 contains the address of variable t1. Note that p2 was unaffected by the reassignment of pointer p1.

Pointer association status

The **association status** of a pointer indicates whether or not the pointer currently points to a valid target. The three possible statuses are **undefined, associated,** and **disassociated.** When a pointer is first declared in a type declaration statement, its pointer association status is *undefined.* Once a pointer has been associated with a target by a pointer assignment statement, its association status becomes *associated.* If a pointer is later disassociated from its target and is not associated with any new target, then its association status becomes *disassociated.*

How can a pointer be disassociated from its target? It can be disassociated from one target and simultaneously associated with another target by executing a pointer assignment statement. In addition, a pointer can be disassociated from all targets by executing a NULLIFY statement. A NULLIFY statement has the form

$$\text{NULLIFY} \ (\ ptr1[, \ ptr2, \ ...] \ )$$

where *ptr1*, *ptr2*, and so on are pointers. After the statement is executed, the pointers listed in the statement are disassociated from all targets.

A pointer can only be used to reference a target when it is associated with that target. Any attempt to use a pointer when it is not associated with a target will result in an error, and the program containing the error will abort. Therefore, we must be able to tell whether or not a particular pointer is associated with a particular target or with any target at all. We can determine the pointer's association status by using the logical intrinsic function ASSOCIATED. The function comes in two forms, one containing a pointer as its only argument and one containing both a pointer and a target. The first form is

```
status = ASSOCIATED ( pointer )
```

This function returns a true value if the pointer is associated with any target and a false value if it is not associated with any target. The second form is

```
status = ASSOCIATED ( pointer, target )
```

This function returns a true value if the pointer is associated with the particular target included in the function and a false value otherwise.

A pointer's association status can only be undefined from the time that it is declared until it is first used. Thereafter, the pointer's status will always be either associated or disassociated. Because the undefined status is ambiguous, it is recommended that every pointer's status be clarified as soon as it is created by either assigning it to a target or nullifying it. For example, pointers could be declared and nullified in a program as follows:

```
REAL, POINTER :: p1, p2
INTEGER, POINTER :: i1
...
(additional specification statements)
...
NULLIFY (p1, p2, i1)
```

Good Programming Practice
Always nullify or assign all pointers in a program unit as soon as they are created. This process eliminates any possible ambiguities associated with the undefined state.

Fortran 95 provides an intrinsic function NULL() that can be used to nullify a pointer at the time it is declared (or at any time during the execution of a program). In Fortran 95, pointers can be declared and nullified as follows:

```
REAL, POINTER :: p1 = NULL(), p2 = NULL()
INTEGER, POINTER :: i1 = NULL()
...
(additional specification statements)
```

The NULL() function is described in Appendix B.

The simple program shown in Figure 9–7 illustrates the use of the NULLIFY statement and the ASSOCIATED intrinsic function.

FIGURE 9–7
Program to illustrate the use of the NULLIFY statement and the ASSOCIATED function.

```
PROGRAM test_ptr3
IMPLICIT NONE
REAL, POINTER :: p1, p2, p3
REAL, TARGET :: a = 11., b = 12.5, c = 3.141592
NULLIFY ( p1, p2, p3)        ! Nullify pointers
WRITE (*,*) ASSOCIATED(p1)
p1 => a                            ! p1 points to a
p2 => b                            ! p2 points to b
p3 => c                            ! p3 points to c
WRITE (*,*) ASSOCIATED(p1)
WRITE (*,*) ASSOCIATED(p1, b)
END PROGRAM
```

The pointers p1, p2, and p3 will be nullified as soon as program execution begins. Thus the result of the first ASSOCIATED(p1) function will be false. Then the pointers are associated with targets a, b, and c. When the second ASSOCIATED(p1) function is executed, the pointer will be associated, so the result of the function will be true. The third ASSOCIATED(p1,b) function checks to see if pointer p1 points to variable b. It doesn't, so the function returns false.

9.2.2 Using Pointers in Assignment Statements

Whenever a pointer appears in a Fortran expression where a value is expected, *the value of the target pointed to is used* instead of the pointer itself. This process is known as **dereferencing** the pointer. We have already seen an example of dereferencing in the previous section: Whenever a pointer appeared in a WRITE statement, the value of the target pointed to was printed out instead. As another example, consider two pointers p1 and p2 that are associated with variables a and b, respectively. In the ordinary assignment statement

$$p2 = p1$$

both p1 and p2 appear in places where variables are expected; therefore, they are dereferenced, and this statement is exactly identical to the statement

$$b = a$$

By contrast, in the pointer assignment statement

$$p2 => p1$$

p2 appears in a place where a pointer is expected, while p1 appears in a place where a target (an ordinary variable) is expected. As a result p1 is dereferenced, while p2 refers to the pointer itself. The result is that the target pointed to by p1 is assigned to the pointer p2.

The program shown in Figure 9–8 provides another example of using pointers in place of variables:

FIGURE 9-8

Program to illustrate the use of pointers in place of variables in assignment statements.

```
PROGRAM test_ptr4
IMPLICIT NONE
REAL, POINTER :: p1, p2, p3
REAL, TARGET :: a = 11., b = 12.5, c
NULLIFY (p1, p2, p3)           ! Nullify pointers
p1 => a                        ! p1 points to a
p2 => b                        ! p2 points to b
p3 => c                        ! p3 points to c
p3 = p1 + p2                   ! Same as c = a + b
WRITE (*,*) 'p3 = ', p3
p2 => p1                       ! p2 points to a
p3 = p1 + p2                   ! Same as c = a + a
WRITE (*,*) 'p3 = ', p3
p3 = p1                        ! Same as c = a
p3 => p1                       ! p3 points to a
WRITE (*,*) 'p3 = ', p3
WRITE (*,*) 'a, b, c = ', a, b, c
END PROGRAM
```

In this example the first assignment statement p3 = p1 + p2 is equivalent to the statement c = a + b, since the pointers p1, p2, and p3 point to variables a, b, and c, respectively, and since ordinary variables are expected in the assignment statement. The pointer assignment statement p2 => p1 causes pointer p1 to point to a, so the second assignment statement p3 = p1 + p2 is equivalent to the statement c = a + a. Finally, the assignment statement p3 = p1 is equivalent to the statement c = a, while the pointer assignment statement p3 => p1 causes pointer p3 to point to a. The output of this program is

```
C>test_ptr4
p3 =       23.500000
p3 =       22.000000
p3 =       11.000000
a, b, c =      11.000000      12.500000      11.000000
```

We will now show one way that pointers can improve the efficiency of a program. Suppose that it is necessary to swap two 100 × 100 element real arrays array1 and array2 in a program. To swap these arrays, we would normally use the following code:

```
REAL, DIMENSION(100,100) :: array1, array2, temp
...
temp = array1
array1 = array2
array2 = temp
```

The code is simple enough, but note that we are moving 10,000 real values in each assignment statement! All of that moving requires a lot of time. By contrast, we could perform the same manipulation with pointers and only exchange the *addresses* of the target arrays:

```
REAL, DIMENSION(100,100), TARGET :: array1, array2
REAL, DIMENSION(:,:), POINTER :: p1, p2, temp
p1 => array1
```

```
                          p2 => array2
                          ...
                          temp => p1
                          p1 => p2
                          p2 => temp
```

In the latter case we only swapped the addresses—not the entire 10,000-element arrays! This example is enormously more efficient than the previous example.

Good Programming Practice
When sorting or swapping large arrays or derived data types, it is more efficient to exchange pointers to the data than it is to manipulate the data itself.

9.2.3 Using Pointers with Arrays

A pointer can point to an array as well as a scalar. A pointer to an array must declare the type and the rank of the array that it will point to, but does *not* declare the extent in each dimension. Thus the following statements are legal:

```
             REAL, DIMENSION(100,1000), TARGET :: mydata
             REAL, DIMENSION(:,:), POINTER :: pointer
             pointer => array
```

A pointer can point not only to an array but also to a *subset* of an array (an array section). Any array section that can be defined by a subscript triplet can be used as the target of a pointer. For example, the program in Figure 9–9 declares a 16-element integer array `info` and fills the array with the values 1 through 16. This array serves as the target for a series of pointers. The first pointer `ptr1` points to the entire array, while the second one points to the array section defined by the subscript triplet `ptr1(2::2)`. This array section will consist of the even subscripts 2, 4, 6, 8, 10, 12, 14, and 16 from the original array. The third pointer also uses the subscript triplet 2::2, and it points to the even elements from the list pointed to by second pointer. This array section will consist of the subscripts 4, 8, 12, and 16 from the original array. This process of selection continues with the remaining pointers.

FIGURE 9–9
Program to illustrate the use of pointers with array sections defined by subscript triplets.

```
             PROGRAM array_ptr
             IMPLICIT NONE
             INTEGER :: i
             INTEGER, DIMENSION(16), TARGET :: info = (/ (i, i=1,16) /)
             INTEGER, DIMENSION(:), POINTER :: ptr1, ptr2, ptr3, ptr4, ptr5
             ptr1 => info
             ptr2 => ptr1(2::2)
             ptr3 => ptr2(2::2)
```

(continued)

(concluded)

```
      ptr4 => ptr3(2::2)
      ptr5 => ptr4(2::2)
      WRITE (*,'(A,16I3)') ' ptr1 = ', ptr1
      WRITE (*,'(A,16I3)') ' ptr2 = ', ptr2
      WRITE (*,'(A,16I3)') ' ptr3 = ', ptr3
      WRITE (*,'(A,16I3)') ' ptr4 = ', ptr4
      WRITE (*,'(A,16I3)') ' ptr5 = ', ptr5
      END PROGRAM
```

When this program is executed, the results are

```
C>array_ptr

ptr1 =   1  2  3  4  5  6  7  8  9 10 11 12 13 14 15 16
ptr2 =   2  4  6  8 10 12 14 16
ptr3 =   4  8 12 16
ptr4 =   8 16
ptr5 =  16
```

Be aware that although pointers work with array sections defined by subscript triplets, they do not work with array sections defined by vector subscripts. Thus the code in Figure 9–10 is illegal and will produce a compilation error.

FIGURE 9–10

Program to illustrate invalid pointer assignments to array sections defined with vector subscripts.

```
      PROGRAM bad
      IMPLICIT NONE
      INTEGER :: i
      INTEGER, DIMENSION(3) :: subs = (/ 1, 8, 11 /)
      INTEGER, DIMENSION(16), TARGET :: info = (/ (i, i=1,16) /)
      INTEGER, DIMENSION(:), POINTER :: ptr1
      ptr1 => info(subs)
      WRITE (*,'(A,16I3)') ' ptr1 = ', ptr1
      END PROGRAM
```

9.2.4 Dynamic Memory Allocation with Pointers

One of the most powerful features of pointers is that they can be used to dynamically create variables or arrays whenever they are required and then to release the space used by the dynamic variables or arrays once they are no longer needed. This procedure is similar to that used to create allocatable arrays. Memory is allocated using an ALLOCATE statement, and it is deallocated using a DEALLOCATE statement. The ALLOCATE statement for a pointer has the same form as it does for an allocatable array. The syntax is

$$\text{ALLOCATE } (pointer(size),[\ ...,] \ \text{STAT}=status)$$

where *pointer* is the name of a pointer to the variable or array being created, *size* is the dimension specification if the object being created is an array, and *status* is the result of the operation. If the allocation is successful, then the status will be 0. If it fails, a processor-dependent positive integer will be returned in the status variable. The STAT= clause is optional but should always be used, since a failed allocation statement without a STAT= clause will cause a program to abort.

This statement creates an unnamed data object of the specified size and the pointer's type and also sets the pointer to point to the object. Because the new data object is unnamed, it can only be accessed by using the pointer. After the statement is executed, the association status of the pointer will become *associated*. If the pointer had been associated with another data object before the ALLOCATE statement is executed, then that association is lost.

Note that the data object created by using the ALLOCATE statement with a pointer is unnamed and so can only be accessed by the pointer. If all pointers to that memory are either nullified or reassociated with other targets, then the data object will no longer be accessible by the program. The object will still be present in memory, but it will no longer be possible to use it. Thus careless programming with pointers can result in memory being filled with unusable space. This unusable memory is commonly referred to as a "memory leak." One symptom of this problem is that a program seems to grow larger and larger as it continues to execute until it either fills the entire computer or uses all available memory. An example of a program with a memory leak is shown in Figure 9–11. This program allocates 10-element arrays using both ptr1 and ptr2. The two arrays are initialized to different values, and those values are printed out. Then ptr2 is assigned to point to the same memory as ptr1 in a pointer assignment statement. After that statement, the memory that was assigned to ptr2 is no longer accessible to the program. That memory has been "lost" and will not be recovered until the program stops executing.

FIGURE 9–11
Program to illustrate memory leaks in a program.

```
PROGRAM mem_leak
IMPLICIT NONE
INTEGER :: i, istat
INTEGER, DIMENSION(:), POINTER :: ptr1, ptr2

! Check associated status of ptrs.
WRITE (*,'(A,2L5)') ' Are ptr1, ptr2 associated? ', &
      ASSOCIATED(ptr1), ASSOCIATED(ptr2)

! Allocate and initialize memory
ALLOCATE (ptr1(1:10), STAT=istat)
ALLOCATE (ptr2(1:10), STAT=istat)
ptr1 = (/ (i, i = 1,10 ) /)
ptr2 = (/ (i, i = 11,20 ) /)

! Check associated status of ptrs.
WRITE (*,'(A,2L5)') ' Are ptr1, ptr2 associated? ', &
      ASSOCIATED(ptr1), ASSOCIATED(ptr2)

WRITE (*,'(A,10I3)') ' ptr1 = ', ptr1    ! Write out data
WRITE (*,'(A,10I3)') ' ptr2 = ', ptr2
```

(continued)

(concluded)

```
            ptr2 => ptr1                                    ! Reassign ptr2

            WRITE (*,'(A,10I3)') ' ptr1 = ', ptr1           ! Write out data
            WRITE (*,'(A,10I3)') ' ptr2 = ', ptr2

            NULLIFY(ptr1)                                    ! Nullify pointer
            DEALLOCATE(ptr2, STAT=istat)                     ! Deallocate memory

            END PROGRAM
```

When program mem_leak executes, the results are

```
C>mem_leak
Are ptr1, ptr2 associated?       F    F
Are ptr1, ptr2 associated?       T    T
ptr1 =    1  2  3  4  5  6  7  8  9 10
ptr2 =   11 12 13 14 15 16 17 18 19 20
ptr1 =    1  2  3  4  5  6  7  8  9 10
ptr2 =    1  2  3  4  5  6  7  8  9 10
```

Memory that has been allocated with an ALLOCATE statement should be deallocated with a DEALLOCATE statement when the program is finished using it. If it is not deallocated, then that memory will be unavailable for any other use until the program finishes executing. When memory is deallocated in a pointer DEALLOCATE statement, the pointer to that memory is nullified at the same time. Thus the statement

```
DEALLOCATE(ptr2, STAT=istat)
```

both deallocates the memory pointed to and nullifies the pointer ptr2.

The pointer DEALLOCATE statement can only deallocate memory that was created by an ALLOCATE statement. It is important to remember this fact. If the pointer in the statement happens to point to a target that was not created with an ALLOCATE statement, then the DEALLOCATE statement will fail and the program will abort unless the STAT= clause was specified. The association between such pointers and their targets can be broken by the use of the NULLIFY statement.

A potentially serious problem can occur when deallocating memory. Suppose that two pointers ptr1 and ptr2 both point to the same allocated array. If pointer ptr1 is used in a DEALLOCATE statement to deallocate the array, then that pointer is nullified. However, ptr2 will *not* be nullified. It will continue to point to the memory location where the array used to be, even if the program reuses that memory location for some other purpose. If that pointer is used to either read data from or write data to the memory location, it will be either reading unpredictable values or overwriting memory used for some other purpose. In either case using that pointer is a recipe for disaster! If a piece of allocated memory is deallocated, then *all* the pointers to that memory should be nullified or reassigned. One of them will be automatically nullified by the DEALLOCATE statement, and any others should be nullified in NULLIFY statement(s).

Figure 9–12 illustrates the effect of using a pointer after the memory to which it points has been deallocated. In this example two pointers ptr1 and ptr2 both point to the same 10-element allocatable array. When that array is deallocated with ptr1, that pointer becomes disassociated. Pointer `ptr2` remains associated, but now it points to a piece of memory that can be freely reused by the program for other purposes. When `ptr2` is accessed in the next WRITE statement, it points to an unallocated part of memory that could contain anything. Then a new two-element array is allocated using `ptr1`. Depending on the behavior of the compiler, this array could be allocated over the freed memory from the previous array, or it could be allocated somewhere else in memory.

FIGURE 9–12
Program to illustrate the effect of using a pointer after the memory to which it points has been deallocated.

```
PROGRAM bad_ptr
IMPLICIT NONE
INTEGER :: i, istat
INTEGER, DIMENSION(:), POINTER :: ptr1, ptr2

! Allocate and initialize memory
ALLOCATE (ptr1(1:10), STAT=istat)       ! Allocate ptr1
ptr1 = (/ (i, i = 1,10 ) /)             ! Initialize ptr1
ptr2 => ptr1                            ! Assign ptr2

! Check associated status of ptrs.
WRITE (*,'(A,2L5)') ' Are ptr1, ptr2 associated? ', &
      ASSOCIATED(ptr1), ASSOCIATED(ptr2)

WRITE (*,'(A,10I3)') ' ptr1 = ', ptr1   ! Write out data
WRITE (*,'(A,10I3)') ' ptr2 = ', ptr2

! Now deallocate memory associated with ptr1
DEALLOCATE(ptr1, STAT=istat)            ! Deallocate memory

! Check associated status of ptrs.
WRITE (*,'(A,2L5)') ' Are ptr1, ptr2 associated? ', &
      ASSOCIATED(ptr1), ASSOCIATED(ptr2)

! Write out memory associated with ptr2
WRITE (*,'(A,10I3)') ' ptr2 = ', ptr2

ALLOCATE (ptr1(1:2), STAT=istat)        ! Reallocate ptr1
ptr1 = (/ 21, 22 /)

WRITE (*,'(A,10I3)') ' ptr1 = ', ptr1   ! Write out data
WRITE (*,'(A,10I3)') ' ptr2 = ', ptr2

END PROGRAM
```

The results of this program will vary from compiler to compiler, since different processors may treat deallocated memory in different ways. When this program is executed on the Lahey Fortran 90 Compiler, the results are

```
C>bad_ptr
Are ptr1, ptr2 associated?      T    T
ptr1 =   1  2  3  4  5  6  7  8  9 10
ptr2 =   1  2  3  4  5  6  7  8  9 10
```

```
Are ptr1, ptr2 associated?      F    T
ptr2 =    1  2  3  4  5  6  7  8  9 10
ptr1 =   21 22
ptr2 =   21 22  3  4  5  6  7  8  9 10
```

After `ptr1` was used to deallocate the memory, its pointer status changed to *disassociated* while the status of `ptr2` remained *associated*. When `ptr2` was then used to examine memory, it pointed to the memory location *where the array used to be* and saw the old values because the memory had not yet been reused. Finally, when `ptr1` was used to allocate a new two-element array, some of the freed-up memory was reused.

It is also possible to mix pointers and allocatable arrays in a single `ALLOCATE` statement or `DEALLOCATE` statement.

Good Programming Practice

Always nullify or reassign *all* pointers to a memory location when that memory is deallocated. One of them will be automatically nullified by the `DEALLOCATE` statement, and any others should be manually nullified in `NULLIFY` statement(s) or reassigned in pointer assignment statements.

9.2.5 Using Pointers as Components of Derived Data Types

Pointers may appear as components of derived data types. Pointers in derived data types may even point to the derived data type being defined. This feature is very useful, since it permits us to construct various types of dynamic data structures linked together by successive pointers during the execution of a program. The simplest such structure is a **linked list,** which is a list of values linked together in a linear fashion by pointers. For example, the following derived data type contains a real number and a pointer to another variable of the same type:

```
TYPE :: real_value
    REAL :: value
    TYPE (real_value), POINTER :: p
END TYPE
```

A *linked list* is a series of variables of a derived data type with the pointer from each variable pointing to the next variable in the list. The pointer in the last variable is nullified, since there is no variable after it in the list. Two pointers (say, `head` and `tail`) are also defined to point to the first and last variables in the list. Figure 9–13 illustrates this structure for variables of type `real_value`.

Linked lists are much more flexible than arrays are. Recall that a static array must be declared with a fixed size when a program is compiled. As a result we must size each such array to be large enough to handle the *largest problem* that a program will ever be

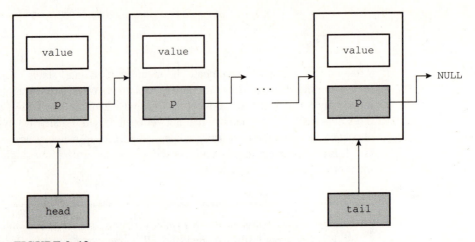

FIGURE 9–13
A typical linked list. Note that pointer in each variable points to the next variable in the list.

required to solve. This large memory requirement can result in a program being too large to run on some computers and also results in a waste of memory most of the time that the program is executed. Even allocatable arrays don't completely solve the problem. Allocatable arrays prevent memory waste by allowing us to allocate only the amount of memory needed for a specific problem, but we must know before we allocate the memory just how many values will be present during a particular run. In contrast, linked lists permit us to add elements one at a time, and we do not have to know in advance how many elements will ultimately be in the list.

When a program containing a linked list first starts to execute, the list is empty. In that case the `head` and `tail` pointers have nothing to point to, so they are both nullified (see Figure 9–14a). When the first value is read in, a variable of the derived data type is created, and the value is stored in that variable. The *head* and *tail* pointers are set to point to the variable, and the pointer in the variable is nullified (Figure 9–14b).

When the next value is read in, a new variable of the derived data type is created, the value is stored in that variable, and the pointer in the variable is nullified. The pointer in

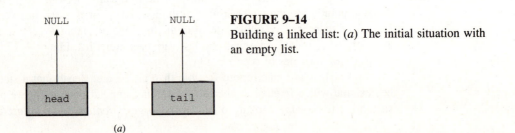

FIGURE 9–14
Building a linked list: (*a*) The initial situation with an empty list.

(*a*)

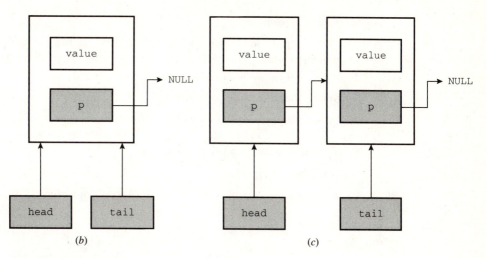

FIGURE 9–14
Building a linked list: (*b*) After adding one value to the list. (*c*) After adding a second value to the list.

the previous variable is set to point to the new variable, and the `tail` pointer is set to point to the new variable. Note that the `head` pointer does not change (Figure 9–14*c*). This process is repeated as each new value is added to the list.

Once all of the values are read in, the program can process them by starting at the `head` pointer and following the pointers in the list until it reaches the `tail` pointer.

EXAMPLE 9–2 *Creating a Linked List:* In this example we will write a simple program that reads in a list of real numbers and then writes them out again. The number of values that the program can handle should only be limited by the amount of memory in the computer.

This program doesn't do anything interesting by itself, but building a linked list in memory is a necessary first step in many practical problems. You will learn how to create the list in this example and then start using lists to do useful work in later examples.

SOLUTION

We will use a linked list to hold the input values, since the size of a linked list can keep growing as long as we can allocate additional memory for new values. Each input value will be stored in a variable of the following derived data type, where the element p points to the next item in the list and the element `value` stores the input real value.

```
TYPE :: real_value
   REAL :: value
   TYPE (real_value), POINTER :: p
END TYPE
```

1. **State the problem.**

Write a program to read an arbitrary number of real values from a file and to store them in a linked list. After all of the values have been read, the program should write them to the standard output device.

2. **Define the inputs and outputs.**

The input to the program will be a file name and a list of real values arranged one value per line in that file. The output from the program will be the real values in the file listed to the standard output device.

3. **Describe the algorithm.**

This program can be broken down into four major steps:

```
Get the input file name
Open the input file
Read the input data into a linked list
Write the data to the standard output device
```

The first three major steps of the program are to get the name of the input file, to open the file, and to read in the data. We must prompt the user for the input file name, read in the name, and open the file. If the file open is successful, we must read in the data, keeping track of the number of values read. Since we don't know how many data values to expect, a while loop is appropriate for the READ. The pseudocode for these steps follows.

```
Prompt user for the input file name "filename"
Read the file name "filename"
OPEN file "filename"
IF OPEN is successful THEN
    WHILE
        Read value into temp
        IF read not successful EXIT
        nvals ← nvals + 1
        (ALLOCATE new list item & store value)
    End of WHILE
    ...                        (Insert writing step here)
End of IF
```

The step of adding a new item to the linked list needs to be examined more carefully. When we add a new variable to the list, there are two possibilities: either the list is still empty or else values are already in the list. If there is nothing in the list yet, then the head and tail pointers are nullified, so we will allocate the new variable using the head pointer and point the tail pointer to the same place. The pointer p within the new variable must be nullified because there is nothing to point to yet, and the real value will be stored in the element value of the variable.

If values already appear in the list, then the tail pointer points to the last variable in the list. In that case we will allocate the new variable using the pointer p within the last variable in the list and then point the tail pointer to the new variable. The pointer p within the new variable must be nullified because there is nothing to point to, and the real value will be stored in the element value of the new variable.

These corresponding pseudocode follows.

```
Read value into temp
IF read not successful EXIT
nvals ← nvals + 1
IF   head is not associated THEN
     ! The list is empty
     ALLOCATE head
     tail => head              ! Tail points to first value
     NULLIFY tail%p            ! Nullify p within 1st value
     tail%value ← temp         ! Store new number
ELSE
     ! The list already has values
     ALLOCATE tail%p
     tail => tail%p            ! Tail now points to new last value
     NULLIFY tail%p            ! Nullify p within new last value
     tail%value ← temp         ! Store new number
END of IF
```

The final step is to write out the values in the linked list. We must go back to the head of the list and follow the pointers in it to the end of the list. We will define a local pointer `ptr` to point to the value currently being printed out. The corresponding pseudocode follows.

```
ptr => head
WHILE ptr is associated
    WRITE ptr%value
    ptr = ptr%p
END of WHILE
```

4. **Turn the algorithm into Fortran statements.**

The resulting Fortran subroutine is shown in Figure 9–15.

FIGURE 9–15
Program to read in a series of real values and store them in a linked list.

```
PROGRAM linked_list
!
! Purpose:
!   To read in a series of real values from an input data file
!   and store them in a linked list.  After the list is read in,
!   it will be written back to the standard output device.
!
! Record of revisions:
!    Date        Programmer           Description of change
!    ====        ==========           =====================
!   01/28/95   S. J. Chapman          Original code
!
IMPLICIT NONE

! Derived data type to store real values in
TYPE :: real_value
   REAL :: value
   TYPE (real_value), POINTER :: p
END TYPE
```

(continued)

(concluded)

```
! List of variables:
TYPE (real_value), POINTER :: head      ! Pointer to head of list
CHARACTER(len=20) :: filename           ! Input data file name
INTEGER :: nvals = 0                     ! Number of data read
TYPE (real_value), POINTER :: ptr       ! Temporary pointer
TYPE (real_value), POINTER :: tail      ! Pointer to tail of list
INTEGER :: istat                         ! Status: 0 for success
REAL :: temp                             ! Temporary variable

! Get the name of the file containing the input data.
WRITE (*,*) 'Enter the file name with the data to be read: '
READ (*,'(A20)') filename

! Open input data file.
OPEN ( UNIT=9, FILE=filename, STATUS='OLD', ACTION='READ', &
       IOSTAT=istat )

! Was the OPEN successful?
fileopen: IF ( istat == 0 ) THEN              ! Open successful

   ! The file was opened successfully, so read the data from
   ! it, and store it in the linked list.
   input: DO
      READ (9, *, IOSTAT=istat) temp           ! Get value
      IF ( istat /= 0 ) EXIT                    ! Exit on end of data
      nvals = nvals + 1                         ! Bump count

      IF (.NOT. ASSOCIATED(head)) THEN     ! No values in list
         ALLOCATE (head,STAT=istat)        ! Allocate new value
         tail => head                      ! Tail pts to new value
         NULLIFY (tail%p)                  ! Nullify p in new value
         tail%value = temp                 ! Store number
      ELSE                                 ! Values already in list
         ALLOCATE (tail%p,STAT=istat)      ! Allocate new value
         tail => tail%p                    ! Tail pts to new value
         NULLIFY (tail%p)                  ! Nullify p in new value
         tail%value = temp                 ! Store number
      END IF
   END DO input

   ! Now, write out the data.
   ptr => head
   output: DO
      IF ( .NOT. ASSOCIATED(ptr) ) EXIT    ! Pointer valid?
      WRITE (*,'(1X,F10.4)') ptr%value     ! Yes: Write value
      ptr => ptr%p                         ! Get next pointer
   END DO output

ELSE fileopen

   ! Else file open failed.  Tell user.
   WRITE (*,'(1X,A,I6)') 'File open failed--status = ', istat

END IF fileopen

END PROGRAM
```

5. **Test the resulting Fortran programs.**

To test this program, we must generate a file of input data. If the following 10 real values are placed in a file called `input.dat`, then we can use that file to test the program: 1.0, 3.0, −4.4, 5., 2., 9.0, 10.1, −111.1, 0.0, −111.1. When the program is executed with this file, the results are

```
C>linked_list
Enter the file name with the data to be read:
input.dat
    1.0000
    3.0000
   -4.4000
    5.0000
    2.0000
    9.0000
   10.1000
 -111.1000
     .0000
 -111.1000
```

The program appears to be working properly. Note that the program does not check the status of the `ALLOCATE` statements. This omission was deliberate to make the manipulations of the linked list as clear as possible. In any real program, these statuses should be checked to detect memory problems so that the program can shut down gracefully.

EXAMPLE 9–3 The Insertion Sort: We introduced the selection sort in Chapter 5. That algorithm sorted a list by searching for the smallest value in the list and placing it at the top. Then it searched for the smallest value in the remaining portion of the list and placed it in the second position, and so forth until all of the values were sorted.

Another possible sorting algorithm is the *insertion sort*. The insertion sort works by placing each value in its proper position in the list as it is read in. If the value is smaller than any previous value in the list, then it is placed at the top. If the value is larger than any previous value in the list, then it is placed at the bottom. If the value is in between, then the number is inserted at the appropriate place in the middle of the list.

An insertion sort of the values 7, 2, 11, −1, and 3 is shown in Figure 9–16. The first value read is a 7. Since there are no other values in the list, it is placed at the top. The next value read is a 2. Since it is smaller than the 7, it is placed above the 7 in the list. The third value read is an 11. Since it is larger than any other value in the list, it is placed at the bottom. The fourth value read is a −1. Since it is smaller than any other value in the list, it is placed at the top. The fifth value read is a 3. Since it is larger than 2 and smaller than 7, it is placed between them in the list. In the insertion sort, the list is always kept sorted as each value is read.

Linked lists are ideally suited for implementing an insertion sort, since new values can be added at the front, at the end, or anywhere in the middle of the list

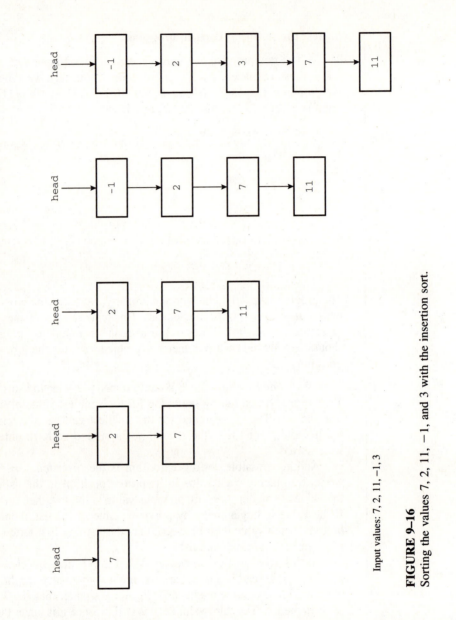

Input values: 7, 2, 11, −1, 3

FIGURE 9-16
Sorting the values 7, 2, 11, −1, and 3 with the insertion sort.

by simply changing pointers. We will now use a linked list to implement an insertion sort algorithm to sort an arbitrary number of integer values.

SOLUTION

We will use a linked list to hold the input values, since it is easy to insert new values anywhere in the linked list by simply changing pointers. Each input value will be read and stored in a variable of the following derived data type, where the pointer next_value points to the next item in the list and the element value stores the input integer value.

```
TYPE :: int_value
   INTEGER :: value
   TYPE (int_value), POINTER :: next_value
END TYPE
```

Each value will be read, compared to all previous values, and inserted at the proper point in the list.

1. State the problem.

Write a program to read an arbitrary number of integer values from a file and to sort them using an insertion sort. After all of the values have been read and sorted, the program should write the sorted list out to the standard output device.

2. Define the inputs and outputs.

The input to the program will be a file name and a list of integer values arranged one value per line in that file. The output from the program will be the sorted integer values listed to the standard output device.

3. Describe the algorithm.

The pseudocode for this program follows.

```
Prompt user for the input file name "filename"
Read the file name "filename"
OPEN file "filename"
IF OPEN is successful THEN
   WHILE
      Read value into temp
      IF read not successful EXIT
      nvals ← nvals + 1
      ALLOCATE new data item & store value
      Insert item at proper point in list
   End of WHILE
   Write the data to the standard output device
End of IF
```

The step of adding a new item to the linked list needs to be examined in more detail. When we add a new variable to the list, there are two possibilities: either the list is still empty or else values are already in the list. If there is nothing in the list yet, then the head and tail pointers are nullified, so we will allocate the new variable using the head pointer and point the tail pointer to the same place. The pointer next_value within the new variable must be nullified because there is nothing to point to yet, and the integer will be stored in the element value of the variable.

If values already appear in the list, then we must search to find the proper place to insert the new value into the list. We have three possibilities. If the number is smaller than the first number in the list (pointed to by the head pointer), then we will add the value at the front of the list. If the number is greater than or equal to the last number in the list (pointed to by the `tail` pointer), then we will add the value at the end of the list. If the number is between those values, we will search until we locate the two values that it lies between and insert the new value there. Note that we must allow for the possibility that the new value is equal to one of numbers already in the list. The pseudocode for these steps is

```
Read value into temp
IF read not successful EXIT
nvals ← nvals + 1
ALLOCATE ptr
ptr%value ← temp
IF head is not associated THEN
   ! The list is empty
   head => ptr
   tail => head
   NULLIFY tail%next_value
ELSE
   ! The list already has values.  Check for
   ! location for new value.
   IF ptr%value < head%value THEN
      ! Add at front
      ptr%next_value => head
      head => ptr
   ELSE IF ptr%value >= tail%value THEN
      ! Add at rear
      tail%next_value => ptr
      tail => ptr
      NULLIFY tail%next_value
   ELSE
      ! Find place to add value
      ptr1 => head
      ptr2 => ptr1%next_value
      DO
         IF ptr%value >= ptr1%value AND
            ptr%value < ptr2%value THEN
            ! Insert value here
            ptr%next_value => ptr2
            ptr1%next_value => ptr
            EXIT
         END of IF
         ptr1 => ptr2
         ptr2 => ptr2%next_value
      END of DO
   END of IF
END of IF
```

The final step is to write the values in the linked list. We must go back to the head of the list and follow the pointers to the end of the list. We will use pointer `ptr` to point to the value currently being printed out. The pseudocode for steps is

```
ptr => head
WHILE ptr is associated
   WRITE ptr%value
   ptr = ptr%next_value
END of WHILE
```

4. **Turn the algorithm into Fortran statements.**

The resulting Fortran subroutine is shown in Figure 9–17.

FIGURE 9–17
Program to read in a series of integer values and sort them using the insertion sort.

```
PROGRAM insertion_sort
!
! Purpose:
!   To read a series of integer values from an input data file
!   and sort them using an insertion sort.  After the values
!   are sorted, they will be written back to the standard
!   output device.
!
! Record of revisions:
!     Date        Programmer          Description of change
!     ====        ==========          =====================
!   01/30/95    S. J. Chapman         Original code
!
IMPLICIT NONE

! Derived data type to store real values in
TYPE :: int_value
   INTEGER :: value
    TYPE (int_value), POINTER :: next_value
END TYPE

! List of variables:
TYPE (int_value), POINTER :: head    ! Pointer to head of list
CHARACTER(len=20) :: filename        ! Input data file name
INTEGER :: istat                     ! Status: 0 for success
INTEGER :: nvals = 0                 ! Number of data read
TYPE (int_value), POINTER :: ptr     ! Ptr to new value
TYPE (int_value), POINTER :: ptr1    ! Temp ptr for search
TYPE (int_value), POINTER :: ptr2    ! Temp ptr for search
TYPE (int_value), POINTER :: tail    ! Pointer to tail of list
INTEGER :: temp                      ! Temporary variable

! Get the name of the file containing the input data.
WRITE (*,*) 'Enter the file name with the data to be sorted: '
READ (*,'(A20)') filename

! Open input data file.
OPEN ( UNIT=9, FILE=filename, STATUS='OLD', ACTION='READ', &
       IOSTAT=istat )

! Was the OPEN successful?
fileopen: IF ( istat == 0 ) THEN          ! Open successful

   ! The file was opened successfully, so read the data value
   ! to sort, allocate a variable for it, and locate the proper
   ! point to insert the new value into the list.
   input: DO
      READ (9, *, IOSTAT=istat) temp      ! Get value
      IF ( istat /= 0 ) EXIT input        ! Exit on end of data
      nvals = nvals + 1                   ! Bump count
```

(continued)

(concluded)

```
        ALLOCATE (ptr,STAT=istat)              ! Allocate space
        ptr%value = temp                       ! Store number

        ! Now find out where to put it in the list.
        new: IF (.NOT. ASSOCIATED(head)) THEN ! No values in list
            head => ptr                        ! Place at front
            tail => head                       ! Tail pts to new value
            NULLIFY (ptr%next_value)           ! Nullify next ptr
        ELSE
            ! Values already in list.  Check for location.
            front: IF ( ptr%value < head%value ) THEN
                ! Add at front of list
                ptr%next_value => head
                head => ptr
            ELSE IF ( ptr%value >= tail%value ) THEN
                ! Add at end of list
                tail%next_value => ptr
                tail => ptr
                NULLIFY ( tail%next_value )
            ELSE
                ! Find place to add value
                ptr1 => head
                ptr2 => ptr1%next_value
                search: DO
                    IF ( (ptr%value >= ptr1%value) .AND. &
                         (ptr%value < ptr2%value) ) THEN
                        ! Insert value here
                        ptr%next_value => ptr2
                        ptr1%next_value => ptr
                        EXIT search
                    END IF
                    ptr1 => ptr2
                    ptr2 => ptr2%next_value
                END DO search
            END IF front
        END IF new
    END DO input

    ! Now, write out the data.
    ptr => head
    output: DO
        IF ( .NOT. ASSOCIATED(ptr) ) EXIT      ! Pointer valid?
        WRITE (*,'(1X,I10)') ptr%value         ! Yes: Write value
        ptr => ptr%next_value                  ! Get next pointer
    END DO output

ELSE fileopen

    ! Else file open failed.  Tell user.
    WRITE (*,'(1X,A,I6)') 'File open failed--status = ', istat

END IF fileopen

END PROGRAM
```

5. Test the resulting Fortran programs.

To test this program, we must generate a file of input data. If the following seven integer values are placed in a file called `input1.dat`, then we can use that file to test the program: 7, 2, 11, −1, 3, 2, and 0. When the program is executed with this file, the results are

```
C>insertion_sort
Enter the file name with the data to be sorted:
input1.dat
        -1
         0
         2
         2
         3
         7
        11
```

The program appears to be working properly. Note that this program also does not check the status of the ALLOCATE statements. This omission was deliberate to make the manipulations as clear as possible. (At one point in the program, the DO and IF structures are nested six deep!) In any real program, these statuses should be checked to detect memory problems so that the program can shut down gracefully.

Quiz 9–1

This quiz provides a quick check to see if you understand the concepts introduced in sections 9.1 and 9.2. If you have trouble with the quiz, reread the sections, ask your instructor, or discuss the material with a fellow student. The answers to this quiz appear in Appendix F.

1. What is an allocatable array? How does it differ from an ordinary array?

2. What will be printed out by the following WRITE statements?

   ```
   REAL, ALLOCATABLE, DIMENSION(:,:,:) :: values
   . . .
   ALLOCATE( values(3,-1:2,5), STAT=istat )
   WRITE (*,*) UBOUND(values,2)
   WRITE (*,*) SIZE(values)
   WRITE (*,*) SHAPE(values)
   ```

3. What is a pointer? What is a target? What is the difference between a pointer and an ordinary variable?

4. What is a pointer assignment statement? What is the difference between a pointer assignment statement and an ordinary assignment statement?

5. What are the possible association statuses of a pointer? How can the association status be changed?

(continued)

(concluded)

6. What is dereferencing?

7. How can memory be dynamically allocated with pointers? How can it be deallocated?

Are the following code segments valid or invalid? If a code segment is valid, explain what it does. If it is invalid, explain why.

8.
```
REAL, DIMENSION(:), ALLOCATABLE :: time
time = (/ 0.00,  0.25,  1.00,  2.25,  4.00,  6.25, &
             9.00, 12.25, 16.00, 20.25/)
WRITE (*,*) time
```

9.
```
REAL, DIMENSION(:,:), ALLOCATABLE :: test
WRITE (*,*) ALLOCATED(test)
```

10.
```
REAL :: value = 35.2
REAL, POINTER :: ptr1
ptr1 => value
```

11.
```
REAL, TARGET :: value = 35.2
REAL, POINTER :: ptr2
ptr2 = value
```

12.
```
INTEGER, DIMENSION(10,10), TARGET :: array
REAL, DIMENSION(:,:), POINTER :: ptr3
ptr3 => array
```

13.
```
INTEGER, TARGET :: i1 = 10, i2 = -123
INTEGER, POINTER :: p1, p2
p1 => i2
p2 => i1
WRITE (*,*) ASSOCIATED(p1)
WRITE (*,*) ASSOCIATED(p1,i1)
NULLIFY (p1)
WRITE (*,*) ASSOCIATED(p1)
```

14.
```
INTEGER, POINTER :: ptr
WRITE (*,*) ASSOCIATED(ptr)
ALLOCATE (ptr)
ptr = 137
WRITE (*,*) ASSOCIATED(ptr), ptr
NULLIFY (ptr)
```

15.
```
INTEGER, DIMENSION(:), POINTER :: ptr1, ptr2
INTEGER :: istat
ALLOCATE (ptr1(10), STAT=istat)
ptr1 = 0
ptr1(3) = 17
ptr2 => ptr1
DEALLOCATE (ptr1)
WRITE (*,*) ptr2
```

9.2.6 Using Pointers in Procedures

Pointers may be used as dummy arguments in procedures and may be passed as actual arguments to procedures. In addition, a function result can be a pointer. The following restrictions apply if pointers are used in procedures:

1. If a procedure has dummy arguments with either the POINTER or TARGET attributes, then the procedure must have an explicit interface.
2. If a dummy argument is a pointer, then the actual argument passed to the procedure must be a pointer of the same type, kind, and rank.
3. A pointer dummy argument cannot have an INTENT attribute.

We must be very careful when passing pointers to procedures. As programs get larger and more flexible, we will often get to a situation where pointers are allocated in one procedure, used in others, and finally deallocated and nullified in yet another. In such a complex program, it is *very* easy to make errors such as attempting to work with disassociated pointers or allocating new arrays with pointers that are already in use. Therefore, always check the status results for ALLOCATE and DEALLOCATE statements and always use the ASSOCIATED function to check the status of pointers.

When a pointer is used to pass data to a procedure, we automatically know the type of the data associated with the pointer from the type of the pointer itself. If the pointer points to an array, we will know the rank of the array, but not its extent or size. If we need to know the extent or size of the array, then we can use the intrinsic functions LBOUND and UBOUND to determine the lower and upper bounds of each dimension of the array.

EXAMPLE 9–4 *Extracting the Diagonal Elements from a Matrix:* To illustrate the proper use of pointers, we will write a subroutine that accepts a pointer to a square matrix and then returns a pointer to an array containing the diagonal elements of the matrix.

SOLUTION

A subroutine with appropriate error checking is shown in Figure 9–18. This sample subroutine accepts a pointer to a two-dimensional square array and returns the diagonal elements of the array in a one-dimensional array that it allocates on a separate pointer. Note that the subroutine checks the association status of the input pointer to ensure that it is currently associated, checks the array to make sure that it is square, and checks the association status of the output pointer to ensure that it is *not* currently associated. (The last test ensures that we don't accidentally reuse a pointer that is currently in use. Reusing the pointer might leave the original data inaccessible if there were no other pointer to it.) If any of the conditions fail, then an appropriate error flag is set and the subroutine returns to the calling program unit.

FIGURE 9–18

Subroutine to extract the diagonal elements from a square array. This subroutine illustrates the proper technique for working with pointers passed as calling arguments.

```
SUBROUTINE get_diagonal ( ptr_a, ptr_b, error )
!
!  Purpose:
!    To extract the diagonal elements from the rank-2
!    square array pointed to by ptr_a, and store them in
!    a rank-1 array allocated on ptr_b.  The following
!    error conditions are defined:
!    0 — No error
!    1 — ptr_a not associated on input
!    2 — ptr_b already associated on input
!    3 — Array on ptr_a not square
!    4 — Unable to allocate memory for ptr_b
!
!  Record of revisions:
!    Date          Programmer          Description of change
!    ====          ==========          =====================
!    01/31/96      S. J. Chapman       Original code
!
IMPLICIT NONE

! Declare calling arguments:
INTEGER, DIMENSION(:,:), POINTER :: ptr_a  ! Ptr to square array
INTEGER, DIMENSION(:), POINTER :: ptr_b    ! Ptr to output array
INTEGER, INTENT(OUT) :: error              ! Errors flag

! Declare local variables:
INTEGER :: i                               ! Loop counter
INTEGER :: istat                           ! Allocate status
INTEGER, DIMENSION(2) :: l_bound           ! Lower bounds on ptr_a
INTEGER, DIMENSION(2) :: u_bound           ! Upper bounds on ptr_a
INTEGER, DIMENSION(2) :: extent            ! Extent of array on ptr_a

! Check error conditions
error_1: IF ( .NOT. ASSOCIATED ( ptr_a ) ) THEN
   error = 1
ELSE IF ( ASSOCIATED ( ptr_b ) ) THEN
   error = 2
ELSE
   ! Check for square array
   l_bound = LBOUND ( ptr_a )
   u_bound = UBOUND ( ptr_a )
   extent = u_bound - l_bound + 1
   error_3: IF ( extent(1) /= extent(2) ) THEN
      error = 3
   ELSE
      ! Everything is ok so far, allocate ptr_b.
      ALLOCATE ( ptr_b(extent(1)), STAT=istat )
      error_4: IF ( istat /= 0 ) THEN
         error = 4
      ELSE
         ! Everything is ok, extract diagonal.
         ok: DO i = 1, extent(1)
            ptr_b(i) = ptr_a(l_bound(1)+i-1,l_bound(2)+i-1)
```

(continued)

(concluded)
```
        END DO ok

          ! Reset error flag.
          error = 0
       END IF error_4
    END IF error_3
END IF error_1

END SUBROUTINE get_diagonal
```

A test driver program for this subroutine is shown in Figure 9–19. This program tests the first three possible error conditions and also the proper operation of the subroutine when no error occurs. Note that there is no easy way to get the memory allocation of `ptr_b` to fail, so there is no explicit test in the driver for that.

This program assumes that subroutine `get_diagonal` has been placed in a module called `subs` to create an explicit interface.

FIGURE 9–19

Test driver program for subroutine `get_diagonal`.

```
PROGRAM test_diagonal
!
! Purpose:
!    To test the diagonal extraction subroutine.
!
! Record of revisions:
!    Date        Programmer           Description of change
!    ====        ==========           =====================
!    01/31/96    S. J. Chapman        Original code
!
USE subs
IMPLICIT NONE

! Declare local variable:
INTEGER :: i, j, k                        ! Loop counter
INTEGER :: istat                          ! Allocate status
INTEGER, DIMENSION(:,:), POINTER :: ptr_a ! Ptr to square array
INTEGER, DIMENSION(:), POINTER :: ptr_b   ! Ptr to output array
INTEGER :: error                          ! Errors flag

! Call diagonal with nothing defined to see what happens.
CALL get_diagonal ( ptr_a, ptr_b, error )
WRITE (*,*) 'No pointers allocated: '
WRITE (*,*) ' Error = ', error

! Allocate both pointers, and call the subroutine.
ALLOCATE (ptr_a(10,10), STAT=istat )
ALLOCATE (ptr_b(10), STAT=istat )
CALL get_diagonal ( ptr_a, ptr_b, error )
WRITE (*,*) 'Both pointers allocated: '
WRITE (*,*) ' Error = ', error

! Allocate ptr_a only, but with unequal extents.
```

(continued)

```
(concluded)
DEALLOCATE (ptr_a, STAT=istat)
DEALLOCATE (ptr_b, STAT=istat)
ALLOCATE (ptr_a(-5:5,10), STAT=istat )
CALL get_diagonal ( ptr_a, ptr_b, error )
WRITE (*,*) 'Array on ptr_a not square: '
WRITE (*,*) ' Error = ', error

! Allocate ptr_a only, initialize, and get results.
DEALLOCATE (ptr_a, STAT=istat)
ALLOCATE (ptr_a(-2:2,0:4), STAT=istat )
k = 0
DO j = 0, 4
   DO i = -2, 2
      k = k + 1                       ! Store the numbers 1 .. 25
      ptr_a(i,j) = k                  ! in row order in the array
   END DO
END DO
CALL get_diagonal ( ptr_a, ptr_b, error )
WRITE (*,*) 'ptr_a allocated & square; ptr_b not allocated: '
WRITE (*,*) ' Error = ', error
WRITE (*,*) ' Diag  = ', ptr_b

END PROGRAM
```

When the test driver program is executed, the results are

```
C>test_diagonal
No pointers allocated:
 Error =             1
Both pointers allocated:
 Error =             2
Array on ptr_a not square:
 Error =             3
ptr_a allocated & square; ptr_b not allocated:
 Error =             0
 Diag  =             1           7          13          19          25
```

All errors were flagged properly, and the diagonal values are correct, so the subroutine appears to be working properly.

Good Programming Practice

Always test the association status of any pointers passed to procedures as calling arguments. In a large program you can easily make mistakes that result in an attempt to use an unassociated pointer or an attempt to reallocate an already associated pointer. (The latter case will produce a memory leak.)

It is also possible for a function to return a pointer value. If a function is to return a pointer, then the RESULT clause must be used in the function definition and the RESULT variable must be declared to be a pointer. For example, the function in Figure 9–20 accepts a pointer to a rank-1 array and returns a pointer to every fifth value in the array.

FIGURE 9–20
A pointer-valued function.

```
FUNCTION every_fifth (ptr_array) RESULT (ptr_fifth)
!
! Purpose:
!   To produce a pointer to every fifth element in an
!   input rank-1 array.
!
! Record of revisions:
!     Date          Programmer         Description of change
!     ====          ==========         =====================
!   01/31/96       S. J. Chapman       Original code
!
IMPLICIT NONE

! Declare calling arguments:
INTEGER, DIMENSION(:), POINTER :: ptr_array
INTEGER, DIMENSION(:), POINTER :: ptr_fifth

! Declare local variables:
INTEGER :: low          ! Array lower bound
INTEGER :: high         ! Array upper bound

low = LBOUND(ptr_array,1)
high = UBOUND(ptr_array,1)
ptr_fifth => ptr_array(low:high:5)

END FUNCTION every_fifth
```

A pointer-valued function must always have an explicit interface in any procedure that uses it. The explicit interface may be specified by placing the function in a module and then using the module in the procedure. Once the function is defined, it can be used any place that a pointer expression can be used. For example, it can be used on the right side of a pointer assignment statement as follows:

```
ptr_2 => every_fifth( ptr_1 )
```

The function can also be used in a location where an integer array is expected. In that case the pointer returned by the function will automatically be dereferenced, and the values pointed to will be used. Thus the following statement is legal and will print out the values pointed to by the pointer returned from the function.

```
WRITE (*,*) every_fifth( ptr_1 )
```

As with any function, a pointer-valued function can *not* be used on the left-hand side of an assignment statement.

■ 9.3
SUMMARY

Allocatable arrays are arrays whose rank is declared at compilation time, but whose shape is not determined until the program is executed. Memory is allocated for allocatable arrays with an ALLOCATE statement and is deallocated with a DEALLOCATE statement.

A pointer is a special type of variable that contains the address of another variable instead of containing a value. A pointer has a specified data type and (if it points to an array) rank, and it can only point to data items of that particular type and rank. Pointers are declared with the POINTER attribute in a type declaration statement or in a separate POINTER statement. The data item pointed to by a pointer is called a target. Pointers can point only to data items declared with the TARGET attribute in a type declaration statement or in a separate TARGET statement.

A pointer assignment statement places the address of a target in a pointer. The form of the statement is

```
pointer => target
pointer1 => pointer2
```

In the latter case, the address currently contained in *pointer2* is placed in *pointer1*, and both pointers independently point to the same target.

A pointer can have one of three possible association statuses: undefined, associated, or disassociated. When a pointer is first declared in a type declaration statement, its pointer association status is undefined. Once a pointer has been associated with a target by a pointer assignment statement, its association status becomes associated. If a pointer is later disassociated from its target and is not associated with any new target, then its association status becomes disassociated. A pointer should always be nullified or associated as soon as it is created. The function ASSOCIATED() can be used to determine the association status of a pointer.

Pointers can be used to dynamically create and destroy variables or arrays. Memory is allocated for data items in an ALLOCATE statement and deallocated in a DEALLOCATE statement. The pointer in the ALLOCATE statement points to the data item that is created and is the *only* way to access that data item. If that pointer is disassociated or is associated with another target before another pointer is set to point to the allocated memory, then the memory becomes inaccessible to the program. This condition is called a memory leak.

When dynamic memory is deallocated in a DEALLOCATE statement, the pointer to the memory is automatically nullified. However, if other pointers are pointing to that same memory, they must be manually nullified or reassigned. If not, the program might attempt to use them to read or write to the deallocated memory location, with potentially disastrous results.

Pointers may be used as components of derived data types, including the data type being defined. This feature permits us to create dynamic data structures such as linked lists, where the pointers in one dynamically allocated data item point to the next item in the chain. This flexibility is extraordinarily useful in many problems.

Pointers may be passed to procedures as calling arguments provided that the procedure has an explicit interface in the calling program. A dummy pointer argument must not have an INTENT attribute. A function can also return a pointer value if the RESULT clause is used and the result variable is declared to be a pointer.

9.3.1 Summary of Good Programming Practice

The following guidelines should be adhered to when working with the pointers:

1. Always include the STAT= clause in any ALLOCATE statement and always check the returned status so that a program can be shut down gracefully if there is insufficient memory to allocate the necessary arrays.
2. Always deallocate dynamic arrays with a DEALLOCATE statement as soon as you are through using them.
3. Always nullify or assign all pointers in a program unit as soon as they are created. This technique eliminates any possible ambiguities associated with the undefined allocation status.
4. When sorting or swapping large arrays or derived data types, it is more efficient to exchange pointers to the data than it is to manipulate the data itself.
5. Always nullify or reassign *all* pointers to a memory location when that memory is deallocated. One pointer will be automatically nullified by the DEALLOCATE statement, and any others must be manually nullified in NULLIFY statement(s) or reassigned in pointer assignment statements.
6. Always test the association status of any pointers passed to procedures as calling arguments. Mistakes can result in an attempt to use an unassociated pointer or an attempt to reallocate an already associated pointer. (The latter case will produce a memory leak.)

9.3.2 Summary of Fortran Statements and Structures

ALLOCATABLE Attribute

```
        type, ALLOCATABLE, DIMENSION(:, [:, ...]) :: array1, ...
```

Example:

```
        REAL, ALLOCATABLE, DIMENSION(:) :: array1
        INTEGER, ALLOCATABLE, DIMENSION(:,:,:) :: indices
```

Description:

The ALLOCATABLE attribute declares that the size of an array is dynamic. The size will be specified in an ALLOCATE statement at run time. The type declaration statement must specify the rank of the array, but not the extent in each dimension. Each dimension is specified using a colon as a placeholder.

ALLOCATE Statement

        ALLOCATE (*array1*(*[i1:]i2, [j1:]j2, ...*), ... , STAT=*status*)

Example:

        ALLOCATE (array1(10000), STAT=istat)
        ALLOCATE (indices(-10:10,-10:10,5), STAT=allocate_status)

Description:

The ALLOCATE statement dynamically allocates memory to an allocatable array or pointer. The extent of each dimension is specified in the ALLOCATE statement. The returned status will be zero for successful completion and will be a processor-dependent positive number in the case of an error.

DEALLOCATE Statement

        DEALLOCATE (*array1*, ... , STAT=*status*)

Example:

        DEALLOCATE (array1, indices, STAT=status)

Description:

The DEALLOCATE statement dynamically deallocates the memory that was assigned by an ALLOCATE statement to one or more allocatable arrays or pointers. After the statement executes, the memory associated with those arrays is no longer accessible. The returned status will be zero for successful completion and will be a processor-dependent positive number in the case of an error.

NULLIFY Statement

        NULLIFY (ptr1 *[, ptr2, ...]*)

Example:

        NULLIFY (pointer1)

Description:

The NULLIFY statement disassociates the pointers in its list from any targets. After the statement is executed, the status of each pointer is DISASSOCIATED.

POINTER Attribute

        type, POINTER :: ptr1 [, ptr2, ...]

Example:

        INTEGER, POINTER :: next_value
        REAL, DIMENSION(:), POINTER :: array

Description:

   The POINTER attribute declares the variables in the type definition statement to be pointers.

TARGET Attribute

        type, TARGET :: var1 [, var2, ...]

Example:

        INTEGER, TARGET :: num_values
        REAL, DIMENSION(100), TARGET :: array

Description:

   The TARGET attribute declares the variables in the type definition statement to be legal targets for pointers.

■ **9.4**

EXERCISES

9–1 What is an allocatable array? How is it used, and why would you want to use one?

9–2 What is the difference between a pointer variable and an ordinary variable?

9–3 How does a pointer assignment statement differ from an ordinary assignment statement? What happens in each of the following statements a = z and a => z?

```
INTEGER :: x = 6, z = 8
INTEGER, POINTER == a
a => x
a = z
a => z
```

9–4 Is the following program fragment correct or incorrect? If it is incorrect, explain what is wrong with it. If it is correct, what does it do?

```
REAL, POINTER :: p1
REAL:: x1 = 11.
INTEGER, POINTER :: p2
INTEGER :: x2 = 12
p1 => x1
p2 => x2
WRITE (*,'(A,4G8.2)') ' p1, p2, x1, x2 = ', p1, p2, x1, x2
p1 => p2
p2 => x1
WRITE (*,'(A,4G8.2)') ' p1, p2, x1, x2 = ', p1, p2, x1, x2
END PROGRAM
```

9–5 What are the possible association statuses of a pointer? How can you determine the association status of a given pointer?

9–6 Is the following program fragment correct or incorrect? If it is incorrect, explain what is wrong with it. If it is correct, what does the WRITE statement print?

```
REAL, POINTER :: p1, p2
REAL, TARGET :: x1 = 11.1, x2= -3.2
p1 => x1
WRITE (*,*) ASSOCIATED(p1), ASSOCIATED(p2), ASSOCIATED(p1,x2)
```

9–7 What are the proper Fortran statements to declare a pointer to an integer array and then point that pointer to every 10th element in a 1000-element target array called my_data?

9–8 What does the following program print? (*Note:* Intrinsic functions SUM and SIZE are described in Appendix B.)

```
PROGRAM ex9_8
IMPLICIT NONE
INTEGER :: i
REAL, DIMENSION(-25:25), TARGET :: info = (/ (2.1*i, i=-25,25) /)
REAL, DIMENSION(:), POINTER :: ptr1, ptr2, ptr3
ptr1 => info(-25:25:5)
ptr2 => ptr1(1::2)
ptr3 => ptr2(3:5)
WRITE (*,'(A,11F6.1)') ' ptr1 = ', ptr1
WRITE (*,'(A,11F6.1)') ' ptr2 = ', ptr2
WRITE (*,'(A,11F6.1)') ' ptr3 = ', ptr3
WRITE (*,'(A,11F6.1)') ' ave of ptr3 = ', SUM(ptr3)/SIZE(ptr3)
END PROGRAM
```

9–9 How is dynamic memory allocated and deallocated using pointers? How does memory allocation using pointers differ from memory allocation using allocatable arrays?

9–10 What is a memory leak? Why is it a problem, and how can it be avoided?

9–11 Is the following program correct or incorrect? If it is incorrect, explain what is wrong with it. If it is correct, what does the WRITE statement print?

```
MODULE my_sub
CONTAINS
    SUBROUTINE running_sum (sum, value)
```

```
                    REAL, POINTER :: sum, value
                    ALLOCATE (sum)
                    sum = sum + value
                    END SUBROUTINE running_sum
                END MODULE
                PROGRAM sum_values
                USE my_sub
                IMPLICIT NONE
                INTEGER :: istat
                REAL, POINTER :: sum, value
                ALLOCATE (sum, value, STAT=istat)
                WRITE (*,*) 'Enter values to add: '
                DO
                    READ (*,*,IOSTAT=istat) value
                    IF ( istat /= 0 ) EXIT
                    CALL running_sum (sum, value)
                    WRITE (*,*) ' The sum is ', sum
                END DO
                END PROGRAM
```

9–12 Modify the test driver program `test_simul` in Figure 6–7 to use allocatable arrays so that it will function properly regardless of the size of the input system of equations.

9–13 Is the following program correct or incorrect? If it is incorrect, explain what is wrong with it. If it is correct, what do the `WRITE` statements print? What happens when this program is compiled and executed on your computer?

```
                PROGRAM ex9_13
                IMPLICIT NONE
                INTEGER :: i, istat
                INTEGER, DIMENSION(:), POINTER :: ptr1, ptr2

                ALLOCATE (ptr1(1:10), STAT=istat)
                ptr1 = (/ (i, i = 1,10 ) /)
                ptr2 => ptr1

                WRITE (*,'(A,10I3)') ' ptr1 = ', ptr1
                WRITE (*,'(A,10I3)') ' ptr2 = ', ptr2

                DEALLOCATE(ptr1, STAT=istat)

                ALLOCATE (ptr1(1:3), STAT=istat)
                ptr1 = (/ -2, 0, 2 /)

                WRITE (*,'(A,10I3)') ' ptr1 = ', ptr1
                WRITE (*,'(A,10I3)') ' ptr2 = ', ptr2

                END PROGRAM
```

9–14 Create a version of the insertion sort program that will sort a set of input character values in a case-insensitive manner (that is, uppercase and lowercase are to be treated as equivalent.)

9–15 Write a function that accepts a real input array and returns a pointer to the largest value in the array.

9–16 Linear Least- Squares Fit Write a program that reads in an unknown number of real (x,y) pairs from a file and stores them in a linked list. When all the values have been read in, the list should be passed to a subroutine that will compute the linear least-squares fit of the data to a straight line. (The equations for the linear least squares fit were introduced in Example 4–5.)

9–17 Doubly Linked Lists Linked lists have the limitation that in order to find a particular element in the list, you must always search the list from the top down. There is no way to work up the list to find a particular item. For example, suppose that a program has examined the 1000th item in a list and now wants to examine the 999th item in the list. The only way to do so would be to return to the top of the list and start over, working from item 1 down! We can get around this problem by creating a doubly linked list. A *doubly linked list* has pointers both to the next item in the list and to the previous item in the list, permitting searches to be conducted in either direction. Write a program that reads in an arbitrary number of real numbers and adds them to a doubly linked list. Then write out the numbers both in input order and in reverse input order using the pointers. Test the program by creating and processing 20 random values between -100.0 and 100.0.

9–18 Insertion Sort with Doubly Linked Lists Write a version of the insertion sort program that inserts the real input values into a doubly linked list. Test the program by creating and sorting 50 random values between -1000.0 and 1000.0. Print out the sorted values in both ascending and descending order.

ASCII and EBCDIC Coding Systems

Each character in the default Fortran character set is stored in 1 byte of memory, so there are 256 possible values for each character variable. The following table contains the characters corresponding to each possible decimal, octal, and hexadecimal value in both the ASCII and the EBCDIC coding systems. Where characters are blank, they either correspond to control characters or are not defined.

Decimal	Octal	Hex	ASCII character	EBCDIC character
0	0	0	NUL	NUL
...		...	...	...
32	40	20	space	
33	41	21	!	
34	42	22	"	
35	43	23	#	
36	44	24	$	
37	45	25	%	
38	46	26	&	
39	47	27	'	
40	50	28	(	
41	51	29	)	
42	52	2A	*	
43	53	2B	+	
44	54	2C	,	
45	55	2D	-	
46	56	2E	.	

Decimal	Octal	Hex	ASCII character	EBCDIC character
47	57	2F	/	
48	60	30	0	
49	61	31	1	
50	62	32	2	
51	63	33	3	
52	64	34	4	
53	65	35	5	
54	66	36	6	
55	67	37	7	
56	70	38	8	
57	71	39	9	
58	72	3A	:	
59	73	3B	;	
60	74	3C	<	
61	75	3D	=	
62	76	3E	>	
63	77	3F	?	
64	100	40	@	blank
65	101	41	A	
66	102	42	B	
67	103	43	C	
68	104	44	D	
69	105	45	E	
70	106	46	F	
71	107	47	G	
72	110	48	H	
73	111	49	I	
74	112	4A	J	¢
75	113	4B	K	.
76	114	4C	L	<
77	115	4D	M	(
78	116	4E	N	+
79	117	4F	O	|

Decimal	Octal	Hex	ASCII character	EBCDIC character
80	120	50	P	&
81	121	51	Q	
82	122	52	R	
83	123	53	S	
84	124	54	T	
85	125	55	U	
86	126	56	V	
87	127	57	W	
88	130	58	X	
89	131	59	Y	
90	132	5A	Z	!
91	133	5B	[	$
92	134	5C	\	*
93	135	5D	]	)
94	136	5E	^ (or ↑)	;
95	137	5F	_	¬
96	140	60	`	_
97	141	61	a	/
98	142	62	b	
99	143	63	c	
100	144	64	d	
101	145	65	e	
102	146	66	f	
103	147	67	g	
104	150	68	h	
105	151	69	i	
106	152	6A	j	
107	153	6B	k	,
108	154	6C	l	%
109	155	6D	m	_
110	156	6E	n	>
111	157	6F	o	?
112	160	70	p	

Decimal	Octal	Hex	ASCII character	EBCDIC character
113	161	71	q	
114	162	72	r	
115	163	73	s	
116	164	74	t	
117	165	75	u	
118	166	76	v	
119	167	77	w	
120	170	78	x	
121	171	79	y	
122	172	7A	z	:
123	173	7B	{	#
124	174	7C	|	@
125	175	7D	}	'
126	176	7E	~	=
127	177	7F	DEL	"
128	200	80		
129	201	81		a
130	202	82		b
131	203	83		c
132	204	84		d
133	205	85		e
134	206	86		f
135	207	87		g
136	210	88		h
137	211	89		i
...	...	...	...	...
145	221	91		j
146	222	92		k
147	223	93		l
148	224	94		m
149	225	95		n
150	226	96		o
151	227	97		p

Decimal	Octal	Hex	ASCII character	EBCDIC character
152	230	98		q
153	231	99		r
...	...	...	...	...
162	242	A2		s
163	243	A3		t
164	244	A4		u
165	245	A5		v
166	246	A6		w
167	247	A7		x
168	250	A8		y
169	251	A9		z
...	...	...	...	...
192	300	C0		}
193	301	C1		A
194	302	C2		B
195	303	C3		C
196	304	C4		D
197	305	C5		E
198	306	C6		F
199	307	C7		G
200	310	C8		H
201	311	C9		I
...	...	...	...	...
208	320	D0		}
209	321	D1		J
210	322	D2		K
211	323	D3		L
212	324	D4		M
213	325	D5		N
214	326	D6		O
215	327	D7		P
216	330	D8		Q
217	331	D9		R

Decimal	Octal	Hex	ASCII character	EBCDIC character
...	...	...	...	...
224	340	E0		\
225	341	E1		
226	342	E2		S
227	343	E3		T
228	344	E4		U
229	345	E5		V
230	346	E6		W
231	347	E7		X
232	350	E8		Y
233	351	E9		Z
...	...	...	...	...
240	360	F0		0
241	361	F1		1
242	362	F2		2
243	363	F3		3
244	364	F4		4
245	365	F5		5
246	366	F6		6
247	367	F7		7
248	370	F8		8
249	371	F9		9
...	...	...	...	...
255	377	FF		

Fortran 90/95 Intrinsic Procedures

This appendix describes the intrinsic procedures built into the Fortran 90/95 languages and provides some suggestions for their proper use. All intrinsic procedures that are present in Fortran 90 are also present in Fortran 95, although some have additional arguments. Procedures that are only in Fortran 95 and procedures that have additional arguments in Fortran 95 are highlighted in Table B–1.

B.1

CLASSES OF INTRINSIC PROCEDURES

Fortran 90/95 intrinsic procedures can be broken down into three classes: elemental, inquiry, or transformational.

An **elemental function** is specified for scalar arguments but may also be applied to array arguments. If the argument of an elemental function is a scalar, then the result of the function will be a scalar. If the argument of the function is an array, then the result of the function will be an array of the same shape as the input argument. If there is more than one input argument, all the arguments must have the same shape. If an elemental function is applied to an array, the result will be the same as if the function were applied to each element of the array on an element-by-element basis. Thus the following two sets of statements are equivalent:

```
REAL, DIMENSION(4) :: x = (/ 0., 3.141593, 1., 2. /), y
INTEGER :: i

y = SIN(x)                       ! Whole array at once

DO i = 1, 4
   y(i) = SIN(x(i))              ! Element by element
END DO
```

If the KIND argument is specified in an elemental function, it must correspond to a kind defined on the particular processor being used.

An **inquiry function** or **inquiry subroutine** is a procedure whose value depends on the properties of an object being investigated. For example, the function

PRESENT(A) is an inquiry function that returns a true value if the optional argument A is present in a procedure call. Other inquiry functions can return properties of the system used to represent real numbers and integers on a particular processor.

A **transformational function** has one or more array-valued arguments or an array-valued result. Unlike elemental functions that operate on an element-by-element basis, transformational functions operate on arrays as a whole. The output of a transformational function will often not have the same shape as the input arguments. For example, the function DOT_PRODUCT has two vector input arguments of the same size and produces a scalar output.

■ B.2
ALPHABETICAL LIST OF INTRINSIC PROCEDURES

Table B–1 contains an alphabetical listing of the intrinsic procedures included in Fortran 90 and Fortran 95. The first column of the table contains the generic name of each procedure and its calling sequence. The calling sequence is represented by the keywords associated with each argument. Mandatory arguments appear in roman type, and optional arguments appear in italics. The use of keywords is optional, but they must be supplied for optional arguments if earlier optional arguments in the calling sequence are missing or if the arguments are specified in a nondefault order (see section 8.3). For example, the function SIN has one argument, and the keyword of the argument is X. This function can be invoked either with or without the keyword, so the following two statements are equivalent:

```
result = sin(X=3.141593)
result = sin(3.141593)
```

Another example is the function MAXVAL. This function has one required argument and two optional arguments:

```
MAVXAL ( ARRAY, DIM, MASK )
```

If all three calling values are specified in that order, then they may be simply included in the argument list without the keywords. However, if the MASK is to be specified without DIM, then keywords must be used. For example:

```
value = MAVXAL ( array, MASK=mask )
```

The types of the most common argument keywords follow (any kind of the specified type may be used):

A	Any
BACK	Logical
DIM	Integer
I	Integer

KIND	Integer
MASK	Logical
STRING	Character
X, Y	Numeric (integer, real, or complex)
Z	Complex

The second column contains the specific name of an intrinsic function. If this column is blank, then the procedure does not have a specific name and so may not be used as a calling argument. The types of arguments used with the specific functions are

c, c1, c2, ...	Default complex
d, d1, d2, ...	Double-precision real
i, i1, i2, ...	Default integer
r, r1, r2, ...	Default real
l, l1, l2, ...	Logical
str1, str2, ...	Character

The third column contains the type of the value returned by the procedure if it is a function. Obviously, intrinsic subroutines do not have a type associated with them. The fourth column is for notes that follow the table.

The descriptions of these procedures are abbreviated due to space constraints. A more detailed description of each procedure may be downloaded from the book's Website.

■   **TABLE B—1**
Specific and generic names for all Fortran 90/95 intrinsic procedures

Generic name, keyword(s), and calling sequence	Specific name	Function type	Description
ABS(A)		Argument type	Take absolute value of a number (Note 2)
	ABS(r)	Default real	
	CABS(c)	Default real	
	DABS(d)	Double Prec.	
	IABS(i)	Default integer	
ACHAR(I)		Character(1)	Return ASCII character in position I of collating sequence
ACOS(X)		Argument type	Inverse cosine
	ACOS(r)	Default real	
	DACOS(d)	Double Prec.	
ADJUSTL(STRING)		Character	Left-justify characters in STRING
ADJUSTR(STRING)		Character	Right-justify characters in STRING

Generic name, keyword(s), and calling sequence	Specific name	Function type	Description
AIMAG(Z)	AIMAG(c)	Real	Return imaginary part of complex value Z
AINT(A,*KIND*)		Argument type	Truncates A to a whole number
	AINT(r) DINT(d)	Default Real Double Prec.	
ALL(MASK,*DIM*)		Logical	Returns true if all values in dimension *DIM* of MASK are true
ALLOCATED(ARRAY)		Logical	Returns true if ARRAY is allocated
ANINT(A,*KIND*)	ANINT(r) DNINT(d)	Argument type Real Double Prec.	Rounds A to the nearest whole number
ANY(MASK,*DIM*)		Logical	Returns true if any values in dimension *DIM* of MASK are true
ASIN(X)	ASIN(r) ASIN(r) DASIN(d)	Argument type Real Double precision	Inverse sine
ASSOCIATED(POINTER,*TARGET*)		Logical	Returns true if POINTER is associated. If *TARGET* is present, returns true of POINTER is associated with *TARGET*
ATAN(X)	ATAN(r) DATAN(d)	Argument type Real Double precision	Inverse tangent
ATAN2(Y,X)	ATAN2(r2,r1) DATAN2(d2,d1)	Argument type Real Double precision	Inverse tangent, correct over the full circle
BIT_SIZE(I)		Integer	Number of bits in I
BTEST(I,POS)		Logical	Returns true if bit POS of I is 1, and false otherwise
CEILING(A,*KIND*)		Integer	Returns nearest integer above A (Note 4)
CHAR(I,*KIND*)		Character(1)	Returns character at position I in collating sequence
CMPLX(X,*Y*,*KIND*)		Complex	Converts input values to complex, with kind *KIND*.

Generic name, keyword(s), and calling sequence	Specific name	Function type	Description
CONGJ(X)	CONJG(c)	Complex	Calculate complex conjugate
COS(X)	CCOS(c) COS(r) DCOS(d)	Argument type Complex Real Double Prec.	Cosine
COSH(X)	COSH(r) DCOSH(d)	Argument type Real Double Prec.	Hyperbolic cosine
COUNT(MASK, *DIM*)		Integer	Returns number of true values in MASK
CPU_TIME(TIME)		Subroutine	Get elapsed CPU time of current program in seconds
CSHIFT(ARRAY, *SHIFT*, *DIM*)		Array type	Circular shift elements in ARRAY by *SHIFT* positions.
DATE_AND_TIME(*DATE*, *TIME*, *ZONE*, *VALUES*)		Subroutine	Get current date and time.
DBLE(A)		Double Prec.	Convert to double prec.
DIGITS(X)		Integer	Returns number of significant binary digits to A
DIM(X,Y)	DDIM(d1,d2) DIM(r1,r2) IDIM(i1,i2)	Argument type Double Prec. Real Integer	Returns X-Y if > 0; otherwise returns to 0.
DOT_PRODUCT(VECTOR_A, VECTOR_B)		Argument type	Returns dot product of two vectors.
DPROD(X,Y)	DPROD(x1,x2)	Double Prec.	Calculates the double prec. Result of two single precision values.
EOSHIFT(ARRAY, SHIFT, *BOUNDARY*, *DIM*)		Array type	Performs end-off shift of elements in ARRAY
EPSILON(X)		Real	Returns a positive number that is almost negligible compared to 1.0 of the same type and kind as X.
EXP(X)	CEXP(c) DEXP(d) EXP(r)	Argument type Complex Double Prec. Real	Returns e^x
EXPONENT(X)		Integer	Returns the exponent of X in the base of the computer numbering system (usually base2)

Generic name, keyword(s), and calling sequence	Specific name	Function type	Description
FLOOR(A, *KIND*)		Integer	Returns nearest integer below A
FRACTION(X)		Real	Returns the mantissa of X in the base of the computer numbering system (usually base2).
HUGE(X)		Argument type	Returns the largest number of the same type and kind as X
IACHAR(C)		Integer	Returns the position in the ASCII collating sequence of C
IAND(I,J)		Integer	Bitwise AND of I and J
IBCLR(I,POS)		Argument type	
IBITSI,POS,LEN)		Argument type	
IBSET(I,POS)		Argument type	
ICHAR(C)		Integer	Returns the position in the processor's collating sequence of C
IEOR(I,J)		Argument type	Bitwise exclusive OR of I and J
INDEX(STRING, SUBSTRING, *BACK*)	INDEX (str1,str2)	Integer	Finds position of first occurrence of SUBSTRING in STRING
INT(A,*KIND*)	IDINT(i) IFIX(r)	Integer Integer Integer	Truncates A to integer, with kind *KIND*. (Note 1)
IOR(I,J)		Argument type	Bitwise OR of I and J
ISHFT(I,SHIFT)		Argument type	Returns I logically shifted to the left (if SHIFT > 0) or right (if SHIFT < 0) by SHIFT bits. The empty bits are filled with zeros.
ISHFTC(I,SHIFT,*SIZE*)		Argument type	Returns I circularly shifted to the left (if SHIFT > 0) or right (if SHIFT < 0) by SHIFT bits.
KIND(X)		Integer	Returns kind number of X
LBOUND(ARRAY,*DIM*)		Integer	Returns lower bounds of dimensions in ARRAY. If *DIM* is specified, returns that lower bound only.

Generic name, keyword(s), and calling sequence	Specific name	Function type	Description
LEN(STRING)	LEN(str)	Integer	Returns declared length of STRING
LEN_TRIM(STRING)		Integer	Returns length of STRING less trailing blanks
LGE(STRING_A,STRING_B)		Logical	Returns true if STRING_A≥ STRING_B in the ASCII collating sequence.
LGT(STRING_A,STRING_B)		Logical	Returns true if STRING_A> STRING_B in the ASCII collating sequence.
LLE(STRING_A,STRING_B)		Logical	Returns true if STRING_A≤ STRING_B in the ASCII collating sequence.
LLT(STRING_A,STRING_B)		Logical	Returns true if STRING_A< STRING_B in the ASCII collating sequence.
LOG(X)	ALOG(r) CLOG(c) DLOG(d)	Argument type Real Complex Double Prec.	Calculates natural logarithm of X
LOG10(X)	ALOG10(r) DLOG10(d)	Argument type Real Double Prec.	Calculates base-10 logarithm of X
LOGICAL(L,*KIND*)		Logical	Converts the logical value L to the specified kind.
MATMUL(MATRIX_A, MATRIX_B)		Argument type	Matrix multiplication.
MAX(A1,A2,*A3*,...)	AMAX0 (i1,i2, ...) AMAX1 (r1,r2, ...) DMAX1 (d1,d2,...) MAX0 (i1,i2,...) MAX1 (r1,r2,...)	Argument type Real Real Double Prec. Integer Integer	Return maximum value of A1,A2,*A3* ... (See note 1 below)
MAXEXPONENT(X)		Integer	Returns the maximum exponent of the same type and kind as X
MAXLOC(ARRAY,*DIM*,*MASK*)		Integer	Returns the location of the maximum value of the elements in ARRAY along dimension *DIM* (if present) cooresponding to the true elements of *MASK* (if present). (Note 6)

Generic name, keyword(s), and calling sequence	Specific name	Function type	Description
MAXVAL(ARRAY, *DIM*, *MASK*)		Argument type	Returns the maximum value of the elements in ARRAY along dimension *DIM* (if present) corresponding to the true elements of *MASK* (if present)
MERGE(TSOURCE, FSOURCE, MASK)		Argument type	Selects one of two alternative values according to MASK. If a given element of MASK is true, then the corresponding element of the result comes from array TSOURCE; otherwise, the element comes from array FSOURCE.
MIN(A1,A2,*A3*, ...)		Argument type	Return maximum value of A1,A2,*A3*, ... (See note 1 below)
	AMIN0 (i1,i2, ...)	Real	
	AMIN1 (r1,r2, ...)	Real	
	DMIN1 (d1,d2,...)	Double Prec.	
	MIN0 (i1,i2,...)	Integer	
	MIN1 (r1,r2,...)	Integer	
MINEXPONENT(X)		Integer	Returns the minimum exponent of the same type and kind as X
MINLOC(ARRAY, *DIM*, *MASK*)		Integer	Returns the location of the minimum value of the elements in ARRAY along dimension *DIM* (if present) corresponding to the true elements of *MASK* (if present). (Note 6)
MINVAL(ARRAY, *DIM*, *MASK*)		Argument type	Returns the minimum value of the elements in ARRAY along dimension *DIM* (if present) corresponding to the true elements of *MASK* (if present).
MOD(A,P)		Argument type	Returns the value MOD(A,P) = A - P*INT(A/P)
	AMOD(r1,r2)	Real	
	MOD(i,j)	Integer	
	DMOD(d1,d2)	Double Prec.	
MODULO(A,P)		Argument type	Modulo function

Generic name, keyword(s), and calling sequence	Specific name	Function type	Description
MVBITS(FROM,FROMPOS,LEN,TO,TOPOS)		Subroutine	Copies a sequence of LEN bits starting at FROMPOS in integer FROM, and stores them starting at TOPOS in integer TO.
NEAREST(X,S)		Real	Returns the nearest machine-representable number different from X in the direction of S.
NINT(A,*KIND*)		Integer	Returns nearest integer to A.
	IDNINT(i)	Integer	
	NINT(x)	Integer	
NOT(I)		Argument type	Bitwise compliment of the bits in I
NULL(*MOLD*)		Pointer	Function to return a null value for a pointer (Note 5)
PACK(ARRAY,MASK,*VECTOR*)		Argument type	Packs an array into a rank-1 array under the control of a mask.
PRECISION(X)		Integer	Returns the number of significant decimal digits in X.
PRESENT(A)		Logical	Returns true if optional argument A is present.
PRODUCT(ARRAY,*DIM*,*MASK*)		Argument type	Takes the product of all elements in ARRAY for which *MASK* is true, along dimension *DIM* if present.
RADIX(X)		Integer	Returns base of number system (usually 2).
RANDOM_NUMBER(HARVEST)		Subroutine	Returns one or more values in the range [0,1) from a uniform random number sequence.
RANDOM_SEED(*SIZE*,*PUT*,*GET*)		Subroutine	Provides initial values for subroutine RANDOM_NUMBER.
RANGE(X)		Integer	Returns the decimal exponent range for X.
REAL(A,*KIND*)		Real	Converts A to real, with kind *KIND*. (Note 1)
	FLOAT(i)	Real	
	SNGL(d)	Real	
REPEAT(STRING,NCOPIES)		Character	Returns a character string formed by concatenating NCOPIES copies of STRING one after another

Generic name, keyword(s), and calling sequence	Specific name	Function type	Description
RESHAPE(SOURCE,SHAPE, PAD,ORDER)		Argument type	Constructs an array of shape SHAPE from the elements of another array SOURCE.
RRSPACING(X)		Argument type	Returns the reciprocal of the relative spacing of the numbers near X.
SCALE(X,I)		Argument type	Returns the value $x \times b^I$, where b is the base of the model used to represent X. The base b can be found with the RADIX(X) function; it is almost always 2.
SCAN(STRING,SET,BACK)		Integer	Scans STRING for the first occurrence of any one of the characters in SET, and returns the position of that occurrence.
SELECTED_INT_KIND(R)		Integer	Returns the kind number for the smallest integer kind which can represent all integers n whose values satisfy the condition ABS(n) < 10**R.
SELECTED_REAL_KIND(P,R)		Integer	Returns the kind number for the smallest real kind which has a decimal precision of at least P digits and an exponent range of at least R powers of 10. (Note 3)
SET_EXPONENT(X,I)		Argument type	Returns the number whose fractional part is the fractional part of the number X, and whose exponent part is I.
SHAPE(SOURCE)		Integer	Returns the shape of SOURCE as a rank-1 array whose elements are the extents of the corresponding dimensions of SOURCE.
SIGN(A,B)	DSIGN(d1,d2) ISIGN(i1,i2) SIGN(r1,r2)	Argument type Double Prec. Integer Real	Returns the value of A with the sign of B.
SIN(X)	CSIN(c) DSIN(d) SIN(r)	Argument type Complex Double Prec. Real	Sine

Generic name, keyword(s), and calling sequence	Specific name	Function type	Description
SINH(X)	DSINH(d) SINH(r)	Argument type Double Prec. Real	Hyperbolic sine
SIZE(ARRAY,*DIM*)		Integer	Returns the extent of ARRAY along a particular dimension if *DIM* is present; or else the total number of elements in the array.
SPACING(X)		Argument type	Returns the absolute spacing of the numbers near X in the model used to represent real numbers.
SPREAD(SOURCE,DIM,NCOPIES)		Argument type	Duplicates NCOPIES copies of SOURCE along dimension *DIM*.
SQRT(X)	CSQRT(c) DSQRT(d) SQRT(r)	Argument type Complex Double Prec. Real	Square root of X
SUM(ARRAY,*DIM*,*MASK*)		Argument type	Takes the sum of all elements in ARRAY for which *MASK* is true, along dimension DIM if present.
SYSTEM_CLOCK(COUNT, COUNT_RATE,COUNT_MAX)		Subroutine	Returns raw counts from the processor's real-time clock.
TAN(X)	DTAN(d) TAN(r)	Argument type Double Prec. Real	Tangent
TANH(X)	DTANH(d) TANH(r)	Argument type Double Prec. Real	Hyperbolic tangent
TINY(X)		Real	Returns the smallest positive number of the same type and kind as X.
TRANSFER(SOURCE,MOLD,*SIZE*)		Argument type	Returns a value with the same bit pattern as SOURCE, but interpreted with the type and kind of MOLD.
TRANSPOSE(MATRIX)		Argument type	Returns the transpose of MATRIX
TRIM(STRING)		Character	Returns STRING with trailing blanks removed.

Generic name, keyword(s), and calling sequence	Specific name	Function type	Description
UBOUND(ARRAY,*DIM*)			Returns upper bounds of dimensions in ARRAY. If *DIM* is specified, returns that upper bound only.
UNPACK(VECTOR,MASK,FIELD)		Argument type	Unpacks an array from a rank-1 array under the control of a mask.
VERIFY(STRING,SET,*BACK*)		Integer	

Notes:

1. These intrinsic functions cannot be passed to procedures as calling arguments.
2. The result of function CABS is real with the same kind as the input complex argument.
3. At least one of P and R must be specified in any given call.
4. Argument KIND is only available only in Fortran 95 for this function.
5. These procedures are available only in Fortran 95.
6. The argument *DIM* is available only in the Fortran 95 version of functions MAXLOC and MINLOC.

The following information applies to all intrinsic procedures in the table:

1. Optional arguments are shown in italics in all calling sequences.

2. When a function has an optional KIND dummy argument, then the function result will be of the kind specified in that argument. If the KIND argument is missing, then the result will be of the default kind. If the KIND argument is specified, it must correspond to a legal kind on the specified processor, or the function will abort. The KIND argument is always an integer.

3. When a procedure has two arguments of the same type, it is understood that they must also be of the same kind.

Order of Statements in a Fortran 90/95 Program

Fortran programs consist of one or more program units, each of which contains at least two legal Fortran statements. A Fortran program may include any number and type of program units, except that there must be one and only one main program.

All Fortran statements belong to one of 17 possible categories, which are listed below. (In this list, all undesirable, obsolescent, or deleted Fortran statements are shown in small type.)

1. Initial statements (PROGRAM, SUBROUTINE, FUNCTION, MODULE, and BLOCK DATA).

2. Comments.

3. USE statements.

4. IMPLICIT NONE statement.

5. Other IMPLICIT statements.

6. PARAMETER statements.

7. DATA statements.

8. Derived type definitions.

9. Type declaration statements.

10. Interface blocks.

11. Statement function declarations.

12. Other specification statements (PUBLIC, PRIVATE, SAVE, etc.).

13. FORMAT statements.

14. ENTRY statements.

15. Executable statements and constructs.

16. CONTAINS statement.

17. END statements (END PROGRAM, END FUNCTION, etc.).

The order in which these statements may appear in a program unit is specified in Table C–1. Horizontal lines indicate varieties of statements that may not be mixed, while vertical lines indicate types of statements that may be interspersed.

TABLE C–1
Requirements on statement ordering

PROGRAM, FUNCTION, MODULE, SUBROUTINE, or BLOCK DATA statement		
USE statements		
IMPLICIT NONE statement		
FORMAT and ENTRY statements	PARAMETER statements	IMPLICIT statements
	PARAMETER and DATA statements	Derived type definitions Interface blocks Type declaration statements Specification statements Statement function statements
	DATA statements	Executable statements and constructs
CONTAINS statement		
Internal subprograms or module subprograms		
END statement		

Note from this table that nonexecutable statements generally precede executable statements in a program unit. The only nonexecutable statements that may be legally mixed with executable statements are FORMAT statements, ENTRY statements, and DATA statements. (The mixing of DATA statements among executable statements has been declared obsolescent in Fortran 95.)

In addition to the above constraints, not every type of Fortran statement may appear in every type of Fortran scoping unit. Table C–2 shows which types of Fortran statements are allowed in which scoping units.

■   **TABLE C–2**
Statements allowed in scoping units

Kind of scoping unit	Main program	Module	Block data	External subprogram	Module subprogram	Internal subprogram	Interface body
USE statement	Yes	Yes	Yes	Yes	Yes	Yes	Yes
ENTRY statement	No	No	No	Yes	Yes	No	No
FORMAT statement	Yes	No	No	Yes	Yes	Yes	No
Misc. declarations (see notes)	Yes	Yes	Yes	Yes	Yes	Yes	Yes
DATA statement	Yes	Yes	Yes	Yes	Yes	Yes	No
Derived-type definition	Yes	Yes	Yes	Yes	Yes	Yes	Yes
Interface block	Yes	Yes	No	Yes	Yes	Yes	Yes
Executable statement	Yes	No	No	Yes	Yes	Yes	No
CONTAINS statement	Yes	Yes	No	Yes	Yes	No	No
Statement function statement	Yes	No	No	Yes	Yes	Yes	No

Notes:
1. Miscellaneous declarations are PARAMETER statements, IMPLICIT statements, type declaration statements, and specification statements such as PUBLIC, SAVE, etc.
2. Derived type definitions are also scoping units. However, they do not contain any of the above statements and do not appear in the table.
3. The scoping unit of a module does not include any module subprograms that the module contains.

Summary of Format Descriptors and I/O Statements

$\blacksquare$ **D.1**

SUMMARY OF FORMAT DESCRIPTORS

Table D–1 contains a complete list of all Fortran 90/95 format descriptors. The shaded format descriptors are obsolete and/or undesirable and should not be used in any new programs.

$\blacksquare$ **TABLE D–1**
Complete list of Fortran 90/95 format descriptors

FORMAT	Descriptors	Usage
Real data I/O descriptors		
D$w.d$		Double-precision data in exponential notation
E$w.d$	E$w.d$ Ee	Real data in exponential notation
EN$w.d$	EN$w.d$ Ee	Real data in engineering notation
ES$w.d$	ES$w.d$ Ee	Real data in scientific notation
F$w.d$		Real data in decimal notation
Integer data I/O descriptor		
Iw	I$w.m$	Integer data in decimal format
Real or integer data I/O descriptors		
Bw	B$w.m$	Data in binary format
Ow	O$w.m$	Data in octal format
Zw	Z$w.m$	Data in hexadecimal format
Logical data I/O descriptor		
Lw		Logical data

FORMAT	Descriptors	Usage
Character data I/O descriptors		
A	Aw	Character data
'x...x'	nHx...x	Character constants (the nHx...x form is
"x...x"		*obsolescent* in Fortran 90 and *deleted* in Fortran 95)
Generalized I/O descriptor		
G$w.d$	G$w.d$Ee	Generalized edit descriptor for any type of data
Positioning descriptors		
nX		Horizontal spacing: skip n spaces
/		Vertical spacing: move down 1 line
Tc		TAB: move to column c of current line
TLn		TAB: move left n columns in current line
TRn		TAB: move right n columns in current line
Scanning control descriptor		
:		Format scanning control character
Miscellaneous descriptors (Undesirable)		
kP		Scale factor for display of real data
BN		Blank null: ignore blanks in numeric input fields
BZ		Blank zero: interpret blanks in a numeric input field as zeros.
S		Sign control: use default system convention
SP		Sign control: display + before positive numbers
SS		Sign control: suppress + before positive numbers

Notes:

c	column number
d	number of digits to right of decimal place
e	number of digits in exponent
k	scale factor (number of places to shift decimal point)
m	minimum number of digits to be displayed
r	repetition count
w	field width in characters

■ **D.2**

SUMMARY OF I/O STATEMENTS

A summary of Fortran 90/95 I/O statements is shown in Table D–2. The lists of possible clauses for each statement are shown in Tables D–3 through D–8.

TABLE D-2
Fortran 90/95 I/O statements

Statement	Function
OPEN	Open a file (connect it to an i/o unit).
CLOSE	Close a file (disconnect it from an i/o unit).
INQUIRE	Check on properties of a file.
READ	Read data from a file (via an i/o unit).
PRINT	Write data to the standard output device.
WRITE	Write data to a file (via an i/o unit).
REWIND	Rewind a sequential file to the beginning.
BACKSPACE	Move back one record in a sequential file.
ENDFILE	Move to the end of a sequential file.

TABLE D-3
Clauses allowed in the OPEN statement

Clause	Input or output	Purpose	Possible values
[UNIT=]int_expr	INPUT	I/O unit to open file on. The UNIT= phrase is optional.	Processor-dependent integer.
FILE=char_expr	INPUT	Name of file to open.[1]	Character string.
STATUS=char_expr	INPUT	Specifies status for file to be opened.	'OLD', 'NEW', 'SCRATCH', 'REPLACE', 'UNKNOWN'
IOSTAT=int_var	OUTPUT	I/O status at end of operation.	Processor-dependent integer int_var. 0= success; positive= open failure.
ACCESS=char_expr	INPUT	Specified sequential or direct access.	'SEQUENTIAL', 'DIRECT'
FORM=char_expr	INPUT	Specified formatted or unformatted data.	'FORMATTED', 'UNFORMATTED'
ACTION=char_expr	INPUT	Specifies whether file is read only, write only, or read/write.	'READ', 'WRITE', 'READWRITE'
RECL=int_expr	INPUT	For a formatted direct access file, the number of characters in each record. For an unformatted direct access file, the number of processor-dependent units in each record.[2]	Processor-dependent positive integer.

Clause	Input or output	Purpose	Possible values
POSITION=*char_expr*	INPUT	Specifies the position of the file pointer after the file is opened.	`'REWIND'`, `'APPEND'`, `'ASIS'`
BLANK=*char_expr*	INPUT	Specifies whether blanks are to be treated as nulls or as zeros. Nulls are the default case.[3]	`'NULL'`, `'ZERO'`
DELIM=*char_expr*	INPUT	Specifies whether list-directed character output is to be delimited by apostrophes, by quotation marks, or by nothing. (Default value is `'NONE'`.)	`'APOSTROPHE'`, `'QUOTE'`, `'NONE'`
PAD=*variable*	INPUT	Specifies whether formatted input records are padded with blanks. (Default value is `'YES'`.)	`'YES'`, `'NO'`
ERR=*label*	INPUT	Statement label to transfer control to if open fails.	Statement labels in current scoping unit.

[1]The `FILE=` clause is not allowed for scratch files.
[2]The `RECL=` clause is defined only for files connected for direct access.
[3]The `BLANK=` clause is defined only for files connected for formatted I/O.

TABLE D–4
Clauses allowed in the CLOSE statement

Clause	Input or output	Purpose	Possible values
[UNIT=]*int_expr*	INPUT	I/O unit to close. The `UNIT=` phrase is optional.	Processor-dependent integer.
STATUS=*char_expr*	INPUT	Specifies whether file is to be kept or deleted after closing.	`'KEEP'`, `'DELETE'`
IOSTAT=*int_var*	OUTPUT	I/O status at end of operation.	Processor-dependent integer *int_var*. 0= success; positive=close failure.
ERR=*label*	INPUT	Statement label to transfer control to if open fails.	Statement labels in current scoping unit.

■   **TABLE D-5**
Clauses allowed in the INQUIRE statement

Clause	Input or output	Purpose	Possible values
[UNIT=]*int_expr*	INPUT	I/O unit of file to check.[1]	Processor-dependent integer.
FILE=*char_expr*	INPUT	Name of file to check.[1]	Processor-dependent character string.
IOSTAT=*int_var*	OUTPUT	I/O status.	Returns 0 for success; processor-dependent positive number for failure.
ERR=*statement label*	INPUT	Statement to branch to if statement fails.	Statement label in current program unit.
EXIST=*log_var*	OUTPUT	Does the file exist?	.TRUE., .FALSE.
OPENED=*log_var*	OUTPUT	Is the file opened?	.TRUE., .FALSE.
NUMBER=*int_var*	OUTPUT	I/O unit number of file if opened. If file is not opened, this value is undefined.	Processor-dependent positive number.
NAMED=*log_var*	OUTPUT	Does the file have a name? (Scratch files are unnamed.)	.TRUE., .FALSE.
NAME=*char_var*	OUTPUT	Name of file if file is named; undefined otherwise.	File name.
ACCESS=*char_var*	OUTPUT	Specifies type of access if the file is currently open.[2]	'SEQUENTIAL', 'DIRECT'
SEQUENTIAL=*char_var*	OUTPUT	Specifies if file *can be opened* for sequential access.[2]	'YES', 'NO', 'UNKNOWN'
DIRECT=*char_var*	OUTPUT	Specifies if file *can be opened* for direct access.[2]	'YES', 'NO', 'UNKNOWN'
FORM=*char_var*	OUTPUT	Specifies type of formatting for a file if the file is open.[3]	'FORMATTED', 'UNFORMATTED'
FORMATTED=*char_var*	OUTPUT	Specifies if file can be connected for unformatted I/O.[3]	'YES', 'NO', 'UNKNOWN'
UNFORMATTED=*char_var*	OUTPUT	Specifies if file *can be* connected for unformatted I/O.[3]	'YES', 'NO', 'UNKNOWN'
RECL=*int_var*	OUTPUT	Specifies the record length of a direct access file; undefined for sequential files.	Record length is in processor-dependent units.
NEXTREC=*int_var*	OUTPUT	For a direct access file, one more than the number of the last record read from or written to the file; undefined for sequential files.	

Clause	Input or output	Purpose	Possible values
BLANK=*char_var*	OUTPUT	Specifies whether blanks in numeric fields are treated as nulls or zeros.[4]	'ZERO', 'NULL'
POSITION=*char_var*	OUTPUT	Specifies location of file pointer when the file is first opened. This value is undefined for unopened files or for files opened for direct access.	'REWIND', 'APPEND', 'ASIS', 'UNDEFINED'
ACTION=*char_var*	OUTPUT	Specifies read, write, or read-write status for opened files. This value is undefined for unopened files.[5]	'READ', 'WRITE', 'READWRITE', 'UNDEFINED'
READ=*char_var*	OUTPUT	Specifies whether file *can be* opened for read-only access.[5]	'YES', 'NO', 'UNKNOWN'
WRITE=*char_var*	OUTPUT	Specifies whether file *can be* opened for write-only acces.[5]	'YES', 'NO', 'UNKNOWN'
READWRITE=*char_var*	OUTPUT	Specifies whether file can be opened for read-write access.[5]	'YES', 'NO', 'UNKNOWN'
DELIM=*char_var*	OUTPUT	Specifies type of character delimiter used with list-directed and namelist I/O to this file.	'APOSTROPHE', 'QUOTE', 'NONE', 'UNKNOWN'
PAD=*char_var*	OUTPUT	Specifies whether or not input lines are to be padded with blanks. This value is always Yes unless a file is explicitly opened with PAD='NO'.	'YES', 'NO'
IOLENGTH=*int_var*	OUTPUT	Returns the length of an unformatted record in processor-dependent units. This clause is special to the third type of INQUIRE statement (see text).	

[1]One and only one of the FILE= and UNIT= clauses may be included in any INQUIRE statement.
[2]The difference between the ACCESS= clause and the SEQUENTIAL= and DIRECT= clauses is that the ACCESS= clause tells what sort of access *is being used,* while the other two clauses tell what sort of access *can be used.*
[3]The difference between the FORM= clause and the FORMATTED= and UNFORMATTED= clauses is that the FORM= clause tells what sort of I/O *is being used,* while the other two clauses tell what sort of I/O *can be used.*
[4]The BLANK= clause is defined only for files connected for formatted I/O.
[5]The difference between the ACTION= clause and the READ=, WRITE=, and READWRITE= clauses is that the ACTION= clause specifies the action for which the file *is* opened, while the other clauses specify the action for which the file *can be* opened.

TABLE D–6
Clauses allowed in the READ statement

Clause	Input or output	Purpose	Possible values
[UNIT=]*int_expr*	INPUT	I/O unit to read from.	Processor-dependent integer.
[FMT=]*statement_label* [FMT=]*char_expr* [FMT=]*	INPUT	Specifies the format to use when reading formatted data.	
IOSTAT=*int_var*	OUTPUT	I/O status at end of operation.	Processor-dependent integer *int_var*: 0=success positive=failure −1=end of file −2=end of record
END=*statement_label*	INPUT	Statement label to transfer control to if end of file is reached.	Statement labels in current scoping unit.
ERR=*statement_label*	INPUT	Statement label to transfer control to if an error occurs.	Statement labels in current scoping unit.
REC=*int_expr*	INPUT	Specifies the record number to read in a direct access file.	
ADVANCE=*char_expr*	INPUT	Specifies whether to perform advancing or nonadvancing I/O. Valid for sequential files only.	'YES', 'NO'
SIZE=*int_var*	OUTPUT	Specifies number of characters read during nonadvancing I/O. Valid for nonadvancing I/O only.	
EOR=*label*	INPUT	Statement label to transfer control to if end of record is reached during nonadvancing I/O. Valid for non-advancing I/O only.	Statement labels in current scoping unit.
NML=*namelist*	INPUT	Specifies name list of I/O entities to read.	Name lists defined in the current scoping unit or accessed through use or host association.

TABLE D–7
Clauses allowed in the `WRITE` statement

Clause	Input or output	Purpose	Possible values
`[UNIT=]`*int_expr*	INPUT	I/O unit to write to.	Processor-dependent integer.
`[FMT=]`*statement_label* `[FMT=]`*char_expr* `[FMT=]*`	INPUT	Specifies the format to use when writing formatted data.	
`IOSTAT=`*int_var*	OUTPUT	I/O status at end of operation.	Processor-dependent integer *int_var*. 0=success positive=failure
`ERR=`*statement_label*	INPUT	Statement label to transfer control to if an error occurs.	Statement labels in current scoping unit.
`REC=`*int_expr*	INPUT	Specifies the record number to write in a direct access file.	
`ADVANCE=`*char_expr*	INPUT	Specifies whether to perform advancing or nonadvancing I/O. Valid for sequential files only.	`'YES'`, `'NO'`
`NML=`*namelist*	INPUT	Specifies name list of I/O entities to write.	Name lists defined in the current scoping unit or accessed through use or host association.

TABLE D–8
Clauses allowed in the `REWIND`, `BACKSPACE`, or `ENDFILE` statements

Clause	Input or output	Purpose	Possible values
`[UNIT=]`*int_expr*	INPUT	I/O unit to operate on. The `UNIT=` phrase is optional.	Processor-dependent integer.
`IOSTAT=`*int_var*	OUTPUT	I/O status at end of operation.	Processor-dependent integer *int_var*. 0=success positive=failure
`ERR=`*statement_label*	INPUT	Statement label to transfer control to if an error occurs.	Statement labels in current scoping unit.

Glossary

This appendix contains a glossary of Fortran terms. Many of the definitions here are paraphrased from the definitions of terms in the Fortran 90 and 95 Standards, ISO/IEC 1539: 1991 and ISO/IEC 1539:1997.

actual argument   An expression, a variable, or a procedure that is specified in a procedure invocation (a subroutine call or a function reference). It is associated with the dummy argument in the corresponding position of the procedure definition unless keywords are used to change the order of arguments.

algorithm   The "formula" or sequence of steps used to solve a specific problem.

allocatable array   An array specified as ALLOCATABLE with a certain type and rank. It can later be allocated a certain extent with the ALLOCATE statement. The array cannot be referenced or defined until it has been allocated. When no longer needed, the corresponding storage area can be released with the DEALLOCATE statement.

allocation statement   A statement that allocates memory for an allocatable array or a statement that allocates memory for a pointer.

allocation status   A logical value indicating whether or not an allocatable array is currently allocated. It can be examined using the ALLOCATED intrinsic function.

argument   A placeholder for a value or variable name that will be passed to a procedure when it is invoked (a dummy argument) or the value or variable name that is actually passed to the procedure when it is invoked (an actual argument). Arguments appear in parentheses after a procedure name both when the procedure is declared and when the procedure is invoked.

argument association   The relationship between an actual argument and a dummy argument during the execution of a procedure reference. Argument association is performed either by the relative position of actual and dummy arguments in the procedure reference and the procedure definition or by means of argument keywords.

argument keyword   A dummy argument name. It may be used in a procedure reference followed by the equals symbol provided the procedure has an explicit interface.

argument list   A list of values and variables that are passed to a procedure when it is invoked. Argument lists appear in parentheses after a procedure name both when the procedure is declared and when the procedure is invoked.

array   A set of data items, all of the same type and kind, which are referred to by the same name. Individual elements within an array are accessed by using the array name followed by one or more subscripts.

array constructor   An array-valued constant.

array element   An individual data item within an array.

array element order   The order in which the elements of an array appear to be stored in memory.

array section   A part of an array that can be used and manipulated as an array in its own right.

array valued   Having the property of being an array.

array-valued function   A function whose result is an array.

ASCII   The American Standard Code for Information Interchange (ANSI X3.4 1977), a widely used internal character coding set. This set is also known as ISO 646 (International Reference Version).

ASCII collating sequence   The collating sequence associated with the ASCII character set.

assignment operator   The equal (=) sign, which indicates that the value of the expression to the right of the equal sign should be assigned to the variable named on the left of the sign.

assignment statement   A Fortran statement that causes the value of an expression to be stored into a variable. The form of an assignment statement is "variable=expression."

associated   A pointer is associated with a target if it currently points to that target.

association status   A logical value indicating whether or not a pointer is currently associated with a target. The possible pointer association status values are undefined, associated, and unassociated. It can be examined using the ASSOCIATED intrinsic function.

assumed-length character declaration   The declaration of a character dummy argument with an asterisk for its length. The actual length is determined from the corresponding actual argument when the procedure is invoked. For example:

```
CHARACTER(len=*) :: string
```

assumed-shape array   An array-valued dummy argument whose upper bounds in each dimension are represented by colons, with the actual bounds being obtained from the corresponding actual argument when the procedure is invoked. An assumed-shape array has a declared data type and rank, but its size is unknown until the procedure is actually executed. For example:

```
SUBROUTINE ( a, ... )
REAL, DIMENSION(:,:) :: a
```

attribute   A property of a variable or constant that may be declared in a type declaration statement. Examples are PARAMETER, DIMENSION, and POINTER.

automatic array   An explicit-shape array in a procedure, which is not a dummy argument, some or all of whose bounds are provided when the procedure is invoked, thus allowing the array to have a different size and shape each time the procedure is invoked. When the procedure is invoked, the array is automatically allocated with the proper size, and when the procedure terminates, the array is automatically deallocated. In the following example, scratch is an automatic array:

```
SUBROUTINE my_sub ( a, rows, cols )
INTEGER :: rows, cols
...
REAL, DIMENSION(rows,cols) :: scratch
```

binary operator   An operator that is written between two operands. Examples include +, -, *, /, >, <, and .AND..

bit   A binary digit.

block   A sequence of executable statements embedded in an executable construct, bounded by statements that are particular to the construct, and treated as an integral unit. For example, the statements between IF and END IF are a block:

```
IF ( x > 0. ) THEN
   ...
   (code block)
   ...
END IF
```

block IF construct A program unit in which the execution of one or more blocks of statements is controlled by a block IF statement, and optionally by one or more ELSE IF statements and up to one ELSE statement.

bound An upper bound or a lower bound; the maximum or minimum value permitted for a subscript in an array.

bounds checking The process of checking each array reference before it is executed to ensure that the specified subscripts are within the declared bounds of the array.

branch (*a*) A transfer of control within a program, as in an IF or CASE structure. (*b*) A linked list that forms part of a binary tree.

bug A programming error that causes a program to behave improperly.

byte A group of 8 bits.

central processing unit The part of the computer that carries out the main data processing functions. It usually consists of one or more *control units* to select the data and the operations to be performed on it and *arithmetic logic units* to perform arithmetic calculations.

character (*a*) A letter, digit, or other symbol. (*b*) An intrinsic data type used to represent characters.

character context Characters that form a part of a character literal constant or a character constant edit descriptor. Any legal character in a computer's character set may be used in a character context, not just those in the Fortran character set.

character length parameter The type parameter that specifies the number of characters for an entity of type character.

character set A collection of letters, numbers, and symbols that may be used in character strings. Two common character sets are ASCII and EBCDIC.

character string A sequence of one or more characters.

character variable A variable that consists of one or more character storage units and that may be used to store one or more characters.

close The process of terminating the link between a file and an input/output unit.

collating sequence The order in which a particular character set is sorted by relational operators.

combinational operator An operator whose operand(s) are logical values, and whose result is a logical value. Examples include .AND., .OR., and .NOT..

comment Text within a program unit that is ignored by a compiler but provides information for the programmer.

compilation error An error that is detected by a Fortran compiler during compilation.

compiler A computer program that translates a program written in a computer language such as Fortran into the machine code used by a particular computer. The compiler usually translates the code into an intermediate form called object code, which is then prepared for execution by a separate linker.

complex An intrinsic data type used to represent complex numbers.

component One of the elements of a derived data type.

component selector   The method of addressing a specific component within a structure. It consists of the structure name and the component name, separated by a percent (%) sign, for example, `student%age`.

concatenation   The process of attaching one character string to the end of another by means of a concatenation operator.

concatenation operator   An operator (`//`) that combines two characters strings to form a single character string.

conformable   Two arrays are said to be conformable if they have the same shape. A scalar is conformable with any array. Intrinsic operations are only defined for conformable data items.

constant   A data object whose value is unchanged throughout the execution of a program. Constants may be named (i.e. parameters) or unnamed.

construct   A sequence of statements starting with a `DO`, `IF`, `SELECT CASE`, or `WHERE` statement and ending with the corresponding terminal statement.

control character   The first character in an output buffer, which is used to control the vertical spacing for the current line.

control mask   In a `WHERE` statement or construct, an array of type logical whose value determines which elements of an array will be operated on. This definition also applies to the `MASK` argument in many array intrinsic functions.

counting loop   A `DO` loop that executes a specified number of times based on the loop control parameters (also known as an iterative loop).

data   Information to be processed by a computer.

data abstraction   The ability to create new data types, with associated operators, and to hide the internal structure and operations from the user.

data dictionary   A list of the names and definitions of all named variables and constants used in a program unit. The definitions should include both a description of the contents of the item and the units in which it is measured.

data hiding   The idea that some items in a program unit may not be accessible to other program units. Local data items in a procedure are hidden from any program unit that invokes the procedure. Access to the data items and procedures in a module may be controlled using `PUBLIC` and `PRIVATE` statements.

data object   A constant or a variable.

deallocation statement   A statement that frees memory previously allocated for an allocatable array or a pointer.

debugging   Locating and eliminating bugs from a program.

declaration statement   *See* type declaration statement.

default character set   The set of characters available for use by programs on a particular computer if no special action is taken to select another character set.

default kind   The kind type parameter used for a specific data type when no kind is explicitly specified. The default kinds of each data type are known as default integer, default real, default complex, etc. Default kinds vary from processor to processor.

default real   The kind of real value used when no kind type parameter is specified.

default typing   The type assigned to a variable when no type declaration statement is present in a program unit, based on the first letter of the variable name.

deferred-shape array   An allocatable array or a pointer array. The type and rank of these arrays are declared in type declaration statements, but the shape of the array is not determined until memory is allocated in an `ALLOCATE` statement.

defined assignment   A user-defined assignment that involves a derived data type. This is done with the `INTERFACE ASSIGNMENT` construct.

defined operation   A user-defined operation that either extends an intrinsic operation for use with derived types or defines a new operation for use with either intrinsic types or derived types. This is done with the INTERFACE OPERATOR construct.

deleted feature   A feature of older versions of Fortran that has been deleted from later versions of the language. An example is the Hollerith (H) format descriptor.

dereferencing   The process of accessing the corresponding target when a reference to a pointer appears in an operation or assignment statement.

derived type (or **derived data type**)   A user-defined data type consisting of components, each of which is either of intrinsic type or of another derived type.

dimension attribute   An attribute of a type declaration statement used to specify the number of subscripts in an array and the characteristics of those subscripts such as their bounds and extent. This information can also be specified in a separate DIMENSION statement.

direct access   Reading or writing the contents of a file in arbitrary order.

direct access file   A form of file in which the individual records can be written and read in any order. Direct access files must have records of fixed length so that the location of any particular record can be quickly calculated.

disassociated   A pointer is disassociated if it no longer points to a valid target.

DO construct   A loop that begins with a DO statement and ends with an END DO statement.

DO loop   A loop that is controlled by a DO statement.

DO loop index   The variable that controls the number of times the loop is executed in an iterative DO loop.

DO statement   The first statement of a DO loop.

double precision   A method of storing floating-point numbers on a computer that uses twice as much memory as single precision, resulting in more significant digits and (usually) a greater range in the representation of the numbers.

dummy argument   An argument used in a procedure definition that will be associated with an actual argument when the procedure is invoked.

dynamic variable   A variable that is created when it is needed during the course of a program's execution and destroyed when it is no longer needed. Examples of dynamic variables are automatic arrays, allocatable arrays, and allocated pointer targets.

EBCDIC   Extended Binary Coded Decimal Interchange Code. This is an internal character coding scheme used by IBM mainframes.

edit descriptor   An item in a format that specifies the conversion between the internal and external representations of a data item (identical to format descriptor).

elemental   An adjective applied to an operation, procedure, or assignment that is applied independently to the elements of an array or corresponding elements of a set of conformable arrays and scalars. Elemental operations, procedures, or assignments may be easily partitioned among many processors in a parallel computer.

elemental intrinsic procedure   An intrinsic procedure that is defined for scalar inputs and outputs but that can accept an array-valued argument or arguments and will deliver an array-valued result obtained by applying the procedure to the corresponding elements of the argument arrays in turn.

end-of-file condition   A condition set when an endfile record is read from a file, which can be detected by an IOSTAT clause in a READ statement.

endfile record   A special record that occurs only at the end of a sequential file. It can be written by an ENDFILE statement.

error flag   A variable returned from a subroutine to indicate the status of the operation performed by the subroutine.

executable statement   A statement that causes the computer to perform some action during the execution of a program.

execution error   An error that occurs during the execution of a program (also called a run-time error).

explicit interface   A procedure interface known to the program unit that will invoke the procedure. An explicit interface to an external procedure may be created by placing the external procedures in modules and then accessing them by USE association.

explicit-shape array   A named array that is declared with explicit bounds in every dimension.

exponent   (*a*) In a binary representation, the power of 2 by which the mantissa is multiplied to produce a complete floating-point number. (*b*) In a decimal representation, the power of 10 by which the mantissa is multiplied to produce a complete floating-point number.

exponential notation   Representing real or floating-point numbers as a mantissa multiplied by a power of 10.

expression   A sequence of operands, operators, and parentheses, where the operands may be variables, constants, or function references.

extent   The number of elements in a particular dimension of an array.

external file   A file that is stored on some external medium. This contrasts with an internal file, which is a character variable within a program.

external function   A function that is not an intrinsic function or an internal function.

external subprogram (or **external procedure**)   A function subprogram or a subroutine subprogram that is not a part of any other program unit.

field width   The number of characters available for displaying an output formatted value or reading an input formatted value.

file   A unit of data that is held on some medium outside the memory of the computer. It is organized into records, which can be accessed individually using READ and WRITE statements.

fixed-source form   An obsolescent method of writing Fortran programs in which fixed columns were reserved for specific purposes (compare with free-source form).

floating point   A method of representing numbers in which the memory associated with the number is divided into separate fields for a mantissa (fractional part) and an exponent.

format   A sequence of edit descriptors that determine the interpretation of an input data record or specify the form of an output data record. A format may be found in a FORMAT statement or in a character constant or variable.

format descriptor   An item in a format that specifies the conversion between the internal and external representations of a data item (identical to edit descriptor).

format statement   A labeled statement that defines a format.

formatted file   A file containing data stored as recognizable numbers, characters, and so on.

Fortran character set   The 86 characters that can be used to write a Fortran program.

free format   List-directed I/O statements, which do not require formats for either input or output.

free-source form   The newer and preferred method of writing Fortran programs in which any character position in a line can be used for any purpose (compare with fixed-source form).

function   A procedure that is invoked in an expression and computes a single result, which is then used in evaluating the expression.

function reference   The use of a function name in an expression, which invokes (executes) the function to carry out some calculation and returns the result for use in evaluating the expression. A function is invoked or executed by naming it in an expression.

function subprogram   A program unit that begins with a FUNCTION statement and ends with an END FUNCTION statement.

function value   The value that is returned when the function executes.

generic function   A function that can be called with different types of arguments. For example, the intrinsic function ABS is a generic function, since it can be invoked with integer, real, or complex arguments.

generic interface block   A form of interface block used to define a generic name for a set of procedures.

generic name   A name that is used to identify two or more procedures, with the required procedure being determined by the compiler determined at each invocation from the types of the non-optional arguments in the procedure invocation. A generic name is defined for a set of procedures in a generic interface block.

hexadecimal   The base 16 number system in which the legal digits are 0 through 9 and A through F.

host   A main program or subprogram that contains an internal subprogram is called the host of the internal subprogram. A module that contains a module subprogram is called the host of the module subprogram.

host association   The process by which data entities in a host scoping unit are made available to an inner scoping unit.

host program unit   See host.

host scoping unit   A scoping unit that surrounds another scoping unit.

IF statement   A block IF statement or a logical IF statement.

ill-conditioned system   A system of equations whose solution is highly sensitive to small changes in the values of its coefficients or to truncation and round-off errors.

imaginary part   The second of the two numbers that make up a COMPLEX data value.

implicit interface   A procedure interface that is not fully known to the program unit that invokes the procedure. A Fortran program cannot detect type, size, or similar mismatches between actual arguments and dummy arguments when an implicit interface is used, so the compiler will not catch all programming errors. All pre-Fortran 90 interfaces were implicit (compare with explicit interface).

implicit type declaration   Determining the type of a variable from the first letter of its name. Implicit type declaration should never be used in any modern Fortran program.

implied DO loop   A shorthand loop structure used in input/output statements, array constructors, and DATA statements, which specifies the order in which that statement uses the elements of an array.

implied DO variable   A variable used to control an implied DO loop.

index array   An array containing indices to other arrays. Index arrays are often used in sorting to avoid swapping large chunks of data.

infinite loop   A loop that never terminates, typically because of a programming error.

initial statement   The first statement of a program unit: a PROGRAM, SUBROUTINE, FUNCTION, MODULE, or BLOCK DATA statement.

initialization expression   A restricted form of constant expression that can appear as an initial value in a declaration statement. For example, the initialization expression in the following type declaration statement initializes PI to 3.141592:

```
REAL :: PI = 3.141592
```

input buffer   A section of memory used to hold a line of input data as it is entered from an input device such as a keyboard. When the entire line is available, the input buffer is made available for processing by the computer.

input device   A device used to enter data into a computer for example, a keyboard.

input format   A format used in a formatted input statement.

input list   The list of variable, array, and/or array element names in a READ statement into which data is to be read.

input statement   A READ statement.

input/output unit   A number, asterisk, or name in an input/output statement referring to either an external unit or an internal unit. A number is used to refer to an external file unit, which may be connected to a specific file using an OPEN statement and disconnected using a CLOSE statement. An asterisk is used to refer to the standard input and output devices for a processor. A name is used to refer to an internal file unit, which is just a character variable in the program's memory.

inquiry intrinsic function   An intrinsic function whose result depends on properties of the principal argument other than the value of the argument.

integer   An intrinsic data type used to represent whole numbers.

integer division   Division of one integer by another integer. In integer division, the fractional part of the result is lost. Thus the result of dividing an integer 7 by an integer 4 is 1.

interface assignment block   An interface block used to extend the meaning of the assignment operator (=).

interface block   A means of defining a generic procedure, operator, or assignment.

interface operator block   An interface block used to define a new operator or to extend the meaning of a standard Fortran operator (+,-,*,/,>, etc.).

internal file   A character variable that can be read from and written to by normal formatted READ and WRITE statements.

internal procedure   A subroutine or function that is contained within another program unit and can only be invoked from within that program unit.

intrinsic data type   One of the predefined data types in Fortran: integer, real, double precision, logical, complex, and character.

intrinsic procedure   A procedure that is defined as a part of the standard Fortran language (see Appendix B).

invoke   To CALL a subroutine or to reference a function in an expression.

i/o unit   See input/output unit.

iteration count   The number of times that an iterative DO loop is executed.

iterative DO loop   A DO loop that executes a specified number of times based on the loop control parameters (also known as a counting loop).

keyword   A word that has a defined meaning in the Fortran language.

keyword argument   A method of specifying the association between dummy arguments and actual arguments of the form: DUMMY_ARGUMENT=actual_argument. Keyword arguments permit arguments to be specified in any order when a procedure is invoked and are especially useful with optional arguments. Keyword arguments may be used only in procedures with explicit interfaces. An example of the use of a keyword argument is

```
kind_value = SELECTED_REAL_KIND(r=100)
```

kind All intrinsic data types except for DOUBLE PRECISION may have multiple processor-dependent representations. Each representation is known as a different kind of that type and is identified by a processor-dependent integer called a *kind type parameter.*

kind selector The means of specifying the kind type parameter of a variable or named constant.

kind type parameter An integer value used to identify the kind of an intrinsic data type.

language extension The ability to use the features of a language to extend the language for other purposes. The principal language extension features of Fortran are derived types, user-defined operations, and data hiding.

lexical functions Intrinsic functions used to compare two character strings in a character-set–independent manner

librarian A program that creates and maintains libraries of compiled object files.

library A collection of procedures that are made available for use by a program. They may be in the form of modules or separately linked object libraries.

line printer A type of printer used to print Fortran programs and output on large computer systems. Large line printers print an entire line at a time.

link The process of combining object modules produced from program units to form an executable program.

linked list A data structure in which each element contains a pointer that points to the next element in the structure. (It sometimes contains a pointer to the previous element as well.)

list-directed input A special type of formatted input in which the format used to interpret the input data is selected by the processor in accordance with the type of the data items in the input list.

list-directed I/O statement An input or output statement that uses list-directed input or output.

list-directed output A special type of formatted output in which the processor selects the format used to display the output data according to the type of the data items in the output list.

literal constant A constant whose value is written directly, as opposed to a named constant. For example, 14.4 is a literal constant.

logical A data type that can have only two possible values: TRUE or FALSE.

logical error A bug or error in a program caused by a mistake in program design (improper branching, looping, etc.).

logical IF statement A statement in which a logical expression controls whether or not the rest of the statement is executed.

logical operator An operator whose result is a logical value. The two types of logical operators are combinational (.AND., .OR., .NOT., etc.) and relational (>, <, etc.).

loop A sequence of statements repeated multiple times and usually controlled by a DO statement.

loop index An integer variable that is incremented or decremented each time an iterative DO loop is executed.

lower bound The minimum value permitted for a subscript of an array.

machine language The collection of binary instructions (also called op codes) actually understood and executed by a particular processor.

main memory The computer memory used to store programs that are currently being executed and the data associated with them; typically semiconductor memory. Main memory is usually much faster than secondary memory is but also much more expensive.

main program unit A program unit that starts with a PROGRAM statement. Execution begins here when a program is started. A program can have only one main program unit.

mantissa (*a*) In a binary representation, the fractional part of a floating-point number that, when multiplied by a power of 2, produces the complete number. The power of 2 required is known as the exponent of the number. The value of the mantissa is always between 0.5 and 1.0. (*b*) In a decimal representation, the fractional part of a floating-point number that, when multiplied by a power of 10, produces the complete number. The power of 10 required is known as the exponent of the number. The value of the mantissa is always between 0.0 and 1.0.

many-one array section   An array section with a vector subscript having two or more elements with the same value. Such an array section cannot appear on the left side of an assignment statement.

mask   (*a*) A logical expression that controls assignment of array elements in a masked array assignment (a WHERE statement or a WHERE construct). (*b*) A logical argument in several array intrinsic functions that determines which array elements will be included in the operation.

masked array assignment   An array assignment statement whose operation is controlled by a logical MASK that is the same shape as the array. The operation specified in the assignment statement is applied only to those elements of the array corresponding to true elements of the MASK. Masked array assignments are implemented as WHERE statements or WHERE constructs.

matrix   A rank-2 array.

mixed-mode expression   An arithmetic expression involving operands of different types. For example, the addition of a real value and an integer is a mixed-mode expression.

module   A program unit that allows other program units to access constants, variables, derived type definitions, interfaces, and procedures declared within it by USE association.

module procedure   A procedure contained within a module.

name   A lexical token consisting of a letter followed by up to 30 alphanumeric characters (letters, digits, and underscores). The named entity could be a variable, a named constant, a pointer, or a program unit.

named constant   A constant that has been named by a PARAMETER attribute in a type declaration statement or by a PARAMETER statement.

nested   The inclusion of one program construct as a part of another program construct, such as nested DO loops or nested block IF constructs.

nonexecutable statement   A statement used to configure the program environment in which computational actions take place. Examples include the IMPLICIT NONE statement and type declaration statements.

numeric type   Integer, real or complex data type.

object module   The file output by most compilers. Multiple object modules are combined with libraries in a linker to produce the final executable program.

octal   The base 8 number system, in which the legal digits are 0 through 7.

one-dimensional array   A rank-1 array, or vector.

operand   An expression that precedes or follows an operator.

operation   A computation involving one or two operands.

operator   A character or sequence of characters that defines an operation. Unary operators have one operand, and binary operators have two operands.

optional argument   A dummy argument in a procedure that does not need to have a corresponding actual argument every time the procedure is invoked. Optional arguments may exist only in procedures with an explicit interface.

out-of-bounds reference   A reference to an array using a subscript either smaller than the lower bound or larger than the upper bound of the corresponding array dimension.

output buffer   A section of memory used to hold a line of output data before it is sent to an output device.

output device   A device used to output data from a computer, for example, a printer and a CRT display.

output format   A format used in a formatted output statement.

parameter attribute   An attribute in a type declaration statement that specifies that the named item is a constant instead of a variable.

parameterized variable   A variable whose kind is explicitly specified.

pointer   A variable that has the POINTER attribute. A pointer may not be referenced or defined unless it is pointer associated with a target. If it is an array, it does not have a shape unless it is pointer associated, although it does have a rank. When a pointer is associated with a target, it contains the memory address of the target and thus "points" to it.

pointer array   An array that is declared with the POINTER attribute. Its rank is determined in the type declaration statement, but its shape and size are not known until memory is allocated for the array in an ALLOCATE statement.

pointer assignment statement   A statement that associates a pointer with a target. Pointer assignment statements take the form pointer => target.

pointer association   The process by which a pointer becomes associated with a target. The association status of a pointer can be checked with the ASSOCIATED intrinsic function.

pointer attribute   An attribute in a type declaration statement that specifies that the named item is a pointer instead of a variable.

precision   The number of significant decimal digits that can be represented in a floating-point number.

present   A dummy argument is present in a procedure invocation if it is associated with an actual argument, and the corresponding actual argument is present in the invoking program unit. The presence of a dummy argument can be checked with the PRESENT intrinsic function.

printer control character   The first character of each output buffer. When it is sent to the printer, it controls the vertical movement of the paper before the line is written.

private   An entity in a module that is not accessible outside the module by USE association; declared by a PRIVATE attribute or in a PRIVATE statement.

procedure   A subroutine or function.

processor   A processor is the combination of a specific computer with a specific compiler. Processor-dependent items can vary from computer to computer or from compiler to compiler on the same computer.

program   A sequence of instructions on a computer that causes the computer to carry out some specific function.

program unit   A main program, a subroutine, a function, a module, or a block data subprogram. Each of these units is separately compiled.

pseudocode   A set of English statements structured in a Fortran-like manner and used to outline the solution to a problem without getting buried in the details of Fortran syntax.

public   An entity in a module that is accessible outside the module by USE association; declared by a PUBLIC attribute or in a PUBLIC statement. An entity in a module is public by default.

random access   Reading or writing the contents of a file in arbitrary order.

random access file   Another name for a direct access file: a form of file in which the individual records can be written and read in any order. Direct access files must have records of fixed length so that the location of any particular record can be quickly calculated.

random access memory (RAM)   The semiconductor memory used to store the programs and data that are actually being executed by a computer at a particular time.

range   The difference between the largest and smallest numbers that can be represented on a computer with a given data type and kind. For example, on most computers a single-precision real number has a range of 10^{-38} to 10^{38}, 0, and -10^{-38} to -10^{38}.

rank   The number of dimensions of an array. The rank of a scalar is zero. The maximum rank of a Fortran array is seven.

rank-1 array   An array having only one dimension, where each array element is addressed with a single subscript.

rank-2 array   An array having two dimensions, where each array element is addressed with two subscripts.

rank-*n* array   An array having *n* dimensions, where each array element is addressed with *n* subscripts.

real   An intrinsic data type used to represent numbers with a floating-point representation.

real part   The first of the two numbers that make up a COMPLEX data value.

record   A sequence of values or characters that is treated as a unit within a file. (A record is a "line" or unit of data from a file.)

record number   The index number of a record in a direct access (or random access) file.

recursion   The invocation of a procedure by itself, either directly or indirectly. Recursion is only allowed if the procedure is declared with the RECURSIVE keyword.

reference   The appearance of a data object name in a context requiring the value at that point during execution; the appearance of a procedure name, its operator symbol, or a defined assignment statement in a context requiring execution of the procedure at that point; or the appearance of a module name in a USE statement. Neither the act of defining a variable nor the appearance of the name of a procedure as an actual argument is regarded as a reference.

relational expression   A logical expression in which two nonlogical operands are compared by a relational operator to give a logical value for the expressions.

relational operator   An operator that compares two nonlogical operands and returns a TRUE or FALSE result. Examples include >, >=, <, <=, ==, and /=.

repeat count   The number before a format descriptor or a group of format descriptors that specifies the number of times they are to be repeated. For example, the descriptor 4F10.4 is used four times.

result variable   The variable that returns the value of a function.

save attribute   An attribute in the type declaration statement of a local variable in a procedure that specifies that the value of the named item is to be preserved between invocations of the procedure. This attribute can also be specified in a separate SAVE statement.

scalar variable   A variable that is not an array variable. The variable name refers to a single item of an intrinsic or derived type, and no subscripts are used with the name.

scratch file   A temporary file that a program uses during execution and is automatically deleted when it is closed. A scratch file may not be given a name.

secondary memory   The computer memory used to store programs that are not currently being executed and the data that is not currently needed; typically a disk. Secondary memory is usually much slower and less expensive than main memory is.

sequential access   Reading or writing the contents of a file in sequential order.

sequential file   A form of file in which each record is read or written in sequential order. Sequential files do not require a fixed record length. The default file type in Fortran.

shape   The rank and extent of an array in each of its dimensions. The shape can be stored in a rank-1 array with each element of the array containing the extent of one dimension.

single precision   A method of storing floating-point numbers on a computer that uses less memory than double precision, resulting in fewer significant digits and (usually) a smaller range in the representation of the numbers. Single-precision numbers are the "default real" type, the type of real number that results if no kind is specified.

size   The total number of elements in an array.

source form   The style in which a Fortran program is written—either free form or fixed form.

specific function   A function that must always be called with a single type of argument. For example, the intrinsic function `IABS` is a specific function, while the intrinsic function `ABS` is a generic function.

specification expression   A restricted form of scalar integer constant expression that can appear in a type specification statement as a bound in an array declaration or as the length in a character declaration.

specifier   An item in a control list that provides additional information for the input/output statement in which it appears. Examples are the input/output unit number and the format specification for `READ` and `WRITE` statements.

statement entity   An entity whose scope is a single statement or part of a statement, such as the index variable in the implied `DO` loop of an array constructor.

statement label   A number preceding a statement that can be used to refer to that statement.

static variable   A variable allocated at compilation time and remaining in existence throughout the execution of a program.

stride   The increment specified in a subscript triplet.

structure   (a) An item of a derived data type. (b) An organized, standard way to describe an algorithm.

structure component   A part of an object of derived type that may be referenced by a component selector. A component selector consists of the object's name followed by the component's name, separated by a percent sign (%).

structure constructor   An unnamed (or literal) constant of a derived type. It consists of the name of the type followed by the components of the type in parentheses. The components appear in the order in which they were declared in the definition of the derived type. For example, the following line declares a constant of type `person`:

```
john = person('John','R','Jones','323-6439',21,'M','123-45-6789')
```

subprogram   A function subprogram or a subroutine.

subroutine   A procedure that is invoked by a `CALL` statement and that returns its result through its arguments.

subscript   One of the integer values in parentheses following an array name, which are used to identify a particular element of the array. There is one subscript value for each dimension of the array.

subscript triplet   A method of specifying one dimension of an array section by means of the initial and final values and a stride. The three components of the subscript triplet are separated by colons, and some of them may be defaulted. For example, the following array section contains two subscript triplets: `array(1:3:2,2:4)`.

substring   A contiguous portion of a scalar character string.

substring specification   The specification of a substring of a character string. The specification takes the form `char_var(istart:iend)`, where `char_var` is the name of a character variable, `istart` is the first character in `char_var` to include in the substring, and `iend` is the first character in `char_var` to include in the substring.

syntax error   An error in the syntax of a Fortran statement, detected by the compiler during compilation.

target   A variable that has the TARGET attribute and can be the destination of a pointer.

test driver program   A small program that is written specifically to invoke a procedure for the purpose of testing it.

top-down design   The process of analyzing a problem by starting with the major steps and successively refining each step until all the small steps are easy to implement in Fortran code.

transformational intrinsic function   An intrinsic function that is neither an elemental function nor an inquiry function. It usually has array arguments and an array result whose elements have values that depend on the values of many of the elements of the arguments.

type declaration statement   A statement that specifies the type and optionally the attributes of one or more variables or constants: an INTEGER, REAL, DOUBLE PRECISION, COMPLEX, CHARACTER, LOGICAL, or TYPE (type_name) statement.

type parameter   A parameter of an intrinsic data type. KIND and LEN are the type parameters.

unary operator   An operator that has only one operand, such as .NOT. or the unary minus.

undefined   A data entity that does not have a defined value.

unicode   An internal character coding scheme that uses 2 bytes to represent each character. The unicode system can represent 65,536 different characters. The first 128 unicode characters are identical to the ASCII character set, and other blocks of characters are devoted to various languages such as Chinese, Japanese, Hebrew, Arabic, and Hindi.

uninitialized array   An array, some or all of whose elements have not been initialized.

uninitialized variable   A variable that has been defined in a type declaration statement, but for which no initial value has been assigned.

unit   An input/output unit.

unit specifier   A specifier that specifies the unit on which input or output is to occur.

unit testing   The process of testing individual procedures separately and independently before they are combined into a final program.

upper bound   The maximum value permitted for a subscript of an array.

USE association   The manner in which the contents of a module are made available for use in a program unit.

USE statement   A statement that references a module in order to make the contents of the module available for use in the program unit containing it.

variable   A data object whose value may be changed during program execution.

variable declaration   The declaration of the type and, optionally, the attributes of a variable.

vector subscript   A method of specifying an array section by a rank-1 array containing the subscripts of the elements to include in the array section.

well-conditioned system   A system of equations whose solution is relatively insensitive to small changes in the values of its coefficients, or to truncation and round-off errors.

while loop   A loop that executes indefinitely until some specified condition is satisfied.

whole array   An array that has a name.

word   The fundamental unit of memory on a particular computer. The size of a word varies from processor to processor, but it typically is 16, 32, or 64 bits.

work array   A temporary array used for the storage of intermediate results; can be implemented as an automatic array in Fortran 90/95.

Answers to Quizzes

Quiz 1–1

1. (a) 11011_2 (b) 1011_2 (c) 100011_2 (d) 1111111_2
2. (a) 14_{10} (b) 85_{10} (c) 9_{10}
3. $131_{10} = 10000011_2$, so the 4th bit is a zero.
4. (a) ASCII: M; EBCDIC: ((b) ASCII: {; EBCDIC: # (c) ASCII: (unused); EBCDIC: 9
5. (a) $-32,768$ (b) $32,767$
6. Yes, a 4-byte variable of the real data type can be used to store larger numbers than a 4-byte variable of the integer data type. The 8 bits of the exponent in a real variable can represent values as large as 10^{38}. A 4-byte integer can only represent values as large as 2,147,483,647 (about 10^9). The real variable is restricted to 6 or 7 decimal digits of precision, while the integer variable has 9 or 10 decimal digits of precision.

Quiz 2–1

1. Valid real constant.
2. Invalid—commas not permitted within constants.
3. Invalid—real constants must have a decimal point. However, many compilers will accept this form.
4. Invalid—single quotes within a character string delimited by single quotes must be doubled. Correct forms are `'That''s ok!'` or `"That's ok!"`.
5. Valid integer constant.
6. Valid real constant.
7. Invalid—mismatched apostrophe and quote.
8. Valid logical constant.
9. Valid character constant.
10. Invalid—character constants must be enclosed by single or double quotes.
11. Valid character constant.
12. Valid real constant.
13. Invalid—Logical constants must be surrounded by periods.
14. Invalid—real exponents are expressed using the E symbol instead of ^.
15. Same
16. Same
17. Different
18. Different

19. Valid program name.
20. Invalid—program name must begin with a letter.
21. Valid integer variable.
22. Valid real variable.
23. Invalid—name must begin with a letter.
24. Valid real variable.
25. Invalid—name must begin with a letter.
26. Invalid—no double colons (::) present.
27. Valid.

Quiz 2–2

1. The order is (*1*) exponentials, working from right to left; (*2*) multiplications and divisions, working from left to right; (*3*) additions and subtractions, working from left to right; (*4*) relational operators (==, /=, >, >=, <, <=), working from left to right; (*5*) .NOT. operators, (*6*) .AND. operators, working from left to right; (*7*) .OR. operators, working from left to right; (*8*) .EQV. and .NEQV. operators, working from left to right. Parentheses modify this order—terms in parentheses are evaluated first, starting from the innermost parentheses and working outward.

2. (*a*) Legal: Result=12; (*b*) Legal: Result=42; (*c*) Legal: Result=2; (*d*) Legal: Result=2; (*e*) Illegal: Division by 0; (*f*) Legal: Result=−40.5 Note that this result is legal because exponentiation precedes negation in operator precedence. It is equivalent to the expression `-(3.**(4./2.))` and does *not* involve taking the real power of a negative number.; (*g*) Legal: Result=0.111111; (*h*) Illegal: Two adjacent operators.

3. (*a*) 7; (*b*) −21; (*c*) 7; (*d*) 9

4. (*a*) Legal: Result=256; (*b*) Legal: Result=0.25; (*c*) Legal: Result=4; (*d*) Illegal: Negative real number raised to a real power.

5. The statements are illegal, since they try to assign a value to named constant k.

6. RESULT=44.16667

7. a=3.0; n=3.

Quiz 2–3

1. `r_eq = r1 + r2 + r3 + r4`
2. `r_eq = 1. / ( 1./r1 + 1./r2 + 1./r3 + 1./r4 )`
3. `t = 2. * pi * SQRT( l / g )`
4. `v = v_max * EXP( - alpha * t ) * COS( omega * t )`
5. $d = \frac{1}{2} a t^2 + v_0 t + x_0$
6. $f = \dfrac{1}{2\pi\sqrt{LC}}$
7. $E = \frac{1}{2} L\, i^2$
8. The results are

$$126 \quad 5.000000E-02 \quad T$$

Make sure that you can explain why a is equal to 0.05!

9. (*a*) Legal: Result=.FALSE.; (*b*) Illegal: .NOT. only works with logical values; (*c*) Legal: Result=.TRUE.; (*d*) Legal: Result .FALSE.; (*e*) Legal: Result=.TRUE.; (*f*) Legal: Result=.TRUE.; (*g*) Legal: Result=.FALSE.; (*h*) Illegal: .OR. only works with logical values.

10. (*a*) Legal: Result='bcd'; (*b*) Legal: Result='ABCd'; (*c*) Legal: Result=.FALSE.; (*d*) Legal: Result=.TRUE.; (*e*) Illegal: can't compare strings with numbers; (*f*) Legal: Result=.TRUE.; (*f*) Legal: Result=.FALSE.

11. The results are shown below. Can you explain why each value was assigned to a given variable by the READ statements?

```
1   3   180   2.000000   30.000000   3.489839E-02
```

Quiz 3–1

1.
```
IF ( x >= 0. ) THEN
    sqrt_x = SQRT( x )
    WRITE (*,*) 'The square root of x is ', sqrt_x
ELSE
    WRITE (*,*) 'Error--x < 0!'
    sqrt_x = 0.
END IF
```

2.
```
IF   ( ABS(denominator) < 1.0E-10) THEN
    WRITE  (*,*) 'Divide by zero error!'
ELSE
    fun = numerator / denominator
    WRITE (*,*) 'FUN = ', fun
END IF
```

3.
```
IF ( distance > 300. ) THEN
    cost = 110. + 0.20 * (distance - 300. )
ELSE IF ( distance > 100. ) THEN
    cost = 50. + 0.30 * ( distance - 100. )
ELSE
    cost = 0.50 * distance
END IF
average_cost = cost / distance
```

4. These statements are incorrect. There is no ELSE in front of IF (VOLTS < 105.).

5. These statements are correct. They will print out the warning because warn is true, even though the speed limit is not exceeded.

6. These statements are incorrect, since a real value is used to control the operation of a CASE statement.

7. These statements are correct. They will print out the message 'Prepare to stop.'.

8. These statements are technically correct, but they are unlikely to do what the user intended. If the temperature is greater than 100°, then the user probably wants 'Boiling point of water exceeded' to be printed out. Instead, the message 'Human body temperature exceeded' will be printed out, since the IF structure executes the first true branch that it comes to. If the temperature is greater than 100°, it is also greater than 37°.

Quiz 3–2

1. 4
2. 0
3. 1
4. 7
5. 9
6. 0
7. ires = 10
8. ires = 55
9. ires = 10
10. ires = 100
11. ires = 21

12. Invalid. These statements redefine DO loop index i within the loop.
13. Valid.
14. Illegal: DO loops overlap.

Quiz 4–1

Note: The following answers represent one of many possible correct answers to these questions.

1. `WRITE (*,100)`
`100 FORMAT ('1',24X,'This is a test!')`

2. `WRITE (*,110) i, j, data1`
`100 FORMAT ('0',2I10,F10.2)`

3. `WRITE (*,110) result`
`110 FORMAT ('1',T13,'The result is ',ES12.4)`

4.
```
   -.0001**********   3.1416
  ──┼───┼───┼───┼───┼───┼──
    5   10  15  20  25  30
```

5.
```
       .000    .602E+24   3.14159
  ──┼───┼───┼───┼───┼───┼──
    5   10  15  20  25  30
```

6.
```
  ********** 6.0200E+23   3.1416
  ──┼───┼───┼───┼───┼───┼──
    5   10  15  20  25  30
```

7.
```
32767
   24
*****

  ──┼───┼───┼───┼───┼───┼──
    5   10  15  20  25  30
```

8.
```
   32767 00000024 -1010101
  ──┼───┼───┼───┼───┼───┼──
    5   10  15  20  25  30
```

9.
```
ABCDEFGHIJ    12345
  ──┼───┼───┼───┼───┼───┼──
    5   10  15  20  25  30
```

10.
```
                 ABC12345IJ
  ──┼───┼───┼───┼───┼───┼──
    5   10  15  20  25  30
```

11.
```
ABCDE 12345
  ──┼───┼───┼───┼───┼───┼──
    5   10  15  20  25  30
```

12. Correct. All format descriptors match variable types.
13. Incorrect. Format descriptors do not match variable types for test and ierror.
14. This program skips to the top of a page and writes the following data.

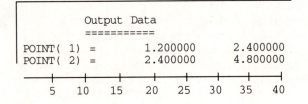

```
              Output Data
              ===========
  POINT( 1) =        1.200000      2.400000
  POINT( 2) =        2.400000      4.800000

  ──┼───┼───┼───┼───┼───┼───┼───┼──
    5   10   15   20   25   30   35   40
```

Quiz 4–2

Note: The following answers represent one of many possible correct answers to these questions.

1. `READ (*,100) amplitude, count, identity`
   `100 FORMAT (9X,F11.2,T30,I6,T60,A13)`
2. `READ (*,110) title, i1, i2, i3, i4, i5`
   `110 FORMAT (T10,A25,/(4X,I8))`
3. `READ (*,120) string, number`
   `120 FORMAT (T11,A10,///,T11,I10)`
4. i=−35, j=6705, k=3687
5. `string1 = 'FGHIJ'`, `string2 = 'KLMNOPQRST'`, `string3 = 'UVWXYZ0123`
   `string4 = ' _TEST_ 1'`.
6. Correct.
7. Correct. These statements read integer `junk` from columns 60–74 of one line and then read real variable `scratch` from columns 1–15 of the next line.
8. Incorrect. Real variable `elevation` will be read with an `I6` format descriptor.

Quiz 4–3

1. `OPEN (UNIT=25, FILE='IN052691', ACTION='READ', IOSTAT=istat)`
   `IF ( istat /= 0 ) THEN`
   `    WRITE (*,'(1X,A,I6)') 'Open error on file.  IOSTAT = ', istat`
   `ELSE`
   `    ...`
   `END IF`
2. `OPEN (UNIT=4, FILE=out_name, STATUS='NEW', ACTION='WRITE', &`
   `       IOSTAT=istat)`
3. `CLOSE (UNIT=24)`
4. `READ (8,*,IOSTAT=istat) first, last`
   `IF ( istat <0 ) THEN`
   `    WRITE (*,*) 'End of file encountered on unit 8.'`
   `END IF`
5. `DO i = 1, 8`
   `    BACKSPACE (UNIT=13)`
   `END DO`
6. Incorrect. File `data1` has been replaced, so there is no data to read.
7. Incorrect. You cannot specify a file name with a scratch file.
8. Incorrect. There is nothing in the scratch file to read, since the file was created when it was opened.
9. Incorrect. You cannot use a real value as an i/o unit number.
10. Correct.

Quiz 5–1

1. 15
2. 256
3. 41
4. Valid. The array will be initialized with the values in the array constructor.
5. Valid. All 10 values in the array will be initialized to 0.
6. Valid. Every `tenth` value in the array will be initialized to 1000, and all other values will be initialized to `zero`. The values will then be written out.

7. Invalid. The arrays are not conformable, since `array1` is 11 elements long and `array2` is 10 elements long.

8. Valid. Every `tenth` element of array `in` will initialized to 10, 20, 30, etc. All other elements will be `zero`. The 10-element array `sub1` will be initialized to 10, 20, 30, . . . , 100, and the 10-element array `sub2` will be initialized to 1, 2, 3, . . . , 10. The multiplication will work because arrays `sub1` and `sub2` arc conformable.

9. Mostly valid. The values in array `error` will be printed out. However, since `error(0)` was never initialized, we don't know what will be printed out, or even whether printing that array element will cause an I/O error.

10. Valid. Array `ivec1` will be initialized to 1, 2, . . . , 10, and array `ivec2` will be initialized to 10, 9, . . . , 1. Array `data1` will be initialized to 1., 4., 9., . . . , 100. The `WRITE` statement will print out 100., 81., 64., . . . , 1., because of the vector subscript.

11. Probably invalid. These statements will compile correctly, but they probably do *not* do what the programmer intended. A 10-element integer array `mydata` will be created. Each `READ` statement reads values into the entire array, so array `mydata` will be initialized 10 times over (using up 100 input values!). The user probably intended for each array element to be initialized only once.

Quiz 5–2

1. 645 elements. The valid range is `data_input(-64,0)` to `data_input(64,4)`.

2. 210 elements. The valid range is `filenm(1,1)` to `filenm(3,70)`.

3. 294 elements. The valid range is `in(-3,-3,1)` to `in(3,3,6)`.

4. Invalid. The array constructor is not conformable with array `dist`.

5. Valid. `dist` will be initialized with the values in the array constructor.

6. Valid. Arrays `data1`, `data2`, and `data_out` are all conformable, so this addition is valid. The first `WRITE` statement prints the five values 1., 11., 11., 11., 11., and the second `WRITE` statement prints the two values 11., 11.

7. Valid. These statements initialize the array and then select the subset specified by `list1=(/1,4,2,2/)`, and `list2=(/1,2,3/)`. The resulting array section is

$$
\texttt{array(list1,list2)} = \begin{bmatrix} \texttt{array(1,1)} & \texttt{array(1,2)} & \texttt{array(1,3)} \\ \texttt{array(4,1)} & \texttt{array(4,2)} & \texttt{array(4,3)} \\ \texttt{array(2,1)} & \texttt{array(2,2)} & \texttt{array(2,3)} \\ \texttt{array(2,1)} & \texttt{array(2,2)} & \texttt{array(2,3)} \end{bmatrix}
$$

$$
\texttt{array(list1,list2)} = \begin{bmatrix} 11 & 21 & 31 \\ 14 & 24 & 34 \\ 12 & 22 & 32 \\ 12 & 22 & 32 \end{bmatrix}
$$

8. Invalid. There is a many-one array section on the left-hand side of an assignment statement.

9. The data on the first three lines would be read into array `input`. However, the data is read in column order, so `mydata(1,1)=11.2`, `mydata(2,1)=16.5`, `mydata(3,1)=31.3`, *etc.* `mydata(2,4)=15.0`

10. The data on the first three lines would be read into array `input`. The data is read in column order, so `mydata(0,2)=11.2`, `mydata(1,2)=16.5`, `mydata(2,2)=31.3`, *etc.* `mydata(2,4)=17.1`

11. The data on the first three lines would be read into array `input`. This time, the data is read in row order, so `mydata(1,1)=11.2`, `mydata(1,2)=16.5`, `mydata(1,3)=31.3`, *etc.* `mydata(2,4)=17.1`

12. The data on the first three lines would be read into array `input`. The data is read in row order, but only the first five values on each line are read by each `READ` statement. The next `READ` statement begins with the first value on the next input line. Therefore, `mydata(2,4)`=11.0

13. 9.0

14. The rank of array `mydata` is 2.

15. The shape of array `mydata` is 3×5.

16. The extent of the first dimension of array `data_input` is 129.

17. 7

Quiz 5–3

1. `LBOUND(values,1)` = -3, `UBOUND(values,2)` = 50, `SIZE(values,1)` = 7, `SIZE(values)` = 357, `SHAPE(values)` = 7,51.

2. The output from these statements will be

6	0	-3	10	-8	4

3. Invalid. The control mask for the `WHERE` construct (`time > 0.`) is not the same shape as the array `dist` in the body of the `WHERE` construct.

Quiz 6–1

1. The call to `ave_sd` is incorrect. The second argument is declared as an integer in the calling program, but it is a real within the subroutine.

2. These statements are valid. When the subroutine finishes executing, `string2` contains the mirror image of the characters in `string1`.

3. These statements are incorrect. Subroutine `sub3` uses 30 elements in array `iarray`, but only 25 values in the array are passed from the calling program. Also, the subroutine uses an assumed-size dummy array, which should not be used in any new programs.

Quiz 6–2

1. The `SAVE` statement or the `SAVE` attribute should be used in any procedure that depends on local data values being unchanged between invocations of the procedure. All local variables that must remain constant between invocations should be declared with the `SAVE` attribute.

2. An automatic array is a local array in a procedure whose extent is specified by variables passed to the procedure when it is invoked. The array is automatically created each time the procedure is invoked and is automatically destroyed each time the procedures exits. Automatic arrays should be used for temporary storage within a procedure.

3. If procedures are placed in a module and accessed by `USE` association, then they will have explicit interfaces, allowing the compiler to catch many errors in calling sequence.

4. Assumed-shape dummy arrays are simpler than explicit-shape dummy arrays because the bounds of each array do not have to be passed to the procedure. The only disadvantage associated with them is that they must be used with an explicit interface.

5. This program will work on many processors, but it has two potentially serious problems. First, the value of variable `isum` is never initialized. Second, `isum` is not saved between calls to `sub1`. When it works, it will initialize the values of the array to 1, 2, . . . , 10.

6. There is no error in this program. The main program and the subroutine share data using a module. The output from the program is `a(5)` = `5.0`.

7. The calling sequence to subroutine `sub3` is in error, and the error will be caught by the compiler since `sub3` has an explicit interface. The second argument of `sub3` is `INTENT(OUT)`, and the corresponding argument in the calling sequence is a constant.

8. This program is invalid. Subroutine `sub4` uses assumed-shape arrays but does not have an explicit interface.

Quiz 6–3

1.
```
REAL FUNCTION f2(x)
IMPLICIT NONE
REAL, INTENT(IN) :: x
f2 = (x - 1.) / (x + 1.)
END FUNCTION
```

2.
```
REAL FUNCTION tanh(x)
IMPLICIT NONE
REAL, INTENT(IN) :: x
tanh = (EXP(x)-EXP(-x)) / (EXP(x)+EXP(-x))
END FUNCTION
```

3.
```
FUNCTION fact(n)
IMPLICIT NONE
INTEGER, INTENT(IN) :: n
INTEGER :: fact
INTEGER :: i
fact = 1.
DO i = n, 1, -1
    fact = fact * i
END DO
END FUNCTION
```

4.
```
LOGICAL FUNCTION compare(x,y)
IMPLICIT NONE
REAL, INTENT(IN) :: x, y
compare = (x**2 + y**2) > 1.0
END FUNCTION
```

5. This function is incorrect because `sum` is never initialized. The sum must be set to `zero` before the `DO` loop is executed.

6. This function is invalid. Argument `a` is `INTENT(IN)`, but its value is modified in the function.

7. This function is valid.

Quiz 7–1

1. This answer to this question processor-dependent. You must consult the manuals for your particular compiler.

2. `(-1.980198E-02,-1.980198E-01)`

3.
```
PROGRAM complex_math
!
!   Purpose:
!     To perform the complex calculation:
!         D = ( A + B ) /C
!     where A = ( 1., -1.)
!           B = (-1., -1.)
!           C = (10., 1.)
!     without using the COMPLEX data type.
!
 IMPLICIT NONE
!
REAL :: ar = 1.,  ai = -1.
REAL :: br = -1., bi = -1.
REAL :: cr = 10., ci = 1.
REAL :: dr, di
REAL :: tempr, tempi

CALL complex_add ( ar, ai, br, bi, tempr, tempi )
```

```
CALL complex_divide ( tempr, tempi, cr, ci, dr, di )

WRITE (*,100) dr, di
100 FORMAT (1X,'D = (',F10.5,',',F10.5,')' )

END PROGRAM
SUBROUTINE complex_add ( x1, y1, x2, y2, x3, y3 )
!
!   Purpose:
!      Subroutine to add two complex numbers (x1, y1) and
!      (x2, y2), and store the result in (x3, y3).
!
IMPLICIT NONE

REAL, INTENT(IN) :: x1, y1, x2, y2
REAL, INTENT(OUT) :: x3, y3

x3 = x1 + x2
y3 = y1 + y2


END SUBROUTINE complex_add

SUBROUTINE complex_divide ( x1, y1, x2, y2, x3, y3 )

!
!   Purpose:
!      Subroutine to divide two complex numbers (x1, y1) and
!      (x2, y2), and store the result in (x3, y3).
!
IMPLICIT NONE

REAL, INTENT(IN) :: x1, y1, x2, y2
REAL, INTENT(OUT) :: x3, y3
REAL :: denom

denom = x2**2 + y2**2
x3 = (x1 * x2 + y1 * y2) / denom
y3 = (y1 * x2 - x1 * y2) / denom

END SUBROUTINE complex_divide
```

It is much easier to use the complex data type to solve the problem than it is to use the definitions of complex operations and real numbers.

Quiz 7–2

1.
```
WRITE (*,100) points(7)%plot_time%day, points(7)%plot_time%month, &
              points(7)%plot_time%year, points(7)%plot_time%hour, &
              points(7)%plot_time%minute, points(7)%plot_time%second
100 FORMAT (1X,I2.2,'/',I2.2,'/',I4.4,' ',I2.2,':',I2.2,':',I2.2)
```

2.
```
WRITE (*,110) points(7)%plot_position%x, &
              points(7)%plot_position%y, &
              points(7)%plot_position%z
110 FORMAT (1X,' x = ',F12.4, ' y = ',F12.4, ' z = ',F12.4 )
```

3. To calculate the time difference, we must subtract the times associated with the two points, taking into account the different scales associated with hours, minutes, and seconds. The following code converts the times to seconds before subtracting them and also assumes that both points occur on the same day, month, and year. (You can easily extend this calculation to handle arbi-

trary days, months, and years as well, but double-precision real arithmetic must be used for the calculations.) To calculate the position difference, we use the equation

$$dpos = \sqrt{(x_2 - x_1)^2 + (y_2 - y_1)^2 + (z_2 - z_1)^2}$$

```
time1 = points(2)%plot_time%second + 60.*points(2)%plot_time%minute &
      + 3600.*points(2)%plot_time%hour
time2 = points(3)%plot_time%second + 60.*points(3)%plot_time%minute &
      + 3600.*points(3)%plot_time%hour
dtime = time2 - time1

dpos = SQRT ( &
          (points(3)%plot_position%x - points(2)%plot_position%x )**2 &
        + (points(3)%plot_position%y - points(2)%plot_position%y )**2 &
        + (points(3)%plot_position%z - points(2)%plot_position%z )**2 )

rate = dpos / dtime
```

4. Valid. This statement prints out all the components of the first element of array points.
5. Invalid. The format descriptors do not match the order of the data in points(4).
6. Invalid. Intrinsic operations are not defined for derived data types, and component plot_position is a derived data type.

Quiz 8–1

1. An internal subroutine is a subroutine that is contained within a main program or procedure and that is compiled together with that program unit. It is placed after the last executable statement in the program unit and is preceded by a CONTAINS statement. The internal subroutine is accessible only from the program unit that contains it. By contrast, an external subroutine is separately compiled and can be called from any program unit.
2. Recursive procedures are procedures that can invoke themselves. They are declared using the RECURSIVE keyword in SUBROUTINE or FUNCTION statement. If the recursive procedure is a function, then the FUNCTION statement should also include a RESULT clause.
3. This function is illegal because it contains a type declaration for the function name sum_1_n and no type declaration for the result variable sum. When a RESULT clause is used, only the type of the result variable should be declared, not the type of the function name.
4. Keyword arguments are calling arguments of the form KEYWORD=value, where KEYWORD is the name used to declare the dummy argument in the procedure definition and value is the value to be passed to that dummy argument when the procedure is invoked. Keyword arguments may only be used if the procedure being invoked has an explicit interface. Keyword arguments may be used to allow calling arguments to be specified in a different order or to specify only certain optional arguments.
5. Optional arguments do not have to be present when a procedure is invoked but will be used if they are present. Optional arguments may be used only if the procedure being invoked has an explicit interface. They may be used for input or output data that is not needed every time a procedure is invoked.

Quiz 8–2

1. A generic procedure is defined using a named interface block. The name of the generic procedure is specified in the INTERFACE statement, and all possible specific procedures are listed in MODULE PROCEDURE statements in the body of the interface block. Each specific procedure must be distinguishable from all other specific procedures by some combination of its non-optional calling arguments.

2. A `MODULE  PROCEDURE` statement is used to specify that a specific procedure is a part of a generic procedure (or operator definition) when both the specific procedure and the generic procedure definition (or operator definition) appear within the same module.

3. A user-defined operator is declared using the `INTERFACE  OPERATOR` block, while a user-defined assignment is declared using the `INTERFACE  ASSIGNMENT` block. A user-defined operator is implemented by a one- or two-argument function (for unary and binary operators, respectively). The arguments of the function must have `INTENT(IN)`, and the result of the function is the result of the operation. A user-defined assignment is implemented using a two-argument subroutine. The first argument must be `INTENT(OUT)` or `INTENT(INOUT)`, and the second argument must be `INTENT(IN)`. The first argument is the result of the assignment operation.

4. Access to the contents of a module may be controlled using `PUBLIC` and `PRIVATE` statements or attributes. It might be desirable to restrict access to the internal components of some user-defined data types, or to restrict direct access to procedures used to implement user-defined operators or assignments, so these items can be declared to be `PRIVATE`.

5. The default type of access for items in a module is `PUBLIC`.

Quiz 9–1

1. An allocatable array is an array whose rank is declared at compilation time but whose size is not determined until a program is executed. When the program is executed, an `ALLOCATE` statement may be used to allocate memory to the array, and a `DEALLOCATE` statement may be used to deallocate the memory. The size of an allocatable array is variable, while the size of an ordinary array is fixed.

2. `UBOUND(values,2)` = 2, `SIZE(values)` = 60, `SHAPE(values)` = 3, 4, 5.

3. A pointer is a Fortran variable that contains the *address* of another Fortran variable or array. A target is an ordinary Fortran variable or array that has been declared with the `TARGET` attribute so that a pointer can point to it. The difference between a pointer and an ordinary variable is that a pointer contains the address of another Fortran variable or array, while an ordinary Fortran variable contains data.

4. A pointer assignment statement assigns the address of a target to a pointer. The difference between a pointer assignment statement and an ordinary assignment statement is that a pointer assignment statement assigns the address of a Fortran variable or array to a pointer, while an ordinary assignment statement assigns the value of an expression to the target pointed to by the pointer.

```
ptr1 => var      ! Assigns address of var to ptr1
ptr1 = var       ! Assigns value of var to target of ptr1
```

5. The possible association statuses of a pointer are associated, disassociated, and undefined. When a pointer is first declared, its status is undefined. It may be associated with a target using a pointer assignment statement or an `ALLOCATE` statement. The pointer may be disassociated from a target by the `NULLIFY` statement, by the `DEALLOCATE` statement, by assigning a null pointer to it in a pointer assignment statement, or by using the `NULL()` function (Fortran 95 only).

6. Dereferencing is the process of accessing the corresponding target when a reference to a pointer appears in an operation or assignment statement.

7. Memory may be dynamically allocated with pointers using the `ALLOCATE` statement. Memory may be deallocated using the `DEALLOCATE` statement.

8. Invalid. This is an attempt to use array `time` before memory is allocated to it.

9. Valid. These statements print out an `F`, since array test is not allocated.

10. Invalid. This is an attempt to associate `ptr1` with a variable that is not declared with the TARGET attribute.

11. Invalid. This is an attempt to use `ptr2` before it is associated with a target.

12. Valid. This statement assigns the address of the target variable `value` to pointer `ptr2`.

13. Invalid. A pointer must be of the same type as its target.

14. Valid. The first WRITE statement will print out a T because pointer p1 is associated. The second WRITE statement will print out an F because pointer p1 is not associated with target i1. The final WRITE statement will print out an F because pointer p1 is no longer associated.

15. Valid but with a memory leak. The first WRITE statement will print out an F because pointer ptr is not associated. The second WRITE statement will print out a T followed by the value 137 because a memory location was allocated using the pointer and the value 137 was assigned to that location. The final statement nullifies the pointer, leaving the allocated memory location inaccessible.

16. Invalid. These statements allocate a 10-element array using `ptr1` and assign values to it. The address of the array is assigned to `ptr2`, and then the array is deallocated using `ptr1`. This leaves `ptr2` pointing to an invalid memory location. When the WRITE statement is executed, the results are unpredictable.

■ Quick Summary of Common Attributes Used in Type Declaration Statements

Statement	Description (page in text)	Example of usage
ALLOCATABLE	Declares that an array is allocatable (449)	`REAL,ALLOCATABLE,DIMENSION(:) :: a`
DIMENSION	Declares the rank and shape of an array (212)	`REAL,DIMENSION(10,10) :: matrix`
EXTERNAL	Declares that a name is a function external to a program unit (340)	`REAL,EXTERNAL :: fun1`
INTENT	Specifies the intended use of a dummy argument (292)	`INTEGER,INTENT(IN) :: ndim`
OPTIONAL	Declares that a dummy argument is optional (414)	`REAL,OPTIONAL,INTENT(IN) :: maxval`
PARAMETER	Defines a named constant (24)	`REAL,PARAMETER :: pi = 3.141593`
POINTER	Declares that a variable is a pointer (455)	`INTEGER,POINTER :: ptr`
PRIVATE	Declares that an object is private to a module (438)	`REAL,PRIVATE :: internal_data`
PUBLIC	Declares that an object in a module is visible outside the module (438)	`REAL,PUBLIC :: pi = 3.141593`
SAVE	Preserves local variables in a procedure between invocations of the procedure (311)	`REAL,SAVE :: sum` `SAVE`
TARGET	Declares that a variable may be pointed to by a pointer (455)	`INTEGER,TARGET :: val1`